LOVE
in the
HOLY QUR'AN

LOVE
—in the—
HOLY QUR'AN

8ᵀᴴ EDITION

HRH Prince Ghazi bin Muhammad

Copyright © HRH Prince Ghazi bin Muhammad 1431 AH/2010 CE
Copyright seventh English edition © The Prince Ghazi Trust for Islamic Thought
1435 AH/2014 CE
Copyright eighth English edition © The Prince Ghazi Trust for Islamic Thought
1440 AH/2019 CE

First edition published by Kazi Publications 2010

This eighth edition published 2019 by
The Islamic Texts Society
Miller's House
Kings Mill Lane
Great Shelford
Cambridge CB22 5EN, U.K.

British Library Cataloguing-in-Publication Data.
A catalogue record for this book is
available from the British Library.

ISBN 978 1911141 419

The right of Ghazi bin Muhammad to be identified as author of this work
has been asserted by him in accordance with the
Copyright, Designs and Patents Act 1988.

All rights reserved. No part of this publication may be produced,
installed in retrieval systems, or transmitted in any form
or by any means, electronic, mechanical, photocopying,
recording, or otherwise, without the prior written
permission of the publishers.

Cover design and typesetting by Besim Bruncaj
Title set in Garamond Premiere Pro
Text set in Minion Pro

CONTENTS

Epigraph   ix
Dedication   x
Acknowledgements   xi
About the Author   xiii
Executive Summary   xv

INTRODUCTORY CHAPTERS

Chapter 1:	Prologue: The Goals and Methodology of this Work	3
	The goals of this work	3
	The methodology of this work	7
	A note to the reader about the English translation	7
	A note on the tenth edition	8
Chapter 2:	Introduction: The Secret of Love	10
Chapter 3:	The Definition of Love	12

PART ONE: DIVINE LOVE

Chapter 4:	God and Love	17
	Love as a Divine Quality	17
	Love and mercy are of the Divine Essence	18
Chapter 5:	Love is the Root of Creation	22
Chapter 6:	The Universe and Love	29
Chapter 7:	God's Love for Humanity	32
	God's favour and love for all human beings in general	32
	God's particular love for the virtuous	34
	The hierarchy of the virtuous	37
	God's bounty to all human beings	42
Chapter 8:	God's Love for His Messengers and Prophets	44
	The prophets	44
	The messengers	45
	The five 'resolute' messengers	46
	God's beloved	50
Chapter 9:	Those whom God does not Love	54

PART TWO: THE MESSENGER OF GOD'S ☸ LOVE

Chapter 10:	The Messenger of God's ☸ Love for God	61
Chapter 11:	The Messenger of God's ☸ Love for the Believers	63

PART THREE: HUMAN LOVE

Chapter 12:	Humanity's Love for God	69
	Why human beings should love God	69
	How human beings should love God	73
	What intentions and motives human beings must have in loving God	77
	On love for what reminds one of God	82
Chapter 13:	The Believer's Love for the Messenger of God ☸	85
Chapter 14:	Love for the Family and Kin of the Messenger of God ☸	90
Chapter 15:	The Effects of Love of God on Human Beings	97
Chapter 16:	Family Love	106
Chapter 17:	Love of Others (All Humanity; the 'People of the Scripture'; Believers, and Friends)	113
	All humanity	113
	The people of the scripture	118
	The believers	121
	Friends	121
Chapter 18:	Conjugal and Sexual Love	124
	The need spouses have for one another in order to procreate	126
	Non-physical conjugal love and 'soulmates'	126
	Sexual conjugal love	129
	Spiritual conjugal love	132
	The preservation of conjugal love	135
Chapter 19:	Love and Extra-marital Sex	139
Chapter 20:	Love and the Eyes	142

PART FOUR: LOVE

Chapter 21:	The Different Kinds of Love	147
Chapter 22:	The Stages of Love	168
	The stages of love that occur in human beings' love for God as well as human beings' love for each other	168
	The stages of human beings' love for God	180
	The stages of human beings' love for each other	189
Chapter 23:	Falling in Love	197
	The constituent parts and faculties of human beings	197

CONTENTS

	The secret of falling in love	202
Chapter 24:	The Growth of Love	205
	How love grows	205
	How to control one's love	208
Chapter 25:	The Two Circles of Love	213
Chapter 26:	The Triangle of Love	219
	Why does love require prior 'adornment'?	219
	How do human beings come to know God?	224
Chapter 27:	The Hierarchies of Beauty and of Love	227
	The levels and hierarchies of beauty	227
	The hierarchy of love	231
Chapter 28:	The Opposites of Beauty and of Love	235
	The opposite of beauty (ugliness and vileness)	235
	The opposite of love (hatred and loathing)	235
Chapter 29:	The End of Love	238
	God's love for human beings	238
	Human love for God	239
	Human love for everything other than God	241
Chapter 30:	The Nature of Love	245
	Human love is always changing	245
	The need in love	246
	The exclusion in love	246
	The power of love	247
Chapter 31:	Love and Happiness	249
Chapter 32:	Love and Beauty in Paradise	253

PART FIVE: THE BELOVED
(Beauty; the Meeting with God; Beatitude)

Chapter 33:	Beauty and its Components	259
	The meaning of 'beauty' (jamal and husn)	259
	The components of beauty	260
Chapter 34:	Taste	263
Chapter 35:	The Nature of Beauty	265
	The objectivity of beauty	265
	The power of beauty	265
	The way beauty works	266
	The benefit of beauty (and love)	268
Chapter 36:	Love and Death	270
	The death of the 'soul which incites evil'	270

	The death of the 'soul which incites evil' by means of God's Love	273
	The torment of the soul which loves but does not die in God	274
	Life in God after the soul's death	275
Chapter 37:	The Meeting with God and Beatitude	278
Chapter 38:	The True Intended Object behind All Love	281

SUMMARY

Chapter 39:	Conclusion	287
Chapter 40:	Synopsis	288

Notes   299

Bibliography: *(A) The Holy Qur'an*   347

(B) Primary sources in Arabic   347

(C) Secondary sources in Arabic   350

(D) Primary sources on love in English and French   352

(E) Secondary sources on love in English and French   353

Index of Qur'anic Verses Cited by Chapter*   355

Index of Qur'anic Verses Cited by Qur'anic Chapter   363

Index of Prophetic Hadiths Cited by Chapter   367

Alphabetical Index of Prophetic Hadiths Cited   370

General Index   373

Postscript   385

Reviews of the English Edition   387

Reviews of the Arabic Edition   390

In the Name of God, the Compassionate, the Merciful,

Praise be to God, Lord of all Worlds.

The Compassionate, the Merciful.

Master of the Day of Judgement.

You [alone] we worship, and You [alone] we ask for help.

Guide us to the straight path,

The path of those upon whom You have bestowed Your grace, not [the path] of those against whom there is wrath, nor of those who are astray.

Amen

(Al-Fatihah, 1:1–7)

… But those who believe love God more ardently …

(Al-Baqarah, 2:165)

Dedicated, with love, to Areej,
my wife and soulmate.

ACKNOWLEDGEMENTS

And He is God, there is no god but He! To Him belongs praise at the beginning and at the end. To Him belongs judgment, and unto Him shall you be returned. (Al-Qasas, 28:70).

Writing this book; doing it as a PhD at the thousand year-old Al-Azhar University, the bastion of Sunni Orthodoxy, and above all thinking about it and researching it, was really a gift from God to me—as of course is every good thing in life—but this was so in an extraordinary way. I count it gratefully as one of the great blessings of my life.

I have also many people to thank for making this book possible: H.M. King Abdullah II bin Al-Hussein, not only allowed me to write this work whilst officially working for him, but also supported and encouraged it as well. My thesis supervisor—now the Grand Imam of the Azhar, H.E. Professor Ahmad al-Tayyib—not only accepted me as his student, but edited the work and shepherded me through the Azhar system. It is hard to describe the personal simplicity and humility of this great scholar, to whom I shall always be grateful, as I am to the Azhar and to Egypt itself, for PhDs there are free, even for foreigners. Mr. Khalid Williams translated it in its entirety from the Arabic in three months with impeccable dedication and professionalism, before I reworked it into my own idiom in English—its faults are mine not Khalid's. Mr. Haitham Malkawi did most of the typing in Arabic; Sheikh Hassan Saqqaf and Prof. Abd Al-Maqsud Hamid edited it and gave excellent critical advice in Arabic; Mr. Mahdi Al-Rawadiya proofread the Arabic with great diligence. Mr. Aftab Ahmed, Mrs. Zeinab Asfour and Miss Lamya Al-Khraisha of MABDA copy-edited the translation, and Lamya did so more than once, with great accuracy and dedication. Mr. Sulayman Hart gave invaluable technical help with the computer. My friend, Mr. Samir Al-Saheb, looked after dozens of things for me when I was working, thereby allowing me to get on with the thesis, and Mr. Lotfi Asfour and Mr. Rami Qteishat kept things going at the office during my work. I must thank, from the bottom of my heart, all the great scholars, Muslim and Christian, who took the time to read and review this book. I have included their comments herein—all of which are remarkably different—as much for what they say about this book or about love, as for what they reveal about their generous souls and noble preoccupations. Most of all I must thank my wife Areej for reading and rereading the book; for her love; for her sagacious advice, and for her ardent and constant encouragement and enthusiasm. Last but not least, I must thank my children Tasneem, Abdullah, Jennah, and Salsabeel for the love, joy and life they always bring me, each in their own different way.

ABOUT THE AUTHOR

H.R.H. Prince Ghazi bin Muhammad bin Talal (born in Amman on the 15th of October 1966) is the nephew of the late King Al-Hussein bin Talal of Jordan and a Professor of Islamic Philosophy. He was educated at Harrow School; received his BA from Princeton University in 1988 Summa cum laude; his first PhD from Cambridge University, U.K., in 1993, and his second PhD from Al-Azhar University in Cairo 2010.

Prince Ghazi has held many official positions in Jordan including: *Cultural Secretary* to H.M. King Al-Hussein; *Advisor for Tribal Affairs* to H.M. King Al-Hussein; *Personal Envoy of* and *Special Advisor* to H.M. King Abdullah II, and *Chief Advisor for Religious and Cultural Affairs* to H.M. King Abdullah II.

In 1996 Prince Ghazi founded the Al-Balqa Applied University, and in 2008 he founded the World Islamic Sciences and Education University (WISE). In 1997 he founded the National Park of the Site of the Baptism of Jesus Christ ﷺ, and in 2000 he established the Great Tafsir Project (www.Altafsir.com), the largest online project for exegesis of the Holy Qur'an. He was the author of 'Three Articles of the Amman Message' in 2005; the author of the historic open letter 'A Common Word Between Us and You' in 2007, and the author of the World Interfaith Harmony Week United Nations General Assembly Resolution in October 2010. In 2012 he established the Al-Ghazali Integral Professorial Chair in Al-Aqsa Mosque and Al-Quds University, and the Al-Razi Integral Professorial Chair in the King Hussein Mosque and Jordan University. Prince Ghazi is also Chairman of the Board of Trustees of The Royal Aal al-Bayt Institute for Islamic Thought. In 2012 he founded the Prince Ghazi Trust for Qur'anic Thought, and in 2013 he set up www.FreeIslamicCalligraphy.com.

Prince Ghazi is the author of a number of books and articles—including the widely-acclaimed work Love in the Holy Qur'an—as well as the recipient of a number of awards and decorations including the Eugen Biser Prize (2008) and the St. Augustine Award for Interfaith Dialogue (2012).

Prince Ghazi is married to Princess Areej (née Areej Omar bin Abdul-Munim al-Zawawi of Oman), and they have four children: Princess Tasneem, Prince Abdullah, Princess Jennah and Princess Salsabeel.

Love in the Holy Qur'an is a translation of his Al-Azhar University PhD thesis. In the first year after its publication in Arabic it was downloaded over 485,000 times on the internet and went through four different printed editions.

EXECUTIVE SUMMARY OF
LOVE IN THE HOLY QUR'AN

PREAMBLE

Love in the Holy Qur'an proceeds from the assertion in the Qur'an itself that God has *dispensed* and *struck* in the Qur'an *every [kind of] similitude* (Al-Isra 17:89; Al-Kahf 18:54; Al-Rum 30:58; Al-Zumar 39:27–28); that the Qur'an *is a clarification of all things* (Al-Nahl, 16:89); and that it contains *the details for all things* (Yusuf, 12:111). This is understood as referring not only to the basic religious sciences of Islamic doctrine, theology, sacred law and spiritual practices and ethics, but also all the major topics of philosophy such as: love, language, time, logic, cognition, ethics, psychology, anthropology, epistemology, hermeneutics, cosmology, metaphysics, oneirology and so on.

For the purposes of the synopsis, we will divide the topic into four parts: (I) Divine Love; (II) Human Love; (III) Love and (IV) Beauty.

(I): DIVINE LOVE

In the Qur'an, love is not merely one of God's acts or actions, but one of God's very own Divine Names and Qualities. The Divine Name 'the Loving' ('*Al-Wadud*'), occurs twice in the Qur'an: *And ask forgiveness of your Lord, then repent to Him. Truly my Lord is Merciful, Loving.* (Hud, 11:90) *And He is the Forgiving, the Loving.* (Al-Buruj, 85:14)

There are many other Divine Names in the Qur'an which denote God's loving qualities and imply love (by Arabic linguistic definition), such as: 'the Gentle'—'*Al-Latif*'; 'the Kind'—'*Al-Raouf*'; 'the Generous'—'*Al-Kareem*'; 'the Forbearing'—'*Al-Haleem*'; 'the Absolutely Reliable'—'*Al-Wakil*'; 'the Friend'—'*Al-Wali*'; 'the Good'—'*Al-Barr*'; 'the Forgiving'—'*Al-Ghafur*'; 'the Forgiver'—'*Al-Ghaffar*'; 'the Granter and Accepter of Repentance'—'*Al-Tawwab*', 'the Pardoner'—'*Al-ʿAfu*' and others. This is true *a fortiori* for the two Divine Names 'the Compassionate' ('*Al-Rahman*') and 'the Merciful' ('*Al-Rahim*'), because the stem of these two Divine Names is the tri-letter root *R-H-M*, which means 'womb', and thus implies maternal mercy and love together. Thus God's Loving is inseparable from His Mercy, and indeed love usually comes with mercy, and mercy usually comes with love—though evidently they do not mean exactly the same thing.

This also means that God's Love is twice implied—along with the double mention of Divine Mercy—at the beginning of the Qur'an itself and the beginning of every one of its one hundred and fourteen chapters except the ninth.

Moreover, since God says in the Qur'an ... *He has prescribed for Himself [nafsihi—His Self] mercy...* (Al-An'am, 6:12), this means that Divine Mercy—and with it Divine Love—is not just a Divine Quality, but of the very Divine Essence Itself.

Furthermore, God, as *Al-Rahman*, created the world and human beings *out of* His Mercy. God says: *The Compassionate One / has taught the Qur'an. / He created man, / teaching him [coherent] speech.* (Al-Rahman, 55:1–4)

This means that God created the world and human beings *out of* love as well. Indeed, God loves all beings and all things—apart from evildoers as such, as we will shortly discuss, God willing—*before* and *more* than they could possibly love Him.

God also created human beings *for* his Mercy. God says: *.... [E]xcept those on whom your Lord has mercy; and for that did He create them...* (Hud, 11:119)

This means that God created the world and human beings *for* love as well. In other words, God created the world and human beings *out of* His Love and *for* His Love.

That is the reason why everything in the world—save only the souls of disbelievers—loves God. God says: *The seven heavens and the earth and all that is therein proclaim His glory. And there is not a thing, but glorifies Him in praise; but you do not understand their glorification. Lo! He is Forbearing, Forgiving.* (Al-Isra', 17:44)

Thus the entire universe praises—and therefore innately loves—God. And thus even the most evil person committing the most evil deed—with his or her consciousness rejecting or hating God at that moment—nevertheless loves God innately in every atom of their being and in their deepest heart.

As regards human beings in particular, God's love for them is seen first of all in His great and innumerable favours to them in their creation, their superior faculties and intelligence and above all in the possibility of their knowing Him through His guidance. God says: *And if you were to count God's grace you could never reckon it. Indeed God is Forgiving, Merciful.* (Al-Nahl, 16:18)

However, God loves those who are the most virtuous and good—those whose souls are the most beautiful—with a particular or special love, starting with the best and most virtuous of them, His messengers and prophets, of whom He says: *... [A]ll of them We favoured (faddalna) above the worlds.* (Al-An'am, 6:85)

As regards the Seal of the Prophets and Messenger, the Prophet Muhammad ﷺ, God says that He has sent him as *a mercy to all the worlds.* (Al-Anbiya', 21:107) and that God will love more (*'yuhbibkum'*) those who follow him (*Aal*

Executive Summary of Love in the Holy Qur'an

'Imran, 3:31), which necessarily implies—as is explicitly stated in a *hadith*[1]—that the Prophet Muhammad ﷺ is 'God's Beloved'.

As regards other people, God mentions eight types of people whom He loves as such:

(1) 'Those who rely' (on God) ('*al-mutawakkilin*' or '*al-mutawakkilun*') (Aal 'Imran, 3:159);
(2) 'Those who cleanse themselves' ('*al-mutatahhirin*') or 'purify themselves' ('*al-muttahhirin*) (Al-Baqarah, 2:222; Al-Tawbah, 9:109);
(3) 'Those who repent' ('*al-tawwabin*') (Al-Baqarah, 2:222);
(4) 'The just' ('*al-muqsitin*') (Al-Ma'idah, 5:42; Al-Hujurat, 49:9; Al-Mumtahanah, 60:8);
(5) 'Those who fight for His cause in ranks, as if they were a solid structure' ('*al-ladhina yuqatiluna fi sabilihi saffan ka'annahum bunyanun marsus*') (Al-Saff, 61:4);
(6) 'The patient' ('*al-sabirin*') (Aal 'Imran, 3:146);
(7) 'The God-fearing' ('*al-muttaqin*') (Aal 'Imran, 3:76; Al-Tawbah, 9:4; Al-Tawbah, 9:7); and
(8) 'The virtuous' ('*al-muhsinin*') (Al-Baqarah, 2:195; Aal 'Imran, 3:134; Aal 'Imran, 3:148; Al-Ma'idah, 5:13; Al-Ma'idah, 5:93).

In short, even though God's bounty is extended to all creation and all people (whether they deserve it or not), God particularly loves the virtuous and those whose souls are beautiful, in varying degrees, according, precisely, to the very measure of their beauty of soul and their virtue. God says: ... *Truly the noblest of you in the sight of God is the most God-fearing among you* ... (Al-Hujurat, 49:13)

Conversely, God mentions twelve kinds of people as such who He 'does not love' ('*la yuhibb*'). These are:

1. 'The disbelievers' ('*al-kafirin*') (Aal 'Imran, 3:32; Al-Rum, 30:45)
2. 'Every guilty ingrate' ('*kulla kaffarin athim*') (Al-Baqarah, 2:276)
3. 'The aggressors'/ ('*al-mu'tadin*') (Al-Baqarah, 2:190; Al-Ma'idah, 5:87; Al-A'raf, 7:55)
4. 'The conceited and boastful' ('*al-mukhtal al-fakhur*'), or 'every swaggering braggart' ('*kulla mukhtalin fakhurin*') (Al-Nisa', 4:36; Luqman, 31:18; Al-Hadid, 57:23)
5. 'The treacherous ingrate' ('*al-khawwan al-athim*') (Al-Hajj, 22:38)
6. 'Every treacherous and sinful [person]' ('*kulla khawwanin kafur*') (Al-Nisa', 4:107)

---

[1] The Prophet Muhammad ﷺ said: '*I am God's beloved, and [I say so] without pride*'. Darimi, *Sunan*, Hadith no. 47; Tirmidhi, *Sunan*, Hadith no. 3616, *Kitab al-Manaqib*.

7. 'The treacherous' ('*al-kha'inin*') (*Al-Anfal*, 8:58)
8. 'The corrupters' ('*al-mufsidin*') (*Al-Ma'idah*, 5:64; *Al-Qasas*, 28:77)
9. 'The excessive' ('*al-musrifin*') (*Al-An'am*, 6:141; *Al-A'raf*, 7:31)
10. 'Those who exult' ('*al-farihin*') (*Al-Qasas*, 28:76)
11. 'The evildoers' ('*al-dhalimin*') (*Aal 'Imran*, 3:57; *Aal 'Imran*, 3:140; *Al-Shura*, 42:40), and
12. 'The arrogant' ('*al-mustakbirin*') (*Al-Nahl*, 16:23)

In addition to this, God does not love certain evil deeds such as the utterance of evil words (*Al-Nisa'*, 4:148) and corruption (*Al-Baqarah*, 2:205).

Nevertheless, God never states—not even once—in the whole Qur'an that He *hates* anyone or any type of evildoer. He only says that He 'does not love' them: not loving is neutral; hatred is negative. Moreover, He does not even say that He 'does not love' anyone personally or individually or as such: He merely says that He does not love them insofar as they are evildoers as such, or do evil things. Admittedly, He says that certain evil deeds are hateful to him[2], and that He is angry with, combats, punishes and even curses, certain evil doers, but that is still not the same as hatred because it can be done with mercy and love—as many a parent can attest! Indeed, a lesson can be inferred herein to hate the sin but not the sinners.

Moreover, in the Qur'an, God never once proscribes punishment for apostasy, but rather merely says that if people turn away from their religion, He will instead love others, and they will love Him: *O you who believe, whoever of you apostatises from his religion, God will assuredly bring a people whom He loves and who love Him* .... (*Al-Ma'idah*, 5:54)

From all this it follows that God's love is: *first, the free gift of existence and of countless other favours (including beauty of various kinds) to every created thing, and, second, love of beauty as such*. As an authentic *hadith* says: 'God is Beautiful, and He loves beauty'.[3]

(II): HUMAN LOVE

There are a number of important aspects to the question of human love, including: (a) the definition of human love; (b) human love for God (including the question of loving God *most ardently*); (c) love for the Messenger of God ﷺ and the sacred; (d) family love; (e) love of other human beings; (f) conjugal and sexual love; and (g) love and extra-marital sex.

---

2 God says: *If they had desired to go forth, they would have made some preparation for it, but God hated that they should be sent forth, So He slowed them down, and it was said: 'Stay back with those who stay back!'* (*Al-Tawbah*, 9:46) ❋ *And do not walk in the earth exultantly. Indeed you will not rend the earth, nor attain the mountains in height. / All of that—the evil of it is hateful in the sight of your Lord.* (*Al-Isra'*, 17:37-38; see also 17:22-36).
3 Muslim, *Sahih*, Hadith no. 99, *Kitab al-Iman*.

Executive Summary of Love in the Holy Qur'an

THE DEFINITION OF (HUMAN) LOVE

Human love can be defined simply as *'an inclination towards beauty after being pleased[4] by it.'* This definition can be constructed from two Qur'anic verses, wherein God says (referring to conjugal love): *... do not incline altogether away...* (Al-Nisa', 4:129) And: *... even though their beauty please you [aʿjabatkum] ...* (Al-Ahzab, 33:52)

Putting them together, we can thus deduce that love is an 'inclination towards beauty after being pleased by it'. There were various debates among Islamic classical scholars as to whether love can truly be defined and known through words or not, so we will just say that this definition does not pretend to convey the experience of love, merely how it is recognised and known, and how it works.

Love requires an object, and there are many objects of human love mentioned in the Qur'an. The superior kinds include (in descending order): love of God; love of the Messenger of God ﷺ and all that is sacred including paradise; conjugal and sexual love; family love; love of other human beings; love for all that is good and beautiful (from nature, to words and poetry, to the world in general).

There are also inferior kinds of love. These include (in descending order): love of material wealth; love of passions and lusts; love of ego, and love of evil actions, to the extent that these seem like they are good.

There is thus a complete metaphysical and cosmological hierarchy of love, depending on the hierarchy of beauty that is loved. The highest is Divine Beauty; then sacred beauty (starting with the beauty of the Messenger of God ﷺ); then inner beauty (which implies love of others); then outer beauty (physical beauty); then outer lusts (passions), and finally, inner lusts (ego and pride). This hierarchy means that not every love is praiseworthy, and not every beauty should be loved. God says: *.... Yet it may happen that you hate a thing which is good for you; and it may happen that you love a thing which is bad for you; God knows, and you know not.* (Al-Baqarah, 2:216)

B)(I) HUMAN LOVE FOR GOD

Whilst human love starts as an emotion—God says: *And long for your Lord (farghab)* (Al-Sharh, 94:8)—it must involve the soul being virtuous. God says to the Prophet ﷺ: *Say: 'If you love God, follow me, and God will love you more [yuhbibkum], and forgive you your sins; God is Forgiving, Merciful.'* (AalʿImran, 3:31)

Now following the Prophet ﷺ, means, first of all, being virtuous and doing good deeds—God says of the Prophet ﷺ: *And assuredly you possess a magnificent nature.* (Al-Qalam, 68:4)

---

4 The word 'pleased' is used for the Arabic *'iʿjab'* for want of a better term in English: *'iʿjab* means to wonder, to marvel, to be pleased, to be astonished, and to be amazed.

Then it means emulating the Prophet ﷺ in 'hoping for' the encounter with God and remembering Him as often as possible. God says: *Verily there is for you a beautiful example in the Messenger of God for whoever hopes for God and the Last Day, and remembers God often.* (Al-Ahzab, 33:21)

Only then does the believer's love of God become like that of the Prophet ﷺ, for whom every action and every thought was done out of love of God. God says: *Say: 'My prayer and my rituals, and my living, and my dying, are all for God, the Lord of the Worlds.'* (Al-An'am, 6:162)

Thus the essential point about love of God is that it is not a mere sentiment, but rather an inclination of the whole being of a person towards virtue, good deeds and the worship of God. God says: *Truly those who believe and perform righteous deeds—for them the Compassionate One shall ordain love.* (Maryam, 19:96)

B)(II) LOVING GOD *MOST ARDENTLY*

Love for God can become stronger and more ardent than any other love in the world, and can become an experience of intensity beyond what anyone who does not believe in God could possibly imagine, let alone experience. This is, of course, due to the Power and Beauty of the Divine Beloved. God says: *Yet there be people who take to themselves rivals besides God, loving them as God is loved; but those who believe love God most ardently ....* (Al-Baqarah, 2:165)

Thus though it is possible to love other things (such as in romantic love) to a degree that should be reserved for the love of God, believers can nevertheless experience a love for God 'more ardent' than any other love could ever be.

LOVE FOR THE MESSENGER OF GOD ﷺ AND THE SACRED

If one truly loves God, one cannot help but love what leads to God, or reminds one of God, as part of that love of God. This applies to the Qur'an; to Holy Places; to Paradise, and of course to the Prophets and Messengers of God, their families, and other blessed personages. The Prophet Muhammad ﷺ himself was '*full of pity; merciful*' (*raoufun rahim*; Al-Tawbah, 9:128) towards believers, and believers must return that love. God says: *The Prophet is closer to the believers than their [own] souls ...* (Al-Ahzab, 33:6)

FAMILY LOVE

God describes, defines and regulates family relations, family rights and family love in many verses of the Qur'an. All familial relations, rights and love are subject to a single general principle, namely '*affection for kinsfolk*' ('*al-mawadata fil qurba*') (Al-Shura, 42:23) for God says: '*those related by blood are nearer to one another, according to the Book of God*', (Al-Ahzab, 33:6; Al-Anfal, 8:75)

Thus the closer family members are to each other by blood, the stronger their love should be. However, God stresses that people's love for God must remain greater and stronger than all family love[5].

LOVE OF OTHER HUMAN BEINGS

The love one has for one's family should be extended to all human beings since all human beings are distantly related. God says: *O people, fear your Lord, Who created you of a single soul, and from it created its mate, and from the pair of them scattered many men and women; and fear God by whom you claim [your rights] from one another and kinship ties (arham)....* (Al-Nisa', 4:1)

Accordingly, God has bestowed upon each and every human being inalienable rights, and has obliged Muslims to have respect for all human beings; not to commit aggression against anyone; to be peaceful and to be just; to be merciful; to empathize with all human beings; to forgive them; to pardon them; to restrain themselves from anger; and even to repay evil deeds with kindness and 'turn the other cheek'—and to do this with all people, whoever they may be and regardless of their faith (or lack of it) all the time, as long as they are not first waging war against Muslims. God says: *And worship God, and associate nothing with Him. Be kind to parents, and near kindred, and to orphans, and to the needy, and to the neighbour who is near, and to the neighbour who is a stranger....* (Al-Nisa', 4:36)

F) CONJUGAL AND SEXUAL LOVE

Conjugal love obviously differs from other forms of inter-human love because it involves the body. The Qur'an is quite clear, and indeed, evocative about conjugal relations. God says (about spouses): *... they are a garment for you, and you are a garment for them....* (Al-Baqarah, 2:187)

Indeed, men need women, and women need men, and without each other they are generally incomplete. This mutual need can be clearly seen in three (distinct) things: in (a) the need men and women have for each other in order to procreate; in (b) the need men and women have for each other psychologically and emotionally during marriage; and in (c) conjugal and sexual love between spouses. God says: *And of His signs is that He created for you from your selves mates that you might take rest in them, and He ordained between you affection and mercy. Surely in that there are signs for a people who reflect.* (Al-Rum, 30:21)

However, this need is not just a generic need for any compatible spouse. A careful reading of the Qur'anic text reveals that every soul (the word '*nafs*'

---

[5] God says: *Say: 'If your fathers, and your sons, and your brothers, and your wives, and your clan, and the possessions which you have acquired, and merchandise for which you fear there may be no sale, and dwellings which you love, are dearer to you than God and His Messenger and struggling in His way, then wait until God brings about His command. And God does not guide the wicked folk'.* (Al-Tawbah, 9:24)

in Arabic means both 'self' and 'soul') has a particular spouse—a unique, individual 'soulmate'—which is exactly compatible with it either by a divine 'creation' ('*khalq*') before terrestrial life, or by a special divine 'making' ('*jaʿal*') ordained after birth. God says: ... *He has created (khalaqa) for you from your souls (anfusikum), mates* ... (*Al-Rum*, 30:21) *He has made (jaʿala) for you, from your souls (anfusikum), mates* ... (*Al-Shura*, 42:11)

Thus every soul has a particular spouse—a unique, individual 'soulmate'—which was created for it either by a divine 'creation' ('*khalq*') *a priori*, or by a special divine 'making' ('*jaʿal*') *a posteriori* (the former perhaps being more perfect).

Hence between some people, and between some spouses, there is a perfect relationship such that each person completes the other, as though they are a single person or a single soul. In such a case, we could call this 'a marriage of souls'. Other spouses, however, may enjoy peace, affection and mercy without their relationship being perfect and complete, even though they have been married for many years. Indeed, only some people are able to find their soulmates in this worldly life.

Howbeit, whatever love there is between a husband and a wife, it is a grievous thing for that love to be withheld or to be allowed to wither. God says: *How shall you take it, when each of you has gone in unto the other, and they have taken from you a solemn covenant?* (*Al-Nisa'*, 4:21)

Thus God holds the sexual act an irrevocable bond of sorts, and even when the act—or the marriage in which it occurs—has come to an end, this bond necessitates kindness and respect forever.

Finally, it should be said that there are clear indications in the Qur'an that sexual beauty, created, as it was by God, can lead to a profound spiritual experience if it is kept within a licit context. God says: *Your women are a tillage for you; so come to your tillage as you wish; and offer for your souls; and fear God; and know that you shall meet Him; and give good tidings to the believers.* (*Al-Baqarah*, 2:223)

We understand from this that in the 'annihilation' during the conjugal act there may be—for certain people at least—a spiritual experience or 'meeting', for God says: *and know that you shall meet Him* in the middle of a verse describing the conjugal act. Thus, every aspect of married life can be consonant with the spiritual life in Islam. Actually, this must be the case, since God says to the Prophet Muhammad ﷺ: *Say: 'My prayer and my rituals, and my living, and my dying, are all for God, the Lord of the Worlds. / No associate has He. And to this, I have been commanded, and I am the first of those who submit'.* (*Al-Anʿam*, 6:162–163)

Executive Summary of Love in the Holy Qur'an

LOVE AND EXTRA-MARITAL SEX

The Qur'an does not deny there can be real love in lust, or in any kind of worldly passion. God says: *Beautified for humankind is love of things they covet—of women, children, stored-up heaps of gold and silver, horses of mark, cattle, and tillage. That is the pleasure of the life of this world; but God—with Him is the most excellent abode.* (Aal 'Imran, 3:14)

Nevertheless, God forbids even approaching fornication, calling it not only 'an indecency' in itself—but more unusually—'an evil way'. God says: *And do not come [anywhere] near fornication. It is indeed an indecency and an evil way.* (Al-Isra', 17:32)

In other words, fornication drags the whole person into an integral movement *away* from the love of God. God says: *God has not placed two hearts inside any man,* (Al-Ahzab, 33:4)

Thus fornication excludes love of God, and as such it is not just a sin, but a potential reversal of the whole momentum of the spiritual life.

(III): LOVE

There are many different aspects to love. These include: (a) the different kinds of love; (b) the stages of love; (c) falling in love; (d) love and happiness; and (e) love and death.

THE DIFFERENT KINDS OF LOVE

In the Qur'an, God mentions at least thirty-eight different kinds of '*hubb*': 'love' or 'liking'—the word '*hubb*' means both things indicating that the difference between them is essentially a question of intensity.

Each of the thirty-eight different kinds of love linguistically defined (according to the lexicons and etymology of Classical Arabic) as forms of love, differs subtly in meaning from each of the others so that there is no tautology in Arabic, but in English translation, we often are forced to resort to reusing the same word for different Arabic terms for *hubb*. These include[6] such forms of love as: love (*mahabba*); preference (*istihbab*); love (*wudd*); affection (*mawaddah*); love

---

6 These are: 1. love (*hubb*); 2. love (*mahabba*); 3. preference (*istihbab*); 4. mercy (*rahmah*); 5. pity (*ra'fah*); 6. love (*wudd*); 7. affection (*mawaddah*); 8. love (*widad*); 9. will / desire (*iradah*); 10. to be smitten (*shaghaf*); 11. impulse (*hawa*); 12. infatuation (*istihwa'*); 13. to stray in love (*ghawa*); 14. desire (*hamm*); 15. longing (*raghab*); 16. to draw near (*taqarrub*); 17. anguish (*gharam*); 18. to wander distracted (*huyam*); 19. close friendship (*khullah*); 20. friendship (*sadaqah*); 21. companionship (*suhbah*); 22. preference to another over oneself (*ithar*); 23. going astray (*dalal*); 24. contentment (*rida*); 25. compassion (*hanan*); 26. admiration (*i'jab*); 27. inclination (*mayl*); 28. lust (*shahwah*); 29. tendency towards (*saba*); 30. seeking (*ibtigha*); 31. favour (*tafdil*); 32. extra-marital sex (*zina*); 33. graciousness (*hafawah*); 34. concern (*shafaqah*); 35. protecting friendship (*wilayah*); 36. inclination (*sagha*); 37. intimate friendship/'penetrating' friendship (*walijah*) and familiar love (*ulfah*).

(*widad*); being smitten (*shaghaf*); impulse (*hawa*); infatuation (*istihwa'*) and so on. There are thus in the Qur'an many subtly different ways to experience love, in accordance with the different kinds of souls that lovers have.

THE STAGES OF LOVE

On the other hand, all human beings experience the same stages of love as such. There are at least one hundred[7] of these in the Qur'an. These include stages like:

---

[7] These can be divided into stages that occur in love for God *and* love for human beings; stages that occur in love for God (and may or may not occur in love for human beings); and stages that occur in human beings' love for each other (and may or may not occur in love for God).

(I) The stages of love that occur in both human beings' love for God and human beings' love for each other are: 1. Emptiness (*al-Faragh*); 2. Neediness (*al-Faqr*); 3. Adornment (*al-Tazayyun*); 4. Admiration (*al-I'jab*); 5. Love (*al-Hubb*) and Intense Love (*al-Ihbab*); 6. Contentment (*al-Rida*); 7. Drawing Near (*al-Taqarrub*); 8. Will or Desire (*al-Iradah*); 9. Seeking (*al-Ibtigha'*); 10. Longing (*al-Raghab*); 11. Protecting Friendship (*al-Wilayah*); 12. Close Friendship (*al-Khullah*); 13. Joy (*al-Farah*); 14. Tranquillity (*al-Sakan*); 15. Hope or Expectancy (*al-Raja'*) 16. Action (*al-'Amal*) 17. Remembrance (*al-Dhikr*); 18. Communion (*al-Najwa*); 19. Trial (*al-Ibtila'*); 20. Serenity (*al-Itmi'nan*); 21. Knowledge (*al-'Ilm*); 22. Recognition (*al-Ma'rifah*); 23. Will or Wish (*al-Mashi'ah*); 24. Fear (*al-Khawf*); 25. Grief (*al-Huzn*); 26. Suffering (*al-Alam*); 27. Weeping (*al-Buka'*); 28. Change (*al-Taghyir*); 29. Contraction (*al-Qabd*); 30. Expansion (*al-Bast*); 31. Need for Seclusion (*al-Hajah ila al-Khalwah*); 32. Patience (*al-Sabr*); 33. Hope (*al-Amal*); 34. Jealousy (*al-Ghirah*); 35. Meeting (*al-Liqa'*); 36. Company (*al-Ma'iyyah*); 37. Comfort of the Eye (*Qurrat al-'Ayn*).

(II) The stages of love that occur in human beings' love for God (and may or may not apply to human love for other human beings. are: 38. Love (*al-Wudd*); 39. Concern (*al-Shafaqah*); 40. Comfortable Familiarity (*al-Uns, al-Isti'nas*); 41. Peace (*al-Salam*); 42. Sufficiency (*al-Iktifa'*); 43. Gratitude or Thankfulness (*al-Shukr*); 44. Trust (*al-Tawakkul*); 45. 'Expansion of the Breast' (*Inshirah al-Sadr*); 46. 'Softening of Skin' (*Layn al-Jild*); 47. 'Softening of the Heart' (*Layn al-Qalb*); 48. 'Quivering of the Skin' (*Qash'arirat al-Jild*); 49. 'Trembling of the Heart' (*Wajl al-Qalb*); 50. Devotion (al-Tabattul); 51. Humble Obedience (*al-Ikhbat*); 52. Turning in Penitence (*al-Inabah*); 53. Humility (*al-Tadarru'*); 54. Repentance (*al-Tawbah*); 55. Asking Forgiveness (*al-Istighfar*); 56. 'Hastening to Please' (*al-'Ajal lil-Tardiyah*); 57. Calling upon or Supplication (*al-Du'a'*); 58. Remembrance (*al-Tadhakkur*); 59. Following (*al-Ittiba'*); 60. 'Proving what is in the Heart' (*Tamhis al-Qalb*); 61. Uncertainty (*al-Shakk*); 62. Doubt (*al-Rayb*); 63. Entertaining Thoughts (*al-Zhann*); 64. Looking (*al-Nazhar*); 65. Contemplation (*al-Tafakkur*); 66. Meditation (*al-Tadabbur*); 67. 'Using Reason' / ratiocination (*Isti'mal al-'Aql*); 68. Perception (*al-Tabassur*); 69. Certainty (*al-Yaqin*) which include: Certain Knowledge ('*Ilm al-Yaqin*); Certain Vision ('*Ayn al-Yaqin*); Certain Truth (*Haqq al-Yaqin*); 70. Ardent Hope (*al-Tama'*); 71. Need for Human Company (*al-Hajah ila al-Jalwah*); 72. Imploring or Tender-heartedness (*al-Ta'awwuh*); 73. Penitence (*al-Awb*); 74. Devoutness (*al-Qunut*); 75. Being Overwhelmed (*al-Qahr*); 76. Submission (*al-Islam*); 77. Faith (*al-Iman*); 78. Virtue (*al-Ihsan*); 79. Sincerity (*al-Ikhlas*).

(III) The stages of love that occur in human beings' love for each other (and may or may not apply to human love for God) are: (80. Love (*al-Mahabbah*); 81. 'The Presence of (physical) Beauty' (*Wujud al-Jamal*); 82. Mutual Knowledge (*al-Ta'aruf*); 83. Inclination (*al-Mayl*); 84. Affection (*al-Mawaddah*); 85. Pity (*al-Ra'fah*); 86. Lust (*al-Shahwah*); 87. Impulse (*al-Hawa*); 88. Desire (*al-Hamm*); 89. Pleasure (*al-Mut'ah*); 90. Enjoyment (*al-Istimta'*); 91. Generosity emptiness (*faragh*); neediness (*faqr*); adornment (*tazayyun*); admiration (*i'jab*); will or desire (*iradah*); joy (*farah*); hope or expectancy (*raja'*); action (*'amal*); remembrance (*dhikr*); communion (*najwa*); trial (*ibtila'*); knowledge (*'ilm*); recognition (*ma'rifah*); fear (*khawf*); grief (*huzn*); and suffering (*alam*), and so on.

C) FALLING IN LOVE

In order to understand what falling in love is, it is first necessary to understand what all the stages of love have in common. And in order to understand this, it is first necessary to understand what a human being is and consists of.

The Qur'an, in fact, identifies all the different constituent parts and faculties of human beings. These include a body; a soul as such (*nafs*); a 'soul that incites to evil' (i.e. an ego); a 'self-reproaching soul' (i.e. a conscience); a 'soul at peace'; an intelligence; a faculty of learning and imitation; a faculty of speech; a will; sentiment; a memory; an imagination; intuition; feeling; sense; insight; a breast (*sadr*); a (subtle) heart (*qalb*); an inner (subtle) heart (*fuad*); a (subtle) heart's core (*lubb*); and a spirit (*ruh*). We will not here explain all of these and the differences between them, but broadly speaking we may say that human beings have three basic dimensions with nexuses between them: (i) a body which is physical and material, and has senses; (ii) a soul which is subtle but personal, and has faculties such as the will, intelligence and sentiment, and modes such as a 'soul that incites evil'; a 'self-reproaching soul', and a 'soul at peace', and (iii) the spirit, which is supra-personal, but comprises degrees 'reaching down' to the 'subtle heart'. The soul is the personal inner witness of the body, and the spirit is the supra-individual inner witness of the soul and body taken together.

Upon examination, it transpires that every single stage of love is connected to one of the constituent parts or faculties of human beings. For example, the stage of 'enjoyment' is connected to the body; the stage of 'emptiness' to the soul; the stages of 'ratiocination' and 'recognition' to the intelligence; 'communion' to the faculty of speech; 'remembrance' to the memory; 'action' to the will and so on. In fact, all of the stages of love—and indeed the growth of love as such—are nothing other than the process of inclination and attachment of the various human faculties and constituents parts towards a beloved. Thus falling in love as such can be defined as '*the systematic inclination of a person's constituent parts and faculties towards beauty, after having been pleased by it*'. We have already cited, God says: *Truly those who believe and perform righteous deeds—for them the Compassionate One shall ordain love.* (Maryam, 19:96)

From this verse, we do not necessarily understand that a supernatural grace

---

(al-Karam); 92. Mercy (al-Rahmah); 93. Tenderness (al-Lutf); 94. Forgiveness (al-Maghfirah, al-Ghufran); 95. Pardoning (al-'Afu); 96. Overlooking (al-Safh); 97. Kindness (al-Ma'ruf); 98. Seduction (al-Murawadah); 99. Shyness (al-Istihya'); 100. Obliviousness to Oneself ('Adam al-Ihsas bil-Hal).

is granted after the requisite amount of righteous deeds and faith is achieved (although this can surely happen), but rather, that belief in God (and hence the intelligence exercised, as it were, 'towards' God) and righteous deeds (and hence the will exercised, as it were, 'towards' God) naturally lead to an increase in sentiment 'towards' God. Thus the involvement of other faculties increases love.

To give an illustration: popular books about how to increase memory are all essentially the same thing: in order to remember things more or better or with greater ease, they advise people to do things like: use rational constructs about the information they want to remember; become emotional about it; contemplate how important it is to remember it; mention it a lot; imagine a story from the information, and eat or drink whilst studying, and then eat or drink the same thing before the exam. In other words, memory naturally grows when reason, sentiment, the will, the faculty of speech, imagination and / or the physical senses are harnessed to its cause. So, too, with love: it naturally grows when the other faculties are harnessed to its cause. Conversely, it is halted by not allowing any of the other faculties to incline towards a given object. This is how love works, and it is remarkable how few people—including philosophers, psychologists and scientists—understand this, although it can be clearly observed every day in every soul in the world.

D) LOVE AND HAPPINESS

The Qur'an shows that there cannot be joy (*farah*), contentment (*rida*), peace (*salam*) or pleasure (*mutʿa*) without love, in one way or another, because joy, contentment, peace and pleasure are all *kinds* of love and / or *stages* of love. Indeed, how can one find joy, pleasure, peace and contentment in something without loving it?

Moreover, there cannot be true happiness without love of God specifically, and only love of God. The word 'happiness' only occurs twice in the whole of the Holy Qur'an (in *Surat Hud*), both times referring to Paradise. This implies that worldly love is not sufficient to lead to happiness, because it does not fill one completely, perfectly and eternally, and that nothing can completely suffice to make human beings happy except the love of God. God says: *Say: 'In the bounty of God, and in His mercy in that let them rejoice: it is better than what they hoard'.* (*Yunus*, 10:58)

E) LOVE AND DEATH

As the soul's faculties incline, one by one, towards a beloved, it naturally becomes gradually less attached to its own ego, until the point where the lover no longer cares or even thinks about him (or her) self, and cares instead only for his or her beloved. If this goes on, the ego will die in itself, 'in' the beloved, and for the sake of the beloved. To be clear: the end of love is death. Love eventually leads to the death of (a part of) the lover. 'Amore' leads to 'mort'—this etymological connection exists in most languages: in Arabic we have 'sakra' which means 'drunkenness' and 'death'; and 'ishq, which means 'passionate love' and derives its name from a desert convolvulus (i.e. a bindweed) that grows around other plants until it becomes one with its object of love. How this 'death' turns out depends upon what the beloved is. We already cited part of God's words:

> Yet there be people who take to themselves rivals besides God, loving them as God is loved; but those who believe love God most ardently; If those who did evil could but see, as they shall when they behold the chastisement, that power altogether belongs to God, and that God is terrible in chastisement. (Al-Baqarah, 2:165)

God's 'terrible chastisement' at the end of this verse refers back to the ardent love of those who love—to the extent of worshiping—something other than God (and unbridled romantic love is included here). This is quite simply because such souls can never fully be one with their beloveds whilst ignoring the love of God, simply because both they, and their beloveds, will inevitably change, separate and die. Herein lies the whole drama of all the lovers—all the Romeos and Juliets—in history who have committed suicide; they commit suicide because they have ceased to live in themselves and then are deprived of their beloveds: the pain and 'terrible chastisement' is too great for them to bear, so that they can no longer live. For many people, this kind of love is instinctively beautiful because it is in fact the only time in their lives they see people transcend their own egos and pettiness out of love, but unless this love is reintegrated into love of God, it remains a beautiful but futile mirage, and not eternal bliss.

By contrast, those whose egos die out of love of God, enter into the Paradise of God's love. God says: *O soul at peace! / Return to your Lord, pleased, pleasing. / Then enter among My servants! / And enter My Paradise!* (Al-Fajr, 89:27–30)

Thus the death of the ego or the 'soul which incites evil', out of love for God is the ultimate aim of the spiritual life. God says: *Go forth, light and heavy! Struggle in the way of God with your possessions and your lives: that is better for you, if only you knew.* (Al-Tawbah, 9:41)[8]

(IV): BEAUTY

There are many aspects to the question of beauty, including: (a) the nature of beauty, (b) taste, (c) the power of beauty, and (d) love and beauty in Paradise.

---

[8] The 'possessions' and 'lives' in this verse can also be understood to be referring to people's passions and egos respectively, because the Qur'an itself establishes that there is 'mirror-imaging' between the outer and the inner worlds of human beings (see: *Fussilat* 41:53, and *Al-Dhariyat*, 51:20–21).

THE NATURE OF BEAUTY

God says that it is He ... *Who beautified everything that He created....* (*Al-Sajdah*, 32:7)

This means that every natural thing objectively possesses some kind of beauty, even if it is only in its possessing the quality of life or of being, although obviously, some things are more beautiful than others.

But what is beauty? And what is it comprised of?

Beauty is a 'quality'. The qualities of created things come ultimately from the Creator's Qualities or Names, albeit in a distant and refracted way. God's Most Beautiful Names (*Al-Asma Al-Husna*) can be thought of as either Names of the Essence, Qualities of Majesty and Rigour, and Qualities of Munificence and Gentleness. The final verse of *Surat Al-Rahman*, called 'the Bride of the Qur'an' by the Prophet ﷺ, is: *'Blessed be the Name of your Lord, He of Majesty and Munificence (Dhul Jalal wal-Ikram)'* (*Al-Rahman*, 55:78).

From this Divine Name, which summarizes God's Most Beautiful Names (and therefore also the very roots of beauty), we understand that the components of beauty are: majesty, munificence and the harmony between them all these together constituting the perfection of beauty.

TASTE

If beauty is objective, how can different people disagree about what they find beautiful? The answer is that different people have slightly different souls and therefore also different spiritual states so that they are bound to look at one and the same object slightly differently. In other words, beauty is objective, but most people are inevitably slightly subjective, and therefore taste is subjective. Thus strictly speaking it is not beauty but taste that is in the eye of the beholder. God says: *Say: 'Everyone acts according to his [own] character, and your Lord knows best who is better guided as to the way'.* (*Al-Isra'*, 17:84)

THE POWER OF BEAUTY

Beauty has a tremendous power. Dazzling beauty can distract those who see it from everything around them; from their own senses; from their own selves; even from pain, and ultimately even from death. God says (referring to Potiphar's wife, the Egyptian townswomen and Joseph ﷺ):

> *And when she heard of their machinations, she sent for them and prepared for them a banquet. She then gave each one of them a knife and said: 'Come out before them!' And when they saw him, they were in awe of him and cut their hands, and they exclaimed: 'God preserve us! This is no human being: this is but a noble angel!'* (*Yusuf*, 12:31)

The townswomen were so attracted and captivated by the mere sight of Joseph ﷺ, that they cut their hands without even feeling it. Thus beauty can dazzle those who see it, and interrupt their actions (hands symbolize action), and it can distract them from everything else so that they no longer feel even pain; such is the power of beauty.

This power can work in two diametrically opposed ways: it can draw its beholder 'outwards', as it were, to seek to possess an exterior object, even by means of force and violence, or it can bring its beholder back to his or her true inner self, away from the world and away from lust, and in the process even transform the outward world itself into a reminder and 'spiritual proof' of God. We see these two ways in Potiphar's wife and Joseph ﷺ themselves. God says: *And she certainly desired him, and he would have desired her [too], had it not been that he saw the proof (burhan) of his Lord. So it was that We might ward off from him evil and lewdness. Truly he was of Our devoted servants.* (*Yusuf*, 12:24)

Thus Joseph's ﷺ beauty affected Potiphar's wife to such an extent that it made her desperately want to commit adultery with him, and even to force him to do so. For Joseph ﷺ, however, the beauty of Potiphar's wife was completely interiorized by him such that it became itself a '*proof of his Lord*' that '*warded off*' '*lewdness*'. In other words, beauty—even physical beauty—is a two-edged sword: it can exteriorise or interiorise; it can disperse or gather the soul; it can give lust or peace; and it can be carnal or spiritual. This explains why it is so precious—and why, by the way, Islam insists on guarding beauty through modesty in dress.

LOVE, BEAUTY AND BEATITUDE IN PARADISE

Paradise contains all that its inhabitants love, and all those whom they love—without any privation or limitation, but the physical aspects of these delights are exaggerated by non-Muslims. The Qur'an does not shy away—as we have seen—from describing conjugal love-making in this life, but love-making is never once mentioned as occurring as such in Paradise. Neither is sleeping, lying down or 'reclining'—as some translators have suggested for '*mutaki'in*', which actually means 'firmly seated' (on couches)—and eating and drinking are never followed by expressions of physical enjoyment, but rather by expressions of gratitude, wonder and praise for God. In short, beauty and love in Paradise are blissful but spiritual, peaceful, contemplative and free of the imperfection, need, suffering and contraction that love in this world entails. God says: *They will not hear therein any vain talk or any sinful words, / but only the saying, 'Peace!' 'Peace!'* (*Al-Waqi'ah*, 56:25–26)

Moreover, obviously the greatest felicities of Paradise are the vision of God—in His Infinite Beauty and Glory—and His Beatitude which is, as it were, a special mode of 'being with' God. God says:

Some faces on that day will be radiant, / looking upon their Lord. (*Al-Qiyamah*, 75:22–23) ● *God has promised the believers, both men and women,*

Gardens underneath which rivers flow, to abide therein, and blessed dwellings in the Gardens of Eden, and beatitude (ridwan) from God is greater. That is the supreme triumph. (Al-Tawbah, 9:72)

The Arabic word for 'beatitude' ('*ridwan*'), comes from '*rida*', meaning 'contentment'—and thus implying love—but it is greater than mere 'contentment', it is felicity by being with He who Himself has Absolute, Infinite and Perfect Love, Beauty, Happiness and Peace, for all eternity, with no end. God says: *'Peace!'—a word from a Lord [Who is] Merciful.* (Ya Sin, 36:58)

CONCLUSION

In conclusion, God is the Compassionate (*Al-Rahman*), the Merciful (*Al-Rahim*), and the Loving (*Al-Wadud*). He created the world and human beings *through love* and *for love*. Thus through love, human beings can return to God in the most beautiful and easiest way. God says: *So flee unto God (fafiru illa Allah)....* (Al-Dhariyat, 51:50)

INTRODUCTORY CHAPTERS

CHAPTER ONE

PROLOGUE: THE GOALS AND METHODOLOGY OF THIS WORK

THE GOALS OF THIS WORK

We will attempt to achieve five goals in this work, God willing.

FIRST GOAL

The Holy Qur'an comes from God and all that it says is true, as God Almighty says: *The truth comes from your Lord; then be not among the doubters.* (Al-Baqarah, 2:147)[1] *And say, 'The truth comes from your Lord…* (Al-Kahf, 18:29)

It is not only true, it is the Truth, for He who revealed the Qur'an revealed it with the Truth: *That is because God has revealed the Book with the truth; and those that are at variance regarding the Book are in schism, far removed.* (Al-Baqarah, 2:176) ❊ *With the truth have We revealed it, and with the truth has it been revealed.* (Al-Isra', 17:105) And since it is the Truth, it is must be the entire truth. God says:

> *And verily We have dispensed for people in this Qur'an every [kind of] similitude, but most people insist on disbelieving.* (Al-Isra', 17:89) ❊ *And verily We have dispensed for humankind in this Qur'an [an example] of every kind of similitude. But man is most disputatious.* (Al-Kahf, 18:54) ❊ *And verily We have struck for humankind in this Qur'an every [kind of] similitude. And if you were to bring them a [miraculous] sign, those who disbelieve will certainly say, 'You are nothing but followers of falsehood'.* (Al-Rum, 30:58) ❊ *And verily We have struck for humankind in this Qur'an every [kind of] similitude, that perhaps they may remember / an Arabic Qur'an without any deviation that perhaps they may guard themselves.* (Al-Zumar, 39:27–28) ❊ *And the day [when] We shall raise up from every community a witness against them from among themselves, and We shall bring you as a witness against these. And We have revealed to you the Book as a clarification of all things and as a guidance, and a mercy and good tidings to those who submit.* (Al-Nahl, 16:89) ❊ *And this Qur'an is not such as could ever be produced [by anyone] besides God; but it is a confirmation of what is before it, and a detailing of the Book, wherein is no doubt from the Lord of the Worlds.* (Yunus, 10:37) ❊ *And indeed We have brought them a Book, which We have detailed with knowledge, a guidance and a mercy for a people who believe.* (Al-A'raf, 7:52) ❊ *Verily*

> there is in their stories a lesson for people of cores. It is not a fabricated discourse but a confirmation of what was [revealed] before it, and the details for all things, and a guidance, and a mercy for a folk who believe. (Yusuf, 12:111) ❊ And We made the night and the day two signs. Then We effaced the sign of the night and made the sign of the day sight-giving that you may seek bounty from your Lord, and that you may know the number of years and the reckoning, and everything We have detailed very distinctly. (Al-Isra', 17:12) ❊ There is no animal on the earth and no bird that flies with its wings, but they are communities like to you. We have neglected nothing in the Book; then to their Lord they shall be gathered. (Al-An'am, 6:38)

Thus God makes it clear that the Holy Qur'an is the entire truth; and indeed it is more than that, for God says that He has *dispensed* and *struck* in it *every [kind of] similitude*. Moreover, God says that the Holy Qur'an is: *a clarification of all things*; and that it contains *the details for all things*. Finally God says: *We have neglected nothing in the Book*.

The classical scholars of Islam have differed as to the interpretation of these verses. From the words *the details for all things*, Tabari understands the following: 'It is a detailing of all the clarification humankind could need of God's commandments and prohibitions; what is lawful and what is unlawful, and His obedience and disobedience'.[2]

On the other hand, al-Razi (in his Great Commentary *Al-Tafsir al-Kabir*) understands '*a clarification of all things*' to refer only to 'all the fundamentals of religious knowledge': 'Some say that [what is meant by] the Qur'an being a *clarification of all things* is that all knowledge is either religious or non-religious; as for the non-religious forms of knowledge, this verse is not concerned with them, because it is plain that God would only praise the Qur'an for encompassing all religious knowledge; and as for non-religious knowledge, it is irrelevant. Now religious knowledge consists of roots and branches; the roots are found in their entirety in the Qur'an. As for the branches, [some say] that there is no law unless its basis has been detailed in this Qur'an. This would mean that God has issued no responsibilities to man save those found in this Qur'an. But if this were indeed the case, then all analogy would be prohibited, and the Qur'an would be enough to fully explain all laws. [Thus] the jurists say that the Qur'an is a *clarification of all things* in that it indicates that consensus, individual reports and analogy are all valid sources of law, such that when someone rules by any of these principles, his ruling may be supported by the Qur'an'.[3]

However, al-Zamakhshari (in *Al-Kashshaf*) understands God's words *a clarification of all things* to mean 'all forms of religious knowledge', saying: 'This means that it clarifies all religious matters, explicitly in some cases and by

Prologue: The Goals and Methodology of this Work

referring them to the *Sunnah* in others, commanding us to follow and obey the Messenger of God ﷺ.[4]

We ourselves believe, however—and hope to demonstrate over the course of this work—that God's Book contains not only all forms of religious knowledge but all the principles of the sciences of philosophy[5] as well[6]. This is one of the wondrous and miraculous features of the Holy Qur'an. Moreover, just as the Holy Qur'an contains linguistic and rhetorical miracles—and perhaps scientific miracles as well—it also contains philosophical miracles (that is to say, it miraculously contains all the answers to the great questions of philosophy). This perhaps explains the Qur'an's challenges as regards its own uniqueness and inimitability:

> *Or do they say, 'He has improvised it?' Rather they do not believe. Then let them bring a discourse like it, if they are truthful.* (Al-Tur, 52:33–34) ❈ *Say: 'Verily, should mankind and jinn come together to produce the like of this Qur'an, they could not produce the like thereof, even if they backed one another'.* (Al-Isra', 17:88) ❈ *Or do they say, 'He has invented it?' Say: 'Then bring ten surahs the like thereof, invented, and call upon whom you can beside God if you are truthful'. / Then, if they do not answer you, know that it has been revealed only in God's knowledge, and that there is no god save Him. Will you then submit?* (Hud, 11:13–14) ❈ *And if you are in doubt concerning what We have revealed to Our servant, then bring a surah like it; and call your witnesses besides God if you are truthful. / And if you do not, and you will not, then fear the Fire, whose fuel is men, and stones, prepared for disbelievers.* (Al-Baqarah, 2:23–24) ❈ *And most of them follow nothing but conjecture; truly conjecture avails nothing against truth. Surely God is Knower of what they do. / And this Qur'an is not such as could ever be produced [by anyone] besides God; but it is a confirmation of what is before it, and a detailing of the Book, wherein is no doubt from the Lord of the Worlds. / Or do they say, 'He has invented it?' Say: 'Then bring a surah like it; and call upon whom you can besides God if you are truthful'. / Nay, but they denied that, the knowledge whereof they did not comprehend; and whereof the interpretation has not yet come to them, as those who were before them denied. Behold then what was the consequence for the evildoers!* (Yunus, 10:36–39)

Hence our first goal in this work is to show that everything that can be said in truth about love is contained in the Holy Qur'an, in detail and not only in a general way. We will therefore limit ourselves in this work to the subject of love in the Qur'an alone, and not love according to the *Hadith* (sayings of the Messenger of God ﷺ), the *Sunnah* (the example of the Messenger of God ﷺ), or the wisdom of Islamic scholars, philosophers, and mystics.

SECOND GOAL

Our second goal is to summarise all that has been said before by others about love in the Holy Qur'an in a single volume. We also hope to add—God willing, and in so far as we are able—some of the secrets of love; secrets that have been known in the past but have not been collected, as far as we know, in a single source, focusing on the topic of love in the Holy Qur'an. It is worth mentioning that in the past when certain Islamic philosophers discussed love, they did not cite even a single verse of the Qur'an. These include—regrettably—Ibn Sina (Avicenna) in his *Treatise on Love*. Other Muslim scholars, such as Abu Hamid Al-Ghazali in his *Ihya 'ulum al-din* (in Chapter 36 on 'Love, Desire, Familiarity and Pleasure'), Muhyi al-Din ibn Arabi (in his *Al-Futuhat al-makkiyyah*, section 178, 'Epistle on Love'), and Ibn Hazm (in *Tawq al-hamamah*), frequently cited the Qur'an and *Hadith* together or sometimes the Qur'an alone or sometimes the *Hadith* alone in the same work. However, our intention here God willing is to give a complete explanation of love using the Qur'an as our only reference and systematically making it the foundation and logical proof of every single point we make. That is not to say, however, that we do not cite *Hadith* herein— we do frequently—but when we do so, we do it only to further strengthen and clarify the points we make.

THIRD GOAL

Our third goal is to give a full and adequate explanation of love and its secrets from the Holy Qur'an alone, although we cannot hope—nor could anyone—to say all that can be said about this subject. Indeed, how could God's words ever be exhausted, when He says:

> Say: 'If the sea were ink for the Words of my Lord, the sea would be spent before the Words of my Lord were spent even though We brought the like of it as replenishment'. (Al-Kahf, 18:109)   And if all the trees on earth were pens, and the sea replenished with seven more seas, the Words of God would not be spent. Truly God is Mighty, Wise. (Luqman, 31:27)

FOURTH GOAL

The fourth goal of this work is to impart to the reader some of the hitherto unexamined mysteries, secrets and wonders of love. Indeed, love may well be the greatest secret in the modern world, especially since most people's acts and hopes are motivated by love and / or the desire for happiness. Moreover, happiness itself is born out of love—as God willing we will see—but since most people do not understand love, they do not know anything about what they are really doing. However, someone who understands love has the ability to cultivate a particular love, or bring it to an end. Therefore, God willing, this work could potentially be of great benefit to people by helping them to love what is good and avoid the love of vain passions. We have endeavoured to spread this subject over short, independent chapters, so that perhaps these chapters might be used as teaching resources in universities or elsewhere; and ...*my success is only with God. In Him I trust and to Him I turn.* (*Hud*, 11:88)

FIFTH GOAL

Many non-Muslims have a common misperception about the subject of love in Islam and the Holy Qur'an: many non-Muslims—from respected intellectuals and thinkers to ordinary people—imagine that there is no mention or attention given to love in the Holy Qur'an. They believe that if Islam has any concern for love it is only because of the Sufis, or perhaps certain *Hadith*s (whose authenticity they in any case doubt), and not the Holy Qur'an itself. The fifth goal of this work, therefore, is to show that, contrary to non-Muslim misperceptions, not only does the Holy Qur'an treat of love repeatedly and extensively, but also all that one may know or understand about love is explained in the Book of God—the Holy Qur'an.

THE METHODOLOGY OF THIS WORK

The methodology of this work is systematic logic based on two major principles of Qur'anic exegesis. The first major principle is that: 'the Qur'an explains itself', and the second major principle is that: 'there is no self-contradiction in the Qur'an'. Concerning the first principle, Suyuti says in *Al-Durr al-manthur*: 'Ibn Abi Hatim reported that Ibn 'Abbas ﷺ said (with reference to God's words *in coupled phrases* [*Al-Zumar*, 39:23]): "The different parts of the Qur'an resemble one another, and refer to one another." And Jarir and Ibn al-Mundhir reported that Sa'id ibn Jubayr said (with reference to God's word *consimilar* [*Al-Zumar*, 39:23]): "One part of it explains the other, and indicates the other".7

The second principle—namely, that 'there is no contradiction in the Qur'an'—is derived from God's own words:

> *What, do they not meditate [upon] the Qur'an? If it had been from other than God, surely they would have found therein much inconsistency.* (*Al-Nisa'*, 4:82) ❋ *[This is] a Book whose verses have been set clear, and then detailed from One [Who is] Wise, Informed.* (*Hud*, 11:1) ❋ *Praise belongs to God [alone], Who has revealed to His servant the Book, and has not placed it in any deviation,* (*Al-Kahf*, 18:1) ❋ *An Arabic Qur'an without any deviation that perhaps they may guard themselves.* (*Al-Zumar*, 39:28)

A NOTE TO THE READER ABOUT THE ENGLISH TRANSLATION

Throughout this book—with the exception perhaps of this paragraph—we deliberately rigorously maintain an impersonal and anonymous narrative voice.

This of course is absolutely appropriate when discussing the Holy Qur'an. In the original Arabic, the incomparable beauty and mystery of the Arabic Qur'an itself—not to mention the Holy Qur'an's own explicit injunctions which every reader of the Qur'an in Arabic will know—forces the reader into 'meditation' (*tadabbur*—4:82; 23:68; 38:29; 47:24; see also 50:37) of the Holy Qur'an; 'contemplation' (*tafakkur fi*—16:43–44; 59:21; 13:3; 3:190–192) upon God's signs [*ayat*] in the Holy Qur'an (as well as in His other great work, creation), and consideration (*nazhar*—30:50; 50:6; 88:17–21 et al) of the nature of all things as described in the Holy Qur'an. In translation, however, the reader runs the risk of understanding this book merely as a harmonious philosophical theory about an important natural process, like, for example, photosynthesis. This may be valuable in itself, but it is not sufficient to fully comprehend love. Love—human love at any rate—is not mere photosynthesis. Therefore, we humbly suggest to the reader that during the course of reading this book, he or she periodically put it down and carefully consider its theories and conclusions, and then meditate upon his or her own experiences to see if and how they relate and bear out what we assert. Without such an introspective reflective process, the reader may attain herein only a theoretical understanding of love; that is obviously not the sole point of this book.

A NOTE ON THE TENTH EDITION, 1439 AH, 2018 CE

This expanded 'tenth edition' of *Love in the Holy Qur'an* contains a number of changes to the previous English (sixth and seventh) editions including: (1) a number of corrections and clarifications were made to the text and in particular to the translations, references and endnotes; (2) a number of Qur'anic verses were added in various passages for the sake of completeness; (3) some important issues were expounded upon largely as a result of some of the discussions that ensued from my lectures on the book in various universities over the last two years, such as the meaning of '*shayy*' ('thing') in Arabic (Chapter 1, endnotes); the difference between love (*hubb*) and mercy (*rahmah*) (Chapter 4); the references to God's Face and His Self in the Qur'an (Chapter 4, endnotes); the question of loving one's enemies (Chapter 11, endnotes); the microcosmic-macrocosmic mirrorplay (Chapter 12, endnotes); the different interpretations of the crucial Qur'anic words '*ala hubbihi*' (which literally mean 'on its love') in verse 2:177 (Chapter 12, endnotes); jealousy (Chapter 22), and the human faculties (Chapter 23); (4) '*ulfah*' ('affinity') has been added as a kind of love mentioned in the Qur'an—it had been there in my original notes but somehow was omitted along the way (making thirty-eight in total—see Chapter 21); (5) a proper subject index was made and added to the end of the book; (6) some of the chapters were given subtitles, in order to make their subjects easier to understand; (7) an entirely new section was added to the end of the chapter on conjugal love (Chapter 18); and (8) most importantly—an executive summary based strictly on the book was added at the beginning.

—Ghazi bin Muhammad, 2018

CHAPTER TWO

INTRODUCTION: THE SECRET OF LOVE

God says: *Beautified for humankind is love of lusts—of women, children, stored-up heaps of gold and silver, horses of mark, cattle, and tillage. That is the comfort of the life of this world; but God—with Him is the most excellent abode.* (Aal 'Imran, 3:14)

Most of human beings' basic concerns are indicated in this Qur'anic verse, for most people either spend their lives in search of sex, family, children, prestige and glory, wealth and possessions, or else in search of God's love and the Hereafter. Most modern music and film is concerned with sexual love; most people's work is done to earn money and meet family needs; the purpose of most social relationships is the search for glory; and the purpose of most worship is the search for Paradise and God's grace. Moreover, most of what people say and think is connected to something they want, and thus something they love. This applies even to food and drink; the search for comfort and ease; working for a living, and how people express their states and emotions. Equally, the purpose of most of what people say and do is to obtain something they want—and hence something they love—or to seek to avoid something they do not want and hence do not love. Yet how many people really perceive this? How many people really perceive that every intention they and others make is born of either love for self, love for the body, love for passion, love for another, or love for God? Even when people seek happiness, they are really seeking nothing but contentment in possessing something they love (as we will discuss later, God willing). Thus love is the intention behind most actions and most things, if not everything.

But what is love? And why are human beings so concerned with love, or indeed, so governed by love? Where does love come from, and where does it go? What is its purpose, and how is this purpose achieved? How many young people have suffered, cried, or committed suicide, because of love? How many older people have wept or felt pain because of their fear of losing those they love? Yet how many people have the power to rationally control what and how much they love? We would not be exaggerating if we said that most of life's activity and effort is expended on the search for love, without people even perceiving what they are doing, and why. For all that, however, there does not exist today anywhere in the world—as far as we know—a single mainstream school or college offering love as a subject of study and thus teaching people about what they will in reality spend their lives thinking about and doing. This

Introduction: The Secret of Love

makes people as follows: *Their likeness is as the likeness of one who kindled a fire, and when it illumined all about him God took away their light and left them in darkness, unable to see, / deaf, dumb, blind, [so that] they shall not return.* (Al-Baqarah, 2:17–18)

God willing, in this work we will convey what God says about love, the greatest secret in life; the secret which people actually spend their lives in pursuit of, although few ever really know anything about it. God says: *They know [merely] an outward aspect of the life of this world; but they, of the Hereafter, they are oblivious.* (Al-Rum, 30:7)

CHAPTER THREE

THE DEFINITION OF LOVE

It is in the nature of things that love cannot be defined exactly, because there is something in love—as there is in pain—which cannot be portrayed or conveyed by description alone. Love is not a tangible thing: one can recognise a chair or a lion by its name alone, but one cannot come to know the entire truth of love by means of its description alone. Because of this, some have said that love cannot be defined at all. Despite this, however, we can derive a specific definition of love from God's words in the Holy Qur'an which comes very close to conveying the meaning of love.

God says: *You will never be able to be just to your wives, even if you be eager; yet do not incline altogether away, so that you leave her like one suspended…* (Al-Nisa' 4:129) And He says: *Women are not lawful for you beyond that, nor [is it lawful] for you to change them for other wives, even though their beauty please you [aʿjabatkum]…* (Al-Ahzab 33:52) The first verse describes love after it has matured and developed. The second verse describes the beginning of love. Together they describe the beginning, development and maturity of love. Describing the beginning, development and maturity of something means describing all of it. Consequently, by putting these two verses together we can describe love as such. However, since these verses are God's words and not human words, and since of course God is Omniscient, we can take this description of love as such a definition. We can thus define love as *'an inclination towards beauty after being pleased (iʿjab) by it.'* This definition, which we have derived directly from God's words cited above, is not essentially different from the definitions many Muslim scholars have offered for love.[8]

This definition applies to all human beings since it applies to the Messenger of God ﷺ, but we do not know if the words 'pleased by' and 'incline' befit a description of God's love. Ghazali says, as we have already cited in the previous endnote: 'In its ordinary use, "love" means the *soul's inclination to something which suits it and pleases it*. Such a thing can only be envisaged for an imperfect being, which inclines towards something it lacks and is made complete by attaining it, and delights in having attained it; and this is impossible for God…. God's love for man, then, *is for Him to draw him nearer to Himself by warding off distractions and sins from him, and purifying his inner being from the turbidity of this worldly life, and drawing back the veil from his heart so that he may behold Him, as though he sees Him with his heart*. As for man's love for God, *it is his inclination towards attaining the perfection which he utterly lacks and needs*, for he will doubtless yearn for what he lacks, and delight in attaining any part of it. This kind of yearning and love is impossible for God.'[9]

Thus Ghazali describes God's love for human beings as being 'for Him to draw [them] nearer to Himself by warding off distractions and sins from [them]…' He uses the word '*mahabbah*' for 'love' here, and there may be a difference between the words '*mahabbah*' and '*hubb*', as we will see later, God willing. But how do we arrive at an understanding of God's love ('*hubb*') from the Holy Qur'an?

As will be seen later (in Chapter 7: God's Love for Humanity), God loves—and therefore gives—all human beings (and indeed all creation) countless favours (*fadl*; pl. *afdal*) out of his Mercy and Love, but specifies eight or nine categories of people (such as 'the patient', 'the God-fearing' and 'the virtuous' etc.) whom He loves in particular. What these people have in common is beauty of soul, and therefore it can be said that whilst God loves everything He has created in general, He loves beauty of soul in particular. Now God has placed beauty in all His creation, for He says: *Who beautified everything that He created. And He began the creation of man from clay.* (Al-Sajdah, 32:7)

Therefore it can be said that God *loves particular beauty of soul in particular, but general beauty in general*. This amounts to saying that *God loves beauty as such, or beauty according to its degree.*

However, since God created every thing in the first place—including all beauty in existence—this means that He gave every thing its particular nature as a free gift from Him. When Moses ﷺ was asked by Pharaoh about God, the following discussion occurred: *He said, 'So who is your Lord, O Moses?' He said, 'Our Lord is He Who gave to every thing its [particular] nature and then guided [them]'*. (Ta Ha, 20:49–50)

Thus God is known first of all as He who gives every thing its particular creation, and then gives them something else—His guidance (which, in the case of human beings, means beauty of soul). Therefore *God's love is knowable to human beings as, first of all, the free gift of existence and countless other favours (including beauty of various kinds) to every created thing, and, second, love of beauty as such*. This is perfectly summarised in the famous Hadith of the Messenger of God ﷺ: 'God is Beautiful, and He loves beauty.'[10]

That God 'is Beautiful'—or rather: 'The Beautiful' (*Al-Jamil*) in another Hadith[11]—means that all beauty comes from Him as a *free gift*, and therefore that He is, first of all, the Giver[12] *of existence and countless other favours to every created thing*. That God 'loves beauty' means that His love is *love of beauty as such* (*not forgetting that all created beauty is from Him*). This exactly confirms our description of God's love above. Indeed, a similar definition could be deduced for God's Mercy.[13]

The definition of Divine love as: *first, the free gift of existence and of countless other favours (including beauty of various kinds) to every created thing, and, second, love of beauty as such* is not opposed in meaning to the definition of human love as '*inclination towards beauty*', except that it must be remembered that God created all things and all beauty in the first place as a gratuitous gift from Him, and that it cannot be said that God 'inclines'. And God knows best.

Our previous definition of love is confirmed by the etymological root of the word '*hubb*' ('love'), which comes from the word '*habb*' ('seed') thus implying a seed which falls into the ground, grows, then brings forth a new and beautiful plant. God makes this clear in the Holy Qur'an with His words: *The likeness of those who expend their wealth in the way of God is as the likeness of a grain ('habb') that sprouts seven ears, in every ear a hundred grains; so God multiplies for whom He will; God is Embracing, Knowing. (Al-Baqarah, 2:261)*

Thus love is like a seed from which comes forth a plant which God multiplies as He wills for whom He wills. Indeed, classical scholars of the Arabic language have affirmed that this is the lexical root of the word '*hubb*', but have also mentioned other roots from which the word might also be derived.[14]

PART ONE: DIVINE LOVE

PART ONE: PRIMITIVE

CHAPTER FOUR

GOD AND LOVE

LOVE AS A DIVINE QUALITY

God speaks of the great reality of love many times in the Holy Qur'an. He mentions those whom He loves, such as, for example, those who rely on Him: *And when you are resolved, rely on God; for God loves those who rely [upon Him].* (Aal 'Imran, 3:159)

However, God's Love is not merely one of God's acts or actions, but one of God's very Own Divine Qualities or Names. This can be seen by the many Divine Names in the Holy Qur'an which denote God's loving qualities (such as: 'the Gentle'—'*Al-Latif*'; 'the Kind'—'*Al-Raouf*'; 'the Generous'—'*Al-Kareem*'; 'the Forbearing'—'*Al-Haleem*'; 'the Absolutely Reliable'—'*Al-Wakil*'; 'the Friend'—'*Al-Wali*'; 'the Good'—'*Al-Barr*'; 'the Forgiving'—'*Al-Ghafur*'; 'the Forgiver'—'*Al-Ghaffar*'; 'the Granter and Accepter of Repentance'—'*Al-Tawwab*', and 'the Pardoner'—'*Al-'Afu*'), and in particular by His Name 'the Loving' ('*Al-Wadud*'), which occurs twice in the Holy Qur'an: *And ask forgiveness of your Lord, then repent to Him. Truly my Lord is Merciful, Loving.* (Hud, 11:90) ❋ *And He is the Forgiving, the Loving.* (Al-Buruj, 85:14)

Here we see the connection between love and mercy: the Divine Name 'the Loving' is mentioned alongside the Divine Names 'the Merciful' and 'the Forgiving' in the two Qur'anic verses (and never without them) indicating that God's Love is inseparable from His Mercy.[15] Thus Love comes with Mercy, and Mercy comes with Love.

Indeed, some of God's other Divine Names that indicate the 'gentle' Divine Qualities—such as the Divine Name 'the Kind' (*Al-Raouf*), which occurs in the Holy Qur'an ten times,[16] and other certain Names as previously mentioned—also imply *both* God's Love and His Mercy together. We may even say that Mercy engenders Love; for the word *rahmah* ('mercy') is derived from *rahim* ('womb'), and God says in a '*Hadith Qudsi*' (that is, a *Hadith* where the Messenger of God ﷺ is quoting God Himself as Speaker):

"I am God (*Allah*), I am the Compassionate One (*Al-Rahman*). I created the womb ('*rahim*') and named it after My Name. He who keeps its ties, I shall keep [my ties with] him; and he who cuts its ties, I shall cut him off [from Me]."[17]

Indeed, if we reflect on the womb, we will realize that the womb produces mercy just as it produces children, because when a child is born from the womb he or she already naturally enjoys his or her mother's love. This is a law of nature: mercy produces love, even though love has special qualities which mercy does not necessarily share.

The natural connection between love and mercy is not confined to the keeping of family ties alone, for God also alludes to the connection between affection—which is a form of love, as God willing we will see later—with mercy, in the following verse: *And of His signs is that He created for you from yourselves mates that you might find peace by their side, and He ordained between you affection (mawaddah) and mercy. Surely in that there are signs for a people who reflect.* (Al-Rum, 30:21)

LOVE AND MERCY ARE OF THE DIVINE ESSENCE

God equates His Name 'the Compassionate' ('*Al-Rahman*') with His Divine Name 'God' ('*Allah*') in His words: *Say: 'Invoke God or invoke the Compassionate One; whichever you invoke, to Him belong the Most Beautiful Names'...* (Al-Isra', 17:110) Since the Divine Name '*Allah*' refers to the Divine Essence, this means that Divine Mercy is of the very Divine Essence—the Godhead or the Self—Itself, without and before any relation to any created being[18]. This is also proved by God's words: *...He has prescribed for Himself [nafsihi—His Self] mercy...* (Al-An'am, 6:12) And His words: *...Your Lord has prescribed for Himself [nafsihi—His Self] mercy...* (Al-An'am, 6:54)

Thus God has made mercy incumbent upon Himself or rather His Self—the Arabic word '*nafsihi*' means both Himself (reflexively) and 'His Self' (thus referring to the Divine Essence or Self or Godhead)—which is to say that Divine Mercy is of the Divine Essence Itself. God's Mercy is thus incumbent on God by His own very Being. Consequently, God is bound by Himself to be Merciful, and His Mercy embraces everything. This is affirmed by His words: *...My mercy embraces all things...* (Al-A'raf, 7:156)

Moreover, this is what the angels affirm when they pray for forgiveness for the believers: *...Our Lord, You embrace all things in [Your] mercy and knowledge...* (Ghafir, 40:7)

We must also mention that every one of the one hundred and fourteen chapters of the Holy Qur'an begins with the sacred formula '*In the Name of God, the Compassionate, the Merciful*' ('*Bism Illah Al-Rahman Al-Rahim*') except the ninth (*Surat Al-Tawbah*)—albeit that Islamic scholars point out that the 'missing' basmallah of *Surat Al-Tawbah* reappears in *Surat Al-Naml* wherein God says: *...And lo! it is: In the Name of God, the Compassionate, the Merciful.* (Al-Naml, 27:30) Thus the fact that practically every chapter in the Holy Qur'an begins with '*In the Name of God, the Compassionate, the Merciful*', further indicates the connection between the Divine Name 'God' ('*Allah*') and mercy.[19]

All of this allows us to say that since Divine Love, like Divine Mercy, is a Divine Quality; and since God's Loving is inseparable from His Mercy; and since Divine Mercy is of the very Divine Essence Itself, then we can conclude that Divine Love, like Divine Mercy, is of[20] the Divine Essence Itself, as well as

God and Love

being a Divine Quality. This is seen in the *Ayat al-Kursi*—which the Messenger of God ﷺ called: 'the greatest verse in the Holy Qur'an'[21]—which speaks of the Divine Essence, and of the Qualities of God in relation to His Creation. God says:

> God, there is no god, except Him, the Living (Al-Hayy), the Eternal Sustainer (Al-Qayyum). Slumber does not seize Him, neither sleep; to Him belongs all that is in the heavens and the earth; who is there, that shall intercede with Him save by His leave? He knows what lies before them, and what is after them; and they encompass nothing of His knowledge, save such as He wills. His throne embraces the heavens and the earth; the preserving of them wearies Him not; He is the Sublime, the Tremendous. (Al-Baqarah, 2:255)

After mentioning two of His Names ('*Al-Hayy*' and '*Al-Qayyum*') and some of His Qualities, God says: *who is there, that shall intercede with Him save by His leave?*. Now intercession is evidently a function and a reflection of mercy, so we understand from this sacred verse not only that Divine Mercy is of the Divine Essence, but also that all mercy—even the mercy of God's creatures to each other—is ultimately from God, for it is *by His leave*. Indeed, God says:

> And how many an angel there is in the heavens whose intercession cannot avail in any way except after God gives permission for whomever He wills, and He is satisfied. (Al-Najm, 53:26) ❋ And warn therewith those who fear they shall be gathered to their Lord: apart from Him they have no protector and no intercessor so that they might fear [God]. (Al-An'am, 6:51) ❋ God is He Who created the heavens and the earth and whatever is between them in six days, then He presided upon the Throne. You do not have besides Him any protector or intercessor. Will you not then remember? (Al-Sajdah, 32:4) ❋ Or have they taken besides God intercessors? Say: 'What! even though they have no power whatever and are unable to comprehend?' / Say: 'All intercession belongs [solely] to God. To Him belongs the kingdom of the heavens and the earth; then to Him you will be brought back'. (Al-Zumar, 39:43–44)

Muslim scholars and exegetes have disagreed about the exact differences between 'the Compassionate' (*Al-Rahman*) and 'the Merciful' (*Al-Rahim*), but they all affirm that the Divine Name 'the Compassionate' does not require an object, whilst the Divine Name 'the Merciful' does require an object to receive the mercy. This means that 'the Compassionate' is compassionate in His Essence, and 'the Merciful' is merciful in His actions. However, since love comes with mercy, and since mercy exists in both the Divine Names 'the Compassionate' and 'the Merciful', then love too is implied in both the Divine Names 'the Compassionate' and 'the Merciful'. Thus God's Love is twice implied—along with the double mention of Divine Mercy—at the beginning of the Holy Qur'an itself and the beginning of every one of its one hundred and fourteen chapters except the ninth (which is later compensated for).[22]

A Question: Since God's mercy embraces all things (*My mercy embraces all things*); and since God *has prescribed for Himself mercy*; and since God's mercy outstrips His wrath (according to the *Hadith Qudsi* which says: 'My mercy outstrips My wrath'), then how can God punish sinners with painful and severe punishment for their sins? God says:

> *The Jews and Christians say: 'We are the sons of God and His beloved ones'. Say: 'Why then does He chastise you for your sins? Nay; you are mortals from among those He created. He forgives whom He wills, and He chastises whom He wills'. For to God belongs the kingdom of the heavens and of the earth, and all that is between them; to Him is the journey's end.* (Al-Ma'idah, 5:18)
> *And whoever slays a believer deliberately, his requital is Hell, abiding therein, and God is angry with him and has cursed him, and has prepared for him a mighty chastisement.* (Al-Nisa', 4:93)

Fakhr al-Din al-Razi says: 'There are many opinions about His words '*My mercy embraces all things*'. It is said that '*My mercy embraces all things*' means that His mercy in the life of the lower world is granted universally to all, whilst in the Hereafter it is granted only to the believers. This is indicated by His words: '*and so I shall prescribe it for those who are God-fearing*'.²³

And Qurtubi says, commenting on this verse: 'His words '*My mercy embraces all things*' are universal, meaning infinite; meaning that it will not fail to reach all those to whom it applies. It is said that it means that [His mercy] embraces all in creation, in that even animals have mercy and affection for their young. Some exegetes say that all beings were given hope by this verse, even Iblis [Satan], who said, 'I am a thing!' But then God says: '*and so I shall prescribe it for those who are God-fearing*'.²⁴

In any case, God says: *My mercy embraces all things*, He does not say: 'My tenderness embraces all things', but rather (elsewhere): *God is Tender with His servants. He provides for whomever He will. And He is the Strong, the Mighty* (Al-Shura, 42:19). God, then, is tender with His servants in a general way, and *He provides for whomever He will*. This does not mean for all, and does not mean that His tenderness—and therefore gentleness—embraces all things all the time, otherwise there would never be any suffering or pain in the world. There is thus a big difference between mercy and tenderness. Indeed, we may have mercy on something by temporarily doing something harsh to it to save it from something even worse and more permanent (as, for example, does the surgeon or veterinarian who performs surgery); yet this mercy (or this surgery) might not be that gentle or involve any tenderness at all. God's Mercy embracing all things thus does not mean that nothing will ever suffer, but that God will guide every existing thing to what will enable it to suffer the least, and God knows best.

Another Question: What is the difference between love (*hubb*) and mercy (*rahmah*)?

As will later be seen, mercy (*rahmah*) is both a kind of love (see Chapter 21: The Different Kinds of Love) and a stage of inter-human love (see Chapter 22: The Stages of Love). Nevertheless, there are a number of important differences—or perhaps distinctions—between the two in the Holy Qur'an.

First, love necessary means having mercy towards that which is 'associated with' the beloved, (for the sake of the beloved). God says: *Muhammad is the Messenger of God, and those who are with him are hard against the disbelievers, merciful among themselves...* (Al-Fath, 48:29). Those 'with the Messenger of God' ﷺ are *par excellence* those who love God. Their love of God necessarily involves mercy towards each other since they recognize that they all love God. By contrast, mercy does not necessarily entail love. Love is thus more complete than mercy, and includes it.

Second, God's mercy *embraces all things...* (Al-A'raf, 7:156), but He is only referred to as having love ('*hubb*') for (particular) human beings. Similarly, God's Name 'the Loving' ('*Al-Wadud*') refers only to all of creation (which is His throne, precisely): *And He is the Forgiving, the Loving / Possessor of the Throne, the Glorious* (Al-Buruj, 85:14-15), not to individual parts within creation. Thus God's love applies only to totalities, not to parts: a human being is a totality and (as will later be discussed in the endnotes of Chapter 12) potentially an image of the whole of creation, which itself is obviously a totality. By contrast, God's Mercy, as just cited, applies to particular things—and indeed to every particular thing—and even to incomplete things. Thus love requires a 'total' object, whereas mercy does not.

Third, whereas God may exercise both love and mercy towards human beings, human beings can feel love towards God, but not mercy. Of course, God is in need of neither human beings' mercy nor their love—*on the contrary, God is the Independent One, while you are the needy...* (Muhammad, 47:38)—so this can only be because true love itself involves the totality of the subject or lover, whereas mercy does not. Indeed, God says: *God has not placed two hearts inside any man...* (Al-Ahzab, 33:4).

Earlier we defined human love as: '*an inclination towards beauty after being pleased (i'jab) by it*', and Divine love as: '*first, the free gift of existence and of countless other favours (including beauty of various kinds) to every created thing and, second, love of beauty as such*'. Since, as we have just seen: (1) love is more complete than mercy and includes it; (2) love requires a 'total' object, whereas mercy does not, and (3) love involves the totality of the subject or lover, whereas mercy does not, we can therefore deduce that *the difference between love and mercy is that love involves a total gift, whereas mercy involves a partial gift*. Consequently, it might even be said that *love involves the gift of self, whereas mercy involves a gift of 'other'*. And God knows best.

CHAPTER FIVE

LOVE IS THE ROOT OF CREATION

God created human beings *out of* His mercy, for He says: *The Compassionate One / has taught the Qur'an. / He created man, / teaching him [coherent] speech.* (Al-Rahman, 55:1–4) And He says: *Had your Lord willed, He would have made humankind one community, but they continue to differ, / except those on whom your Lord has mercy; and for that did He create them...* (Hud, 11:118–119)

Fakhr al-Din al-Razi says about God's words '*and for that did He create them*': 'There are three opinions about these words. The first opinion: Ibn ʿAbbas ؓ said: "He created them for mercy"; and this is the opinion of the majority of Muʿtazilites, who say that it cannot be that God created them so that they would differ. There are several proofs for this: firstly, pronouns should be assumed to refer to their nearest possible antecedent, and the nearest possible antecedent here is "mercy", whilst "to differ" is further away. Secondly, had He created them to differ and wanted them to believe this, He could not then punish them for it, since they would be obeying Him by differing. Thirdly, if we understand the verse in this way, it is in harmony with what He says elsewhere: "*and I did not create the jinn and humankind except that they may worship Me*" (Al-Dhariyat, 51:56). If it is said, "If the meaning were that He created them because of His mercy, the pronoun 'that' would be feminine in Arabic (since *rahmah* ['mercy'] is a feminine noun in Arabic), not masculine", we respond that the feminine status of the word *rahmah* is not a true feminine, since the word means "favour" and "forgiveness" [respectively '*fadl*' and '*ghufran*' in Arabic, which are both masculine], as He says: "*Said he, 'This ('hadha'*—a masculine pronoun) *is a mercy (rahmah) from my Lord...*" (Al-Kahf, 18:98), and He says: "*... surely the mercy (rahmah) of God is near (qarib*, masculine adjective) *to the virtuous* (Al-Aʿraf, 7:56)". The second opinion is that these words mean that He created them so that they would differ. The third opinion, which is the most satisfactory one, is that He created the people of mercy for mercy, and the people of differing for differing.'[25]

Accordingly, we ourselves believe that the opinion of Ibn ʿAbbas ؓ is the one that corresponds best with the literal meaning of the verse. Indeed, we cannot ignore the opinion of Ibn ʿAbbas ؓ—who learnt the Holy Qur'an personally from his cousin the Prophet Muhammad ﷺ himself—even if al-Razi does not concur. Moreover, as al-Razi himself says, linguistically speaking, the word '*rahmah*' may be considered either feminine or masculine—and therefore the word can indeed apply to it. At most, it might be said—to accommodate al-Razi's opinion—that God created people as such for mercy, but also created them as 'people of differing' for differing and 'people of mercy' for mercy—in other words, that God wants to grant His Mercy to everyone, but created them free and thus allowed them not to choose His Mercy. However, this seems an unnecessary, complicated quibble with Ibn Abbas's commentary. Moreover, logically speaking, God prescribes mercy for Himself: *… Your Lord has prescribed for Himself mercy…* (Al-An'am, 6:54) And this mercy is linked to the very creation of the heavens and the earth: *Say: 'To whom belongs what is in the heavens and in the earth?' Say: 'To God. He has prescribed for Himself mercy. He will surely gather you together on the Day of Resurrection of which there is no doubt. Those who have forfeited their own souls, they do not believe.* (Al-An'am, 6:12)

And the Messenger of God ﷺ said: 'When God created the world, He wrote above His Throne: "My mercy outstrips My wrath."'[26]

How, then, could God have 'created the people of differing for differing' as al-Razi says, and not for mercy? Rather, God created human beings *for* His mercy but some of them 'differed', and as a result of this they closed themselves off from Divine mercy, despite the vastness of His mercy about which God says: *My mercy embraces all things…* (Al-A'raf, 7:156).[27]

Furthermore, how could God have created 'the people of differing' for 'differing', when God has actually stated that the reason for creation elsewhere in the Holy Qur'an, and it is precisely not for 'differing' as such. God says: *And I did not create the jinn and humankind except that they may worship Me.* (Al-Dhariyat, 51:56)

Now the worship of God is a mercy, and it leads to more mercy; and God does not say here that He created some of humanity and the jinn for worship, and others for something else (i.e. 'differing'), but rather that He created them *all* for worshipping Him, and therefore for attaining His Mercy. Indeed, there are more than twenty-five verses in the Holy Qur'an which indicate that God created human beings for mercy, and for that which leads to mercy. In what follows we consider these.

God says that He created human beings to be God-fearing: *O people, worship your Lord Who created you and those that were before you, so that you may be God-fearing.* (Al-Baqarah, 2:21)

And 'to know the names of all things', for He says:

> *And when your Lord said to the angels, 'I am appointing on earth a vicegerent', they said, 'What, will You appoint therein one who will do corruption therein and shed blood, while we glorify You with praise and sanctify You?'; He said, 'Assuredly, I know what you know not'. / And He taught Adam the*

names, *all of them; then He presented them to the angels and said, 'Now tell Me the names of these if you speak truly'.* (Al-Baqarah, 2:30–31)

And He created human beings 'to reward them with the best reward', for He says: *And to God belongs whatever is in the heavens and whatever is in the earth that He may requite those who do evil for what they have done, and reward those who are virtuous with the best [reward].* (Al-Najm, 53:31)

And 'to test which of them is best in conduct', for God says: *[He] Who created death and life, that He may try you [to see] which of you is best in conduct, and He is the Mighty, the Forgiving.* (Al-Mulk, 67:2)

And 'to reward those who believe and perform good deeds', for God says:

To Him is the return of all of you: God's promise, in truth. Truly He originates creation, then recreates it that He may requite those who believe and perform righteous deeds, justly. And those who disbelieve, for them will be a draught of boiling water and a painful chastisement because they disbelieved. (Yunus, 10:4)

And 'so that human beings may be certain about the encounter with God', for He says:

God is He Who raised up the heavens without visible supports then presided upon the Throne and disposed the sun and the moon, each one moving, until [the conclusion of] an appointed time. He directs the command. He details the signs so that you might be certain of the encounter with your Lord. (Al-Ra'd, 13:2)

And 'so that human beings may seek His favour; give thanks to Him; reflect on His signs; understand them, and be guided', for God says:

He created the heavens and the earth with the Truth. Exalted be He above what they associate. / He created man from a drop of fluid, yet behold! he is disputatious, openly. / And the cattle, He created them for you. In them there is warmth, as well as [other] uses, and of them you eat; / and for you there is in them beauty, when you bring them [home] to rest, and when you drive them forth to pasture. / And they bear your burdens to a land which you could not reach, save with great trouble to yourselves. Indeed your Lord is Gentle, Merciful. / And [He created] horses and mules and asses, that you may ride them, and for adornment; and He creates what you do not know. / And God's is the direction of the way, and some of them are deviant. And had He willed, He would have guided you all. / He it is Who sends down water from the heaven, whence you have drink, and whence are trees, whereat you let your animals graze. / With it He makes the crops grow for you, and olives and date-palms and vines and all kinds of fruit. Surely in that there is a sign for people who reflect. / And He disposed for you the night and the day, and the sun and the moon and the stars are disposed by His command. Surely in that there are signs for people who understand. / And whatever He has created for you in the earth, diverse in hue. Surely in that there is a sign for people who remember. / And He it is Who disposed the sea, that you may eat from it fresh meat, and bring forth from it ornaments which you wear. And you see the ships ploughing therein; and that you may seek of His favour, and that you might be thankful. / And He cast into the earth firm mountains, lest it should shake with you, and rivers and ways so that you might be guided /— and landmarks [as well], and by the stars, they are guided. (Al-Nahl, 16:3–16)

And 'so that human beings remember Him and thank Him', for God says: *And He it is Who made the night and day [to appear] in succession for him who desires to remember or desires to be thankful.* (Al-Furqan, 25:62)

And 'so that human beings supplicate Him', for God says: *Say, 'My Lord would not be concerned with you were it not for your supplications. But you have denied, and so that will remain binding'.* (Al-Furqan, 25:77) And 'so that He might relent to the believing men and women', for God says: *So that God may chastise the hypocrites, men and women, and the idolaters, men and women, and that God may relent to the believing men and believing women. And God is Forgiving, Merciful.* (Al-Ahzab, 33:73)

And 'so that human beings may complete an appointed term, and understand', for God says:

> *He it is Who created you from dust, then from a drop [of sperm], then from a blood-clot, then He brings you forth as infants, then that you may come of age, then that you may become aged, though there are some of you who die earlier, and that you may complete an appointed term that perhaps you might understand.* (Ghafir, 40:67)

And 'so that human beings might seek God's favour, and thank Him, and reflect upon His signs', for God says:

> *God it is Who disposed for you the sea so that the ships may sail upon it by His command, and that you may seek of His favour, and that perhaps you may give thanks. / And He has disposed for you whatever is in the heavens, and whatever is in the earth, all being from Him. Surely in that there are signs for a people who reflect.* (Al-Jathiyah, 45:12–13)

And 'to requite each soul justly', for God says: *And God created the heavens and the earth with the truth and so that every soul may be requited for what it has earned, and they will not be wronged.* (Al-Jathiyah, 45:22)

And 'so that human beings may come to know one another', for God says: *O humankind! We have indeed created you from a male and a female, and made you nations and tribes that you may come to know one another. Truly the noblest of you in the sight of God is the most God-fearing among you. Truly God is Knower, Aware.* (Al-Hujurat, 49:13)

And 'so that human beings might have insight and be people of remembrance and penitence', for God says: *As an insight and a reminder for every penitent servant.* (*Qaf*, 50:8)

And 'so that human beings might keep the balance with justice', for God says:

The Compassionate One / has taught the Qur'an. / He created man, / teaching him [coherent] speech. / The sun and the moon follow a reckoning, / and the grass and the trees prostrate. / And He has raised the heaven and set up the balance, / [declaring] that you should not contravene with regard to the balance. / And observe the weights with justice and do not skimp the balance. (*Al-Rahman*, 55:1–9)

And 'so that human beings might be guided to the way, and be grateful to God', for God says: *Verily We created man from a drop of mixed fluid, so that We may test him. So We made him hearing, seeing. / Verily We have guided him to the way, whether he be grateful or ungrateful.* (*Al-Insan*, 76:2–3)

And that 'God created the earth as sustenance for human beings', for God says:

Are you harder to create or the heaven which He has built? / He made it rise high and levelled it, / and darkened its night, and brought forth its day; / and after that He spread out the earth; / from it He has brought forth its waters and its pastures, / and has set firm the mountains / as a [source of] sustenance for you and your flocks. (*Al-Nazi'at*, 79:27–33)

What all these verses have in common is the fact that God creates human beings, gives them freedom and tests them in this life so that they might attain His mercy, although those who fail and do evil things are requited for their own evil deeds.

It should also be mentioned that in addition to all the verses from the Holy Qur'an cited above there are twenty-five other verses in the Holy Qur'an in which God describes the wisdom behind His creating *certain parts* of creation (and not all of it). These parts of creation were *specifically* made for the service of humanity, to help achieve their purpose in life, which is to attain God's mercy by worshipping Him. These verses include, for example: *It is He Who made the earth tractable for you, so walk in its flanks and eat of His provision; and to Him is the resurrection.* (*Al-Mulk*, 67:15)[28]

Thus it is clear and beyond doubt that God created human beings and the world *out of mercy* and *for mercy*; and since Divine Mercy is inseparable from Divine love (as we have already discussed in Chapter 4: God and Love), this means that the world and human beings were created *out of love* and *for love* as well.

A Question: If the world and human beings were created *out of* mercy, and thus love, and *for* mercy and thus love, then how can it be that God does not love certain (evil) people?

As we will later see, God willing, the only creatures and things which God does not love are the evildoers and disbelievers and certain evil deeds. The answer to this question therefore is limited to an examination of the states of the evildoers, disbelievers and certain evil deeds with respect to God's love and mercy.

As regards evildoers and the disbelievers, God in His mercy and love created them in a state of primordial purity, and in the best stature and the best form.[29] God says:

> *By the fig and the olive, / and [by] the Mount Sinai, / and [by] this secure land, / Verily We created man in the best stature. / Then, We reduced him to the lowest of the low, / except those who believe and perform righteous deeds, for they shall have an unfailing reward. / So what makes you deny thereafter the Judgement? / Is not God the fairest of all judges? (Al-Tin, 95:1–8)* ❈ *God it is Who made for you the earth as a [stable] abode and the heaven as a canopy. And He formed you and perfected your forms, and provided you with [all] the wholesome things. That then is God, your Lord, so blessed be God, the Lord of the Worlds. (Ghafir, 40:64)* ❈ *He created the heavens and the earth with the truth, and He shaped you and made your shapes excellent; and to Him is the journey's end. (Al-Taghabun, 64:3)* ❈ *O man! What has deceived you with regard to your generous Lord? / Who created you, then made you upright, then proportioned you, / assembling you in whatever form He wishes? (Al-Infitar, 82:6–8)*

But this does not mean that God, who created human beings *in the best of statures*, still loves them if and after they become *the lowest of the low*. Abu Hurayrah ❦ reported that the Messenger of God ❀ said: 'Every child is born primordially pure, and then his parents make him Jewish, or Christian, or Magian....'[30] And 'Iyad ibn Majashi'i reported that the Messenger of God ❀ said: 'God Almighty says: "… And I created all My servants in a righteous state, and then demons came to them and drew them away from their religion…."'[31]

This means that although God created human beings out of mercy, He made them free and able to choose between good and evil. God says:

> *Verily We have guided him to the way, whether he be grateful or ungrateful. (Al-Insan, 76:3)* ❈ *And We guided him to the two paths. (Al-Balad, 90:10)* ❈ *And as for Thamud, We offered them guidance, but they preferred blindness to guidance. So the thunderbolt of the humiliating chastisement seized them on account of what they used to earn. (Fussilat, 41:17)*

If a person chooses goodness, virtue, or the like, then God will love him or her more. However, if they choose the way of evil and sin, and close themselves off from God's guidance, then they will not attain God's mercy and love. Thus

God—out of mercy and love—creates people free, but some use this freedom to choose not to accept God's mercy and love. The inevitable price to be paid for freedom is the possibility of evil and thus the rejection of God's mercy. Indeed, God cites the Prophet Noah ﷺ in the Holy Qur'an saying: *He said, 'O my people, have you considered if I am [acting] upon a clear proof from my Lord and He has given me mercy from Him, and you have remained blind to it, can we force it on you, even though you are averse to it?* (*Hud*, 11:28)

It is thus not a question of God not loving evil people and acts, but rather of evil people freely refusing to be loved by God. And God knows best.

CHAPTER SIX

THE UNIVERSE AND LOVE

What is the difference between glorification of God ('*tasbih*') and praise of God ('*hamd*')? When glorifying God, one evokes His magnificence and His Qualities of Majesty, for to glorify God implies declaring His transcendence. When praising God—which is essentially giving thanks in a general way for everything[32]—one evokes God's Qualities of Beauty or Gentleness, for to praise implies declaring the immanence of God's Qualities. Everything in the heavens and the earth innately and naturally both glorifies and praises God with their very beings: *The seven heavens and the earth and all that is therein proclaim His praise. And there is not a thing, but glorifies Him in praise; but you do not understand their glorification. Lo! He is Forbearing, Forgiving.* (Al-Isra', 17:44)[33]

This praise includes the primordial and natural love which all creatures feel for God. Thus the entire universe innately loves God. We do not see the effects of this love, and we do not understand the universe's glorification of God, for He says: '*but you do not understand their glorification*'. However, the Messenger of God ﷺ did understand and hear the love of inanimate objects—although they have no hearts—for God, and even their love for the Messenger of God himself. This is clear in the *Hadith* of the weeping tree-trunk, which is related in Bukhari's *Sahih*:

> Jabir ibn 'Abdullah ؓ reported that on Fridays the Prophet ﷺ used to stand by a tree or a palm [to deliver the sermon]. A woman (or a man) of the Helpers said, 'O Messenger of God, shall we not make you a pulpit?' He said, 'If you will.' So they made him a pulpit, and the next Friday he was shown to the pulpit, and the palm let out a cry like that of a baby. The Prophet ﷺ descended [from the pulpit] and embraced the tree, and it sobbed like a baby being comforted. He said: 'You weep for the remembrance you used to hear there.'[34]
>
> And Ibn 'Umar ؓ said: 'The Prophet ﷺ gave a sermon by a palm-trunk, and went to it and he stroked it with his hand.'[35]

The reality of this universal love for God is affirmed by the Creator's dominion over all creation, for He is the King and the Owner of Creation (and therefore it innately praises Him): *Why, surely to God belongs all that is in the heavens and the earth. Why, surely God's promise is true, but most of them do not* know. (Yunus, 10:55) ❋ *Why, surely to God belongs all who are in the heavens and all who are in the earth... (Yunus, 10:66)*

This reality is also confirmed by creation's obedience of God: *And to Him belongs whoever is in the heavens and the earth. All are obedient to Him. (Al-Rum, 30:26)* It is also confirmed by creation's submission to God: *What! Do they desire other than God's religion, when to Him has submitted whoever is in the heavens and the earth, willingly, or unwillingly, and to Him they shall be returned? (Aal 'Imran, 3:83)*

This fact is also confirmed by how all of creation—save disobedient human beings—prostrates before God, for He says:

> *Have you not seen that to God prostrates whoever is in the heavens and whoever is in the earth, together with the sun and the moon, and the stars and the mountains, and the trees and the animals, as well as many of humankind? And for many the chastisement has become due. And he whom God abases, there is none to give him honour. Indeed God does whatever He wishes. (Al-Hajj, 22:18)*

And God says: *And to God prostrates whoever is in the heavens and the earth, willingly or unwillingly, and also their shadows in the mornings and the evenings. (Al-Ra'd, 13:15)*

And finally, this reality is also reflected in the way everything asks—and makes requests of—God. This is what is understood from the Divine Name 'Al-Samad'—as He says: *Say: He, God, is One. / God, the Self-Sufficient Besought of all (Al-Samad). (Al-Ikhlas, 112:1–2)* In the *Tafsir Al-Jalalayn*, this is explained as follows: '[This means that God is] always and constantly besought in needs.'[36]

Moreover, God says: *All that is in the heavens and the earth implore Him. Every day He is upon some matter. (Al-Rahman, 55:29)*

Evil human beings who are disobedient to God are the only beings that do not love God—in the moment of their disobedience at least, but not in their being as such or their individual parts, which all glorify God all the time. In other words, even the most evil person committing the most evil deed—with his or her consciousness rejecting or hating God at that moment—nevertheless loves God in every atom of their being and in their deepest heart. This is one of the meanings of God's words: *...And there is not a thing, but proclaims His praise... (Al-Isra', 17:44)*

The proof that a person loves God with all his being, even if his or her soul is disobedient, lies in the fact that the very skins and senses of humanity will testify against them, for God says: *On the day when their tongues and their hands and their feet shall testify against them concerning what they used to do. (Al-Nur, 24:24)* And God says: *Today We shall seal up their mouths, and their hands shall speak to Us, and their feet shall bear witness concerning what they used to earn. (Ya Sin, 36:65)* And God says:

> *Until, when they reach it, their hearing and their eyes and their skins will bear witness against them concerning what they used to do. / And they will say to their skins, 'Why did you bear witness against us?' They will say, 'God made us speak, Who gave speech to all things. And He created you the first time, and to Him you will be returned.* (Fussilat, 41:20–21)

Thus the whole universe loves God, and how could it not, when He is its Creator, Maker and Shaper? God says: *He is God, the Creator, the Maker, the Shaper. To Him belong the Most Beautiful Names. All that is in the heavens and the earth glorify Him, and He is the Mighty, the Wise.* (Al-Hashr, 59:24)

As for God's love of His creation, we mentioned previously that God says: *…My mercy embraces all things…* (Al-Aʿraf, 7:156)

Now although God does not love the evildoers, disbelievers, hypocrites and the like as such—as we will later see God willing—apart from these people, God loves all beings and all things, before and more than they could possibly love Him—since His mercy *embraces all things*. This does not mean, of course, that He is gentle with all things at all times, for He says: '*My mercy embraces all things*', not '*My tenderness embraces all things.*' Rather, He says: *God is Tender [Latif] towards His servants. He provides for whomever He will. And He is the Strong, the Mighty.* (Al-Shura, 42:19) Thus God is tender or gentle to whom He will, but His mercy is greater and vaster than His Gentleness.

The proof that God loves everything that He created (except the evildoers, disbelievers, and hypocrites as such) is that He gave them the gift of existence (and countless other favours) and that beauty is present in everything He created, for He says: *Who beautified everything that He created…* (Al-Sajdah, 32:7)

God loves thus the beauty inherent in the creation He adorned with His beauty, because He 'loves beauty'. But of course this does not mean that God's love is like human love, for He says: *There is nothing like Him. He is the Hearer, the Seer.* (Al-Shura, 42:11)

In summary: God loves the universe and humanity for the beauty He placed in them, and thus God loves His own beauty in the universe. This means that He loves the universe ultimately for His own sake. Humanity, on the other hand, loves God (or should), not for their own sakes, but for God's sake only. This is necessarily so because: *…God is the Independent One, while you are the needy…* (Muhammad, 47:38) And God says: *O humankind! You are the ones who are indigent to God. And God, He is the Independent, the Praised.* (Fatir, 35:15)

Thus God is loved for His own Beauty, and the beauty of the Universe and humanity—which is not its own but is, as it were, 'lent to it' by God—is also loved for God's sake. And God knows best.

CHAPTER SEVEN

GOD'S LOVE FOR HUMANITY

GOD'S FAVOUR AND LOVE FOR ALL HUMAN BEINGS IN GENERAL

God's favour ('*fadl*') is an aspect of His mercy, and Divine mercy itself—as we saw earlier—is inseparable from Divine love. Hence we must mention here God's completely gratuitous favour upon humanity in general as an aspect of God's love.

After creating human beings from dust, God breathed His spirit into Adam:

> *So when I have proportioned him, and breathed in him My spirit, then fall down in prostration before him! (Sad, 38:72)* ❊ *Who beautified everything that He created. And He began the creation of man from clay, / then He made his progeny from an extract of a base fluid, / then He proportioned him, and breathed into him of His spirit. And He made for you hearing, and sight and hearts. Little thanks do you give. (Al-Sajdah, 32:7–9)* ❊ *And when your Lord said to the angels, 'Indeed I am going to create a mortal out of dry clay [drawn] from malleable mud. / So, when I have proportioned him and breathed of My spirit in him, fall down in prostration before him!' / And so the angels prostrated, all of them together, / except Iblis, he refused to be among those prostrating. / He [said]: 'O Iblis what is wrong with you that you are not among those prostrating?' / Said he, 'I was not about to prostrate myself before a mortal whom You have created out of a dry clay [drawn] from malleable mud'. / Said He, 'Then be gone from hence; for you are indeed accursed. (Al-Hijr, 15:28–34)*

And God created human beings in the best of forms ('*surah*'):

> *God it is Who made for you the earth as a [stable] abode and the heaven as a canopy. And He formed you and perfected your forms, and provided you with [all] the wholesome things. That then is God, your Lord, so blessed be God, the Lord of the Worlds. (Ghafir, 40:64)* ❊ *He created the heavens and the earth with the truth, and He shaped you and made your forms excellent; and to Him is the journey's end. (Al-Taghabun, 64:3)* ❊ *O man! What has deceived you with regard to your generous Lord? / Who created you, then made you upright, then proportioned you, / assembling you in whatever form He wishes? (Al-Infitar, 82:6–8)*

And God created human beings in the best of statures ('*taqwim*'):

> By the fig and the olive, / and [by] the Mount Sinai, / and [by] this secure land, / Verily We created man in the best of statures. / Then, We reduced him to the lowest of the low, / except those who believe and perform righteous deeds, for they shall have an unfailing reward. / So what makes you deny thereafter the Judgement? / Is not God the fairest of all judges? (Al-Tin, 95:1–8)

And He created human beings in the primordial state of purity ('*fitra hanifa*'):

> Nay, but those who do evil follow their own desires without any knowledge. So who will guide him whom God has led astray? And they have no helpers. / So set your purpose for religion, as a hanif—a nature (fitra) given by God, upon which He originated humankind. There is no changing God's creation. That is the upright religion, but most people do not know (Al-Rum, 30:29–30)

So by God's spirit; by the best of forms; by the best of statures; and by the primordial state of purity, God has favoured or preferred (*faddala*) humanity in general above many other creatures.[37] God says: *And verily We have honoured the Children of Adam, and carried them over land and sea, and provided them with good things; and We have preferred (faddalnahum) them above many of those whom We created with a marked preferment.* (Al-Isra', 17:70)

Indeed, by these favours, God has ennobled human beings above even the angels, and made them His vicegerent on earth:

> And We created you, then shaped you, then said to the angels: 'Prostrate yourselves before Adam!' So they fell prostrate, all save Iblis [Lucifer], he was not of those who make prostration. (Al-A'raf, 7:11) ❋ He it is Who created for you all that is in the earth; then He turned to heaven and levelled them seven heavens and He has knowledge of all things. / And when your Lord said to the angels, 'I am appointing on earth a vicegerent', they said, 'What, will You appoint therein one who will do corruption therein and shed blood, while we glorify You with praise and sanctify You?'; He said, 'Assuredly, I know what you know not'. / And He taught Adam the names, all of them; then He presented them to the angels and said, 'Now tell Me the names of these if you speak truly'. / They said, 'Glory be to You! We know not except what You have taught us. Surely You are the Knower, Wise'. / He said, 'Adam, tell them their names'; And when he had told them their names He said, 'Did I not tell you that I know the Unseen in the heavens and the earth?, And I know what you reveal and what you were hiding. / And when We said to the angels, 'Prostrate yourselves to Adam; so they prostrated themselves, except Iblis, he refused and disdained; and so he became one of the disbelievers [kafirin]. (Al-Baqarah, 2:29–34)[38]

Through all these Divine favours, human beings were given a trust greater than could have been borne by the heavens, the earth and the mountains: *Indeed We offered the Trust to the heavens and the earth and the mountains, but they refused to bear it and were apprehensive of it; but man undertook it. Truly he is a wrongdoer, ignorant.* (Al-Ahzab, 33:72)

Finally, we must mention that in addition to all the gratuitous favours which God has granted every human being in general, He has also granted gratuitous graces (*ni'ma*; pl. *ni'am*) to every single human being individually. God says:

> *And if you were to count God's grace you could never reckon it. Indeed God is Forgiving, Merciful* (Al-Nahl, 16:18) ❋ *Whatever grace you have, it is from God. Then when misfortune befalls you, to Him you cry for help.* (Al-Nahl, 16:53) ❋ *Do you not see that God has disposed for you whatever is in the heavens and whatever is in the earth, and He has showered His graces upon you, [both] outwardly and inwardly? Yet among people there are those who dispute concerning God without any knowledge or guidance or an illuminating scripture.* (Luqman, 31:20) ❋ *Each We supply [to] these and [to] those from your Lord's bounty. And your Lord's bounty is not confined.* (Al-Isra', 17:20)

GOD'S PARTICULAR LOVE FOR THE VIRTUOUS

As we have seen, God has greatly favoured human beings in general and individually—more than He has favoured other creatures. Divine favour comes from Divine Mercy, and Divine Mercy is inseparable from Divine Love. Thus God's great favour to human beings is also a result of His love for them in general or as such.

In addition to all that, moreover, God says that He loves people more if they follow the Messenger of God ﷺ: *Say: 'If you love God, follow me, and God will love you more [yuhbibkum], and forgive you your sins; God is Forgiving, Merciful.'* (Aal 'Imran, 3:31)

Moreover, God mentions that a people may come in the future whom God loves and who love God, and who are characterised by the following attributes:

> *O you who believe, whoever of you apostatises from his religion, God will assuredly bring a people whom He loves and who love Him: humble towards believers, stern towards disbelievers, struggling in the way of God, and fearing not the reproach of any reproacher. That is God's favour; He gives it to whom He will; and God is Embracing, Knowing.* (Al-Ma'idah, 5:54)

God also specifically mentions eight general kinds of people whom He says (in the present tense) that He 'loves'. They are as follows:

1. 'Those who rely' (on God) ('*al-mutawakkilin*' or '*al-mutawakkilun*'—depending on the word's grammatical case):

> *It was by the mercy of God that you were lenient with them; had you been harsh and fierce of heart, they would have dispersed from about you. So pardon them, and ask forgiveness for them, and consult them in the matter.*

And when you are resolved, rely on God; for God loves those who rely. (Aal 'Imran, 3:159)

2. 'Those who cleanse themselves' ('*al-mutatahhirin*') or 'purify themselves' ('*al-muttahhirin*'):

They will ask you about the monthly period. Say: 'It is an ailment; so part with women in the monthly period, and do not approach them until they are pure; when they have cleansed themselves, then come to them, as God has commanded you'. Truly, God loves those who repent, and He loves those who cleanse themselves. (Al-Baqarah, 2:222) ❂ *Never stand there. A mosque which was founded upon piety from the first day is worthier for you to stand therein; in it are men who love to purify themselves; and God loves those who purify themselves. (Al-Tawbah, 9:109)*

3. 'Those who repent' ('*al-tawwabin*'):

They will ask you about the monthly period. Say: 'It is an ailment; so part with women in the monthly period, and do not approach them until they are pure; when they have cleansed themselves, then come to them, as God has commanded you'. Truly, God loves those who repent, and He loves those who cleanse themselves. (Al-Baqarah, 2:222)

4. 'The just' ('*al-muqsitin*'):

Listeners to calumny and consumers of unlawful gain. If they come to you, then judge between them or turn away from them. If you turn away from them, they cannot harm you at all; and if you judge, then judge justly between them; God loves the just. (Al-Ma'idah, 5:42) ❂ *And if two parties of believers fall to fighting, make peace between them. And if one of them aggresses against the other, fight the one which aggresses until it returns to God's ordinance. Then, if it returns, reconcile them, and act justly. Surely God loves the just. (Al-Hujurat, 49:9)* ❂ *God does not forbid you in regard to those who did not wage war against you on account of religion and did not expel you from your homes, that you should treat them kindly and deal with them justly. Surely God loves the just. (Al-Mumtahanah, 60:8)*

5. 'Those who fight for His cause in ranks, as if they were a solid structure' ('*al-ladhina yuqatiluna fi sabilihi saffan kanuhum bunyanun marsus*')³⁹: *Indeed God loves those who fight for His cause in ranks, as if they were a solid structure. (Al-Saff, 61:4)*

6. 'The patient' ('*al-sabirin*'): *How many a prophet has been killed and with him thousands manifold [fought], but they fainted not in the face of what afflicted them in God's way; they neither weakened, nor did they humble themselves. And God loves the patient. (Aal 'Imran, 3:146)*

7. 'The God-fearing' ('*al-muttaqin*'):

Nay, but whoever fulfils his covenant, and has fear, for truly God loves the

God-fearing. (Aal 'Imran, 3:76) ⁕ *Excepting those of the idolaters with whom you have made a pact, and who have not diminished [their commitment to] you in anyway, nor supported anyone against you; [as for these] fulfil your pact with them until the term. Truly God loves the God-fearing. (Al-Tawbah, 9:4)* ⁕ *How can the idolaters have a pact with God and His Messenger, except for those with whom you made a pact at the Sacred Mosque? So long as they are true to you, be true to them. Truly God loves the God-fearing (Al-Tawbah, 9:7)*

8. 'The virtuous' ('al-muhsinin'):

And spend in the way of God; and do not cast yourselves by your own hands into destruction; but be virtuous; God loves the virtuous. (Al-Baqarah, 2:195) ⁕ *Who expend in prosperity and adversity, and restrain their rage, and pardon their fellow-men; and God loves those who are virtuous. (Aal 'Imran, 3:134)* ⁕ *And God gave them the reward of this world, and the fairest reward of the Hereafter, and God loves the virtuous. (Aal 'Imran, 3:148)* ⁕ *So because of their breaking their covenant, We cursed them and made their hearts hard; they distort words from their contexts; and they have forgotten a portion of what they were reminded of; and you will never cease to discover some treachery on their part, except for a few of them. Yet pardon them, and forgive; surely God loves the virtuous. (Al-Ma'idah, 5:13)* ⁕ *Those who believe and perform righteous deeds are not at fault in what they may have consumed, so long as they fear, and believed and performed righteous deeds, and then were God-fearing and believed, and then were God-fearing and virtuous; God loves the virtuous. (Al-Ma'idah, 5:93)*

What do all these eight types of people have in common? The answer is that they are all characterised by certain good and virtuous characteristics of the soul. Reliance; purity; repentance; justice; fighting in God's cause; patience; fear of God and virtue are all good and virtuous characteristics of the soul. They are thus all aspects of 'beauty of soul' or of human beings' 'inner beauty'.[40] This confirms our definition (in Chapter 3: The Definition of Love) of God's love as the *'love of beauty'*, as per the *Hadith* wherein it is stated: 'God is Beautiful, and He loves beauty.'[41]

However, 'virtue' ('*ihsan*') is more than one single good characteristic in the soul; it encompasses the entire soul and all its traits. This is evident from the '*Hadith* of Gabriel' ﷺ, which says: 'Virtue (*al-ihsan*) means to worship God as though you see Him; for [even] if you see Him not, He assuredly sees you.'[42]

Sincere worship—'as though we see God'—requires the whole soul because people cannot be fully aware of God and worship Him as if they saw Him, without giving Him all that they are with all their hearts, with all their souls, with all their minds and with all their strengths. God's Oneness and Absoluteness requires people's unanimity and totality. This is reflected in the root meaning of the word *'ihsan'* ('virtue'): *'ihsan'* comes from *'husn'*, which means 'beauty', or 'the opposite of ugliness'.[43] Virtue, then, is the beauty of the soul, or human beings' inner beauty, in its entirety. This conforms perfectly to the description of God's love as from the *Hadith*, namely that God's love is 'love for beauty.' Thus in all of the aforementioned verses (about those whom God loves), it is as though God were saying that He *particularly* loves those who adorn themselves with virtue or beauty of soul, in varying degrees; and God knows best.

Certainly, this is what we understand from God's words: *Say: 'If you love God, follow me, and God will love you more [yuhbibkum], and forgive you your sins; God is Forgiving, Merciful.'* (Aal 'Imran, 3:31)[44] God 'loves more' (*'yuhbibkum'*)—that is, God loves them greatly and loves them more than others[45]—those who follow the way of the Messenger of God ﷺ; and those who follow the way of the Messenger of God ﷺ are necessarily the righteous and the virtuous, because the Messenger of God ﷺ had a 'magnificent nature': *And assuredly you possess a magnificent nature.* (Al-Qalam, 68:4)

God's words *'Say: If you love God, follow me, and God will love you more'* imply that God does not necessarily promise His greatest love to anyone but His Messenger ﷺ. As for everyone else, He promises to love them more if they follow the *Sunnah*, without necessarily promising them ultimate success therein. God knows best, but there may be herein a great mystery to the effect that the person who loves God and is loved by Him in the most perfect way is the Messenger of God ﷺ. This is also suggested by the fact that in the Holy Qur'an there is no other specific, individual mention of anyone who 'loves God and God loves him' in the present tense as such, and on the only occasion when this phrase is used, it is used in the future tense. This occurs in the following Qur'anic verse, which we have already cited:

> *O you who believe, whoever of you apostatises from his religion, God will assuredly bring a people whom He loves and who love Him: humble towards believers, stern towards disbelievers, struggling in the way of God, and fearing not the reproach of any reproacher. That is God's favour; He gives it to whom He will; and God is Embracing, Knowing.* (Al-Ma'idah, 5:54)

Howbeit, we will discuss God's love for His Messenger ﷺ in the following chapter, God willing, and will content ourselves here with this mere allusion to the subject.

THE HIERARCHY OF THE VIRTUOUS

Among the types of virtuous people mentioned above it appears that there are differences of degree and rank, for God mentions that He loves 'the virtuous' (*'al-muhsinun'*) five times in the Holy Qur'an; 'the God-fearing' (*'al-muttaqun'*) and 'the just' ('*al-muqsitun*') three times each, and all the other categories of people once only.

On the other hand, God only specifically says that He is 'with' (*ma*') 'the virtuous' ('*al-muhsinun*'), 'the God-fearing' ('*al-muttaqun*'), and 'the patient' ('*al-sabirun*')—and does not specifically say this about the other five categories mentioned.[46] The meaning of 'God's Companionship' (literally: 'God's being with someone', '*ma'iyyat Allah*') is a delicate issue over which Muslim scholars have differed; but Muslim scholars have generally distinguished between two kinds of 'Divine Companionship' in the Holy Qur'an[47]:

1. 'General Divine Companionship'. This refers to God's being with all things: *And We shall narrate to them with knowledge; for verily We were not absent.* (Al-A'raf, 7:7) And with every group of people:

> *Have you not seen that God knows all that is in the heavens and all that is in the earth? No secret conversation of three takes place but He is their fourth [companion], nor of five but He is their sixth, nor of fewer than that or more but He is with them wherever they may be. Then He will inform them of what they did, on the Day of Resurrection. Assuredly God has knowledge of all things.* (Al-Mujadilah, 58:7)

And even with the sinners: *They hide themselves from people, but they do not hide themselves from God; for He is with them while they plot at night with discourse displeasing to Him. God is ever Encompassing what they do.* (Al-Nisa', 4:108)

2. 'Special Divine Companionship'. This refers to God's being with the messengers, the prophets, and the believers in particular:

> *If you have sought a judgement, the judgement has now come to you; and if you desist, it will better for you. But if you return, We shall return, and your host will not avail you in any way, however numerous it be; and verily God is with the believers.* (Al-Anfal, 8:19) ❖ *God had made a covenant with the Children of Israel, and We raised up from among them twelve leaders. And God said: 'I am with you. Surely if you establish the prayer, and pay the alms, and believe in My messengers and succour them, and lend to God a goodly loan, I will absolve you of your evil deeds, and I will admit you to gardens underneath which rivers flow. So whoever of you disbelieves after that, surely he has strayed from the right way'.* (Al-Ma'idah, 5:12) ❖ *It is He Who created the heavens and the earth in six days, then presided upon the Throne. He knows what enters the earth, and what issues from it, and what comes down from the heaven. And He is with you wherever you may be; and God is Seer of what you do.* (Al-Hadid, 57:4) ❖ *So do not falter, and [do not] call for peace when you have the upper hand; and God is with you, and He will not stint you in [the reward for] your works.* (Muhammad, 47:35) ❖ *If you do not help him, [know that] God has already helped him, when the disbelievers*

drove him forth—the second of two; when the two were in the cave—when he said to his companion, 'Do not despair; verily God is with us'. Then God sent down His spirit of peace (sakinatahu) upon him and supported him with legions you did not see; and He made the word of those who disbelieved the nethermost, and the Word of God was the uppermost. And God is Mighty, Wise. (Al-Tawbah, 9:40)

And with Moses ﷺ and Aaron ﷺ: *Said He, 'Certainly not! Go both of you with Our signs. We will indeed be with you, hearing.* (Al-Shu'ara', 26:15) *He said, 'Do not fear, for I shall be with the two of you, hearing and seeing.'* (Ta Ha, 20:46) And with Moses ﷺ individually: *He said, 'Certainly not! Indeed I have my Lord with me. He will guide me'.* (Al-Shu'ara', 26:62)

Thus there are two distinct kinds of 'God's Companionship'. Otherwise, what did the Messenger of God ﷺ mean by saying *'Do not despair; verily God is with us'*? If there were no difference between God's being with His Messenger ﷺ and Abu Bakr ؓ inside the cave of Thawr, and God's being with the disbelievers who were trying to kill them outside the cave of Thawr, then these words would be redundant. Similarly, what did the Prophet Moses ﷺ mean by saying *'Certainly not'* (in response to his people's saying that they would be caught by Pharaoh and his army)? If there were no difference between God's being with Moses and the Children of Israel and His being with Pharaoh and his army, then these words too would be redundant.

This leads us to distinguish between the five aforementioned types of people whom God loves but does not specifically say He is 'with' them (namely: 'those who rely'; 'those who purify themselves' or 'cleanse themselves'; 'those who repent'; 'the just', and 'those who fight for His cause in ranks, as if they were a solid structure'), and the three types of people whom God loves *and* whom God says He is with, namely:

1. 'The patient'[48] ('*al-sabirin*'):

O you who believe, seek help through patience and prayer; surely God is with the patient. (Al-Baqarah, 2:153) ❊ *And when Saul went forth with the hosts, he said, 'God will try you with a river; whoever drinks of it, is not of me, and whoever tastes it not, he is of me, except for him who scoops up with his hand. But they drank of it, except a few of them; and when he crossed it, with those who believed, they said, 'We have no power today against Goliath and his troops'. Those who thought they would meet God, said, 'How often a little company has overcome a numerous one, by God's leave; and God is with the patient'.* (Al-Baqarah, 2:249) ❊ *And obey God and His Messenger, and do not quarrel with one another, lest you falter and your strength fade; and be patient. Surely God is with the patient.* (Al-Anfal, 8:46) ❊ *Now God has lightened [the burden] for you, for He knows that there is weakness in you. So if there be a hundred of you, steadfast, they will overcome two hundred;*

and if there be a thousand of you, they will overcome two thousand by the leave of God. And God is with the patient. (Al-Anfal, 8:66)

2. 'The God-fearing' ('*al-muttaqin*'):

The sacred month for the sacred month; holy things demand retaliation; whoever commits aggression against you, then commit aggression against him in the manner that he aggressed against you; and fear God, and know that God is with the God-fearing. (Al-Baqarah, 2:194) ❋ *Verily the number of months with God is twelve months in the Book of God from the day that He created the heavens and the earth; four of them are sacred. That is the right religion. So do not wrong yourselves during them. And fight the idolaters altogether, even as they fight you altogether; and know that God is with the God-fearing.* (Al-Tawbah, 9:36) ❋ *O you who believe, fight those of the [aggressive] disbelievers who are near to you, and let them find harshness in you, and know that God is with the God-fearing.* (Al-Tawbah, 9:123)

3. 'The virtuous' ('*al-muhsinin*'): *But as for those who struggle for Our sake, We shall assuredly guide them in Our ways, and truly God is indeed with the virtuous.* (Al-ʿAnkabut, 29:69)

In addition to all the above, God mentions 'the virtuous' and 'the God-fearing'—and alludes to 'the patient'—all together in the following two passages in the Holy Qur'an:

So be patient, and your patience is only by [the help of] God. And do not grieve for them, nor be in distress because of that which they scheme. / Truly God is with those who fear [Him], and those who are virtuous. (Al-Nahl, 16: 127–128) ❋ *They said: 'Is it really you, Joseph?' He said, 'I am [indeed] Joseph, and this is my brother. God has truly shown favour to us. Verily if one fears and is patient, God does not waste the wage of those who are virtuous'.* (Yusuf, 12:90)

This means—and God knows best—that the three types of believers whom God loves ('the patient', 'the God-fearing' and 'the virtuous') are, as it were, a degree more distinguished than the other five types of believers whom God loves ('those who rely'; 'those who purify themselves' or 'cleanse themselves'; 'those who repent'; 'the just'; and 'those who fight for His cause in ranks, as if they were a solid structure').

This is remarkably confirmed in God's mention of those whom He rewards '*without reckoning*'—that is to say: without limit, and without any common measure with the good they have done—this reward obviously being an important indication of God's favour, if not His love. In six different verses in the Holy Qur'an, God mentions rewarding '*without reckoning*':

Decked out fair to the disbelievers is the life of this world; and they deride the believers; but those who fear (ittaqu) shall be above them on the Day of Resurrection; and God sustains whomever He will without reckoning. (Al-Baqarah,

God's Love for Humanity

2:212) ❋ *You make the night to pass into the day and You make the day to pass into the night; You bring forth the living from the dead, and You bring forth the dead from the living, and You provide whom You will without reckoning'.* (Aal 'Imran, 3:27) ❋ *Her Lord accepted the child with gracious acceptance, and made her grow excellently, and Zachariah took charge of her. Whenever Zachariah went into the sanctuary, where she was, he found her with provisions. 'O Mary', he said, 'Whence comes this to you?' She said, 'From God. Truly God provides for whomever He will without reckoning'.* (Aal 'Imran, 3:37) ❋ *[M]en whom neither trading, nor sale distracts from the remembrance of God and the observance of prayer and payment of the alms. They fear a day when hearts and eyes will be overturned, / so that God may reward them for the best of what they did, and give them more out of His favour; and God provides whomever He will without reckoning.* (Al-Nur, 24: 37–38) ❋ *Say: 'O servants of Mine who believe! Fear (ittaqu) your Lord. For those who are virtuous (ahsanu) in this world, there will be good, and God's earth is vast. Truly the steadfast (al-sabirun) will be paid their reward in full without any reckoning'.* (Al-Zumar, 39:10) ❋ *Whoever commits an evil deed shall not be requited except with the like of it; but whoever acts righteously, whether male or female, and is a believer—such shall be admitted into Paradise wherein they will be provided without any reckoning.* (Ghafir, 40:40)

The first verse alludes to 'the God-fearing' (*ittaqu*); the second verse does not define those who receive the reward '*without reckoning*'; the third verse concerns the Blessed Virgin Mary; the fourth verse refers to those who remember God constantly; the fifth verse refers to 'the patient', 'the God-fearing' and 'the virtuous'—all three of the virtues mentioned earlier together here in one verse; and the sixth and last verse refers to those who 'act righteously', which perhaps implies 'the virtuous' in action. In short, the only virtues that are specifically mentioned as being rewarded by God '*without reckoning*' are the same three virtues mentioned earlier—'the patient', 'the God-fearing' and 'the virtuous'—as 'the elite' among those whom God loves.⁴⁹

There seems to be a hierarchy even within 'the patient', 'the God-fearing' and' the virtuous', with the latter two seeming to be slightly more excellent than the former: this is seen in the fact that the only promise that God has explicitly 'bound Himself' (*kana 'ala rabbika wa'dan masula*) as such to fulfil in the Holy Qur'an is to the 'God-fearing' (*al-muttaqun*). God says:

> *Say: 'Is that better, or the Garden of Immortality which has been promised to the God-fearing, which will be their requital and journey's end?' / For them therein is that which they desire, forever and ever—a promise that your Lord has bound Himself to fulfil (kana 'ala rabbika wa'dan masula).* (Al-Furqan, 25:15–16)

This of course is very significant, and is reminiscent of God's 'prescribing for Himself Mercy' (*Surat Al-Anʿam*, 6:12 and 6:54), as something so important that God has deigned to 'make it incumbent upon Himself', because, in fact (as we have seen in Chapter 4: God and Love) Divine Mercy is of the Divine Essence Itself. In other words, God loves 'the God-fearing' to the degree that rewarding them with the *Garden of Immortality* is necessitated by God's own Essence.[50]

On the other hand, the paramount importance of virtue (*ihsan*) is seen in the use of the word 'indeed with' ('*la-ma*'') in Gods words: a*nd truly God is indeed with the (la-ma') virtuous*. (*Al-ʿAnkabut*, 29:69), indicating additional emphasis on God's being with the virtuous. Furthermore, 'the virtuous'—and only 'the virtuous'—are described in the Holy Qur'an as being 'near to God's mercy': *And work not corruption in the land, after it has been set right, and call upon Him in fear, and in hope—surely the mercy of God is near to the virtuous.* (*Al-Aʿraf*, 7:56)

All of this confirms our earlier definition of 'virtue' as the combination and culmination of all the good character traits of the soul. In other words, God particularly loves those whose souls are beautiful and virtuous *according to the very measure of the level* of their beauty of soul and virtue. And the sum of virtue is synonymous with a sound (spiritual) heart, for God says: *The day when neither wealth nor children will avail, / except him who comes to God with a heart that is sound* (*Al-Shuʿara'*, 26:88–89)

GOD'S BOUNTY TO ALL HUMAN BEINGS

Although God particularly loves the patient, the God-fearing and the virtuous, His mercy embraces all things, as we have mentioned. To this it should be added that God's generous bounty reaches also all things and all people, whether they deserve it or not—the virtuous and the sinners—as a free gift from Him, for He says (referring to the people who only want this world and to the believers, as mentioned in the preceding verses): *Each We supply [to] these and [to] those from your Lord's bounty. And your Lord's bounty is not confined.* (*Al-Isra'*, 17:20)

Even in the case of the most virtuous people, there is no common measure between God's grace and their worthiness to receive it:

And He gives you all that you ask of Him. And if you were to enumerate God's graces, you could never number them. Lo! man is verily a wrong-doer and unthankful! (*Ibrahim*, 14:34) • *Do you not see that God has disposed for you whatever is in the heavens and whatever is in the earth, and He has showered His graces upon you, [both] outwardly and inwardly? Yet among people there are those who dispute concerning God without any knowledge or guidance or an illuminating scripture.* (*Luqman*, 31:20)

And even the evildoers, disbelievers, idolaters and hypocrites receive God's mercy and bounty:

And if God were to take humankind to task for their wrongdoing, He would not leave upon it any living being; but He gives them respite until an appointed term; and when their term comes they will not defer it by a single hour nor advance it. (Al-Nahl, 16:61) ❖ *Were God to take humankind to task for what they have acquired, He would not leave on its surface a single creature. But He reprieves them to an appointed term. And when their term comes—then truly [they will know that] God is ever Seer of His servants.* (Fatir, 35:45)

Hence all praise belongs to God: *And He is God; there is no god except Him. To Him belongs [all] praise in the former and in the latter. And to Him belongs the judgement, and to Him you will be returned.* (Al-Qasas, 28:70)

CHAPTER EIGHT

GOD'S LOVE FOR HIS MESSENGERS AND PROPHETS

THE PROPHETS

God favours His messengers and prophets to the rest of humanity (including His saints): *And Ishmael and Elisha, and Jonah and Lot, all We favoured (faddalna) above all the worlds. (Al-An'am, 6:85)* And God has sent a messenger or warner to every community:

> *And verily We sent messengers before you. Of them are those whom We have recounted to you, and of them are those whom We have not recounted to you. And it was never [permitted] for any messenger to bring a sign except with God's permission. Hence when God's command comes, judgement is passed justly; and it is thence that the advocates of falsehood become losers. (Ghafir, 40:78)* ❋ *Truly We have sent you with the truth, as a bearer of good tidings, and a warner. And there is not a community but there has passed in it a warner. (Fatir, 35:24)* ❋ *And We have not destroyed any town but it had warners. (Al-Shu'ara', 26:208)* ❋ *By God, We verily sent [messengers] to communities before you. But Satan adorned for them their deeds. So he is their patron today, and for them there will be a painful chastisement. (Al-Nahl, 16:63)* ❋ *Nothing is said to you, except what has already been said to the messengers before you. Surely your Lord is One of forgiveness and [also] One of painful punishment. (Fussilat, 41:43)* ❋ *Say: 'I am not a novelty among the messengers. Nor do I know what will be done with me or with you. I only follow what is revealed to me. And I am only a plain warner'. (Al-Ahqaf, 46:9)*

And God names twenty-five messengers and prophets in the Holy Qur'an, eighteen of them in the following verses:

> *That argument of Ours We bestowed upon Abraham against his people. We raise up in degrees whom We will; surely your Lord is Wise, Knowing. / And We bestowed upon him Isaac and Jacob; each one We guided. And Noah We guided before, and of his seed, David and Solomon and Job and Joseph, and Moses and Aaron; and so We requite the virtuous. / And Zachariah and John, and Jesus, and Elijah; all were of the righteous. / And Ishmael and Elisha, and Jonah and Lot, all We preferred above all the worlds. / And of their fathers, and of their seed, and of their brethren; and We chose them and We guided them to a straight path. (Al-An'am, 6:83–87)*

The remaining seven prophets not mentioned in the above verses but nevertheless mentioned by name elsewhere in the Holy Qur'an are: Enoch (*Idris*), Ezekiel (*Dhul-Kifl*), Jethro (*Shu'ayb*), Hud, Salih, and the Prophet Muhammad ﷺ—may peace and blessings be upon them all. In addition to these, Muslim scholars differ as to whether *Khadir*, the man mentioned as meeting Moses ﷺ (in *Surat Al-Kahf*, 18:60–82) was a prophet or merely a saint ('*wali Ullah*').

THE MESSENGERS

Every messenger is a prophet, but not every prophet is a messenger. Various *Hadiths* report that throughout history there were a total of one hundred and twenty-four thousand prophets, and three hundred and fifteen messengers.[51] A messenger is someone who brings forth a new law, whereas a prophet is someone who is inspired by God to inform people of a law brought by a messenger.[52] We know that twelve of the prophets named in the Holy Qur'an were also messengers. Five of these are mentioned in the following Qur'anic verse:

> *He has prescribed for you as a religion that which He enjoined upon Noah and that which We have revealed to you, and that which We enjoined upon Abraham, and Moses, and Jesus [declaring], 'Establish religion and do not be divided in it'. Dreadful is for the idolaters that to which you summon them. God chooses for it whomever He will, and He guides to it whomever turns penitently.* (Al-Shura, 42:13)

These five are known as 'the resolute' among the messengers: Noah, Abraham, Moses, Jesus and Muhammad—may peace and blessings be upon them all. God also says that the following prophets were also messengers:

1. Hud ﷺ: *When Hud, their brother, said to them, 'Will you not fear God? / Truly I am a trusted messenger [sent] to you.'* (Al-Shu'ara', 26:124–125)

2. Salih ﷺ: *When Salih, their brother, said to them, 'Will you not fear God? / Truly I am a trusted messenger [sent] to you.* (Al-Shu'ara', 26:142–143)

3. Lot (*Lut*) ﷺ: *When Lot, their brother, said to them, 'Will you not fear God? / Truly I am a trusted messenger [sent] to you.'* (Al-Shu'ara', 26:161–162)

4. Ishmael (*Ismail*) ﷺ: *And mention in the Book Ishmael. Indeed he was true to his promise, and he was a messenger, a prophet [likewise].* (Maryam, 19:54)

5. Joseph (*Yusuf*) ﷺ: *And verily Joseph brought you, before clear signs, but you continued to be in doubt concerning what he had brought you until, when he died, you said: "God will never send any messenger after him". So God leads astray one who is a prodigal, a sceptic'.* (Ghafir, 40:34)

6. Jethro (Shu'ayb) ﷺ: *When Shu'ayb said to them, 'Will you not fear God? / Truly I am a trusted messenger [sent] to you.'* (Al-Shu'ara', 26:177–178)

7. Elijah (*Elias*) ﷺ: *And truly Elijah was [also] one of the messengers* (Al-Saffat, 37:123)

8. Jonah (*Yunus*) ﷺ: *And indeed Jonah was one of the messengers.* (Al-Saffat, 37:139)

9. Aaron (*Harun*) ※: *So go to him and say, "Truly we are two messengers of your Lord, so let the Children of Israel go with us and do not [continue to] chastise them. We have verily brought you a sign from your Lord, and may peace be upon him who follows [right] guidance.* (Ta Ha, 20:47)

10. David (*Dawud*) ※: *We have revealed to you as We revealed to Noah, and the prophets after him, and We revealed to Abraham and Ishmael and Isaac, and Jacob, and the Tribes, and Jesus and Job and Jonah and Aaron, and Solomon, and We gave to David the Inscribed Book.* (Al-Nisa', 4:163) *And your Lord knows best all who are in the heavens and the earth. And verily We have preferred some of the prophets above others; and We gave David the Psalms.* (Al-Isra', 17:55)

THE FIVE 'RESOLUTE' MESSENGERS

The believers may not make any division between any of God's messengers:

The Messenger believes in what was revealed to him from his Lord, and the believers; each one believes in God and His angels, and in His Books, and His messengers, 'we make no division between any of His messengers'. And they say, 'We hear and obey; Your forgiveness, our Lord! To You is the homecoming'. (Al-Baqarah, 2:285) ❋ *Say: 'We believe in God, and in that which has been revealed to us, and revealed to Abraham, Ishmael, Isaac, Jacob, and the Tribes, and that which was given to Moses, and Jesus, and the prophets, from their Lord; we make no division between any of them, and to Him we submit'.* (Al-Baqarah, 2:136) ❋ *Say, 'We believe in God, and that which has been revealed to us, and that which has been revealed to Abraham and Ishmael, and Isaac and Jacob, and the Tribes; and in that which was given to Moses and Jesus, and the prophets, from their Lord; we make no division between any of them; and to Him we submit'.* (Aal 'Imran, 3:84) ❋ *Those who disbelieve in God and His messengers and seek to divide between God and His messengers, and say, 'We believe in some, and disbelieve in some', and seek to adopt a way between them. / Those are the disbelievers truly; and We have prepared for the disbelievers a humiliating chastisement. / And those who believe in God and His messengers and do not seek to divide between any of them, those—We shall surely give them their wages. God is ever Forgiving, Merciful.* (Al-Nisa', 4:150–152)

Despite this, one cannot but notice that God Himself favours some messengers over others:

Those messengers some We have favoured above others; some there are to whom God spoke, and some He raised in rank. And We gave Jesus son of Mary the clear proofs, and confirmed him with the Holy Spirit. And had God willed, those who came after them would not have fought against one another after the clear proofs had come to them; but they fell into variance, and some of them believed, and some disbelieved, and had God willed they would not have fought against one another, but God does whatever He desires. (Al-Baqarah, 2:253)

We noted earlier that God mentions 'the resolute' among the messengers:

So endure [with patience] just as the resolute from among the messengers endured [with patience]. And do not seek to hasten [it] for them. It shall seem for them, on the day when they see what they are promised, as though they had tarried only an hour of a day. A communication. So shall any be destroyed, but the immoral folk? (Al-Ahqaf, 46:35)

And an authentic *Hadith*[55] says that 'the resolute' from among the messengers are the five messengers mentioned in the following two verses:

He has prescribed for you as a religion that which He enjoined upon Noah and that which We have revealed to you, and that which We enjoined upon Abraham, and Moses, and Jesus [declaring], 'Establish religion and do not be divided in it'. Dreadful is for the idolaters that to which you summon them. God chooses for it whomever He will, and He guides to it whomever turns penitently. (Al-Shura, 42:13) ❋ *And when We took a pledge from the prophets and from you, and from Noah and Abraham and Moses and Jesus son of Mary. And We took from them a solemn pledge. (Al-Ahzab, 33:7)*

These five are the 'resolute' from among the messengers, and are the best of the best of humanity and of all creation. God shows His love for each of them in a different way, as we will show:

1. Noah (*Nuh*) ﷺ:

God mentions that Noah was 'beneath His eyes', and He says that Noah built the Ark based upon Divine Revelation: *So We revealed to him [saying], 'Build the Ark beneath Our eyes and [by] Our revelation...' (Al-Mu'minun, 23:27)* ❋ *Build the Ark beneath Our eyes and by Our revelation... (Hud, 11:37)*

2. Abraham (*Ibrahim*) ﷺ:

God says that He gave (Revealed) 'scrolls' to Abraham: *Truly this is in the former scrolls, / the scrolls of Abraham and Moses. (Al-A'la, 87:18–19)* And God says that Abraham was His 'close friend' ('*khalil*'): *...And God took Abraham for a close friend. (Al-Nisa', 4:125)*

And God says that Abraham ﷺ in turn was ardent in his love ('*awwah*') for God: *...Truly Abraham was ardent, forbearing. (Al-Tawbah, 9:114)* ❋ *Assuredly Abraham was forbearing, ardent, penitent. (Hud, 11:79)*

3. Moses (*Musa*) ﷺ:

God says that He gave Moses 'scrolls', 'tablets' and the Torah:

Truly this is in the former scrolls, / the scrolls of Abraham and Moses. (Al-A'la, 87:18–19) ❋ *Or has he not been informed of what is in the scrolls of Moses? (Al-Najm, 53:36)* ❋ *And when Moses returned to his people, angry and bitterly grieved, he said, 'Evil is that which you have followed in my place, after I* had gone. Would you hasten on the judgement of your Lord?' And he cast down the Tablets, and he seized his brother by the head, dragging him toward him. He said, 'Son of my mother! Truly the people judged me weak and they were close to killing me. Do not make my enemies gloat over my misfortune, and do not count me among the folk who have done evil'. (Al-A'raf, 7:150) ❋ And when Moses's anger abated, he took the tablets, and in their copy, there was guidance, and mercy for all those who hold their Lord in awe. (Al-A'raf, 7:154) ❋ He has revealed to you the Book, by the truth, confirming what was before it, and He revealed the Torah and the Gospel. (Aal 'Imran, 3:3)

And God says that Moses was 'near to Him in communion': *...And We brought him near in communion* (*Maryam*, 19:52)

And God says that Moses ﷺ was 'honourable' ('*wajih*') in God's sight: *O you who believe, do not behave as did those who harmed Moses, whereat God absolved him of what they alleged. And he was honourable in God's sight* (*Al-Ahzab*, 33:69)

And God 'cast His love' upon him and he was reared 'beneath God's eyes': *'Cast him in the ark, then cast him into the river, and then the river shall throw him up onto the shore; [there] an enemy of Mine and an enemy of his shall take him'. And I cast upon you a love from Me and that you might be reared beneath My eyes.* (*Ta Ha*, 20:39)

And God chose Moses ﷺ for Himself: *And I chose you for Myself.* (*Ta Ha*, 20:41) Consequently Moses ﷺ was 'the first of the believers': *...And I am the first of the believers.* (*Al-A'raf*, 7:143)

And as seen earlier, God says that He was 'with' Moses ﷺ and Aaron ﷺ, and with Moses ﷺ especially: *Said He, 'Certainly not! Go both of you with Our signs. We will indeed be with you, hearing.* (*Al-Shu'ara'*, 26:15) ❋ *He said, 'Certainly not! indeed I have my Lord with me. He will guide me'.* (*Al-Shu'ara'*, 26:62)

4. Jesus Christ ('*Isa*) ﷺ:

God says that He gave Jesus Christ ﷺ the Gospel:

And We caused Jesus son of Mary to follow in their footsteps, confirming the Torah before him; and We gave to him the Gospel, wherein is guidance and light, confirming the Torah before it, and as a guidance and an admonition to the God-fearing. (*Al-Ma'idah*, 5:46) ❋ *When God said, 'O Jesus, son of Mary, remember My favour to you and to your mother, when I strengthened you with the Holy Spirit to speak to people in the cradle and in maturity, and when I taught you the Scripture, and wisdom, and the Torah, and the Gospel; and how you created out of clay the likeness of a bird by My permission, and you breathed into it and it became a bird by My permission, and you healed the blind and the leper by My permission, and you raised the dead by My permission; and how I restrained the Children of Israel from you, when you brought them clear proofs, and the disbelievers among them said, "This is nothing but manifest sorcery".* (*Al-Ma'idah*, 5:110) ❋ *Then We sent to follow in their footsteps Our messengers, and We sent to follow, Jesus son of*

God's Love for His Messengers and Prophets

Mary, and We gave him the Gospel, and We placed in the hearts of those who followed him kindness and mercy. But [as for] monasticism, they invented it—We had not prescribed it for them—only seeking God's beatitude. Yet they did not observe it with due observance. So We gave those of them who believed their reward; but many of them are immoral. (Al-Hadid, 57:27)

And God says that He made Jesus ﷺ an 'exemplar' ('*mathal*') for the Children of Israel: *He is only a servant [of Ours] on whom We bestowed favour, and We made him an exemplar for the Children of Israel.* (Al-Zukhruf, 43:59) And God says that He gave Jesus ﷺ 'signs' ('*ayah*'; pl.: '*ayat*') from Him, just as He gave them to other prophets and messengers before him[56]:

Likewise, confirming that which was before me of the Torah, and to make lawful for you some of that which was forbidden to you. I have come to you with a sign from your Lord: so fear God, and obey me. (Aal 'Imran, 3:50)
Jesus, son of Mary, said: 'O God, our Lord, send down upon us a Table from the heaven, that it shall be a celebration for us for the first and the last of us and a sign from You. And provide for us; You are the Best of Providers'. (Al-Ma'idah, 5:114)

But while some messengers and prophets were given one or two 'signs', God made Jesus ﷺ himself a 'sign' (along with his mother, the Blessed Virgin Mary): *And the one who guarded her virginity, so We breathed into her of Our spirit. And We made her and her son a sign for all the worlds.* (Al-Anbiya', 21:91)
And We made the son of Mary and his mother a sign. And We gave them refuge on a height watered by springs. (Al-Mu'minun, 23:50)

And God says that He made Jesus ﷺ a 'sign' for humankind and a mercy from Him: *He said, 'It shall be so! Your Lord has said: "It is easy for Me, and so that We may make him a sign for humankind, and a mercy from Us. And it is a thing [already] decreed"'.* (Maryam, 19:21)

And God says that Jesus ﷺ was the Messiah, and God's word, and a spirit from Him: *...The Messiah, Jesus the son of Mary, was only the Messenger of God, and His Word which He cast to Mary, and a spirit from Him...* (Al-Nisa', 4:171)

And God says that Jesus ﷺ was honoured ('*wajih*') in this world and the Hereafter, and was one of those 'brought close' ('*muqarrab*'); and in fact he is the only human being mentioned by name as 'one of those brought close' in the Holy Qur'an: *When the angels said, 'O Mary, God gives you good tidings of a Word from Him, whose name is the Messiah, Jesus, son of Mary, honoured shall he be in this world, and the Hereafter, and of those brought close.* (Aal 'Imran, 3:45)

And God says that Jesus ﷺ was 'protected'—together with his mother, the Blessed Virgin Mary—from Satan:

And when she gave birth to her, she said, 'Lord, I have given birth to a female'—and God knew very well what she had given birth to; and the male is not as the female. 'And I have named her Mary, and commend her to You with her seed to protect them from the accursed Satan'. Her Lord accepted the child with gracious acceptance, and made her grow excellently, and Zachariah took charge of her. Whenever Zachariah went into the sanctuary, where she was, he found her with provisions. 'O Mary', he said, 'Whence comes this to you?' She said, 'From God. Truly God provides for whomever He will without reckoning'. Then Zachariah prayed to his Lord, saying, 'Lord, bestow upon me from You a goodly offspring, verily You are the Hearer of supplication'. And the angels called to him, standing in the sanctuary at worship, that 'God gives you good tidings of John, who shall confirm a Word from God; a lord, and one chaste, and a prophet of the righteous'. (Aal 'Imran, 36:39)

And God says that He 'raised up' Jesus ﷺ to Him: *Nay, God raised him up to Him. God is ever Mighty, Wise.* (Al-Nisa', 4:158)

And perhaps in the following verse we can see an indication that Jesus ﷺ was favoured above all the messengers—and thus of course all humanity—who came before him: *Those messengers: some We have favoured above others; some there are to whom God spoke, and some He raised in rank. And We gave Jesus son of Mary the clear proofs, and confirmed him with the Holy Spirit...* (Al-Baqarah, 2:253)

5. Muhammad ﷺ: The Prophet Muhammad ﷺ is the fifth of the five 'Resolute' Messengers (see following section).

GOD'S BELOVED

God gave Prophet Muhammad ﷺ the Holy Qur'an: *And verily We have given you seven of the oft-repeated [verses] and the great Qur'an.* (Al-Hijr, 15:87)

And God made the Prophet Muhammad ﷺ the Seal of the prophets and messengers: *... But [he is] the Messenger of God and the Seal of the Prophets...* (Al-Ahzab, 33:40; see also: al-An'am, 6:19; Yusuf, 12:3; Ta Ha, 20:2, 114; Al-Qasas, 28:85; Al-Insan, 76:25)

'Seal' ('*khatim*') in Arabic implies both 'final' and 'pinnacle'. Thus the Prophet Muhammad ﷺ is also 'the first' Muslim as well as the last Prophet and Messenger. Hence, he is 'the first to submit'; 'the first of those who submit' and 'the first of the worshippers'. God says in the Holy Qur'an that the Prophet Muhammad ﷺ is: *...the first to submit...* (Al-An'am, 6:14) *...the first of those who submit...* (Al-Zumar, 39:12) *...first among the worshippers...* (Al-Zukhruf, 43:81)

All this is proof of God's great love for the Prophet Muhammad ﷺ. Moreover, if God says about the Prophet Moses ﷺ: '*that you might be reared beneath My eyes*' (*Ta Ha*, 20:39), and to the Prophet Noah ﷺ: '*Build the Ark beneath Our eyes and by Our revelation...*' (*Hud*, 11:37), then He says to the Prophet Muhammad ﷺ: '*...for surely you are beneath Our eyes...*' (*Al-Tur*, 52:48), without any additional qualification or limitation.[57]

Furthermore, God and His angels bless the Prophet Muhammad ﷺ with

God's Love for His Messengers and Prophets

a special blessing: *Indeed God and His angels bless the Prophet. O you who believe, invoke blessings on him and invoke peace upon him in a worthy manner.* (Al-Ahzab, 33:56)

And God was 'with' the Prophet Muhammad ﷺ with his companion Abu Bakr ؓ, as mentioned before, with a 'special companionship' in the cave of Thawr:

> *If you do not help him, [know that] God has already helped him, when the disbelievers drove him forth—the second of two; when the two were in the cave—when he said to his companion, 'Do not despair; verily God is with us'. Then God sent down His spirit of peace (sakinatahu) upon him and supported him with legions you did not see; and He made the word of those who disbelieved the nethermost, and the Word of God was the uppermost. And God is Mighty, Wise. (Al-Tawbah, 9:40)*

And God exalted his very mention: *Did We not exalt your mention?* (Al-Sharh, 94:4)

And God favoured him (*'fadl'*) and revealed to him the Book and wisdom, and taught him what he did not know:

> *Were it not for God's favour to you and His mercy, a party of them would have intended to lead you astray; but they lead only themselves astray; they will not hurt you at all. God has revealed to you the Book and wisdom, and He has taught you what you did not know; and God's favour to you is ever great. (Al-Nisa', 4:113)*

And God calls him 'noble': *It is indeed the speech of a noble messenger* (Al-Haqqah, 69:40)

And God praises his nature: *And assuredly you possess a magnificent nature* (Al-Qalam, 68:4)

And God describes him as an 'illuminating lamp': *O Prophet! Indeed We have sent you as a witness, and as a bearer of good tidings,/ and as a warner, and as a summoner to God by His leave, and as an illuminating lamp.* (Al-Ahzab, 33:45–46)

And God describes him as a light: *O People of the Scripture, now there has come to you Our Messenger, making clear to you much of what you used to conceal of the Scripture, and pardoning much. There has verily come to you from God a light, and a Book, lucid.* (Al-Ma'idah, 5:15)

And God describes him as a 'beautiful example' for those who 'hope for God' (and the Arabic word for 'hope'—'*raja*'—implies the concept of love, as will later be seen): *Verily there is for you a beautiful example in the Messenger of God for whoever hopes for [the encounter with] God and the Last Day, and remembers God often.* (Al-Ahzab, 33:21)

The only other occasion in the Holy Qur'an when God describes someone other than the Prophet Muhammad ﷺ as a 'beautiful example' is the Prophet

Abraham ﷺ and his companions in the following verse (but it will be noted that whereas the Prophet Muhammad ﷺ by himself is called a 'beautiful example', the Prophet Abraham ﷺ is only a 'beautiful example' together with those with him):

Verily there is for you a beautiful example in [the person of] Abraham, and those who were with him, when they said to their people, 'We are indeed innocent of you and of what you worship besides God. We repudiate you, and between us and you there has arisen enmity and hate forever until you [come to] believe in God alone'; except for Abraham's saying to his father, 'I shall ask forgiveness for you, but I cannot avail you anything against God'. 'Our Lord, in You we put our trust, and to You we turn [penitently], and to You is the journeying. (Al-Mumtahanah, 60:4)

The Prophet Muhammad ﷺ is also the only person to be called by God in the Holy Qur'an a 'remembrance of God':

God has prepared for them a severe chastisement. So fear God, O you who have cores who believe! God has certainly revealed to you a remembrance, a messenger, / reciting to you the clear signs of God that He may bring forth those who believe and perform righteous deeds from darkness to light. And those who believe in God and act righteously, He will admit them into gardens underneath which rivers flow, wherein they will abide forever. God has verily made a good provision for him. (Al-Talaq, 65:10–11)

Raghib al-Isfahani explains these two verses as follows: 'Concerning His words '*God has certainly revealed to you a remembrance*', it is said that 'remembrance' here describes the Prophet ﷺ just as 'the Word [of God]' describes Jesus ﷺ such that glad tidings of him [the Prophet Muhammad ﷺ] were given in the previous scriptures; thus His words '*a messenger*' refer back to '*a remembrance*'. It is also said that the word 'messenger' is the object of 'remembrance'; that is, as though He were saying: "We have revealed to you a Book wherein there is remembrance of a messenger, reciting…"'⁵⁸

In addition to all of the above, to pledge allegiance to the Prophet Muhammad ﷺ is to pledge allegiance to God Himself, and when one places one's hand in the Prophet Muhammad's, God's Hand is above both, for God says: *Truly those who pledge allegiance to you, in fact pledge allegiance to God. The Hand of God is above their hands. So whoever reneges, reneges against his own soul; and whoever fulfils the covenant which he has made with God, He will give him a great reward. (Al-Fath, 48:10)*

Thus the Messenger of God ﷺ was—and is—a mercy to the worlds: *We did not send you, except as a mercy to all the worlds. (Al-Anbiya', 21:107)*

Finally, God shows the extent of His love for His Messenger Muhammad ﷺ in the following verse, as previously cited: *Say: 'If you love God, follow me, and God will love you more [yuhbibkum], and forgive you your sins; God is Forgiving, Merciful.' (Aal 'Imran, 3:31)*

God's Love for His Messengers and Prophets

From this verse we understand that the Prophet Muhammad ﷺ is not only 'God's Beloved' as such, but also the only person who is referred to unequivocally and definitively in the Holy Qur'an as 'loved more' by God ('*ahbaba*' meaning not merely 'to love', but 'to love more', according to Raghib Al-Isfahani, as explained earlier in Chapter 7: God's Love for Humanity). This is confirmed in the well-known *Hadith* wherein the Prophet Muhammad ﷺ says: 'I am God's beloved, and [I say so] without pride.'[59]

In summary then: it can be said that God favours his prophets more than the rest of humanity (including the saints); that God favours His messengers more than the prophets; that God especially loves the five 'resolute' messengers; and that God made the Prophet Muhammad ﷺ His beloved.

CHAPTER NINE

THOSE WHOM GOD DOES NOT LOVE

Despite the fact that God has favoured humanity in general and that He created human beings *out of* His Mercy and *for* His Mercy, God mentions twelve kinds of people in the Holy Qur'an whom He does not love. It will be noted, however, that God does not say—and in fact never says—that He does not love them *as people*, but rather that He does not love them *in so far as they are identified with* (and indentify themselves with) *certain unlovable traits*. These twelve kinds of people are:

1. 'The disbelievers' ('*al-kafirin*'): *Say: 'Obey God, and the Messenger'. But if they turn their backs, God does not love the disbelievers.* (Aal 'Imran, 3:32) ❋ *That He may requite those who believe and perform righteous deeds out of His favour. Indeed He does not love the disbelievers.* (Al-Rum, 30:45)

2. 'Every guilty ingrate' ('*kulla kaffarin athim*'): *God effaces usury, but He augments voluntary almsgivings with interest. God does not love any guilty ingrate.* (Al-Baqarah, 2:276)

3. 'The aggressors'/'transgressors' ('*al-muʿtadin*'):

> *And fight in the way of God with those who fight against you, but aggress not; God does not love the aggressors.* (Al-Baqarah, 2:190) ❋ *O you who believe, do not forbid the good things that God has made lawful for you and do not transgress; God does not love transgressors.* (Al-Maiʾdah, 5:87) ❋ *Call upon your Lord humbly and quietly. Truly, He does not love the aggressors.* (Al-Aʿraf, 7:55)

4. 'The conceited and the boastful' ('*al-mukhtal al-fakhur*'), or 'every swaggering braggart' ('*kulla mukhtalin fakhurin*'):

> *And worship God, and associate nothing with Him. Be kind to parents, and near kindred, and to orphans, and to the needy, and to the neighbour who is near, and to the neighbour who is a stranger, and to the friend at your side, and to the wayfarer, and to what your right hands own. Surely God does not love the conceited, and the boastful.* (Al-Nisa', 4:36) ❋ *And do not turn your cheek disdainfully from people and do not walk upon the earth exultantly. Truly God does not love any swaggering braggart.* (Luqman, 31:18) ❋ *So that you may not grieve for what escapes you, nor exult at what He has given you. For God does not love any swaggering braggart.* (Al-Hadid, 57:23)

5. 'The treacherous ingrate' ('*al-khawwan al-athim*'): *Indeed God protects*

those who believe. Indeed God does not love the treacherous, the ungrateful. (Al-Hajj, 22:38)

6. 'Every treacherous and sinful [person]' ('*kulla khawwanin kafur*'): *And do not dispute on behalf of those who betray themselves; surely God loves not one who is treacherous and sinful.* (Al-Nisa', 4:107)

7. 'The treacherous' ('*al-kha'inin*'): *And if you fear, from any folk some treachery, then cast it back to them with fairness. Truly God does not love the treacherous.* (Al-Anfal, 8:58)

8. 'The corrupters' ('*al-mufsidin*'):

The Jews said: 'God's hand is fettered'. Fettered be their hands, and they are cursed for what they have said. Nay, but His hands are extended out wide. He expends how He wills. And what has been revealed to you from your Lord will surely increase many of them in insolence and disbelief; and We have cast between them enmity and hatred until the Day of Resurrection. Every time they light the fires of war, God extinguishes them. And they hasten about the earth in corruption, and God does not love corrupters. (Al-Ma'idah, 5:64) ❊ *But seek, in that which God has given you, the Abode of the Hereafter, and do not forget your share of this world, and be good just as God has been good to you. And do not seek to cause corruption in the earth. Surely God does not love the agents of corruption'.* (Al-Qasas, 28:77)

9. 'The prodigal' / 'the excessive' ('*al-musrifin*'):

And He it is Who produces gardens, trellised and untrellised, and palm-trees, and crops diverse in flavour, and olives, and pomegranates, alike and unlike. Eat of the fruit thereof when it ripens, and pay the due thereof on the day of its harvest, and do not be prodigal. Truly, God does not love the prodigal. (Al-An'am, 6:141) ❊ *O Children of Adam! Don your adornment at every place of worship, and eat and drink, but do not be excessive; He truly does not love those who are excessive.* (Al-A'raf, 7:31)

10. 'Those who exult' ('*al-farihin*'): *Indeed Korah belonged to the people of Moses but he became insolent towards them. For We had given him so many treasures that [the number of] their keys would verily have burdened a group of strong men. When his people said to him, 'Do not exult; truly God does not love those who exult.* (Al-Qasas, 28:76)

11. 'The evildoers' ('*al-dhalimin*'):

But as for the believers, who do deeds of righteous, He will pay them in full their wages. God loves not the evildoers. (Aal 'Imran, 3:57) ❊ *If a wound touches you, a like wound already has touched the other people. Such days We deal out in turn among humankind, and that God may know those who believe; and that He may take witnesses from among you, and God does not love the evildoers.* (Aal 'Imran, 3:140) ❊ *For the requital of an evil deed is an evil deed like it. But whoever pardons and reconciles, his reward will be with God. Truly He does not love evildoers.* (Al-Shura, 42:40)

12. 'The arrogant' ('*al-mustakbirin*'): *Without doubt God knows what they keep secret and what they disclose. Indeed He does not love the arrogant.* (*Al-Nahl*, 16:23)

In addition to this, God does not love evil deeds as such, the utterance of evil words and corruption: *God does not love the utterance of evil words out loud, unless a person has been wronged. God is ever Hearer, Knower.* (*Al-Nisa'*, 4:148) *…And God does not love corruption.* (*Al-Baqarah*, 2:205)[60]

Hence God does not love twelve kinds of people who do evil things (in so far as they are people who do evil things), whereas He loves eight or nine kinds of people who do good things. What the twelve kinds of people who do evil things share in common is evidently their evil deeds and thus, *a priori*, *ugliness of soul* as such, which is then manifested in committing sins, the refusal to obey God, and disobedience to His commands—in a similar way to the common denominator of *beauty of soul* shared by the eight kinds of people whom God loves.

Does the fact that there are more categories of people that God does not love than categories of who He does love mean that God hates more than He loves? And does this mean that God's love for the virtuous is symmetrical—and thus comparable with—a hatred of the evildoers? Of course not, because the absence of love is something neutral, and the opposite of love is hatred. Thus God's *lack of love* for the various types of evildoers as such does not mean that God hates them, and thus God's love for the virtuous is in no way symmetrical to His lack of love for evildoers. God never says—not even once—in the Holy Qur'an that He hates anyone or any type of evildoer. God only says that He hates evil *deeds*, or the evil that they cause. The closest thing in the Holy Qur'an to evoking God's hatred is a particular action by treacherous hypocrites (who were pretending to be Muslims) and '*…will be in the lowest level of the Fire…*' (*Al-Nisa*, 4:145). God says about these hypocrites: *If they had desired to go forth, they would have made some preparation for it, but God hated that they should be sent forth, so He slowed them down, and it was said: 'Stay back with those who stay back!'* (*Al-Tawbah*, 9:46)

God hates that the hypocrites should 'go forth' with the Muslims and later betray them—that is all; God does not say that He hates those hypocrites themselves. Similarly, God calls some deeds 'evil' and 'hateful' in His sight but does *not* say that He hates those who commit them:

Do not set up another god besides God, or you will sit blameworthy, forsaken. / And your Lord has decreed that you worship none save Him, and [have] kindness to parents. If they should reach old age with you, one of them or both then do not say to them 'Fie' nor repulse them, but speak to them gracious words. / And lower to them the wing of humility out of mercy and say: 'My Lord, have mercy on them, just as they reared me when I was little'. / Your Lord knows best what is in your hearts. If you are righteous, then truly, to those who are penitent He is Forgiving. / And give the kinsman his due, and the needy and the traveller [as well]; and do not squander. / Indeed squanderers are brothers of devils, and the Devil was ever ungrateful to his Lord. / But if you [have to] overlook them, seeking mercy from your Lord, [a mercy] which you expect [in the future], then speak to them gentle words. / And do not keep your hand chained to your neck, nor open it completely, or you will sit blameworthy and denuded. / Truly your Lord expands provision for whomever He will and He straitens it. Indeed He is ever Aware and Seer of His servants. / And do not slay your children, fearing penury. We shall provide for them and for you. Slaying them is truly a great sin. / And do not come [anywhere] near fornication. It is indeed an indecency and an evil way. / And do not slay the soul [whose life] God has made inviolable, except with due cause. Whoever is slain wrongfully, We have certainly given his heir, a warrant; but let him not commit excess; for he is supported [by the Law]. / And do not come [anywhere] near an orphan's property, except in the fairest manner until he comes of age. And fulfil the covenant. Indeed the covenant will be enquired into. / And give full measure when you measure, and weigh with a right balance: that is better and fairer in return. / And do not pursue that of which you have no knowledge. Indeed the hearing and the sight and the heart—of each of these it will be asked. / And do not walk in the earth exultantly. Indeed you will not rend the earth, nor attain the mountains in height. / All of that—the evil of it is hateful in the sight of your Lord. / This is [part] of the wisdom which your Lord has revealed to you. And do not set up with God any other god, or you will be cast into Hell, blameworthy, abandoned. (Al-Isra', 17:22–39)

In the Qur'anic verse above which says '*All of that—the evil of it is hateful in the sight of your Lord*', there are two indications that God does not hate evildoers and disbelievers. The first is that it says that the 'evil of sin' is hateful to God, not the act of sin itself—much less the sinner. The second is that God says the evil of sin is 'hateful' to Him, and does not say that He *hates* sin—something being hateful to a subject, does not necessarily imply that the subject will let himself hate it. And God knows best.

Thus God shows in the Holy Qur'an that He does not hate anyone, but rather that He loves all beings and things except certain types of evildoers, disbelievers, idolaters and hypocrites, and certain of their actions. This holds true even when God sternly condemns disbelievers for their most evil deeds, and even when He curses them:

And whoever slays a believer deliberately, his requital is Hell, abiding therein, and God is angry with him and has cursed him, and has prepared for him a mighty chastisement. (Al-Nisa', 4:93) ❊ Say: 'Shall I tell you of what is worse than that by way of requital from God? Those whom God has cursed and with whom He is angry, and some of whom He has turned into apes and swine, and worship the false deity. They are worse situated and further astray from the even way'. (Al-Ma'idah, 5:60) ❋ *And so that He may chastise the hypocrites, men and women, and the idolaters, men and women, and those who make evil assumptions about God. For them will be an evil turn of fortune, and God is angry with them, and He has cursed them, and has prepared for them Hell—and it is an evil destination!* (Al-Fath, 48:6)

These Qur'anic verses contain mention of a divine curse; divine wrath; a mighty chastisement and a lack of love for them on God's part. However, they do not say that God hates the disbelievers themselves. And since God does not say that He hates the disbelievers, Muslims may not say so either[61] for God says: *So do not strike any similitude for God. Truly God knows, and you do not know.* (Al-Nahl, 16:74)

Equally, God never says—*in the Holy Qur'an* at least—that He 'abhors' ('*yabghad*') anyone, or even any specific deed, although 'abhorrence' ('*bughd*') as such is mentioned in the Qur'an: *Satan desires only to precipitate enmity and abhorrence between you through wine and games of chance and to bar you from the remembrance of God and from prayer. So will you then desist?* (Al-Ma'idah, 5:91)

As regards 'loathing' ('*maqt*')—which, like 'abhorrence', is one of the opposites of love—God's 'loathing' is mentioned four times in the Holy Qur'an:

It is greatly loathsome to God that you say what you do not do. (Al-Saff, 61:3) ❋ *Those who dispute the signs of God without any warrant that has come to them—greatly loathsome [is that] in the sight of God and in the sight of those who believe. So God sets a seal on the heart of every arrogant tyrant.* (Ghafir, 40:35) ❋ *It is He Who made you successors in the earth. So whoever disbelieves, his disbelief will be to his own detriment. And their disbelief does not increase the disbelievers with their Lord [in anything] except loathing. And their disbelief does not increase the disbelievers [in anything] except loss.* (Fatir, 35:39) ❋ *Indeed to those who disbelieve it will be proclaimed [to them]: 'Surely God's loathing is greater than your loathing of yourselves, as you were called to faith but you used to disbelieve'.* (Ghafir, 40:10)

However, as is the case with 'hatred' and 'abhorrence', nowhere in the Holy Qur'an is it stated that God 'loathes' anyone. God 'loathes' only certain deeds, and although disbelief increases the loathsomeness of people in the sight of God, God never says in the Holy Qur'an that disbelief actually takes evildoers to the level of God's 'loathing' as such.[62] This is an aspect of God's mercy, and perhaps there is herein a great lesson about mercy for humanity: namely that people should love good people, and hate certain evil deeds, but not hate people as such, even when they commit these evil deeds.

PART TWO: THE MESSENGER OF GOD'S ﷺ LOVE

CHAPTER TEN

THE MESSENGER OF GOD'S ﷺ LOVE FOR GOD

We mentioned previously that the Messenger of God ﷺ was '... *first to submit...*' (*Al-An'am*, 6:14); '...*first of those who submit*' (*Al-Zumar*, 39:12), and '...*first among the worshippers*' (*Al-Zukhruf*, 43:81). These descriptions constitute clear evidence of the Messenger's absolute love for God. We also mentioned that the Messenger of God ﷺ 'hoped for' God (and that 'hope'—'*raja*'—implies a kind of love): *Verily there is for you a beautiful example in the Messenger of God for whoever hopes for God and the Last Day, and remembers God often.* (*Al-Ahzab*, 33:21)

However, the clearest proof of the Messenger of God's ﷺ love for his Lord is found in the following beautiful verses:

Say: 'As for me, my Lord has guided me to a straight path, a right religion, the creed of Abraham, a hanif; and he was not of the idolaters'. / Say: 'My prayer and my rituals, and my living, and my dying, are all for God, the Lord of the Worlds. / No associate has He. And to this, I have been commanded, and I am the first of those who submit'. / Say: 'Shall I seek any other than God for a lord, when He is the Lord of all things?' Every soul earns only against itself; and no burdened soul shall bear the burden of another. Then to your Lord shall you return, and He will inform you of that over which you differed. (*Al-An'am*, 6:161–164)

The Messenger of God's ﷺ prayer, rituals, life and death all being for God is the ultimate expression of the highest possible level of love. It means that the Messenger of God's ﷺ love for God went beyond mere emotion, and even beyond the 'ardent love' of which God speaks in the following verse: '...*but those who believe love God more ardently...*' (*Al-Baqarah*, 2:165) so that he was completely immersed with all of his being in the ocean of God's love. It is as though God were saying—after affirming that the Messenger ﷺ was *first of those who submit*—that the Messenger of God ﷺ had become unable to desire or seek anything but God. Thus God calls on His Messenger to say: *Say: 'Shall I seek any other than God for a lord, when He is the Lord of all things?'*

Thus just as the Messenger ﷺ is the beloved of God (as we saw earlier), God is the Beloved of His Messenger. This reciprocity of love means that the Messenger is included in the promise of mutual love of which the following verse speaks:

O you who believe, whoever of you apostatises from his religion, God will assuredly bring a people whom He loves and who love Him: humble towards believers, stern towards disbelievers, struggling in the way of God, and fearing not the reproach of any reproacher. That is God's favour; He gives it to whom He will; and God is Embracing, Knowing. (Al-Ma'idah, 5:54)

We can now understand the following *Hadith*: 'There have been made beloved to me, of your world, three things: perfume, women, and the coolness of my eye in the prayer.'[63]

Perfume and women reminded the Messenger of God ﷺ of Paradise (where they are promised—see for example *Surat Al-Waqi'ah*, 56:22 and 89) and thus of nearness to God; and prayer is a direct invocation of God. Perfume, women and prayer were thus all beloved to the Messenger of God ﷺ only because they reminded him of God, who was the Messenger's ﷺ real Beloved. Thus the Messenger of God ﷺ was completely infused in all his being with love for God, even in this world and even in his love of natural things. Indeed, God says: *Indeed God and His angels bless the Prophet. O you who believe, invoke blessings on him and invoke peace upon him in a worthy manner.* (Al-Ahzab, 33:56)

CHAPTER ELEVEN

THE MESSENGER OF GOD'S ﷺ LOVE FOR THE BELIEVERS

God made His Messenger ﷺ a witness, a bearer of good tidings, and a warner to humankind: *O Prophet! Indeed We have sent you as a witness, and as a bearer of good tidings, and as a warner.* (Al-Ahzab, 33:45) *Indeed We have sent you as a witness, and a bearer of good tidings, and a warner.* (Al-Fath, 48:8)

And He commanded His Messenger ﷺ to pray for forgiveness for the believers and the Muslims:

Know, then, that there is no god except God, and ask forgiveness for your sin and for the believing men and believing women. And God knows your going to and fro and your place of rest. (Muhammad, 47:19) ❋ *O Prophet, if believing women come to you, pledging allegiance to you that they will not ascribe anything as partner to God, and that they will not steal, nor commit adultery, nor slay their children, nor bring any lie that they have invented [originating] between their hands and their legs, nor disobey you in what is decent, then accept their allegiance and ask God to forgive them; surely God is Forgiving, Merciful.* (Al-Mumtahanah, 60:12) ❋ *It was by the mercy of God that you were lenient with them; had you been harsh and fierce of heart, they would have dispersed from about you. So pardon them, and ask forgiveness for them, and consult them in the matter. And when you are resolved, rely on God; for God loves those who rely.* (Aal 'Imran, 3:159) ❋ *Only they are believers who believe in God and His Messenger and who, when they are with him in a collective affair do not leave until they have asked leave of him. Truly those who ask leave of you—it is they who believe in God and His Messenger. So when they ask leave of you for some affair, of theirs, give permission to whom you will of them, and ask God to forgive them. Truly God is Forgiving, Merciful.* (Al-Nur, 24:62)

God allowed His Messenger ﷺ to pray for forgiveness for the hypocrites: *Ask forgiveness for them, or do not ask forgiveness for them. If you ask forgiveness for them seventy times, God will not forgive them. That is because they disbelieved in God and His Messenger; and God does not guide the wicked folk.* (Al-Tawbah, 9:80)

The Messenger of God ﷺ chose to pray for forgiveness for the hypocrites more than seventy times, saying: 'I hear that my Lord has given me leeway in their affair; so by God, I shall pray for forgiveness more than seventy times, that perhaps God will forgive them!'⁶⁴

Nevertheless God says, in His knowledge of them: *It will be the same for them, whether you ask forgiveness for them or do not ask forgiveness for them: God will never forgive them. Indeed God does not guide the immoral folk.* (Al-Munafiqun, 63:6)

The Messenger of God ﷺ also almost consumed himself with worry for humankind:

> *Perhaps, you might consume yourself that they will not become believers.* (Al-Shuʿaraʾ, 26:3) ۝ *Is he, the evil of whose deeds is made [to seem] fair to him, so that he deems it good [...]? Indeed God leads astray whomever He will and guides whomever He will. So do not let your soul expire through woes for their sake. Indeed God is Knower of what they do.* (Fatir, 35:8)

Moreover, not only did the Messenger of God ﷺ nearly consume himself with grief because he wanted people to believe in God, he nearly consumed himself with grief about people even when they would not believe, and he knew that they would not believe: *Yet it may be that you will consume yourself in their wake if they should not believe in this discourse out of grief.* (Al-Kahf, 18:6)

This is a very subtle but beautiful point: the Messenger of God ﷺ continued to care for people and feel mercy towards them even when they rejected him. He did not care about them only as potential believers: he cared about them even when they stayed in disbelief (and thus presumably in enmity towards him) to the point where he nearly consumed himself about them—that is to say, nearly died of grief—out of care for his enemies.

This shows the universal mercy⁶⁵ the Messenger of God ﷺ felt towards all people, not only the believers. God affirms this by stating that He sent the Messenger as a mercy to *all the worlds*: *We did not send you, except as a mercy to all the worlds* (Al-Anbiyaʾ, 21:107)

But of course, the Messenger ﷺ was a special mercy for those who believe:

> *And of them are those who injure the Prophet, saying, 'He is only a listener!' Say: 'A listener to good for you, one who believes in God and has faith, in the believers, and who is a mercy to those of you who believe. Those who injure God's Messenger, for them there is a painful chastisement'.* (Al-Tawbah, 9:61)

And his prayers were a comfort for the believers: *Take of their wealth some alms, to purify them and to cleanse them thereby, and pray for them; truly your prayers are a comfort for them. And God is Hearer, Knower.* (Al-Tawbah, 9:103)

And indeed God commanded him to be kind to the believers: *Do not extend your glance toward that which We have given different groups of them to enjoy, and do not grieve for them, and lower your wing for the believers.* (Al-Hijr, 15:88) *And lower your wing to the believers who follow you.* (Al-Shuʿaraʾ, 26:215)

And God indicates that the Messenger was full of pity and mercy for the believers: *Verily there has come to you a messenger from among yourselves for whom it is grievous that you should suffer; who is full of concern for you, to the believers full of pity, merciful.* (Al-Tawbah, 9:123)

And God praises His Messenger's ﷺ tenderness of heart towards the believers:

> *It was by the mercy of God that you were lenient with them; had you been harsh and fierce of heart, they would have dispersed from about you. So pardon them, and ask forgiveness for them, and consult them in the matter. And when you are resolved, rely on God; for God loves those who rely.* (Aal ʿImran, 3:159)

Indeed, the Messenger ﷺ was so tender with the believers that he was shy of them:

> *O you who believe, do not enter the Prophet's houses unless permission is granted you to [share] a meal without waiting for the [right] moment. But when you are invited, enter, and, when you have had your meal, disperse, without any [leisurely] conversation. Indeed that is upsetting for the Prophet, and he is [too] shy of you, but God is not shy of the truth. And when you ask anything of [his] womenfolk, ask them from behind a screen. That is purer for your hearts and their hearts. And you should never cause the Messenger of God hurt; nor ever marry his wives after him. Assuredly that in God's sight would be very grave.* (Al-Ahzab, 33:53)

This shyness he felt towards the believers—and the way he would prefer them to himself—is a clear proof of the Messenger of God's ﷺ love for the believers, for God links love to preferring others to oneself, even if one's need is great:

> *And those who had settled in the hometown, and [had abided] in faith before them, love those who have emigrated to them, and do not find in their breasts any need of that which those [others] have been given, but prefer [others] to themselves, though they be in poverty. And whoever is saved from the avarice of his own soul, those—they are the successful.* (Al-Hashr, 59:9)

All of this shows that the Messenger of God ﷺ felt a great love for the believers especially, and for all humanity in general.

PART THREE: HUMAN LOVE

CHAPTER TWELVE

HUMANITY'S LOVE FOR GOD

WHY HUMAN BEINGS SHOULD LOVE GOD

We mentioned earlier (in Chapter 6: The Universe and Love) that everything loves God. In addition to this innate, natural love, there is also a special love which believers feel for God's Beauty, His Names, and His Qualities. God says:

> *God—there is no god save Him. To Him belong the Most Beautiful Names. (Ta Ha, 20:8)* ❋ *And to God belong the Most Beautiful Names—so invoke Him by them, and leave those who blaspheme His Names. They will be requited for what they did. (Al-A'raf, 7:180)* ❋ *Say: 'Invoke God or invoke the Compassionate One, whichever you invoke, to Him belong the Most Beautiful Names'. And be not loud in your prayer, nor be silent therein, but seek between that a way. (Al-Isra', 17:110)*

Indeed, since human beings love beauty, they cannot help but love the absolute and perfect beauty which is in God's Names and Qualities.

It is also natural for human beings to love God because of the mercy He shows them, for humanity was created *out of* God's mercy as well as *for* God's Mercy, as we saw earlier (in Chapter 5: Love is the Root of Creation). We might also add that it is natural for human beings to love God for the blessings He has given them, for God has showered human beings with blessings both open and hidden:

> *Do you not see that God has disposed for you whatever is in the heavens and whatever is in the earth, and He has showered His favours upon you, [both] outwardly and inwardly? Yet among people there are those who dispute concerning* ❋ *God without any knowledge or guidance or an illuminating scripture. (Luqman, 31:20)*

Human beings also cannot but love God because of the tenderness He shows them: *God is tender with His servants. He provides for whomever He will. And He is the Strong, the Mighty. (Al-Shura, 42:19)*

And human beings cannot but love God because He is 'the Loving': *And ask forgiveness of your Lord, then repent to Him. Truly my Lord is Merciful, Loving. (Hud, 11:90) And He is the Forgiving, the Loving. (Al-Buruj, 85:14)*

And likewise, human beings cannot but love God because of how He forgives them, pardons them and relents towards them for all their sins (except idolatry):

Tell My servants that verily I am the Forgiving, the Merciful. (Al-Hijr, 15:49) ❋ *Your Lord knows best what is in your hearts. If you are righteous, then truly, to those who are penitent He is Forgiving. (Al-Isra', 17:25)* ❋ *[T]hen glorify with praise of your Lord and seek forgiveness from Him; for verily He is ever Ready to Relent (Tawwab). (Al-Nasr, 110:3)* ❋ *And they would have you hasten on the evil, rather than the good, when there have indeed occurred before them exemplary punishments. Truly your Lord is forgiving to humankind despite their evil-doing; and truly your Lord is severe in retribution. (Al-Raʿd, 13:6)* ❋ *And He it is Who accepts repentance from His servants, and pardons evil deeds, and knows what they do. And He answers those who believe and perform righteous deeds, and He enhances them of His favour. And as for the disbelievers, for them there will be a severe chastisement. (Al-Shura, 42:25–26)* ❋ *And [there are] others, who have confessed their sins; they have mixed a righteous deed with another that was bad. It may be that God will relent to them. Truly God is Forgiving, Merciful. / Take of their wealth some alms, to purify them and to cleanse them thereby, and pray for them; truly your prayers are a comfort for them. And God is Hearer, Knower. / Do they not know that God is He Who accepts repentance from His servants and takes the voluntary alms, and that God is He Who is the Relenting and the Merciful? (Al-Tawbah, 9:102–104)* ❋ *And vie with one another hastening to forgiveness from your Lord, and to a garden as wide as the heavens and the earth that has been prepared for those who fear. / Who expend in prosperity and adversity, and restrain their rage, and pardon their fellow-men; and God loves those who are virtuous. / And who, when they commit an indecency or wrong themselves, remember God, and pray forgiveness for their sins—and who shall forgive sins but God?—and who do not persist in what they did, knowing. / Those—their requital is forgiveness from their Lord, and Gardens beneath which rivers flow, abiding therein; excellent is the wage of those workers! (Aal ʿImran, 3:133–136)* ❋ *Whoever does evil, or wrongs himself, and then prays for God's forgiveness, he shall find God is Forgiving, Merciful. (Al-Nisa', 4:110)* ❋ *Say [that God declares]: 'O My servants who have been prodigal against their own souls, do not despair of God's mercy. Truly God forgives all sins. Truly He is the Forgiving, the Merciful. / And turn [penitently] to your Lord and submit to Him, before the chastisement comes on you, whereupon you will not be helped. / And follow the best of what has been revealed to you from your Lord before the chastisement comes on you suddenly while you are unaware. (Al-Zumar, 39:53–55)* ❋ *God forgives not that anything should be associated with Him. But He forgives other than that to whomever He wills. Whoever associates anything with God, then he has indeed invented a tremendous sin. (Al-Nisa', 4:48)* ❋ *God does not forgive* that anything should be associated with Him; He forgives all except that, to whomever He will. Whoever associates anything with God, verily he has strayed far away. (Al-Nisa', 4:116)⁶⁶

Furthermore, human beings cannot but love God because He answers their prayers:

If misfortune should befall a man, he calls upon Us [lying] on his side, or sitting or standing; but when We have relieved him of his misfortune, he passes on, as if he had never called upon Us because of a misfortune that befell him. So is adorned for the prodigal that which they do. (Yunus, 10:12) ❋ *Nay; upon Him you will call, and He will remove that for which you call upon Him, if He wills, and you will forget what you associate with Him. (Al-Anʿam, 6:41)* ❋ *Whatever grace you have, it is from God. Then when misfortune befalls you, to Him you cry for help. Then when He has rid you of the misfortune, behold, a group of you attribute partners to their Lord. (Al-Nahl, 16:53–54)* ❋ *Or He Who answers the desperate one when he calls to Him and Who removes [his] distress and makes you successors in the earth. Is there a god with God? Little do you remember. (Al-Naml, 27:62)*

God even asks human beings to call upon Him so that He will give to them. God says:

Do not covet that in which God has favoured some of you above others. To men a share from what they have earned and to women a share from what they have earned. And ask God of His favour; God is ever Knower of all things. (Al-Nisa', 4:32) ❋ *And your Lord has said, 'Call on Me and I will respond to you. Surely those who disdain to worship Me shall enter Hell [utterly] humiliated'. (Ghafir, 40:60)* ❋ *And when My servants question you concerning Me, I am near; I answer the call of the caller when he calls to Me; so let them respond to Me, and let them believe in Me that they might go aright. (Al-Baqarah, 2:186)*

We notice here God's 'nearness' to human beings; God mentions this 'nearness' again in the following Qur'anic verse: *And verily We created man and We know what his soul whispers to him, and We are nearer to him than his jugular vein. (Qaf, 50:16)*

This 'nearness' exists despite the fact that God is free of need from the whole of creation, for He says:

Therein are clear signs, the station of Abraham; and whoever enters it is in security. It is the duty of people towards God to make the pilgrimage to the House, all who are able to make their way there. As for the one who disbelieves, God is Independent of all the worlds. (Aal ʿImran, 3:97) ❋ *And whoever struggles, struggles only for his own sake. For truly God is Independent of [the creatures of] all the worlds. (Al-ʿAnkabut, 29:6)* ❋ *And Moses said: 'If you are thankless, you and all who are on earth, lo! assuredly God is Independent,*

Praised'. (Ibrahim, 14:8) ❋ *If you are ungrateful, indeed God is Independent of you, though He does not approve of ingratitude for His servants. And if you give thanks, He will approve of it for you. And no burdened soul shall bear the burden of another [soul]. Then to your Lord will be your return, whereat He will inform you of what you used to do. Indeed He is Knower of what is in the breasts.* (Al-Zumar, 39:7)

Equally, this 'nearness' exists despite the fact that God is absolutely free of need for human beings (though they, on the other hand, are always in abject need of Him):

O humankind! You are the ones who are in need of God. And God, He is the Independent, the Praised. (Fatir, 35:15) ❋ *Lo! there you are those who are being called to expend in the way of God; yet among you there are those who are niggardly; and whoever is niggardly is niggardly only to his own soul. For God is the Independent One, while you are the needy. And if you turn away, He will replace you with another people, and they will not be the likes of you.* (Muhammad, 47:38)

Thus despite God's absolute independence from human beings, and human beings' utter need for God, God answers all sincere petitions human beings put to Him, for He says: *And He gives you of all that you ask of Him. And if you were to enumerate God's graces, you could never number them. Lo! man is verily a wrong-doer and unthankful!* (Ibrahim, 14:34)

Furthermore, God promises a goodly life to the righteous who call upon Him: *Whoever acts righteously, whether male or female, and is a believer, him verily We shall revive with a goodly life. And We shall surely pay them their reward according to the best of what they used to do.* (Al-Nahl, 16:97)

And He promises to deliver them from distress: *Then We shall deliver Our messengers and the believers. In like manner it is incumbent upon Us to deliver the believers.* (Yunus, 10:103) And to succour them: *And verily We sent before you messengers to their people and they brought them clear signs. Then We took vengeance upon those who were guilty; and it was ever incumbent upon Us to succour the believers.* (Al-Rum, 30:47)

In summary: God is loved first for His Beauty in Itself, then for the beauty, mercy, goodness and favour that He shows to human beings (and in fact all creatures). Indeed, God's Qualities include Absolute Beauty, Mercy and Generosity, and He has graced human beings with beautiful gifts and blessings beyond measure, and is always answering their needs and prayers; so how could human beings not love God? God says: *Whatever grace you have, it is from God. Then when misfortune befalls you, to Him you cry for help.* (Al-Nahl, 16:53)

HOW HUMAN BEINGS SHOULD LOVE GOD

Now after all we have said above, it remains to say that God does not accept the mere sentiment of love alone from human beings. God says: *Say: 'If you love God, follow me, and God will love you more [yuhbibkum], and forgive you your sins; God is Forgiving, Merciful.'* (Aal 'Imran, 3:31)

God expects human beings—if they truly love Him—to follow the example of the Messenger of God ﷺ; and to follow Messenger of God ﷺ means that human beings must truly love God with all their beings and souls, and in all their actions. God says;

> *Say: 'As for me, my Lord has guided me to a straight path, a right religion, the creed of Abraham, a hanif; and he was not of the idolaters'. / Say: 'My prayer and my rituals, and my living, and my dying, are all for God, the Lord of the Worlds. / No associate has He. And to this, I have been commanded, and I am the first of those who submit'.* (Al-An'am, 6:161-4)

In order to reach this level of totally devoted and absorbed love, human beings must follow the Messenger of God ﷺ in: (a) his character, and (b) his actions.

(a) As regards his character, we have seen that the Messenger of God ﷺ possessed a magnificent nature: *And assuredly you possess a magnificent nature.* (Al-Qalam, 68:4) This 'magnificent nature' includes all the good qualities which God loves (namely: reliance, purity, repentance, justice, fighting in God's cause, patience, fear of God, and especially virtue, as we saw earlier).

(b) As regards his actions, the best of all actions is the remembrance of God, since God says: '*...the remembrance of God is surely greater...*' (Al-'Ankabut, 29:45); and since the '*beautiful example*' of the Messenger of God ﷺ in action is to '*hope for God*' and to '*remember God often*', for God says: *Verily there is for you a beautiful example in the Messenger of God for whoever hopes for [the encounter with] God and the Last Day, and remembers God often.* (Al-Ahzab, 33:21)

If a person follows the Messenger of God ﷺ in his character and his actions (and in particular by remembering God often), he or she will become one of those who truly love God and whom God 'loves more' ('ahbaba'). This is reflected in God's affirmation that prayer without sacrifice for others is not enough:

> *And they give food, despite [their] love of it to the needy, and the orphan, and the prisoner.* (Al-Insan, 76:8) ❊ *Have you seen him who denies the Judgement? / That is he who repels the orphan / and does not urge the feeding of the needy. / So woe to them who pray, / those who are heedless of their prayers, / those who make a pretence, / and deny aid.* (Al-Ma'un, 107:1-7) ❊ *It is not piety that you turn your faces to the East and to the West. True piety is [that of] the one who believes in God and the Last Day and the angels and the Book and the prophets, and who gives of his substance, however cherished[67], to kinsmen and orphans and the needy and the traveller and beggars, and for slaves, and who observes prayer and pays the alms, and those who fulfil*

their covenant when they have engaged in a covenant, those who endure with fortitude misfortune, hardship, and peril. These are the ones who are truthful, and these are the ones who are God-fearing. (Al-Baqarah, 2:177)

As regards this last verse, in the Qur'anic Commentary *Tafsir al-Jalalayn* it is explained that the phrase '*that you turn your faces to the East and to the West*' means 'in prayer', and that '*however cherished*' means 'despite his [or her] love for his [or her] own wealth'.[68] These meanings are also clear in the following verse: *You will not attain piety until you expend of what you love; and whatever thing you expend, God knows of it.* (Aal 'Imran, 3:92)

By following the *Sunnah* with all his or her being and actions (and in particular by remembering God often), the believer begins to truly love God. When this happens, love of God and *struggling in His way* becomes dearer to the believer than everything else on earth:

Say: 'If your fathers, and your sons, and your brothers, and your wives, and your clan, and the possessions which you have acquired, and merchandise for which you fear there may be no sale, and dwellings which you love, are dearer to you than God and His Messenger and struggling in His way, then wait until God brings about His command. And God does not guide the wicked folk'. (Al-Tawbah, 9:24)

In this state the believer seeks to 'rise up' for God, alone or with another of a similar disposition: *Say: 'I will give you just one [piece of] admonition: that you rise up for God in twos and individually, and then reflect: there is no madness in your companion. He is just a warner to you before [the befalling of] a severe chastisement'.* (Saba, 34:46)

The believer then 'flees' to God. God says: *So flee unto God. Truly I am a clear warner to you from Him.* (Al-Dhariyat, 51:50)

Thereafter the believer becomes empty of worldly desires, longs for God and toils in devotion to Him. God says:

So when you are empty, strive hard (fa'nsab). / And long for (fa'rghab) your Lord. (Al-Sharh, 94:7–8) ❋ *And mention the Name of your Lord, and devote yourself [exclusively] to Him with complete devotion. / Lord of the east and the west; there is no god except Him, so take Him for a Guardian (Wakil), / and bear patiently what they say, and part with them in a beautiful manner (hajran jamilan).* (Al-Muzzammil, 73:8–10)

Parting from people *in a beautiful manner (hajran jamilan)* implies not only taking leave of people graciously, but also (and more importantly) that being alone with God and taking God as sole Guardian (*Al-Wakil*)—after the initial difficulties of 'striving hard' (*nasab*), and on condition that one remembers God with utter devotion and emptiness—is an experience of unspeakable beauty and mystery. This is true Beauty, and it explains the true manner of parting from people in a beautiful way (*hajran jamilan*): parting is beautiful because of the Beauty of the destination. Indeed, God is the Absolutely Beautiful (*Al-Jamil*), and He may grant the believer ever more 'longing for' (*raghab*) Him or some knowledge of His Beauty and an experience of His Grace. Thus, if a believer goes to God as a servant and alone—and hence having left everything and everyone else behind completely and being utterly destitute and in need—God 'appoints love' for the believer. God says:

> *There is none in the heavens and the earth but he comes to the Compassionate One as a servant. / Verily He knows their number and has counted them precisely. / And each one of them will come to Him on the Day of Resurrection, [each one] alone. / Truly those who believe and perform righteous deeds—for them the Compassionate One shall appoint love.* (*Maryam*, 19:93–96)

This no doubt holds true in both this world and the hereafter, for in the Holy Qur'an we see that Joseph said that being in prison (where he would be alone and free to worship God) would be more *lovable* (*ahabb*) to him—and not simply ultimately 'better for him'—than the (adulterous) embraces of beautiful women: *He said, 'My Lord, prison is more lovable (ahabb) to me than that to which they are urging me. And if You do not fend off their wiles from me, then I shall tend towards them and become of the ignorant.* (*Yusuf*, 12:33)

However, in the Holy Qur'an, the beauty of loving, remembering and worshipping God in isolation is perhaps characterised most by the person of the Blessed Virgin Mary, who, whilst worshipping God within the sanctuary alone as a child, was miraculously given, as a Divine Grace, summer fruits in winter and winter fruits in summer[69] and provision *without reckoning*. God says:

> *Her Lord accepted the child with gracious acceptance, and made her grow excellently, and Zachariah took charge of her. Whenever Zachariah went into the sanctuary, where she was, he found her with provisions. 'O Mary', he said, 'Whence comes this to you?' She said, 'From God. Truly God provides for whomever He will without reckoning'.* (*Aal 'Imran*, 3:37)

Of course not every believer is given supernatural graces and experiences like the Blessed Virgin Mary, but nevertheless every believer can, by God's leave, attain both serenity of heart (*itmi'nan al-qalb*) and God's spirit of peace (*al-sakinah*)[70] through love of God and through the remembrance and worship of God. God says:

> *[T]hose who believe and whose hearts are reassured (tatma'innu) by God's remembrance. Verily by God's remembrance are hearts reassured;* (*Al-Ra'd*, 13:28) ❁ *He it is Who sent down the spirit of Peace into the hearts of the believers, that they might add faith to their faith. And to God belong the hosts of the heavens and the earth. And God is ever Knower, Wise;* (*Al-Fath*, 48:4; see also: *Al-Fath*, 48:18 and 26, and *Al-Tawbah*, 9:26)

Thus when the believer devotes himself or herself to God *with complete devotion*, he or she eventually, but inevitably, becomes completely satisfied—and indeed, utterly delighted—with what God has given him or her, for God says:

If only they had been content with what God and His Messenger have given them, and had said, 'Sufficient for us is God; God will give us from His favour, and His Messenger [will also give us]; to God we are suppliants'. (Al-Tawbah, 9:59) ❋ *Does God not suffice His servant? Yet they would frighten you of those besides Him. And whomever God leads astray, for him there is no guide. (Al-Zumar, 39:36)*

This is the state—and God knows best—wherein God 'purchases' the soul of the believer in return for Paradise and 'the supreme triumph'. God says:

Indeed God has purchased from the believers their lives and their possessions, so that theirs will be [the reward of] Paradise: they shall fight in the way of God and they shall kill and be killed; that is a promise which is binding upon Him in the Torah, and the Gospel and the Qur'an; and who fulfils his covenant better than God? Rejoice then in this bargain of yours which you have made, for that is the supreme triumph. (Al-Tawbah, 9:111)

In this state, the believer also becomes one of those who truly follow the Messenger ﷺ to the extent that they are considered to be 'with' the Messenger ﷺ:

Muhammad is the Messenger of God, and those who are with him are hard against the disbelievers, merciful among themselves. You see them bowing, prostrating [in worship]. They seek favour from God and beatitude. Their mark is on their faces from the effect of prostration. That is their description in the Torah, and their description in the Gospel is as a seed that sends forth its shoot and strengthens it, and it grows stout and rises firmly upon its stalk, delighting the sowers, so that He may enrage the disbelievers by them. God has promised those of them who believe and perform righteous deeds forgiveness and a great reward. (Al-Fath, 48:29)

In this state also the believer loves God 'ardently', as one ought to love one's Lord. None but the believer can have such a love, or reach its degree of 'ardour'. God says:

Yet there be people who take to themselves rivals besides God, loving them as God is loved; but those who believe love God more ardently; If those who did evil could but see, as they shall when they behold the chastisement, that power altogether belongs to God, and that God is terrible in chastisement. (Al-Baqarah, 2:165)

God summarises this kind of love and all it entails in the following Qur'anic verse: *Truly those who believe and perform righteous deeds—for them the Compassionate One shall appoint love. (Maryam, 19:96)*

Faith and righteous deeds are tantamount to following the Messenger of

God ﷻ. After this, the Compassionate One ('*Al-Rahman*') graces a person with 'love' ('*wudd*'). No one can reach this level of love without faith and righteous deeds because this 'love' is a divine 'appointment' or 'gift', not a human deed, though it nevertheless requires belief and righteous deeds. Thus human beings' love for God begins as an emotion, and then—by following the Messenger of God ﷺ through righteous deeds, virtuous character and remembrance of God— it becomes part of the believer's very being and soul. Then the believer attains unto Paradise and the 'supreme triumph', and tastes the reality of God's love as a 'divine appointment' or 'gift'. This love is then stronger and more ardent than any worldly love, and stronger and more ardent than any love which anyone who does not believe in God could ever experience, or even imagine. This explains the allusion to God's power in His words: *…but those who believe love God more ardently; If those who did evil could but see, as they shall when they behold the chastisement, that power altogether belongs to God, and that God is terrible in chastisement.* (*Al-Baqarah*, 2:165)

Thus the Messenger of God ﷺ taught the following supplication: 'O God, make Your love more beloved to me than myself, my family, and cool water.'[71] And he also taught the supplication:

> 'O God, provide me with Your love and the love of all that will benefit me in Your sight. O God, make all those things that I love which you have given me a source of strength for me to do what You love. O God, make all those things that I love which You have not given me a space for me to fill with what You love.'[72]

WHAT INTENTIONS AND MOTIVES HUMAN BEINGS MUST HAVE IN LOVING GOD

God warns against insincere worship in the Holy Qur'an: *And their worship at the [holy] house is naught but whistling and hand-clapping. Therefore [it is said unto them]: 'Taste of the doom because you disbelieve'.* (*Al-Anfal*, 8:35)

Thus the Messenger of God ﷺ said:

> 'The first person to be judged on the Day of Judgment will be a man who was martyred. He will be brought forth, shown the favours he enjoyed, and he will recognize them. He [God] will say, 'What did you do concerning these?' He will say, 'I fought for Your sake until I was martyred.' He will say, 'You have lied. Rather, you fought so that it would be said, "He was bold," and it was said.' Then it will be commanded that he be dragged along on his face until he is thrown into the Fire. Then there will be a man who acquired and dispensed knowledge and recited the Qur'an. He will be brought forth, shown the favours he enjoyed, and he will recognize them. He will say, 'What did you do concerning these?' He will say, 'I acquired and dispensed knowledge and recited the Qur'an for Your sake.' He will

say, 'You have lied. Rather, you acquired knowledge so that it would be said, "He is learned," and you recited the Qur'an so that it would be said, "He is a reciter," and it was said.' Then it will be commanded that he be dragged along on his face until he is thrown into the Fire. Then there will be a man whom God enriched and gave all manner of wealth. He will be brought forth, shown the favours he enjoyed, and he will recognize them. He will say, 'What did you do concerning these?' He will say, 'I left no path upon which you ordered that a bestowal be made without giving something there for Your sake.' He will say, "You have lied. Rather, you did that so that it would be said, "He is generous," and it was said.' Then it will be commanded that he be dragged along on his face and then thrown into the Fire'.[73]

Thus we must ask: 'what makes worship as such true and sincere', and, above all, 'what makes it acceptable to God'? Now, no matter what human beings do, God knows what is going on inside them: *Lo! now they fold up their breasts that they may hide [their thoughts] from Him. At the very moment when they cover themselves with their clothing, God knows that which they keep hidden and that which they proclaim. Lo! He is Aware of what is in the breasts [of people].* (Hud, 11:5)

Furthermore, He judges human beings on what is in their souls: *Unto God [belongs] whatsoever is in the heavens and whatsoever is in the earth; and whether you make known what is in your souls or hide it, God will bring you to account for it. He will forgive whom He will and He will punish whom He will. God is Able to do all things.* (Al-Baqarah, 2:284)

Thus it is people's secret intentions that God looks at in whatever they do: *Lo! those who fear their Lord in secret, theirs will be forgiveness and a great reward. / And keep your opinion secret or proclaim it, lo! He is Knower of all that is in the breasts [of people]. / Should He not know what He created? And He is the Subtle, the Aware.* (Al-Mulk, 67:12–14)

For this reason, worship of God—including, most importantly, love of God—must be sincere. God says:

Indeed We have revealed to you the Book with the truth; so worship God, devoting your religion sincerely to Him. / Surely to God belongs sincere religion. And those who take besides Him patrons, [say]: 'We only worship them so that they may bring us near to God'. God will indeed judge between them concerning that about which they differ. Truly God does not guide one who is a liar, a disbeliever. (Al-Zumar, 39:2–3) ❊ *Say: 'God [alone] I worship, devoting [my] religion sincerely to Him.* (Al-Zumar, 39:14) ❊ *So supplicate God, devoting [your] religion sincerely to Him, however much the disbelievers be averse.* (Al-Ghafir, 40:14) ❊ *He is the Living; there is no god except Him. So supplicate Him, devoting [your] religion sincerely to Him. Praise be to God, the Lord of the Worlds.* (Al-Ghafir, 40:65)[74]

Indeed, the Messenger of God ﷺ said: 'Actions are in their intentions. Every person shall have what he intended'.[75]

Thus the following question must be asked: *exactly what secret intentions and motives must human beings have in acts of worship (and other righteous deeds) in order that they be acceptable to God?* In other words: *what intentions and motives are not just vanity and hypocrisy?* As applied to love which someone experiences subjectively and therefore knows it is present (to some degree at least), the question becomes: *how can the lover know if his or her love for God is truly sincere and thus acceptable to God?* In other words, *what intentions and motives must human beings have in loving God?* God Himself answers these questions a number of times in the Holy Qur'an:

(1) *Lo! your Lord is God Who created the heavens and the earth in six Days, then mounted He the Throne. He covers the night with the day, which is in haste to follow it, and has made the sun and the moon and the stars subservient by His command. His verily is all creation and commandment. Blessed be God, the Lord of the Worlds! / [O mankind!] Call upon your Lord humbly and in secret. Lo! He loves not aggressors. / Work not confusion in the earth after the fair ordering [thereof], and call on Him in fear and ardent hope. Lo! the mercy of God is near to the virtuous. / And He it is Who sends the winds as tidings heralding His mercy, till, when they bear a cloud heavy [with rain)], We lead it to a dead land, and then cause water to descend thereon and thereby bring forth fruits of every kind. Thus bring We forth the dead that perhaps you may remember. / As for the good land, its vegetation comes forth by permission of its Lord; while as for that which is bad, only the useless comes forth (from it). Thus do We recount the tokens for people who give thanks. / As for the good land, its vegetation comes forth by permission of its Lord; while as for that which is bad, only the useless comes forth (from it). Thus do We recount the tokens for people who give thanks. (Al-Aʿraf, 7:54–58)*

(2) *Only those believe in Our revelations who, when they are reminded of them, fall down prostrate and hymn the praise of their Lord, and they are not scornful, / Who forsake their beds to cry unto their Lord in fear and ardent hope, and spend of that We have bestowed on them. / No soul knows what is kept hid for them of joy, as a reward for what they used to do. / Is he who is a believer like unto him who is an evil-liver? They are not alike. / But as for those who believe and do good works, for them are the Gardens of Retreat - a welcome [in reward] for what they used to do. (Al-Sajdah, 32:15–19)*

(3) *Is he who pays adoration in the watches of the night, prostrate and standing, being wary of the hereafter and hoping for the mercy of his Lord, [to be accounted equal with a disbeliever]? Say [unto them, O Muhammad]: are those who know equal with those who know not? But only men of understanding will pay heed. (Al-Zumar, 39:9)*

(4) *And Zachariah, when he cried unto his Lord: 'My Lord! Leave me not childless, though You are the Best of inheritors'. / Then We heard his prayer, and bestowed upon him John, and adjusted his wife [to bear a child] for him. Lo! they used to vie one with the other in good deeds, and they cried unto Us in longing and in awe, and were humble (khashi'in) before Us.* (Al-Anbiya, 21:89–90)

One of the remarkable things about these four passages is the way they *each depict the same three motives for sincere worship—albeit from different* perspectives. They depict two of these motives clearly, and the third motive more subtly: we observe that in the first passage (in *Surat Al-A'raf) fear (khaufan)* and *ardent hope (tama'an)* are mentioned after *humility (tadarru'an)*[76] and *secrecy (khufyatan).* In the second *passage* (in *Surat Al-Sajdah) fear (khaufan)* and *ardent hope (tama'an)* are also mentioned. In the third passage (in *Surat Al-Zumar) being wary (yahdhar)* of the hereafter and *hoping (yarju)* for mercy (and hence also *fear* and *hope*—although in fact in Arabic the two words for 'being wary' *[yahdhar]* and 'hoping' *[yarju]* are different from the Arabic words for 'fear' *[khaufan]* and 'ardent hope' *[tama'an]* in the previous two passages) are mentioned. In the fourth passage—which describes the Prophets Zachariah ﷺ, John (the Baptist, *Yahya*) ﷺ and Zachariah's wife and John's mother (Elisabeth)—*fear* has deepened into *awe (rahaban),* and *hope* has deepened into *longing (raghaban).*

The third motive is more subtle. In the first passage: God starts by mentioning some of the great phenomena of the universe and then asks rhetorically if their existence does not necessarily imply creation by God and (hence) God's dominion over that creation. Then God mentions how humanity should worship, starting with *humility* and *secrecy,* these being states of the soul imposed by knowledge or awareness of God's Greatness, and consequently by awareness of the greatness of being able to worship Him. Then *fear* and *hope* are mentioned. Then, finally, God returns to mentioning the phenomena of the universe, starting with the tidings of the winds and ending with the fruits of the land. Thus before worship there is the Truth of God as seen through His creation, and after worship there are the tidings of the fruits of His creation. Hence *knowledge* comes before *fear* and *hope,* and after them, but is linked to them.

This is more evident in the second passage. There, after mentioning the worshippers, their fear, their hope and their reward, God suddenly—and at first glance, surprisingly—asks if the believers and the evil-livers are alike, and then says that they are not. Belief in God, or faith *(iman),* is evidently a mode of knowledge of God's existence (depending on the degree of certainty and enlightenment behind that belief) and good works are an extrinsic proof of true faith and certainty. Thus God then mentions the reward of those who believe and do good works.

In the third passage, the connection between fear, hope and knowledge is clearer still: God starts by comparing the (sincere) worshiper with his (or her) fear and hope; then there is an ellipsis (whose very void expresses the futility of the non-worshiper), and then God asks if 'those who know' are equal to 'those who do not know'? Finally, God says that only those *of understanding will pay heed*. Thus knowledge is clearly bound to fear and hope.

In the fourth passage, which describes the more exalted state of the prophets, faith and knowledge have deepened into humility before God: true faith and knowledge of God necessarily bring knowledge of human beings' nothingness before Him, and thus humility before Him.

All this is to say then that God accepts only three motives for people's worship: (1) that they fear Him and that they fear punishment for their sins—and this fear opens onto awe of God; (2) that they have hope in God, and hope to be forgiven for their sins—and this hope opens onto longing, and thus love, since they can only hope for (and *a fortiori* long for) something they love (and indeed, as we see later in Chapters 21: The Different Kinds of Love and 22: The Stages of Love, ardent hope [*tamaʿ*] is a stage of love, and longing [*raghab*] is a kind of love); and (3) that they have faith in, or *know*, God. Knowing that God is God, and that human beings are what they are, how can human beings not worship Him, and how can they not be humble before Him?

Fear, hope and knowledge are the intentions which God accepts for worship because they affect and motivate the three main faculties of the human soul which was created by God to worship Him. These three faculties are: the will, sentiment and the intelligence. The will was created for freedom of choice; sentiment was created for loving the good and the beautiful, and the mind or the intelligence was created for comprehending the truth.

This is seen in the *Fatihah* itself, the 'opening' and—according to the Messenger of God ﷺ himself—'the greatest Surah in the Holy Qur'an', whose second half consists of the supplication: *You [alone] we worship, and You [alone] we ask for help. / Guide us to the straight path, / The path of those upon whom You have bestowed Your grace, not [the path] of those against whom there is wrath, nor of those who are astray.* (Al-Fatihah, 1: 5–7)

You [alone] we worship: this is a prayer of adoration and love. *[A]nd You [alone] we ask for help*: this is a prayer of fear and will. *The path of those upon whom You have bestowed Your grace, not [the path] of those against whom there is wrath, nor of those who are astray*: this is a prayer of truth and knowledge. The *Fatihah* is recited of necessity in every single cycle (*rakʿah*) of every single canonical prayer of every day—thus at least seventeen times by every practicing Muslim in history—and its second half (quoted above) is the quintessence not only of personal supplication but of human prayer as such. Thus its predication upon the sentiment, the will and the intelligence shows perfectly that the only motives God accepts from human beings are fear, love (or hope) and knowledge.[77]

We will see later God willing (in Chapter 23: Falling in Love) how all three faculties are necessarily involved in falling in love, and how each of these faculties gives rise to specific stages of love as they incline towards the beloved. This is in a sense obvious because in true love everything in the heart, soul, mind, and will or strength—and indeed the whole person, with all its faculties—of a human being must eventually be involved. However, it also means that there is no such thing as true love of God without some fear of Him or some without knowledge of Him. Of course the starting point of worship of God can be either one of three motives (or any combination of them), but by the time worship of God becomes true love of God, it must involve fear and knowledge. This explains why loving God (with sentiment) means following the Messenger of God ﷺ, obeying him (with the will) and not being a disbeliever (with the intelligence). God says: *Say: 'If you love God, follow me, and God will love you more, and forgive you your sins; God is Forgiving, Merciful. / Say: 'Obey God, and the Messenger'. But if they turn their backs, God loves not the disbelievers.* (Aal 'Imran, 3:31–32)

ON LOVE FOR WHAT REMINDS ONE OF GOD

A person's love for God requires—and inevitably leads to—love for what reminds him or her of God, and this means love of the Messenger ﷺ (as we will see in a coming chapter, God willing)—as well as: (a) love for religion and worship in general; (b) love for prayer and invocation in particular; (c) love for the Holy Qur'an; (d) love for nature as God's creation wherein one can see God's works and creatures, and (e) love even for fate and destiny, wherein one can see God's will manifested.

(a) On love for religion and worship in general, God says:

Say: 'If your fathers, and your sons, and your brothers, and your wives, and your clan, and the possessions which you have acquired, and merchandise for which you fear there may be no sale, and dwellings which you love, are dearer to you than God and His Messenger and struggling in His way, then wait until God brings about His command. And God does not guide the wicked folk'. (Al-Tawbah, 9:24) ❈ *Say: 'If you love God, follow me, and God will love you more [yuhbibkum], and forgive you your sins; God is Forgiving, Merciful.'* (Aal 'Imran, 3:31) ❈ *That [is his state]. And whoever venerates the sacraments of God, then that derives from the piety of the hearts.* (Al-Hajj, 22:32) ❈ *[That is] that. And whoever venerates the sacraments of God—that shall be better for him with his Lord. And cattle are lawful for you, except for that which* has been recited to you. So avoid the abomination of idols and avoid false speech. (Al-Hajj, 22:30)

(b) On love for prayer and invocation in particular, God says:

Verily there is for you a beautiful example in the Messenger of God for whoever hopes for [the encounter with] God and the Last Day, and remembers God often. (Al-Ahzab, 33:21) ❊ *Recite what has been revealed to you of the Book, and maintain prayer; truly prayer prevents against lewd acts and indecency. And the remembrance of God is surely greater, and God knows what you do. (Al-ʿAnkabut, 29:45)* ❊ *The believers are only those who, when God is mentioned, their hearts tremble, and when His verses are recited to them, they increase their faith, and who rely upon their Lord. (Al-Anfal, 8:2)* ❊ *Say: 'My prayer and my rituals, and my living, and my dying, are all for God, the Lord of the Worlds.' (Al-Anʿam, 6:162)*

And as already cited, the Messenger of God ﷺ said: 'Three have been made beloved to me, of this world, perfume and women; and the coolness of my eye is in the prayer.'[78]

(c) On love for the Holy Qur'an, God says:

Is he whose breast God has opened to Islam, so that he follows a light from his Lord [like he who disbelieves]? So woe to those whose hearts have been hardened against the remembrance of God. Such are in manifest error. / God has revealed the most beautiful of discourses, a Book, consimilar in coupled phrases—whereat quiver the skins of those who fear their Lord; then their skins and their hearts soften to the remembrance of God. That is God's guidance, by which He guides whomever He wishes; and whomever God leads astray, for him there is no guide. (Al-Zumar, 39:22–23) ❊ *Truly my Protector is God Who reveals the Book, and He takes charge of the righteous. (Al-Aʿraf, 7:196)* ❊ *The believers are only those who, when God is mentioned, their hearts tremble, and when His verses are recited to them, they increase their faith, and who rely upon their Lord. (Al-Anfal, 8:2)* ❊ *And whenever a surah is revealed, there are some of them who say: 'Which of you has this increased in faith?' As for those who believe, it has increased them in faith and they rejoice. (Al-Tawbah, 9:124)* ❊ *Messengers bearing good tidings and warning so that people might have no argument against God after the messengers. God is ever Mighty, Wise. / But God bears witness with what He has revealed to you; He has revealed it through His knowledge; and the angels also bear witness; and God suffices as a Witness. (Al-Nisa', 4:165–166)*

(d) On love for nature as God's creation and wherein one can see God's works and creatures, God says:

So behold the effects of God's mercy, how He revives the earth after it has died. Surely He is the Reviver of the dead, and He has power over all things. (Al-Rum, 30:50) ❊ *To God belongs the kingdom of the heavens and of the earth, and God has power over all things. / Surely in the creation of the heavens and the earth, and in the alternation of night and day, there are signs for people of cores. / Those who remember God, standing and sitting and on their sides, and reflect upon the creation of the heavens and the earth: 'Our Lord, You have not created this in vain. Glory be to You! So guard us against the chastisement of the Fire. (Aal 'Imran, 3:189–191)* ❋ *Say: 'Behold what is in the heavens and in the earth!' But signs and warners do not avail a folk who will not believe. (Yunus, 10:101)* ❋ *Surely in the creation of the heavens and the earth, and the alternation of the night and day, and the ships that run in the sea with what profits men, and the water God sends down from the heaven with which He revives the earth after it is dead, and He scatters abroad in it all manner of crawling things; and the disposition of the winds, and the clouds compelled between heaven and the earth—surely therein are signs for a people who comprehend. / Yet there be people who take to themselves rivals besides God, loving them as God is loved; but those who believe love God more ardently. If those who did evil could but see, as they shall when they behold the chastisement, that power altogether belongs to God, and that God is terrible in chastisement. (Al-Baqarah, 2:164–165; see also: Al-Rum, 30:20–27; Al-Rahman, 55:1–13.)*

Nature reminds one of its Creator, and therefore it is natural for people to love nature and see God's signs in it. People can also see God's signs within themselves as they are also a part of nature, or at least of creation. God says:

And in the earth there are signs for those who know with certainty, and in your souls. Will you not then perceive? (Al-Dhariyat, 51:20–21) ❋ *We shall show them Our signs in the horizons and in their own souls until it becomes clear to them that it is the truth. Is it not sufficient that your Lord is witness to all things? (Fussilat, 41:53)*[79]

(e) On love for fate and destiny, wherein one can see God's will manifested, God says:

Those who, when they are struck by an affliction, say, 'Surely we belong to God, and to Him we will return'. (Al-Baqarah, 2:156) ❋ *If only they had been content with what God and His Messenger have given them, and had said, 'Sufficient for us is God; God will give us from His favour, and His Messenger [will also give us]; to God we are suppliants'. (Al-Tawbah, 9:59)*

All of this shows that love of God necessarily means love for all that leads to God as love—or at least to appreciation, thanks and gratitude for it: if one truly loves God, one cannot help but love what leads to God as well, as part of that love of God.

CHAPTER THIRTEEN

THE BELIEVER'S LOVE FOR THE MESSENGER OF GOD ﷺ

Just as a believer must love God for His Beauty and because of the blessings He has given him (or her), so also he (or she) must also love the Messenger of God ﷺ for his beauty of soul and because of his love and care for believers as previously discussed (in Chapter 11: The Messenger of God's ﷺ Love for the Believers), for God says: *Verily there has come to you a messenger from among yourselves for whom it is grievous that you should suffer; who is full of concern for you, to the believers full of pity, merciful.* (Al-Tawbah, 9:128)

It is this being 'full of pity' ('*raouf*') and mercy ('*rahim*')—this love—that will make the Messenger of God ﷺ intercede for the believers on the Day of Judgment (according to the *Hadith*). This is the explanation of the 'praiseworthy station' of which God speaks in the following Qur'anic verse: *And for a part of the night, keep vigil therewith as a supererogatory [devotion] for you. It may be that your Lord will raise you to a praiseworthy station.* (Al-Isra', 17:79)

Ibn Kathir narrates the following *Hadith* about this 'praiseworthy station' on the Day of Judgment in his Qur'anic Commentary (*Tafsir*):

> A *Hadith* of Anas ibn Malik ؓ: Imam Ahmad ibn Hanbal narrated, from Yahya ibn Sa'id, from Sa'id ibn Abi 'Aruba, from Anas ؓ that the Prophet ﷺ said: 'The believers will be gathered on the Day of Resurrection, and will be inspired to say, "Were we to seek intercession from our Lord, He might relieve us from this position of ours!" They will go to Adam and say, "You are the father of humankind; God created you with His hand, and bade the angels prostrate before you, and taught you the names of all things. Intercede for us with your Lord, that He might give us relief from this position of ours!" Adam will say to them, "Not I", and he will tell of the sin he committed, and will feel shame before his Lord because of it; and he will say, "But go to Noah, for he was the first messenger God sent to the people of the earth." They will go to Noah, and he will say, "Not I", and will tell of the mistake he made in questioning his Lord about something of which he had no knowledge; and he will feel shame before his Lord because of that. "But go to Abraham, the Friend (*khalil*) of the Compassionate One". They will go to Abraham, and he will say, "Not I; but go to Moses, a servant to whom God spoke, and gave the Torah." They will go to Moses, and he will say, "Not I", and tell them of how he killed a man who had killed no one,

and will feel shame before his Lord because of that. 'But go to Jesus, God's Servant and Messenger, and His Word and His Spirit'. They will go to Jesus, and he will say, 'Not I, but go to Muhammad, a servant whose sins past and future were forgiven for him.' They will come to me, and I will stand and walk between two throngs of believers, until I seek leave of my Lord. And when I see my Lord, I will fall down prostrate before Him, and He will leave me as long as God wills to leave me. Then it will be said, 'Arise, Muhammad. Speak and it shall be heard; intercede and your intercession shall be granted; ask and you shall be given.' I will raise my head, and praise Him with words of praise He will teach me. Then I will intercede, and He will set a limit for me, and I will place them in Paradise. Then I will return to Him a second time, and when I see my Lord, I will fall down prostrate before Him, and He will leave me as long as God wills to leave me. Then it will be said, 'Arise, Muhammad. Speak and it shall be heard; ask and you shall be given; intercede and your intercession shall be granted.' I will raise my head, and praise Him with words of praise He will teach me. Then I will intercede, and He will set a limit for me, and I will place them in Paradise. Then I will return a third time, and when I see my Lord, I will fall down prostrate before Him, and He will leave me as long as God wills to leave me. Then it will be said, 'Arise, Muhammad. Speak and it shall be heard; ask and you shall be given; intercede and your intercession shall be granted.' I will raise my head, and praise Him with words of praise He will teach me. Then I will intercede, and He will set a limit for me, and I will place them in Paradise. Then I will return a fourth time, and say: 'My Lord, no one remains but those whom the Qur'an has confined.'

Equally, Anas ibn Malik related that the Prophet said:

'And there will be taken out of hell all those who say 'There is no god but God' and have but a barley grain's weight of goodness in their hearts; and then there will be taken out of hell all those who say 'There is no god but God' and have but a wheat grain's weight of goodness in their hearts; and then there will be taken out of hell all those who say 'There is no god but God' and have but an atom's weight of goodness in their hearts.' This was narrated in the two *Sahih* collections [of Bukhari and Muslim] on the authority of Sa'id. Imam Ahmad narrated the entire event on the authority of 'Affan, who heard it from Hammad ibn Salamah, who heard it from Thabit, who heard it from Anas.[80]

In addition to this great mercy that the Messenger of God will extend to the believers on the Day of Judgment—and in addition to the love which the Messenger of God showed in his lifetime—believers should also love the

Messenger of God ﷺ for his beauty of character to which God Himself attests when He says: *And assuredly you possess a magnificent nature* (*Al-Qalam*, 68:4)

If a believer does not feel love—or feels insufficient love—for the Messenger of God ﷺ, this can only mean that he or she has not fully perceived or understood the beauty of the Messenger's character and the perfection of his virtue (and consequently that he or she has misunderstood the Messenger's nature and intentions). This in turn means that he or she has not fully perceived or understood the meaning and value of good character and virtue in general. In this case, there is a fault in the believer's soul and a flaw in his faith. The Messenger ﷺ said: 'None of you [truly] believes until I am more beloved to him than his father, his son, and all humankind.'[81]

And the Messenger of God ﷺ also said:

'Three [things] there are which, if they are a found in a person, he tastes the sweetness of faith: For God and His Messenger to be more beloved to him than everything else; for him to love a man for nothing but God's sake; and for him to hate to return to unbelief as he would hate to be cast into a fire.'[82]

And God explains this in the following Qur'anic verses:

The Prophet is closer to the believers than their [own] souls, and his wives are their mothers. And those related by blood are more entitled, [from] one another in the Book of God than the [other] believers and the Emigrants, barring any favour you may do your friends. This is written in the Book. (*Al-Ahzab*, 33:6) ❈ *It is not for the people of Medina and for the Bedouins [who dwell] around them to stay behind God's Messenger, and to prefer their lives to his life; that is because neither thirst nor toil nor hunger afflicts them in the way of God, nor tread they any tread that enrages the disbelievers, nor gain any gain from the enemy, but a righteous deed is therefore recorded for them. Truly God does not leave the wage of the virtuous to go to waste.* (*Al-Tawbah*, 9:120)

Thus the believer should love the Messenger of God ﷺ—in whose noble person all virtue is perfected—more than the believer loves his or her own self, full, as it is bound to be, with faults and sins. Indeed, when a believer venerates the Messenger of God ﷺ, this reflects a depth of understanding of his or her own soul and state before God; and when a believer further honours the Messenger, this reflects a depth of love for goodness as such, and thus for God, who is the Good ('*Al-Barr*'—see: the Holy Qur'an, *Surat Al-Tur*, 52:28) and hence the Source of all goodness. In other words, understanding and loving the Messenger of God ﷺ is the first step towards truly understanding and loving virtue as such, because, precisely, the Messenger of God was the embodiment of perfect virtue; and understanding and loving virtue is the first step towards *practicing* virtue and *being* virtuous.

The Messenger of God ﷺ implied this when he said: 'I have been sent to complete the beauty of virtuous character'.⁸³

The mere emotion of love for the Messenger of God ﷺ is not necessarily sufficient in itself. It must be accompanied by deeds. The deed which accompanies sincere love of the Messenger of God ﷺ is so important that God Himself commands the believer to perform it and does so Himself first followed by His angels. This deed is of course to invoke blessings and peace upon the Messenger of God ﷺ: *Indeed God and His angels bless the Prophet. O you who believe, invoke blessings on him and invoke peace upon him in a worthy manner.* (Al-Ahzab, 33:56)

Now good deeds as such are rewarded tenfold: *Whoever brings a good deed shall receive tenfold the like of it, and whoever brings an evil deed shall only be requited the like of it; and they shall not be wronged.* (Al-An'am, 6:160)

But the good deed of invoking blessings upon the Messenger of God ﷺ is rewarded with ten blessings from God Himself, for the Messenger said: 'Whosoever invokes one blessing on me, God sends ten blessings to him.'⁸⁴

And constantly invoking blessings upon the Messenger of God ﷺ is rewarded with the forgiveness of all sins:

> Ubayy ibn Ka'b ؓ said: 'When two thirds of the night had passed, the Messenger of God ﷺ would get up and say: "O People! Remember God, remember God! The Tremor which is followed by the Aftershock has come! Death has come, with all that it contains! Death has come, with all that it contains!" I said, "O Messenger of God, I invoke blessings upon you a great deal; how much of my prayer should I devote to you?" He said, "As you wish." I said, "A quarter?" He said, "As you wish; and if you increased, it would be better for you." I said, "Half?" He said, "As you wish; and if you increased, it would be better for you." I said, "Two thirds?" He said, "As you wish; and if you increased, it would be better for you." I said, "Shall I devote to you all of my prayer?" He said, "If so, then all your worries shall be relieved, and all your sins shall be forgiven."'⁸⁵

Moreover, constant invoking of blessings upon the Messenger of God ﷺ allows the believer to be 'with' the Messenger of God in thought. In this case, the believer will be as described in the Qur'anic verse:

> *Muhammad is the Messenger of God, and those who are with him are hard against the disbelievers, merciful among themselves. You see them bowing, prostrating [in worship]. They seek favour from God and beatitude. Their mark is on their faces from the effect of prostration. That is their description in the Torah, and their description in the Gospel is as a seed that sends forth its shoot and strengthens it, and it grows stout and rises firmly upon its stalk, delighting the sowers, so that He may enrage the disbelievers by them. God has*

promised those of them who believe and perform righteous deeds forgiveness and a great reward. (Al-Fath, 48:29)

And when the believer is 'with' the Messenger ﷺ, he does not desire merely God's forgiveness, but also God's beatitude ('*ridwan*'), as the verse cited above says. This is one of the meanings of the Messenger of God's words: 'You shall be with those you love.'[86]

Therefore the believer should be careful never to commit any offence against the Messenger of God ﷺ:

O you who believe, do not venture ahead of God and His Messenger, and fear God. Surely God is Hearer, Knower. / O you who believe, do not raise your voices above the voice of the Prophet, and do not shout words at him, as you shout to one another, lest your works should be invalidated without your being aware. / Truly those who lower their voices in the presence of God's Messenger—they are the ones whose hearts God has tested for God-fearing. For them will be forgiveness and a great reward. / Truly those who call you from behind the apartments—most of them do not understand. / And had they been patient until you came out to them, it would have been better for them; and God is Forgiving, Merciful. (Al-Hujurat, 49:1–5)

Love and respect for the Messenger of God ﷺ—and the invoking of blessings and peace upon him—constitute a great test of the heart's God-fearingness, as the Qur'anic verse (cited above) makes clear: '*they are the ones whose hearts God has tested for God-fearing.*' This explains why love for the Messenger of God ﷺ is an essential duty of every believer, not as a mere emotion, but as a state of understanding of the reality of God's Messenger and the great mercy he shows believers. This also explains why it is also obligatory to invoke blessings and peace upon the Messenger of God ﷺ. God emphasises this, and indeed summarises the whole issue of love (or at least affection) for the Messenger of God in His words:

That is the good tidings which God gives to His servants who believe and perform righteous deeds. Say: 'I do not ask of you any reward for it, except affection for kinsfolk. And whoever acquires a good deed, We shall enhance for him its goodness. Surely God is Forgiving, Appreciative. (Al-Shura, 42:23)

CHAPTER FOURTEEN

LOVE FOR THE FAMILY AND KIN OF THE MESSENGER OF GOD ﷺ

God says:

> *That is the good tidings which God gives to His servants who believe and perform righteous deeds. Say: 'I do not ask of you any reward for it, except affection for kinsfolk [qurba]. And whoever acquires a good deed, We shall enhance for him its goodness. Surely God is Forgiving, Appreciative.* (Al-Shura, 42:23)

This means two things: (1) that the tribe of Quraysh were obliged to love the Messenger of God ﷺ because he was related to them; and (2) that believers must love the kin ('*qurba*') of the Messenger of God ﷺ. Ibn Kathir says in his Commentary: 'God Almighty's words "*Say: 'I do not ask of you any reward for it, except the affection for [my] kinsfolk'*" mean: Say, Muhammad, to the idolaters of Quraysh: "I do not ask you to give me anything in return for this message and counsel; I ask only that you keep your evil from me and allow me to deliver the messages of my Lord. If you do not wish to help me, then at least do not harm me, for the sake of the kinship we share." ... And do not neglect the counsel you have been given about the Prophet's Household, and the command to treat them well, respect them and honour them; for they are of pure lineage, members of the noblest household ever to exist on earth, in terms of dignity, rank and pedigree. This is especially true if they are followers of the pure and noble prophetic *Sunnah*, as were their forefathers such as 'Abbas and his sons, and 'Ali and his household and progeny ﷺ. It is authentically related that the Messenger of God ﷺ said in his sermon at Ghadir Khumm: "I leave with you the two weighty things: The Book of God, and my progeny; and they shall never be divided until they come to me at the Pool [in Paradise].'"[87]

And Qurtubi says (after citing what Ibn Kathir says above): '*Kinsfolk*' ('*qurba*') here means the kin of the Messenger ﷺ; that is: 'I ask no reward of you save that you have affection for my kinsfolk and my household', just as they were commanded to honour their own kinsfolk. This is the opinion of 'Ali ibn Husayn, 'Amr ibn Shu'ayb, and Suddi.[88]

And Fakhr al-Din al-Razi says: 'The upshot is that this verse proves that it is obligatory to love the family of the Messenger of God ﷺ and his Companions.'[89]

So who are the 'kinsfolk'[90] ('*qurba*') of the Messenger of God ﷺ? The Messenger of God ﷺ is seen to have different degrees of 'kinship' in the Holy Qur'an. These are (in descending order):

(a) The 'People of the Cloak' of the Messenger of God ﷺ (namely: ʿAli, Fatimah, Al-Hasan and Al-Husayn ؓ).
(b) The Household ('*Ahl Bayt*') of the Messenger of God ﷺ including his wives.
(c) The Closest Companions to the Messenger of God ﷺ (including Zayd ibn Harithah ؓ and Abu Bakr ؓ).
(d) The Companions who were 'with' the Messenger of God ﷺ.
(e) The Emigrants and Helpers.
(f) The Tribe of Quraysh in general.
(g) The Arabs in general.
(h) All believers (as we will see in a coming chapter, God willing).

(a) Concerning the 'People of the Cloak' of the Messenger of God ﷺ (namely ʿAli ؓ, the Lady Fatimah Al-Zahra, Hasan and Husayn ؓ), God says: *And whoever disputes with you concerning him, after the knowledge that has come to you, say: 'Come! Let us call our sons and your sons, our women and your women, our selves and your selves, then let us humbly pray and invoke God's curse upon those who lie'.* (Aal ʿImran, 3:61)

The 'People of the Cloak' are naturally those of the first degree of proximity to the Messenger of God ﷺ. The Lady ʿAishah, the Messenger of God's ﷺ wife, related:

> The Prophet ﷺ went out one morning in a striped cloak of black hair. Hasan, the son of Ali, came along, and [the Prophet] brought him underneath it. Then Husayn came along and went underneath with him. Then Fatimah came along, and he brought her under it. Then ʿAli came along, and he brought him under it. Then he said: '*Indeed God wishes but to rid you of sin, People of the House, and to purify you with a thorough purification.*' (Al-Ahzab, 33:33)[91]

And ʿUmar ibn Abi Salamah, the stepson of the Messenger of God ﷺ, said:

> This verse, '*Indeed God wishes but to rid you of sin, People of the House, and to purify you with a thorough purification.*' (Al-Ahzab, 33:33) was revealed to the Prophet ﷺ in the house of Umm Salamah. The Prophet ﷺ then called Fatimah, Hasan and Husayn and covered them in a cloak; he also covered ʿAli, who was behind him. Then he said: 'O God, these are my Household, so rid them of sin and purify them with a thorough purification!' Umm Salamah said: 'And am I with them, O Prophet of God?' He said, 'You are in your own place; and yours shall be a good end'[92]

And concerning the Lady Fatimah, God says: *We have assuredly given you Abundance. / So pray to your Lord and sacrifice. / Indeed it is your antagonist who is the severed one.* (Al-Kawthar, 108:1–3)

Fakhr al-Din al-Razi comments on this verse: … 'The third opinion is that

'Abundance' means his [the Prophet's ﷺ] children. They say this is because this chapter was revealed in response to those who criticised [the Prophet ﷺ] for having no sons. It meant that God would give him progeny who would remain as time passed; and look at how many of the Prophetic Family were killed, yet the world is still full of them, and not a single noteworthy member of the tribe of Umayy remains in the world. And look at how many great scholars were from the Household, such as al-Baqir, al-Sadiq, al-Kazim, al-Rida and Nasf al-Zakiyya, and their like.'[93]

And concerning ʿAli bin Abi Talib ؈, God says: *Your patron is God only, and His Messenger, and the believers who establish prayer and pay the alms, bowing down. / Whoever affiliates with God and His Messenger and the believers; for verily the party of God, they are the victors.* (Al-Maʾidah, 5:55–56)

Fakhr al-Din al-Razi comments: 'Concerning His words "*and the believers*", there are two opinions: the first is that it means all the believers…. The second opinion is that this verse is speaking about a specific person; there are several opinions about this person's identity. ʿIkrimah related that this verse was revealed about Abu Bakr ؈. The second opinion, related by ʿAta' on the authority of Ibn ʿAbbas, is that it was revealed about ʿAli ibn Abi Talib ؈. It is related that ʿAbdullah ibn Salam said: "When this verse was revealed, I said, 'O Messenger of God, I saw ʿAli give his ring in charity to a poor person even as he bowed in prayer, and we passed it to him.'" It is related that Abu Dharr ؈ said: "I prayed the midday prayer with the Messenger of God ﷺ one day, and a beggar came into the mosque to beg but no one gave him anything. The beggar raised his hands to the sky and said, 'O God, bear witness that I begged in the mosque of the Messenger ﷺ but no one gave me anything!' ʿAli was bowing at the time, and he gestured to the beggar with his little finger, upon which there was a ring. The beggar came forward and took the ring, as the Messenger of God ﷺ looked on."'[94]

And Abu Tufayl ؈ reported that the Messenger of God ﷺ said: 'Whose master I am, his master this man is [meaning ʿAli]. O God, be the friend of him who is his friend, and the foe of him who is his foe.'[95]

And Saʿd ibn Abi Waqqas ؈ reported that the Messenger of God ﷺ said to ʿAli ؈: 'Are you not content to have the position next to me as Aaron had next to Moses, save that there will be no prophet after me?'[96]

Moreover, God says: *But there are other men who sell themselves, desiring God's pleasure; and God is Gentle with His servants.* (Al-Baqarah, 2:207) Fakhr al-Din al-Razi comments on this verse: 'There are several narrations concerning the circumstances behind this verse's revelation…. The third narration states that it was revealed about ʿAli ibn Abi Talib ؈, who slept in the bed of the Messenger of God ﷺ the night he went out to the Cave.'[97]

Love for the Family and Kin of the Messenger of God ﷺ

Concerning his grandsons Al-Hasan ؓ and Al-Husayn ؓ, the Messenger of God ﷺ said: 'Al-Hasan and Al-Husayn are the lords of the youths of Paradise.'[98]

Al-Hasan ؓ and Al-Husayn ؓ were also considered to be the 'sons' (*'abna'*) of the Messenger of God ﷺ in the verse mentioned above which laid down a challenge (*'ayat al-mubahala'*) to the sincerity of (Aal 'Imran, 3:61). Their being the Messenger's 'sons' might seem to contradict God's words: *'Muhammad is not the father of any man among you, but the Messenger of God and the Seal of the Prophets. And God has knowledge of all things'* (Al-Ahzab, 33:40) In fact, however, there is no contradiction because Al-Hasan ؓ and Al-Husayn ؓ were not yet men at that time (being only young children), and the verse specifies *'any man among you'*.

(b) Concerning the Household (*'Ahl Bayt'*) of the Messenger of God ﷺ, including his wives, God honours them by mentioning them in the Holy Qur'an:

> *And bid your family to prayer, and be steadfast in [the maintenance of] it. We do not ask of you any provision. We [it is Who] provide you, and the [best] sequel will be in favour of God-fearing.* (Ta Ha, 20:132) ❊ *And when you went forth at dawn from your family to assign the believers their places for battle, and God hears, knows.* (Aal 'Imran, 3:121)

And God says that He wishes to rid the Household of the Messenger of God ﷺ of sin, saying:

> *And stay in your houses and do not flaunt your finery in the [flaunting] manner of the former Time of Ignorance. And maintain prayer and pay the alms, and obey God and His Messenger. Indeed God wishes but to rid you of sin, People of the House, and to purify you with a thorough purification.* (Al-Ahzab, 33:33)

And Zayd ibn Arqam ؓ reported that the Messenger of God ﷺ said:

> 'I leave with you that which, if you cleave to it, you shall never go astray after me; one of the two is greater than the other: The Book of God, a rope extended from Heaven to earth; and my progeny, the People of my House (*'itrati, ahl bayti'*). These two shall never be divided until they come to me at the Pool. Mind, then, how you look after them in my stead!'[99]

And it is reported that Abu Juhayfa said:

> I said to 'Ali ibn Abi Talib: 'Have you a book [from the Prophet]?' 'No,' he said, 'save for the Book of God, or understanding given to a Muslim man, or what is in this page here: Blood indemnities, the freeing of captives, and that a Muslim is not executed for a disbeliever.'[100] ('Blood indemnity' means the money which must be paid in compensation for murder or assault.)

And Abu Bakr al-Siddiq ؓ said: 'Watch over Muhammad by [watching over] his Household.'[101]

Some scholars say that the Messenger of God's wives are not part of 'the

Household', but the Holy Qur'an affirms that they are indeed part of the Household, for God says of the wives of Abraham ﷺ: *They said, 'Are you astonished by God's command? The mercy of God and His blessings be upon you, people of the House [Ahl al-Bayt]! Truly He is Praised, Glorious!'* (Hud, 11:73)

In any case, God honours the wives of the Messenger of God ﷺ by calling them the 'Mothers of the Believers':

> *The Prophet is closer to the believers than their [own] souls, and his wives are their mothers. And those related by blood are more entitled, [from] one another in the Book of God than the [other] believers and the Emigrants, barring any favour you may do your friends. This is written in the Book.* (Al-Ahzab, 33:6) ◉ *O wives of the Prophet! You are not like any other women. If you fear [God], then do not be complaisant in your speech, lest he in whose heart is a sickness aspire [to you], but speak honourable words. / And stay in your houses and do not flaunt your finery in the [flaunting] manner of the former Time of Ignorance. And maintain prayer and pay the alms, and obey God and His Messenger. Indeed God wishes but to rid you of sin, People of the House, and to purify you with a thorough purification.* (Al-Ahzab, 33:32–33)

(c) Concerning the closest of the Companions to the Messenger of God ﷺ (including Zayd ؓ and Abu Bakr ؓ), God says of Zayd ibn Harithah ؓ (who is the only Companion mentioned by name in the Holy Qur'an):

> *And when you said to him to whom God had shown grace, and to whom you [too] had shown grace. 'Retain your wife for yourself and fear God'. But you had hidden in your heart what God was to disclose, and you feared people, though God is worthier that you should fear Him. So when Zayd had fulfilled whatever need he had of her, We joined her in marriage to you so that there may not be any restriction for the believers in respect of the wives of their adopted sons, when the latter have fulfilled whatever wish they have of them. And God's commandment is bound to be realised.* (Al-Ahzab, 33:37)

And the Lady 'Aishah reported that Quraysh were incensed by a woman of the Makhzum tribe who stole, and they said (showing that Zayd was the most beloved of the Messenger of God ﷺ, for he was the one *whom God had shown favour, and to whom you [too] had shown favour*): 'Who will speak to the Messenger of God ﷺ?; and no one dared but Usamah, son of Zayd, the most beloved [*'hibb'*] of the Messenger of God ﷺ.[102]

As for Abu Bakr al-Siddiq ؓ, God singles him out for His Own Companionship in the company of His Messenger ﷺ in the following Qur'anic verse:

> *If you do not help him, [know that] God has already helped him, when the disbelievers drove him forth—the second of two; when the two were in the cave—when he said to his companion, 'Do not despair; verily God is with us'. Then God sent down His spirit of peace (sakinatahu) upon him and supported him with legions you did not see; and He made the word of those who*

disbelieved the nethermost, and the Word of God was the uppermost. And God is Mighty, Wise. (Al-Tawbah, 9:40)

(d) Concerning the Companions who were 'with' the Messenger of God ﷺ, God says:

Muhammad is the Messenger of God, and those who are with him are hard against the disbelievers, merciful among themselves. You see them bowing, prostrating [in worship]. They seek favour from God and beatitude. Their mark is on their faces from the effect of prostration. That is their description in the Torah, and their description in the Gospel is as a seed that sends forth its shoot and strengthens it, and it grows stout and rises firmly upon its stalk, delighting the sowers, so that He may enrage the disbelievers by them. God has promised those of them who believe and perform righteous deeds forgiveness and a great reward. (Al-Fath, 48:29) ❋ *You are the best community brought forth to men, enjoining decency, and forbidding indecency, and believing in God. Had the People of the Scripture believed, it would have been better for them; some of them are believers; but most of them are wicked.* (Aal ʿImran, 3:110)

(e) Concerning the Emigrants and Helpers, God says:

And the first to lead the way, of the Emigrants and the Helpers, and those who follow them by being virtuous—God will be pleased with them, and they will be pleased with Him; and He has prepared for them Gardens with rivers flowing beneath them to abide therein forever: that is the supreme triumph. (Al-Tawbah, 9:100) ❋ *God has truly relented to the Prophet and the Emigrants and the Helpers who followed him in the hour of hardship, after the hearts of a party of them had almost deviated, then He relented to them. Truly He is Gentle, Merciful to them.* (Al-Tawbah, 9:117) ❋ *And those who believed and emigrated and strove for the way of God, and those who provided refuge and assisted—those are the true believers, and for them is forgiveness and a generous provision. / And those who believed afterwards, and emigrated and strove with you—they are of you; and those related by blood are nearer to one another, according to the Book of God. Truly God is Knower of all things.* (Al-Anfal, 8:74–75) ❋ *It is for the poor emigrants, who were expelled from their habitations and their possessions, seeking favour from God and good pleasure, and helping God and His Messenger. Those—they are the sincere. / And those who had settled in the hometown, and [had abided] in faith before them, love those who have emigrated to them, and do not find in their breasts any need of that which those [others] have been given, but prefer [others] to themselves, though they be in poverty. And whoever is saved from the avarice of his own soul, those—they are the successful. / And those who will come after them say, 'Our Lord, forgive us and our brethren who preceded us in [embracing] the faith, and do not place any rancour in our hearts toward those who believe. Our Lord, You are indeed Kind, Merciful!'* (Al-Hashr, 59:8–10)

(f) Concerning (the tribe of) Quraysh in general, God says:

[In gratitude] for the security of Quraysh, / their security for the journey of winter and of summer, / let them worship the Lord of this House, / Who has fed them against hunger and made them secure from fear. (Quraysh, 106:1–4)
* *And warn the nearest of your kinsfolk. (Al-Shuʿaraʾ, 26:214)*

Since Quraysh were the descendants of Abraham ﷺ through Ishmael ﷺ who lived in Mecca by the Kaʿbah and established the prayer there, then it could be said that God made people love them—or at least made 'their inner hearts yearn towards them'—since God cites the prayer of Abraham ﷺ (which He surely granted): *Our Lord, indeed I have made some of my seed to dwell in a valley where there is no sown land, by Your Sacred House; our Lord, that they may establish prayer. So make some of the inner hearts of men yearn towards them. And provide them with fruits, that they might be thankful. (Ibrahim, 14:37)*

This applies to all the believers from the tribe of Quraysh (and any other believers living there descended from Ishmael ﷺ), but of course a fortiori to the Prophet Muhammad ﷺ and his family.

(g) Concerning the Arabs in general, God says:

And of the Bedouins (al-aʾrab) there is he who believes in God and the Last Day, and takes what he expends as [pious] offerings to bring [him] nearer to God, and to [secure] the prayers of the Messenger. Surely these will bring them nearer. God will admit them into His mercy. Truly God is Forgiving, Merciful. (Al-Tawbah, 9:99)

Moreover, we need hardly also say that the Holy Qurʾan was revealed in the Arabic language.[103]

(h) Concerning all believers, we will see (in a coming chapter) what the Holy Qurʾan says about them, God willing.

In summary then: it is obligatory to love the family and kin of the Messenger of God ﷺ according to the different degrees of their proximity to him. This love is obligatory in the Holy Qurʾan for all those who love the Messenger of God ﷺ, and thus it is obligatory for all those who love God.

All this explains why the invocation of blessings upon the family and kin of the Messenger of God ﷺ is an indispensable part of Muslim prayer:

Kaʿb ibn ʿAjaza reported that the Companions asked the Messenger of God ﷺ: 'O Messenger of God, how do we invoke blessings upon you and your Household; for God has taught us how to send greetings of peace upon you?' He replied: 'Say: O God, invoke blessings upon Muhammad and the family of Muhammad, as You invoked blessings upon Abraham and the family of Abraham; indeed You are Praised, Glorious. O God, bless Muhammad and the family of Muhammad, as You blessed Abraham and the family of Abraham; indeed, You are Praised, Glorious.'[104]

CHAPTER FIFTEEN

THE EFFECTS OF LOVE OF GOD ON HUMAN BEINGS

Does faith in God as such have visible effects on human beings? It must do, because faith in God is a mercy from God[105], and God says: *So behold the effects of God's mercy, how He revives the earth after it has died. Surely He is the Reviver of the dead and He has power over all things.* (Al-Rum, 30:50)

This is the only verse in the entire Holy Qur'an in which God speaks of the 'effects of His mercy'. It will be noticed that God uses the word '*behold*' ('*undhur*'), meaning that the effects of God's mercy may be physically seen, if He wills. Moreover, God describes sincere faith in Him as having a '*mark*' ('*sibghah*'), saying:

> *Say: 'We believe in God, and in that which has been revealed to us, and revealed to Abraham, Ishmael, Isaac, Jacob, and the Tribes, and that which was given to Moses, and Jesus, and the prophets, from their Lord, we make no division between any of them, and to Him we submit'. / And if they believe in the like of what you believe in, then they are truly guided; but if they turn away, then they are clearly in schism; God will suffice you against them; He is the Hearer, the Knower. / The mark of God ['sibghatullah']; and who has a better mark than God? And Him we worship.* (Al-Baqarah, 2:136–138)

In the *Tafsir al-Jalalayn* it is stated: 'The words '*The mark of God*' are meant to add emphasis to the words '*We believe*'; the word 'mark' is in the [Arabic] accusative case because it is the object of an elided verb; that is, 'God marked us'. This alludes to His religion, for which he created in all humankind a natural disposition, so that its effect would be clearly visible on its follower, just as dye makes a clear mark on cloth.'[106]

In the Holy Qur'an, God describes the signs, marks and states of the believers precisely and beautifully in several verses. God says:

> *Indeed successful are the believers, / those who in their prayers are humble, / and who shun vain talk, / and who fulfil payment of alms, / and who guard their private parts, / except from their spouses, and what their right hands possess, for then they are not blameworthy. / But whoever seeks [anything] beyond that, those, they are transgressors. / And who are keepers of their trusts and covenants. / And who are watchful of their prayers. / Those—they are the inheritors who shall inherit Paradise, wherein they will abide.* (Al-Mu'minun, 23:1–11)

Surely those who, for fear of their Lord, are apprehensive, / and who believe in the signs of their Lord, / and who do not associate others with their Lord, / and who give what they give, while their hearts tremble [with awe], because they are going to return to their Lord /—those [are the ones who] hasten to [perform] good works, and they [are the ones who] shall come out ahead in them. / And We do not task any soul beyond its capacity, and with Us is a Record that speaks the truth; and they will not be wronged. / Nay, but their hearts are in ignorance of this, and they have other deeds which they will perpetrate, besides, which they are doing. (Al-Mu'minun, 23:57–63)

That [is his state]. And whoever venerates the sacraments of God, then that derives from the piety of the hearts. / You may benefit from them until a specified time; thereafter its lawful sacrifice is by the Ancient House. / And for every community, We have appointed a [holy] rite that they might mention God's Name over the livestock that He has provided them. For your God is One God, so submit to Him. And give good tidings to the humbly obedient, / who, when God is mentioned, their hearts tremble, and who endure [patiently] whatever may befall them, and who observe prayer, and who, from that which We have provided them, expend. (Al-Hajj, 22:32–35)

The believers are only those who, when God is mentioned, their hearts tremble, and when His verses are recited to them, they increase their faith, and who rely upon their Lord. / Those who observe the prayers, and who, from that with which We have provided them, expend. / Those are the true believers. For them are ranks with their Lord, and forgiveness, and generous provision. (Al-Anfal, 8:2–4)

God has promised the believers, both men and women, Gardens underneath which rivers flow, to abide therein, and blessed dwellings in the Gardens of Eden; and beatitude from God is greater. That is the supreme triumph. (Al-Tawbah, 9:72)

Does every believer love God? And consequently are the signs and marks of faith the same as the signs and marks of God's love for the servant and the servant's love for God? God says: *Truly those who believe and perform righteous deeds—for them the Compassionate One shall appoint love [wudd]. (Maryam, 19:96)*

This Qur'anic verse indicates that every believer who does righteous deeds will be granted some measure of love. This means that the signs and marks of sincere faith also indicate—to a certain extent—the effects of God's love for His servant, and the servant's love for God. However, it appears that sincere love for God requires something more than faith and righteous deeds alone. God says: *Say: 'If you love God, follow me, and God will love you more [yuhbibkum], and forgive you your sins; God is Forgiving, Merciful.' (Aal 'Imran, 3:31)*

In this Qur'anic verse, God addresses the believers[107] with the words: 'If *you love God'*. This means that the believers do not necessarily love God truly and fully simply by virtue of their having faith in Him: the word '*If*' evidently implies that there are two possibilities—either something is the case, or it is not. However, as we saw earlier, this does not mean that the believers do not have any love for God at all: they *do* all have some love for God by virtue of believing in Him, but they have not—at least during the initial stages of faith—yet reached the highest and most complete degrees of love with the full immersion of their whole hearts, souls, wills, minds—and indeed their very beings—in the love of God. However, God promises that as they follow the Messenger of God ﷺ, their love for God will increase degree by degree and stage by stage until God loves them. Thus God describes His Messenger's 'hope[108] for God' as a *'beautiful example'* for the believers in the following Qur'anic verse: *Verily there is for you a beautiful example in the Messenger of God for whoever hopes for [the encounter with] God and the Last Day, and remembers God often.* (Al-Ahzab, 33:21)

All we have just said is supported by the well-known *Hadith Qudsi*—known as '*Hadith al-Nawafil*' (the *Hadith* of 'voluntary deeds of devotions')—which explains that the servant's love for God, and God's love for the servant, increase degree by degree and stage by stage:

> The Messenger of God ﷺ said: 'God says: "Whosoever shows enmity to a friend of Mine, I declare war upon him. My servant does not draw nigh unto Me with anything more beloved to Me than what I have made obligatory upon him; and My servant continues to draw nearer unto Me with voluntary deeds until I love him—and when I love him, I am his Hearing wherewith he hears, his Sight wherewith he sees, his Hand wherewith he grasps, and his Foot wherewith he walks. If he asks Me, I will surely give unto him; if he seeks My refuge, I will surely give him refuge. I hesitate in nought of all that I do as I hesitate in taking the believer's soul: he hates to die, and I hate to hurt him."'[109]

God also mentions, in the Holy Qur'an, the recognizable attributes of those whom He loves and who love Him completely, describing them precisely with His words:

> *O you who believe, whoever of you apostatises from his religion, God will assuredly bring a people whom He loves and who love Him: humble towards believers, stern towards disbelievers, [they] struggle in the way of God, and fear not the reproach of any reproacher. That is God's favour; He gives it to whom He will; and God is Embracing, Knowing.* (Al-Ma'idah, 5:54)

It may be observed in this Qur'anic verse that those '*whom He loves and who love Him*' have four attributes:

(a) They are *'humble towards believers'*,
(b) They are *'stern towards disbelievers'*,
(c) They *'struggle in the way of God'*,
(d) They *'fear not the reproach of any reproacher'*.

(a) Concerning the first attribute (*'humble towards believers'*), God makes the meaning and importance of this sublime virtue clear in other verses in the Holy Qur'an (and thus by way of 'exegesis *through* exegesis'—'*tafsir bil-tafsir*'). Part of 'humility towards believers' is to be merciful with them, and to join the Messenger of God ﷺ in prostrating before God and seeking God's beatitude ('*ridwan*'), thereby becoming like a seed which gives forth fruit after humbly burying itself in the earth. God says:

> *Muhammad is the Messenger of God, and those who are with him are hard against the disbelievers, merciful among themselves. You see them bowing, prostrating [in worship]. They seek favour from God and beatitude. Their mark is on their faces from the effect of prostration. That is their description in the Torah, and their description in the Gospel is as a seed that sends forth its shoot and strengthens it, and it grows stout and rises firmly upon its stalk, delighting the sowers, so that He may enrage the disbelievers by them. God has promised those of them who believe and perform righteous deeds forgiveness and a great reward.* (Al-Fath, 48:29)

Another aspect of 'humility towards believers' is to prefer them to oneself, even if one is in need. God says:

> *And those who had settled in the hometown, and [had abided] in faith before them, love those who have emigrated to them, and do not find in their breasts any need of that which those [others] have been given, but prefer [others] to themselves, though they be in poverty. And whoever is saved from the avarice of his own soul, those—they are the successful.* (Al-Hashr, 59:9)

Preferring others to oneself makes the believer able also to give '*of his wealth, however cherished*'.[110] God says:

> *It is not piety that you turn your faces to the East and to the West. True piety is [that of] the one who believes in God and the Last Day and the angels and the Book and the prophets, and who gives of his wealth, however cherished, to kinsmen and orphans and the needy and the traveller and beggars, and for slaves, and who observes prayer and pays the alms, and those who fulfil their covenant when they have engaged in a covenant, those who endure with fortitude misfortune, hardship, and peril are the ones who are truthful, and these are the ones who are God-fearing.* (Al-Baqarah, 2:177)

And this all leads to piety and goodness ('*birr*')[111], for piety and goodness require that believers fear God and spend from what they love. God says: ...*But piety is to fear...* (*Al-Baqarah*, 2:189) *You will not attain piety until you expend of what you love; and whatever thing you expend, God knows of it.* (*Aal 'Imran*, 3:92)

Thus part of loving God—and hence also part of humility towards the believers—is to prefer them to oneself; to give to them; to favour them; to honour them, and to be good to them both materially and morally; for as we mentioned earlier, God says:

> *And those who had settled in the hometown, and [had abided] in faith before them, love those who have emigrated to them, and do not find in their breasts any need of that which those [others] have been given, but prefer [others] to themselves, though they be in poverty. And whoever is saved from the avarice of his own soul, those—they are the successful.* (*Al-Hashr*, 59:9)

Since love of God is accompanied by preferring others to oneself, this explains why God's love is accompanied by gentleness ('*rifq*') towards others—Jarir bin 'Abdullah reported that the Messenger of God ﷺ said: 'If God loves a servant, He gives him gentleness.'[112]

The servant whom God loves and who loves God is humble and gentle towards people, and because of this precisely will inevitably be loved and accepted by people in return. Abu Hurayrah ؓ reported that the Messenger of God ﷺ said: 'If God loves a servant, He calls Gabriel: "God loves so-and-so, so love him!", so he loves him. Then Gabriel calls out to the folk of Heaven: "God loves so-and-so, so love him!", so the folk of Heaven love him; and then he is given acceptance and is loved by the people of earth.'[113]

(b) Concerning the second attribute ('*stern towards disbelievers*'), God also makes this clear in the Qur'anic verse:

> *Muhammad is the Messenger of God, and those who are with him are hard against the disbelievers, merciful among themselves. You see them bowing, prostrating [in worship]. They seek favour from God and beatitude. Their mark is on their faces from the effect of prostration. That is their description in the Torah, and their description in the Gospel is as a seed that sends forth its shoot and strengthens it, and it grows stout and rises firmly upon its stalk, delighting the sowers, so that He may enrage the disbelievers by them. God has promised those of them who believe and perform righteous deeds forgiveness and a great reward.* (*Muhammad*, 48:29)

Similarly, God makes it clear that sternness towards the disbelievers also requires harshness, saying:

> *O you who believe, fight those of the disbelievers who are near to you, and let them find harshness in you, and know that God is with the God-fearing.* (*Al-Tawbah*, 9:123) ❈ *O Prophet! Struggle against the disbelievers and the hypocrites, and be harsh with them. For their abode will be Hell—and [what] an evil journey's end!* (*Al-Tahrim*, 66:9)

(c) Concerning the third attribute (*'struggling in the way of God'*), God speaks of struggle (*jihad*) in a number of verses in the Qur'an, such as:

O you who believe, what is wrong with you that, when it is said to you, 'Go forth in the way of God', you sink down heavily to the ground. Are you so content with the life of this world, rather than with the Hereafter? Yet the enjoyment of the life of this world compared with the Hereafter is but little. (Al-Tawbah, 9:38)

In the second verse God makes the connection between struggle and love clear through two vivid images in the following verses:

Say: 'If your fathers, and your sons, and your brothers, and your wives, and your clan, and the possessions which you have acquired, and merchandise for which you fear there may be no sale, and dwellings which you are content in (tardaunaha), are more lovable (ahabb) to you than God and His Messenger and struggling in His way, then wait until God brings about His command. And God does not guide the wicked folk'. (Al-Tawbah, 9:24) ⁕ As for the weak, and the sick, and those who find nothing to expend, no blame falls upon them if they remain true to God and to His Messenger. There is no way [of blame] against those who are virtuous. And God is Forgiving, Merciful. / Nor against those who, when they came to you so that you might give them a mount—you having said to them, 'I cannot find [a mount] whereon to mount you' turned back, their eyes flowing with tears for sorrow that they could not find the means to expend. (Al-Tawbah, 9:91–2)

In the first passage, we see love of everything in the world opposed to love of God, His Messenger ﷺ and struggle in the way of God, and in the second passage there is a reference to those Companions who were too poor to find camels to mount for war and actually wept because they loved God, His Messenger ﷺ and struggle in the way of God so much. This explains how in the Qur'anic economy of language and symbolism both being *'stern towards disbelievers'* and *'struggling in the way of God'* are attributes of love: love for God which manifests itself as struggling for God and opposition to that which opposes God.

Nevertheless, there are two kinds of struggle in the way of God: (1) to struggle, with the aid of the Holy Qur'an[114], against one's own ego, and this is the 'Greater Struggle'[115] (*'al-Jihad al-Akbar'*); and (2) to struggle against those disbelievers who aggress against Muslims, and this is the 'Lesser Struggle' (*'al-Jihad al-Asghar'*). God says: *So do not obey the disbelievers, but struggle against them therewith with a great endeavour. (Al-Furqan, 25:52)*

Hence the third attribute of those who love God—*'struggling in the way of God'*—implies, first and foremost, a constant struggle for self-improvement and constant battle against the ego with all one's strength. Moreover, whilst the struggle against the disbelievers takes place only at certain times and in certain circumstances, the struggle for self-improvement is limitless and does

The Effects of Love of God on Human Beings

not end until death, never ceasing or being interrupted for a single moment in life. And God Almighty warns those who neglect this struggle, saying: *And whoever withdraws from the remembrance of the Compassionate One, We assign for him a devil and he becomes his companion.* (Al-Zukhruf, 43:36)[116]

(d) Concerning the fourth attribute (*'fearing not the reproach of any reproacher')*, this means to be sincere to God and not obey anything other than God (or His Will). God says:

> And do not drive away those who call upon their Lord at morning and evening desiring His countenance. You are not accountable for them in anything; nor are they accountable for you in anything, that you should drive them away and be of the evildoers. (Al-An'am, 6:52) ❊ And restrain yourself along with those who call upon their Lord at morning and evening, desiring His Countenance; and do not let your eyes overlook them desiring the glitter of the life of this world. And do not obey him whose heart We have made oblivious to Our remembrance, and who follows his own whim, and whose conduct is [mere] prodigality. (Al-Kahf, 18:28)

Such is the state of people who are so sincere that they pay no heed to anything but God: they are completely immersed with all their hearts, souls, minds and wills in the love of God and care about nothing except God and what God enjoins. Thus they pray to God morning and evening, and remember God standing, sitting and reclining on their sides, for God says: *Those who remember God, standing and sitting and [lying] on their sides, and reflect upon the creation of the heavens and the earth: 'Our Lord, You have not created this in vain. Glory be to You! So guard us against the chastisement of the Fire.* (Aal 'Imran, 3:191)[117]

For this reason, the Messenger of God ﷺ can be understood to be alluding to people who truly *'fear not the reproach of any reproacher'* in his words: 'Invoke God until they say: "Madman!"'[118]

Such, then, is the state of those whom God loves and who love Him. They are: *humble towards believers, stern towards disbelievers, [they] struggle in the way of God, and fear not the reproach of any reproacher.* Thus they are pious and humble; they are proud of their faith but struggle constantly against their egos and obey none but God.[119] And these attributes, which encompass their whole beings, can be concretely recognised by others, for God says: '... *Their mark is on their faces...*'

God Almighty says:

> O you who believe, whoever of you apostatises from his religion, God will assuredly bring a people whom He loves and who love Him: humble towards believers, stern towards disbelievers, struggling in the way of God, and fearing

not the reproach of any reproacher. That is God's favour; He gives it to whom He will; and God is Embracing, Knowing. (Al-Ma'idah, 5:54)

Summarising what we have discussed above, we may say that four attributes mentioned in this Qur'anic verse constitute a precise overview of all that can be said about the visible effects of love on those whom God loves and who love God. This verse also gives a synopsis of all that God says in the Holy Qur'an about those whom God loves and who love God, as we have seen. The signs of their love will inevitably show themselves as particular, recognizable qualities because their whole beings are immersed in love of God, and this cannot but manifest itself.

A Question: Can those of whom God says '*He loves [them] and [they] love Him*' be considered to be among God's 'friends' or 'saints' ('*awliya*')? If so, what is the evidence for this in the Holy Qur'an?

God describes His 'friends' by saying:

Assuredly God's friends, no fear shall befall them, neither shall they grieve. / Those who believe and fear [God]. / Theirs are good tidings in the life of this world and in the Hereafter. There is no changing the Words of God; that is the supreme triumph. / And let not what they say grieve you. Truly power belongs wholly to God. He is the Hearer, the Knower. (Yunus, 10:62–65)

God's 'friends', then, are those for whom '*no fear shall befall them, neither shall they grieve*'. Moreover, God says to His Messenger ﷺ: '*And let not what they say grieve you. Truly power belongs wholly to God*'. From this we can understand that the Messenger ﷺ is the epitome of all God's friends who 'do not grieve'[120], and that he is thus the epitome of all those who are 'mighty' and 'stern against the disbelievers', for true might belongs to God and then to His Messenger: *They say, 'Surely if we return to Medina, the powerful will [soon] expel from it the weaker'. Yet [the real] might belongs to God and to His Messenger, and to the believers, but the hypocrites do not know.* (Al-Munafiqun, 63:8)

This means that there is a certain equivalence between 'God's friends' and those of whom He says '*He loves [them] and [they] love Him*': neither of them fear, and they are both mighty and stern before the disbelievers, by the might of God.

In addition to this, God gives another definition of His 'friends' in His words: *Say: 'O you of Jewry, if you claim that you are the [favoured] friends of God, to the exclusion of other people, then long for death, if you are truthful'. / But they will never long for it, because of what their hands have sent ahead; and God is Knower of the evildoers.* (Al-Jumu'ah, 62:6–7)

These two verses indicate that God's 'friend' is someone who longs for death[121], because he or she is at peace with his or her deeds. God makes the state of His friends clear (and also the state of those who are not His friends) in His words:

> *Say: 'If the Abode of the Hereafter with God is purely yours, and not for other people, then long for death—if you speak truly'. / But they will never long for it, because of that which their own hands have sent before them. God knows the evildoers. / And you shall find them the people most covetous of life, and the idolaters; any one of them would love that he might be given life for a thousand years; yet, his being given life shall not budge him from the chastisement. God sees what they do.* (Al-Baqarah, 2:94–96)[122]

Likewise, in His words God describes the sincerity of people who await death impassibly and stoically: *Among the believers are men who are true to the covenant they made with God. Some of them have fulfilled their vow, and some are still awaiting; and they have not changed in the least.* (Al-Ahzab, 33:23)

This, then, is how God's 'friends' are: they prefer the meeting with God and the Hereafter to this worldly life—through their faith and their deeds—and they do not fail nor change. This description might well apply to some of those of whom God says '*He loves [them] and [they] love Him*', for the degree of love which God describes with the words '*He loves [them] and [they] love Him*' is a state of virtue near to that of God's 'friends' or 'saints' (*awliya*'). In other words, those who truly love God and whom God loves are His saints, or at least close to being so; and God knows best.

CHAPTER SIXTEEN

FAMILY LOVE

God Almighty describes, defines and regulates family relations, family rights[123] and family love in many verses of the Holy Qur'an. All familial relations, rights and love are subject to a single general principle, namely '*affection for kinsfolk*' ('*al-mawadata fil qurba*'). God says:

> *That is the good tidings which God gives to His servants who believe and perform righteous deeds. Say: 'I do not ask of you any reward for it, except affection for kinsfolk. And whoever acquires a good deed, We shall enhance for him its goodness. Surely God is Forgiving, Appreciative. (Al-Shura, 42:23)*

The reason behind this principle is that '*those related by blood are nearer to one another, according to the Book of God*', for God says:

> *The Prophet is closer to the believers than their [own] souls, and his wives are their mothers. And those related by blood are nearer to one another, according to the Book of God, than the [other] believers and the Emigrants, barring any favour you may do your friends. This is written in the Book.* (Al-Ahzab, 33:6) ❂ *And those who believed afterwards, and emigrated and strove with you—they are of you; and those related by blood are nearer to one another, according to the Book of God. Truly God is Knower of all things.* (Al-Anfal, 8:75)

Nevertheless, God defines different specific degrees of blood relations, and honours them by naming them in the following Qur'anic verses:

> *And do not marry women whom your fathers married, unless it be a thing of the past; surely that is obscene and abominable, an evil way. / Forbidden to you are your mothers, and daughters, your sisters, your paternal aunts, and maternal aunts, your brother's daughters, your sister's daughters, your foster mothers who have given you milk, your foster sisters, your mothers-in-law, your step-daughters, who are in your care being born of your wives you have been in to—but if you have not yet been in to them you are not at fault—and the spouses of your sons who are of your loins, and that you should take to you two sisters together unless it be a thing of the past. God is ever Forgiving, Merciful. / And wedded women, save what your right hands own, this is what God has prescribed for you. Lawful for you beyond all that is that you seek using your wealth, in wedlock and not in illicitly. Such wives as you enjoy thereby, give them their wages as an obligation; you are not at fault in agreeing together, after the obligation. God is ever Knowing, Wise.* (Al-Nisa', 4:22–24)

Family Love

And tell believing women to lower their gaze and to guard their private parts, and not to display their adornment except for what is apparent, and let them draw their veils over their bosoms and not reveal their adornment, except to their husbands or their fathers, or their husbands' fathers, or their sons, or their husbands' sons, or their brothers, or their brothers' sons, or their sisters' sons, or their women, or what their right hands own, or such men who are dependant, not possessing any sexual desire, or children who are not yet aware of women's private parts. And do not let them thump with their feet to make known their hidden ornaments. And rally to God in repentance, O believers, so that you might be prosperous. (Al-Nur, 24:31)

There is no blame upon the blind, nor any blame upon the lame, nor any blame upon the sick, nor upon yourselves if you eat from your own houses, or your fathers' houses, or your mothers' houses, or your brothers' houses, or your sisters' houses, or the houses of your paternal uncles or the houses of your paternal aunts, or the houses of your maternal uncles or the houses of your maternal aunts, or [from] that whereof you hold the keys, or [from] those of your [faithful] friends. You would not be at fault whether you eat together, or separately. But when you enter houses, bid peace to yourselves with a salutation from God, blessed and good. So God clarifies the signs for you that perhaps you might comprehend. (Al-Nur, 24:61)

And God gives rights to 'kinsmen' ('*al-qurba*') in general:

It is not piety that you turn your faces to the East and to the West. True piety is [that of] the one who believes in God and the Last Day and the angels and the Book and the prophets, and who gives of his substance, however cherished, to kinsmen and orphans and the needy and the traveller and beggars, and for slaves, and who observes prayer and pays the alms, and those who fulfil their covenant when they have engaged in a covenant, those who endure with fortitude misfortune, hardship, and peril are the ones who are truthful, and these are the ones who are God-fearing. (Al-Baqarah, 2:177) ❊ *They will ask you about what they should expend. Say, 'Whatever you expend of good it is for parents and kinsmen, orphans, the needy, and the traveller; and whatever good you may do, God has knowledge of it'. (Al-Baqarah, 2:215)* ❊ *And give the kinsman his due, and the needy and the traveller [as well]; and do not squander. / Indeed squanderers are brothers of devils, and the Devil was ever ungrateful to his Lord. / But if you [have to] overlook them, seeking mercy from your Lord, [a mercy] which you expect [in the future], then speak to them gentle words. (Al-Isra', 17:26–28)*

As for the closest of kin, God affirms and stresses the importance of close kinship through both blood and marriage: *And He it is Who created man from water, and made for him ties of blood and ties of marriage. For your Lord is ever Powerful. (Al-Furqan, 25:54)*

This is evidently because marriage is the (licit) cause of children and grandchildren, and thus the basis of ties of kinship: *And God made for you mates from your own selves, and made for you, from your mates, children and grandchildren, and He provided you with the good things. Is it then in falsehood that they believe and in the grace of God that they disbelieve?* (Al-Nahl, 16:72)

God also specifically mentions children—both male and female—in the Holy Qur'an, and stresses that they are a gift from Him:

> *To God belongs the kingdom of the heavens and the earth. He creates whatever He will; He gives to whomever He will females, and He gives to whomever He will males. / Or He combines them, males and females; and He makes whomever He will infertile. Surely He is Knower, Powerful.* (Al-Shura, 42:49–50)

And naturally, God gives children rights over their parents:

> *Mothers suckle their children for two full years for such as desire to fulfil the suckling. It is for the father to provide them and clothe them honourably. No soul is charged save to its capacity; a mother shall not be harmed by her child; neither a father by his child. The heir has a similar duty. But if the two desire by mutual consent and consultation to wean, then they would not be at fault. And if you desire to seek nursing for your children, you would not be at fault, provided you hand over what you have given honourably, and fear God, and know that God sees what you do.* (Al-Baqarah, 2:233)[124]

One of the most beautiful descriptions of love between children and parents is the expression '*go round attendant*' ('*tawwafun*') which occurs in the verse from the Holy Qur'an cited below. It describes the mutual care and love parents and children should have for each other—and the joy in their nearness to each other—in a way which alludes to and evokes the love the pilgrim feels as he 'goes around' ('*tawaf*') the Blessed Ka'bah, God's Ancient House:

> *O you who believe, let those whom your right hands own, and those of you who have not reached puberty, ask leave of you three times: before the dawn prayer, and when you put off your garments at noon, and after the night prayer. [These are] three periods of privacy for you. Neither you nor they would be at fault at other times; they go round attendant upon you [as] some of you [do] with others. So God clarifies for you the signs; and God is Knower, Wise.* (Al-Nur, 24:58)

Ibn Kathir says, commenting on this verse: '"*They go round attendant upon you*"; that is, to serve you and the like; and those who go round [their kin] in this manner are excused things that no one else is excused. In this regard, Imam Malik, Ahmad ibn Hanbal and the authors of the *Sunan* collections report that the Messenger of God ﷺ said about cats: "They are not filthy; for they are among those beings, male and female, who go round attendant upon you."'[125]

Just as God mentions children's rights in the Holy Qur'an, He also mentions parents' rights, and the honour they are due from their children:

And worship God, and associate nothing with Him. Be kind to parents, and near kindred, and to orphans, and to the needy, and to the neighbour who is near, and to the neighbour who is a stranger, and to the friend at your side, and to the wayfarer, and to what your right hands own. Surely God loves not the conceited, and the boastful. (Al-Nisa', 4:36)

God says that this honour was also mentioned in the Torah:

And when We made a covenant with the Children of Israel: 'You shall not worship any other than God; and to be good to parents, and the near of kin; and to orphans, and to the needy; and speak well to men; and observe prayer and pay the alms', then you turned away; all but a few of you, rejecting. (Al-Baqarah, 2:83)

And God teaches people how they ought to pray for their parents:

And your Lord has decreed that you worship none save Him, and kindness to parents. If they should reach old age with you, one of them or both then do not say to them 'Fie' nor repulse them, but speak to them gracious words. / And lower to them the wing of humility out of mercy and say: 'My Lord, have mercy on them, just as they reared me when I was little'. / Your Lord knows best what is in your hearts. If you are righteous, then truly, to those who are penitent He is Forgiving. (Al-Isra', 17:23–25)

Through the supplication, '*My Lord, have mercy on them, just as they reared me when I was little*', God reminds people of the mercy their parents showed them when they were young—however remiss they may have been in certain details—because every living person is alive only due to God's grace and mercy, and then due to the mercy of his or her parents. For no newborn would survive if his or her parents (or foster parents) had not reared, fed, protected and nurtured her baby, starting with the newborn's mother, who nourished her baby from her own body and then bore them with great difficulty. This explains why God honours mothers above fathers in the following verses:

And We have enjoined man concerning his parents—his mother bears him in weakness after weakness, and his weaning is in two years. 'Give thanks to Me and to your parents. To Me is the journey's end. / But if they urge you to ascribe to Me as partner that whereof you have no knowledge, then do not obey them. And keep them company in this world honourably, and follow the way of him who returns to Me [in penitence]. Then to Me will be your return, and I will inform you of what you used to do. (Luqman, 31:14–15)

And We have enjoined man to be kind to his parents. His mother carries him in travail, and gives birth to him in travail, and his gestation and his weaning take thirty months. So that when he is mature and reaches forty years he says, 'My Lord! Inspire me to give thanks for Your favour with which You have favoured me and my parents, and that I may act righteously in a way that will please You, and invest my seed with righteousness. Indeed I repent to You and I am truly of those who submit [to You]'. / Those are they from whom We accept the best of what they do, and overlook their misdeeds, [as they stand] among the inhabitants of Paradise—[this is] the true promise which they were promised. / As for him who says to his parents: 'Fie on you both. Do you threaten me that I shall be raised, when already generations have passed away before me?' And they call on God for succour, 'Woe to you. Believe! Surely God's promise is true'. But he says, 'This is nothing but the fables of the ancients'. Such are the ones against whom the Word is due concerning communities of jinn and humans that have passed away before them. Truly they are losers. (Al-Ahqaf, 46:15–18)[126]

The prayer said when a man reaches forty (cited above)—this being the age when '*he is mature*', meaning that a man has reached 'his full capacity of strength, intellect and reasoning'[127]—is a prayer which combines love and appreciation for one's parents with love and (legitimate) hope for one's children. In another verse, God teaches human beings that they do not know whether their parents or their children are closest to them and which of them benefits them the most:

God charges you concerning your children, to the male the equivalent of the portion of two females; and if they be women more than two, then for them two-thirds of what he leaves; but if she be one then to her a half; and to his parents, to each one of the two the sixth of what he leaves, if he has a child; but if he has no child, and his heirs are his parents, then to his mother a third; or, if he has siblings, to his mother a sixth after any bequest that he may bequeathe, or any debt. Your parents and children—you know not which of them is nearer in benefit to you, a prescription from God; surely God is ever Knowing, Wise. (Al-Nisa', 4:11)

In other words, God gave parents and children each certain rights and considerations, and made these rights and considerations second in importance only to His own rights (that no partner be associated with Him), and thus more important than all other rights. This indicates the great importance of loving one's parents and children in God's sight.[128] God says:

Say: 'Come, I will recite that which your Lord has made a sacred duty for you: that you associate nothing with Him, that you be dutiful to parents, and that you do not slay your children, because of poverty—We will provide for you and them—and that you do not draw near any acts of lewdness, whether it be manifest or concealed, and that you do not slay the life which God has made sacred, except rightfully. This is what He has charged you with, that perhaps you will understand. (Al-An'am, 6:151)

Although God commands human beings to love their parents and honour their rights, He warns them that these rights must not impinge on His own rights; and His first right over human beings is that they worship no other gods but Him, nor 'associate partners with Him' (i.e. idolatry). Therefore, God warns against the danger of respecting one's parents so much that one obey them if they demand that one associate partners with God:

And We have enjoined on man kindness to his parents, but if they urge you to ascribe to Me as partner that of which you do not have any knowledge, then do not obey them. To Me will be your return whereat I will inform you of what you used to do. (Al-ʿAnkabut, 29:8) ❈ *And We have enjoined man concerning his parents—his mother bears him in weakness after weakness, and his weaning is in two years. 'Give thanks to Me and to your parents. To Me is the journey's end. / But if they urge you to ascribe to Me as partner that whereof you have no knowledge, then do not obey them. And keep them company in this world honourably, and follow the way of him who returns to Me [in penitence]. Then to Me will be your return, and I will inform you of what you used to do. (Luqman, 31:14–15)*

Moreover, God makes it clear that believers must love God more than they love anything else in this world, even their parents:

Say: 'If your fathers, and your sons, and your brothers, and your wives, and your clan, and the possessions which you have acquired, and merchandise for which you fear there may be no sale, and dwellings which you love, are dearer to you than God and His Messenger and struggling in His way, then wait until God brings about His command. And God does not guide the wicked folk'. (Al-Tawbah, 9:24) ❈ *O you who believe, be upright in justice; witnesses for God, even though it be against yourselves; or parents and kinsmen, whether the person be rich or poor; God is closer to the two. So do not follow any whim, lest you swerve; for if you twist, or refrain, surely God is ever aware of what you do. (Al-Nisaʾ, 4:135)*

And naturally, if one's parents are idolaters it is difficult for a believer to love them fully, despite all that they have done for them:

You will not find a people who believe in God and the Last Day loving those who oppose God and His Messenger, even though they were their fathers or their sons or their brothers or their clan. [For] those He has inscribed faith upon their hearts and reinforced them with a spirit from Him, and He will admit them into gardens underneath which rivers flow, wherein they will abide, God being pleased with them, and they being pleased with Him. Those [they] are God's confederates. Assuredly it is God's confederates who are the successful. (Al-Mujadilah, 58:22)

For this reason, God makes it clear that when Abraham ﷺ—who was 'soft of heart' and 'forbearing'—asked forgiveness for his 'father', he did so more to honour his promise, rather than out of any love for idolaters: *Abraham's prayer for the forgiveness of his father was only because of a promise he had made to him;*

but when it became clear to him that he was an enemy of God, he declared himself innocent of him; truly Abraham was soft of heart, forbearing. (Al-Tawbah, 9:114)

If respecting and loving one's parents too much carries the risk of infringing on God's right (that no partner be associated with Him), loving one's children too much carries a different risk. Loving one's children too much can lead to vanity and worldliness. God says:

Wealth and children are an adornment of the life of this world. But the enduring things, the righteous deeds—[these] are better with your Lord for reward and better in [respect of] hope. (Al-Kahf, 18:46) ❈ *Know that the life of this world is merely play and diversion and glitter, and mutual vainglory in respect of wealth and children; as the likeness of rain whose vegetation the disbelievers admire; [but] then it withers, and you see it turn yellow, then it becomes chaff. And in the Hereafter there is a severe chastisement and forgiveness from God and beatitude; and the life of this world is but the comfort of delusion. (Al-Hadid, 57:20)*

Thus God warns human beings that children, like wealth, can be a trial: *And know that your wealth and your children are a trial; and that with God is a tremendous wage. (Al-Anfal, 8:28)*

This trial is itself 'an enemy' to believers, drawing them towards this worldly life and leading them away from what is good for them as regards the Hereafter:

O you who believe! Indeed among your wives and children there are enemies for you, so beware of them. And if you pardon, and overlook [such enmity] and forgive, then assuredly God is Forgiving, Merciful. / Your possessions and your children are only a trial, and God—with Him is a great reward. (Al-Taghabun, 64:14–15)

Therefore God warns believers not to let their children cause them to forget Him or His remembrance: *O you who believe, do not let your possessions and your children divert you from the remembrance of God; for whoever does that—it is they who are the losers. (Al-Munafiqun, 63:9)*

Thus God has made it clear that believers must love their children, but in a certain way and within certain limits, as we have seen.

To summarise: God has established a natural, licit, good and praiseworthy love between every human being and his or her family. God has established this love in accordance with the degree of closeness between family members: the closer they are to each other by blood, the stronger the love should be. However, God stresses that people's love for God must remain greater and stronger than all family love.

CHAPTER SEVENTEEN

LOVE OF OTHERS (ALL HUMANITY; THE 'PEOPLE OF THE SCRIPTURE'; BELIEVERS, AND FRIENDS)

ALL HUMANITY

God does not limit love only to family and relatives alone. On the contrary, because God's mercy *'embraces all things'* (*Al-A'raf*, 7:156), He creates mercy and love between all people, albeit in differing degrees and with specific conditions. Perhaps one of the reasons for this is that every person is ultimately related to every other person, since all human beings are the progeny of Adam ﷺ and Eve and thus the 'sons [or daughters] of Adam' (*'bani adam'*).[129] This thus constitutes a degree of kinship, although distant. God reminds human beings of this in the Holy Qur'an, and warns them to fear God whenever they deal with their brothers and sisters from the womb (*rahm*) of their common mother, Eve:

> *O people, fear your Lord, Who created you of a single soul, and from it created its mate, and from the pair of them scattered many men and women; and fear God by whom you claim [your rights] from one another and kinship ties (arham). Surely God has been watchful over you.* (*Al-Nisa'*, 4:1) ❁ *And He it is Who produced you from a single soul, such that some are established and some are deposited. Verily We have distinguished the signs for a people who understand.* (*Al-An'am*, 6:98)

God also tells human beings that they were created, and they will be resurrected, as a single soul. Human beings thus share not only the same beginning but the same end as well: *Your creation and your resurrection are only as [that of] a single soul. Truly God is Hearer, Seer.* (*Luqman*, 31:28)

Moreover, although God created human beings as different nations and tribes, they are nonetheless all equal before God. The only thing that differentiates one person from another in 'the sight of God' is how God-fearing he or she is (and therefore how good they are): *O humankind! We have indeed created you from a male and a female, and made you nations and tribes that you may come to know one another. Truly the noblest of you in the sight of God is the most God-fearing among you. Truly God is Knower, Aware.* (*Al-Hujurat*, 49:13)

Indeed, the ethnic and linguistic differences and variety between peoples and nations reflect divine wisdom and manifest divine 'signs' (*'ayat'*) which people must respect, contemplate and appreciate: *And of His signs is the creation of the heavens and the earth and the differences of your tongues and your colours. Surely in that there are signs for all peoples. (Al-Rum, 30:22)*

Human beings must value and rejoice in the way people differ. This is one of the meanings of *'that you may come to know one another'*, and God knows best. Moreover, God forbids the killing of any human soul, saying: *And do not slay the soul [whose life] God has made inviolable, except with due cause… (Al-Isra', 17:33) …do not slay the life which God has made sacred, except rightfully. This is what He has charged you with that perhaps you will understand. (Al-An'am, 6:151)*

Furthermore, God values every single soul as if it were all humanity, when it comes to saving its life or not causing its death:

Because of that, We decreed for the Children of Israel that whoever slays a soul for other than a soul, or for corruption in the land, it shall be as if he had slain humankind altogether; and whoever saves the life of one, it shall be as if he had saved the life of all humankind. Our messengers have already come to them with clear proofs, but after that many of them still commit excesses in the land. (Al-Ma'idah, 5:32)

Thus God commands Muslims in the Holy Qur'an not to aggress against any individual soul. God says:

And fight in the way of God with those who fight against you, but aggress not; God loves not the aggressors. (Al-Baqarah, 2:190) ❈ *O you who believe, do not profane God's sacraments, nor the sacred month, nor the offering, nor the garlands; nor those repairing to the Sacred House, seeking favour from their Lord, and beatitude. But when you are discharged, then hunt for game. And let not hatred of a people that, barred you from the Sacred Mosque cause you to commit aggression. Help one another to righteousness and piety; do not help one another to sin and enmity. And fear God; surely God is severe in retribution. (Al-Ma'idah, 5:2)* ❈ *O you who believe, be upright before God, witnesses in equity. Let not hatred of a people cause you not to be just; be just, that is nearer to God-fearing. And fear God; surely God is aware of what you do. (Al-Ma'idah, 5:8)*

Muslims may not even commit verbal aggression against anyone, for God says: *Woe to every backbiter, [who is a] slanderer, (Al-Humazah, 104:1)*

Nor even may Muslims insult anyone in their beliefs, even if they be idolaters[130]: *Do not revile those whom they call upon, besides God, lest they then revile God out of spite, through ignorance. So, We have adorned for every community their deeds; then to their Lord they shall return, and He will tell them what they used to do. (Al-An'am, 6:108)*

Thus God commands Muslims to be peaceful and to be just towards every single human being, except those who wage war upon them, destroy their places of worship and drive them out of their homes (this being the sufficient justification for a just, defensive war in the Holy Qur'an[131]):

It may be that God will bring about between you and those of them with whom you are at enmity, affection. For God is Powerful, and God is Forgiving, Merciful. / God does not forbid you in regard to those who did not wage war against you on account of religion and did not expel you from your homes, that you should treat them kindly and deal with them justly. Assuredly God loves the just. (Al-Mumtahanah, 60:7–8) ❊ *How can the idolaters have a pact with God and His Messenger, except for those with whom you made a pact at the Sacred Mosque? So long as they are true to you, be true to them. Truly God loves the God-fearing.* (Al-Tawbah, 9:7)

In addition to this, God enjoins mercy and empathy *upon all* human beings *to* all human beings and not merely to particular groups of people, in the following verse (although ʿAli ibn Abi Talib ؑ, the Lady Fatimah, Al-Hasan and Al-Husayn ؑ were all the specific cause of its revelation): *And they give food, despite [their] love of it to the needy, and the orphan, and the prisoner.* (Al-Insan, 76:8)

Fakr al-Din al-Razi comments, in his *Al-Tafsir al-kabir*: 'His words, "*And they give food, despite [their] love of it to the needy, and the orphan, and the prisoner*", refer to the story we have related in which ʿAli ؑ fed the needy, the orphan and the prisoner. Others say that the verse refers generally to the all pious people, and that 'giving food' symbolises all acts of kindness and benevolence towards the needy, of whatever kind, even if not giving food specifically.'[132]

Thus God says elsewhere:

It is not piety that you turn your faces to the East and to the West. True piety is [that of] the one who believes in God and the Last Day and the angels and the Book and the prophets, and who gives of his substance, however cherished, to kinsmen and orphans and the needy and the traveller and beggars, and for slaves, and who observes prayer and pays the alms, and those who fulfil their covenant when they have engaged in a covenant, those who endure with fortitude misfortune, hardship, and peril. These are the ones who are truthful, and these are the ones who are God-fearing. (Al-Baqarah, 2:177)

And: *Have you seen him who denies the Judgement? / That is he who repels the orphan / and does not urge the feeding of the needy. / So woe to them who pray, / those who are heedless of their prayers, / those who make a pretence, / and deny aid.* (Al-Maʿun, 107:1–7)

As if to confirm this, God mentions a prayer said by believers which evinces mercy even towards disbelievers:

Our Lord, do not make us a cause of beguilement for those who disbelieve, and forgive us. Our Lord, You are indeed the Mighty, the Wise'. / Verily there is for you in them a beautiful example, for those [of you] who hope for God and the Last Day. And whoever turns away, [should know that] God is the Independent, the Worthy of Praise. (Al-Mumtahanah, 60:5–6) ❊ *So they* said, 'In God we have put our trust. Our Lord, make us not a [cause of] temptation for the evildoing folk'; (Yunus, 10:85)¹³³

God also says:

And worship God, and associate nothing with Him. Be kind to parents, and near kindred, and to orphans, and to the needy, and to the neighbour who is near, and to the neighbour who is a stranger, and to the friend at your side, and to the wayfarer, and to what your right hands own. Surely God loves not the conceited, and the boastful. (Al-Nisa', 4:36)

In the Qur'anic Commentary *Tafsir al-Jalalayn*, it is explained that '*the neighbour who is near*' means 'the one who is near to you either in terms of residence, or of family ties', and that '*the neighbour who is a stranger*' means 'the one who is distant from you, either in terms of residence, or of family ties'.¹³⁴ In other words, according to *Tafsir al-Jalalayn*, the 'neighbour' means every person on the face of the earth, whether Muslim or disbeliever.

Likewise, it is stated in the Qura'nic Commentary *Tafsir al-Qurtubi* that '*the neighbour who is near*' means the 'nearby neighbour', and that '*the neighbour who is a stranger*' means the 'unknown neighbour'¹³⁵; and God knows best.

The Messenger of God ﷺ emphasised this when he said: 'By Him in whose hand is my soul, no servant believes until he loves for his neighbour (or he said: 'his brother') what he loves for himself.'¹³⁶

Similarly, the Messenger of God ﷺ said: 'The Compassionate One has mercy upon those who have mercy; have mercy upon those on earth, and He who is in Heaven will have mercy upon you.'¹³⁷ The Messenger of God ﷺ also said: 'God does not have mercy on those who have no mercy on people.'¹³⁸

Thus mercy and empathy should be shown to all people—every single human being—whether they be believers or not. And mercy and empathy towards all humanity, even disbelievers, necessarily means to forgive them, just as it means to forgive Muslims. God says:

Tell those who believe to forgive those who do not hope for the days of God that He may requite a people for what they used to earn. (Al-Jathiyah, 45:14) ❈ *It was by the mercy of God that you were lenient with them; had you been harsh and fierce of heart, they would have dispersed from about you. So pardon them, and ask forgiveness for them, and consult them in the matter. And when you are resolved, rely on God; for God loves those who rely. (Aal 'Imran, 3:159)*

And forgiveness, in turn, means to pardon people. God says:

We did not create the heavens and the earth and all that is between them save with the Truth. And truly the Hour shall come. So pardon them with a gracious pardoning. / Truly your Lord, He is the Creator, the Knowing. (Al-Hijr, 15:85–86) ❈ *Then pardon them and say, 'Peace!' For they will [soon] come* to know. (Al-Zukhruf, 43:89) ❊ *But verily he who is patient and forgives—surely that is [true] constancy in [such] affairs.* (Al-Shura, 42:43)

And pardon and forgiveness are the way—or part of the way—of God's prophets, for the Prophet Joseph ﷺ said:

They said: 'Is it really you, Joseph?' He said, 'I am [indeed] Joseph, and this is my brother. God has truly shown favour to us. Verily if one fears and endures, God does not waste the wage of those who are virtuous'. / They said, 'By God, truly God has preferred you over us, and indeed we have been erring'. / He said, 'There shall be no reproach on you this day. May God forgive you, and He is the Most Merciful of the merciful. (Yusuf, 12:90–92)

Similarly, the Prophet Abraham ﷺ said: *My Lord, truly they have led many of humankind astray. So whoever follows me, verily belongs with me, and whoever disobeys me, truly You are Forgiving, Merciful.* (Ibrahim, 14:36)

Equally, the Prophet and Messenger of God Muhammad ﷺ pardoned the Meccans on the Day of the Conquest, saying:

'What say you, and what think you?' They said: 'We say: The son of a noble and generous brother, and the son of a noble and generous uncle.' The Messenger of God ﷺ said: 'I say, as Joseph said: There shall be no reproach upon you this day. May God forgive you, and He is the Most Merciful of the merciful.' So they went out, as though they had been brought out of their graves.[139]

To pardon, in turn, means to stop oneself from growing angry. God says:

And vie with one another hastening to forgiveness from your Lord, and to a garden as wide as the heavens and the earth that has been prepared for those who fear. / Who expend in prosperity and adversity, and restrain their rage, and pardon their fellow-men; and God loves those who are virtuous. / And who when they commit an indecency or wrong themselves, remember God, and pray forgiveness for their sins—and who shall forgive sins but God?—and who do not persist in what they did, knowing. / Those—their requital is forgiveness from their Lord, and Gardens beneath which rivers flow, abiding therein; excellent is the wage of those workers! (Aal 'Imran, 3:133–136)

So whatever you have been given is [but] the enjoyment of the life of this world. But what is with God is better and more lasting for those who believe and put their trust in their Lord, / and those who avoid grave sins and indecencies and [who], when they are angry, forgive, / and those who answer their Lord, and whose courses of action are [a matter of] counsel between them, and who, of what We have bestowed on them, expend, / and those who, when they suffer aggression defend themselves: / For the requital of an evil deed is an evil deed like it. But whoever pardons and reconciles, his reward will be with God. Truly He does not love wrongdoers. / And whoever defends himself after he

> has been wronged, for such, there will be no course [of action] against them. / A course [of action] is only [open] against those who wrong people and seek [to commit] in the earth what is not right. For such there will be a painful chastisement. (Al-Shura, 42:36–42)

Furthermore, pardon on its own is not enough, for Muslims are asked to repay an ill turn with a good one, to 'turn the other cheek'. God says:

> Ward off with that which is better the evil [act]. We know best what they allege. (Al-Mu'minun, 23:96) ❈ And they are not equal, the good deed and the evil deed. Repel with that which is better then, behold, he between whom and you there was enmity will be as though he were a dear friend. / But none is granted it, except those who are steadfast; and none is granted it except one [deserving] of a great reward. (Fussilat, 41:34–35) ❈ And such as cement what God has commanded should be cemented, and fear their Lord, and dread an awful reckoning; / such as are patient, desiring their Lord's countenance; and maintain the prayer and expend of that which We have provided them, secretly and openly, and repel evil with good; those, theirs shall be the sequel of the [heavenly] Abode: / Gardens of Eden, which they shall enter along with those who were righteous from among their fathers and their spouses and their descendants; and the angels shall enter to them from every gate. / 'Peace be upon you for your patience'. How excellent is the sequel of the [heavenly] Abode! (Al-Ra'd, 13:21–24) ❈ And if you retaliate, retaliate with the like of what you have been made to suffer; and yet if you endure patiently, verily that is better for the patient. (Al-Nahl, 16:126) ❈ And the [true] servants of the Compassionate One are those who walk upon the earth modestly, and who, when the ignorant address them, say [words of] peace. (Al-Furqan, 25:63)

In summary: God has given each and every human being inalienable rights, and has obliged Muslims to have respect for all human beings; not to commit aggression against anyone; to be peaceful and to be just; to be merciful; to empathize with all human beings; to forgive them; to pardon them; to restrain themselves from anger; and even to repay evil deeds with kindness and 'turn the other cheek'—and to do this with all people, whoever they may be and regardless of their faith (or lack of it) all the time, so long as they are not first waging war against Muslims.

THE 'PEOPLE OF THE SCRIPTURE'

God has enjoined mercy, justice and forgiveness upon people in general, even as He has commanded people to be kind to all their neighbours, whether near or far, regardless of the neighbour's religion. God says:

> And worship God, and associate nothing with Him. Be kind to parents, and near kindred, and to orphans, and to the needy, and to the neighbour who is near, and to the neighbour who is a stranger, and to the friend at your side,

and to the wayfarer, and to what your right hands own. Surely God loves not the conceited, and the boastful. (Al-Nisa', 4:36)

As we mentioned earlier, according to the commentaries of Qurtubi and the Jalalayn, 'the neighbour' means every human being whether near or far. It is worth adding here that Ibn Kathir says the following in his own commentary: 'It is related from 'Ikrimah, Mujahid, Maymun ibn Mahran, Dahhak, Zayd ibn Aslam, Muqatil bin Hayyan, Qatada, and Nawf Bakkali (according to Abu Ishaq) that *'the neighbour who is near'* means the Muslim, and *'the neighbour who is a stranger'* means the Jew and the Christian'.[140]

It is also worth mentioning that God calls the Christians of Najran 'believers', and curses those who tortured them, in the Holy Qur'an: *Perish the men of the ditch! / Of the fire abounding in fuel, / when they sat by it, / and they themselves were witnesses, to what they did to the believers. / And they ill-treated them for no other reason than that they believed in God, the Mighty, the Praised.* (Al-Buruj, 85:4–8)

Qurtubi said, commenting on this verse: 'This refers to those who made the ditches and cast into them the believers who dwelt in Najran in the time between Jesus ﷺ and Muhammad ﷺ; the narrators differ in their exact words, but the meaning of what they say is essentially the same'.[141]

God also refers to the joy of the Muslims when the Christians of Byzantium defeated the pagan Persians: *Alif lam mim. / The Byzantines have been vanquished / in the nearer [part of the] land. But they, after their vanquishing, shall be the victors / in a few years. To God belongs the command before and after, and on that day, the believers shall rejoice.* (Al-Rum, 30:1–4)

God knew full well of course that Muslims would later face the same Christians of Byzantium in battle (including at the Battle of Mu'tah during the Messenger's ﷺ own lifetime in 630 CE), yet He immortalised the Muslims' joy about the Christian victory over the idolaters in the Holy Qur'an. Moreover, God speaks of their victory in the form of a happy promise to the Muslims that would cause the Muslims to rejoice, and so this means that there is special affection between Muslims and Christians. Indeed, this is precisely what God promises in the following verse:

> *You will truly find the most hostile of people to those who believe to be the Jews and the idolaters; and you will truly find the nearest of them in love to those who believe to be those who say 'Verily, we are Christians'; that is because some of them are priests and monks, and because they are not proud.* (Al-Ma'idah, 5:82)

Although God warns His Messenger about the hostility of some Jews towards him[142], and praises Christians in this verse, in other verses God praises the Children of Israel (or at least the faithful and pious among them[143]) and says that they were His most favoured people:

> O Children of Israel, remember My grace wherewith I graced you, and that I have favoured you above all the worlds; (Al-Baqarah, 2:47) ❋ He said, 'Shall I seek other than God as a god for you, when He has favoured you above all the worlds?' (Al-A'raf, 7:140) ❋ And when Moses said to his people, 'O my people, remember God's favour to you, when He established among you prophets, and established you as kings, and gave you such as He had not given to any in all the worlds. (Al-Ma'idah, 5:20) ❋ And verily We gave the Children of Israel the Scripture, and [the means of] judgement, and prophethood, and We provided them with the good things, and We favoured them above [all] worlds. / And We gave them clear illustrations of the commandment. And they did not differ, except after the knowledge had come to them, out of rivalry among themselves. Surely your Lord will judge between them on the Day of Resurrection concerning that in which they used to differ. (Al-Jathiyah, 45:16–17) ❋ And verily We favoured them with a knowledge over [all] the worlds. / And We gave them signs in which there was a manifest trial. (Al-Dukhan, 44:32–33) ❋ And verily We gave Moses the Scripture; so do not be in doubt concerning the encounter with Him; and We appointed him a guidance for the Children of Israel. / And We appointed among them leaders who guided by Our command, when they had endured [patiently] and had conviction in Our signs. / Surely your Lord will judge between them on the Day of Resurrection concerning that wherein they used to differ. (Al-Sajdah, 32:23–25)

Moreover, God tells Muslims that among all the People of the Scripture there are righteous and exemplary people (who should be admired):

> Yet they are not all alike; some of the People of the Scripture are a community upright, who recite God's verses in the watches of the night, prostrating themselves. / They believe in God and in the Last Day, enjoining decency and forbidding indecency, vying with one another in good works; those are of the righteous. / And whatever good you do, you shall not be denied it, and God knows the God-fearing. (Aal 'Imran, 3:113–115) ❋ And those who adhere to the Scripture, and have established prayer—verily We shall not let the wages of reformers go to waste. (Al-A'raf, 7:170)

In summary: God enjoins upon Muslims—in addition to having respect, justice and mercy in general towards all humanity—to have affection and admiration for the People of the Scripture in general (notably Christians and Jews). God says in the Holy Qur'an that the Jews were His most favoured people and that Muslims have a special affinity with Christians in particular; and God knows best.

THE BELIEVERS

In addition to respect, justice, mercy, pardon, forgiveness,[144] kindness, affection and admiration, God requires believers to maintain special ties of brotherhood between them: *The believers are indeed brothers. Therefore [always] make peace between your brethren, and fear God, so that perhaps you might receive mercy.* (*Al-Hujurat*, 49:10)

Thus God makes believers brothers (and sisters), and reminds them of the rights of this brotherhood by saying '*and fear God*'. God then makes His mercy conditional upon fearing Him and maintaining the bond of brotherhood and peace between believers. In other words, God says that He will have mercy on those who love their brethren in faith and keep peace with them and between them.

Now, 'brotherhood' means love—and nothing less than love—between believers:

> *And those who had settled in the hometown, and [had abided] in faith before them, love those who have emigrated to them, and do not find in their breasts any need of that which those [others] have been given, but prefer [others] to themselves, though they be in poverty. And whoever is saved from the avarice of his own soul, those—they are the successful.* (*Al-Hashr*, 59:9)

In this beautiful verse, God Almighty makes it clear that the love that believers should have for one another is not a matter of mere sentiment that does not oblige the believer to *do* anything. Rather, this love presupposes a state of soul which sincerely and altruistically puts the good of others above oneself, and thus overcomes '*the avarice of his [or her] own soul*'.[145]

In summary: in addition to respect, justice, mercy, affection and kindness, God requires believers to love one another more than they love themselves. This love is what is sometimes called 'love for the sake of God' or 'love in God' ('*al-hubb fi'Llah*').

FRIENDS

In addition to the brotherhood of faith just discussed, God mentions various degrees of friendship in the Holy Qur'an. 'Company' or 'companionship' ('*suhbah*') is the lowest level of friendship, and God mentions it in many verses of the Holy Qur'an, such as the following two verses:

> *[Moses] said, 'If I ask you about anything after this, then do not keep me in your company (tusahibni), for truly you [will] have found from me' [sufficient] excuse.* (*Al-Kahf*, 18:76) ❈ *O my two fellow-prisoners (sahibayy al-sijni)!: Are several lords better, or God, the One, the Almighty?* (*Yusuf*, 12:39)

Generally, the word 'company' ('*suhbah*') in the Holy Qur'an does not imply a special affection or friendship, but suggests the notion of fellowship or companionship in a particular thing. The 'companions of hell' ('*ashab al-nar*') do not love one another, but they are together in hell:

> He will say, 'Enter into the Fire among communities of jinn and humankind who passed away before you'. Every time a community enters, it curses its sister-community, until, when they have all followed one another there, the last of them shall say to the first of them, 'Our Lord, these led us astray; so give them a double chastisement of the Fire.' He will say, 'For each will be double but you do not know'. / And the first of them shall say to the last of them, 'You have no advantage over us. So taste the chastisement for what you used to earn'. (Al-A'raf, 7:38–39)

Sometimes '*suhba*' can simply mean 'ownership', as with '*ashab al-fil*' ('*owners of an elephant*'—the army of the Abyssinian King Abrahah who owned an elephant and tried to attack the Ka'bah in pre-Islamic times). God says: *Have you not considered the way in which your Lord dealt with the Men of the Elephant (ashab al-fil)? (Al-Fil, 105:1)*

Despite this, the word 'company' ('*suhbah*') can also mean 'friendship' and imply a certain kind of affection, as is the case in the following two verses:

> If you do not help him, [know that] God has already helped him, when the disbelievers drove him forth—the second of two; when the two were in the cave—when he said to his companion, 'Do not despair; verily God is with us'. Then God sent down His spirit of peace (sakinatahu) upon him and supported him with legions you did not see; and He made the word of those who disbelieved the nethermost, and the Word of God was the uppermost. And God is Mighty, Wise. (Al-Tawbah, 9:40) ❊ Or did you think that the Companions of the Cave and the Inscription were a [unique] marvel from among Our signs? (Al-Kahf, 18:9)

Beyond 'companionship' lies 'friendship' ('*sadaqah*'). 'Friendship' ('*sadaqah*') implies a specific level of sincere mutual love ('*mahabbah*') and brotherhood. God mentions 'friendship', clarifies its meaning, honours it, and grants it a special status by acknowledging it even in His Laws:

> There is no blame upon the blind, nor any blame upon the lame, nor any blame upon the sick, nor upon yourselves if you eat from your own houses, or your fathers' houses, or your mothers' houses, or your brothers' houses, or your sisters' houses, or the houses of your paternal uncles or the houses of your paternal aunts, or the houses of your maternal uncles or the houses of your maternal aunts, or [from] that whereof you hold the keys, or [from] those of your [faithful] friends. You would not be at fault whether you eat together, or separately. But when you enter houses, bid peace to yourselves with a salutation from God, blessed and good. So God clarifies the signs for you that perhaps you might comprehend. (Al-Nur, 24:61)

Above 'friendship' we can discern 'close friendship' ('*sadaqah hamimiyya*') in the Holy Qur'an, for God says: *Tell My servants who believe that they establish prayers and expend of that which We have provided them, secretly and openly, before a day comes wherein there will be neither bargaining, nor befriending (khilal). (Ibrahim, 14:31) Nor any intimate friend. (Al-Shuʿara', 26:101)*[146]

Finally, there is a degree of friendship that is even higher than 'close friendship' ('*sadaqah hamimiyya*'). God calls this '*khullah*' or 'intimate friendship'.[147] God says: *[Intimate] Friends (al-akhilla) will, on that day, be foes of one another, except for the God-fearing. (Al-Zukhruf, 43:67)*

In summary: God mentions, affirms and blesses four different degrees of 'friendship'—over and above the love which exists between believers—in the Holy Qur'an: (1) 'Company' or 'companionship' ('*suhbah*'); (2) 'friendship' ('*sadaqah*'); (3) 'close friendship' ('*sadaqah hamimiyya*'), and (4) 'intimate friendship' ('*khullah*'). These constitute, in ascending order, the gamut of friendship between believers, and the highest degrees of (non-sexual) love between those who are not related[148]; and God knows best.

CHAPTER EIGHTEEN

CONJUGAL AND SEXUAL LOVE

God Almighty created all human beings from a single soul—the soul of Adam ﷺ. First, God created a mate from Adam ﷺ (Eve), and then He created all humanity from Adam ﷺ and Eve together. God says:

> *O people, fear your Lord, Who created you of a single soul, and from it created its mate, and from the pair of them scattered many men and women; and fear God by whom you claim [your rights] from one another and kinship ties. Surely God has been watchful over you. (Al-Nisa', 4:1)* ❊ *He created you from a single soul, then made from it its mate; and He sent down for you of the cattle, eight kinds. He creates you in your mothers' wombs, creation after creation in a threefold darkness. That is God, your Lord. To Him belongs [all] sovereignty. There is no god except Him. Why then are you being turned away? (Al-Zumar, 39:6)*

And He created human beings (generally speaking[149]) as two mates ('*zawj*'), male and female[150]:

> *And that He [Himself] creates the two mates, the male and the female. (Al-Najm, 53:45)* ❊ *And He made of it the two mates, the male and the female. (Al-Qiyamah, 75:39)* ❊ *Glory be to Him Who created all the pairs of what the earth produces, and of themselves, and of what they do not know. (Ya Sin, 36:36)* ❊ *To God belongs the kingdom of the heavens and the earth. He creates whatever He will; He gives to whomever He will females, and He gives to whomever He will males. / Or He combines them, males and females; and He makes whomever He will infertile. Surely He is Knower, Powerful. (Al-Shura, 42:49–50)*

And in the creation and existence of the two genders, male and female, there is a remembrance for humanity: *And of all things We created pairs that perhaps you might remember. (Al-Dhariyat, 51:49)*

In one way, God distinguishes males: *Men are caretakers of women because of that with which God has preferred the one over the other, and because of what they expend of their property. Therefore righteous women are obedient, guarding in the unseen because of what God has guarded…. (Al-Nisa', 4:34)*

And in another way, God distinguishes females: *And when she gave birth to her, she said, 'Lord, I have given birth to a female'—and God knew very well what she had given birth to; the male is not as the female. 'And I have named her*

Mary, and commend her to You with her seed to protect them from the accursed Satan'. (Aal 'Imran, 3:36)

Indeed, God has given a woman's testimony in her own defence greater weight than her husband's:

> And those who accuse their wives, but have no witnesses, except themselves, then the testimony of one of them shall be to testify [swearing] by God four times that he is indeed being truthful, / and a fifth time that God's wrath shall be upon him if he were lying. / And the punishment shall be averted from her if she testify [swearing] by God four times that he is indeed lying, / and a fifth time that God's wrath shall be upon her if he were being truthful. (Al-Nur, 24:6–9)

But He makes all human beings—both males and females—part of each other:

> And their Lord answers them, 'I do not let the labour of any labourer among you go to waste, be you male or female—You are members, one of another; and those who emigrated, and were expelled from their habitations, those who suffered hurt in My way, and fought, and were slain—them I shall surely absolve of their evil deeds, and I shall admit them to Gardens underneath which river flow'. A reward from God! And God—with Him is the fairest reward. (Aal 'Imran, 3:195)

And thus He rewards males and females equally:

> Indeed the men who have submitted [to God] and the women who have submitted [to God], and the believing men and the believing women, and the obedient men and the obedient women, and the men who are truthful and the women who are truthful, and the patient men and the patient women, and the humble men and the humble women, and the charitable men and the charitable women, and the men who fast and the women who fast, and the men who guard their private parts and the women who guard their private parts, and the men who remember God often and the women who remember God often—for them God has prepared forgiveness and a great reward. (Al-Ahzab, 33:35)

Males and females, therefore, share a common human nature despite the differences between them: every human being has a father and a mother (except Jesus Christ ﷺ, who had no father, and Adam ﷺ, who had neither mother nor father); and every human being (who enjoys normal health) may have a male or a female child.

Human beings' common human nature also means that they cannot be complete without each other. Males need females, and females need males, and without each other they are generally incomplete. This need for each other—and the deficiency that exists when the need is not met—can be clearly seen in three things: (a) the need males and females have for each other in order to procreate; (b) the need males and females have for each other psychologically and emotionally during marriage; and (c) conjugal and sexual love between spouses. (It is also worth mentioning that these three needs might all combine in a relationship, or they might be separate from each other, or they might occur in any combination.)

THE NEED SPOUSES HAVE FOR ONE ANOTHER IN ORDER TO PROCREATE

Naturally, no human being can (naturally) produce a child without a mate: *And God made for you mates from your own selves, and made for you, from your mates, children and grandchildren, and He provided you with the good things. Is it then in falsehood that they believe and in the grace of God that they disbelieve?* (*Al-Nahl*, 16:72)

This is obvious, even today when there are 'test-tube babies', because even test-tube babies require a 'gushing fluid' wherein is combined that which comes from the 'loins' ('*sulb*') of a man and the 'pelvic arch' ('*tara'ib*') of a woman:

> *And We certainly created man from an extraction of clay. / Then We made him a drop in a secure lodging. / Then We transformed the drop [of semen] into a clot. Then We transformed the clot into a [little] lump of flesh. Then We transformed the lump of flesh into bones. Then We clothed the bones with flesh. Then We produced him as [yet] another creature. So blessed be God, the best of creators!* (*Al-Mu'minun*, 23:12–14) ❋ *Did We not create you from a base fluid, / then lodged it in a secure abode / for a known span? / Thus We were able; so [how] excellent able ones We are!* (*Al-Mursalat*, 77:20–23) ❋ *So let man consider from what he was created. / He was created from a gushing fluid, / issuing from between the loins and the pelvic arch.* (*Al-Tariq*, 86:5–7)

Regarding this last verses, *Tafsir al-Jalalayn* says:

'*So let man consider*' and reflect '*from what he was created*', i.e. from what substance. And the answer is: '*He was created from a gushing fluid*' which flows from the man and woman in her womb; '*issuing from between the loins*' in the case of men, '*and the pelvic arch*' in the case of women.'[151]

NON-PHYSICAL CONJUGAL LOVE AND 'SOULMATES'

People need each other not only for procreation, but for natural psychological reasons as well:

> *He it is Who created you from a single soul, and made from him his spouse that he might take rest in her. Then, when he covered her, she bore a light burden, and moved to and fro with it; but when she became heavy, they cried*

to God their Lord, *'If You give us one that is sound, we indeed shall be of the thankful'*. (Al-A'raf, 7:189)

It may be observed in this Qur'anic verse that God says *'that he might take rest in her'*, and not *'that he dwell with her'*, nor *'that he might dwell near her'*. This indicates that a man's life with his spouse is a source of rest (and *vice versa*) as well as cohabitation, and rest is a profound psychological need. And God shows the blessings of this 'rest' in the fact the two spouses pray together (at the end of the verse): *'If You give us one that is sound, we indeed shall be of the thankful.'*

Moreover, in another verse, God says: *And of His signs is that He created for you from yourselves mates that you might take rest in them, and He ordained between you affection and mercy. Surely in that there are signs for a people who reflect.* (Al-Rum, 30:21)

This verse contains many secrets, as is implied by the sacred words: *'Surely in that there are signs for a people who reflect.'* In what follows we consider some of these secrets:

(a) God tells people that their spouses are *'from yourselves'*. Now in the Holy Qur'an the word *'yourselves'* (*'anfusikum'*) has two meanings: firstly, it can mean 'you' (in the plural form), and therefore *'from yourselves'* would mean simply 'from you'. Secondly, 'yourselves' can mean 'your souls' (*nufusikum*). God mentions the 'soul' (*'nafs'*) in the Holy Qur'an as that part of human beings which is non-bodily and thus eternal. For example, God speaks of the *'soul which incites to evil'* (Yusuf, 12:53); the *'self-reproaching soul'* (Al-Qiyamah, 25:2), and the *'soul at peace'* (Al-Fajr, 89:27).

So what is the meaning of *'He created (khalaqa) for you from yourselves (anfusikum) mates that you might find peace by their side'* according to these two definitions of the word 'self' (*'nafs'*)? To understand this we have to turn to another Qur'anic verse which uses the same word. The word *'yourselves'* (*'anfusikum'*) is used in conjunction with the word *'made'* (*'ja'ala'*) in the following Qur'anic verse: *The Originator of the heavens and the earth. He has made (ja'ala) for you, from yourselves (anfusikum), pairs, and [also] pairs of the cattle: He multiplies you by such [means]. There is nothing like Him. He is the Hearer, the Seer.* (Al-Shura, 42:11)

The first meaning of *'from yourselves'* is thus plain, namely that God created for people spouses who, like themselves, are from the progeny of Adam ﷺ and Eve.

The second (and more subtle) meaning of *'from yourselves'* (*'min anfusikum'*) is that every soul has a particular spouse—a unique, individual 'soulmate'— which was created for it *a priori* either by divine 'creation' (*'khalq'*), or by special divine 'making' (*'ja'al'*) ordained after creation. Sometimes, people are able to find their 'soulmate' through original divine creation' (*'khalq'*) in this worldly life—or alternatively they become 'soulmates' with someone whom they find in life, (this being perhaps is what is meant by soulmates who are made ['*ja'al*'] by God). Sometimes they never find him or her. In either case, however, their soulmate has been created, or does exist. The soulmate which has been created as such *a priori* by God may be considered to be more complete and more perfect as a soulmate than the soulmate which has been made as such a *posteriori* by God; and God knows best. According to this understanding of '*from yourselves*', the Qur'anic words '*and [also] pairs of the cattle*' symbolise bodies: cattle resemble human bodies in that their function is limited to the natural activities of life such as eating and drinking; and moreover, they resemble also the disbelievers who have no higher concerns except to satisfy their bodily and personal desires, for God says:

> *And We have indeed urged unto Hell many of the jinn and humankind, having hearts wherewith they do not understand, and having eyes wherewith they do not perceive, and having ears wherewith they do not hear. These, they are like cattle—nay, rather they are further astray. These—they are the heedless.* (Al-A'raf, 7:179) ⁕ ...*As for those who disbelieve, they take their enjoyment and eat as the cattle eat; and the Fire will be their habitation.* (Muhammad, 47:12)

The pairs of cattle, then, symbolise the marriages of those people who are overwhelmed by the urge to satisfy their bodily desires and who do not possess real love, or whose hearts do not '*perceive*' and do not remember God. In this case, God's words '*He multiplies you by such [means]*' allude to the placement of souls and spirits in human bodies; in other words, it may be understood from this that God gathered up the souls and spirits which existed before the bodies were created, and then placed them in this world in material bodies akin to cattle; and God knows best.

The benefit of understanding this subtle point here is to know that between some people, and between some spouses, there is a perfect relationship such that each person completes the other, as though they are a single person or a single soul. In such a case, we could call this 'a marriage of souls'. Other spouses, however, may enjoy peace, affection and mercy without their relationship being perfect and complete, even though they have been married for many years. And God knows best.

(b) God tells people (in: *Al-Rum*, 30:21) that they take rest '*in*' their spouses. We touched on the meaning of the word '*in*' here earlier. We add here to that discussion only what Fakhr al-Din al-Razi says in his *Al-Tafsir al-Kabir*: '"To take rest in" means the rest of the heart, whilst "to take rest with" means the rest of the body; this is because the word "with" suggests a spatial relationship, which is for bodies, whilst the word "in" suggests the final destination, which is the heart.'[152]

Thus God also says:

> *He it is Who created you from a single soul, and made from him his spouse that he might take rest in her. Then, when he covered her, she bore a light burden, and moved to and fro with it; but when she became heavy, they cried to God their Lord, 'If You give us one that is sound, we indeed shall be of the thankful'.* (Al-A'raf, 7:189)

(c) God tells people (in: *Al-Rum*, 30:21) that He has made '*affection*' ('*mawaddah*') between them. We will later discuss, God willing, the meaning of '*affection*' as a form of love, so it suffices to observe here that '*affection*' is not a physical love and need, but rather a kind of 'emotional love'. God says: *But if a favour from God befalls you, he will surely cry as if there had never been any affection (mawaddah) between you and him: 'Oh, would that I had been with them, so that I might have won a great triumph!'* (Al-Nisa', 4:73)

(d) God tells people (in: *Al-Rum*, 30:21) that He has made '*mercy*' between them. Earlier on we discussed the meaning of '*mercy*' ('*rahmah*'), and the connection between '*mercy*' and the womb ('*rahm*'). It suffices here to say that '*mercy*', like '*affection*', is also not a physical need nor physical love.

Finally, in the following verse wherein God describes the ideal spouse, it may be observed that the majority (if not all) of the attributes mentioned in this description are related to the soul and nature of the spouse, not her face, figure or physical beauty, and this confirms both the existence and importance of extra-physical love in marriage. God says: *It may be that, if he divorces you, his Lord will give him in [your] stead wives better than you—women submissive [to God], believing, obedient, penitent, devout, given to fasting, widows or virgins.* (Al-Tahrim, 66:5)

In summary: all of this allows us to say that in the aforementioned Qur'anic verse (in: *Al-Rum*, 30:21), God affirms that in marriage there is a love which can be entirely separate from physical relations, and that the souls of both spouses naturally need this love just as much as their bodies need physical love.

SEXUAL CONJUGAL LOVE

What is it that makes conjugal love and the conjugal relationship completely different from all other kinds of love? The answer is evidently that conjugal love involves the human body's participation in love (for males as well as for females). Family love and the love between believers and friends do not involve the body's participation as such. In conjugal love, by contrast, couples touch one another and their bodies intermingle and are temporarily conjoined in a (normally) amorous act. In other words, all other forms of love between human beings occur primarily between their souls, whilst conjugal love involves both souls and bodies. God describes (or alludes to) the components and the secrets of this 'meeting of bodies' during conjugal relations in several verses of the Qur'an. It suffices here—since this subject is obviously particularly sensitive—to mention the way these secrets are symbolically alluded to a number of times in the Holy Qur'an. God says: *And do not extend your glance toward the pleasure We have given to some pairs among them, [as] the flower of the life of this world that We may try them thereby. And your Lord's provision is better and more enduring.* (Ta Ha, 20:131)

We understand from this verse, firstly, that in spouses there is (or should be) beauty, for flowers are beautiful; and secondly that marriage holds love and delight, for flowers evoke love and delight. We also understand from the words '*the pleasure We have given*' that marriage involves a particular 'pleasure' ('*mutʿa*'). God also says:

> *...And wedded women, save what your right hands own; this is what God has prescribed for you. Lawful for you beyond all that is that you seek using your wealth, in wedlock and not in illicitly. Such wives as you enjoy (istamta'tum) thereby, give them their wages as an obligation; you are not at fault in agreeing together, after the obligation. God is ever Knowing, Wise.* (Al-Nisa', 4:24)

We understand from this verse that in sexual relations, in addition to the 'pleasure' we have mentioned, there is also 'enjoyment' (*istimtaʿ*). God also says:

> *They will ask you about the monthly period. Say: 'It is an ailment; so part with women in the monthly period, and do not approach them until they are pure; when they have cleansed themselves, then come to them, as God has commanded you'. Truly, God loves those who repent, and He loves those who cleanse themselves. / Your women are a tillage for you; so come to your tillage as you wish (shi'tum); and offer for your souls; and fear God; and know that you shall meet Him; and give good tidings to the believers.* (Al-Baqarah, 2:222–223)

The words '*a tillage for you*' evoke two things: firstly, the notion of fertility, as is needed in farming; and secondly, there is an obvious sexual symbolism in tilling between the earth which is tilled and the plough which tills it. From the words '*as you wish*' ('*anna shi'tum*'), we understand that in sexual relations there is a particular 'wish' or 'urge', and a particular liberty in satisfying this urge. This is where the aforementioned pleasure and enjoyment come from. This urge is naturally strong, and is thus considered a 'desire'. God says: *And she certainly desired him, and he would have desired her [too], had it not been that he saw the proof of his Lord. So it was that We might ward off from him evil and lewdness. Truly he was of Our devoted servants.* (Yusuf, 12:24)

And because of the intensity of this 'desire', God permits—and indeed, enjoins—sexual relations during the night in Ramadan, after the Companions had at first abstained from them in the first years of Islam. God says:

> *Permitted to you, upon the night of the Fast, is to go in to your wives; they are a garment for you, and you are a garment for them; God knows that you have*

been betraying yourselves, and so He has turned to you [relenting], and He has pardoned you. So now, lie with them and seek what God has prescribed for you, and eat and drink until the white thread is distinct to you from the black thread at daybreak; then complete the fast to the night; and do not lie with them, while you cleave to the mosques in devotion [to God]. Those are God's bounds; do not approach them. So, God makes clear His signs to people so that they might fear. (Al-Baqarah, 2:187)

The word '*garment*' evokes two things: firstly, the 'covering' which garments provide; and secondly, the way in which garments touch and rub the body. Thus, in marriage, satisfying one's natural desire; taking pleasure and enjoyment in this, and being protected by this act (from wrong-doing and shame) is like donning a 'garment'. God also says: *How shall you take it, when each of you has gone in unto the other, and they have taken from you a solemn covenant?* (Al-Nisa', 4:21)[153]

We understand from the Qur'anic words '*when each of you has gone in unto the other*' that in sexual relations, firstly each spouse lets out something (of their fluids), and secondly that the husband literally goes into the wife. In other words, the sexual act involves an entering, an emptying, and then relaxation and comfort. Moreover, God holds the sexual act an irrevocable bond of sorts in the above verse—even when that act, or the marriage in which it occurs, has come to end—and that this bond necessitates kindness and respect forever; hence His question: *How shall you take it, when each of you has gone in unto the other [?].*

But these things—and *a priori* an over-attachment to these things—present a particular danger to the individual, who should remember God and the Last Day more than this worldly life, for God says: *O you who believe! Indeed among your wives and children there are enemies for you, so beware of them. And if you pardon, and overlook [such enmity] and forgive, then assuredly God is Forgiving, Merciful.* (Al-Taghabun, 64:14)

In summary: the Holy Qur'an contains a complete but subtle description of natural physical needs and sexual desires in conjugal love, and a description of how sexual relations between men and women naturally proceed. Hence God ordains marriage whenever possible. God says:

And marry such of you as are solitary and the pious of your slaves and maid-servants. If they be poor, God will enrich them of His bounty. God is Embracing, Aware. / And let those who cannot find a match keep chaste till God give them independence by His grace. And such of your slaves as seek a writing (of emancipation), write it for them if ye are aware of aught of good in them, and bestow upon them of the wealth of God which He hath bestowed upon you. Force not your slave-girls to whoredom that ye may seek enjoyment of the life of the world, if they would preserve their chastity. And if one force them, then (unto them), after their compulsion, lo! God will be Forgiving, Merciful. (Al-Nur, 24:32–33)

SPIRITUAL CONJUGAL LOVE

Is there more to sexual relations than procreation and physical pleasure? In other words, is there also a spiritual experience in the sexual act, in addition to the physical one? Now we know that the Messenger of God ﷺ was devoted to God in his entire being, for God says: *Say: 'My prayer and my rituals, and my living, and my dying, are all for God, the Lord of the Worlds. / No associate has He. And to this, I have been commanded, and I am the first of those who submit'.* (*Al-An'am*, 6:162–163)

And yet he was married, and loved women: 'There have been made beloved to me, of your world, three [things]: perfume, women, and the coolness of my eye placed in prayer.'[154]

But his wives were not entirely like other women: *O wives of the Prophet! You are not like any other women. If you fear [God], then do not be complaisant in your speech, lest he in whose heart is a sickness aspire [to you], but speak honourable words.* (*Al-Ahzab*, 33:32)

Should it, then, be understood from all this that the Messenger ﷺ loved women for their own sake as women, or that he loved them (who were *not like any other women* precisely) for the sake of God and His remembrance?

God says: *And she certainly desired him, and he would have desired her [too], had it not been that he saw the proof (burhan) of his Lord. So it was that We might ward off from him evil and lewdness. Truly he was of Our devoted servants.* (*Yusuf*, 12:24)

What was it that stopped Joseph ﷺ from 'desiring' the Chief of the Court's (Potiphar) wife in the above verse from the Holy Qur'an? The answer is that *'he saw the proof (burhan) of his Lord'*. But Potiphar's wife did not see *'the proof of her Lord'*. She only saw Joseph ﷺ and his great beauty, and so she desired him even though she was married to another, and this was adultery. She, too, however, was beautiful, so what exactly was the 'proof' that Joseph ﷺ saw and she did not? The very fact that the verse mentions nothing else implies that Joseph saw the *'proof of his Lord'* in the very beauty of Potiphar's wife. God says elsewhere in the Holy Qur'an: *O people, a proof has now come to you from your Lord, and We have revealed to you a manifest light.* (*Al-Nisa'*, 4:147) And as we mentioned before, God says: *Verily We created man in the best of statures.* (*Al-Tin*, 95:4) And God also says: *So behold the effects of God's mercy, how He revives the earth after it has died. Surely He is the Reviver of the dead and He has power over all things.* (*Al-Rum*, 30:50)

So, did Joseph ﷺ behold the beauty of Potiphar's wife and see therein *'the proof of his Lord'* Who created her *'in the best of statures'*. Did seeing her thus cause him, rather than forgetting God, to remember Him and thus refrain from 'desiring' her adulterously? If the answer is 'yes', this means that it is possible for

Conjugal and Sexual Love

physical beauty to remind one of God in such a way that it distances one from physical 'desire' (rather than increasing physical desire, as is usually the case). This then means that the Messenger of God ﷺ—who is the best example *'for whoever hopes for [the encounter with] God and the Last Day, and remembers God often'* (Al-Ahzab, 33:21)—would have himself had to have seen the 'proof of his Lord' in his wives. God knows best, but there may be an allusion here in the Holy Qur'an to the idea that beholding physical beauty can sometimes be—or bring about—a state of spiritual contemplation, which is diametrically opposed to physical lust. Otherwise, how could the figures of the hypocrites please the Messenger of God ﷺ despite their moral deviation? God says:

> *And when you see them, their figures please you; and if they speak, you listen to their speech. [Yet] they are like blocks of timber [that have been] propped-up. They assume that every cry is [directed] against them. They are the enemy, so beware of them. May God assail them! How can they deviate?* (Al-Munafiqun, 63:4)

God says:

> *They will ask you about the monthly period. Say: 'It is an ailment; so part with women in the monthly period, and do not approach them until they are pure; when they have cleansed themselves, then come to them, as God has commanded you'. Truly, God loves those who repent, and He loves those who cleanse themselves. / Your women are a tillage for you; so come to your tillage as you wish; and offer for your souls; and fear God; and know that you shall meet Him; and give good tidings to the believers.* (Al-Baqarah, 2:222–223)

It is assumed from the Holy Qur'an that the 'meeting' (*'liqa''*) with God will take place in the Hereafter, for God says:

> *Then We gave Moses the Scripture, complete for him who does good, and a detailing of all things, and as a guidance and a mercy, that perhaps they might believe in the meeting with their Lord.* (Al-An'am, 6:154) ❋ *And on the day when He shall gather them as if they had not tarried, but an hour of the day, recognising one another; those will verily have lost who denied the meeting with God, for they were not guided.* (Yunus, 10:45)[155]

However, in three other Qur'anic verses, it is unclear whether the meeting with God will take place in the Hereafter only, or whether it also takes place in this life as well, for God says:

> *O man! Verily you are labouring toward your Lord laboriously, and you will meet Him.* (Al-Inshiqaq, 84:6) ❋ *And when Saul went forth with the hosts, he said, 'God will try you with a river; whoever drinks of it, is not of me, and whoever tastes it not, he is of me, except for him who scoops up with his hand.*

But they drank of it, except a few of them; and when he crossed it, with those who believed, they said, 'We have no power today against Goliath and his troops'. Those who thought they would meet God, said, 'How often a little company has overcome a numerous one, by God's leave; and God is with the patient'. / So, when they went forth against Goliath and his troops, they said, 'Our Lord, pour out upon us patience, and make firm our feet, and grant us victory over the disbelieving folk!' (Al-Baqarah, 2:249-250)

The third verse is the one we have already cited: *Your women are a tillage for you; so come to your tillage as you wish; and offer for your souls; and fear God; and know that you shall meet Him; and give good tidings to the believers.* (Al-Baqarah, 2:223)

What the mentions of 'meeting' ('*liqa*'') with God have in common in these three verses is that they all take place after a kind of destruction: in the first verse, 'laborious labour' is mentioned before the meeting with God; in the second verse, the meeting with God is mentioned before a battle; and in the third verse, the meeting with God is mentioned after the sexual act. What does this mean? Is there an indication here that in 'destructions' of various kinds there is a meeting with God, and that in the sexual act—and in the ecstasy of sex and the '*going into*' as discussed earlier—there is a kind of destruction? And if there is no indication of this, then why does God mention the meeting with Him right after the sexual act '*as you wish*'? Is all this an indication that in the sexual act—by God's grace, and for whom He wills—there is sometimes a spiritual element or 'meeting' in the Spirit? In other words, can the annihilation in sexual climax lead—for certain people at least—to a spiritual experience and 'meeting'?

In any case, if this is indeed true, such a meeting, spiritual though it may be, could not be like the meeting with God in the Hereafter, for God says: *The Originator of the heavens and the earth. He has made for you, from your own selves, pairs, and [also] pairs of the cattle: He multiplies you by such [means]. There is nothing like Him. He is the Hearer, the Seer* (Al-Shura, 42:11)

In this verse, God—after speaking of spouses and pairs—categorically denies that He resembles His creation through His words '*There is nothing like Him*'. This means that even if there is a spiritual element to the sex act, it does not resemble the meeting with God in the Hereafter; and God knows best.

All of this allows us to say that there may be indications in the Holy Qur'an that one may remember God when looking lawfully at the beauty of another person's body—or rather that this physical beauty may be the cause of remembrance of God and contemplation of a 'proof' of God—and that thus there may be, for certain people, a profound spiritual element to sexual beauty; and God knows best.

Conjugal and Sexual Love

THE PRESERVATION OF CONJUGAL LOVE

We have discussed at length the *affection and mercy* (*Al-Rum*, 30:21) that God has placed between spouses. It remains to be said that these have to be deliberately and carefully cultivated and maintained. Indeed, God cites (and thus commends) the supplication (by believers): *[A]nd those who say, 'Our Lord! Grant us in our spouses and our offspring the joy of our eyes, and make us paragons for the God-fearing'.* (*Al-Furqan*, 25:74)

Thus believers *should* desire that their conjugal love be preserved and that they continue to love their spouses (even in the next world, as will be discussed in Chapter 32). However, for conjugal love to be preserved irrespective of physical beauty (and indeed long after physical beauty has faded), beauty of soul and beautiful actions must be maintained and practiced between a husband and wife. Inner beauty can—and should—more than make up for the lack of physical beauty or for its inevitable loss over time.

More specifically, God orders ten principles (at least) in the Qur'an to be assiduously mutually observed in marriage: (1) kindness and honour (*ma'ruf*); (2) goodness or virtue or excellence (*ihsan*); (3) generosity (*fadl*); (4) mutual consultation (*tashawur*); (5) mutual agreement (*taradi*); (6) justice and equity (*'adl* and / or *qist*); (7) not harming (*la darar*); (8) keeping the 'bounds' (*hudud*) that God sets and not transgressing (*la i'tida*); (9) not harassing (*la diq*), and (10) mutual 'protecting friendship' (*wilayah*). All of this is a vast topic of great importance—indeed, of paramount importance to the harmonious functioning of the Muslim family and of Islamic society—and many long books and studies have (rightly) been written on it, so we can only cover it briefly here.

The emphasis God places on kindness and honour (*ma'ruf*) in marriage—and even in divorce—in the Qur'an is remarkable. In the following passage of ten verses it is mentioned ten times, in addition to (2) goodness (*ihsan*)—twice; (3) generosity (*fadl*); (4) mutual consultation (*tashawur*); (5) mutual agreement (*taradi*)—twice; (6) justice and equity (*'adl* and / or *qist*)—this is implied in the principles of: *No soul is charged save to its capacity*, and: *women shall have rights similar to those due from them*; (7) not harming (*la darar*)—twice; (8) keeping the 'bounds' (*hudud*) that God sets and not transgressing (*i'tida*)—nine times, and (9) not harassing (*la diq*)—this is implied in God's words: *do not debar them...* :

> *Divorced women shall wait by themselves for three periods. And it is not lawful for them to hide what God has created in their wombs if they believe in God and the Last Day. Their mates have a better right to restore them in such time if they desire to set things right; women shall have rights similar to those due from them with kindness and honour (bil ma'ruf); but their men have a degree [of right] over them; God is Mighty, Wise. / Divorce is twice; then kind and honourable (bi ma'ruf) retention; or setting free with goodness (ihsan). It is not lawful for you to take of what you have given them unless the couple*

fear that they may not maintain God's bounds (hudud). If you fear they may not maintain God's bounds (hudud), neither of them would be at fault if she were to ransom herself. Those are God's bounds (hudud); do not transgress them (ta'tadu). Whoever transgresses (ya'tadu) God's bounds (hudud)—those are the evildoers. / If he divorces her, she shall not be lawful to him after that, until she marries another husband. If he divorces her, then neither of them would be at fault to return to each other, if they think that they will maintain God's bounds (hudud). Those are God's bounds (hudud), which He makes clear to a people who have knowledge. / When you divorce women, and they have reached their term, then retain them kindly and honourably (bi ma'ruf), or set them free kindly and honourably (bi ma'ruf); do not retain them in harm (dirar) to transgress (ta'tadu); whoever does that has wronged his soul; take not God's verses in mockery, and remember God's grace upon you, and the Book, and the wisdom He has revealed to you, to exhort you therewith; and fear God, and know that God has knowledge of all things. / When you divorce women, and they have reached their term, do not debar them from marrying their husbands when they have agreed (taradu) together kindly and honourably (bil ma'ruf). That is an admonition for whoever of you believe in God and the Last Day; that is purer for you, and cleaner. God knows, and you know not. / Mothers suckle their children for two full years for such as desire to fulfil the suckling. It is for the father to provide them and clothe them kindly and honourably (bil ma'ruf). No soul is charged save to its capacity; a mother shall not be harmed (tudar) by her child; neither a father by his child. The heir has a similar duty. But if the two desire by mutual consent (taradin) and consultation (tashawur) to wean, then they would not be at fault. And if you desire to seek nursing for your children, you would not be at fault, provided you hand over what you have given kindly and honourably (bil ma'ruf), and fear God, and know that God sees what you do. / And those of you who pass away, leaving wives, they shall wait by themselves for four months and ten. When they have reached their term, then you would not be at fault regarding what they may do with themselves, kindly and honourably (bil ma'ruf); God is aware of what you do. / You would not be at fault regarding the proposal you present or hide in your hearts to women. God knows that you will be mindful of them; but do not make arrangements with them secretly, unless you speak kind and honourable (ma'rufan) words. And do not resolve on the knot of marriage until that which is written has reached its term; and know that God knows what is in your souls; so be fearful of Him; and know that God is Forgiving, Forbearing. / You would not be at fault if you divorce women while you have not touched them, nor appointed any obligation for them; yet make provision of comforts for them kindly and honourably (bil ma'kiruf), the one of ample means, according to his means, and the needy man, according to his means—an obligation on the virtuous (muhsinin). / And if you divorce them before you have touched them, and you have already appointed for them an obligation, then one-half of what you have appointed, unless it be that they make remission, or he makes remission, the one in whose hand is the knot of marriage; yet that you should remit is nearer to piety. Forget not to be generous (al-fadl) between yourselves; surely God sees what you do. (Al-Baqarah, 2:228–237)

The same principles are also evident in the following two Qur'anic passages (among others):

O Prophet, when you [men] divorce women, divorce them by their prescribed period. And count the prescribed period, and fear God your Lord. Do not expel them from their houses, nor let them go forth, unless they commit a blatant [act of] indecency. And those are God's bounds; and whoever transgresses the bounds of God has verily wronged his soul. You never know: it may be that God will bring something new to pass afterwards. / Then, when they have reached their term, retain them kindly and honourably, or separate from them kindly and honourably. And call to witness two just men from among yourselves, and bear witness for the sake of God. By this is exhorted whoever believes in God and the Last Day. And whoever fears God, He will make a way out for him; / and He will provide for him from whence he never expected. And whoever puts his trust in God, He will suffice him. Indeed God fulfils His command. Verily God has ordained for everything a measure. / And [as for] those of your women who no longer expect to menstruate, if you have any doubts, their prescribed [waiting] period shall be three months, and [also for] those who have not yet menstruated. And those who are pregnant, their term shall be when they deliver. And whoever fears God, He will make matters ease for him. / That is God's command which He has revealed to you. And whoever fears God, He will absolve him of his misdeeds and magnify the reward for him. / Lodge them where you dwell in accordance with your means and do not harass them so as to put them in straits. And if they are pregnant, then maintain them until they deliver. Then, if they suckle for you, give them their wages, and consult together, kindly and honourably. But if you both make difficulties, then another woman will suckle [the child] for him. / Let the affluent man expend out of his affluence. And let he whose provision has been straitened for him, expend of what God has given him. God does not charge any soul save except with what He has given it. God will assuredly bring about ease after hardship. (Al-Talaq, 65:1–7)

O you who believe, it is not lawful for you to inherit women against their will; neither debar them, so that you may go off with part of what you have given them, except when they commit flagrant lewdness. Consort with them in kindness and honour; for if you hate them, it may happen that you hate a thing wherein God has set much good. / And if you desire to exchange a wife in place of another, and you have given to one a hundredweight, take of it nothing. Would you take it by way of calumny and manifest sin? / How shall *you take it, when each of you has been privily with the other, and they have taken from you a solemn covenant. (Al-Nisa, 4:19–21)*

Equal justice for both spouses is also particularly evident in the following rules for arbitration in the Qur'an: *And if you fear a breach between the two, send forth an arbiter from his folk, and an arbiter from her folk, if they desire to set things right, God will grant them success. Surely God is ever Knower, Aware. (Al-Nisa, 4:35)*

We should also mention the remarkable verse, where God Himself says that He has heard the complaints of a woman about her husband (and is thus a salutary warning to husbands and men): *God has certainly heard the words of her who disputes with you concerning her husband and complains to God. And God hears your conversation. Assuredly God is Hearer, Seer. (Al-Mujadilah, 58:1)*

Finally, we should mention the mutual 'protecting friendship' (*wilayah*) between men and women in the Qur'an that protects conjugal love, marriage and society as a whole—God Himself says He will have mercy on those who are *'protecting friends'* of one another: *And the believers, both men and women, are 'protecting friends' of one another; they enjoin decency and forbid indecency; they observe prayer and pay the alms, and they obey God and His Messenger. Those, God will have mercy on them. Truly God is Mighty, Wise. (Al-Tawbah, 9:71)*

The Prophet Muhammad ﷺ tersely summed up all these principles when he said: 'The best of you is the best to his wife.'[156] And also: 'The best money is the money spent by a man on his family [his wife and children], and money spent by a man on his horse in God's way, and money spent by a man on his companions in God's way.'[157]

CHAPTER NINETEEN

LOVE AND EXTRA-MARITAL SEX

Is there any love in extra-marital—and hence illicit—sex, or is it merely a case of satisfying lust and a physical urge? Can believers truly love what God does not love? Extra-marital sex is condemned in the Holy Qur'an, and is punished with grave chastisement in this life and the next, for God says:

> *A Surah which We have revealed and prescribed and wherein We have revealed manifest signs that perhaps you might remember. / As for the adulterer and the adulteress, strike each of them a hundred lashes. And do not let any pity for them overcome you in God's religion, if you believe in God and the Last Day. And let their punishment be witnessed by a group of the believers. / The adulterer shall not marry anyone but a adulteress or an idolatress, and the adulteress shall be married by none except a adulterer or an idolater, and that is forbidden to believers. / And those who accuse honourable women [in wedlock], and then do not bring four witnesses, strike them eighty lashes, and do not accept any testimony from them ever; and those, they are the immoral, / except those who repent thereafter and make amends, for God is indeed Forgiving, Merciful.* (Al-Nur, 24:1–5)

However, despite this, it is obvious that an untold amount of extra-marital sex exists in the world, even in Islamic societies, and that it existed even at the time of the Messenger of God ﷺ. So what is the motivation in illicit sex that makes it so powerful and irresistible that those who commit it are willing to disregard God's commandments, and risk social opprobrium and even legal punishment? God says: *And she certainly desired him, and he would have desired her [too], had it not been that he saw the proof of his Lord. So it was that We might ward off from him evil and lewdness. Truly he was of Our devoted servants* (*Yusuf*, 12:24)

And after 'desiring' Joseph, Potiphar's wife did the following: *And they raced to the door, and she tore his shirt from behind, whereupon they encountered her master at the door. She said, 'What is to be the requital of him who intends evil against your folk, but that he should be imprisoned, or [suffer] a painful chastisement?'* (*Yusuf*, 12:25)

And even after failing and being exposed, she still persisted in her adulterous desires and deliberately and brazenly kept on planning for the same thing, even in front of the women of the city: *She said, 'This is he on whose account you blamed me. Indeed I did attempt to seduce him, but he withheld himself. Yet if he does not do what I bid him, he verily shall be imprisoned, and verily shall be of those brought low'.* (*Yusuf*, 12:32)

All of this makes us ask: aside from this 'desire' (and thus this physical urge), what made Potiphar's wife act this way? There must have been something else as well, because physical urges sometimes fade with the passing of time and in the presence of fear, yet this woman continued to be attached to Joseph ﷺ even after he was imprisoned for several years (according to *Yusuf* 12:42): '*That is so that he may know I did not betray him in his absence, and that truly God does not guide [to success] the guile of the treacherous.*' (*Yusuf*, 12:52)

This means that it was not only 'desire' and physical lust that drove Potiphar's wife, but also another motive, namely an 'inclination towards beauty', and thus a love, according to our definition of love. And God says: *And God desires to turn [forgivingly] towards you, but those who follow their passions, desire that you incline with a terrible inclination.* (*Al-Nisa'*, 4:27)

Tafsir al-Jalalayn says, about this Qur'anic verse: ' *"And God desires to turn [forgivingly] towards you"*: He repeats this to give it emphasis; *"but those who follow their passions"*: namely the Jews and Christians, or the Magians, or the adulterers; *"desire that you incline with a terrible inclination"*: i.e. that you should deviate from the truth by committing what has been forbidden for you, thus becoming like them.'[158]

God thus makes it clear here that illicit sex involves '*passions*' and '*a terrible inclination*'; or in other words, there is—or can be—love in fornication, in addition to the passion and the physical desire. This is also clear from the use of the word 'love' in God's words: *Beautified for humankind is love of lusts—of women, children, stored-up heaps of gold and silver, horses of mark, cattle, and tillage. That is the comfort of the life of this world; but God—with Him is the most excellent abode.* (*Aal 'Imran*, 3:14)

This is where the great and '*terrible*' danger inherent in fornication comes from: illicit sex is not only an evil 'indecency', but it is also a forbidden form of love which drags the person who indulges in it with the full force of love into a circle of emotions and deeds which take him or her further and further away from God's guidance and His straight path. God warns people clearly of this danger when He says: *And do not come [anywhere] near fornication. It is indeed an indecency and an evil way.* (*Al-Isra'*, 17:32)

With the words '*an evil way*', God emphasizes the power and danger of fornication on the soul of the person who commits it and on his or her prospects in the Hereafter. Thus extra-marital love could sometimes become so ardent and intense that it almost reaches the level of worship, although it can never actually reach the level of true worship of God, for God says:

> *Yet there be people who take to themselves rivals besides God, loving them as God is loved; but those who believe love God more ardently. If those who*

did evil could but see, as they shall when they behold the chastisement, that power altogether belongs to God, and that God is terrible in chastisement! (Al-Baqarah, 2:165)

We see here that it is possible that a person can love something which God does not love, and love this thing very deeply, even if it is bad for him or her and their beloved[159] (and this is exactly the state of a person who engages in extra-marital sex). God says: .... *Yet it may happen that you hate a thing which is good for you; and it may happen that you love a thing which is bad for you; God knows, and you know not.* (Al-Baqarah, 2:216)

'*God knows, and you know not*'; so the fornicator should beware of their love, and the believer should stay well clear of a fancy which might lead to illicit sex or to something which does not please God. God says:

> *Do not marry idolatresses until they believe; a believing slavegirl is better than an idolatress, though you may admire her. And do not marry idolaters, until they believe. A believing slave is better than an idolater, though you may admire him. Those call to the Fire; and God calls to Paradise and pardon by His leave; and He makes clear His signs to the people so that they might remember.* (Al-Baqarah, 2:221)

Finally, those who engage in extra-marital sex had best cling to what God loves for them, because God's love will not lead them away from what is truly good for them, but their own love might. Indeed, God, in His Mercy, says about spouses: ...*Consort with them in kindness; for if you hate them, it may happen that you hate a thing wherein God has set much good.* (Al-Nisa', 4:19)

CHAPTER TWENTY

LOVE AND THE EYES

A believer may come to know the reality of another person either through his or her face, or through his or her words. God says: *And if We wish, We could show them to you, then you would recognise them by their mark. And you will certainly recognise them by [their] tone of speech, and God knows your deeds.* (*Muhammad*, 47:30)

And the Messenger of God ﷺ said: 'Beware the insight of the believer, for he [or she] sees by the light of God.'[160]

This is generally the case with the believers, but there is something special—a great mystery—about a person's eyes which may: (1) express love; or (2) engender love in the beholder himself or herself[161], or (3) engender love in the one who looks into their eyes. In other words, love may: (1) be seen by others in a person's eyes; (2) 'enter' a person through his or her eyes into his or her soul and heart as they look at someone else, or (3) cause another person to love them as a result of a meeting of the eyes—of 'eye-contact'. God alludes to all of this with His words: *He knows the treachery of the eyes and what the breasts hide.* (*Ghafir*, 40:19)

Thus the eyes betray love in the soul and heart, and make it plain to see; and the eyes can also cause love to grow, when there is prolonged eye-contact. This allows us to understand the two *Hadiths*: Ibn Mas'ud and Hudhayfah both reported that the Messenger of God ﷺ said: 'The glance of the eye is a poison dart fired by Iblis [the Devil]; whosoever leaves it through fear of Me, I shall replace it for him with a faith whose sweetness he shall experience in his heart.'[162]

And 'Ali bin Abi Talib ؓ reported that the Messenger of God ﷺ said: 'O 'Ali, do not follow one glance with another, for you are permitted the first one but not the second.'[163]

Conversely, when Mughirah ibn Shu'bah wanted to ask for a woman's hand in marriage, the Messenger of God ﷺ said to him: 'Look upon her, for it is more likely that you will bond with each other.'[164]

This explains the importance of lowering one's gaze[165], which God commands the believers to do, with His words:

> *Tell believing men to lower their gaze and to guard their private parts. That is purer for them. Truly God is Aware of what they do. / And tell believing women to lower their gaze and to guard their private parts, and not to display*

their adornment except for what is apparent, and let them draw their veils over their bosoms and not reveal their adornment, except to their husbands or their fathers, or their husbands' fathers, or their sons, or their husbands' sons, or their brothers, or their brothers' sons, or their sisters' sons, or their women, or what their right hands own, or such men who are dependant, not possessing any sexual desire, or children who are not yet aware of women's private parts. And do not let them thump with their feet to make known their hidden ornaments. And rally to God in repentance, O believers, so that you might be successful. (Al-Nur, 24:30–31)

Similarly, God warns His Messenger ﷺ as follows:

And do not extend your glance toward what We have given to some pairs among them to enjoy, [as] the flower of the life of this world that We may try them thereby. And your Lord's provision is better and more enduring (Ta Ha, 20:131) ❖ *Do not extend your glance toward that which We have given different groups of them to enjoy, and do not grieve for them, and lower your wing for the believers.* (Al-Hijr, 15:88)

In summary: the eyes play a special role in love that makes them like 'windows' to the soul and heart, through which love can enter and exit. Moreover, love appears in the eyes, just as a person's love for God appears on his or her entire person, as we saw earlier (in Chapter 15: The Effects of God's Love on Human Beings), and God knows best.

PART FOUR: LOVE

CHAPTER TWENTY-ONE

THE DIFFERENT KINDS OF LOVE

God mentions many different kinds of love (*hubb*)[166] in the Holy Qur'an[167] (some of which are also 'degrees' of love). They are defined as 'kinds of love' according to their lexical semantic and etymological meanings as given in the most authoritative Classical Arabic dictionaries and lexicons (such as: Muhibb al-Din Zabidi's *Taj al-a'rus min jawahir al-qamus*; Jamal al-Din Ibn Manzhur's *Lisan 'Arab*, and Raghib al-Isfahani's *Al-Mufradat fi gharib al-Qur'an*). In what follows in this chapter we enumerate thirty-eight different kinds of love mentioned in the Holy Qur'an, giving an English translation of their Arabic dictionary and lexical definitions in so far as this is possible.

The different kinds of love—defined linguistically and etymologically as such—mentioned in the Holy Qur'an, include:

1. LOVE (*AL-HUBB*):
Love (*hubb*) is obviously a kind of love, as we discussed previously in Chapter 3: The Definition of Love. As noted in an endnote earlier '*hubb*' also means 'to like'.

2. LOVE (*MAHABBAH*):
God says: *…And I cast upon you a love (mahabbah) from Me and that you might be reared under My eyes.* (*Ta Ha*, 20:39) Raghib al-Isfahani explains: 'Love (*mahabbah*) means the desire for what you know or deem to be good, and it has three aspects: Love for pleasure, such as a man's love for a woman, as in: '*And they give food, despite [their] love of it to the needy, and the orphan, and the prisoner*' (*Al-Insan*, 76:8); love for benefit, such as one's love for something that benefits one, as in: '*And, another which you love: help from God and a victory near at hand. And give good tidings to the believers*' (*Al-Saff*, 61:13); and love for virtue, such as the love knowledgeable people have for one another because of knowledge itself. Perhaps love ('*mahabbah*') may be thought to mean 'desire' in such statements of God as: '*…in it are men who love to purify themselves…*' (*Al-Tawbah*, 9:108), but this is not the case, because love is more than just desire, as was just stated. Every love is desire, but not every desire is love.'[168] Ibn

Manzhur explains: '*Mahabbah* is another word for *hubb* (love)'.[169] Zabidi[170] explains: '*Hubb* means affection (*widad*) and *mahabbah*.'[171]

3. PREFERENCE (AL-ISTIHBAB):

God says: *That is because they have preferred (istahabu) the life of this world to the Hereafter, and because God does not guide the disbelieving folk.* (Al-Nahl, 16:107) Raghib explains: 'God says: *O you who believe, do not take your fathers and brothers for your friends, if they prefer disbelief over belief; whoever of you takes them for friends, such are the evildoers* (Al-Tawbah, 9:23); and *the true meaning of 'preference' is to pursue something to gain its love*'.[172] Ibn Manzhur explains: '*To prefer* is like to love, and preference is like approval.'[173] Zabidi[174] explains: '*To prefer* is like to love, and preference is like approval.'[175]

4. MERCY (AL-RAHMAH):

We have discussed *mercy* previously in Chapter 4: God and Love.

God says:

> *And of His signs is that He created for you from yourselves mates that you might find peace by their side, and He ordained between you affection and mercy (rahmah). Surely in that there are signs for a people who reflect.* (Al-Rum, 30:21) ❊ *And ask forgiveness of your Lord, then repent to Him. Truly my Lord is Merciful (Rahim), Loving.* (Hud, 11:90)

Raghib explains: '*Mercy (rahmah) is tenderness (riqqa) which engenders kindness towards its object: the word can be used to mean tenderness on its own, or kindness without tenderness, as in: 'May God have mercy upon him'. When the word is ascribed to the Creator, it means nothing other than kindness without tenderness. In this regard, it is related that mercy from God means blessing and generous bounty, whereas from human beings it means tenderness and compassion*'.[176] Ibn Manzhur explains: '*Mercy* means tenderness and compassion ... human mercy, as understood by the Arabs, means *the tenderness and compassion of the heart*, whilst God's mercy is His compassion, kindness and provision'.[177] Zabidi explains: '*Mercy* is tenderness ... Harali said: "Mercy means to give someone something that he needs both outwardly and inwardly; the least mercy is to prevent harm and ward off hurt, and the highest mercy is to favour with [spiritual] unveiling"'.[178]

5. PITY (AL-RA'FAH):

God says:

> *Then We sent to follow in their footsteps Our messengers, and We sent to follow, Jesus son of Mary, and We gave him the Gospel, and We placed in the hearts of those who followed him pity (ra'fah) and mercy. But [as for] monasticism, they invented it—We had not prescribed it for them—only seeking God's*

beatitude. Yet they did not observe it with due observance. So We gave those of them who believed their reward; but many of them are immoral. (Al-Hadid, 57:27) ❂ As for the adulteress and the adulterer, strike each of them a hundred lashes. And do not let any pity (ra'fah) for them overcome you in God's religion, if you believe in God and the Last Day. And let their punishment be witnessed by a group of the believers. (Al-Nur, 24:2) ❂ Verily there has come to you a messenger from among yourselves for whom it is grievous that you should suffer; who is full of concern for you, to the believers full of pity (raouf), merciful. (Al-Tawbah, 9:128)

Raghib explains: 'Pity is mercy ... God says: ...And do not let any pity (ra'fah) for them overcome you in God's religion....'[179] Ibn Manzhur explains: 'Pity is mercy; and it is said that it means especially strong mercy ... One of God's Qualities is *Al-Raouf*, 'Full of Pity' or 'Gentle'; this means He has mercy and compassion for His servants, and is kind to them. *Pity is more specific than mercy, and more tender.*'[180] Zabidi[181] explains: '*Pity is especially strong mercy, or especially tender mercy*, as *al-Sihah* has it. *Al-Mujmal* defines it as a mercy which is absolute and especially strong, so that it cannot occur where there is hatred; for one might show mercy to one he hates if there is a beneficial reason for doing so. Fakhr al-Din al-Razi says: '*Pity is an intense form of mercy* ... It may be added that *Al-Raouf, Full of Pity*, is one of the Most Beautiful Names, meaning: 'He who is full of mercy and compassion for His servants'; and *tara'afa* means the pity a father has for his son.'[182]

6. LOVE (AL-WUDD):

God says: *Truly those who believe and perform righteous deeds—for them the Compassionate One shall appoint love (wudd).* (*Maryam*, 19:96) Raghib explains: '*Wudd* means *to love something* and hope for it, and it is used for both meanings, since hope comprises love in that it means to desire to obtain what you love.'[183] Ibn Manzhur explains: '*Wudd* comes from the root *mawaddah* (*affection*), and Ibn Sayyidih said that it means love for all good things.'[184] Zabidi explains: 'The words *wudd* and *widad* mean love and friendship, and are then used metaphorically to mean hope. Ibn Sayyidih said that *wudd* means love for all good things.'[185]

7. AFFECTION (AL-MAWADDAH):

God says:

> And of His signs is that He created for you from yourselves mates that you might find peace by their side, and He ordained between you affection (mawaddah) and mercy. Surely in that there are signs for a people who reflect. (Al-Rum, 30:21) ❂ ...Say: 'I do not ask of you any reward for it, except affection (mawaddah) for kinsfolk... (Al-Shura, 42:23)

Raghib explains: 'Concerning the kind of *affection* which implies pure love

(...*Say: 'I do not ask of you any reward for it, except the affection* (mawaddah) *for [my] kinsfolk...*), it is said that God's affection for His servants means the care He shows them'.[186] Ibn Manzhur explains: '*Wudd* comes from the root *mawaddah* ... and it is said it is named after *mawaddah*, which means 'love''. Zabidi explains: 'It is said that it is named after *mawaddah*, which means 'love'.

8. LOVE (AL-WIDAD):
God says:

> You will not find a people who believe in God and the Last Day loving (yu-waddun) those who oppose God and His Messenger, even though they were their fathers or their sons or their brothers or their clan. [For] those He has inscribed faith upon their hearts and reinforced them with a spirit from Him, and He will admit them into gardens underneath which rivers flow, wherein they will abide, God being pleased with them, and they being pleased with Him. Those [they] are God's confederates. Assuredly it is God's confederates who are the successful. (Al-Mujadilah, 58:22)

Raghib explains: '*Wudd* means to love something ... And God's words '*You will not find a people who believe in God and the Last Day loving those who oppose God and His Messenger...*' mean that it is forbidden to take the disbelievers as loving allies and to support them [militarily]'.[187] Ibn Manzhur explains: 'Ibn Anbari said that God's Name *Al-Wadud* ('The Loving') means He who loves His servants; it is derived from the verb *wadda*, which means 'to love', and whose gerund is *widad*'.[188] Zabidi explains: '*Widadah*, as given by Ibn Sayyid in *al-Muthallath* (others spell it *wudadah*) is based on the three-letter root *w-d-d*, as our own teacher affirmed. Ibn Qatta' (in *Al-Af'al*) says that the verb *wadda* with the gerund *wudd* means 'to love', whilst the gerund *widadah* means 'to hope'; this is how the Arabs use the word. The verb *waadda*, gerund *widad/widadah/wadadah*, describes a reciprocal love between two people. Thus it seems that the words *widad*, *wadadah* and *widadah* are all gerunds of the verb *waadah*, in the morphological form *mafa'alah* [form III]'.[189]

9. WILL OR DESIRE[190] (AL-IRADAH):
God says:

> Divorced women shall wait by themselves for three periods. And it is not lawful for them to hide what God has created in their wombs if they believe in God and the Last Day. Their mates have a better right to restore them in such time if they will (yuridu) to make things right; women shall have rights similar to those due from them, with justice; but their men have a degree above them; God is Mighty, Wise. (Al-Baqarah, 2:228)

Raghib explains: 'Will is essentially a force composed of desire, need and hope; it is used to describe the soul's desire for something to happen or not to happen. To 'seduce' (*murawadah*) means to attempt to influence someone else's will to make them want what they do not want ... God says: '...*It was she who attempted to seduce me...*' (*Yusuf*, 12:26), and '...*The Chief of the Court's wife has been seducing her boy...*' (*Yusuf*, 12:30)'.[191] Ibn Manzhur explains: 'To *will something means to love it* and be concerned with it'.[192] Zabidi[193] explains: 'Tha'lab said that a person's will might involve love, or it might not'.[194]

10. TO BE SMITTEN (AL-SHAGHAF):

God says: *And some of the women in the city said, 'The Chief of the Court's wife has been seducing her boy. Indeed he has smitten her heart (shaghafaha) with love. Lo! we see her to be plainly astray.'* (*Yusuf*, 12:30) Raghib explains: 'He has smitten (*shaghafa*) her heart with love' means that he has touched the *shaghghaf* of her heart, meaning its core'.[195] Ibn Manzhur explains: 'The *shaghghaf* is the inner skin, like the inner fold of a curtain ... To make someone 'smitten with love' means to reach the inside of his heart. Ibn ʿAbbas said that it means for love to penetrate the heart'.[196] Zabidi explains: 'The *Sihah* defines 'smitten with love' (*shaghafa*) as love's penetrating the heart; this is also the opinion of Ibn Sikkit. Farra' says that it means to break the seal of the heart. Ibn ʿAbbas said that it means for love to penetrate the heart. Layth said it means for love to touch the inside of the heart'.[197]

11. IMPULSE (AL-HAWA):

God says:

> And We made a covenant with the Children of Israel, and We sent messengers to them. Every time a messenger came to them with what their souls did not desire (tahwa); some they denied, and some they slay. (Al-Ma'idah, 5:70) ❋ Have you seen him who has taken as his god his own impulse (hawahu)? Will you be a guardian over him? (Al-Furqan, 25:43) ❋ These are nothing but names which you have named, you and your fathers. God has not revealed any warrant for them. They follow nothing but conjecture and that which [ignoble] souls desire (tahwa), even though guidance has already come to them from their Lord. (Al-Najm 53:23) ❋ Nay, but those who do evil follow their own impulses (ahwahum) without any knowledge. So who will guide he whom God has led astray? And they have no helpers. (Al-Rum, 30:29)

Raghib explains: 'Impulse means the soul's inclination to lust; it is said that it is called *hawa* because it causes one to fall (*yahwa*) into every calamity in this life, and into the Pit (*al-hawiyah*) in the next'.[198] Ibn Manzhur explains: 'Ibn Sayyidih said that *impulse means devotion*, and it can be for both good and evil things'.[199] Zabidi explains: 'Impulse means the *soul's inclination to lust*. Layth said it means *the conscience's desire*. Azhari said that it means *to love something and for this love to overwhelm the heart*. An example of it is the Almighty's words: '...*and forbade the soul from [pursuing] impulse...*' (*Al-Naziʿat*, 79:40), that is, from pursuing its lusts and all the sins that tempt it. Ibn Sayyidih says that it can be for both good and evil things. Others say that when one speaks of 'impulse' generally, it means something bad unless it is qualified, such as by saying 'good impulse' or 'right impulse'.[200]

12. INFATUATION (*AL-ISTIHWA*'):
God says:

> Say: 'Shall we call upon, instead of God, that which neither profits us, nor hurts us; and so be turned back after God has guided us?—Like one whom the devils have infatuated (istahwathu) in the earth, bewildered; he has companions, who call him to guidance: "Come to us!" Say: 'Truly, God's guidance is [the true] guidance and we have been commanded to submit to the Lord of the Worlds. (*Al-Anʿam*, 6:71)

Raghib explains: '*One whom the devils have infatuated*' means one whom they have incited to follow his impulse.'[201] Ibn Manzhur explains: 'To be infatuated by devils means *for one's impulse and mind to be overcome*; the Mighty Revelation says: '*Like one whom the devils have infatuated*'. It is said that to be infatuated means to be enthralled and bewildered. It is also said that it means for the devils to make one's impulse seem goodly to one and bewilder him or her thereby. Someone in the thrall of the jinn is said to be 'infatuated by devils'. Qatibi said that 'to be infatuated by devils' means to be caused to fall and snatched away by them; he based this on the root word *hawa/yahwa*, 'to fall'. Zajjaj was of the opinion that it is derived from the root *hawa/yahwa*, 'to desire'; that is, the devils make one's impulse seem goodly to him.'[202] Zabidi explains: 'The Almighty's words '*...Like one whom the devils have infatuated in the earth, bewildered...*' mean 'one whose impulse and mind have been overcome'. Qatibi said it means to be caused to fall and snatched away; he based this on the root word *hawà/yahwa*, 'to fall'. Or it may mean to be enthralled and bewildered, or for one's impulse to be made to seem goodly to one; this is the opinion of Zajjaj, who deemed it to be derived from the root *hawa/yahwa*, 'to desire'.'[203]

13. TO STRAY (*AL-GHAWA*):
God says: *As for the poets, [only] the stray (ghawun) follow them.* (*Al-Shuʿara*', 26:224) Raghib explains: 'It is said that 'to stray' (*ghawa*) means to spoil one's life, from the verb *ghawiya*, which describes how a young camel gets indigestion from drinking milk.'[204] Ibn Manzhur explains: 'Regarding the Almighty's words '*As for the poets, [only] the stray follow them*', it is said that 'the stray' means the devils, and it is also said it means those human beings who are astray. Zajjaj said it means that when the poet composes satire in an unlawful manner, people desire this and love him for it, thereby going astray'.[205] Zabidi[206] explains:

'Regarding the Almighty's words '*As for the poets, [only] the stray follow them*', it is said in the exegesis literature that this means the devils, or those human beings who fall into error, or *those who love the poet* when he satirises people in an unlawful manner (as Zajjaj noted), *or who love him for praising them* for qualities they do not posses; and they follow him for this reason'.[207]

14. DESIRE (AL-HAMM):

God says: *And she certainly desired (hammat) him, and he would have desired (hamma) her [too], had it not been that he saw the proof of his Lord. So it was that We might ward off from him evil and lewdness. Truly he was of Our devoted servants.* (*Yusuf*, 12:24) Raghib explains: 'Desire is what the soul is concerned with.'[208] Ibn Manzhur explains: 'Tha'lab was asked about the Almighty's words '*And she certainly desired him, and he would have desired her [too], had it not been that he saw the proof of his Lord...*', and answered: 'Zulaykhah desired to commit sin and insisted on it, whilst Yusuf ﷺ desired sin but did not commit it, nor insist upon it; thus there was a difference between the two desires'.... Abu 'Ubaydah said: 'There is inversion here; it is as though what He means is that she desired him, and were it not that he saw the proof of his Lord, he would have desired her.'[209] Zabidi explains: 'Desire means what your soul is concerned with, that is, what it intends, wills, and resolves on. Tha'lab was asked about the Almighty's words '*And she certainly desired him, and he would have desired her [too], had it not been that he saw the proof of his Lord...*', and answered: 'Zulaykhah desired to commit sin and insisted on it, whilst Yusuf ﷺ desired sin but did not commit it, nor insist upon it; thus there was a difference between the two desires.' Abu Hatim reported that Abu 'Ubaydah said: 'There is inversion here; it is as though what He means is that she desired him, and were it not that he saw the proof of his Lord, he would have desired her.'[210]

15. LONGING (AL-RAGHAB):

God says:

> *They will ask you for a pronouncement concerning women. Say: 'God pronounces to you concerning them, and what is recited to you in the Book, concerning the orphan women to whom you do not give what is prescribed for them, for you long to (targhabun) marry them, and the oppressed children, and that you deal justly with orphans. Whatever good you do, God is ever Knower of it'.* (*Al-Nisa'*, 4:127) ❉ *So We responded to him, and gave him John, and We restored [fertility to] his wife for him. Truly they would hasten to good works, and supplicate Us out of longing (raghaban) and in awe, and they were submissive before Us.* (*Al-Anbiya'*, 21:90) ❉ *If only they had been content with what God and His Messenger have given them, and had said, 'Sufficient for us is God; God will give us from His favour, and His Messenger*

[will also give us]; for God we long (raghibun)'. (*Al-Tawbah*, 9:59) ❋ *And long your for Lord (fa'rghab).* (*Al-Sharh*, 94:8)

Raghib explains: 'Longing means: a *deep will*; the Almighty says: '*...and supplicate Us out of longing and in awe...*'. To 'long for' means: '*to be avid for*', God says: '*...for God we long*'.'²¹¹ Ibn Manzhur explains: 'To long for something means *to be avid for it and to desire it*; 'longing' means a supplication and a desire; and the verbs *raghghaba* and *arghaba* mean 'to give someone what he or she desires'.'²¹² Zabidi explains: 'To long for something means ... to will it, or ... to request it.'²¹³

16. TO DRAW NEAR (*AL-TAQARUB, AL-MUQARABAH* OR *AL-QURB*):
God says:

And We called him from the right side of the Mount and We brought him near (qarrabnahu) in communion. (*Maryam*, 19:52) ❋ *The Messiah would never disdain to be a servant of God, neither would the angels who are near [to God] (muqarrabun). Whoever disdains to worship Him, and waxes proud, He will assuredly muster them to Him, all of them.* (*Al-Nisa'*, 4:172) ❋ *You will truly find the most hostile of people to those who believe to be the Jews and the idolaters; and you will truly find the nearest (aqrab) of them in love to those who believe to be those who say 'Verily, we are Christians'; that because some of them are priests and monks, and because they are not disdainful.* (*Al-Ma'idah*, 5:82) ❋ *And when My servants question you concerning Me, I am near (qarib); I answer the call of the caller when he calls to Me; so let them respond to Me, and let them believe in Me that they might go aright.* (*Al-Baqarah*, 2:186)

Raghib explains: 'Nearness and farness are opposites, ... and this may be applied to space, time, relation, rank and custody ... In the case of rank, there are, for example: *the angels who are near (al-muqarrabun)*; and God said of Jesus ﷺ: '*...honoured shall he be in this world, and the Hereafter, and of those brought near*' (*Aal 'Imran*, 3:45)'.²¹⁴ Ibn Manzhur explains: 'The *Hadith* says: 'Whosoever draws nearer to Me by a hand's span, I draw nearer to him by an arm's length.' The meaning of a person's nearness to God is to draw near to Him with remembrance and good deeds, not to be near in a spatial sense, since this is the attribute of physical bodies, and God is transcendently above such a thing. And the meaning of God's nearness to people is the nearness of His blessings, kindnesses, goodness and favours to them, and the showering of His gifts upon them'.²¹⁵ Zabidi explains: 'To draw near (*taqarrub*) means to approach something, and to have contact with someone by a tie of kinship or right. The word *iqrab* also means 'to draw near'. The verb *qaraba* can mean 'to have sexual relations' (literally 'to cover')'.

17. ANGUISH (AL-GHARAM):

God says: *And who say, 'Our Lord, avert from us from the chastisement of Hell. Truly its chastisement is abiding anguish (gharama)'. (Al-Furqan, 25:65)* ❊ *We have indeed suffered anguish (la-mughramun)! (Al-Waqi'ah, 56:66)* Raghib explains: 'The Almighty says: '... *Truly its chastisement is abiding anguish*'[216], derived from the word *mughram*, which means a person who is obsessed with women and follows them around like a zealous creditor (*gharim*)'.[217] Ibn Manzhur explains: '*Anguish* (*gharam*) means abiding torment and constant suffering, *and overwhelming love and devotion*'.[218] Zabidi explains: '*Anguish* means passion, and *aghrama* means 'to love passionately' ... The word *mughram* means a prisoner of love, or someone deep in debt; and the kind of love meant by this is love of women, as Abu 'Ubaydah stated'.[219]

18. TO WANDER DISTRACTED (AL-HUYAM):

God says: *Have you not noticed that in every valley they wander distracted (yahimun)? (Al-Shu'ara', 26:225)* Raghib explains: 'The words *hayman* and *ha'im* mean someone who is extremely thirsty, and the verb *hama* means to wander aimlessly about. *Huyam* is also the name of an illness camels contract from thirst. *It is used metaphorically to mean someone who feels intense devotion, and to wander in the land feeling intense yearning and thirst*'.[220] Ibn Manzhur explains: '*Huyam* means a kind of madness; the *Tahdhib* says that it means the madness of love ... The *ha'im* ... is the one who wanders around distracted by his love'.[221] Zabidi explains: '*Huyam* is like the madness of love; it is a metaphor. To wander distracted means to be madly in love.'[222]

19. CLOSE FRIENDSHIP (AL-KHULLAH):

God says:

> *And who is fairer in religion than he who submits his purpose to God and is virtuous, and who follows the creed of Abraham as a hanif? And God took Abraham for a close friend (khalil). (Al-Nisa', 4:125)* ❊ *Close friends (al-akhilla) will, on that day, be foes of one another, except for the God-fearing. (Al-Zukhruf, 43:67)* ❊ *O you who believe, expend of what We have provided you with before there comes a day in which there shall be neither commerce, nor close friendship (khulla), nor intercession. And the disbelievers—they are the evildoers. (Al-Baqarah, 2:254)*

Raghib explains: '*Close friendship* (*khullah*) means love, either because it penetrates and intermingles (*tatakhallal*) the soul, or because it pierces (*tukhill*) the heart like an arrow, or because of the dire need (*khallah*) for it. The verb is *khalala*, and the noun ('close friend') is *khalil* ... the close friend is the one whose soul is penetrated and saturated by love, as the poet said:

> *You have penetrated (takhallal) the cord of my spirit;*

And it was for this that the close friend (khalil) was named so'.[223]

Ibn Manzhur explains: '*Khill* means love, as well as 'friend' ... *Khullah* means friendship and love which penetrates (*takhallal*) the heart and so reaches the inside (*khilal*) of it. The *khalil* is the true friend; the word may have the meaning of either an active or a passive participle. [God called Abraham His friend] because his heart was empty of all but love for God, and had no room for any of the things which may be loved in this life or the next. This is a noble state which cannot be acquired or attained by effort, for human nature does not generally allow this; but God gives it to whom He chooses of His servants, such as the Leader of the Prophets—may God's blessings and peace be upon them all.'[224] Zabidi explains: '*Khullah* also means the special friendship in which there are no defects (*khalal*). It can be used to describe both *chaste love and unchaste love* ... The forms *khull* and *khill* mean 'special friend', and the form *khull* always suggests an element of love, as in the phrase 'he was my love and my true friend' ... God says: '...*And God took Abraham for a close friend*'. Or, it is said that *khalil* means 'truthful', as Ibn al-ʿArabi is reported to have said. Zajjaj said it means the lover whose love is free of defects; he explained the aforementioned verse as meaning that God loved him with a perfect, faultless love.'[225]

20. FRIENDSHIP (AL-SADAQAH):

We have discussed this previously in Chapter 17: Love of Others.
God says:

> *There is no blame upon the blind, nor any blame upon the lame, nor any blame upon the sick, nor upon yourselves if you eat from your own houses, or your fathers' houses, or your mothers' houses, or your brothers' houses, or your sisters' houses, or the houses of your paternal uncles or the houses of your paternal aunts, or the houses of your maternal uncles or the houses of your maternal aunts, or [from] that whereof you hold the keys, or [from] those of your [faithful] friends (sadiqikum). You would not be at fault whether you eat together, or separately. But when you enter houses, bid peace to yourselves with a salutation from God, blessed and good. So God clarifies the signs for you that perhaps you might comprehend. (Al-Nur, 24:61)* ❋ *Nor any sympathetic friend (sadiq hamim). (Al-Shuʿara, 26:101)*

Raghib explains: 'Friendship means true feelings of love; and only human beings experience this.'[226] Ibn Manzhur explains: '*Sadaqah* is the root of the word *sadiq* ('friend'), derived from the verb *sadaqa* meaning 'to be true', i.e. true in love and sincere counsel. The friend is the one who is true to you.'[227] Zabidi explains: 'Your friend is *the one who loves you and is true to you.*'[228]

21. COMPANIONSHIP (AL-SUHBAH):

We have discussed this previously in Chapter 17: Love of Others.

God says:

If you do not help him, [know that] God has already helped him, when the disbelievers drove him forth—the second of two; when the two were in the cave—when he said to his companion (sahibihi), 'Do not despair; verily God is with us'. Then God sent down His Sakinah upon him and supported him with legions you did not see; and He made the word of those who disbelieved the nethermost, and the Word of God was the uppermost. And God is Mighty, Wise. (Al-Tawbah, 9:40)

Raghib explains: 'The companion is that which is constantly with you, whether a person, animal, place or time; this means you are either with it in person, which is the essential meaning, or with it by care and concern ... Generally, it is only used for one you spend a great deal of time with'.[229] Ibn Manzhur explains: 'The word [for 'companion'] is *sahib*, plural *ashab*, from the verb *sahiba/yashabu*, gerund *suhbah*. They say that women are 'the companions of Joseph'; the feminine plural form here is *sawahib* or *sawahibat*, which is a double plural, as Farisi reported Abu Hasan to have said. The word *sihabah* is the gerund of the verb *sahabak Allah*, 'God be with you', or *ahsana sihabatak*, 'may He keep your company well'. When you bid someone farewell, you say *mu'anan musahaban*, 'May you be aided and accompanied [by God]'. The word *mishab* means 'compliant', as in 'he is compliant to us, giving us all that we like'.'[230] Zabidi[231] explains: 'The verb *sahab* means ... 'to accompany' ... *Suhbah* is the gerund of the verb *sahiba/yashabu*. They say that women are 'the companions of Joseph'; the feminine plural form here is *sawahib* or *sawahibat*, which is a double plural, as Farisi reported Abu Hasan to have said. The word *sihabah* is the gerund of the verb *sahabak Allah*, 'God be with you', or *ahsana sihabatak*, 'may He keep your company well'; this is a metaphor. *Istashaba* means 'to ask someone for company' and to accompany them; this word is used for anything which accompanies one.'[232]

22. TO PREFER ANOTHER TO ONESELF (AL-ITHAR):
God says:

And those who had settled in the hometown, and [had abided] in faith before them, love those who have emigrated to them, and do not find in their breasts any need of that which those [others] have been given, but prefer (yu'thirun)[others] to themselves, though they be in poverty. And whoever is saved from the avarice of his own soul, those—they are the successful. (Al-Hashr, 59:9) ❋ *They said, 'By God, truly God has preferred (atharaka) you over us, and indeed we have been erring'.* (Yusuf, 12:91) ❋ *Nay, but you prefer (tuthirun) the life of this world.* (Al-A'la, 87:16)

Raghib explains: '*Ma'athir* is a general terms for human goodness; *athar* is used metaphorically to mean 'goodness', and *ithar* to mean 'to be good to another', or to prefer another to oneself ... *Ista'thara* means to reserve something for oneself and no one else; when they say 'God has reserved so-and-so for Himself' ... it means that He has chosen and elected him or her, out of all mankind, for a special honour.'[233] Ibn Manzhur explains: 'Asma'i says that *ithar* means to prefer someone. Someone may be preferred over another, or he or she may be 'one of the preferred', meaning one of the elite.'[234] Zabidi[235] explains: 'To be 'preferred' means to be especially chosen (*khulasa* or *khulsan*). Someone is said to be preferred by another, or simply 'preferred' if he or she is one of the elite. A preferred person is one who is distinguished and honoured. The Al-Asas says that if you call someone your *athir*, this means you prefer him or her, and always put him first.'[236]

23. GOING ASTRAY (*AL-DALAL*):

God says: *And some of the women in the city said, 'The Chief of the Court's wife has been seducing her boy. Indeed he has smitten her heart with love. Lo! we see her to be plainly astray (fi dalalin mubin).'* (*Yusuf*, 12:30) ⁕ *They said: 'By God, you are certainly astray (dalalika) as of old'.* (*Yusuf*, 12:95) Raghib explains: 'When God tells us that the sons of Jacob ﷺ said of him: *'you are certainly astray as of old'*, they meant: 'Our father is clearly astray', referring to his love and longing for Joseph. The same is the case with: *'Indeed he has smitten her heart with love. Lo! we see her to be plainly astray'.*'[237] Ibn Manzhur explains: 'The word *dallah* has several meanings. It can mean 'lost treasure', as in 'The wise word is the believer's lost treasure', or 'every wise person's lost treasure'; that is, he or she continues to look for it as a man looks for something he has lost.'[238] Zabidi[239] explains: 'Raghib said that it means to swerve from the straight path, and that its opposite is 'to be guided'. God says: *'...So whoever is guided, is guided only for the sake of his own soul, and whoever strays, strays only against it...'* (*Yunus*, 10:108). The word *dalal* can be used to describe any straying from the truth, whether deliberate or accidental, and whether slight or great. For the straight path chosen for us is difficult indeed to follow, and the Prophet ﷺ said: 'Be upright, though you will not [always] be able to'. Therefore the word can be used to describe all those who make mistakes of any kind, and this is why it has been ascribed to the prophets and to the disbelievers, even though there is a huge difference between these two kinds of straying. Thus He said of the Prophet ﷺ: *'And did He not find you astray, and guide you?'* (*Al-Duha*, 93:7), meaning 'guided to the prophethood for which you were destined', and He said of Jacob ﷺ: *'...you are certainly astray as of old'*, and his sons said of him: *'...Lo! our father is plainly astray'* (*Yusuf*, 12:8), alluding to his love and longing for Joseph.'[240]

24. CONTENTMENT (AL-RIDA):
God says:

> God says, 'This is the day those who were truthful shall profit by their truthfulness. Theirs will be Gardens underneath which rivers flow, wherein they shall abide forever. God is content (radiya) with them, and they are content with Him—that is the great triumph'. (Al-Ma'idah, 5:119) ❋ We have indeed seen you turning your face about in the heaven; now We will surely turn you to a direction that shall content (tardahu) you. Turn your face towards the Sacred Mosque, and wherever you are turn your faces towards it. Those who have been given the Scripture know that it is the truth from their Lord; God is not heedless of what you do. (Al-Baqarah, 2:144) ❋ They will swear to you, that you may be content (tarda) with them; but if you are content with them, God will surely not be content (yarda) with the wicked folk. (Al-Tawbah, 9:96) ❋ He used to enjoin upon his kinsfolk prayer and the [payment of] alms, and he was contenting (mardiya) to his Lord. (Maryam, 19:55)

Raghib explains: 'The verb is *Radiya/yarda*, gerund *rida*, participles *mardi* and *mardu*. People are content with God when they do not hate the turns of fate He sends upon them; and God is content with people when He sees them obeying His commandments and prohibitions'.[241] Ibn Manzhur explains: 'Contentment is the opposite of resentment. Quhayf 'Uqayli said:

> If the tribe of Qushayr are content at me,
>> By God, how their contentment does please me!

He said 'content at me' rather than 'with me', because *to be content 'with'* means *to love and to accept*.'[242] Zabidi explains: 'As is reported in *al-Sihah*, Akhfash recited the verses:

> If the tribe of Qushayr are content at me,
>> By God, how their contentment does please me!

Ibn Sayyidih stated that the poet said 'content at me' because had he said 'content with me', this would have meant that they loved him and accepted him ... *Radi* means 'responsible' (*damin*), though one copy of the *Tahdhib* has it as 'lean' (*damir*); and it also means 'lover'—all this according to Ibn al-'Arabi'.[243]

25. COMPASSION (AL-HANAN):
God says: *And compassion (hananan) from Us, and purity, and he was God-fearing.* (Maryam, 19:13) Raghib explains: '*Hanin* means an expression of compassion; *it is said that a woman (or a she-camel) feels compassion (hannat) for her child.* This might involve a sound, and therefore *hanin* is also the word for a cry or moan of emotion and compassion; an instance of this is the sobbing of the palm-trunk [in the famous *Hadith*] ... Since such a cry expresses compassion, and compassion is inseparable from mercy, the word is also used to express mercy, such as is the case when God says: '*And compassion from Us...*'; from

this is derived the Divine Name 'The Compassionate' (*Al-Hannan*), often paired with 'The Bountiful' (*Al-Mannan*).²⁴⁴ Ibn Manzhur explains: '*Al-Hannan* is a Divine Name, which according to Ibn al-ʿArabi means 'The Compassionate'; Ibn Athir says it means 'He who is Compassionate to His servants' ... An example of this is found when God says: '*And compassion from Us...*' ... A *Hadith* relates that the Prophet ﷺ went to see Umm Salamah, God be pleased with her, who had with her a boy named Walid. He said: 'You have come to feel compassion (*hanan*) for [this name] Walid; change his name!' *That is, you have come to feel emotion and love for this name*'.²⁴⁵ Zabidi explains: 'The compassionate person is the one who feels compassion and emotion for something; and 'The Compassionate' (*Al-Hannan*) is a Name of God, derived from *hinnah*, which means compassion and mercy'.²⁴⁶

26. ADMIRATION (*AL-IʿJAB*):

We have discussed this previously in Chapter 3: The Definition of Love. God says:

Do not marry idolatresses until they believe; a believing slavegirl is better than an idolatress, though you may admire (ʿajabatkum) her. And do not marry idolaters, until they believe. A believing slave is better than an idolater, though you may admire (aʾjabakum) him. Those call to the Fire; and God calls to Paradise and pardon by His leave; and He makes clear His signs to the people so that they might remember. (Al-Baqarah, 2:221) ❋ *And when you see them, their figures arouse your admiration (tuʾjibuka); and if they speak, you listen to their speech. [Yet] they are like blocks of timber [that have been] propped-up. They assume that every cry is [directed] against them. They are the enemy, so beware of them. May God assail them! How can they deviate?* (Al-Munafiqun, 63:4) ❋ *Women are not lawful for you beyond that, nor [is it lawful] for you to change them for other wives, even though you may admire (aʾjabaka) their beauty, except those whom your right hand owns. And God is Watcher over all things.* (Al-Ahzab, 33:52) ❋ *They said, "Do you admire (ataʾjabina) God's command? The mercy of God and His blessings be upon you, people of the House! Truly He is Praised, Glorious!'* (Hud, 11:73) ❋ *Say: 'It has been revealed to me that a company of the jinn listened, then said: "We have indeed heard an admirable (ʿajaba) Qur'an".* (Al-Jinn, 72:1)

Raghib explains: '*Taʾajjub* or *ʿujb* means 'astonishment', i.e. a condition which overcomes a person when he or she does not know the cause of something; therefore a wise man said that a marvel is something whose cause is unknown. Thus it is said that God cannot be astonished, since He knows all things and nothing is beyond His ken ... It is also used (metaphorically in Arabic) to mean 'admire' or 'like', as in 'I admire this', i.e. 'I like it'; a person who finds himself pleasing is said to be a 'self-admirer'.²⁴⁷ Ibn Manzhur explains: ' *ʿUjb* or *ʿajab* means 'to marvel', i.e. to express incredulity at something you see because it is so unusual … If the word is ascribed to God, it does not mean the same as it does for human beings … *'Ujb also means a man who loves to talk to women* (but not in a way which arouses suspicion). *'Ujb, 'ajb and 'ijb all mean a man who loves to keep the company of women.*'[248] Zabidi explains: 'The verb *'ujiba* in the passive voice means 'to be pleased with', or 'to admire'.[249]

27. INCLINATION (AL-MAYL):

We have discussed this previously in Chapter 3: The Definition of Love.
God says:

> And God desires to turn [forgivingly] towards you, but those who follow their passions, desire that you incline with a terrible inclination (tamilu maylan). (Al-Nisa', 4:27) ❉ You will never be able to be just to your wives, even if you be eager; yet do not incline (tamilu kulla al-mayl) altogether away, so that you leave her like one suspended. If you set things right, and fear, surely God is ever Forgiving, Merciful. (Al-Nisa', 4:129)

Raghib explains: 'To incline means to turn from the centre to one of the sides, and it is used to mean 'injustice' … One is said to incline to someone when one helps him or her'.[250] Ibn Manzhur explains: *'To incline means to turn towards something and approach it'* … *Tamayala* means to swerve to the side when walking. *Istamala* means to cause someone to incline, or to win someone's heart. *Tamyil* means to compare two things and decide which one is best. Abu Hurayrah reported that the Prophet ﷺ said: 'There are two groups of the denizens of hell whom I have not yet seen: People with whips like the tails of cows with which they scourge the people, and women who are both clothed and naked, inclining and making others incline, with heads like the humps of Bactrian camels. They will not enter Paradise, nor catch its scent, though its scent may be caught from afar.'[251] Zabidi[252] explains: 'To incline … means *to turn towards and approach* … *ma'ilat* means women who incline to lust and passion instead of chastity'.[253]

28. LUST (AL-SHAHWAH):

God says:

> Adorned for mankind is love of lusts (shahawat)—of women, children, stored-up heaps of gold and silver, horses of mark, cattle, and tillage. That is the pleasure of the life of this world; but God—with Him is the most excellent abode. (Aal ʿImran, 3:14) ❉ Do you come lustfully (shahwatan) to men instead of women? Nay, you are a wanton folk'. (Al-Aʿraf, 7:81)

Raghib explains: 'The root of passion is the soul's attraction to what it desires. In the life of this world, it is of two kinds: true and false. The true is that which the body cannot live without, such as lust for food when one is hungry, and the false is that which the body can live without. The word 'lust' can be used to designate both the object of the lust and the feeling of lust itself'.[254] Ibn Manzhur explains: *'To lust for something means to love it* and desire it.'[255] Zabidi[256] explains: *'To lust for something means to love it'* and desire it. The *Misbah* defines 'lust' as the soul's longing for something.[257]

29. TENDENCY (AL-SABA):

God says: *He said, 'My Lord, prison is dearer to me than that to which they are urging me. And if You do not fend off their wiles from me, then I shall tend towards (asbu) them and become of the ignorant.* (*Yusuf*, 12:33) Raghib explains: 'To tend (*saba*) means to incline and yearn as children (*sibyan*) do; God says: '…*then I shall tend towards them and become of the ignorant*'.[258] Ibn Manzhur explains: 'Tendency means the ignorance of youth, and *romantic foolishness*.'[259] Zabidi[260] explains: 'Tendency means the ignorance of youth, and Layth added: romantic foolishness.'[261]

30. SEEKING (AL-IBTIGHA'):

God says:

> *But there are other men who sell themselves, seeking (ibtigha') God's pleasure; and God is Gentle with His servants.* (Al-Baqarah, 2:207) ❋ *Shall I seek (abtaghi) other than God as a judge, when it is He Who revealed to you the Book, clearly explained? Those to whom We have given the Scripture know that it is revealed from your Lord in truth; so do not be of the waverers.* (*Al-An'am*, 6:114) ❋ *Say: 'Shall I seek (abghi) any other than God for a lord, when He is the Lord of all things?' Every soul earns only against itself; and no burdened soul shall bear the burden of another. Then to your Lord shall you return, and He will inform you of that over which you differed.* (*Al-An'am*, 6:164)

Raghib explains: 'The verbs *bagha* and *ibtagha* mean to seek something more than it should be sought; *ibtagha* also means to help someone seek'.[262] Ibn Manzhur explains: '*Bagha* means to examine something to see what it is … and to monitor it and watch it … *Ibtagha, tabagha* and *istabgha* all mean 'to seek'.[263] Zabidi[264] explains: '*Bagha* means to seek something, whether it is good or evil … The same is the case of *Ibtagha, tabagha* and *istabgha* … An example of this is found in God's words: '*But whoever seeks [anything] beyond that…*' (*Al-Mu'minun*, 23:7) … Raghib said that *ibtigha'* implies a certain amount of effort in the seeking; and when something is praiseworthy, then seeking it is also praiseworthy; an example of this is '…*seeking mercy from your Lord, [a mercy] which you expect…*' (*Al-Isra'*, 17:28), and '*but only seeking the pleasure of his Lord the Most High*' (*Al-Layl*, 92:20). And the *baghi* is the one who seeks'.[265]

31. FAVOUR (AL-TAFDIL):
God says:

> See how We have given preference (faddalna) to some of them over others. And truly the Hereafter is greater in degrees and greater in favour (tafdila). (Al-Isra', 17:21) ❋ And verily We have honoured the Children of Adam, and carried them over land and sea, and provided them with good things and We have favoured (faddalnahum) them above many of those whom We created with a marked favouring (tafdila). (Al-Isra', 17:70)

Raghib explains: 'When the word 'favour' is used in the sense of one thing being preferred to another, there are three possibilities: A favouring of class, such as the superiority of the animal class above the plant class; a favouring of type, such as the superiority of mankind above all other animals—and an example of this is found in God's words *'And verily We have honoured the Children of Adam ... with a marked favouring'*; and then there is individual favour, such as the superiority of one man over another. The first two kinds are essential, and the lower has no hope of becoming the higher. As for the third kind, it might be contingent and thus possible to obtain; an example of this is found in God's words: *'And God has favoured some of you above others in [respect of] provision...'* (Al-Nahl, 16:71).'²⁶⁶ Ibn Manzhur explains: 'God's words *'...and We have favoured them above many of those whom We created with a marked favouring'* are said to mean that God favoured them with distinction; now He said *'above many of those whom We created'* and not *'above all'*, for God favoured the angels when He said: *'...neither would the angels who are nigh...'* (Al-Nisa', 4:172). To favour one above another may mean either to judge that one is superior, or to actually make him or her that way.'²⁶⁷ Zabidi explains: 'The meaning of favour (*fadl*) is well known; it is the opposite of inferiority ... *Fadil* means a superior or favoured person, ... one of much favour, kindness, goodness and forbearance. A *fadilah* (virtue) is the opposite of a flaw, and is the highest rank of favour ... *To favour one above another means to affirm a distinction for him or her, meaning a characteristic that distinguishes him or her above others*; or it means to judge that he or she is superior to others, or to make him or her so.'²⁶⁸

32. EXTRA-MARITAL SEX (AL-ZINA):
We have discussed this previously in Chapter 19: Love and Extra-marital Sex, and we established that sometimes extra-marital sex involves love.

God says: *And do not come [anywhere] near fornication (zina). It is indeed an indecency and an evil way.* (Al-Isra', 17:32) Raghib explains: 'Fornication means to have sexual intercourse with someone to whom one is not lawfully wed.'²⁶⁹ Ibn Manzhur explains: '*Zana / yazni* means to engage in extra-marital sex; it applies to both men and women.'²⁷⁰ Zabidi²⁷¹ explains: '*Zana / yazni*, gerund *zina* ... means to fornicate, for both men and women ... Munawi said that legally speaking, extra-marital sex means for the head of the penis to enter the vagina without the parties being lawfully wed, regardless of whether sexual desire is involved'.²⁷²

33. GRACIOUSNESS (AL-HAFAWAH):

God says: *He said, 'Peace be to you. I shall ask forgiveness of my Lord for you. Truly He is ever gracious (hafiya) to me.* (Maryam, 19:47) Raghib explains: 'The gracious person is he (or she) who is a good and kind person. God says: '…*He is ever gracious to me*'. The verbs *hafiya* and *tahaffa* mean to ask after someone often'.²⁷³ Ibn Manzhur explains: '*Hafawah* means to ask after someone often and *show care for him* or her … To be gracious to someone means to treat him or her very generously and kindly'.²⁷⁴ Zabidi explains: 'To be gracious to someone means to be especially generous to him or her, and do one's best to please him or her. *A gracious person means a person who is extremely good and kind, and graciousness means kindly speech and treatment.* Zajjaj said that the Almighty's words '…*He is ever gracious to me*' means ever kind; to be gracious to someone means to be good and kind to him or her'.²⁷⁵

34. CONCERN (AL-SHAFAQAH):

God says: *He knows what is before them and what is behind them, and they do not intercede except for him with whom He is satisfied, and they, for fear of Him, are concerned (mushfiqun).* (Al-Anbiya', 21:28) ❊ *Surely those who, for fear of their Lord, are concerned (mushfiqun).* (Al-Mu'minun, 23:57) Raghib explains: 'Concern is a combination of care and fear, *because the awestruck person loves those he or she is concerned for,* and fears what might happen to them'.²⁷⁶ Ibn Manzhur explains: 'Concern means *fear* … "I am concerned for you" means "I fear for you" … Concern [also] means a tender feeling of sincerity or love which leads to fear'.²⁷⁷ Zabidi explains: 'Concern means the care one feels for the person one counsels; it is said "I am concerned for him", meaning "I feel mercy and tenderness for him, and fear that something bad might happen to him despite my counsel"; or "I am concerned that something bad will happen to him"'.²⁷⁸

35. PROTECTING FRIENDSHIP (AL-WILAYAH):

God says:

> *God is the Friend (Wali) of the believers; He brings them forth from the shadows into the light. And the disbelievers—their protectors are false deities that bring them forth from the light into the shadows; those are the inhabitants of the Fire, therein they shall abide.* (Al-Baqarah, 2:257) ❊ *And they are not equal, the good deed and the evil deed. Repel with that which is better then, behold, he between whom and you there was enmity will be as though he were a dear friend (waliun hamim).* (Fussilat, 41:34)

Raghib explains: '*'Wala'* and *tawali* literally mean 'direct succession', meaning that two or more things follow one another so closely that there is no gap between them. This is used metaphorically to mean 'nearness' in terms of space, kinship, religion, friendship, succour and belief'.[279] Ibn Manzhur explains: 'The Prophet's ﷺ words: 'Lord, be a friend to those who are friends to him' mean 'love those who love him' … *To be a protecting friend to someone means to love him or her.*'[280] Zabidi explains: '*The word 'wali' has many meanings, including 'lover'*; it is the opposite of 'enemy', and describes one who is a protecting friend to another person because of love for him or her'.[281]

36. INCLINATION (SAGHA):

God says: *And that the hearts of those who do not believe in the Hereafter may incline (tasgha) to it, and that they may be pleased with it, and that they may acquire what they are acquiring.* (Al-An'am, 6:113) Raghib explains: ' *'Al-Saghu'* means *inclination (al-mayl)*. It is said: 'the stars and the sun incline (*saghu*) towards setting'.[282] Ibn Manzhur explains: '*Sagha* means 'to incline' … Ibn Sikkit says 'To *sagha* to something means *to incline to it.*' … God says: '*And that the hearts of those who do not believe in the Hereafter tasgha to it…*' (Al-An'am, 6:113), that is, that they may incline to it. And the words *saghw, sighw* and *sagha* all mean 'inclination'. A man's *saghiya* are those people who incline to him and who come to him and seek what he has, and throng around him … Ibn 'Awf is reported to have said: 'I made a written pact with Umayya ibn Khalaf that he would look after me among my *saghiya* in Mecca, and I would look after him among his *saghiya* in Medina.' The *saghiya* are a person's special retinue, and those who incline to him or her … And to *sagha* against a people means to take sides against them, i.e. to desire another people over them.'[283] Zabidi explains: '*Sagha/yasgha/saghan* means *to incline* … The noun *sagha* means 'inclination' … Your *saghiya* are those who incline to you and come to you at their time of need.'[284]

37. INTIMATE FRIENDSHIP / 'PENETRATING' FRIENDSHIP (AL-WALIJAH):

God says: *Or did you suppose that you would be left [in peace] when God does not yet know those of you who have struggled and have not taken, besides God and His Messenger and the believers, an intimate friend? And God is aware of what you do.* (Al-Tawbah, 9:16) Al-Raghib explains: '*Walijah* means everyone on whom a person relies though he or she is not a member of his or her family. A person is said to be *walijah* in a community if he or she joins them but is not originally one of them. The word can apply to humans and non-humans alike. God says: *and [they] have not taken, besides God and His Messenger and the believers, an intimate friend* (Al-Tawbah, 9:16). This is akin to His words: *O you who believe, do not take Jews and Christians as patrons* (Al-Ma'idah, 5:51)'.[285] Ibn

Manzhur explains: '*Walijah* means a person's retinue and close companions, and those in his or her inner circle. The Qur'an says: *and [they] have not taken, besides God and His Messenger and the believers, an intimate friend (Al-Tawbah, 9:16)*. Abu 'Ubaydah says that *walijah* means 'retinue', and is derived from the verb *walaja/yaliju/wuluj*, which means 'to enter'. So this verse means 'they have not admitted the disbelievers into their inner circle of love.' He also said that *wajila* means everything that is placed into something else from the outside, not being an original part of it. If a person lives among a community but is not originally one of them, he or she is a *wajila* in them. He is saying: 'They do not take any non-believers as protecting friends, alongside God and His Messenger'.[286] Al-Zabidi explains: 'Abu 'Ubaydah says that *walijah* means 'retinue', 'inner circle' and 'close companions'. It has the same form in the singular and plural. *Al-'Inaya* says, in the section on *Surat Aal 'Imran*, that it is used symbolically to mean those who are close to you, in the same sense that the Arabs say 'I wore so-and-so' ('*labistu fulanan*') to mean 'I took him as a close companion.' So it is a metaphor. Or, *walijah* means someone you rely on who is not a member of your family'.[287]

38. AFFINITY (*AL-ULFAH*):
God says:

> *And hold fast to God's bond, together, and do not scatter; remember God's grace upon you when you were enemies, and He brought your hearts together (allafa) so that by His grace you became brothers; and you were upon the brink of a pit of fire; but He delivered you from it. So God makes clear to you His signs that you might be guided. (Aal-'Imran, 3:103)* ❋ *And if they desire to trick you, then God is sufficient for you. He it is Who strengthened you with His help and with the believers; / and reconciled (allafa) their hearts. Had you expended all that is in the earth, you could not have reconciled (allafta) their hearts, but God reconciled (allafa) their hearts. Truly He is Mighty, Wise. (Al-Anfal, 8:62–63)*

Al-Raghib explains: '*Al-ilf* is a bringing together with healing, it is said: *allafta baynahum*—he brought their hearts together; and from this is derived *al-ulfah* (affinity). The person with whom there is affinity is called *ilf* and *aalif*. God says: *when you were enemies, and He brought your hearts together*; and God says: *had you expended all that is in the earth, you could not have reconciled their hearts*'. In dialectics (*kalam*) Al-Raghib says, on the subject of affection (*al-mawaddah*): 'affection is to love something and wish for it to be. God says: *and He ordained between you affection and mercy*. And He says: *for them the Compassionate One shall appoint love*. These are references to the affinity (*ulfah*) that has been engendered in their hearts and which is mentioned in God's words: *had you expended all that is in the earth, you could not have reconciled*

The Different Kinds of Love

*their hearts'.*²⁸⁸ Ibn Manzhur explains: 'When one forms an affinity with something (*i'talaf al-shayy'*); this means that one has become familiar with it. And when we say *allafahu*, we mean that one has brought parts back together; and by *ta'allaf* we mean that something has been made organized. Moreover, *ilf* is one who is familiar. We say: the female mate (*al-ilf*) yearned towards the mate (*al-ilf*).'²⁸⁹ Al-Zubaidi explains: 'Referring to the *Hadith* in which the Prophet ﷺ says: 'for it is more likely to engender love between the two of you', Al-Kasa'i said: "The Prophet meant that it would engender affinity and affection".²⁹⁰

In summary, God mentions at least thirty-eight different kinds of '*hubb*'—'love' or 'liking'—in the Holy Qur'an. Each one of these thirty-eight kinds of *hubb* differs subtly in meaning from each of the others so that there is no tautology in Arabic, and each word means something unique and precise but subtly different. In English translation, however, we often are forced to resort to reusing the same word for different Arabic terms for *hubb* (but in these cases we generally provide accompanying transliterations in brackets). The different kinds of '*hubb*' mentioned in the Holy Qur'an include: 1. love (*hubb*); 2. love (*mahabba*); 3. preference (*istihbab*); 4. mercy (*rahmah*); 5. pity (*ra'fah*); 6. love (*wudd*); 7. affection (*mawaddah*); 8. love (*widad*); 9. will or desire (*iradah*); 10. to be smitten (*shaghaf*); 11. impulse (*hawa*); 12. infatuation (*istihwa'*); 13. to stray (*ghawa*); 14. desire (*hamm*); 15. longing (*raghab*); 16. to draw near (*taqarrub*); 17. anguish (*gharam*); 18. to wander distracted (*huyam*); 19. close friendship (*khullah*); 20. friendship (*sadaqah*); 21. companionship (*suhbah*); 22. preference to another over oneself (*ithar*); 23. going astray (*dalal*); 24. contentment (*rida*); 25. compassion (*hanan*); 26. admiration (*i'jab*); 27. inclination (*mayl*); 28. lust (*shahwah*); 29. tendency towards (*saba*); 30. seeking (*ibtigha'*); 31. favour (*tafdil*); 32. extra-marital sex (*zina*); 33. graciousness (*hafawah*); 34. concern (*shafaqah*); 35. protecting friendship (*wilayah*); 36. inclination (*sagha*); 37. intimate friendship / 'penetrating' friendship (*walijah*); and 38. affinity (*ulfah*). We should also mention that there may be other kinds of love mentioned in the Qur'an, such as '*ibadah*' ('worship'); '*ikhbat*' ('humble obedience'); '*ushribu fi qulubihim*' ('their hearts drank', see *Al-Baqarah*, 2:93); '*alaqa* ('to be suspended', see *Al-Nisa* 4:129) and '*waqaar*' ('reverence'), but we found no clear linguistic evidence that these are kinds of love and not merely acts which can occur in love.

CHAPTER TWENTY-TWO

THE STAGES OF LOVE

In the Holy Qur'an, God describes a number of different stages of human love that, in what follows, we divide into three categories and enumerate, citing some of the verses of the Holy Qur'an in which they occur.

THE STAGES OF LOVE THAT OCCUR IN HUMAN BEINGS' LOVE FOR GOD AS WELL HUMAN BEINGS' LOVE FOR EACH OTHER

In this section, we enumerate the stages of love that we have seen occur in the Holy Qur'an in both human beings' love for God and in their love for each other. It is comprised of the following stages[291]:

1. EMPTINESS (AL-FARAGH):

Emptiness is a stage of love, and both human love for God and human beings' love for one another require that the heart first be emptied of any other love. God says:

> *God has not placed two hearts inside any man, nor has He made your wives whom you declare [to be your mothers] your [true] mothers. Nor has He made those whom you claim as [adopted] sons your [true] sons. That is a mere utterance of your mouths. But God speaks the truth and He guides to the way.* (Al-Ahzab, 33:4) ❋ *And the heart of Moses's mother became empty. Indeed she was about to expose him had We not fortified her heart that she might be of the believers.* (Al-Qasas, 28:10) ❋ *So when you are free (faraghta), toil.* (Al-Sharh, 94:7)

2. NEEDINESS (AL-FAQR):

Neediness is a stage of love, and both human love for God and human beings' love for one another require an initial neediness. God says:

> *O mankind! You are the ones who are in need of God. And God, He is the Independent, the Praised.* (Fatir, 35:15) ❋ *Lo! there you are those who are being called to expend in the way of God; yet among you there are those who are niggardly; and whoever is niggardly is niggardly only to his own soul. For God is the Independent One, while you are the needy. And if you turn away, He will replace you with another people, and they will not be the likes of you.* (Muhammad, 47:38)

And Moses ﷺ says in the Holy Qur'an: *So he watered [their flock] for them, then he retreated to the shade and said, 'My Lord, indeed I am in utter need of whatever good You send down to me'.* (Al-Qasas, 28:24)

3. ADORNMENT (AL-TAZAYYUN):

'Adornment' is a stage of love, and both human love for God and human beings' love for one another require that there first be an 'adornment' in the eye, soul or heart of lovers. God says:

> Adorned with beauty for mankind is love of lusts—of women, children, stored-up heaps of gold and silver, horses of mark, cattle, and tillage. That is the pleasure of the life of this world; but God—with Him is the most excellent abode. (Aal 'Imran, 3:14) ❋ Nay, but you thought that the Messenger and the believers would never return to their families, and that [thought] was adorned in your hearts, and you thought evil thoughts, and you were a ruined lot'. (Al-Fath, 48:12) ❋ Said he, 'My Lord, because You have lead me astray, I shall adorn (la-uzayina) for them [evil acts] in the earth and I shall lead them astray, all of them. (Al-Hijr, 15:39) ❋ And know that the Messenger of God is among you. If he were to obey you in many matters, you would surely be in trouble. But God has endeared faith to you, adorning your hearts with it, and He has made odious to you disbelief and immorality and disobedience. Those they are the right-minded. (Al-Hujurat, 49:7) ❋ Adorned with beauty to the disbelievers seems the life of this world; and they deride the believers; but those who fear shall be above them on the Day of Resurrection; and God sustains whomever He will without reckoning. (Al-Baqarah, 2:212)[292]

We will explain this further in Chapter 26: The Triangle of Love.

4. ADMIRATION (AL-I'JAB):

Admiration is a stage of love, and both human love for God and human beings' love for one another require admiration. God says:

> Do not marry idolatresses until they believe; a believing slavegirl is better than an idolatress, though you may admire her. And do not marry idolaters, until they believe. A believing slave is better than an idolater, though you may admire him. Those call to the Fire; and God calls to Paradise and pardon by His leave; and He makes clear His signs to the people so that they might remember. (Al-Baqarah, 2:221) ❋ And when you see them, their figures arouse your admiration; and if they speak, you listen to their speech. [Yet] they are like blocks of timber [that have been] propped-up. They assume that every cry is [directed] against them. They are the enemy, so beware of them. May God assail them! How can they deviate? (Al-Munafiqun, 63:4) ❋ Women are not lawful for you beyond that, nor [is it lawful] for you to change them for other wives, even though you may admire their beauty, except those whom your right hand owns. And God is Watcher over all things. (Al-Ahzab, 33:52) ❋ They said, 'Do you admire God's command? The mercy of God and His blessings be upon you, people of the House! Truly He is Praised, Glorious!' (Hud, 11:73) ❋ Say: 'It has been revealed to me that a company of the jinn listened, then said: "We have indeed heard an admirable Qur'an"'. (Al-Jinn, 72:1)

We have mentioned this previously as one of the kinds of love in Chapter 21: The Different Kinds of Love.

5. LOVE (*AL-HUBB*) AND INTENSE LOVE (*AL-IHBAB*):

Love ('*hubb*') is a word that can be used in both a general and a specific sense, and there is thus a particular stage of love as such which is itself called 'love' ('*hubb*'). God says:

> Yet there be people who take to themselves rivals besides God, loving them as God is loved; but those who believe love God more ardently. If those who did evil could but see, as they shall when they behold the chastisement, that power altogether belongs to God, and that God is terrible in chastisement. (Al-Baqarah, 2:165)

In this Qur'anic verse, we see that the word 'love' is used for two different stages of love and is also used to mean love in general; and God knows best.

We mentioned this previously as a kind of love in Chapter 21: The Different Kinds of Love.

6. CONTENTMENT (*AL-RIDA*):

Contentment is a stage of love, and both human love for God and human beings' love for one another require contentment. God says:

> God says, 'This is the day those who were truthful shall profit by their truthfulness. Theirs will be Gardens underneath which rivers flow, wherein they shall abide forever. God is content with them, and they are content with Him—that is the great triumph'. (Al-Ma'idah, 5:119) ❋ And the first to lead the way, of the Emigrants and the Helpers, and those who follow them by being virtuous, God is content with them, and they are content with Him; and He has prepared for them Gardens—with rivers flowing beneath them to abide therein forever: that is the supreme triumph. (Al-Tawbah, 9:100) ❋ You will not find a people who believe in God and the Last Day loving those who oppose God and His Messenger, even though they were their fathers or their sons or their brothers or their clan. [For] those He has inscribed faith upon their hearts and reinforced them with a spirit from Him, and He will admit them into gardens underneath which rivers flow, wherein they will abide, God being content with them, and they being content with Him. Those [they] are God's confederates. Assuredly it is God's confederates who are the successful. (Al-Mujadilah, 58:22) ❋ Their reward with their Lord will be Gardens of Eden underneath which rivers flow, wherein they shall abide forever. God is content with them, and they are content with Him. That is [the reward] for him who fears his Lord. (Al-Bayyinah, 98:8) ❋ They will swear to you, that you may be content with them; but if you are content with them, God will surely not be content with the wicked folk. (Al-Tawbah, 9:96)

We mentioned this previously as a kind of love in Chapter 21: The Different Kinds of Love.

7. DRAWING NEAR (AL-TAQARRUB):

'Drawing near' is a stage of love, and both human love for God and human beings' love for one another require 'drawing near'. God says:

> *And We called him from the right side of the Mount and We brought him near in communion. (Maryam, 19:52)* ❋ *You will truly find the most hostile of people to those who believe to be the Jews and the idolaters; and you will truly find the nearest of them in love to those who believe to be those who say 'Verily, we are Christians'; that because some of them are priests and monks, and because they are not disdainful. (Al-Ma'idah, 5:82)*

We mentioned this previously as a kind of love in Chapter 21: The Different Kinds of Love.

8. WILL OR DESIRE (AL-IRADAH):

Will (or desire) is a stage of love, and both human love for God and human beings' love for one another require will. God says:

> *Divorced women shall wait by themselves for three periods. And it is not lawful for them to hide what God has created in their wombs if they believe in God and the Last Day. Their mates have a better right to restore them in such time if they wish (aradu) to set things right; women shall have rights similar to those due from them, with justice; but their men have a degree above them; God is Mighty, Wise. (Al-Baqarah, 2:228)* ❋ *And restrain yourself patiently along with those who call upon their Lord at morning and evening, desiring His Countenance; and do not let your eyes overlook them desiring the glitter of the life of this world. And do not obey him whose heart We have made oblivious to Our remembrance, and who follows his own whim, and whose conduct is [mere] prodigality. (Al-Kahf, 18:28)* ❋ *And do not drive away those who call upon their Lord at morning and evening desiring His countenance. You are not accountable for them in anything; nor are they accountable for you in anything, that you should drive them away and be of the evildoers. (Al-An'am, 6:52)*

We mentioned this previously as a kind of love in Chapter 21: The Different Kinds of Love.

9. SEEKING (AL-IBTIGHA'):

'Seeking' is a stage of love, and both human love for God and human beings' love for one another require seeking. God says: *But there are other men who sell themselves, seeking God's pleasure; and God is Gentle with His servants. (Al-Baqarah, 2:207)* ❋ *But only seeking the pleasure of his Lord the Most High. (Al-A'la, 92:20)*

We mentioned this previously as a kind of love in Chapter 21: The Different Kinds of Love.

10. LONGING (AL-RAGHAB):

Longing is a stage of love, and both human love for God and human beings' love for one another require longing. God says:

> *And long your for Lord. (Al-Sharh, 94:8)* ❈ *They will ask you for a pronouncement concerning women. Say: 'God pronounces to you concerning them, and what is recited to you in the Book, concerning the orphan women to whom you do not give what is prescribed for them, for you long to marry them, and the oppressed children, and that you deal justly with orphans. What-ever good you do, God is ever Knower of it'. (Al-Nisa', 4:127)* ❈ *So We responded to him, and gave him John, and We restored [fertility to] his wife for him. Truly they would hasten to good works, and supplicate Us out of longing and in awe, and they were submissive before Us. (Al-Anbiya', 21:90)*

We mentioned this previously as a kind of love in Chapter 21: The Different Kinds of Love.

11. PROTECTING FRIENDSHIP (AL-WILAYAH):

'Protecting friendship' is a stage of love, and both human love for God and human beings' love for one another require 'protecting friendship'. God says:

> *Truly my Protecting Friend is God Who reveals the Book, and He takes charge of the righteous. (Al-A'raf, 7:196)* ❈ *Assuredly God's friends, no fear shall befall them, neither shall they grieve. (Yunus, 10:62)* ❈ *My Lord, indeed You have given me [something] of sovereignty and You have taught me the interpretation of events. Originator of the heavens and the earth! You are my Protecting Friend in this world and the Hereafter. Take me [in death] to You in submission [to You] and join me to the righteous'. (Yusuf, 12:101)* ❈ *Let not the believers take the disbelievers as protecting friends, rather than the believers—for whoever does that, does not belong to God in anyway—unless you protect yourselves against them, as a safeguard. God warns you of His Self; and to God is the journey's end. (Aal 'Imran, 3:28)*

We mentioned this previously as a kind of love in Chapter 21: The Different Kinds of Love.

12. CLOSE FRIENDSHIP (AL-KHULLAH):

'Close friendship' is a stage of love, and both human love for God and human beings' love for one another require close friendship. God says:

> *O you who believe, expend of what We have provided you with before there comes a day in which there shall be neither commerce, nor close friendship, nor intercession. And the disbelievers—they are the evildoers. (Al-Baqarah, 2:254)* ❈ *Close friends will, on that day, be foes of one another, except for the God-fearing. (Al-Zukhruf, 43:67)* ❈ *And God took Abraham for a close friend. (Al-Nisa', 4:125)*

We mentioned this previously as a kind of love in Chapter 21: The Different Kinds of Love.

13. JOY (AL-FARAH):

Joy is a stage of love, and both human love for God and human beings' love for one another require joy. God says:

Say: 'In the bounty of God, and in His mercy in that let them rejoice: it is better than what they hoard'. (Yunus, 10:58) ❊ *Rejoicing in what God has given them of His bounty, and rejoicing, for the sake of those who have not joined them but are left behind, that no fear shall befall them, neither shall they grieve.* (Aal 'Imran, 3:170) ❊ *God expands provision for whom He will, and straitens for whomever He will; and they rejoice in the life of this world, yet the life of this world in the Hereafter, is but [a brief] enjoyment.* (Al-Ra'd, 13:26) ❊ *But they split into sects regarding their affair, each party rejoicing in what it had.* (Al-Mu'minun, 23:53)

14. TRANQUILLITY (AL-SAKAN):

Tranquillity is a stage of love, and both human love for God and human beings' love for one another require tranquillity. God says: *And of His signs is that He created for you from yourselves mates that you might find tranquillity by their side, and He ordained between you affection and mercy. Surely in that there are signs for a people who reflect.* (Al-Rum, 30:21)

15. HOPE OR EXPECTANCY (AL-RAJA'):

Hope (or expectancy) is a stage of love, and both human love for God and human beings' love for one another require hope. God says:

> *Truly those who do not expect to encounter Us, and are content with the life of this world, and feel reassured in it, and those who are heedless of Our signs.* (Yunus, 10:7) ❊ *Be not faint in seeking the enemy; if you are suffering, they are also suffering as you are suffering; and you hope from God that for which they cannot hope. God is ever Knower, Wise.* (Al-Nisa', 4:104) ❊ *Verily there is for you a beautiful example in the Messenger of God for whoever hopes for [the encounter with] God and the Last Day, and remembers God often.* (Al-Ahzab, 33:21) ❊ *And as for menopausal women who do not expect to marry, they would not be at fault if they put off their clothes in such a way as not to display adornment; but to refrain [from doing so] is better for them; and God is Hearer, Knower.* (Al-Nur, 24:60)

16. ACTION (AL-'AMAL):

Action is a stage of love, and both human love for God and human beings' love for one another require action. God says:

> *And they raced to the door, and she tore his shirt from behind, whereupon they encountered her master at the door. She said, 'What is to be the requital of him who intends evil against your folk, but that he should be imprisoned, or [suffer] a painful chastisement?'* (Yusuf, 12:25) ❊ *She said, 'This is he on whose account you blamed me. Indeed I did attempt to seduce him, but he withheld himself. Yet if he does not do (ya'mal) what I bid him, he verily shall be imprisoned, and verily shall be of those brought low'.* (Yusuf, 12:32) ❊ *And say to those who do not believe: 'Act according to your ability, we are acting'.* (Hud, 11:121)

17. REMEMBRANCE (AL-DHIKR):

Remembrance is a stage of love, and both human love for God and human beings' love for one another require remembrance. God says:

> They said, 'By God, you will never cease remembering Joseph until you are consumed, or you are of those who perish'. (Yusuf, 12:85) ❊ O you who believe! Remember God with much remembrance. (Al-Ahzab, 33:41) ❊ So remember Me, I will remember you; and be thankful to Me, and be not ungrateful towards Me. (Al-Baqarah, 2:152) ❊ And when you have performed your holy rites, remember God as you remember your fathers, or yet more intensely. There are some people who say, 'Our Lord, give to us in this world'; such people will have no part in the Hereafter. (Al-Baqarah, 2:200)

18. COMMUNION (AL-NAJWA):

Communion is a stage of love, and both human love for God and human beings' love for one another require communion. God says: *And We called him from the right side of the Mount and We brought him near in communion. (Maryam, 19:52)* ❊ *We know best what they listen to when they listen to you, and when they are in secret communion, when the evildoers say: 'You are only following a man bewitched'. (Al-Isra', 17:47)*

19. TRIAL (AL-IBTILA'):

'Trial' is a stage of love, occurring in both human love for God and human beings' love for one another. God says:

> It was there that the believers were [sorely] tried, and were shaken with a mighty shock. (Al-Ahzab, 33:11) ❊ And when his Lord tested (ibtila) Abraham with certain words, and he fulfilled them, He said: 'I make you a leader for the people'. Said he, 'And of my seed?' He said, 'My covenant shall not reach the evildoers'. (Al-Baqarah, 2:124)

20. SERENITY (AL-ITMI'NAN):

Serenity is a stage of love, and both human love for God and human being's love for one another require serenity. God says:

> Truly those who do not expect to encounter Us, and are content with the life of this world, and feel serene therein, and those who are heedless of Our signs. (Yunus, 10:7) ❊ Those who believe and whose hearts are made serene (tatma'innu) by God's remembrance. Verily by God's remembrance are hearts made serene. (Al-Ra'd, 13:28)

21. KNOWLEDGE (AL-'ILM):

Knowledge (about the beloved) is a stage of love, and both human love for God and human beings' love for one another require knowledge. God says:

> So exalted be God, the King, the Truth. And do not hasten with the Qur'an before its revelation is completed for you, and say, 'My Lord, increase me in

knowledge'. (Ta Ha, 20:114) ❊ *He said, 'What was your business, women, when you solicited Joseph?' 'God preserve us!' they said. 'We know of no evil in him'. The Chief of the Court's wife said, 'Now the truth is out; it was I who attempted to seduce him and he is indeed of the truthful'. / 'That is so that he may know I did not betray him in his absence, and that truly God does not guide [to success] the guile of the treacherous. (Yusuf, 12:51–2)*

Thus the women in the verse above did not solicit Joseph ❊ as they knew he would not respond. Potiphar's wife solicited him but she was not successful as she did not know him well enough (to know that he would never give in to her). Later (after she had finally understood him), she says that she did not betray him in his absence so that he might know that about her (and thus perhaps love her for it).

22. RECOGNITION (AL-MAʿRIFAH):
Recognition is a stage of love, and both human love for God and human beings' love for one another require recognition. God says:

Those to whom We have given the Scripture, they recognise him, as they recognise their sons; even though there is a party of them that conceal the truth, while they know. (Al-Baqarah, 2:146) ❊ *And when they hear what has been revealed to the Messenger, you see their eyes overflow with tears because of what they recognise of the truth. They say, 'Our Lord, we believe, so inscribe us among the witnesses. (Al-Ma'idah, 5:83)* ❊ *And on the day when He shall gather them as if they had not tarried, but an hour of the day, recognising one another; those will verily have lost who denied the encounter with God, for they were not guided. (Yunus, 10:45)* ❊ *O mankind! We have indeed created you from a male and a female, and made you nations and tribes that you may come to recognise one another. Truly the noblest of you in the sight of God is the most God-fearing among you. Truly God is Knower, Aware. (Al-Hujurat, 49:13)* ❊ *And what she worshipped besides God barred her, for she belonged to disbelieving folk. / It was said to her, 'Enter the palace [hallway]'. And when she saw it, she supposed it to be a pool, and so she bared her legs. He said, 'It is a hallway paved [smooth] with crystal'. She said, 'My Lord, indeed I have wronged myself, and I submit with Solomon to God, the Lord of the Worlds'. (Al-Naml, 47:43–44)*

23. WILL OR WISH (AL-MASHI'AH):
Will (or wish) is a stage of love, and both human love for God and human beings' love for one another require will. God says:

Your women are a tillage for you; so come to your tillage as you wish; and offer for your souls; and fear God; and know that you shall meet Him; and give good tidings to the believers. (Al-Baqarah, 2:223) ❊ *You will see the wrongdoers apprehensive because of what they had earned; and it will surely befall them; but those who believe and perform righteous deeds will be in the* lushest Gardens. They will have whatever they wish near their Lord; that is the great favour. (Al-Shura, 42:22) ❊ They shall have whatever they wish with their Lord. That is the reward of those who are virtuous. (Al-Zumar, 39:34)

24. FEAR (AL-KHAWF):

Fear is a stage of love, inevitably occurring in both human love for God and human beings' love for one another. God says:

> And remember your Lord within yourself, humbly, and fearfully, and more quietly than speaking out loud at morning and evening. And do not be among the heedless. (Al-A'raf, 7:205) ❊ They fear their Lord from above them, and they do what they are commanded. (Al-Nahl, 16:50) ❊ And let them fear those who, if they leave behind them weak offspring would be afraid for them; let them fear God and speak pertinent words. (Al-Nisa', 4:9)

25. GRIEF (AL-HUZN):

Grief is a stage of love, inevitably occurring in both human love for God and human beings' love for one another. God says:

> He said, 'Lo! It grieves me that you should go with him, and I fear lest the wolf devour him, while you are heedless of him'. (Yusuf, 12:15) ❊ And he turned away from them and said, 'Alas, my grief for Joseph!' And his eyes turned white with grief, such that he was [filled] with suppressed agony. (Yusuf, 12:84) ❊ You may put off whomever of them you wish and consort whomever you wish, and as for whomever you may desire of those whom you have set aside, you would not be at fault. That makes it likelier that they will be comforted and not grieve, and that they will be satisfied with what you give them, every one of them will be well-pleased with what you give her. And God knows what is in your hearts. And God is Knower, Forbearing. (Al-Ahzab, 33:51) ❊ Nor against those who, when they came to you so that you might give them a mount—you having said to them, 'I cannot find [a mount] whereon to mount you' turned back, their eyes flowing with tears for grief that they could not find the means to expend. (Al-Tawbah, 9:92)

26. SUFFERING (AL-ALAM):

Suffering is a stage of love, inevitably occurring in both human love for God and human beings' love for one another. God says: *Be not faint in seeking the enemy; if you are suffering, they are also suffering as you are suffering; and you hope from God that for which they cannot hope. God is ever Knower, Wise. (Al-Nisa', 4:104)*

27. WEEPING (AL-BUKA'):

Weeping is a stage of love, and both human love for God and human beings' love for one another require weeping. God says:

> Those to whom God has been gracious from among the prophets of the seed of Adam, and of those whom We carried with Noah, and of the seed of Abraham,

and Israel, and from among those whom We guided and chose, when the signs of the Compassionate One were recited to them, they would fall down prostrating and weeping. (Maryam, 19:58) ❊ Nor against those who, when they came to you so that you might give them a mount—you having said to them, 'I cannot find [a mount] whereon to mount you' turned back, their eyes flowing with tears for grief that they could not find the means to expend. (Al-Tawbah, 9:92)

28. CHANGE (AL-TAGHYIR):

Change is a stage of love, and both human love for God and human beings' love for one another require change (in the lover himself or herself). God says:

> And turn [penitently] to your Lord and submit to Him, before the chastisement comes on you, whereupon you will not be helped. / And follow the best of what has been revealed to you from your Lord before the chastisement comes on you suddenly while you are unaware. (Al-Zumar, 39:54–55) ❊ 'That is so that he may know I did not betray him in his absence, and that truly God does not guide [to success] the guile of the treacherous. / Yet I do not exculpate my own soul; verily the soul is ever inciting to evil, except that whereon my Lord has mercy. Truly my Lord is Forgiving, Merciful'. (Yusuf, 12:52–53).

Love produces a change in the one who loves; thus Potiphar's wife (Zulaikhah), after betraying her husband, refuses to betray Joseph ﷺ and admits her earlier wanton behaviour. Similarly, when people love God they submit and turn penitently to Him; and this means that a change takes place in their souls.

29. CONTRACTION (AL-QABD):

Contraction is a stage of love, inevitably occurring in both human love for God and human beings' love for one another. God says: *Who is he that will lend God a loan that is good, and He will multiply it for him manifold? God contracts and expands; and to Him you shall be returned.* (Al-Baqarah, 2:245)

30. EXPANSION (AL-BAST):

Expansion is a stage of love, necessarily occurring in both human love for God and human beings' love for one another. God says: *Who is he that will lend God a loan that is good, and He will multiply it for him manifold? God contracts and expands; and to Him you shall be returned.* (Al-Baqarah, 2:245)

31. NEED FOR SECLUSION (AL-HAJAH ILA AL-KHALWAH):

Having a 'need for seclusion' is a stage of love, and in both human love for God and human beings' love for one another there occurs a need for seclusion. God says: *He said, 'My Lord, prison is dearer to me than that to which they are urging me. And if You do not fend off their wiles from me, then I shall tend towards them and become of the ignorant.* (Yusuf, 12:33)

We note here that Joseph ﷺ, having (earlier) seen *'His Lord's proof*, did not say: 'prison is better for me', but rather said: *'prison is dearer to me'*. Thus

Joseph ﷺ was eager to enter prison because (presumably) he loved to invoke his Lord without any disturbances.

32. PATIENCE (AL-SABR):

Patience is a stage of love, and both human love for God and human beings' love for one another require patience. God says:

> *And they came with false blood on his shirt. He said: 'Nay, but your souls have beguiled you into something. Yet beautiful patience! And God is the One Whose succour is sought in that [predicament] which you describe'. (Yusuf, 12:18)* ❋ *'Nay,' he said, 'but your souls have beguiled you into something. Yet beautiful patience! It may be that God will bring them all [back] to me. Indeed He is the Knower, the Wise'. (Yusuf, 12:83)* ❋ *The Lord of the heavens and the earth and all that is between them. So worship Him and be steadfast (istabir) in His worship. Do you know [of] anyone who could be His namesake? (Maryam, 19:65)* ❋ *And restrain (asbir) yourself patiently along with those who call upon their Lord at morning and evening, desiring His Countenance; and do not let your eyes overlook them desiring the glitter of the life of this world. And do not obey him whose heart We have made oblivious to Our remembrance, and who follows his own whim, and whose conduct is [mere] prodigality. (Al-Kahf, 18:28)*

33. HOPE (AL-AMAL):

Hope is a stage of love, and both human love for God and human beings' love for one another require hope. God says:

> *He said: 'I complain of my anguish and grief only to God, and I know from God what you do not know. / O my sons, go and enquire about Joseph and his brother, and do not despair of God's [gracious] Spirit. Indeed none despairs of the [gracious] Spirit of God save the disbelieving folk'. (Yusuf, 12:86–87)* ❋ *Wealth and children are an adornment of the life of this world. But the enduring things, the righteous deeds—[these] are better with your Lord for reward and better in [respect of] hope. (Al-Kahf, 18:46)* ❋ *Leave them to eat and to enjoy, and that they be diverted by hope, for they will come to know. (Al-Hijr, 15:3)*

34. JEALOUSY (AL-GHIRAH):

Jealousy is a stage of love, and both human love for God and human beings' love for one another require jealousy. God says:

> *You do not worship, apart from Him anything but [mere] names that you have named, you and your fathers. God has not revealed any warrant regarding them. Judgement belongs only to God. He has commanded that you worship none but Him. That is the upright religion, but most people do not know. (Yusuf, 12:40)* ❋ *When they said: 'Surely Joseph and his brother are dearer to our father than we are, though we be a [hardy] band. Lo! our father is in*

plain aberration. / Kill Joseph or cast him away into some land so that your father might be solely concerned with you, and that thereafter you might be a righteous folk'. (Yusuf, 12:8–9) ❂ '…and I am the first of the believers'. (Al-A'raf, 7:143) ❂ And I did not create the jinn and mankind except that they may worship Me. (Al-Dhariyat, 51:56) ❂ Say: 'Shall I take as a protector other than God, the Originator of the heavens and the earth, He Who feeds and is not fed?' Say: 'I have been commanded to be the first to submit, and: "Do not be among those who associate others"'. (Al-An'am, 6:14) ❂ And your Lord has decreed that you worship none save Him, and kindness to parents. If they should reach old age with you, one of them or both then do not say to them 'Fie' nor repulse them, but speak to them gracious words. (Al-Isra', 17:23) ❂ Say: 'If the Compassionate One had a son, I would have been first among the worshippers. (Al-Zukhruf, 43:81)

We note here that Joseph's brothers were jealous of him because of their father's love for him.

We note here also that the Messenger of God was commanded to say: 'I would have been first among the worshippers', and that Moses said: 'I am the first of the believers'. We infer from this that God's messengers experience a certain kind of jealousy because of their ardent love for God; and God knows best. And can we consider that when God forbids that anything be associated with Him, that this is a kind of jealousy towards His servants? God knows best.

Finally, we note that in the Qur'an and in Islamic *Shari'ah* if a husband and wife definitively divorce, they may not be remarried until the wife marries another man first and then divorces him (if she wants to, of course). God says:

> If he divorces her, she shall not be lawful to him after that, until she marries another husband. If he divorces her, then neither of them would be at fault to return to each other, if they think that they will maintain God's bounds. Those are God's bounds, which He makes clear to a people who have knowledge. (Al-Baqarah, 2:230)

Here we see how jealousy (amongst other emotions) helps to rejuvenate love and its mystery.

35. MEETING (AL-LIQA'):

'Meeting' is a stage of love, occurring in both human love for God and human beings' love for man. God says:

> Your women are a tillage for you; so come to your tillage as you wish; and offer for your souls; and fear God; and know that you shall meet Him; and give good tidings to the believers. (Al-Baqarah, 2:223) ❂ And when Saul went forth with the hosts, he said, 'God will try you with a river; whoever drinks of it, is not of me, and whoever tastes it not, he is of me, except for him who scoops up with his hand. But they drank of it, except a few of them; and when

he crossed it, with those who believed, they said, 'We have no power today against Goliath and his troops'. Those who thought they would meet God, said, 'How often a little company has overcome a numerous one, by God's leave; and God is with the patient'. (Al-Baqarah, 2:249) ❋ Who reckon that they shall meet their Lord, and that to Him they are returning. (Al-Baqarah, 2:46)

We mentioned this previously in Chapter 18: Conjugal Love.

36. COMPANY (AL-MA'IYYAH):

Company (literally, 'with-ness') is a stage of love, occurring in both human love for God and human beings' love for one another. God says:

> Muhammad is the Messenger of God, and those who are with him are hard against the disbelievers, merciful among themselves. You see them bowing, prostrating [in worship]. They seek favour from God and beatitude. Their mark is on their faces from the effect of prostration. That is their description in the Torah, and their description in the Gospel is as a seed that sends forth its shoot and strengthens it, and it grows stout and rises firmly upon its stalk, delighting the sowers, so that He may enrage the disbelievers by them. God has promised those of them who believe and perform righteous deeds forgiveness and a great reward. (Al-Fath, 48:29) ❋ If you have sought a judgement, the judgement has now come to you; and if you desist, it will better for you. But if you return, We shall return, and your host will not avail you in any way, however numerous it be; and verily God is with the believers. (Al-Anfal, 8:19)

37. COMFORT OF THE EYE (QURRAT AL-ʿAYN):

The beloved's becoming 'the comfort of the lover's eye' is a stage of love, occurring in both human love for God and human being's love for one another. God says:

> And submit patiently to the judgement of your Lord, for surely you are before Our eyes. And glorify with praise of your Lord when you rise. (Al-Tur, 52:48) ❋ And those who say, 'Our Lord! Grant us in our spouses and our offspring a joyful sight (qurata a'yun), and make us paragons for the Godfearing'. (Al-Furqan, 25:74)

THE STAGES OF HUMAN BEINGS' LOVE FOR GOD

In this section, we list the stages of love which pertain to man's love for God. (These may or may not also apply to human beings' love for each other, but we have not found them in that context in the Holy Qur'an). These stages are:

38. LOVE (AL-WUDD):

The type of love called *wudd* is one of the stages of love, and human love for God requires *wudd*. God says: *Truly those who believe and perform righteous deeds—for them the Compassionate One shall appoint love (wudd). (Maryam,*

19:96) We mentioned this previously as a kind of love in Chapter 21: The Different Kinds of Love.

39. CONCERN (*AL-SHAFAQAH*):

Concern is one of the stages of love, and human love for God requires concern. God says: *Surely those who, for fear of their Lord, are concerned.* (Al-Mu'minun, 23:57) We mentioned this previously as a kind of love in Chapter 21: The Different Kinds of Love.

40. COMFORTABLE FAMILIARITY (*AL-UNS, AL-ISTI'NAS*):

'Comfortable familiarity' (in speech) is a stage of love, occurring in human love for God. God says:

> O you who believe, do not enter the Prophet's houses unless permission is granted you to [share] a meal without waiting for the [right] moment. But when you are invited, enter, and, when you have had your meal, disperse, without any seeking comfort in conversation. Indeed that is upsetting for the Prophet, and he is [too] shy of you, but God is not shy of the truth. And when you ask anything of [his] womenfolk, ask them from behind a screen. That is purer for your hearts and their hearts. And you should never cause the Messenger of God hurt; nor ever marry his wives after him. Assuredly that in God's sight would be very grave. (Al-Ahzab, 33:53)

41. PEACE (*AL-SALAM*):

Peace is a stage of love, and human love for God requires peace. God says:

> They will not hear therein any vain talk or any sinful words, / but only the saying, 'Peace!' 'Peace!' (Al-Waqi'ah, 56:25–26) ❖ And God summons to the Abode of Peace, and He guides whomever He wills to a straight path. (Yunus, 10:25) ❖ 'Peace!'—the word from a Lord [Who is] Merciful. (Ya Sin, 36:58) ❖ The Night of Ordainment is better than a thousand months. / The angels and the Spirit descend in it by the leave of their Lord with every command. / Peace—it is until the rising of the dawn. (Al-Qadr, 97:3–5)

42. SUFFICIENCY (*AL-IKTIFA'*):

'Sufficiency' is a stage of love, and human love for God requires having 'sufficiency'. God says:

> And if they believe in the like of what you believe in, then they are truly guided; but if they turn away, then they are clearly in schism; God will suffice you against them; He is the Hearer, the Knower. (Al-Baqarah, 2:137) ❖ Does God not suffice His servant? Yet they would frighten you of those besides Him. And whomever God leads astray, for him there is no guide. (Al-Zumar, 39:36)

43. GRATITUDE OR THANKFULNESS (*AL-SHUKR*):

Gratitude (or thankfulness) is a stage of love, and human love for God requires gratitude. God says:

> And We have enjoined man to be kind to his parents. His mother carries him in travail, and gives birth to him in travail, and his gestation and his weaning take thirty months. So that when he is mature and reaches forty years he says, 'My Lord! Inspire me to give thanks for Your favour with which You have favoured me and my parents, and that I may act righteously in a way that will please You, and invest my seed with righteousness. Indeed I repent to You and I am truly of those who submit [to You]'. (Al-Ahqaf, 46:15) ◉ And when your Lord proclaimed: 'If you are thankful, then assuredly I shall give you more; but if you are thankless, My chastisement is indeed severe'. (Ibrahim, 14:7)

44. TRUST (AL-TAWAKKUL):

Trust is a stage of love, and human love for God requires trust. God says: *And He will provide for him from whence he never expected. And whoever puts his trust in God, He will suffice him. Indeed God fulfils His command. Verily God has ordained for everything a measure.* (Al-Talaq, 65:3)

45. 'EXPANSION OF THE BREAST' (INSHIRAH AL-SADR):

'Expansion of the breast' is a stage of love, and human love for God requires expansion of the breast. God says:

> Is he whose breast God has opened (sharaha) to Islam, so that he follows a light from his Lord [like he who disbelieves]? So woe to those whose hearts have been hardened against the remembrance of God. Such are in manifest error. (Al-Zumar, 39:22) ◉ Did We not expand your breast for you? (Al-Sharh, 94:1)

46. 'SOFTENING OF THE SKIN' (LAYN AL-JILD):

'Softening of skin' is a stage of love, and human love for God requires that the skin soften. God says:

> God has revealed the best of discourses, a Book, consimilar in coupled phrases—whereat quiver the skins of those who fear their Lord; then their skins and their hearts soften to the remembrance of God. That is God's guidance, by which He guides whomever He wishes; and whomever God leads astray, for him there is no guide. (Al-Zumar, 29:23)

47. 'SOFTENING OF THE HEART' (LAYN AL-QALB):

'Softening of the heart' is a stage of love, and human love for God requires that the heart soften. God says:

> God has revealed the best of discourses, a Book, consimilar in coupled phrases—whereat quiver the skins of those who fear their Lord; then their skins and their hearts soften to the remembrance of God. That is God's guidance, by which He guides whomever He wishes; and whomever God leads astray, for him there is no guide. (Al-Zumar, 29:23)

48. 'QUIVERING OF THE SKIN' (QASH'ARIRAT AL-JILD):

'Quivering of the skin' is a stage of love, and human love for God requires that the skin quiver. God says:

> God has revealed the best of discourses, a Book, consimilar in coupled phrases—whereat quiver the skins of those who fear their Lord; then their skins and their hearts soften to the remembrance of God. That is God's guidance, by which He guides whomever He wishes; and whomever God leads astray, for him there is no guide. (Al-Zumar, 29:23)

49. 'TREMBLING OF THE HEART' (WAJL AL-QALB):

'Trembling of the heart' is a stage of love, and human love for God requires that the heart tremble. God says:

> The believers are only those who, when God is mentioned, their hearts tremble, and when His verses are recited to them, they increase their faith, and who rely upon their Lord. (Al-Anfal, 8:2) ❊ Who, when God is mentioned, their hearts tremble, and who endure [patiently] whatever may befall them, and who observe prayer, and who, from that which We have provided them, expend. (Al-Hajj, 22:35)

50. DEVOTION (AL-TABATTUL):

Devotion is a stage of love, and human love for God requires devotion. God says: *And mention the Name of your Lord, and devote yourself [exclusively] to Him with complete devotion.* (Al-Muzzammil, 73:8)

51. HUMBLE OBEDIENCE (AL-IKHBAT):

Humble obedience is a stage of love, and human love for God requires humble obedience. God says: *And for every community, We have appointed a [holy] rite that they might mention God's Name over the livestock that He has provided them. For your God is One God, so submit to Him. And give good tidings to the humbly obedient.* (Al-Hajj, 22:34)

52. TURNING IN PENITENCE (AL-INABAH):

Turning in penitence is a stage of love, and human love for God requires that one turn in penitence to Him. God says:

> And those who disbelieve say, 'Why has not some sign not been revealed him from his Lord?' Say: 'Indeed God sends astray whomever He will, and He guides to Him those who turn in penitence'. (Al-Ra'd, 13:27) ❊ And turn [penitently] to your Lord and submit to Him, before the chastisement comes on you, whereupon you will not be helped. (Al-Zumar, 39:54)

53. HUMILITY (AL-TADARRU'):

Humility is a stage of love, and human love for God requires humility. God says: *Call upon your Lord humbly and quietly. Truly, He loves not the aggressors.*

(Al-A'raf, 7:55) ❊ *And remember your Lord within yourself, humbly, and fearfully, and more quietly than speaking out loud at morning and evening. And do not be among the heedless.* (Al-A'raf, 7:205)

54. REPENTANCE (AL-TAWBAH):
Repentance is a stage of love, and human love for God requires repentance. God says:

> *And when Moses came at Our appointed time, and his Lord spoke with him, he said, 'My Lord! Show me that I may behold You!' Said He, 'You shall not see Me, but behold the mountain, and if it remains, in its place, then you shall see Me'. And when his Lord revealed Himself to the mountain He levelled it to the ground and Moses fell down senseless. And when he recovered his senses he said, 'Glory be to You! I repent to You, and I am the first of the believers'.* (Al-A'raf, 7:143)

55. ASKING FORGIVENESS (AL-ISTIGHFAR):
Asking forgiveness is a stage of love, and human love for God requires that one ask forgiveness. God says:

> *And ask forgiveness of your Lord, then repent to Him. Truly my Lord is Merciful, Loving.* (Hud, 11:90) ❊ *...And seek forgiveness from God; assuredly God is Forgiving, Merciful.* (Al-Muzzammil, 73:20) ❊ *And [bidding you]: 'Ask forgiveness of your Lord, then repent to Him, and He will give you fair enjoyment until a time appointed, and He will give every person of merit, [the due for] his merit. But if you turn away, I fear for you the chastisement of an awful day.* (Hud, 11:3) ❊ *I said, 'Ask your Lord for forgiveness. Assuredly He is ever Forgiving.'* (Nuh, 71:10)

56. 'HASTENING TO PLEASE' (AL-'AJAL LIL-TARDIYAH):
'Hastening to please' the Beloved is a stage of love, occurring in human love for God. God says:

> *He said, 'They are close upon my track, and I hastened to You, my Lord, that You may be pleased'.* (Ta Ha, 20:84) ❊ *And We have enjoined man to be kind to his parents. His mother carries him in travail, and gives birth to him in travail, and his gestation and his weaning take thirty months. So that when he is mature and reaches forty years he says, 'My Lord! Inspire me to give thanks for Your favour with which You have favoured me and my parents, and that I may act righteously in a way that will please You, and invest my seed with righteousness. Indeed I repent to You and I am truly of those who submit [to You]'.* (Al-Ahqaf, 46:15)

57. CALLING UPON OR SUPPLICATION (AL-DU'A'):
To call upon or supplicate God is a stage of love, and human love for God requires that one call upon Him. God says:

The Stages of Love

He it is Who created you from a single soul, and made from him his spouse that he might take rest in her. Then, when he covered her, she bore a light burden, and moved to and fro with it; but when she became heavy, they cried (da'a) to God their Lord, 'If You give us one that is sound, we indeed shall be of the thankful'. (Al-A'raf, 7:189) ❊ *And those who say, 'Our Lord! Grant us in our spouses and our offspring a joyful sight, and make us paragons for the God-fearing'.* (Al-Furqan, 25:74) ❊ *And when My servants question you concerning Me, I am near; I answer the call of the caller when he calls to Me; so let them respond to Me, and let them believe in Me that they might go aright.* (Al-Baqarah, 2:186) ❊ *And your Lord has said, 'Call on Me and I will respond to you. Surely those who disdain to worship Me shall enter Hell [utterly] humiliated'.* (Ghafir, 40:60)

58. REMEMBRANCE (AL-TADHAKKUR):

Remembrance is a stage of love, and human love for God requires remembrance. God says: *Truly the God-fearing, when a visitation from Satan touches them, they remember, and then see clearly.* (Al-A'raf, 7:201)

59. FOLLOWING (AL-ITTIBA'):

'Following' is a stage of love, and human love for God requires 'following'. God says:

> Say: 'If you love God, follow me, and God will love you more, and forgive you your sins; God is Forgiving, Merciful.' (Aal 'Imran, 3:31) ❊ *Verily there is for you a beautiful example in the Messenger of God for whoever hopes for [the encounter with] God and the Last Day, and remembers God often.* (Al-Ahzab, 33:21)

60. 'PROVING WHAT IS IN THE HEART' (TAMHIS AL-QALB):

'Proving what is in the heart' is a stage of love, and human love for God requires that what is in the heart be proved. God says:

> *And that God may prove the believers, and efface the disbelievers.* (Aal 'Imran, 3:141) ❊ *Then He sent down upon you, after grief, security—a slumber overcoming a party of you, and a party whose own souls distressed them, thinking wrongly of God, thoughts of age of ignorance, saying, 'Have we any part whatever in the affair?' Say: 'The affair belongs entirely to God'. They conceal within their hearts what they do not disclose to you, saying, 'Had we had any part in the affair, we would not have been slain here'. Say: 'Even if you had been in your houses, those for whom it had been appointed that they be slain would have sallied forth to the places where they were to lie' that God might try what was in your breasts and that He might prove what was in your hearts; and God knows what is in the breasts.* (Aal 'Imran, 3:154)

61. UNCERTAINTY (AL-SHAKK):

Uncertainty is a stage of love, and being uncertain of the sincerity of one's love (in one's eagerness for it to be completely pure) occurs in human love for God. God says: *So, if you are uncertain concerning what We have revealed to you, then question those who read the Scripture before you. Verily the Truth from your Lord has come to you; so do not be of the waverers.* (Yunus, 10:94)

62. DOUBT (AL-RAYB):

Doubt is a stage of love, and it occurs in human love for God. God says:

> *O mankind, if you are in doubt about the Resurrection, then lo! [consider that] We have created you from dust then, from a drop, then from a clot, then from a [little] lump of flesh, partly formed, and partly unformed, that We may make clear to you. And We establish in the wombs whatever We wish for a specified time, then We bring you forth as infants, and then that you may come of age. And there are some of you who are taken away, and there are some of you who are relegated to the most abject time of life, so that after [having had] some knowledge, he no longer knows anything. And you see the earth torpid, yet when We send down water upon it, it stirs, and swells, and grows [plants of] every delightful kind.* (Al-Hajj, 22:5) ❋ *And if you are in doubt concerning what We have revealed to Our servant, then bring a surah like it; and call your witnesses besides God if you are truthful.* (Al-Baqarah, 2:23) ❋ *And when Abraham said, 'My Lord show me how You give life to the dead'. He said, 'Why, do you not believe?' 'Yes', he said, 'but so that my heart may be re-assured'. Said He, 'Take four birds, and twist them to you, then set a part of them on every hill, then summon them, and they will come to you in haste. And know that God is Mighty, Wise'.* (Al-Baqarah, 2:260)

63. ENTERTAINING THOUGHTS (AL-ZHANN):

Entertaining thoughts and misgivings that one may be rejected by his or her Beloved is a stage of love; and it occurs in human love for God. God says:

> *He said, 'He has certainly wronged you by asking for your ewe that he may add it to his sheep. And indeed many associates infringe upon [the rights of] one other, except such as believe and perform righteous deeds, but few are they!'. And David thought that We had indeed tried him. So he sought forgiveness of his Lord and fell down bowing and repented.* (Sad, 38:24) ❋ *When they came at you from above you and from below you, and when the eyes turned away [in fear], and the hearts leapt to the throats, while you entertained all sorts of thoughts concerning God.* (Al-Ahzab, 33:10)

64. LOOKING (AL-NAZHAR):

Looking is a stage of love (that is, looking with one's heart); and human love for God requires looking. God says:

> *So behold (fa'nzhur) the effects of God's mercy, how He revives the earth after it has died. Surely He is the Reviver of the dead and He has power over all things.* (Al-Rum, 30:50) ❋ *Say: 'Behold (unthuru) what is in the heavens*

and in the earth!' But signs and warners do not avail a folk who will not believe. (Yunus, 10:101)

65. CONTEMPLATION (AL-TAFAKKUR):

Contemplation is a stage of love, and human love for God requires contemplation. God says:

> Have they not contemplated themselves? God did not create the heavens and the earth, and what is between them, except with the truth and an appointed term. But indeed many people disbelieve in the encounter with their Lord. (Al-Rum, 30:8) ❊ Those who remember God, standing and sitting and on their sides, and contemplate the creation of the heavens and the earth: 'Our Lord, You have not created this in vain. Glory be to You! So guard us against the chastisement of the Fire. (Aal 'Imran, 3:191)

66. MEDITATION (AL-TADABBUR):

Meditation is a stage of love, and human love for God requires meditation. God says: *Do they not meditate upon the discourse, or has there come upon them that which has not come upon their forefathers?* (Al-Mu'minun, 23:68) ❊ *A Book that We have revealed to you, full of blessing, that they may meditate upon its signs and that they who have cores may remember.* (Sad, 38:29)

67. 'USING REASON' (ISTI'MAL AL-'AQL):

'Using reason' is a stage of love, and human love for God requires using reason. God says:

> Surely in the creation of the heavens and the earth, and the alternation of the night and day, and the ships that run in the sea with what profits men, and the water, God sends down from the heaven with which He revives the earth after it is dead, and He scatters abroad in it all manner of crawling thing; and the disposition of the winds, and the clouds compelled between heaven and the earth—surely there are signs for a people who have reason (ya'qilun). (Al-Baqarah, 2:164)

68. PERCEPTION (AL-TABASSUR):

Perception is a stage of love, and human love for God requires perception. God says: *Clear proofs have come to you from your Lord; whoever perceives, then it is for his own good; and whoever is blind, then it will be to his own hurt. And I am not a keeper over you.* (Al-An'am, 6:104)

69. CERTAINTY (AL-YAQIN): CERTAIN KNOWLEDGE ('ILM AL-YAQIN); CERTAIN VISION ('AYN AL-YAQIN); CERTAIN TRUTH (HAQQ AL-YAQIN):

Certainty is a stage of love, and human love for God requires certainty. God says: *No indeed! Were you to know with certain knowledge.* (Al-Takathur, 102:5) ❊ *Again, you will surely see it with certain vision.* (Al-Takathur, 102:7) ❊ *This indeed is the certain truth.* (Al-Waqi'ah, 56:95) ❊ And assuredly it is the certain truth. (*Al-Haqqah*, 69:51) And, finally: *[A]nd worship your Lord until Certainty comes to you.* (*Al-Hijr*, 15:99)

70. ARDENT HOPE (*AL-TAMA'*):

To ardently hope to attain one's goal is a stage of love, and human love for God requires that one hope ardently. God says: *And work not corruption in the land, after it has been set right, and call upon Him in fear, and in ardent hope—surely the mercy of God is near to the virtuous.* (*Al-A'raf*, 7:56)

71. NEED FOR HUMAN COMPANY (*AL-HAJAH ILA AL-JALWAH*):

The need for human company is a stage of love; people need other people to share with them their love for God. God says: *And as for your Lord's grace, proclaim [it].* (*Al-Duha*, 93:11) 'Proclaiming' God's grace requires people to proclaim to, and this requires human company.

72. IMPLORING (*AL-TA'AWWUH*):

Imploring—literally 'tender-heartedness'—is a stage of love, and when people love God, they implore Him. God says:

> *Abraham's prayer for the forgiveness of his father was only because of a promise he had made to him; but when it became clear to him that he was an enemy of God, he declared himself innocent of him; truly Abraham was imploring, forbearing.* (*Al-Tawbah*, 9:114) ❋ *Assuredly Abraham was forbearing, imploring, penitent.* (*Hud*, 11:75)

73. PENITENCE (*AL-AWB*):

Penitence is a stage of love, and human love for God requires penitence. God says: *This is what you were promised—[it is] for every penitent one, who is mindful.* (*Qaf*, 50:32) ❋ *Your Lord knows best what is in your hearts. If you are righteous, then truly, to those who are penitent He is Forgiving.* (*Al-Isra'*, 17:25)

74. DEVOUTNESS (*AL-QUNUT*):

Devoutness is a stage of love, and human love for God requires devoutness. God says: *Or is he who is devout [in worship] in the watches of the night, prostrating and standing, apprehensive of the [eventuality of the] Hereafter, and hoping for the mercy of his Lord ... ? Say: 'Are those who know equal with those who do not know?' Only people of cores remember.* (*Al-Zumar*, 39:9)

75. BEING OVERWHELMED (*AL-QAHR*):

Being completely overwhelmed by the irresistible Beloved is a stage of love; and it occurs in human love for God. God says: *O my two fellow-prisoners!: Are several lords better, or God, the One, the Irresistible (Al-Qahhar)?* (*Yusuf*, 12:39)

76. SUBMISSION (*AL-ISLAM*):

Submission is a stage of love, and it means to yield completely to the will of the Beloved. Human love for God requires submission. God says:

It was said to her, 'Enter the palace [hallway]'. And when she saw it, she supposed it to be a pool, and so she bared her legs. He said, 'It is a hallway paved [smooth] with crystal'. She said, 'My Lord, indeed I have wronged myself, and I submit with Solomon to God, the Lord of the Worlds'. (Al-Naml, 27:44) ❂ Whomever God desires to guide, He expands his breast to Islam; and whomever He desires to send astray, He makes his breast narrow and constricted, as if he were engaged in ascent to the heaven. So, God casts ignominy over those who do not believe. (Al-An'am, 6:125) ❂ Is he whose breast God has opened to Islam, so that he follows a light from his Lord [like he who disbelieves]? So woe to those whose hearts have been hardened against the remembrance of God. Such are in manifest error. (Al-Zumar, 39:22)

77. FAITH (AL-IMAN):

Faith is a stage of love, and human love for God requires faith. God says:

> The Bedouins say, 'We believe'. Say: 'You do not believe; but rather say, "We have submitted"; for faith has not yet entered into your hearts'. Yet if you obey God and His Messenger, He will not diminish for you anything of your deeds. God is indeed Forgiving, Merciful. (Al-Hujurat, 49:14) ❂ And know that the Messenger of God is among you. If he were to obey you in many matters, you would surely be in trouble. But God has endeared faith to you, adorning your hearts with it, and He has made odious to you disbelief and immorality and disobedience. Those they are the right-minded. (Al-Hujurat, 49:7)

78. VIRTUE (AL-IHSAN):

Virtue is a stage of love, and human love for God requires virtue. God says:

> But as for those who struggle for Our sake, We shall assuredly guide them in Our ways, and truly God is with the virtuous. (Al-'Ankabut, 29:69) ❂ Truly God is with those who fear [God], and those who are virtuous. (Al-Nahl, 16:128) ❂ And work not corruption in the land, after it has been set right, and call upon Him in fear, and in hope—surely the mercy of God is near to the virtuous. (Al-A'raf, 7:56)

79. SINCERITY (AL-IKHLAS):

Sincerity is a stage of love, and human love for God requires sincerity. God says:

> Indeed We have revealed to you the Book with the truth; so worship God, devoting your religion purely to Him. / Surely to God belongs pure religion. And those who take besides Him patrons, [say]: 'We only worship them so that they may bring us near to God'. God will indeed judge between them concerning that about which they differ. Truly God does not guide one who is a liar, a disbeliever. (Al-Zumar, 39:2–3)

THE STAGES OF HUMAN BEINGS' LOVE FOR EACH OTHER

In this section, we list the stages of love which pertain to human beings' love for other human beings as such. (These stages may or may not apply to human beings' love of God, but we have not found them in that context in the Holy Qur'an.) These stages are:

80. LOVE (AL-MAHABBAH):

The type of love called *mahabbah* is one of the stages of love, and human love for God requires *mahabbah*. God says: *'Cast him in the ark, then cast him into the river, and then the river shall throw him up onto the shore; [there] an enemy of Mine and an enemy of his shall take him'. And I cast upon you a love (mahabbah) from Me and that you might be reared under My eyes. (Ta Ha, 20:39)*

We mentioned this previously as a kind of love in Chapter 21: The Different Kinds of Love, and explained that it is either a kind of love between people, or from God for people.

81. 'THE PRESENCE OF BEAUTY' (WUJUD AL-JAMAL):

'The presence of (physical) beauty' is a stage of love, and human love for other human beings requires the presence of beauty, whether outer or inner. God says:

> *And do not extend your glance toward what We have given to some pairs among them to enjoy, [as] the flower of the life of this world that We may try them thereby. And your Lord's provision is better and more enduring. (Ta Ha, 20:131)* ❋ *And when she heard of their machinations, she sent for them and prepared for them a repast. She then gave each one of them a knife and said: 'Come out before them!' And when they saw him, they were in awe of him and cut their hands, and they exclaimed: 'God preserve us! This is no human being: this is but a noble angel!' (Yusuf, 12:31)*

82. MUTUAL KNOWLEDGE (AL-TAʿARUF):

Mutual knowledge is a stage of love, occurring in human love for other human beings. God says:

> *O mankind! We have indeed created you from a male and a female, and made you nations and tribes that you may come to know one another. Truly the noblest of you in the sight of God is the most God-fearing among you. Truly God is Knower, Aware. (Al-Hujurat, 49:13)* ❋ *And on the day when He shall gather them as if they had not tarried, but an hour of the day, knowing one another; those will verily have lost who denied the encounter with God, for they were not guided. (Yunus, 10:45)*

83. INCLINATION (AL-MAYL):

Inclination is a stage of love, and human love for other human beings requires inclination. God says:

> *And God desires to turn [forgivingly] towards you, but those who follow their passions, desire that you incline with a terrible inclination. (Al-Nisa', 4:27)* ❋ *You will never be able to be just to your wives, even if you be eager; yet do not*

incline altogether away, so that you leave her like one suspended. If you set things right, and fear, surely God is ever Forgiving, Merciful. (Al-Nisa', 4:129)

We mentioned this previously as a kind of love in Chapter 21: The Different Kinds of Love.

84. AFFECTION (AL-MAWADDAH):

Affection is a stage of love, and human love for other human beings requires affection. God says: *And of His signs is that He created for you from yourselves mates that you might find peace by their side, and He ordained between you affection and mercy. Surely in that there are signs for a people who reflect.* (Al-Rum, 30:21)

We mentioned this previously as a kind of love in Chapter 21: The Different Kinds of Love.

85. PITY (AL-RA'FAH):

Pity is a stage of love, and human love for other human beings requires pity. God says: *Verily there has come to you a messenger from among yourselves for whom it is grievous that you should suffer; who is full of concern for you, to the believers full of pity, merciful.* (Al-Tawbah, 9:128) We mentioned this previously as a kind of love in Chapter 21: The Different Kinds of Love.

86. LUST (AL-SHAHWAH):

Lust—meaning 'desire for contact', physically or mentally—is a stage of love, and human love for other human beings requires lust, meaning 'desire for contact'. God says:

> *Adorned for mankind is love of lusts—of women, children, stored-up heaps of gold and silver, horses of mark, cattle, and tillage. That is the pleasure of the life of this world; but God—with Him is the most excellent abode.* (Aal 'Imran, 3:14) ❋ *And God desires to turn [forgivingly] towards you, but those who follow their passions (shahawat), desire that you deviate with a terrible deviation.* (Al-Nisa', 4:27)

We mentioned this previously as a kind of love in Chapter 21: The Different Kinds of Love.

87. IMPULSE (AL-HAWA):

Impulse is a stage of love, and human love for other human beings requires impulse. God says: *Have you seen him who has taken as his god his own impulse? Will you be a guardian over him?* (Al-Furqan, 25:43) *Nor does he speak from [his own] impulse.* (Al-Najm, 53:3) We mentioned this previously as a kind of love in Chapter 21: The Different Kinds of Love.

88. DESIRE (AL-HAMM):

Desire is a stage of love, and human love for other human beings requires desire. God says: *And she certainly desired him, and he would have desired her [too], had it not been that he saw the proof of his Lord. So it was that We might ward off from him evil and lewdness. Truly he was of Our devoted servants.* (*Yusuf*, 12:24) We mentioned this previously as a kind of love in Chapter 21: The Different Kinds of Love.

89. PLEASURE (AL-MUTʿAH):

Pleasure is a stage of love, and human love for other human beings requires pleasure. God says: *Adorned for mankind is love of lusts—of women, children, stored-up heaps of gold and silver, horses of mark, cattle, and tillage. That is the pleasure of the life of this world; but God—with Him is the most excellent abode.* (*Aal ʿImran*, 3:14)

90. ENJOYMENT (AL-ISTIMTAʿ):

Enjoyment is a stage of love, and human love for other human beings requires enjoyment. God says:

> *And wedded women, save what your right hands own, this is what God has prescribed for you. Lawful for you beyond all that is that you seek using your wealth, in wedlock and not in illicitly. Such wives as you enjoy thereby, give them their wages as an obligation; you are not at fault in agreeing together, after the obligation. God is ever Knowing, Wise.* (*Al-Nisa'*, 4:24)

91. GENEROSITY (AL-KARAM):

Generosity is a stage of love, and human love for other human beings requires generosity. God says: *And your Lord has decreed that you worship none save Him, and kindness to parents. If they should reach old age with you, one of them or both then do not say to them 'Fie' nor repulse them, but speak to them reverent (kareem) words.* (*Al-Isra'*, 17:23)

92. MERCY (AL-RAHMAH):

Mercy is a stage of love, and human love for other human beings requires mercy. God says:

> *And of His signs is that He created for you from yourselves mates that you might find peace by their side, and He ordained between you affection and mercy. Surely in that there are signs for a people who reflect.* (*Al-Rum*, 30:21) ⊛ *And prescribe for us in this world good and in the Hereafter. We have turned to You'. He says: 'My chastisement—I smite with it whom I will, and My mercy embraces all things, and so I shall prescribe it for those who are God-fearing and pay the alms, and those who believe in Our signs.* (*Al-Aʿraf*, 7:156) ⊛ *Those who bear the Throne and those around it glorify with praise of their Lord, and they believe in Him, and they ask forgiveness for those who believe: 'Our Lord, You embrace all things in [Your] mercy and knowledge. So forgive those who repent and follow Your way and shield them from the chastisement of Hell-fire.* (*Ghafir*, 40:7)

As God's mercy *embraces all things* and is prescribed for the *God-fearing*, it necessarily encompasses God-fearing human love for other human beings.

93. TENDERNESS (AL-LUTF):

Tenderness is a stage of love, and human love for other human beings requires tenderness. God says: *God is Tender to His servants; He provides for whomever He will. And He is the Strong, the Mighty.* (Al-Shura, 42:19)

Because God is Tender (*Latif*) towards His servants and *provides for whomever He will* among them, we understand that, *for whomever He will* of His servants, their love for other human beings requires tenderness.

94. FORGIVENESS (AL-MAGHFIRAH, AL-GHUFRAN):

Forgiveness is a stage of love, and human love for other human beings requires forgiveness. God says: *O you who believe! Indeed among your spouses and children there are enemies for you, so beware of them. And if you pardon, and overlook [such enmity] and forgive, then assuredly God is Forgiving, Merciful.* (Al-Taghabun, 64:14)

95. PARDONING (AL-ʿAFU):

Pardoning is a stage of love, and human love for other human beings requires pardoning. God says: *O you who believe! Indeed among your spouses and children there are enemies for you, so beware of them. And if you pardon, and overlook [such enmity] and forgive, then assuredly God is Forgiving, Merciful.* (Al-Taghabun, 64:14)

96. OVERLOOKING (AL-SAFH):

Overlooking is a stage of love, and human love for other human beings requires that one overlook the faults of others. God says: *O you who believe! Indeed among your spouses and children there are enemies for you, so beware of them. And if you pardon, and overlook [such enmity] and forgive, then assuredly God is Forgiving, Merciful.* (Al-Taghabun, 64:14)

97. KINDNESS (AL-MAʿRUF):

Kindness is a stage of love, and human love for other human beings requires kindness. God says:

> Lodge them where you dwell in accordance with your means and do not harass them so as to put them in straits. And if they are pregnant, then maintain them until they deliver. Then, if they suckle for you, give them their wages, and consult together with kindness. But if you both make difficulties, then another woman will suckle [the child] for him. (Al-Talaq, 65:6)

98. SEDUCTION (AL-MURAWADAH):

Seduction is a stage of love, occurring in human love for other human beings. God says:

> He said: 'It was she who attempted to seduce me'. And a witness of her own folk testified: 'If his shirt has been torn from the front, then she speaks the truth, and he is of the liars. (Yusuf, 12:26) ❋ And some of the women in the

city said, 'The Chief of the Court's wife has been seducing her boy. Indeed he has smitten her heart with love. Lo! we see her to be in plain aberration'. (Yusuf, 12:30)²⁹³ ● And they had even solicited of him his guests. So We blotted out their eyes. 'So taste [now] My chastisement and My warnings'. (Al-Qamar, 54:37)

99. SHYNESS (AL-ISTIHYA'):

Shyness is a stage of love, occurring in human love for other human beings. God says:

> Then one of the two women came to him, walking shyly, and said, 'My father invites you, that he may pay you a wage for watering [our flock] for us'. So when he came to him and recounted to him the story, he [their father] said, 'Do not be afraid. You have escaped from the evildoing people'. (Al-Qasas, 20:25)

100. OBLIVIOUSNESS TO ONESELF ('ADAM AL-IHSAS BIL-HAL):

Being obliviousness to oneself is a stage of love, occurring in human love for other human beings. God says:

> And when she heard of their machinations, she sent for them and prepared for them a repast. She then gave each one of them a knife and said: 'Come out before them!' And when they saw him, they were in awe of him and cut their hands, and they exclaimed: 'God preserve us! This is no human being: this is but a noble angel!' (Yusuf, 12:31)

In summary: we enumerated herein one hundred stages of human love derived from the Holy Qur'an, and arranged them in three sections as follows:

(A) THE STAGES OF LOVE THAT OCCUR IN BOTH HUMAN BEINGS' LOVE FOR GOD AND HUMAN BEINGS' LOVE FOR EACH OTHER ARE:

1. Emptiness (*al-Faragh*); 2. Neediness (*al-Faqr*); 3. Adornment (*al-Tazayyun*); 4. Admiration (*al-I'jab*); 5. Love (*al-Hubb*) and Intense Love (*al-Ihbab*); 6. Contentment (*al-Rida*); 7. Drawing Near (*al-Taqarrub*); 8. Will or Desire (*al-Iradah*); 9. Seeking (*al-Ibtigha*); 10. Longing (*al-Raghab*); 11. Protecting Friendship (*al-Wilayah*); 12. Close Friendship (*al-Khullah*); 13. Joy (*al-Farah*); 14. Tranquillity (*al-Sakan*); 15. Hope or Expectancy (*al-Raja'*); 16. Action (*al-'Amal*); 17. Remembrance (*al-Dhikr*); 18. Communion (*al-Najwa*); 19. Trial (*al-Ibtila'*); 20. Serenity (*al-Itmi'nan*); 21. Knowledge (*al-'Ilm*); 22. Recognition (*al-Ma'rifah*); 23. Will or Wish (*al-Mashi'ah*); 24. Fear (*al-Khawf*); 25. Grief (*al-Huzn*); 26. Suffering (*al-Alam*); 27. Weeping (*al-Buka'*); 28. Change (*al-Taghyir*); 29. Contraction (*al-Qabd*); 30. Expansion (*al-Bast*); 31. Need for Seclusion (*al-Hajah ila al-Khalwah*);

32. Patience (*al-Sabr*); 33. Hope (*al-Amal*); 34. Jealousy (*al-Ghirah*); 35. Meeting (*al-Liqa'*); 36. Company (*al-Ma'iyyah*); 37. Comfort of the Eye (*Qurrat al-ʿAyn*).

(B) THE STAGES OF LOVE THAT OCCUR IN HUMAN BEINGS' LOVE FOR GOD ARE:

38. Love (*al-Wudd*); 39. Concern (*al-Shafaqah*); 40. Comfortable Familiarity (*al-Uns, al-Isti'nas*); 41. Peace (*al-Salam*); 42. Sufficiency (*al-Iktifa'*); 43. Gratitude or Thankfulness (*al-Shukr*); 44. Trust (*al-Tawakkul*); 45. 'Expansion of the Breast' (*Inshirah al-Sadr*); 46. 'Softening of Skin' (*Layn al-Jild*); 47. 'Softening of the Heart' (*Layn al-Qalb*); 48. 'Quivering of the Skin' (*Qashʿarirat al-Jild*); 49. 'Trembling of the Heart' (*Wajl al-Qalb*); 50. Devotion (*al-Tabattul*); 51. Humble Obedience (*al-Ikhbat*); 52. Turning in Penitence (*al-Inabah*); 53. Humility (*al-Tadarruʿ*); 54. Repentance (*al-Tawbah*); 55. Asking Forgiveness (*al-Istighfar*); 56. 'Hastening to Please' (*al-ʿAjal lil-Tardiyah*); 57. Calling upon or Supplication (*al-Duʿa'*); 58. Remembrance (*al-Tadhakkur*); 59. Following (*al-Ittibaʿ*); 60. 'Proving what is in the Heart' (*Tamhis al-Qalb*); 61. Uncertainty (*al-Shakk*); 62. Doubt (*al-Rayb*); 63. Entertaining Thoughts (*al-Zhann*); 64. Looking (*al-Nazhar*); 65. Contemplation (*al-Tafakkur*); 66. Meditation (*al-Tadabbur*); 67. 'Using Reason' (*Istiʿmal al-ʿAql*); 68. Perception (*al-Tabassur*); 69. Certainty (*al-Yaqin*): Certain Knowledge (*ʿIlm al-Yaqin*); Certain Vision (*ʿAyn al-Yaqin*); Certain Truth (*Haqq al-Yaqin*); 70. Ardent Hope (*al-Tamaʿ*); 71. Need for Human Company (*al-Hajah ila al-Jalwah*); 72. Imploring or Tender-heartedness (*al-Taʿawwuh*); 73. Penitence (*al-Awb*); 74. Devoutness (*al-Qunut*); 75. Being Overwhelmed (*al-Qahr*); 76. Submission (*al-Islam*); 77. Faith (*al-Iman*); 78. Virtue (*al-Ihsan*); 79. Sincerity (*al-Ikhlas*).

(C) THE STAGES OF LOVE THAT OCCUR IN HUMAN BEINGS' LOVE FOR EACH OTHER ARE:

80. Love (*al-Mahabbah*); 81. 'The Presence of (physical) Beauty' (*Wujud al-Jamal*); 82. Mutual Knowledge (*al-Taʿaruf*); 83. Inclination (*al-Mayl*); 84. Affection (*al-Mawaddah*); 85. Pity (*al-Raʾfah*); 86. Lust (*al-Shahwah*); 87. Impulse (*al-Hawa*); 88. Desire (*al-Hamm*); 89. Pleasure (*al-Mutʿah*); 90. Enjoyment (*al-Istimtaʿ*); 91. Generosity (*al-Karam*); 92. Mercy (*al-Rahmah*); 93. Tenderness (*al-Lutf*); 94. Forgiveness (*al-Maghfirah, al-Ghufran*); 95. Pardoning (*al-ʿAfu*); 96. Overlooking (*al-Safh*); 97. Kindness (*al-Maʿruf*); 98. Seduction (*al-Murawadah*); 99. Shyness (*al-Istihya'*); 100. Obliviousness to Oneself (*ʿAdam al-Ihsas bil-Hal*).

Thus, in its totality, human love is composed of (at least) all of these one hundred stages, because human love is what happens within a person when he or she loves, not what happens to the object of his or her love. We cannot say with certainty that these are all the stages of love that are mentioned in the Holy Qur'an, and that no others could be found therein. However, we trust that the stages we have mentioned constitute most of the main stages of love. As such they provide a definite idea of how love develops, and thus also of what happens when someone falls in love. We will discuss this further God willing in the following chapter (23): Falling in Love.

A Question: What is the difference between human love for God, and human love for other human beings?

Answer: There are several differences between these two forms of love.

The first difference is that human love for God is more ardent: '...*but those who believe love God more ardently...*' (*Al-Baqarah*, 2:165).

Another difference is that the two highest faculties which God has given to human beings—the 'inner heart' (*fu'ad*) and the 'heart's core' (*lubb*)—play no part in the love which exists between human beings. Indeed, we mention, in Chapter 23: Falling in Love, that the 'heart's core' (*lubb*) is 'without fault, blindness or doubt', and requires no strengthening, and is always in a state of devotion, remembrance and insight, for God says: '*that they who have cores may remember*' (Sad, 38:29). Thus human love for other human beings does not reach or involve the heart's core, because this kind of love is subject to change and difference. As regards the 'inner heart' (*fu'ad*), its nature means that although it may require 'strengthening', it nevertheless innately inclines towards the good and possesses vision, for God says: '*The inner heart denied not what it saw*' (Al-Najm, 53:11). Thus human love for other human beings does not reach or involve the inner heart (*fu'ad*) either, because human love for other human beings does not involve the vision of the inner heart as illuminated by God's light (as does love for God). As regards the heart as such (*qalb*) and the lower faculties of the breast and the soul, they participate in both love for God and love for other human beings; and God knows best.

As regards sexual love (love involving the human body), it is obviously completely different from human love for God. However, when those who truly love God remember Him, their hearts, their minds, their limbs, their skin and, indeed, every atom in their bodies trembles, quivers, softens or expands (as we have seen in the stages of human love for God). In this sense, even the body is involved in human love for God. This is reflected—and God knows best—in God's words: *Say: 'My prayer and my rituals, and my living, and my dying, are all for God, the Lord of the Worlds. No associate has He. And to this, I have been commanded, and I am the first of those who submit'*. (Al-An'am, 6:162)

CHAPTER TWENTY-THREE

FALLING IN LOVE

THE CONSTITUENT PARTS AND FACULTIES OF HUMAN BEINGS

In order to understand what falling in love is, we must first understand what human beings as such are, as falling in love is something that occurs within—and *to*—human beings. Indeed, it is illogical to seek to understand the actions of something without first understanding the thing itself.

Human beings are composed of three main parts: the body, the soul, and the spirit. The body is individual and physical; the soul is individual but subtle (supra-physical); and the spirit is supra-individual and supra-physical.

(A) THE BODY (*AL-JISM*):
God mentions people's bodies in the Holy Qur'an, saying:

> Then their prophet said to them, 'Verily God has raised up Saul for you as king'. They said, 'How can he be king over us when we have better right than he to kingship, seeing he has not been given amplitude of wealth?' He said, 'God has chosen him over you and has increased him broadly in knowledge and body. God gives the kingship to whom He will'; and God is Embracing, Knowing. (Al-Baqarah, 2:247) ❋ And when you see them, their figures (ajsamuhum) please you; and if they speak, you listen to their speech. [Yet] they are like blocks of timber [that have been] propped-up. They assume that every cry is [directed] against them. They are the enemy, so beware of them. May God assail them! How can they deviate? (Al-Munafiqun, 63:4)

Bodies obviously have senses, such as hearing and sight. God says: *The lightning well-nigh snatches away their sight; whensoever it gives them light, they walk in it; and when the darkness is over them, they stop; had God willed, He would have taken away their hearing and their sight; Truly, God has power over all things.* (Al-Baqarah, 2:20)

God alludes to the other bodily senses, namely taste, smell and touch. In the following two verses, God alludes to taste as such:

> And a tree that grows on Mount of Sinai that produces oil and seasoning for those who eat. (Al-Mu'minun, 23:20) ❋ And on the earth are tracts neighbouring each other, and gardens, of vines and sown fields, and date-palms sharing one root, and date-palms otherwise, watered by the same [source of]

water; and We make some of them to excel others in flavour. Surely in that are signs for a people who understand. (Al- Ra'd, 13:4)

And God mentions touch in the following verse:

> O you who believe, draw not near to prayer, whilst you are inebriated, until you know what you are saying, nor whilst you are defiled, unless you are traversing a way, until you have washed yourselves. But if you are sick, or on a journey, or if any of you comes from the privy, or you have touched women; and you can find no water, [then] wholesome soil, and wipe your faces and your hands [with it]. God is ever Pardoning, Forgiving. (Al-Nisa', 4:43)

And God alludes to smell in the following verse: *And grain with husk, and fragrant herb (rayhan). (Al-Rahman, 55:12)* 'Fragrant herb' ('rayhan') here means: 'a plant with a pleasant smell'.[294]

(B) THE SOUL (AL-NAFS):

God speaks of three 'kinds' or 'parts' of the soul, namely: 'the soul which incites to evil' ('al-nafs al-ammarah bil-su''), 'the self-reproaching soul' ('al-nafs al-lawammah') and 'the soul at peace' ('al-nafs al-mutma'innah'). God says: *Yet I do not exculpate my own soul; verily the soul is ever inciting to evil, except that whereon my Lord has mercy. Truly my Lord is Forgiving, Merciful'. (Yusuf, 12:53) And, nay, I swear by the (self-)reproaching soul. (Al-Qiyamah, 75:2) O soul at peace! (Al-Fajr, 89:27)*[295]

And God speaks of the human soul's faculties; He speaks of the intelligence ('aql):

> Are you then so eager that they should believe you, seeing there is a party of them that heard God's word, and then tampered with it, and that, after they had comprehended it knowingly? (Al-Baqarah, 2:75) ❋ Will you bid others to piety and forget yourselves, while you recite the Book? Do you not use your intelligence? (Al-Baqarah, 2:44) ❋ And they will say, 'Had we listened or used our intelligence, we would not have been among the inhabitants of the Blaze'. (Al-Mulk, 67:10)

And God speaks of the human capacity (to imitate and) learn (ta'lim): *Recite: and your Lord is the Most Generous, / who taught by the pen / taught man what he did not know. (Al-'Alaq, 96:3–5)*

And God speaks of the human faculty of speech (kalam):

> He said, 'Adam, tell them their names'; And when he had told them their names He said, 'Did I not tell you that I know the Unseen in the heavens and the earth?, And I know what you reveal and what you were hiding. (Al-Baqarah, 2:33) ❋ The Compassionate One / has taught the Qur'an. / He created man, / teaching him [coherent] speech. (Al-Rahman, 55:1–4)

And God speaks of human beings' will or desire (iradah) (and it will be remembered from Chapter 21: The Different Kinds of Love that *iradah* is a kind of love): *And whoever wills for the Hereafter and strives for it with the necessary effort, being a believer—for such their effort will find favour. (Al-Isra', 17:19)*

And God speaks of human sentiments (*'atifah*), as we just saw in the last two Chapters (21: The Different Kinds of Love and 22: The Stages of Love), for love is a sentiment in addition to being '*an inclination towards beauty after having been pleased by it*'. God says:

> O you who believe, whoever of you apostatises from his religion, God will assuredly bring a people whom He loves and who love Him: humble towards believers, stern towards disbelievers, struggling in the way of God, and fearing not the reproach of any reproacher. That is God's favour; He gives it to whom He will; and God is Embracing, Knowing. (Al-Ma'idah, 5:54)

And God speaks of human memory (*dhakirah*): *And he of the two who was released, remembering after a time, said, 'I will inform you of its interpretation; so send me forth'. (Yusuf, 12:45)*

And God speaks of human imagination (*khayal*): *He said, 'Nay, you cast!', and lo! their ropes and their staffs made him imagine, by their sorcery, that they were gliding swiftly. (Ta Ha, 20:66)*

And God speaks of human intuition (*ihsas*): *O my sons, go and intuit and enquire (tahassasu) about Joseph and his brother, and do not despair of God's [gracious] Spirit. Indeed none despairs of the [gracious] Spirit of God save the disbelieving folk'. (Yusuf, 12:87)*

And God speaks of human feelings (*shuʿur*): *Their reckoning is only my Lord's concern, if you could but feel it. (Al-Shuʿara', 26:113)*

And God speaks of human 'sense' (*inas*):

> So when Moses had completed the term and was travelling with his family, he saw in the distance on the side of the Mount [Tur] a fire. He said to his family, 'Wait, I sense a fire in the distance. Maybe I will bring you from it news or a brand from the fire, that you may warm yourselves'. (Al-Qasas, 28:29) ❈ When Moses said to his family, 'Assuredly I sense a fire. I will bring you news from there, or bring you a firebrand that perhaps you might warm yourselves'. (Al-Naml, 27:7)

And God speaks of human insight (*basira*):

> Clear insightful proofs have come to you from your Lord; whoever perceives (absara), then it is for his own good; and whoever is blind, then it will be to his own hurt. And I am not a keeper over you. (Al-Anʿam, 6:104) ❈ And when the Prophet confided to one of his wives a certain matter; but when she divulged it and God apprised him of it, he announced part of it, and passed over part. So when he told her about it, she said, 'Who told you this?' He said, 'I was told by the Knower, the Aware'. (Al-Tahrim, 66:3) ❈ He said: 'I complain of my anguish and grief only to God, and I know from God what you do

not know. / O my sons, go and enquire about Joseph and his brother, and do not despair of God's [gracious] Spirit. Indeed none despairs of the [gracious] Spirit of God save the disbelieving folk'. (Yusuf, 12:86–87)[296]

We have already seen (in Chapter 12: Humanity's Love for God; in the section on: What Intentions and Motives Human Beings must have in loving God) that the three main faculties of the soul are the will, sentiment and the intelligence. Accordingly, it could be said that the faculty of speech is part of—or an extension of—the will and of the intelligence; human feelings are part of—or an extension of—sentiment; the faculty of learning (and imitation) is part of—or an extension of—the intelligence; that 'sense' 'connects' the soul to the body; that intuition and insight 'connect' the soul to the spirit; and that memory and the imagination connect the soul to the past and the future respectively, and God knows best.

(C) THE SPIRIT (AL-RUH):

God says that He breathed *of His Spirit* into the first man: *Then He proportioned him, and breathed into him of His Spirit. And He made for you hearing, and sight and hearts. Little thanks do you give.* (Al-Sajdah, 32:9)

However, one cannot hope to mentally know very much about the spirit, because God says: *And they will question you concerning the Spirit. Say: 'The Spirit is of the command of my Lord. And of knowledge you have not been given except a little'.* (Al-Isra', 17:85)

God also speaks of other elements of man, namely: (1) the breast (*sadr*); (2) the heart (*qalb*); (3) the inner heart (*fu'ad*), and (4) the heart's core (*lubb*). These elements seem to lie somewhere between the soul and the spirit.

(1) The breast (*sadr*) is the seat of unbelief and misgivings, but also the seat of 'expansion'. God says:

Whoever disbelieves in God after [having affirmed] his faith—except for him who is compelled, while his heart is at rest in faith—but he who opens up his breast to unbelief, upon such shall be wrath from God, and there is a great chastisement for them. (Al-Nahl, 16:106) ❋ *From the evil of the slinking whisperer, / who whispers in the breasts of mankind, / of the jinn and mankind.* (Al-Nas, 114:4–6) ❋ *Whomever God desires to guide, He expands his breast to Islam; and whomever He desires to send astray, He makes his breast narrow and constricted, as if he were engaged in ascent to the heaven. So, God casts ignominy over those who do not believe.* (Al-An'am, 6:125)

(2) The heart (*qalb*) may be blind, and filled with doubt and rancour; but it may also be filled with faith, tranquillity and peace. God says:

> Have they not travelled in the land so that they may have hearts with which to comprehend, or ears with which to hear? Indeed it is not the eyes that turn blind, but it is the hearts that turn blind within the breasts. (Al-Hajj, 22:46) ❉ They alone ask leave of you who do not believe in God and the Last Day, and whose hearts are doubtful, so in their doubt they waver. (Al-Tawbah, 9:45) ❉ And those who will come after them say, 'Our Lord, forgive us and our brethren who preceded us in [embracing] the faith, and do not place any rancour in our hearts toward those who believe. Our Lord, You are indeed Kind, Merciful!' (Al-Hashr, 59:10) ❉ The Bedouins say, 'We believe'. Say: 'You do not believe; but rather say, "We have submitted"; for faith has not yet entered into your hearts'. Yet if you obey God and His Messenger, He will not diminish for you anything of your deeds. God is indeed Forgiving, Merciful. (Al-Hujurat, 49:14) ❉ He it is Who sent down the Sakinah into the hearts of the believers, that they might add faith to their faith. And to God belong the hosts of the heavens and the earth. And God is ever Knower, Wise. (Al-Fath, 48:4)

(3) The inner heart (*fu'ad*) may be empty and may require 'strengthening'. It innately tends towards the good in believers, although it inclines towards the bad in disbelievers. However, it possesses (inward, spiritual) vision, for God says:

> And the inner heart of Moses's mother became empty. Indeed she was about to expose him had We not fortified her heart that she might be of the believers (Al-Qasas, 28:10) ❉ And all that We relate to you of the accounts of the messengers, that with which We might strengthen your inner heart. And in these, there has come to you the Truth and an admonition and a reminder to the believers. (Hud, 11:120) ❉ And those who disbelieve say, 'Why has the Qur'an not been revealed to him all at once?' Thus, [it is], that We may strengthen your inner heart with it, and We have arranged it in a specific order. (Al-Furqan, 25:32) ❉ Our Lord, indeed I have made some of my seed to dwell in a valley where there is no sown land, by Your Sacred House; our Lord, that they may establish prayer. So make some of the inner hearts of men yearn towards them. And provide them with fruits, that they might be thankful. (Ibrahim, 14:37) ❉ And that the inner hearts of those who do not believe in the Hereafter may incline to it, and that they may be pleased with it, and that they may acquire what they are acquiring. (Al-An'am, 6:113) ❉ As they come hastening with their heads turned upwards, their gaze returning not to them, and their inner hearts as air. (Ibrahim, 14:43) ❉ The inner heart denied not what it saw. (Al-Najm, 53:11)

(4) The heart's core (*lubb*) is completely free of fault, blindness and doubt. It requires no strengthening; it is always in a state of devotion and remembrance, and it possesses insight. God says:

> Say: 'The evil and the good are not equal, even though the abundance of the evil attract you'. So fear God, O you who have cores, that you might prosper.

(Al-Ma'idah, 5:100) ❋ *The Pilgrimage is in months well-known; whoever undertakes the duty of Pilgrimage during them, then no lewdness, nor wickedness, or disputing in the Pilgrimage. Whatever good you do, God knows it. And take provision. But the best provision is piety; and fear you Me, O you who have cores!* (Al-Baqarah, 2:197) ❋ *He gives wisdom to whomever He will, and he who is given wisdom, has been given much good; yet none remembers save they who have cores.* (Al-Baqarah, 2:269) ❋ *This is a Proclamation for mankind, and so that they may be warned thereby, and that they may know that He is One God, and that they who have cores may remember.* (Ibrahim, 14:52) ❋ *A Book that We have revealed to you, full of blessing, that they may meditate [upon] its signs and that they who have cores may remember.* (Sad, 38:29)

Clearly, the heart (*qalb*) is higher and purer than the breast (*sadr*); and the inner heart (*fu'ad*) is higher and purer than the heart; and the heart's core (*lubb*) is higher and purer than the inner heart. Clearly also, the breast, heart, inner heart and heart's core are not physical realities, but metaphysical realities that lie between the soul and the spirit. Thus the breast and the soul share avarice in common; God says:

And if a woman fears from her husband ill-treatment or rejection, they are not at fault if they are reconciled through some agreement; reconciliation is better. But avarice has been made present in the souls. If you are virtuous and fear, surely God is ever aware of what you do. (Al-Nisa', 4:128) ❋ *And those who had settled in the hometown, and [had abided] in faith before them, love those who have emigrated to them, and do not find in their breasts any need of that which those [others] have been given, but prefer [others] to themselves, though they be in poverty. And whoever is saved from the avarice of his own soul, those—they are the successful.* (Al-Hashr, 59:9) ❋ *So fear God as far as you can, and listen, and obey and expend; that is better for your souls. And whoever is shielded from the avarice of his own soul, such are the successful.* (Al-Taghabun, 64:16)

Similarly, the heart's core and the spirit share spiritual knowledge and secrets; God says:

Exalter of ranks, Lord of the Throne, He casts the Spirit of His command upon whomever He wishes of His servants, that he may warn them of the Day of Encounter. (Ghafir, 40:15) ❋ *O my sons, go and enquire about Joseph and his brother, and do not despair of God's [gracious] Spirit. Indeed none despairs of the [gracious] Spirit of God save the disbelieving folk'.* (Yusuf, 12:87)

And God knows best.[297]

THE SECRET OF FALLING IN LOVE

Having identified and discussed the parts and faculties of human beings, we can now, God willing, understand the secret of falling in love, and what happens in all the stages of love (as mentioned in Chapter 22: 'The Stages of Love'). First, however, it will be noticed that all of the one hundred stages of love apply and refer back to one or more of the parts and faculties of human beings in the following way:

(1) The body: *pleasure, enjoyment, suffering, 'the quivering of the skin', 'softness of skin', obliviousness to oneself.*
(2) The soul: *emptiness, neediness, trial, grief, suffering, weeping, change, contraction, expansion, need for seclusion, need for company, imploring (tender-heartedness), being overwhelmed.*
(3) The 'soul that incites evil': *seduction.*
(4) The 'self-reproaching soul': *generosity, mercy, tenderness, forgiveness, pardon, overlooking, kindness, shyness, devotion, humble obedience, turning in penitence, humility, repentance, seeking forgiveness, penitence, devoutness.*
(5) The 'soul at peace': *tranquillity, peace, sufficiency, gratitude, trust.*
(6) The intelligence: *knowledge, recognition, doubt, uncertainty, thought, looking, contemplation, meditation, 'using reason', mutual knowledge.*
(7) The faculty of learning and imitation: *following.*
(8) The faculty of speech: *communion.*
(9) The will: *action, will, fear, patience, hope, jealousy, 'hastening to please', supplication.*
(10) Sentiment: *admiration, inclination, love (hubb, mahabbah and wudd), affection, contentment, concern, pity, drawing near, will, seeking, longing, protecting friendship, lust, impulse, desire, joy, hope, 'comfort of the eye', ardent hope.*
(11) Memory: *remembrance (dhikr and tadhakkur).*
(12) Imagination: *adornment.*
(13) Intuition: *'presence of beauty'.*
(14) Feeling: *pain, knowledge.*
(15) Sense: *certainty (certain knowledge), comfortable familiarity.*
(16) Insight: *insight, certainty (certain vision, certain truth).*
(17) The breast: *'softness of skin', submission.*
(18) The heart: *imploring (tender-heartedness), serenity, 'softness of heart', 'the trembling of the heart', 'proving what is in the heart', faith, looking.*
(19) The inner heart: *virtue, emptiness.*
(20) The heart's core: *sincerity.*
(21) The spirit: *'meeting'.*

From all this, a pattern emerges: all the stages of love apply, and refer perfectly to, all the constituent parts and faculties of human beings, and all the constituent parts and faculties of human beings become involved—each in their own way and according to their nature—in loving. In other words, everything that occurs in falling in love—from hope to fear; joy to jealousy; from contraction and the need for seclusion to expansion and the need for company; and from infatuation, desire and longing to grief, suffering and weeping—is a direct result of the process of the parts of the lover's body, soul or spirit becoming attached to his or her beloved. From this, we can discern and define what falling in love is: falling in love is *'the systematic inclination of a person's constituent parts and faculties towards beauty, after having been pleased by it'*. That is, falling in love means the inclination of, ultimately, every part of a person towards the beloved.

Falling in love may come about gradually, or it may be sudden, depending on the state of the lover and the nature of the beloved. It always, however, comes about in the same way and according to the same process, because the parts and faculties of human beings do not differ in essence from one person to another. And God says: *So set your purpose for religion, as a hanif—a nature given by God, upon which He originated mankind. There is no changing God's creation. That is the upright religion, but most people do not know.* (Al-Rum, 30:30)

Thus all the stages of love—be they pleasure, pain[298], fear, desire, sentiments, thoughts or whatever—are nothing but the workings of the body, soul and spirit's faculties as they incline towards, and attach themselves to, the object of love. Love requires all that is in human beings, and all the constituent parts and faculties of human beings must eventually participate in the inclination towards that person's beloved. This is the great secret of falling in love[299]; and God knows best.

A Question: What is the difference between human love for God, and the love of other beings and inanimate objects for God?

Answer: Human love for God is distinguished by the particular faculties which God has given to human beings (i.e. the soul, the spirit, the intelligence, the heart, the imagination, the will and so on, as we have just seen), whilst the love of other beings and inanimate objects for God is an innate and natural love which does not require the faculties particular to human beings. Human love also consists of stages and of different kinds of love, each one of these stages and kinds of love ultimately deriving from one or more of the faculties particular to human beings. These stages and kinds of love do not exist in the innate and natural love of inanimate objects for God. Thus, for example, angels have no physical bodies and yet they love God, and rocks have no hearts and yet they love God too. This is the difference between human love and the love of other beings, and it shows the central place of human love in relation to the universe's total love for God.

CHAPTER TWENTY-FOUR

THE GROWTH OF LOVE

HOW LOVE GROWS

How does love grow? By this, we mean: how does love strengthen, and become more profound and more ardent? God says:

> Yet there be people who take to themselves rivals besides God, loving them as God is loved; but those who believe love God more ardently. If those who did evil could but see, as they shall when they behold the chastisement, that power altogether belongs to God, and that God is terrible in chastisement. (Al-Baqarah, 2:165)

This verse shows that love comprises degrees, although the definition of love—'*inclination to beauty after being pleased by it*'—applies to all the different kinds and degrees of love. But why does love sometimes grow and become more ardent, and why does it sometimes not do so; and why does it sometimes fade and die?

We saw in Chapter 23: 'Falling in Love' that falling in love can be defined as: '*the systematic inclination of a person's constituent parts and faculties towards beauty, after having been pleased by it*'. This implies that love grows as a person's constituent parts and faculties gradually incline towards the beloved. Indeed, we see in the Holy Qur'an that human faculties nourish and strengthen one another when they share a common goal or object. Thus, sentiment can grow deeper through the will and the intelligence, just as the will can be strengthened through sentiment and the intelligence, and just as the intelligence can understand more through sentiment and the will. This is something that every teacher and every parent knows: a child who loves something, or a certain academic subject, understands it more easily than a child who does not love it. Similarly, a child who wants to understand something understands it more easily than a child who does not want to understand it. There are a number of examples of this psychological principle in the Holy Qur'an, such as the following:

Faith leads to the heart's guidance, hearing, obedience and 'ascendancy':

> No affliction strikes except by the leave of God. And whoever believes in God, He will guide his heart. And God is Knower of all things. (Al-Taghabun, 64:11) ⚬ The Messenger believes in what was revealed to him from his Lord, as do the believers; each one believes in God and His angels, and in His Books,

and His messengers, 'we make no distinction between any of His messengers'. And they say, 'We hear and obey; Your forgiveness, our Lord; to You is the homecoming'. (Al-Baqarah, 2:285) ❊ Faint not, neither grieve, for you shall be ascendant if you are believers. (Aal 'Imran, 3:139)*

Faith in God plus disbelief in idolatry together lead to a 'grasping of the firmest handle': *There is no compulsion in religion. Rectitude has become clear from error; so whoever disbelieves in false gods, and believes in God, has laid hold of the most firm handle, unbreaking; God is Hearing, Knowing. (Al-Baqarah, 2:265)*

Faith plus righteous deeds together lead to guidance and the absolution from sins:

Truly those who believe and perform righteous deeds, their Lord will guide them through their faith. Rivers will flow beneath them in the Gardens of Bliss. (Yunus, 10:9) ❊ The day when He will gather you for the Day of Gathering that will be the Day of Dispossession. And [as for] those who believe in God and act righteously, He will absolve them of their misdeeds and admit them into gardens underneath which rivers flow wherein they will abide. That is the supreme triumph. (Al-Taghabun, 64:9)

Faith plus fear of God or piety (*taqwa*) together lead to discernment or discrimination (between truth and falsehood) and an absolution of sins, and to a twofold portion of God's mercy:

O you who believe, if you fear God, He will grant you a [means of] discrimination, and absolve you of your evil deeds, and forgive you; and God is of tremendous bounty. (Al-Anfal, 8:29) ❊ O you who believe, fear God and believe in His Messenger, and He will give you a twofold portion of His mercy; and He will assign for you a light by which you will walk and forgive you; for God is Forgiving, Merciful. (Al-Hadid, 57:28)

Faith plus knowledge together lead to higher degrees (of spiritual knowledge):

O you who believe, when it is said to you, 'Make room' during the assembly, then make room; God will make room for you. And when it is said, 'Rise up', God will raise those of you who have faith and those who have been given knowledge by degrees. And God is Aware of what you do. (Al-Mujadilah, 58:11)

Fear of God or piety (*taqwa*) leads to knowledge, to 'a way out' and to provision:

…And fear God. God teaches you and God knows all things. (Al-Baqarah, 2:282) ❊ Then, when they have reached their term, retain them honourably, or separate from them honourably. And call to witness two just men from among yourselves, and bear witness for the sake of God. By this is exhorted whoever believes in God and the Last Day. And whoever fears God, He will make a way out for him; / and He will provide for him from whence he never

The Growth of Love

expected. And whoever puts his trust in God, He will suffice him. Indeed God fulfils His command. Verily God has ordained for everything a measure. (Al-Talaq, 65:2–3)

Fear of God plus hearing and obedience, plus expending for God, together shield a person against their soul's own avarice: *So fear God as far as you can, and listen, and obey and expend; that is better for your souls. And whoever is shielded from the avarice of his own soul, such are the successful.* (Al-Taghabun, 64:16)

Fear of God plus giving, plus affirming the truth of what is best, together lead to ease: *As for him who gives and is God-fearing, / and affirms the truth of the best [word], / We shall surely ease his way to [the abode of] ease.* (Al-Layl, 92:5–7)

Fear of God plus virtue together lead to God's being with us: *Truly God is with those who fear, and those who are virtuous.* (Al-Nahl, 16:128)

Virtue leads to knowledge and firm judgment: *And when he reached his prime We gave him [power of] judgement and knowledge. Thus, We reward those who are virtuous.* (Yusuf, 12:22)

Guidance leads to further guidance: *But those who are [rightly] guided, He enhances their guidance and invests them with fear [of Him].* (Muhammad, 47:17) *And fear God. God teaches you and God knows all things.* (Al-Baqarah, 2:282)

Fear of God (*taqwa*) leads to knowledge, and knowledge leads to fear of God (*khashiyat Illah*): *And of humans and beasts and cattle, there are diverse hues likewise. Indeed only those of God's servants who have knowledge fear Him. Truly God is Mighty, Forgiving.* (Fatir, 35:28)

Uprightness plus remembrance of God together lead to the descent of the angels with glad tidings, and to an absence of fear and grief:

> *Truly those who say, 'Our Lord is God!' and then remain upright, the angels descend upon them, [saying to them], 'Do not fear, nor grieve, and rejoice in the good tidings of the paradise which you were promised. / We are your friends in the life of this world, and in the Hereafter, and therein you will have whatever your souls desire, and therein you will have whatever you request, / as a hospitality from One Forgiving, Merciful'.* (Fussilat, 41:30–32)

Struggling for God's sake leads to guidance: *But as for those who struggle for Our sake, We shall assuredly guide them in Our ways, and truly God is with the virtuous.* (Al-ʿAnkabut, 29:69)

Conversely, sickness of the heart plus abominable conduct together lead to further abomination: *But as for those in whose hearts is sickness, it only adds abomination to their abomination, and they die while they were disbelievers.* (Al-Tawbah, 9:125)

As for love as such, God makes the following promise: *Truly those who believe and perform righteous deeds—for them the Compassionate One shall appoint love.* (Maryam, 19:96)

Thus faith plus righteous deeds together lead to love as a 'Divine appointment'. This perhaps explains why God cast 'a (special) love from Him' upon Moses ﷺ (for Moses ﷺ was to be full of faith and righteous deeds[300]): *'Cast him in the ark, then cast him into the river, and then the river shall throw him up onto the shore; [there] an enemy of Mine and an enemy of his shall take him'. And I cast upon you a love from Me and that you might be reared under My eyes.* (*Ta Ha*, 20:39)

Furthermore, love for God plus adherence to the *Sunnah* together lead to love from God. (Indeed, these two elements mean that the entire soul is beautiful because it follows the example of the Messenger of God ﷺ, who himself possessed '*a magnificent nature*' [*Al-Qalam*, 68:4]). God says: *Say: 'If you love God, follow me, and God will love you more, and forgive you your sins; God is Forgiving, Merciful.'* (*Aal 'Imran*, 3:31)

Thus love increases as the other faculties incline towards the beloved. Love for God increases when the *Sunnah* (and thus virtue) is adhered to. In this case, it is rewarded by God with an 'appointment' of love from Him; and God knows best.

HOW TO CONTROL ONE'S LOVE

If love increases as a person's soul—with all its constituent parts and faculties—inclines towards the beloved, then how can anyone deliberately and consciously cultivate a specific love and diminish another? In other words, how can a person choose and control what to love and what not to love? How can the will alone control the inclination of all the other faculties including the ego itself? Someone might want to refrain from loving something in which there is no good or no hope, and not know how to do so. Conversely, someone might want to love something wherein there is a great deal of good, but might not incline to it naturally. God says:

> *...Consort with them in kindness; for if you hate them, it may happen that you hate a thing wherein God has set much good.* (*Al-Nisa'*, 4:19) ❁ *Say: 'The evil and the good are not equal, even though the abundance of the evil attract you'. So fear God O you who have cores, so that you might prosper.* (*Al-Ma'idah*, 5:100) ❁ *Prescribed for you is fighting, though it be hateful to you. Yet it may happen that you hate a thing which is good for you; and it may happen that you love a thing which is bad for you; God knows, and you know not.* (*Al-Baqarah*, 2:216)

In a sense, the whole spiritual and moral life is about controlling what one loves and what one does not love, and so this question can be tremendously complex. Nevertheless, in the Holy Qur'an God speaks of particular keys that show how to more easily strengthen and weaken love as such.

The Growth of Love

Actually, strengthening a beneficial love for something good occurs naturally by means of faith and righteous deeds in general. As previously cited, God says: *Truly those who believe and perform righteous deeds—for them the Compassionate One shall appoint love.* (Maryam, 19:96)

This is thus very simple. The key to strengthening a beneficial love for something that is good is to perform righteous deeds and hence to behave virtuously. Virtue (or goodness—*ihsan*) is truly its own reward. God says: *Is the reward of goodness (ihsan) anything but goodness (ihsan)?* (Al-Rahman, 55:60)

On the other hand, weakening a love for something negative is not so easy. It is, nevertheless, possible with God's help. God says: *Will you bid others to piety and forget yourselves, while you recite the Book? Do you not understand? / Seek help in patience and prayer. For it is indeed hard, except to the humble (al-khashi'in), / who reckon that they shall meet their Lord, and that to Him they are returning.* (Al-Baqarah, 2:44–46)

Thus internal change is hard, but not impossible. It requires *a priori* some faith in God (*who reckon that they shall meet their Lord*), hope in Him and fear of Him (*and that to Him they are returning*). But in addition to faith, hope and fear (and we have already discussed—in Chapter 12: Humanity's Love for God—these three elements as the fundamental three motives that God accepts in loving Him, and indeed in all our actions) internal change then has need of three key virtues or practices, namely: (1) patience; (2) humility; (3) prayer and remembrance of God.

Taking humility ('key' no. 2) first, it must be said that true humility comes from self-knowledge; and self-knowledge requires, practically speaking, careful self-monitoring. God says: *Rather man has insight into his [own] soul, / though he should offer his excuses.* (Al-Qiyamah, 75:14–15)

Self-monitoring means that people must control what they let themselves indulge in. God says:

> *Like those before you, who were far mightier than you, and more abundant in wealth and children. They enjoyed their share. So you enjoy your share, just as those before you enjoyed their share, and you indulge [in vain talk], just as they indulged [in vain talk]. Those, their works have become invalid in this world and in the Hereafter; and those, they indeed are the losers.* (Al-Tawbah, 9:69) ❃ *Woe then on that day to the deniers, / those who indulge in vain talk.* (Al-Tur, 52:11–12)

Thus if a person's soul—with all its constituent parts and faculties—indulges in, and becomes attached to, a 'negative' object of love, then (if they truly wish to stop that harmful love) they must stop letting themselves indulge in it, and *a fortiori* stop thinking about it.

In order to do this they have to think about something else; or rather they have to pray and think of God ('key' no. 3). In particular, they have to remember God. God says:

> *Is it not time for those who believe that their hearts should be humbled to the remembrance of God and [to] what has been revealed of the truth, and that they should not be like those who were given the Scripture before? For the stretch of time was too long for them and so their hearts became hardened, and many of them are immoral.* (Al-Hadid, 57:16) ❖ *Recite what has been revealed to you of the Book, and maintain prayer; truly prayer prevents against lewd acts and indecency. And the remembrance of God is surely greater, and God knows what you do.* (Al-ʿAnkabut, 29:45) ❖ *And those who disbelieve say, 'Why has not some sign not been sent down upon him from his Lord?' Say: 'Indeed God sends astray whomever He will, and He guides to Him those who turn in repentance'; / those who believe and whose hearts are reassured by God's remembrance. Verily by God's remembrance are hearts made serene.* (Al-Raʿd, 13:27–28)

However, even though they start to remember God more, temptation and Satan's voice (inside themselves) will still assail them. God says:

> *'And tempt whomever of them you can with your voice, and rally against them your cavalry and your infantry, and share with them in wealth, and children, and make promises to them'. And Satan promises them nothing but delusion. / 'Truly as for My servants, you shall have no warrant'. And Your Lord suffices as a guardian.* (Al-Isra', 17:64–65) ❖ *God has cursed him. And he said, 'Assuredly I will take to myself an appointed portion of Your servants. And I will surely lead them astray, and surely I will fill them with desires; and surely I will command them and they will cut up the cattle's ears. And surely I will command them and they will change God's creation'. / And whoever takes Satan for a patron, instead of God, has surely suffered a manifest loss. He promises them, and fills them with desires; but what Satan promises them is only delusion.* (Al-Nisa', 4:118–120)

The evil voice of the 'slinking (inner) whisperer' *'who whispers in the breasts of mankind'* (Al-Nas, 114:5) is a powerful obstacle to the spiritual life. It can derail people's best efforts, if they give in to it. Thus the virtue of patience ('key' no. 1) is essential. Without patience and perseverance (the term *'sabr'* covers both concepts) in prayer and in the remembrance of God, there is no way—psychologically and spiritually speaking—to escape harmful and negative thoughts and desires. Indeed, human beings are inevitably caught internally between two alternatives: a 'demonic companion' (*qarin*), or the remembrance of God (*Allah*), who is the Most Compassionate (*Al-Rahman*), the Most Merciful (*Al-Rahim*). God says: *And whoever withdraws from the Remembrance of the Compassionate One, We assign for him a devil (qarin) and he becomes his companion.* (Al-Zukhruf, 43:36)

The Growth of Love

In order to extricate oneself from a negative or evil love, one must simply keep remembering God and invoking Him as much and as often as possible—if not constantly—and simply ignore temptations or negative thoughts. As regards ignoring temptations and negative thoughts, God says:

> ... Say: 'God', then leave them to play in their vain discourse. (Al-An'am, 6:91) ❊ Truly the God-fearing, when a visitation from Satan touches them, they remember, and then see clearly. (Al-A'raf, 7:201) ❊ O you who believe, do not let your possessions and your children divert you from the remembrance of God; for whoever does that—it is they who are the losers. / And expend of that with which We have provided you before death comes to any of you, whereat he will say, 'My Lord, if only You would reprieve me for a short time so that I might give charity and become one of the righteous!' (Al-Munafiqun, 63:9–10) ❊ But whoever disregards My remembrance, his shall be a straitened life. And on the Day of Resurrection We shall bring him to the assembly, blind. (Ta Ha, 20:124)

And as regards remembering God and invoking Him as much and as often as possible, God says:

> O you who believe! Remember God with much remembrance. / And glorify Him morning and evening. (Al-Ahzab, 33:41–42) ❊ And never say regarding something, 'I will indeed do that tomorrow', / without [adding], 'If God will'. And remember your Lord if you forget. And say, 'May be my Lord will guide me to [something] closer [in time] than this by way of guidance. (Al-Kahf, 18:23–24) ❊ Go, you and your brother with My signs, and do not flag in remembrance of Me. (Ta Ha, 20:42) ❊ When you have performed the prayer, remember God, standing and sitting and on your sides. Then, when you are reassured, observe the prayer, surely the prayer is for believers a prescription at specific times. (Al-Nisa', 4:103) ❊ Surely in the creation of the heavens and the earth, and in the alternation of night and day, there are signs for those who have cores. / Those who remember God, standing and sitting and on their sides, and contemplate the creation of the heavens and the earth: 'Our Lord, You have not created this in vain. Glory be to You! So guard us against the chastisement of the Fire. (Aal 'Imran, 3:190–191) ❊ And mention the Name of your Lord at dawn and with the declining of the sun. (Al-Insan, 76:25) ❊ And mention the Name of your Lord, and devote yourself [exclusively] to Him with complete devotion. (Al-Muzzammil, 73:8)[301] ❊ And restrain yourself along with those who call upon their Lord at morning and evening, desiring His Countenance; and do not let your eyes overlook them desiring the glitter of the life of this world. And do not obey him whose heart We have made oblivious to Our remembrance, and who follows his own whim, and whose conduct is [mere] prodigality. (Al-Kahf, 18:28)

Through constant remembrance of God[302]—with humility, and with patience and perseverance—it eventually becomes possible to overcome vain caprice (*hawa*), restrain lusts, false loves and worldly desires. And God will help the God-fearing with an unexpected *way out: ... And whoever fears God, He will make a way out for him; / and He will provide for him from whence he never expected. And whoever puts his trust in God, He will suffice him. Indeed God fulfils His command. Verily God has ordained for everything a measure.* (Al-Talaq, 65:2–3)

Then love becomes love for the good, and love for the good is always beneficial to the lover. Indeed, sincerely loving what is good and not loving what is evil leads to Paradise and Salvation. God says: *But as for him who feared the stance before his Lord, and forbade the soul from [pursuing] desire, / Paradise will indeed be the abode.* (Al-Nazi'at, 79:40–41)

CHAPTER TWENTY-FIVE

THE TWO CIRCLES OF LOVE

We saw in the last chapter (Chapter 24: The Growth of Love) that love grows through the inclination and movement of all the constituent parts and faculties of a person towards the beloved. We also saw, conversely, that sickness of the heart and abominable conduct lead to further abominations. But what happens after this love grows, or this abomination increases? God says: *God is the Protector of the believers; He brings them forth from the shadows into the light. And the disbelievers—their protectors are false deities that bring them forth from the light into the shadows; those are the inhabitants of the Fire, therein they shall abide.* (Al-Baqarah, 2:257)

It will be observed in this verse that the state in which believers begin is, surprisingly, one of shadows—'*He brings them forth from the shadows*'—in comparison with what awaits them: '*into the light*'. Disbelievers, on the other hand, begin, equally surprisingly, in a state of light—'*bring them forth from the light into the shadows*'—in comparison with what awaits them: '*into the shadows*'. Thus believers are initially in darkness, and disbelievers are initially in light, despite the fact that '*God is the Protecting Friend of the believers*', and that '*the disbelievers—their protectors are false deities*'. This may be represented as follows (see right):

What does this mean? The answer is contained within the very same verse: God takes believers out of the shadows into the light, which means that they will be in a state of light *relative to* the shadows in which they were. Thus believers ascend from what seems like shadows *relative to* the light into which they ascend, but this does not mean that the shadows of believers are darker than the light of disbelievers. Similarly, in the case of disbelievers, they begin in what seems like light *relative to* the shadows into which they fall, but this does not mean that the light of disbelievers is brighter than the shadows of believers.[303]

A similar situation can be seen in God's words:

> *There has already been a sign for you in two hosts that met; one company fighting in the way of God; and another unbelieving; they saw them, twice the like of them; for God*

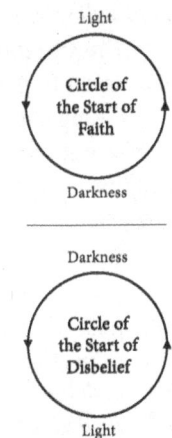

(Believers start at the bottom of the higher circle, and disbelievers start at the bottom of the lower circle.)

confirms with His help whom He will. Surely in that is a lesson for people of vision'. / Adorned for mankind is love of lusts—of women, children, stored-up heaps of gold and silver, horses of mark, cattle, and tillage. That is the comfort of the life of this world; but God—with Him is the most excellent abode. / Say: 'Shall I tell you of something better than that? For those that are fearful with their Lord are Gardens underneath which rivers flow, abiding therein, and spouses purified, and beatitude from God; and God is Seer, of His servants. / Those who say: "O, Our Lord, we believe; so forgive us our sins, and guard us from the chastisement of the Fire"'. (Aal 'Imran, 3:13–16)

In these verses, too, there are two hosts which can be represented by two circles: the circle of faith, God's love, paradise, purified spouses and beatitude; and the circle of love for the life of this world, embodied by love of lusts and preferring them to obeying God. These two circles represent the two hosts who fought one another, one of them composed of believers fighting in God's cause, and the other composed of disbelievers.

From all this, it is clear that both believers and disbelievers are in a state of constant increase of their own situation. Believers are always ascending and attaining ever higher degrees; and the opposite is true for disbelievers: they are constantly sinking to lower and lower levels. What is meant here by 'believers' are the most sincere believers who have not adulterated their faith and obedience with disobedience and mortal sins.[304] Likewise, what is meant by 'disbelievers' here are those who have not done any righteous deeds. The state of those who mix faith with hypocrisy, or faith and obedience with some sin, is different. They are those of whom God says: *And [there are] others, who have confessed their sins; they have mixed a righteous deed with another that was bad. It may be that God will relent to them. Truly God is Forgiving, Merciful.* (Al-Tawbah, 9:102)

The situation of such people is not entirely clear, for '*It may be that God will relent to them*'.

Going back to those who truly believe and those who completely disbelieve, they are each in a state of continual increase of their states, as we have said. We see this in the true believers' continual increase of faith and love of God, or in their being rewarded twofold and more for their good deeds:

Surely God shall not wrong so much as the weight of an atom; and if it be a good deed, He will double it and give from Himself a great wage. (Al-Nisa, 4:40) ❋ *Nor is it your wealth or your children that will bring you near to Us in closeness, except for those who believe and act righteously: those, they shall have a twofold reward for what they did, and they shall be in the lofty abodes, secure.* (Saba, 34:37) ❋ *O you who believe, fear God and believe in His Messenger, and He will give you a twofold portion of His mercy; and He will assign for you a light by which you will walk and forgive you; for God is Forgiving, Merciful.* (Al-Hadid, 57:28)

Or in their being rewarded tenfold for their good deeds: *Whoever brings a good deed, shall receive tenfold the like of it, and whoever brings an evil deed shall only be requited the like of it; and they shall not be wronged.* (*Al-An'am*, 6:160)

Or in their being rewarded many times over:

Who is he that will lend God a loan that is good, and He will multiply it for him manifold? God straitens and enlarges; and to Him you shall be returned. (*Al-Baqarah*, 2:245) ❈ *Who is it that will lend God a goodly loan so that He may multiply it for him, and [so that] there may be for him a generous reward.* (*Al-Hadid*, 57:11) ❈ *Indeed men who give voluntary alms and women who give voluntary alms and [those of them] who have lent God a goodly loan, it will be multiplied for them and they will have a generous reward.* (*Al-Hadid*, 57:18) ❈ *If you lend God a good loan, He will multiply it for you and He will forgive you, and God is Appreciative, Forbearing,* (*Al-Taghabun*, 64:17)

Or in their being rewarded seven hundredfold: *The likeness of those who expend their wealth in the way of God is as the likeness of a grain of corn that sprouts seven ears, in every ear a hundred grains; so God multiplies for whom He will; God is Embracing, Knowing.* (*Al-Baqarah*, 2:261)

Or in their being rewarded beyond reckoning:

Decked out fair to the disbelievers is the life of this world; and they deride the believers; but those who fear shall be above them on the Day of Resurrection; and God sustains whomever He will beyond reckoning. (*Al-Baqarah*, 2:212) ❈ *You make the night to pass into the day and You make the day to pass into the night; You bring forth the living from the dead, and You bring forth the dead from the living, and You provide whom You will beyond reckoning'.* (*Aal 'Imran*, 3:27) ❈ *Her Lord accepted the child with gracious acceptance, and made her grow excellently, and Zachariah took charge of her. Whenever Zachariah went into the sanctuary, where she was, he found her with provisions. 'O Mary', he said, 'Whence comes this to you?' She said, 'From God. Truly God provides for whomever He will beyond reckoning'.* (*Aal 'Imran*, 3:37) ❈ *So that God may reward them for the best of what they did, and give them more out of His bounty; and God provides whomever He will beyond [any] reckoning.* (*Al-Nur*, 24:38) ❈ *Say: 'O servants of Mine who believe! Fear your Lord. For those who are virtuous in this world, there will be good, and God's earth is vast. Truly the steadfast will be paid their reward in full beyond any reckoning'.* (*Al-Zumar*, 39:10) ❈ *Whoever commits an evil deed shall not be requited except with the like of it; but whoever acts righteously, whether male or female, and is a believer—such shall be admitted into Paradise wherein they will be provided beyond any reckoning.* (*Ghafir*, 40:40)

Of course, God's love for believers and their loving Him as well are the best 'provision' or 'reward' imaginable to believers, so by *reward in full beyond any reckoning*, we may understand that God will grant the believers true love of

Him in addition to deeper faith in Him. The 'ascent' of believers is thus also a continuous increase of love—in addition to a continuous increase of faith—and hence may be called 'the higher circle of love'. In it, love of God beautifies the soul of the believer who then has a greater capacity to love, and this in turn leads to greater love and so on, indefinitely, in a self-perpetuating closed circle of ('higher') love. This circle is completely closed to disbelievers, and in it both love of God and faith in Him are rewarded with more love and faith, and this increased love and faith are then rewarded with yet more love and faith, and so on, 'beyond all reckoning'. God says: *Is the reward of goodness anything but goodness?* (Al-Rahman, 55:60) *For those who do good is the fairest reward and more; neither dust, nor ignominy shall overcome their faces. Those, they are the inhabitants of Paradise: therein they will abide.* (Yunus, 10:26)

As for disbelievers, God uses the phrase 'circle of evil' in connection with them as follows:

> *And so that He may chastise the hypocrites, men and women, and the idolaters, men and women, and those who make evil assumptions about God. Upon them is the circle of evil, and God is angry with them, and He has cursed them, and has prepared for them Hell—and it is an evil destination!* (Al-Fath, 48:6)

This constant and self-reinforcing falling is what we saw earlier in the case of adultery. Adultery—even if it involves a kind of love (as discussed in Chapter 19: Love and Extra-marital Sex)—nourishes the 'base' love which engendered it. This is seen in God's words: *And do not come [anywhere] near fornication. It is indeed an indecency and an evil way.* (Al-Isra', 17:32)

'*And an evil way*': the 'way' is evil because extra-marital sex makes fornicators sink deeper and deeper in fornication or adultery (this then becomes a 'way' and no longer a mere 'act'), and this ruins any chance of following a 'way' which leads to God and His love. Fornicators thus become trapped in a vicious 'circle of evil'. This no doubt explains the danger of looking too long at a member of the opposite sex outside the bounds of marriage. God says:

> *And tell believing women to lower their gaze and to guard their private parts, and not to display their adornment except for what is apparent, and let them draw their veils over their bosoms and not reveal their adornment, except to their husbands or their fathers, or their husbands' fathers, or their sons, or their husbands' sons, or their brothers, or their brothers' sons, or their sisters' sons, or their women, or what their right hands own, or such men who are dependant, not possessing any sexual desire, or children who are not yet aware of women's private parts. And do not let them thump with their feet to make known their hidden ornaments. And rally to God in repentance, O believers, so that you might be prosperous.* (Al-Nur, 24:31) ❋ *O Prophet! Tell your wives and daughters and the women of the believers to draw their cloaks closely over*

themselves. That makes it likelier that they will be known and not be molested. And God is Forgiving, Merciful. (Al-Ahzab, 33:59)

There are thus two closed, self-perpetuating circles of love: a higher one of licit love or love for God; and a lower circle of illicit love, or at least negative, love.

Since both of these circles are constantly increasing, does this mean that the lower circle attains the same level of ardour in love as the higher circle? No, because the beloved in the higher circle is God (or something good loved for God's sake), and love for God is always different to love for evil, however intense love for evil may become. God says:

Yet there be people who take to themselves rivals besides God, loving them as God is loved; but those who believe love God more ardently. If those who did evil could but see, as they shall when they behold the chastisement, that power altogether belongs to God, and that God is terrible in chastisement. (Al-Baqarah, 2:165)

In other words, however ardent love for something evil may become, it cannot attain the same strength as can love for God. Love for God can become immeasurable, because this kind of love ultimately comes from God Himself. God says: *'Cast him in the ark, then cast him into the river, and then the river shall throw him up onto the shore; [there] an enemy of Mine and an enemy of his shall take him'. And I cast upon you a love from Me and that you might be reared under My eyes. (Ta Ha, 20:39)*

A Question: Does love benefit the lover, or the beloved?

Answer: We saw above that 'higher' love leads naturally to an increase of high love, whilst 'lower' love leads naturally to an increase of lower love. This means that love either benefits or harms the lover according to his or her intention: 'higher' love increases the believer's faith and love—and this is certainly a benefit; whilst 'lower' love increases the sinner's unbelief and lust—and this is certainly detrimental.

This is counter-intuitive, for many people suppose that love benefits the beloved more than it benefits or harms the lover, as though love were a gift which is given by the lover to the beloved in order to benefit them. Yet in fact the object of love might not even know or be aware that someone loves them, even if they benefit from this love. For example, if someone loves a tree, does the tree know of this love, even if it benefits from the protection and the water the lover gives it? And the beloved might not want to be loved by the one who loves them (and this love might be harmful to them), as was the case with the

Prophet Joseph ﷺ, who preferred jail to the love of Potiphar's wife, and said: *He said, 'My Lord, prison is dearer to me than that to which they are urging me. And if You do not fend off their wiles from me, then I shall tend towards them and become of the ignorant.* (*Yusuf*, 12:33)

The upshot of this is that love always benefits or harms the lover according to the nature of the love; and the beloved might benefit or be harmed, or indeed might not be affected at all. And God knows best.

CHAPTER TWENTY-SIX

THE TRIANGLE OF LOVE

WHY DOES LOVE REQUIRE PRIOR 'ADORNMENT'?

We saw previously (in Chapter 22: The Stages of Love) that 'adornment' is a stage of love, and that human love for God and human love for other human beings both require that the object of love be adorned *a priori* in the sight, mind, soul or heart of the lover. We cited the following verses, and alluded to others:

> *Adorned with beauty for mankind is love of lusts—of women, children, stored-up heaps of gold and silver, horses of mark, cattle, and tillage. That is the pleasure of the life of this world; but God—with Him is the most excellent abode.* (Aal 'Imran, 3:14) ❉ *Nay, but you thought that the Messenger and the believers would never return to their families, and that [thought] was adorned in your hearts, and you thought evil thoughts, and you were a ruined lot.* (Al-Fath, 48:12) ❉ *Said he, 'My Lord, because You have led me astray, I shall adorn for them [evil acts] in the earth and I shall lead them astray, all of them.* (Al-Hijr, 15:39) ❉ *And know that the Messenger of God is among you. If he were to obey you in many matters, you would surely be in trouble. But God has endeared faith to you, adorning your hearts with it, and He has made odious to you disbelief and immorality and disobedience. Those, they are the right-minded.* (Al-Hujurat, 49:7) ❉ *Adorned with beauty to the disbelievers seems the life of this world; and they deride the believers; but those who fear shall be above them on the Day of Resurrection; and God sustains whomever He will beyond reckoning.* (Al-Baqarah, 2:212)[305]

The question that arises here is: why does love require prior adornment? God says:

> *And when your Lord took from the Children of Adam, from their loins their seed and made them testify against themselves, 'Am I not your Lord?' They said, 'Yea, indeed we testify', lest you should say on the Day of Resurrection, 'Truly, of this we were unaware'.* (Al-A'raf, 7:172)

This verse[306] shows that all human beings were given an innate knowledge of God's existence even during Adam's ﷺ creation, and thus long before they came into existence in this world. This verse also shows that innate knowledge exists in the soul—or perhaps the spirit—of every human being. However, when a person is born, he or she does not have knowledge of anything else or any 'thing' in particular. God says: *And God brought you forth from the bellies of your mothers while you did not know anything, and He gave you hearing and sight and hearts that perhaps you might give thanks.* (Al-Nahl, 16:78)

There are perhaps exceptions[307] to this verse—and natural principle—such as Jesus Christ ﷺ, who spoke to the people whilst still in his cradle. God says:

When God said, 'O Jesus, son of Mary, remember My favour to you and to your mother, when I strengthened you with the Holy Spirit to speak to people in the cradle and in maturity and when I taught you the Scripture, and wisdom, and the Torah, and the Gospel; and how you create out of clay the likeness of a bird by My permission, and you breathe into it and it becomes a bird by My permission, and you heal the blind and the leper by My permission, and you raise the dead by My permission; and how I restrained the Children of Israel from you, when you brought them clear proofs, and the disbelievers among them said, "This is nothing but manifest sorcery". (Al-Ma'idah, 5:110)[308]

Humanity in general, on the other hand, has no knowledge when they are born. However, as we discussed previously (in Chapter 23: Falling in Love), every normal person has the ability to learn and imitate. Since they know nothing when they are born, they do not know what the different kinds of beauty are, nor which they should love more. Thus human beings require things to be 'adorned' for them beforehand—or rather, *in them*—before they can love them.

Thus God adorns beauty of faith in believers' hearts. God says:

And know that the Messenger of God is among you. If he were to obey you in many matters, you would surely be in trouble. But God has endeared faith to you, adorning your hearts with it, and He has made odious to you disbelief and immorality and disobedience. Those they are the right-minded. (Al-Hujurat, 49:7)

Conversely, Satan adorns the beauty of the life of this world in order to deceive people:

Said he, 'My Lord, because You have lead me astray, I shall adorn for them [evil acts] in the earth and I shall lead them astray, all of them. (Al-Hijr, 15:39) ❈ *And thus, those associates of theirs have adorned for many of the idolaters the slaying of their children that they may destroy them and to confuse their religion for them. Had God willed, they would not have done so; so leave them and that which they fabricate.* (Al-An'am, 6:137) ❈ *And that Satan adorned their deeds for them and said: 'Today no person shall overcome you, for I shall be your protector'. But when the two armies sighted each other, he turned his back in flight, saying, 'I am quit of you, for I see what you do not see. I fear God; and God is severe in retribution'.* (Al-Anfal, 8:48) ❈ *By God, We verily sent to communities before you [messengers]. But Satan adorned for them their deeds. So he is their patron today, and for them there will be a painful chastisement.* (Al-Nahl, 16:63) ❈ *I found her and her people prostrating to the sun instead of God, and Satan has adorned for them their deeds*

The Triangle of Love

and he has barred them from the Way, so that they are not guided. (Al-Naml, 27:24) ❋ *And 'Ad, and Thamud, it is indeed evident to you from their [former] dwellings. For Satan adorned for them their deeds, and thus barred them from the Way, though they had been discerning. (Al-'Ankabut, 29:38)* ❋ *And We have assigned them companions, who have adorned for them that which is before them, and that which is behind them. And the word became due against them, being among communities that passed away before them of jinn and mankind. Truly they were losers. (Fussilat, 41:25)*

It seems—and God knows best—that even the Satanic adornment of things is part of human nature, since the adornment of disbelievers' evil deeds is also from God, through the people's own souls. God says:

Truly those who do not believe in the Hereafter, We have adorned their deeds for them, and so they are bewildered. (Al-Naml, 27:4) ❋ *Is he, the evil of whose deeds is made [to seem] fair to him, so that he deems it good [...]? Indeed God leads astray whomever He will and guides whomever He will. So do not let your soul expire through woes for their sake. Indeed God is Knower of what they do. (Fatir, 35:8)* ❋ *Is he who follows a clear sign from his Lord like those whose evil deeds have been adorned for them, and who follow their desires? (Muhammad, 47:14)*

Howbeit, whatever the kind of love in question, it requires prior adornment. Moreover, since human beings love by means of prior adornment, we can say that people (at the beginning of love, at least) do not love their beloveds directly as much as they love the prior adornment itself that causes them to love. Thus love, in its development stage, forms a triangle, which may be represented as follows:

In this triangle, we see that at the beginning of love, the lover loves an adorned image (in his or her mind, soul or heart) of the beloved as much as he or she loves the 'beloved' in reality. Thus the lover loves the beloved through a particular (internal) image that he or she has formed of this beloved, regardless

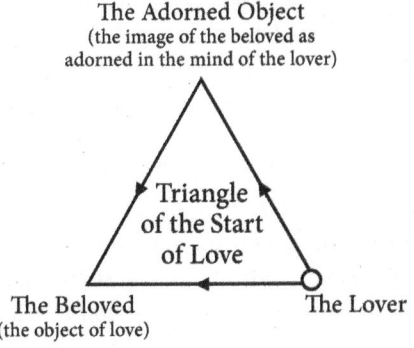

The Adorned Object
(the image of the beloved as adorned in the mind of the lover)

Triangle of the Start of Love

The Beloved
(the object of love)

The Lover

of whether this image truly represents the reality of the beloved or not. In other words, the lover does not at first really know his / her beloved; the lover loves the beloved because he or she imagines that their beloved is identical to an internal image they already love, whether it is so in reality or not. This is the meaning of the arrows in the diagram above. This explains how people can fall in love with other people or things without truly knowing them: they love the image they have in their minds as much as they love the reality of the objects of their love; and they might not even know the things they love at all, but imagine that they do know them because of the love they feel towards the images they hold of them.

For example, let us suppose that a man named 'Qays' is the lover (on the bottom right of the triangle); that a woman named 'Layla' is his beloved (on the bottom left of the triangle); and that the image of Layla in Qays' mind is at the apex of the triangle. The triangle then shows that Qays loves the image he has of Layla as much as he loves Layla herself as how she really is. The image Qays has of Layla is what kindles his love for her, because he does not really know the true reality of Layla (at least at first). Once Qays finds out who Layla truly is (by becoming better acquainted with her) his love for her may diminish if he finds that she is not like the adorned image he has of her in his mind. Indeed, many a love dies when the truth about the beloved is discovered!

This triangle is, broadly speaking, an accurate representation of the beginning of love, when there is a certain degree of 'separation' between the lover and the beloved. Sometimes—for example, where lusts are concerned—the beloved is more than one degree of separation away. God says: *Adorned for mankind is love of lusts—of women, children, stored-up heaps of gold and silver, horses of mark, cattle, and tillage. That is the pleasure of the life of this world; but God—with Him is the most excellent abode.* (Aal 'Imran, 3:14)

In this verse, we see that between humanity and '*women, children, stored-up heaps of gold and silver, horses of mark, cattle, and tillage*', there are at least two degrees of separation: the first is the adornment, the second is the love, and the third is the lust; or perhaps adornment is the first degree of separation, and the 'love of lusts' as such is the second. In other words, people love lusts themselves—or perhaps they even love to love lusts, through prior adornment—before they actually love the '*women, children, stored-up heaps of gold and silver, horses of mark, cattle, and tillage*' themselves.

The point here is: firstly to show that this kind of love has no connection, necessarily, with reality itself; and secondly to show that we are able to inhibit this kind of love by forestalling its prior adornment, as mentioned previously (in Chapter 23: Falling in Love). Indeed, this is something Muslims are obligated to do, for God says (as already cited): *But as for him who feared the stance before*

The Triangle of Love

his Lord, and forbade the soul from [pursuing] desire, / Paradise will indeed be the abode. (Al-Nazi'at, 79:40–41)

A Question: Is a person really 'separated' from his or her beloved even where love for God is concerned? In other words, do we really love God, or are we only really loving what we imagine to be God?

Now, we know that God is Near:

> And when My servants question you concerning Me, I am Near; I answer the call of the caller when he calls to Me; so let them respond to Me, and let them believe in Me that they might go aright. (Al-Baqarah, 2:186) ❊ To God belong the East and the West; whithersoever you turn, there is the Face of God. Lo! God is Embracing, Knowing. (Al-Baqarah, 2:115)

And we know that there is something in human beings which bears witness to the Truth of God: *And when your Lord took from the Children of Adam, from their loins their seed and made them testify against themselves, 'Am I not your Lord?' They said, 'Yea, indeed we testify', lest you should say on the Day of Resurrection, 'Truly, of this we were unaware'. (Al-A'raf, 7:172)*

But we also know that human beings cannot perceive God with their physical eyesight: *Vision cannot encompass Him, but He encompasses [all] vision. And He is the Subtle, the Aware. (Al-An'am, 6:103)*

So how can someone love what he or she cannot perceive? God gives the answer to this question in the Holy Qur'an when He says:

> And know that the Messenger of God is among you. If he were to obey you in many matters, you would surely be in trouble. But God has endeared faith to you, adorning your hearts with it, and He has made odious to you disbelief and immorality and disobedience. Those, they are the right-minded. (Al-Hujurat, 49:7)

In this verse, we see that people first love God through the faith which God adorns for them in their hearts. After this, they begin to come to know God and His Names and Qualities (which hitherto they knew only by name, without understanding their true realities) through God's acts and signs. God says, in the story of Joseph ﷺ in the Holy Qur'an: *Verily in Joseph and his brethren are signs for those who inquire. (Yusuf, 12:7) … We raise by degrees whom We will; and above every man of knowledge is one who knows better. (Yusuf, 12:76)*

But how exactly does this happen? How do human beings come to know God?

HOW DO HUMAN BEINGS COME TO KNOW GOD?

God alludes to twelve categories of His acts and signs by which believers can come to know Him, in Joseph's short prayer:

> *My Lord, indeed You have given me [something] of sovereignty and You have taught me the interpretation of events. Originator of the heavens and the earth! You are my Protecting Friend in this world and the Hereafter. Take me [in death] to You in submission [to You] and join me to the righteous.* (*Yusuf*, 12:101)

Believers, then, begin to know God: first, by faith in God (this is implied in the supplication '*My Lord,*') ; second, by humility (this is implied in calling God '*Lord,*'—for even the devil believes in God, but he has no humility); third, by gratefully considering the blessings God has given them ('*indeed You have given me [something] of sovereignty*'); fourth, through the visions with which God graces His creatures ('*and You have taught me the interpretation of events*'); fifth, by contemplating nature and its beauty, majesty and design ('*Originator of the heavens and the earth*')[309]; sixth, by appreciating God's love for them ('*You are my Protecting Friend*'); seventh, by meditating upon—or at least recognising—God's Qualities and Names in every moment and situation, and their effects upon themselves ('*You are my Protecting Friend in this world and the Hereafter*'); eighth, by pondering the reality of death and everyone's helplessness in the face of death ('*Take me [in death] to You*'); ninth, by submission (*islam*) to God and consequently by performing righteous acts ('*in submission [to You] and join me to the righteous*')[310]; tenth, by the experience of supplication and prayer itself (for this verse is itself a prayer) and in particular by prayer in isolation (and we saw in Chapter 12: Humanity's Love for God, how going to jail was lovable to Joseph because of the beauty of remembrance of God in solitude); eleventh, by observing how God answers prayers (and evidently this is implicit in Joseph's very supplication) and determines destinies; and, twelfth and finally—and this is inherent in the act of reading this verse of the Holy Qur'an—through God's Scripture, and thus *a fortiori*, through the Holy Qur'an. In short, knowledge of God increases through faith, humility, love, good deeds, and meditating and contemplating upon everything inside the soul and the world. In other words, knowledge of God grows in a similar way to love of God: by the gradual exercise and concentration of the heart and soul and all their many faculties and constituent parts upon the object of knowledge—or rather, upon the Object of knowledge. Thus after recognising God's acts and signs in these twelve ways, believers begin to have more knowledge of God and His Names and Qualities, and thus begin to love God more 'directly', or at least with a lesser degree of 'separation'; and God knows best.

The Triangle of Love

In addition to the above, if believers possess sufficient virtue, God will begin to grace them with a special kind of (spiritual) knowledge 'from Himself'. Thus Joseph ﷺ—who was *among the virtuous* (*Yusuf*, 12:26)—*saw the proof of his Lord* (*Yusuf*, 12:24), and received God's *mercy Yusuf*, 12:56):

> *And there entered the prison with him two youths. One of them said: 'I dreamed that I was pressing wine'. The other said: 'I dreamed that I was carrying on my head bread whereof the birds were eating. Tell us its interpretation, for indeed we see you as being among the virtuous'.* (*Yusuf*, 12:26) ◉ *Thus, We established Joseph in the land that he may settle in it wherever he wished. We confer Our mercy on whomever We will and We do not waste the wage of the virtuous.* (*Yusuf*, 12:56)

The same was true of his father, Jacob ﷺ, who knew *from God* what others did not: *He said: 'I complain of my anguish and grief only to God, and I know from God what you do not know. / O my sons, go and enquire about Joseph and his brother, and do not despair of God's [gracious] Spirit. Indeed none despairs of the [gracious] Spirit of God save the disbelieving folk'.* (*Yusuf*, 12:86–87)

It was also true of Noah ﷺ who said: *I convey to you the messages of my Lord, and I am advising you, for I know from God what you know not.* (*Al-A'raf*, 7:62)

And of course it was true with the Messenger of God ﷺ himself, even down to domestic details of his life. God says: *And when the Prophet confided to one of his wives a certain matter; but when she divulged it and God apprised him of it, he announced part of it, and passed over part. So when he told her about it, she said, 'Who told you this?' He said, 'I was told by the Knower, the Aware'.* (*Al-Tahrim*, 66:3)

This special knowledge that comes from God to His prophets and messengers is not, however, reserved exclusively for prophets and messengers, for it was also given to Khadir (and this means it can also be given to other people who are not prophets but saints [*awliya'*], since, unlike prophecy, sanctity has not ended). God says: *So [there] they found one of Our servants to whom We had given mercy from Us and We had taught him knowledge from Us.* (*Al-Kahf*, 18:65)

Ibn Kathir says in his *Tafsir* that many Muslim scholars[311] do not consider Khadir a prophet: 'And many opine that he was not a prophet, but a saint; and God knows best.'[312]

Thus God refers to those believers who are not prophets but have particular 'awareness' of Him: *Who created the heavens and the earth and all that is between them in six days, then presided upon the Throne. The Compassionate One. So ask about Him anyone who is well aware (khabir).* (*Al-Furqan*, 25:59)

Perhaps there is also an allusion to 'special knowledge' from God in the '*witness from Him*' which God mentions in His words:

> *Is he who relies on a clear proof from his Lord—[a clear proof] which is followed by a witness from Him. [—] and before it was the Book of Moses as an*

example and a mercy? Those they believe in it; but he who disbelieves in it of the partisans, the Fire shall be his appointed place. So do not be in doubt concerning it. Truly it is the Truth from your Lord, but most of humankind do not believe. (Hud, 11:17)

We understand 'special knowledge' from God, particular 'awareness' of Him and '*witness from Him*' to be spiritual knowledge—knowledge that comes through the Spirit. Moreover, though we know comparatively little[313] about the Spirit, we do know that God may cast it upon whom He wills, thereby giving knowledge from Him. God says:

He sends down the angels with the Spirit of His command to whomever He will of His servants, [saying]: Warn that there is no God save Me: so fear Me (Al-Nahl, 16:2) ❊ *Exalter of ranks, Lord of the Throne, He casts the Spirit of His command upon whomever He wishes of His servants, that he may warn them of the Day of Encounter.* (Ghafir, 40:15) ❊ *O my sons, go and enquire about Joseph and his brother, and do not despair of the [gracious] Spirit of God. Indeed none despairs of the [gracious] Spirit of God save the disbelieving folk'.* (Yusuf, 12:87)

In summary: love and virtue increase knowledge, just as knowledge and virtue increase love—and this is just what we saw in Chapter 24: The Growth of Love. After knowledge of the Beloved and virtue increase, love becomes direct and no longer acts through the triangle of adornment. This is no doubt why Joseph ﷺ expressed his love for God by saying (with direct knowledge of God): '*You are my Protecting Friend in this world and the Hereafter*' (*Yusuf*, 12:101). And God knows best.

CHAPTER TWENTY-SEVEN

THE HIERARCHIES OF BEAUTY AND OF LOVE

We said previously (in Chapter 25: The Two Circles of Love) that there are two circles of love: a higher circle and a lower circle; a circle of love for good, and a circle of love for evil. However, we said that God placed beauty in everything He created, for He says: *Who beautified everything that He created. And He began the creation of man from clay.* (Al-Sajdah, 32:7)

So if beauty is in all things, and if love is love whatever its object, then why is one kind of love better than another, and why is one kind of beauty better than another? In what follows, we will give and explain the answers to these two questions, God willing.

THE LEVELS AND HIERARCHIES OF BEAUTY

As just cited, God put beauty in all that He created, for He says: *Who beautified everything that He created. And He began the creation of man from clay.* (Al-Sajdah, 32:7)

Moreover, God is *the best of creators*—and thus the most beautiful, and beauty-giving—of creators:

> *Then We transformed the drop [of semen] into a clot. Then We transformed the clot into a [little] lump of flesh. Then We transformed the lump of flesh into bones. Then We clothed the bones with flesh. Then We produced him as [yet] another creature. So blessed be God, the best of creators!* (Al-Mu'minun, 23:14)

God's Names and Qualities are 'the Most Beautiful (*Husna*) Names', for God says:

> *Say: 'Invoke God or invoke the Compassionate One, whichever you invoke, to Him belong the Most Beautiful Names': And do not be loud in your prayer, nor be silent therein, but seek between that a way.* (Al-Isra', 17:110) ❖ *And to God belong the Most Beautiful Names—so invoke Him by them, and leave those who blaspheme His Names. They will be requited for what they did.* (Al-A'raf, 7:180) ❖ *God—there is no god save Him. To Him belong the Most Beautiful Names.* (Ta Ha, 20:8)

God speaks of the beauty of His Book, the Holy Qur'an:

> *Is he whose breast God has opened to Islam, so that he follows a light from his Lord [like he who disbelieves]? So woe to those whose hearts have been hardened against the remembrance of God. Such are in manifest error. / God*

has revealed the most beautiful of discourses, a Book, consimilar in coupled phrases—whereat quiver the skins of those who fear their Lord; then their skins and their hearts soften to the remembrance of God. That is God's guidance, by which He guides whomever He wishes; and whomever God leads astray, for him there is no guide. (Al-Zumar, 39:22–23)

And God speaks about the beauty of the most beautiful story, which is in fact contained in His Holy Book, and is the story[314] of Joseph ﷺ, from which we have cited so many times whilst discussing love. God says: *We will relate to you the most beautiful of stories in what We have revealed to you this Qur'an, though prior to it you were of the heedless.* (Yusuf, 12:3)

God also speaks of the beauty of being in solitude, praying to God (as discussed in Chapter 12: Humanity's Love for God):

So when you are empty, strive hard (fa'nsab). / And long for (fa'rghab) your Lord. (Al-Sharh, 94:7–8) ❊ *And mention the Name of your Lord, and devote yourself [exclusively] to Him with complete devotion. / Lord of the east and the west; there is no god except Him, so take Him for a Guardian (Wakil), / and bear patiently what they say, and part with them in a beautiful manner (hajran jamilan). (Al-Muzzammil, 73:8–10)*

And God speaks of the beauty and virtue of His Messenger ﷺ:

Verily there is for you a good (hasana) example in the Messenger of God for whoever hopes for [the encounter with] God and the Last Day, and remembers God often. (Al-Ahzab, 33:21) ❊ *O People of the Scripture, now there has come to you Our Messenger, making clear to you much of what you used to conceal of the Scripture, and pardoning much. There has verily come to you from God a light, and a Book, lucid. (Al-Ma'idah, 5:15)* ❊ *O Prophet! Indeed We have sent you as a witness, and as a bearer of good tidings, and as a warner, / and as a summoner to God by His leave, and as a illuminating lamp. (Al-Ahzab, 33:45–46)* ❊ *Verily there has come to you a messenger from among yourselves for whom it is grievous that you should suffer; who is full of concern for you, to the believers full of pity, merciful. (Al-Tawbah, 9:128)*

And God speaks of the beauty of the Hereafter:

And whatever things you have been given are [only] the [short-lived] enjoyment of the life of this world and an ornament thereof; and what is with God is better and more lasting. Will you not understand? (Al-Qasas, 28:60)

And God speaks of the beauty of the virtues, such as patience:

And they came with false blood on his shirt. He said: 'Nay, but your souls have beguiled you into something. Yet beautiful patience! And God is the One Whose succour is sought in that [predicament] which you describe'. (Yusuf, 12:18) ❊ *'Nay,' he said, 'but your souls have beguiled you into something. Yet beautiful patience! It may be that God will bring them all [back] to me. Indeed*

He is the Knower, the Wise'. (Yusuf, 12:83) ❂ *So be patient with a beautiful patience. (Al-Maʿarij, 70:5)*

And generosity:

O you who believe if you marry believing women and then divorce them before you have touched them, there shall be no [waiting] period for you to reckon against them. But provide for them and release them in a beautiful manner. (Al-Ahzab, 33:49) ❂ *O Prophet! Say to your wives: 'If you desire the life of this world and its adornment, come [now], I will provide for you and release you in a beautiful manner. (Al-Ahzab, 33:28)*

And God speaks of the virtues of the believers—and thus their beauty—in many verses, including:

Muhammad is the Messenger of God, and those who are with him are hard against the disbelievers, merciful among themselves. You see them bowing, prostrating [in worship]. They seek favour from God and beatitude. Their mark is on their faces from the effect of prostration. That is their description in the Torah, and their description in the Gospel is as a seed that sends forth its shoot and strengthens it, and it grows stout and rises firmly upon its stalk, delighting the sowers, so that He may enrage the disbelievers by them. God has promised those of them who believe and perform righteous deeds forgiveness and a great reward. (Al-Fath, 48:29)

God also says (of believers' virtue):

Do not marry idolatresses until they believe; a believing slavegirl is better than an idolatress, though you may admire her. And do not marry idolaters, until they believe. A believing slave is better (ahsan) than an idolater, though you may admire him. Those call to the Fire; and God calls to Paradise and pardon by His leave; and He makes clear His signs to the people so that they might remember. (Al-Baqarah, 2:221)

And God speaks of the beauty of the human form and image:

He created the heavens and the earth with the truth, and He shaped you and made your shapes excellent; and to Him is the journey's end. (Al-Taghabun, 64:3) ❂ *God it is Who made for you the earth as a [stable] abode and the heaven as a canopy. And He formed you and perfected your forms, and provided you with [all] the wholesome things. That then is God, your Lord, so blessed be God, the Lord of the Worlds. (Ghafir, 40:64)* ❂ *Verily We created man in the best of forms. (Al-Tin, 95:4)*

And God also speaks of the beauty of women in particular:

And do not extend your glance toward what We have given to some pairs among them to enjoy, [as] the flower of the life of this world that We may try them thereby. And your Lord's provision is better and more enduring. (Ta Ha, 20:131) ❂ *Women are not lawful for you beyond that, nor [is it lawful] for you to change them for other wives, even though their beauty impress you, except those whom your right hand owns. And God is Watcher over all things. (Al-Ahzab, 33:52)* ❈ *And tell believing women to lower their gaze and to guard their private parts, and not to display their adornment except for what is apparent, and let them draw their veils over their bosoms and not reveal their adornment, except to their husbands or their fathers, or their husbands' fathers, or their sons, or their husbands' sons, or their brothers, or their brothers' sons, or their sisters' sons, or their women, or what their right hands own, or such men who are dependant, not possessing any sexual desire, or children who are not yet aware of women's private parts. And do not let them thump with their feet to make known their hidden ornaments. And rally to God in repentance, O believers, so that you might be prosperous. (Al-Nur, 24:31)*

And God speaks of the essential positive nature of physical beauty as such, and thus of the permissibility—and even the desirability—of self-adornment during spiritual acts (such as prayer), and natural acts (such as eating):

O Children of Adam! Don your adornment at every place of worship, and eat and drink, but do not be excessive; He truly does not love those who are excessive. / Say, 'Who has forbidden the adornment of God which He has brought forth for His servants, and the good things of [God's] sustenance?' Say: 'These, on the Day of Resurrection, shall be exclusively for those who believed during the life of this world. Thus We detail the signs for a people who know'. (Al-A'raf, 7:31–32)

And God alludes to the beauty of human speech and poetry: *As for the poets, [only] the perverse follow them. / Have you not noticed that in every valley they rove / and that they say what they do not do? (Al-Shu'ara', 26:224–226)*

And God even speaks of the beauty of animals: *And for you there is in them beauty, when you bring them [home] to rest, and when you drive them forth to pasture. (Al-Nahl, 16:6)*

And God speaks of the beauty—and hence tastiness—of food and drink:

… They said, 'Your Lord knows best how long you have tarried. Now send one of you with this silver coin of yours to the city, and let him see which is the purest food, and [let him] bring you a supply thereof. Let him be careful and not make anyone aware of you. (Al-Kahf, 18:19) ❈ *Nor are the two [kinds of] seas alike: this one is extremely sweet, pleasant to drink and that one is salty, extremely bitter. Yet from each, you eat fresh meat, and obtain ornaments which you wear. And you see the ships therein ploughing through that you may seek of His bounty, and that perhaps you may give thanks. (Fatir, 35:12)*

And God speaks of the beauty of the life of this world in general: *And whatever things you have been given are [only] the [short-lived] enjoyment of the life of this world and an ornament thereof; and what is with God is better and more lasting. Will you not understand? (Al-Qasas, 28:60)*

And God speaks of the splendour of material wealth:

And Moses said, 'Our Lord, You have indeed given Pharaoh and his council splendour and riches in the life of this world. Our Lord, that they may lead [people] astray from Your way. Our Lord, obliterate their riches and harden their hearts so that they do not believe until they see the painful chastisement'. (*Yunus*, 10:88)

And God speaks of how evil deeds are adorned to seem beautiful: *And We have assigned them companions, who have adorned for them that which is before them, and that which is behind them. And the word became due against them, being among communities that passed away before them of jinn and mankind. Truly they were losers.* (*Fussilat*, 41:25)

And God speaks of how even vile deeds such as infanticide and idolatry may be adorned to seem 'beautiful' (if indeed the term 'beauty' can be applied here at all): *And thus, those associates of theirs have adorned for many of the idolaters the slaying of their children that they may destroy them and to confuse their religion for them. Had God willed, they would not have done so; so leave them and that which they fabricate.* (*Al-An'am*, 6:137)

In summary, there are many different types of beauty in the different things God has created. How, then, can one know if there is hierarchy in these types of beauty? And how can one know which type of beauty is superior to which?

The answer is that God praises some kinds of love and condemns others, and He makes some superior to others and puts them in a hierarchical order. The worth of something's beauty can be known by the worth of the love by which it is loved. This will become clear in the following section, God willing.

THE HIERARCHY OF LOVE

God promises His love and His grace to the most virtuous:

O you who believe, whoever of you apostatises from his religion, God will assuredly bring a people whom He loves and who love Him: humble towards believers, stern towards disbelievers, struggling in the way of God, and fearing not the reproach of any reproacher. That is God's favour; He gives it to whom He will; and God is Embracing, Knowing. (*Al-Ma'idah*, 5:54)

And God makes it clear that love of Him is stronger and more ardent—or can be—than any other love:

Yet there be people who take to themselves rivals besides God, loving them as God is loved; but those who believe love God more ardently. If those who did evil could but see, as they shall when they behold the chastisement, that power altogether belongs to God, and that God is terrible in chastisement. (*Al-Baqarah*, 2:165)

God also makes it clear that love of Him and the love of His remembrance are better than any other love:

And We bestowed on David, Solomon—what an excellent servant! Truly he was a penitent [soul]. / When one evening there were displayed before him the light-footed coursers. / He said, 'Lo! I have loved the love of [worldly] good things over the remembrance of my Lord', until it disappeared behind the [night's] veil. (Sad, 38:30–32)

Of course, love of the remembrance of God, means, *a fortiori*, love of the Holy Qur'an ... *bearing the Remembrance (Sad, 38:1).* God says: *The believers are only those who, when God is mentioned, their hearts tremble, and when His verses are recited to them, they increase their faith, and who rely upon their Lord. (Al-Anfal, 8:2)*

Second to love of God; love of His Qur'an and love of His remembrance comes love for God's Messenger. God holds love for His Messenger ﷺ higher than people's love for their own selves:

The Prophet is closer to the believers than their [own] souls, and his wives are their mothers. And those related by blood are more entitled, [from] one another in the Book of God than the [other] believers and the Emigrants, barring any favour you may do your friends. This is written in the Book. (Al-Ahzab, 33:6)

After love for God's Messenger ﷺ, God shows that the people ought to love Paradise most:

Indeed God has purchased from the believers their lives and their possessions, so that theirs will be [the reward of] Paradise: they shall fight in the way of God and they shall kill and be killed; that is a promise which is binding upon Him in the Torah and the Gospel and the Qur'an; and who fulfils his covenant better than God? Rejoice then in this bargain of yours which you have made, for that is the supreme triumph. (Al-Tawbah, 9:111) ❋ *And their Lord answers them, 'I do not let the labour of any labourer among you go to waste, be you male or female—the one of you is as the other: and those who emigrated, and were expelled from their habitations, those who suffered hurt in My way, and fought, and were slain—them I shall surely absolve of their evil deeds, and I shall admit them to Gardens underneath which river flow'. A reward from God! And God—with Him is the fairest reward. (Aal 'Imran, 3:195)*

God also makes clear the virtue of love for faith:

And know that the Messenger of God is among you. If he were to obey you in many matters, you would surely be in trouble. But God has endeared faith to you, adorning your hearts with it, and He has made odious to you disbelief and immorality and disobedience. Those they are the right-minded; (Al-Hujurat, 49:7)

The Hierarchies of Beauty and of Love

God also praises love for believers:

And those who had settled in the hometown, and [had abided] in faith before them, love those who have emigrated to them, and do not find in their breasts any need of that which those [others] have been given, but prefer [others] to themselves, though they be in poverty. And whoever is saved from the avarice of his own soul, those—they are the successful. (Al-Hashr, 59:9)

God praises love for all that is good in general: *Say: 'The evil and the good are not equal, even though the abundance of evil attract you'. So fear God O you who have cores, so that you might prosper. (Al-Ma'idah, 5:100)*

And as we mentioned earlier, God speaks of certain kinds of love for (worldly) 'good things' (*khair*), but without praising them:

And We bestowed on David, Solomon—what an excellent servant! Truly he was a penitent [soul]. / When one evening there were displayed before him the light-footed coursers. / He said, 'Lo! I have loved the love of [worldly] good things over the remembrance of my Lord', until it disappeared behind the [night's] veil. (Sad, 38:30–32)

God also speaks of love for lusts, but makes it clear that the beauty of the Hereafter is better: *Adorned for mankind is love of lusts—of women, children, stored-up heaps of gold and silver, horses of mark, cattle, and tillage. That is the pleasure of the life of this world; but God—with Him is the most excellent abode. (Aal 'Imran, 3:14)*

God also condemns love for the life of this world:

No indeed! Rather you love the transitory [life] / and forsake the Hereafter. (Al-Qiyamah, 75:20–21) *Whoever desires the hasty world, We hasten for him therein whatever We wish, for whom We please. Then We appoint for him Hell, to which he will be exposed, condemned, and rejected. (Al-Isra', 17:18)*

God also condemns love for wealth: *And they love wealth with abounding love. (Al-Fajr, 89:20)*

Moreover, God warns against extra-marital sex and illicit love: *And do not come [anywhere] near fornication. It is indeed an indecency and an evil way. (Al-Isra', 17:32)*

Finally, God condemns idolatry and the love of false deities alongside God:

Yet there be people who take to themselves rivals besides God, loving them as God is loved; but those who believe love God more ardently. If those who did evil could but see, as they shall when they behold the chastisement, that power altogether belongs to God, and that God is terrible in chastisement. (Al-Baqarah, 2:165)

From all this—and other verses not cited here—we can clearly see the hierarchy of love, and how the different kinds of love are definitely ranked in worth, beginning with love of God and His Qur'an and remembrance; then His Messenger ﷺ; then Paradise; then faith; then the believers; then love for the good; then love for worldly good things; and then the lower levels of love, which are (from highest to lowest): love for lusts; love for the life of this world; then extramarital sex, and then, finally, love for those rivals which people set up alongside God. In other words, the best kind of love is love for God and for His Beautiful Names; and then consequently love for the Qur'an and the remembrance of Him; then love for the Messenger of God ﷺ; then love for Paradise; then love for a special kind of inner beauty (faith); then love for inner beauty in general (the believers; the good); then love for a special kind of outer beauty (beauty of the opposite sex); then love for natural beautiful things; then love for outer beauty in general (love for worldly good things); then the lower levels of love (from highest to lowest) are: love for lusts; love for evil; and then love for Satan.

This means, consequently, that the highest beauty is the Beauty of God and His Names; then His remembrance; then the beauty of the Messenger of God ﷺ; then the beauty of Paradise; then special inner beauty (faith); then general inner beauty (the believers; the good); then special outer beauty (beauty of the opposite sex); then natural beautiful things; then general outer beauty (love for worldly good things). And the lower levels of 'beauty', or rather the degrees of 'false adornment' (from highest to lowest) are: the adornment of lusts, the adornment of evil, and then the adornment of Satan. In other words, the highest beauty is Divine Beauty; then sacred beauty (starting with the beauty of the Messenger of God ﷺ); then inner beauty; then outer beauty; then inner lusts; then outer lusts. Through God's mention of these kinds of love and beauty throughout the Holy Qur'an, their hierarchy and descending order is made clear. Thus not every love is praiseworthy, and not every beauty should be loved, as we have seen.

The Messenger of God ﷺ implied this exact same hierarchy of love when he described the reasons why one should marry, in the following *Hadith*: 'A woman is married for four things: her wealth, her lineage, her beauty and her piety: so find success by choosing the pious woman!'[315]

'Wealth' is general, outer beauty; the 'beauty' of a woman is a special, outward beauty; 'lineage' is a general, inner beauty; and 'piety' is a special, inner beauty. It is as though the Messenger ﷺ were saying: 'Love means an inclination towards beauty, but love has a hierarchy: love for God is better than love for people; love for people is better than love for physical beauty; and love for physical beauty is better than love for wealth'. And God knows best.

CHAPTER TWENTY-EIGHT

THE OPPOSITES OF BEAUTY AND OF LOVE

THE OPPOSITE OF BEAUTY (UGLINESS AND VILENESS)

In the previous Chapter (Chapter 27: The Hierarchies of Love and Beauty), we saw that the hierarchy of beauty ranges from adorned love for false gods all the way up to love for God. If every existing thing has a beauty of some kind, how could beauty have an opposite? And if beauty does not have an opposite, then what is 'ugliness' or 'vileness'? If God has placed beauty in all that He has created, then where is the ugliness? As we have mentioned, God says: *Who beautified everything that He created. And He began the creation of man from clay.* (Al-Sajdah, 32:7)

Indeed, it may be observed that the word 'ugliness' (*basha'ah*) is not found in the Holy Qur'an at all, which indicates that everything in creation has some kind of beauty, even if some things are less beautiful than other things, according to the hierarchy of beauty as we have seen. Even the word 'vileness' (*qubh*)[316] is not used in the Holy Qur'an to describe anything which God has created, but is only used once, referring to how Pharaoh and his hosts will be viewed on the Day of Resurrection: *And We made a curse pursue them in this world, and on the Day of Resurrection they will be among the reviled.* (Al-Qasas, 28:42)

The vileness of Pharaoh and his hosts is not of God's doing as such, but of their own doing; and God does not say in the Holy Qur'an that He has ever brought anything vile into the universe He created. Thus we can conclude that ugliness or vileness is a privation or absence of beauty and not a thing in itself; and God knows best.

THE OPPOSITE OF LOVE (HATRED AND LOATHING)

We mentioned previously (in Chapter 7: God's Love for Humanity) that God does not hate anyone, but that He hates certain actions. However, God does say that believers hate evil things:

> *O you who believe, shun much suspicion. Indeed some suspicions are sins. And do not spy, nor backbite one another. Would any of you love to eat the flesh of his brother dead? You would abhor it. And fear God; assuredly God is Relenting, Merciful.* (Al-Hujurat, 49:12) ❋ *And know that the Messenger of God is among you. If he were to obey you in many matters, you would surely be in trouble. But God has endeared faith to you, adorning your hearts with*

it, and He has made odious to you disbelief and immorality and disobedience. Those they are the right-minded.* (Al-Hujurat, 49:7)

Conversely, disbelievers and evildoers hate the truth, and hate good things: *And that He might cause the truth to be realised and annul falsehood, however much the sinners hate it.* (Al-Anfal, 8:8)

They also hate God's light: *They desire to extinguish God's light with their tongues; and God refuses but to perfect His light, even though the disbelievers hate it.* (Al-Tawbah, 9:32)

They also hate the religion of truth: *He it is Who has sent His Messenger with the guidance and the religion of truth, that He may manifest it over every religion, even though the disbelievers hate it.* (Al-Tawbah, 9:32)

They hate striving in God's cause: *Those who were left behind rejoiced at remaining behind the Messenger of God, and hated to striving with their wealth and their lives in the way of God. And they said, 'Do not go forth in the heat!' Say: 'The fire of Hell is hotter, did they but understand'.* (Al-Tawbah, 9:81)

They hate the Holy Qur'an: *That is because they hate what God has revealed, so He has made their works fail.* (Muhammad, 47:9)

They even hate God's beatific pleasure or beatitude (*ridwan*): *That is because they followed what angers God, and [because] they hated His ridwan. Therefore He has made their works fail.* (Muhammad, 47:28)

They hate God's beatific pleasure even though God's beatific pleasure is greater than any other good thing for which human beings could strive. God says: *God has promised the believers, both men and women, Gardens underneath which rivers flow, to abide therein, and blessed dwellings in the Gardens of Eden, and beatitude from God is greater. That is the supreme triumph.* (Al-Tawbah, 9:72)

God also says that some of the People of the Scripture hate one another: *And with those who say: 'We are Christians', We made a covenant, and they have forgotten a portion of that they were reminded of. So We have stirred up among them enmity and hatred until the Day of Resurrection; and God will assuredly tell them of what they wrought.* (Al-Ma'idah, 5:14)

Satan would like to make the believers hate one another, too. God says: *Satan desires only to precipitate enmity and hatred between you through wine and games of chance and to bar you from the remembrance of God and from prayer. So will you then desist?* (Al-Ma'idah, 5:91)

Does all this mean, then, that believers only hate evil things, and disbelievers only hate good things? No, because—as we saw in Chapter 25: The Two Circles of Love—between those who have pure faith and those who are in pure unbelief there are those who combine the two: faith and the sins of disbelievers. God says: *And [there are] others, who have confessed their sins; they have mixed a righteous deed with another that was bad. It may be that God will relent to them. Truly God is Forgiving, Merciful.* (Al-Tawbah, 9:102)

The Opposites of Beauty and of Love

Since most people are guilty of some evil deeds, it follows that they must hate some of the things that are good for them. God says:

Prescribed for you is fighting, though it be hateful to you. Yet it may happen that you hate a thing which is good for you; and it may happen that you love a thing which is bad for you; God knows, and you know not. (Al-Baqarah, 2:216) ❋ *O you who believe, it is not lawful for you to inherit women against their will; neither debar them, so that you may go off with part of what you have given them, except when they commit flagrant lewdness. Consort with them in kindness; for if you hate them, it may happen that you hate a thing wherein God has set much good. (Al-Ma'idah, 5:19)*

By contrast, God's messengers and prophets—and the saints (*awliya*) who have overcome the avarice or pettiness (*shuhh*) of their souls—love good and hate evil. They have attained a state where they have no desire in their breasts for any worldly advantage, and thus they obey God unwaveringly:

And those who had settled in the hometown, and [had abided] in faith before them, love those who have emigrated to them, and do not find in their breasts any need of that which those [others] have been given, but prefer [others] to themselves, though they be in poverty. And whoever is saved from the avarice (shuhh) of his own soul, those—they are the successful. (Al-Hashr, 59:9) ❋ *So fear God as far as you can, and listen, and obey and expend; that is better for your souls. And whoever is shielded from the avarice (shuhh) of his own soul, such are the successful. (Al-Taghabun, 64:16)* ❋ *The Messenger believes in what was revealed to him from his Lord, and the believers; each one believes in God and His angels, and in His Books, and His messengers, 'we make no distinction between any of His messengers'. And they say, 'We hear and obey; Your forgiveness, our Lord; to You is the homecoming'. (Al-Baqarah, 2:285)*

In summary: hatred seems to depend on the state of the individual. The believers and the good hate evil, and disbelievers and the evil hate good, but it is possible that those believers who have not completely overcome the avarice of their souls (i.e. their egos) might love something that is bad for them or hate something that is good for them. This means that hatred in itself is not something blameworthy as such, and that it only becomes blameworthy in the case of those people who are themselves already blameworthy. Thus hatred emerges from love of sorts: believers hate evil because of their love for God, and disbelievers hate good because of their love for evil or their love for their own souls' avarice (i.e. because their egos hate goodness). In other words, hatred emerges from love of the thing opposite to what one hates. This means that even if hatred is the opposite of love in an emotional sense, nevertheless, like ugliness, it is not in itself a reality as such, but only an inverted mirror-image of love, which is why it seems ugly. And God knows best.

CHAPTER TWENTY-NINE

THE END OF LOVE

Does love end? If so, for whom? When? Why? And how? We will consider this question in three sections as follows:

GOD'S LOVE FOR HUMAN BEINGS

God's love for those of His creatures who are worthy to be loved (such as His messengers, prophets, saints and the righteous, as discussed in the Chapters 7: God's Love for Humanity and 8: God's Love for His Messengers and Prophets') never ends in itself because it is a Divine Quality (as we discussed in Chapter 4: God and Love), and God's Qualities are eternal and unchanging. God says:

> ...*There is none to change the words of God, and there has already come to you tidings of the messengers.* (Al-Anᶜam, 6:34) ❂ *Perfected is the word of your Lord in truthfulness and justice; none can change His words. He is the Hearing, the Knowing.* (Al-Anᶜam, 6:115) ❂ *Theirs are good tidings in the life of this world and in the Hereafter. There is no changing the Words of God; that is the supreme triumph.* (Yunus, 10:64) ❂ *And recite that which has been revealed to you of the Book of your Lord. There is none who can change His words. And you will not find, besides Him, any refuge.* (Al-Kahf, 18:27) ❂ *God's precedent with those who passed away before, and you will find that there is no changing God's precedent.* (Al-Ahzab, 33:62) ❂ ... *Yet you will never find any change in God's precedent, and you will never find any revision in God's precedent.* (Fatir, 35:43) ❂ *[That is] the way of God which has taken its course before, and you will never find in God's way any change.* (Al-Fath, 48:23) ❂ *The word [that comes] from Me cannot be altered, and I am not unjust to [My] servants.* (Qaf, 50:29) ❂ *[That is] the way in the case of those whom We have sent from among Our messengers before you. And as regards Our [established] way you will not find any change.* (Al-Isra', 17:77)

Thus God's love for people never changes and never ends, unless of course those loved by God change so much that they become evil and reject God's love. Even then, however, it is not God's love that changes, but rather they who have turned their backs on it. Thus God promises:

> *That is because God would never change a grace that He had conferred on a people, until they have changed that which is in themselves; and [know] that God is Hearing, Knowing.* (Al-Anfal, 8:53) ❂ ... *Indeed God does not*

alter the state of a people unless they have altered the state of their souls. ... (Al-Raʿd, 13:11)

HUMAN LOVE FOR GOD

Human beings' love for God is defined (as seen in Chapter 3: The Definition of Love) as '*an inclination towards beauty after having been pleased by it*'. Since God's Beauty is Eternal and Unchanging, this means that the only way a person's love for God will change is if that person changes, so that his or her love and inclination towards the Beloved, changes. However, as we will later see, God willing, (in Chapter 30: The Nature of Love) human beings are in a constant state of change. Thus God makes it clear in the Holy Qur'an that human beings' faith can change, increasing and decreasing, right up until the final moment of a person's life:

> ...*that they might add faith to their faith...* (Al-Fath, 48:4) ❈ ...*and We increased them in guidance.* (Al-Kahf, 18:13) ❈ *And God increases in guidance those who found [right] guidance...* (Maryam, 19:76) ❈ *But those who are [rightly] guided, He enhances their guidance and invests them with fear [of Him].* (Muhammad, 47:17) ❈ ...*That those who believe may increase in faith...* (Al-Muddathir, 74:31) ❈ ...'*Which of you has this increased in faith?' As for those who believe, it has increased them in faith and they rejoice.* (Al-Tawbah, 9:124) ❈ *Those to whom people said, 'The people have gathered against you, therefore fear them'; but that increased them in faith...* (Aal ʿImran, 3:173) ❈ ...*And that only increased them in faith and submission.* (Al-Ahzab, 33:22) ❈ ...*And when His verses are recited to them, they increase their faith...* (Al-Anfal, 8:2) ❈ ...'*Yes', he said, 'but so that my heart may be re-assured'...* (Al-Baqarah, 2:260)

If a person changes and his or her faith lessens, it follows that his or her love for God will also lessen. Similarly, if a person's faith increases, it follows that his or her love for God will also increase (and, indeed, we mentioned both of these possibilities in Chapters 24: The Growth of Love and 25: The Two Circles of Love). In summary, a person's love for God may change, not because his or her Beloved has changed (for God never changes), but because the person themself has changed, in heart and soul. Naturally, this also applies to the love a person feels 'for God's sake', such as the love the believers feel for the Messenger of God ﷺ, the Holy Qur'an, the remembrance of God, and other religious rites.

A person's love for God may come to an end altogether if that person becomes an outright disbeliever; yet even then, as we saw earlier (in Chapter 6: The Universe and Love), every part of his or her body and every atom in it will continue to love God (as long as it exists) with a natural innate love, despite his or her soul being veiled from loving God. We discussed previously that everything in existence loves God except the soul of disbelieving human beings; it remains to add here that the one thing whose love for God can possibly end is the soul of a disbelieving human being.

A Question: What is it that causes change in a person's state, faith, and love?

Answer: People's faith changes when their intentions and deeds change: if their intentions and deeds are righteous, their faith increases; and if their intentions and deeds are evil, their faith decreases. God says: *No indeed, but their earnings are even as rust over their hearts. (Al-Mutaffifin, 83:14)*

Similarly, it is reported that Hudhayfah ibn Yaman ؓ said that he heard the Messenger of God ﷺ say:

'Temptations come to hearts like the weave of a reed mat, stick by stick; the heart which imbibes them is marked with a black mark, and the heart which rejects them is marked with a white mark. So it is that there are at last two hearts: one white like a stone, which no temptation can harm as long as the heavens and the earth endure; the other black as soot, like an overturned jug, recognising no goodness and rejecting no evil, [recognising] only what it has imbibed of its own desire.' [317]

Abu Hurayrah ؓ reports that the Messenger of God ﷺ said:
'When the servant commits a sin, his heart is marked with a black mark; when he desists, seeks forgiveness and repents, his heart is cleansed; and when he persists, [the mark] grows, until it covers his whole heart. This is the rust of which God speaks: *No indeed, but their earnings are even as rust over their hearts. (Al-Mutaffifin, 83:14)*.' [318]

It will be observed that even some of those 'Friends of God' or 'saints' (*awliya*) who are not perfect might stumble from the path of faith and piety (such as the one mentioned in the following verses, whose name allegedly was Bal'am bin Ba'ura)[319]:

And recite to them the tidings of him to whom We gave Our signs, but he cast them off, and Satan pursued him, and he became of the perverse. / And had We willed, We would have raised him up, thereby; but he was disposed to the earth, and followed his whims. Therefore his likeness, is as the likeness of a dog: if you attack it, it lolls its tongue out, and if you leave it, it lolls its tongue out. That is the likeness of those people who deny Our signs. So recount the tale that they might reflect. (Al-A'raf, 7:175–176)

Even righteous believers must beware of committing sins and thereby causing their faith—and thus their love for God—to diminish; for Satan is always waiting for a chance to cause people to slip. God says:

And tell My servants to speak that which is finer. For Satan indeed incites ill feeling between them, and Satan is indeed man's manifest enemy. (Al-Isra', 17:53) ❂ *Said he, 'Do You see this one whom You have honoured above me?*

If You defer me to the Day of Resurrection I shall verily eradicate his seed, [all] save a few'. / Said He: 'Begone. Whoever of them follows you—indeed Hell shall be your requital, a requital [that is indeed] ample. / And tempt whomever of them you can with your voice, and rally against them your cavalry and your infantry, and share with them in wealth, and children, and make promises to them'. And Satan promises them nothing but delusion. (Al-Isra', 17:62–64) ❋ *Said he, 'Now, because You have sent me astray verily I shall sit in ambush for them on Your straight path.' (Al-A'raf, 7:16)* ❋ *Said he, 'My Lord, because You have lead me astray, I shall adorn for them [evil acts] in the earth and I shall lead them astray, all of them. (Al-Hijr, 15:39)* ❋ *He said, 'Now, by Your might, I shall surely pervert them all. (Sad, 38:82)* ❋ *And I will surely lead them astray, and surely I will fill them with desires; and surely I will command them and they will cut up the cattle's ears. And surely I will command them and they will change God's creation'. And whoever takes Satan for a patron, instead of God, has surely suffered a manifest loss. (Al-Nisa', 4:119)*

A lapse or a slip might be the result of a subtle and gradual process of temptation whose source one is not aware of. God says: *And those who deny Our signs, We will draw them on by degrees, whence they do not know. (Al-A'raf, 7:182) So leave Me [to deal] with those who deny this discourse. We will draw them on by degrees, whence they do not know. (Al-Qalam, 68:44)*

Thus there is no way for Muslims to protect themselves from this except to follow the Sacred Law of God (*Shari'ah*) and the example of God's Messenger ﷺ.

HUMAN LOVE FOR EVERYTHING OTHER THAN GOD

Human beings' love for everything other than God is (as we have seen) of the following kinds: (1) love for things; (2) love for lusts; (3) love for one's friends; (4) love for one's spouse; (5) love for one's family and relatives; (6) love for believers; (7) love for the People of the Scripture, and (8) love for all humanity.

As regards the last four kinds of love mentioned above (love for one's family and relatives; love for believers; love for the people of the Scripture, and love for all humanity), these kinds of love are influenced by one's love for God, because God exhorts Muslims to love them, as discussed previously (in Chapter 17: Love of Others: All Humanity, the 'People of the Scripture, Believers and Friends'). Thus, as one's love for God increases, these four kinds of love also increase; and as one's love for God decreases or diminishes, these four kinds of love also decrease[320]. This does not mean, however, that a person cannot have a special inclination to one of his or her family, or the believers, or the People of the Scripture, or any person at all (based on a relation, a special experience or a special circumstance which has nothing directly to do with love for the sake of God). A person can love others in a special way because of a particular temperament or need he or she has that has nothing to do with love for God. God says about the Prophet Jacob ﷺ and his sons:

> *And when they entered in the manner which their father had bidden them, it did not avail them anything against God; it was but a need in Jacob's soul which he [thus] satisfied. And verily he was possessed of knowledge, because We had taught him; but most of mankind do not know.* (*Yusuf*, 12:68)

As regards the first two kinds of love mentioned above (love for things, and love for lusts), they can change, increase, decrease or end at any moment, since human beings and their love are in a constant state of flux. They are among the 'lower' kinds of love (as we discussed previously in Chapter 27: The Hierarchies of Beauty and of Love), and are based on whims and lusts, and thus have no connection to love of God and hence no stability.

The third kind of love, love for one's friends, is divided into two kinds: 'friends in goodness', and 'friends in evil'.

It is easy for 'friendship in evil' to change because it is based on delusion, and delusion is not real. God says:

> *But if a bounty from God befalls you, he will surely cry as if there had never been any affection between you and him: 'Oh, would that I had been with them, so that I might have won a great triumph!'* (*Al-Nisa'*, 4:73) ❃ *It may be that God will bring about between you and those of them with whom you are at enmity, affection. For God is Powerful, and God is Forgiving, Merciful.* (*Al-Mumtahanah*, 60:7) ❃ *And they are not equal, the good deed and the evil deed. Repel with that which is better then, behold, he between whom and you there was enmity will be as though he were a dear friend.* (*Fussilat*, 41:34)

If this kind of 'friendship in evil' does not change in the life of this world, it will certainly come to an end in the Hereafter, because all delusions vanish in the Hereafter. God says:

> *And he said: 'You have adopted mere idols besides God for the sake of [mutual] affection between you in the life of this world. Then on the Day of Resurrection you will disown one another, and you will curse one another, and your abode will be the Fire, and you will have no helpers'.* (*Al-ʿAnkabut*, 29:25) ❃ *O woe to me! Would that I had not taken so and so as friend!* (*Al-Furqan*, 25:28) ❃ *And those who followed say, 'O, if only we might return again and disown them, as they have disowned us!' So, God shall show them their works, anguish for them! Never shall they exit from the Fire.* (*Al-Baqarah*, 2:167)

'Friendship in goodness', however—true friendship—does not change so easily because it is not based on delusion, and because the love in this kind of friendship is born of the attachment of all the faculties to the goodness beloved in one's friend, such that it is a kind of love for the sake of God. God says: *Close friends will, on that day, be foes of one another, except for the God-fearing. (Al-Zukhruf, 43:67)*

In the fourth kind of love mentioned above, love for one's spouse, if there is true love, and not merely physical love, then it is not easily changed because as we saw previously (in Chapter 18: Conjugal Love) true conjugal love for one's soulmate is a 'divine appointment' or a 'divine creation'. Its bonds run deep: not only does it involve all the lovers' component parts and faculties including the body, it was made by a special Divine creation, and ultimately is also a love for God's sake.

This does not mean that the profound conjugal love can never change. It can change due to a change in the inner beauty of the lover or the beloved. If the beloved displays some new ugliness that was not there before when the love began (by committing evil deeds, for example), this might have an effect on their lover's love. God says:

If the two of you repent to God ... for your hearts were certainly inclined, and if you support one another against him, then [know that] God, He is indeed his Protector, and Gabriel, and the righteous among the believers, and the angels furthermore, are his supporters. / It may be that, if he divorces you, his Lord will give him in [your] stead wives better than you—women submissive [to God], believing, obedient, penitent, devout, given to fasting, previously married and virgins. (Al-Tahrim, 60:4–5)

However, the virtue of fidelity (*wafa'*) ensures that such love will not change because of any change in the body or physical beauty of the beloved, as happens naturally with the passage of time, or after an accident. God stresses the value of the virtue of fidelity in the soul:

Nay, but whoever fulfils his covenant, and has fear, for truly God loves the God-fearing. (Aal 'Imran, 3:76) ❋ *And Abraham, who was true. (Al-Najm, 53:37)* ❋ *And do not come [anywhere] near an orphan's property, except in the fairest manner until he comes of age. And fulfil the covenant. Indeed the covenant will be enquired into. (Al-Isra', 17:34)* ❋ *Truly those who pledge allegiance to you, in fact pledge allegiance to God. The Hand of God is above their hands. So whoever reneges, reneges against his own soul; and whoever fulfils the covenant which he has made with God, He will give him a great reward. (Al-Fath, 48:10)*

God also alludes to the great importance of fidelity in conjugal love; the baseness of betraying this love, and the solemn covenant which is an indispensable part of this love, in His words:

And if you desire to exchange a wife in place of another, and you have given to one a hundredweight, take of it nothing. Would you take it by way of calumny and manifest sin? / How shall you take it, when each of you has gone in unto the other, and they have taken from you a solemn covenant? (*Al-Nisa'*, 4:20–21)

Here God shows how sinful it is to take anything away from one's spouse (and this must include love itself—if it was truly there to take away in the first place) after each spouse has 'gone into the other'. Perhaps this is why divorce is the most hateful of all permitted things by God, as the Messenger of God ﷺ said: 'The most hateful of all permitted things to God is divorce.'[321]

In summary: true conjugal love has tremendous value and worth. God Himself attests to its solemn covenant, a covenant which must be honoured. This love—like all the other natural or positive kinds of inter-human love that are ultimately love for God's sake—should not ever change in this life or the next, and will not, unless the inner state of the lover or the beloved changes for the worst. Certainly it should not change merely because the beloved has become less beautiful physically, as all bodies naturally do over time. And God knows best.

CHAPTER THIRTY

THE NATURE OF LOVE

God makes it clear in the Holy Qur'an that the nature of love is based on general principles, some of which we examine below:

HUMAN LOVE IS ALWAYS CHANGING

Naturally, all things change. However, in addition to this general change, all those who experience love change in themselves constantly and continuously (in this world, at least). This is because God is 'every day upon some matter' (in the sense that He reveals it, not that He begins it): *All that is in the heavens and the earth implore Him. Every day He is upon some matter.* (Al-Rahman, 55:29)

This is because God is ever creating new creations:

> *Were We then wearied by the first creation? Nay, yet they are in doubt about a new creation.* (Qaf, 50:15) *Have you not seen that God created the heavens and the earth in truth? If He will, He can take you away and bring [about] a new creation. / And that for God is surely no great matter.* (Ibrahim, 14:19-20)

However, lovers (and, indeed, all things) are not only always changing, they are also 'contracting' and 'expanding', for God contracts and expands: *Who is he that will lend God a loan that is good, and He will multiply it for him manifold? God contracts and expands; and to Him you shall be returned.* (Al-Baqarah, 2:245)

As discussed previously (in Chapter 22: The Stages of Love), in the different stages of love, we can see the effects of this contraction and expansion. Certain stages of love—such as grief, suffering, fear, weeping, adoration, seeking forgiveness, devotion, humble obedience, penitence, humility and 'the trembling of the heart'—are all stages of 'contraction'. Similarly, joy, tranquillity, gratitude, peace, sufficiency, serenity, admiration, love, affection and contentment, are all stages of 'expansion'. Lovers experience the effects of contraction and expansion naturally as they experience the stages of love. Thus all lovers are in a state of continuous change, constantly passing between the states of contraction and expansion of love, in this world at least. Thus God says: *For truly with hardship comes ease. / Truly with hardship comes ease.* (Al-Sharh, 94:5-6)

Perhaps this constant change is the reason why there is no weariness or boredom in real love. Indeed, lovers never tire or grow weary of supplicating for good things, and thus they never tire of supplication (and supplicating God itself is a stage of love, as we have seen). God says: *Man never wearies of supplicating for good, but should any ill befall him, then he becomes despondent, despairing.* (*Fussilat*, 41:49)

Similarly, the inhabitants of Paradise never tire of love, as we will see God willing (in Chapter 32: Love and Beauty in Paradise). God says: *No toil will touch them, nor will they be expelled from thence.* (*Al-Hijr*, 15:48)

Maybe the reason for all of this is that God Himself never grows weary or bored. God says: *And verily We created the heavens and the earth, and all that is between them, in six days, and no weariness touched Us.* (*Qaf*, 50:38)

All this allows us to say that lovers are subject to constant change, but this change does not cause them to grow weary of love; and God knows best.

THE NEED IN LOVE

Lovers have a constant need for their beloved, and need implies imperfection. We have spoken previously about the poverty of human beings, and thus their need. God says:

> O mankind! You are the ones who are poor towards God. And God, He is the Independent, the Praised. (*Fatir*, 35:15) ❋ Lo! there you are those who are being called to expend in the way of God; yet among you there are those who are niggardly; and whoever is niggardly is niggardly only to his own soul. For God is the Independent One, while you are the poor. And if you turn away, He will replace you with another people, and they will not be the likes of you. (*Muhammad*, 47:38)

Naturally, everything needs God: *All that is in the heavens and the earth implore Him. Every day He is upon some matter.* (*Al-Rahman*, 55:29)

But since everything also loves God (as we saw in Chapter 6: The Universe and Love), this means that this constant imploring of God and needing Him is necessarily part of love. Love necessarily means need, and the lover needs his or her beloved.

THE EXCLUSION IN LOVE

Love has a special 'exclusion' to it, for one cannot love two beloveds (of the same kind) with all one's heart. Indeed, God says: *You will never be able to be just to your wives, even if you be eager; yet do not incline altogether away, so that you leave her like one suspended. If you set things right, and fear, surely God is ever Forgiving, Merciful.* (*Al-Nisa'*, 4:129)

The reason for love's 'exclusion' is that each person has only one heart, and love can fill this heart completely, such that it cannot also be filled with love for something else. God says:

The Nature of Love

> *God has not placed two hearts inside any man, nor has He made your wives whom you declare (to be your mothers) your [true] mothers. Nor has He made those whom you claim as [adopted] sons your [true] sons. That is a mere utterance of your mouths. But God speaks the truth and He guides to the way.* (Al-Ahzab, 33:4)

No doubt this general principle is the reason why jealousy occurs: just as people know that their own hearts only have room for one love, they also know that their beloveds, too, can only have one love, and so they feel jealousy when their beloveds seem to incline towards anything but them; and God knows best. In any case, love has an exclusive nature which demands from people all their hearts, all their souls, all their minds, and all their strength. Thus 'ardent love' (*al-hubb al-ashadd*) fills people completely and does not allow anything else to enter the heart. God says to His Messenger ﷺ: *Say: 'My prayer and my rituals, and my living, and my dying, are all for God, the Lord of the Worlds. / No associate has He. And to this, I have been commanded, and I am the first of those who submit'.* (Al-An'am, 6:162–163)

THE POWER OF LOVE

Love has tremendous power, for it changes the lover, (as previously discussed in Chapters 22: The Stages of Love and 24: The Growth of Love). Through this change, love conquers lovers—the 'contraction' mentioned earlier is an element of this conquest—but its conquest is positive. It changes lovers for the better, and detaches them from their lower selves, their avarice and their egos. The Prophet Joseph ﷺ alluded to this 'positive conquest' whilst he was in prison with nothing but God.: *O my two fellow-prisoners! Are several lords better, or God, the One, the Almighty?* (Yusuf, 12:39)

In other words, his state in prison; conquered by Love of God and with only the One God as Lord, was better and happier than those in the world distracted by many things (hence 'lords') from God.

The final stage of the love's 'positive conquest' is the absolute conquest: death. The lover dies in his or her beloved, or for his or her beloved; and we will discuss this in more detail God willing in Chapter 36: Love and Death. It suffices here to point to rejoicing in death through love of God in God's words:

> *Indeed God has purchased from the believers their lives and their possessions, so that theirs will be [the reward of] Paradise: they shall fight in the way of God and they shall kill and be killed; that is a promise which is binding upon Him in the Torah and the Gospel and the Qur'an; and who fulfils his covenant better than God? Rejoice then in this bargain of yours which you have made, for that is the supreme triumph.* (Al-Tawbah, 9:111)

In summary: love has a tremendous power, for love conquers lovers and then leads them on through the stages of love until their deaths through love.

In the case of lovers of God, love leads them from death through love to eternity in their Beloved. Love has the power to annihilate and then to preserve—such is the power of love! God says:

> *And say not of those slain in God's way: 'They are dead'; rather they are living; but you are not aware. Surely We will try you with something of fear and hunger, and diminution of goods and lives; yet give good tidings to the patient; / those who, when they are struck by an affliction, say, 'Surely we belong to God, and to Him we will return'.* (Al-Baqarah, 2:154–156)

CHAPTER THIRTY-ONE

LOVE AND HAPPINESS

There is no joy (*farah*), contentment (*rida*), peace (*salam*) or pleasure (*mut'a*) without love, in one way or another. This is because, as we have seen (in Chapters 21: The Different Kinds of Love and 22: The Stages of Love), joy, contentment, peace and pleasure are all kinds of love and / or stages of love. Indeed, how can one find joy in something without loving it? Or be content with it without loving it? Or find peace in it without loving it? Or take pleasure in it without loving it? God makes this clear through His words: *God has not placed two hearts inside any man...* (Al-Ahzab, 33:4)

Since human beings only have one heart, they cannot be content or find peace in something that they do not love. God also says: *Adorned for mankind is love of lusts—of women, children, stored-up heaps of gold and silver, horses of mark, cattle, and tillage. That is the pleasure of the life of this world; but God—with Him is the most excellent abode.* (Aal 'Imran, 3:14)

Thus we see that all the pleasures, adornments and lusts of the life of this world are connected to love. From a different perspective, we can see that people rejoice in fleeing from that which they do not love or from inclining towards that which they do love. God says:

> *Those who were left behind rejoiced at remaining behind the Messenger of God, and were averse to striving with their wealth and their lives in the way of God. And they said, 'Do not go forth in the heat!' Say: 'The fire of Hell is hotter, did they but understand'. / But let them laugh a little and weep much as a requital for what they used to earn.* (Al-Tawbah, 9:81–82)

Those who were left behind rejoiced at remaining behind because they hated striving and loved what they considered to be safety. This indicates that joy comes from love, even if this love is for something base or evil. This also explains how there can be any pleasure at all in the life of this world despite the fact that death that awaits at its end. God says:

> *And, the day when He shall gather them all together, 'O assembly of jinn, you have garnered much of mankind'. Then their friends from among mankind will say, 'Our Lord, we enjoyed one another, but now we have arrived at the term which You have appointed for us'. He will say, 'The Fire is your lodging to abide therein'—except what God wills. Surely your Lord is Wise, Knowing.* (Al-An'am, 6:128)

Furthermore, this explains how heedless people can find contentment and reassurance in the life of this world: *Truly those who do not expect to encounter Us, and are content with the life of this world, and feel reassured in it, and those who are heedless of Our signs.* (*Yunus*, 10:7)

Thus heedless people find reassurance in the life of this world and are content with it, despite the fact that true peace, tranquillity and serenity of the heart can only be found in the remembrance of God, for God says: *Those who believe and whose hearts are reassured by God's remembrance. Verily by God's remembrance are hearts made serene.* (*Al-Raʿd*, 13:28)

Equally, the heedless are content with the life of this world, despite the true mutual contentment that exists between God and the believers in this life and the next. God says:

> *Their reward with their Lord will be Gardens of Eden underneath which rivers flow, wherein they shall abide forever. God is content with them, and they are content with Him. That is [the reward] for him who fears his Lord.* (*Al-Bayyinah*, 98:8) (See also: *Al-Maʾidah*, 5:119; *Al-Tawbah*, 9:100; *Al-Mujadilah*, 58:22; *Al-Fajr*, 89:27–30)

However despite the joy, pleasure and contentment which disbelievers, idolaters, heedless people and evildoers experience as a result of their inclining towards the things of this life that they love, there is always and inevitably a certain amount of misery when life is bereft of God's remembrance and worship (perhaps because everyone knows that sooner or later the life of this world will end). God says: *But whoever disregards My remembrance, his shall be a straitened life. And on the Day of Resurrection We shall bring him to the assembly, blind'.* (*Ta Ha*, 20:124)

Here we come to a very important point, which the Qur'an miraculously illuminates: the word 'happiness' is not used even once in the Holy Qur'an to describe the life of this world and the life of the disbelievers, the idolaters, the heedless and the evildoers. The word 'happiness' only occurs twice in the whole of the Holy Qur'an, both times referring to Paradise. These both occur in the following passage from *Surat Hud*:

> *The day it comes, no soul shall speak except by His permission. Some of them will be wretched, and [some] happy. / As for those who are damned, they will be in the Fire; their lot therein will be wailing and sighing; / abiding therein for as long as the heavens and the earth endure, except what your Lord may will. Truly your Lord is Doer of what He desires. / And as for those who are happy, they shall be in Paradise, abiding therein for as long as the heavens and the earth endure except what your Lord may will, an endless bounty.* (*Hud*, 11:105–108)

The only people who are truly happy, then, will be those who enter Paradise to abide therein; and none of the disbelievers, idolaters, heedless ones and evildoers will ever be truly happy, neither in this life nor in the next, despite the joy, pleasure and contentment they might feel in the life of this world. In other words, there is no true happiness without the love of God.

A Question: Does the word 'happiness' apply to righteous believers in this life in the Holy Qur'an?

God says:

> And give good tidings to those who believe and perform righteous deeds that theirs shall be Gardens underneath which rivers run; whensoever they are provided with fruits therefrom, they shall say, 'This is what we were provided with before'; they shall be given it in perfect semblance; and there for them shall be spouses purified; therein they shall abide. (Al-Baqarah, 2:25)

Since happiness is a blessing for people and thus a provision from God, and since every provision granted the believers in Paradise will remind them of something they were provided with in the life of this world, this means that there may be a certain happiness in this life for the righteous believer, even though the provision of Paradise is not the same as the provision of earth (and is of course superior to it), but is only a '*semblance*' of it; and God knows best.

A Question: Why can there be no real happiness for the disbelievers, the idolaters, the heedless and the evildoers in the life of this world?

We saw previously that God says: *But whoever disregards My remembrance, his shall be a straitened life. And on the Day of Resurrection We shall bring him to the assembly, blind.* (Ta Ha, 20:124)

We also saw that joy, pleasure, contentment and peace all depend on love. This inevitably means that the love of the disbelievers, idolaters, heedless and evildoers is not enough to lead to the level of complete happiness. Their happiness will always be incomplete, because their love will always be incomplete (compared to the believers' love). Their love will always be incomplete because they can never reach the state of perfect and constant communion with their beloved, because—since their beloved is not God and not Everlasting—it is bound to pass away. This is made plain in God's words:

> Yet there be people who take to themselves rivals besides God, loving them as God is loved; but those who believe love God more ardently. If those who did evil could but see, as they shall when they behold the chastisement, that power altogether belongs to God, and that God is terrible in chastisement. (Al-Baqarah, 2:165)

Thus worldly love is not sufficient to lead to happiness, because it does not fill one completely, perfectly and eternally. Moreover, as we have cited many times, God blew 'something' of His Spirit into human beings (see: *Al-Sajdah*, 32:7–9; *Sad*, 38:72; *Al-Hijr*, 15:28–34), and this explains why nothing can *completely* suffice human beings and fill them except the love of God. God says:

> *And if they believe in the like of what you believe in, then they are truly guided; but if they turn away, then they are clearly in schism; God will suffice you against them; He is the Hearer, the Knower.* (Al-Baqarah, 2:137) ⁕ *Does God not suffice His servant? Yet they would frighten you of those besides Him. And whomever God leads astray, for him there is no guide.* (Al-Zumar, 39:36)

Because of this, human beings' true happiness, love and life are only with God, or in the Hereafter. God says: *And the life of this world is nothing but diversion and play. But surely the Abode of the Hereafter is indeed the [true] Life, if they only knew.* (Al-ʿAnkabut, 29:64)

And God knows best.

CHAPTER THIRTY-TWO

LOVE AND BEAUTY IN PARADISE

Will there be love and beauty in Paradise? With respect to beauty, the answer is clear, for all of Paradise is beautiful, and in it is found the beatific vision of the Beautiful—the vision of God. God says: *Some faces on that day will be radiant, / looking upon their Lord.* (Al-Qiyamah, 75:22–23)

In addition to this, Paradise is filled with those who have beautiful spirits, beginning with the Messenger of God ﷺ. God says: *Whoever obeys God and the Messenger, they are with those whom God has blessed of the prophets and the truthful, and the martyrs, and the righteous. What fine companions they are!* (Al-Nisa', 4:69)

And we should not neglect to mention the beauty of the *houris* of Paradise. God says:

And buxom maidens of equal age. (Al-Naba', 78:33) ❋ *And We made them virgins, / amorous, of equal age.* (Al-Waqi'ah, 56:36–37) ❋ *In them are maidens of restrained glances, [maidens] who have not been touched by any man or jinn before them.* (Al-Rahman, 55:56) ❋ *Houris secluded in pavilions.* (Al-Rahman, 55:72) ❋ *So [shall it be]; and We shall pair them with houris of beautiful eyes.* (Al-Dukhan, 44:54) ❋ *[They will be] reclining on ranged couches, and We will wed them to beautiful houris.* (Al-Tur, 52:20) ❋ *And houris with wide eyes / resembling hidden pearls.* (Al-Waqi'ah, 56:22–23) ❋ *And with them will be maidens of restrained glances with beautiful eyes.* (Al-Saffat, 37:48) ❋ *And with them [there] will be maidens of restrained glances of a like age.* (Sad, 38:52)

But does this mean that there is love in Paradise?[322] As we saw earlier (in Chapter 30: The Nature of Love), love necessarily involves 'contraction'; 'imperfection'; 'need' and 'suffering', and these difficult experiences do not exist in Paradise. God says:

Truly the God-fearing shall be amidst gardens and springs. / 'Enter them in peace, secure!' And We remove whatever rancour may be in their breasts. As brethren, [they shall recline] upon couches, facing one another. No toil will touch them, nor will they be expelled from thence. (Al-Hijr, 15:45–48) ❋ *And they will say, 'Praise be to God who has removed grief from us. Truly our Lord is Forgiving, Appreciative, / who out of His favour has made us to dwell in the Abode of [everlasting] Stay, wherein no toil shall touch us, nor shall we be touched by any fatigue'.* (Fatir, 35:34–35)

Moreover, every 'provision' ('*rizq*') granted to human beings in the life of this world will be present in Paradise (and of course love itself is a 'provision' granted to human beings). God says:

And give good tidings to those who believe and perform righteous deeds that theirs shall be Gardens underneath which rivers run; whensoever they are provided (ruziqu) with fruits therefrom, they shall say, 'This is what we were provided with before'; they shall be given it in perfect semblance; and there for them shall be spouses purified; therein they shall abide. (Al-Baqarah, 2:25)
◉ *So whoever does an atom's weight of good shall see it, (Al-Zalzalah, 99:7)*

And though the provision of Paradise resembles the provision of earth, the provision of Paradise differs from that of earth in a specific way. God says:

Say, 'Who has forbidden the adornment of God which He has brought forth for His servants, and the good things of [God's] sustenance?' Say: 'These, on the Day of Resurrection, shall be purely for those who believed during the life of this world. Thus We detail the signs for a people who know'. (Al-A'raf, 7:32)

Thus the provision and adornment of Paradise are pure, whilst the provision of earth is necessarily imperfect. God says:

A similitude of the Garden promised to the God-fearing: therein are rivers of un-staling water, and rivers of milk unchanging in flavour, and rivers of wine delicious to the drinkers, and [also] rivers of purified honey; and there will be for them therein every fruit and forgiveness from their Lord. [Is such a one] like him who abides in the Fire. And they will be given to drink boiling water which rips apart their bowels. (Muhammad, 47:15)

The same is true of love in Paradise: love in Paradise is pure and unadulterated, and thus it exists only for the God-fearing (*al-muttaqin*). Even the degree of love called 'close friendship' only exists in Paradise if it is accompanied by God-consciousness (*taqwa*): *Are they awaiting anything, but that Hour should come upon them suddenly, while they are unaware? / Friends will, on that day, be foes of one another, except for the God-fearing. (Al-Zukhruf, 43:66–67)*

Therefore, blessed husbands and wives will be reunited in Paradise (with their children as well), because love—which is inherently good and is ultimately for the sake of God—is eternal[323]. God says:

They and their spouses shall be beneath the shade, reclining upon couches. (Ya Sin, 36:56) ◉ *Enter Paradise, you and your spouses to be made joyful. (Al-Zukhruf, 43:70)* ◉ *Our Lord, and admit them into the Gardens of Eden that which You have promised them, along with whoever were righteous among their fathers and their wives and their descendants. Surely You are the One Who is the Mighty, the Wise. (Ghafir, 40:8)* ◉ *Gardens of Eden, which they shall enter along with those who were righteous from among their fathers and their spouses and their descendants; and the angels shall enter to them from every gate*. (*Al-Ra'd*, 13:23) ❉ *And those who believed and whom We made to be followed by their descendants in faith, We will make their descendants join them, and We will not deprive them of anything of their deeds. Every man is subject to what he has earned.* (*Al-Tur*, 52:21)

Conversely, evil husbands and wives will be together in hell, because love stemming from the 'soul which incites evil' always ends. God says: *Gather those who did wrong together with their mates and what they used to worship.* (*Al-Saffat*, 37:22)

In summary: Paradise contains all that its inhabitants love, and all those whom they love. There is love in Paradise, but the love of Paradise differs from the love of this world. Thus love in Paradise is all the soul desires and everything in which the eye rejoices, but without the imperfection, need, suffering and contraction of the love of this world; and God knows best. He says:

> *Are they awaiting anything, but that Hour should come upon them suddenly, while they are unaware? / Friends will, on that day, be foes of one another, except for the God-fearing. / 'O My servants, there is no fear for you this day, nor will you grieve, / those who believed in Our signs and had submitted themselves [to Me]. / Enter Paradise, you and your spouses to be made joyful. / They will be served from all around with [large] dishes of gold and goblets and therein will be whatever souls desire and eyes delight in, and you will abide in it [forever]. / And that is the Paradise which you have been given to inherit [as the reward] for what you used to do.* (*Al-Zukhruf*, 43:66–72)

PART FIVE: THE BELOVED
(BEAUTY; THE MEETING WITH GOD; BEATITUDE)

CHAPTER THIRTY-THREE

BEAUTY AND ITS COMPONENTS

THE MEANING OF 'BEAUTY' (*JAMAL* AND *HUSN*)

What is the difference between the Arabic words '*jamal*' and '*husn*', which both indicate 'beauty'? The following is an overview of what the Muslim scholars have said on this matter:

CONCERNING '*JAMAL*':
Raghib says: '*Jamal* means great beauty (*husn*), and there are two aspects to this: the first is the beauty with which a person is characterised in soul, body or actions; the second is that which connects to something else. In this regard, it is related that the Prophet ﷺ said: 'God is beautiful, and He loves beauty', which indicates that all goodness flows from Him, so He loves those who are characterised by this goodness. And God Almighty says: '*And for you there is in them beauty, when you bring them [home] to rest…*' (*Al-Nahl*, 16:6), and: '*…Yet beautiful patience!…*' (*Yusuf*, 12:18)'.[324] Zabidi says: '*Jamal* means beauty (*husn*), whether of appearance or of character.'[325]

CONCERNING '*HUSN*':
Raghib says: 'The word *husn* describes all that is delightful and desirable, and there are three aspects to this: that which the mind finds attractive, that which the impulse finds attractive, and that which the senses find attractive'.[326] Zabidi says: '*Husn* means beauty (*jamal*), and *it seems that they are synonyms*. Asma'i said that *husn* refers to the beauty the eyes perceive, and *jamal* to the beauty the nose perceives. The *Sihah* says that *husn* is the opposite of ugliness. Azhari said that *husn* describes all that is good and beautiful'.[327]

From the aforementioned lexical definitions, it is clear that the words *jamal* and *husn* are basically synonyms, and that the classical Muslim scholars could not make a decisive judgement upon the matter. Despite this, it may be observed that in the Holy Qur'an and the *Hadith* the word '*jamal*' is used when the beautiful thing is singular: God is beautiful (*Jamil*); patience is beautiful (*jamil*)[328], and there is beauty (*jamal*) in cattle.[329] Whenever the word '*husn*' is used, it describes more than one of something, or a plurality of different types of beauty: God has the Most Beautiful Names (*Al-Asma' al-Husna*);[330] *ihsan* (virtue) means all good characteristics and virtues, as we have seen; and the beauty (*husn*) of a woman means all the aspects of beauty which are combined in her appearance. And God knows best.

THE COMPONENTS OF BEAUTY

Beauty is a quality, and qualities are indivisible and generally cannot be broken down into pieces (in themselves); but does this quality have components? In other words, does beauty have elements which we can name and understand? God says:

> *The Compassionate One / has taught the Qur'an. / He created man, / teaching him [coherent] speech. / The sun and the moon follow a measure, / and the grass and the trees prostrate. / And He has raised the heaven and set up the balance, / [declaring] that you not transgress in the balance. / And set the weight justly, and come not short of the balance. / And the earth, He placed it for [all] creatures. / In it are fruits and date-palms with sheaths, / and grain with husk, and fragrant herb. / So which of your Lord's favours will you deny?* (Al-Rahman, 55:1–13)

We see here, in the opening of *Surat Al-Rahman*, that God mentions 'the balance' ('*al-mizan*') three times. The *Tafsir al-Jalalayn* explains the following: '*And He has raised the heaven and set up the balance*: He has established justice; *that you not transgress*, i.e. that you not be unjust *in the balance*, meaning all that is weighed out. *And set the weight justly* i.e. equitably, *and come not short of the balance* by skimping on that which is weighed out.'³³¹

However, it may be observed that God mentions 'the balance' ('*al-mizan*') in between His mention of the sun, the moon, the stars, the trees, the sky, the earth, and what grows from the earth, and that God does not mention things usually connected with justice before or after speaking of 'the balance'. Rather, God only speaks of the natural phenomena of His creation before and after mentioning 'the balance'. God does not speak of rewards and punishments, or the other things that come to mind when justice is spoken of. Perhaps, then, the mention of 'the balance' here is an allusion to a greater 'balance', namely the natural harmony and equilibrium of God's creation. Our evidence for this is the 'measure' ('*husban*') of which God speaks in connection with 'the balance': '*The sun and the moon follow a measure, / and the grass and the trees prostrate. / And He has raised the heaven and set up the balance.*' (Al-Rahman, 55:5–7)

Moreover, we know—as we have seen several times—that God put beauty into all that He created:

> *Who beautified everything that He created. And He began the creation of man from clay.* (Al-Sajdah, 32:7) ❈ *And you see the mountains, supposing them*

Beauty and its Components

to be still, while they drift like passing clouds. The handiwork of God Who has perfected everything. Truly He is aware of what you do. (Al-Naml, 27:88)

There must therefore also be beauty in the heavens and the earth and in the components of each, of which God mentions in the opening of *Surat Al-Rahman*. Does this mean that 'the balance' is part of beauty? Or indeed, does this mean that 'balance' is the very constitution of beauty?

The Messenger of God ﷺ spoke of the virtues (*fada'il*) of a number of *Surahs* of the Holy Qur'an; but in the case of *Surat Al-Rahman*, he said something unique. 'Ali ؓ reported that the Messenger of God ﷺ said: 'Everything has a bride, and the bride of the Qur'an is [Surat] Al-Rahman.'[332]

The concept of a 'bride' differs from that of a 'woman' or a 'wife' in two ways: firstly, there is a suggestion of a presence of beauty (because a bride is usually adorned to be beautiful), and secondly there is suggestion of celebration (because a bride differs from other women because of the wedding, and a wedding is a celebration). Do these words of the Messenger of God ﷺ therefore allude to the beauty inherent in *Surat Al-Rahman*? Do these words of the Messenger of God ﷺ also imply that *Surat Al-Rahman* contains an exposition, and an explanation, of beauty?

This permits us to say that the concept of 'the balance' mentioned in *Surat Al-Rahman* must contain an allusion to beauty.

Now God speaks (in verse 9 of *Surat Al-Rahman*) of the components of 'the balance', namely: (1) a 'setting-up' ('*iqama*'), (2) a 'weight' ('*wazn*'), and (3) 'justice' ('*qist*') therein.

(1) The notion of 'setting-up' implies verticality, and (2) the notion of 'weight' implies horizontality, and (3) the notion of 'justice' implies a harmony between them. From a different perspective, the notion of 'setting-up' implies majesty (*jalal*—because it requires truth), and the notion of 'weight' implies munificence (*jamal*—because it requires something available and present, and thus a provision from God), and the concept of 'justice' implies perfection. If this suggestion is accurate, we can therefore say that the components of beauty are majesty, munificence and the harmony between them, all these together constituting the perfection of beauty.

There may be another allusion to the components of beauty at the opening and ending of *Surat Al-Rahman*. The first verse of this *Surah* is: '*The Compassionate One*' and The Compassionate is (as we saw in Chapter 4: God and Love) the Source of love and the Source of creation, and thus the Source of beauty. The final verse of this *Surah* is: '*Blessed be the Name of your Lord, He of Majesty and Munificence (Dhul Jalal wal-Ikram)*' (Al-Rahman, 55:78). Thus perhaps this Divine Name ('*Dhul Jalal wal-Ikram*') contains the secret of the components of beauty: the components of beauty are thus majesty, munificence and their blessed combination.

Indeed, Fakhr al-Din al-Razi, divides God's Most Beautiful Names (*Al-Asma Al-Husna*)—and hence beauty itself, by implication—into two categories, Majesty and Munificence. Al-Razi says: 'God's Qualities are of two kinds: '*silbiyya*', which are called in the Holy Qur'an 'Majesty'; and '*idafiyya*', which are called in the Holy Qur'an 'Munificence'; this is alluded to by His words: *He of Majesty and Munificence* (*Al-Rahman*, 55:78).'[333]

Similarly, other Muslim scholars (such as 'Abd al-Karim bin Ibrahim Al-Jili in his book *Al-Insan al-Kamil*, 'The Universal Man') have divided God's Most Beautiful Names (*Al-Asma Al-Husna*) into two categories: The Names of the Divine Essence (such as 'the One'), and the Names of the Divine Qualities. The Names of the Divine Qualities are then divided into three categories: the Names of Beauty (such as: 'The Compassionate' and 'The Beautiful'), the Names of Majesty (such as: 'the Almighty' and 'The Irresistible'), and the Names of Perfection (such as: 'The King' and 'The Lord'). Is all beauty then composed of munificence, majesty and their harmonious combination? God knows best.

CHAPTER THIRTY-FOUR

TASTE

As we will shortly see, God willing (in Chapter 35: The Nature of Beauty) beauty is an objective reality that exists in things themselves. Thus everyone instinctively knows and recognizes beauty in some form. God says:

> And when she heard of their machinations, she sent for them and prepared for them a repast. She then gave each one of them a knife and said: 'Come out before them!' And when they saw him, they were in awe of him and cut their hands, and they exclaimed: 'God preserve us! This is no human being: this is but a noble angel!' (Yusuf, 12:31)

Thus the 'women of the city' (referred to in the verse above) all agreed about Joseph's ﷺ beauty, and were amazed by it.

However, sometimes people differ—or change their opinions—about which things are beautiful and which of the beautiful things they find the most beautiful. For example, the Prophet Abraham ﷺ went from admiring and loving the star to not loving it; and then to admiring the moon; and then to admiring the sun. God says:

> When night descended upon him he saw a star and said, 'This is my Lord'. But when it set, he said, 'I love not those that set'. / And when he saw the moon rising, he said, 'This is my Lord'. But when it set he said, 'Unless my Lord guides me, I shall surely become one of the folk who are astray'. / And when he saw the sun rising, he said, 'This is my Lord; this is greater!' But when it set, he said, 'O my people, surely I am innocent of what you associate. (Al-An'am, 6:76–78)

Thus Abraham's ﷺ admiration changed according to his perception of beauty. This means that the perception of beauty is linked to the state of its beholder, even though beauty exists as a reality in objects as such.

In addition to this, there are natural differences and variances between people, even though all human beings share the same origin. God says: *O mankind! We have indeed created you from a male and a female, and made you nations and tribes that you may come to know one another. Truly the noblest of you in the sight of God is the most God-fearing among you. Truly God is Knower, Aware.* (Al-Hujurat, 49:13)

Since perception of beauty differs from one person to another according to their state, this also means that it will differ from one person to another according to the natural differences and variances between them. God says:

> *Verily this your community is one community and I am your Lord, so fear Me'. / But they split into sects regarding their affair, each party rejoicing in what it had. (Al-Mu'minun, 23:52–53)* ❖ *[Of] those who have divided up their religion, and have become [dissenting] factions, each party rejoicing in what they have. (Al-Rum, 30:32)*

'*Each party rejoicing in what they have*': this Qur'anic phrase means that each party is happy with their lot; but it may also be understood to mean that each party rejoices according to their nature ('*in what they have*'); in other words, that each party rejoices in one particular thing more than another particular thing, according to its individual nature. God says: *Say: 'Everyone acts according to his [own] character, and your Lord knows best who is better guided as to the way'. (Al-Isra', 17:84)*

This Qur'anic verse also indicates that every human being chooses what he or she likes and loves, in accordance with their own nature. Abu Hurayrah ؓ reports that the Messenger of God ﷺ said: 'Spirits are conscripted soldiers: those of them who recognise one another bond; and those of them who do not recognise one another differ.'[334]

This *Hadith* also indicates that taste is an innate and special part of the human spirit; and God knows best.[335]

In summary: despite the objective reality of beauty, there is something in people's natures and in their natural differences that causes each person to have his or her own individual taste. This individual taste is what makes a person prefer one kind of beauty to another. Thus beauty is objective, whereas taste is not objective but subjective, and personal; and God knows best.

CHAPTER THIRTY-FIVE

THE NATURE OF BEAUTY

God makes it clear in the Holy Qur'an that the nature of beauty is based on certain general principles; what follows is an examination of some of these principles.

THE OBJECTIVITY OF BEAUTY

Beauty is an objective reality that exists in things themselves, and therefore it is objectively present in the beloved. It is not true, as the saying goes, that 'beauty is in the eye of the beholder' (although it would be true to say: 'taste is in the eye of the beholder'). Rather beauty is present in things themselves—indeed, it is present in all things, for God says:

> Who beautified everything that He created. And He began the creation of man from clay. (Al-Sajdah, 32:7) ❋ And you see the mountains, supposing them to be still, while they drift like passing clouds. The handiwork of God Who has perfected everything. Truly He is aware of what you do. (Al-Naml, 27:88) ❋ O man! What has deceived you with regard to your generous Lord, / who created you, then made you upright, then proportioned you, / assembling you in whatever form He wishes? (Al-Infitar, 82:6–8) ❋ And for you there is in them beauty, when you bring them [home] to rest, and when you drive them forth to pasture. / And they bear your burdens to a land which you could not reach, save with great trouble to yourselves. Indeed your Lord is Gentle, Merciful. (Al-Nahl, 16:6–7)

THE POWER OF BEAUTY

Beauty has a tremendous power, just as love does. Dazzling beauty can distract those who see it from everything around them; even from their own selves; even from their own senses; even from pain. God says:

> And when she heard of their machinations, she sent for them and prepared for them a repast. She then gave each one of them a knife and said: 'Come out before them!' And when they saw him, they were in awe of him and cut their hands, and they exclaimed: 'God preserve us! This is no human being: this is but a noble angel!' (Yusuf, 12:31)

The women of the city (referred to in the verse above) were so attracted and captivated by the mere sight of Joseph ﷺ, that they cut their hands without even feeling it. Thus beauty can dazzle those who see it, and interrupt their actions (hands symbolise action), and distract them from anything else. There is no other power, save the power of God, which can do this in this way.

THE WAY BEAUTY WORKS

Beauty works on those who behold it in two different ways:

(1) The first way beauty works is that it takes its beholder out of himself or herself, and then draws him or her to love the beautiful object. It then causes its beholder to desire to possess it—even by means of force and violence. Joseph's ﷺ beauty affected Potiphar's wife to such an extent that it made her want to commit adultery with him, and even to force him to do so. God says:

> *And she, in whose house he was attempted to seduce him, and she closed the doors. And she said: 'Come!' 'God forbid!' he said. 'Truly he is my lord, who has given me an honourable place. Truly, evildoers never prosper'. / And she certainly desired him, and he would have desired her [too], had it not been that he saw the proof of his Lord. So it was that We might ward off from him evil and lewdness. Truly he was of Our devoted servants. / And they raced to the door, and she tore his shirt from behind, whereupon they encountered her master at the door. She said, 'What is to be the requital of him who intends evil against your folk, but that he should be imprisoned, or [suffer] a painful chastisement?'* (Yusuf, 12:23–25)

Because of this, God warns His Messenger ﷺ against 'extending his glance' towards beauty, saying:

> *Do not extend your glance toward that which We have given different groups of them to enjoy, and do not grieve for them, and lower your wing for the believers.* (Al-Hijr, 15:88) ❋ *And do not extend your glance toward what We have given to some pairs among them to enjoy, [as] the flower of the life of this world that We may try them thereby. And your Lord's provision is better and more enduring.* (Ta Ha, 20:131)

(2) The second way beauty works is to cause its beholder to return to himself or herself, and thus to virtue of soul, to faith, and to tranquillity. Jacob ﷺ sought the aid of the beauty of patience in the midst of his suffering, and so became tranquil and put his trust in God. This can clearly be seen in the words of Jacob ﷺ in the following verses:

> *'Nay,' he said, 'but your souls have beguiled you into something. Yet beautiful patience! It may be that God will bring them all [back] to me. Indeed He is the Knower, the Wise'.* (Yusuf, 12:83) ❋ *He said: 'I complain of my anguish and grief only to God, and I know from God what you do not know. / O my sons, go and enquire about Joseph and his brother, and do not despair of God's [gracious] Spirit. Indeed none despairs of the [gracious] Spirit of God save the disbelieving folk'.* (Yusuf, 12:86–87)

The Nature of Beauty

The same was true of the Companions of God's Messenger ﷺ when they pledged allegiance to the Messenger ﷺ underneath the tree at Hudaybiyah: they stood before this magnificent sight—the Messenger of God ﷺ, who was even more beautiful in appearance and character than Joseph ﷺ—and '*The Hand of God [was] above their hands*' (*Al-Fath*, 48:10). Thereupon they returned to their true, inner selves, and God graced them with something deeper than tranquillity, namely the *Sakinah*—Peace of Heart. God says: *Verily God was pleased with the believers when they pledged allegiance to you under the tree. And He knew what was in their hearts, so He sent down the Sakinah upon them, and rewarded them with a near victory.* (*Al-Fath*, 48:18)

Similarly, God promises the believers a vision of angels accoutred in beauty ('*musawimin*') to give their hearts serenity ('*itmi'nan*'), even though in the midst of a battle. God says:

> When you were saying to the believers, 'Is it not sufficient for you that your Lord should reinforce you with three thousand angels sent down? / Yea, if you are patient and fear, and they come against you instantly, your Lord will reinforce you with five thousand angels accoutred (musawimin)'. / What God ordained was only as a good tiding to you and that your hearts might be serene (wa li tatma'ina qulubukum bihi). Victory comes only from God, the Mighty, the Wise. (Aal 'Imran, 3:124–126)

In Chapter 18: Conjugal and Sexual Love, we touched briefly on the spiritual element of the sexual act. It remains to be added here that beauty of the opposite sex—the human form being *the best of statures* (*Al-Tin*, 95:4)—can not only bring its beholder (or some of them at least) back to his or her true inner self, away from the world and from lust, but also transform the outward world itself into a reminder and 'spiritual proof' of God. In other words, beauty can not only return someone to their true inner selves, but can also, as it were, transform the world itself into a concrete outward reflection of what is most inward of all: knowledge of God. Thus for Joseph ﷺ, the beauty of Potiphar's wife was completely interiorized by him such that it became a '*proof of his Lord*', unlike Potiphar's wife herself, who saw Joseph's ﷺ beauty as so outside of herself that she had to hunt it down desperately. God says:

> And she certainly desired him, and he would have desired her [too], had it not been that he saw the proof (burhan) of his Lord. So it was that We might ward off from him evil and lewdness. Truly he was of Our devoted servants. / And they raced to the door, and she tore his shirt from behind, whereupon they encountered her master at the door. She said, 'What is to be the requital of him who intends evil against your folk, but that he should be imprisoned, or [suffer] a painful chastisement?' (Yusuf, 12:24–5)

In such a state—when the exterior is transformed and interiorised—the world stops being worldly. This is akin to the state of the Messenger of God ﷺ

himself, of which God says: *To God belong the East and the West; whithersoever you turn, there is the Face of God. Lo! God is Embracing, Knowing. (Al-Baqarah, 2:115) He is the First and the Last, and the Manifest and the Hidden and He has knowledge of all things. (Al-Hadid, 57:3)*

In summary: beauty has a tremendous power that works in two alternative ways: either it draws its beholder out of himself or herself, or draws its beholder back into himself or herself. Indeed, we can see these two diametrically opposed effects in the way women's beauty leads either to lustful attraction to women, or to a 'special mercy' towards women, as the following Qur'anic verse indicates (for the Messenger of God ﷺ is ordered not to look at women as such but rather to 'lower his wing' [in compassion] for all believers as such [including of course women]): *Do not extend your glance toward that which We have given different groups of them to enjoy, and do not grieve for them, and lower your wing for the believers. (Al-Hijr, 15:88)*

THE BENEFIT OF BEAUTY (AND LOVE)

We have previously cited God's words:

And when she heard of their machinations, she sent for them and prepared for them a repast. She then gave each one of them a knife and said: 'Come out before them!' And when they saw him, they were in awe of him and cut their hands, and they exclaimed: 'God preserve us! This is no human being: this is but a noble angel!' (Yusuf, 12:31)

Herein, we see the power of beauty to bring about a state wherein its beholder does not feel pain, and in the next chapter, God willing, we will examine how love is connected to death. Here, however, we must consider God's words: *And for you there is in them beauty, when you bring them [home] to rest, and when you drive them forth to pasture. / And they bear your burdens to a land which you could not reach, save with great trouble to yourselves. Indeed your Lord is Gentle, Merciful. (Al-Nahl, 16:6–7)*

This is the only occasion in the Holy Qur'an where God speaks of 'great trouble to the self' (*shiqq al-nafs*, which literally means 'a splitting of the self' or 'a splitting of the soul'). Is there an allusion here to the way in which love and beauty console human beings and make the hardship of death easier to endure? In other words, although these words speak about cattle and livestock (which is the literal meaning referred to) and how they make travel easier, they also mention beauty, and right after the mention of beauty comes the mention of a journey to a land which no one can reach without enduring great trouble to the soul. May we therefore understand that beauty and love enable human beings to do that which they cannot ordinarily do without 'splitting their souls'? May we understand here that beauty and love enable human beings to endure

The Nature of Beauty

destruction and death? In short, is there an allusion here to the power that beauty and love have to lighten the hardship of death—whether psychological or physical—such that through love and beauty, one may endure the experience of death without any suffering or grief? Indeed, we know for a fact that the Messenger of God ﷺ passed away in a state of longing for God;[336] and likewise, when the Messenger of God ﷺ told his daughter, the Lady Fatimah, that she would die soon after him, she rejoiced because she longed to meet her Lord.[337] Does this not show that beauty (and love) may have the power to make even the hardship of death easier to endure? If the answer is yes, then this is the great benefit of beauty (and love). Beauty (and love) can make human beings feel no pain—physical or emotional—like the women of the city who cut their hands but felt no pain when they saw the Prophet Joseph ﷺ, even when it comes to the hardship of death and destruction. There is perhaps an indication of this in God's words: *As for him who gives and is God-fearing, / and affirms the truth of the best [word] (husna), / We shall surely ease his way to [the abode of] ease.* (*Al-Layl*, 92: 5-7). We have seen that love means giving. Here God says that he who gives with fear of God and affirms beauty—*husna* actually literally means beauty, as we have seen—will be shown ease. And God knows best.

CHAPTER THIRTY-SIX

LOVE AND DEATH

THE DEATH OF THE 'SOUL WHICH INCITES EVIL'

We mentioned previously (in Chapters 22: The Stages of Love and 30: The Nature of Love) that love for God leads gradually—but inevitably—to the lover's death in his or her beloved. This does not mean physical death, of course, but 'psychological death'. In the story of the women of the city who cut their hands upon beholding Joseph ﷺ, we saw the beginning of the process of the death of the soul through love. God says:

> And when she heard of their machinations, she sent for them and prepared for them a repast. She then gave each one of them a knife and said: 'Come out before them!' And when they saw him, they were in awe of him and cut their hands, and they exclaimed: 'God preserve us! This is no human being: this is but a noble angel!' (Yusuf, 12:31)

Thus love, caused by dazzling beauty, takes its beholder out of himself or herself. At the onset of love, this does not lead to the death of the lover. However, as time passes and love becomes ardent, the lover must die, because all his or her constituent parts and faculties incline towards the beloved, so that the lover is entirely transformed and his (or her) 'former self' changes entirely. This then leads to the death of the lover's former self as such.

This does not mean, of course, that the soul comes to an end or that the person no longer has a soul; it means that the soul loses all its egotism and selfishness, such that it could be said that the lover's 'former' soul has died.

Which 'soul' is it that dies? We saw in Chapter 23: Falling in Love that there is a personal 'soul' as such, in addition to which there are three distinct 'parts' or 'kinds' of the soul, which are: 'the soul which incites evil', 'the self-reproaching soul', and the 'soul at peace'. God says, about the 'soul which incites evil': *Yet I do not exculpate my own soul; verily the soul is ever inciting to evil, except that whereon my Lord has mercy. Truly my Lord is Forgiving, Merciful'*. (*Yusuf*, 12:53)

The 'soul which incites evil' is the part of a person that encourages him or her to commit evil. This soul is forever prompting, enticing and enjoining wicked thoughts and actions. God says:

> And they came with false blood on his shirt. He said: 'Nay, but your souls have beguiled you into something. Yet comely patience! And God is the One

Whose succour is sought in that [predicament] which you describe'. (*Yusuf*, 12:18) ❂ *'Nay,'* he said, *'but your souls have beguiled you into something. Yet comely patience! It may be that God will bring them all [back] to me. Indeed He is the Knower, the Wise'*. (*Yusuf*, 12:83) ❂ *He said, 'I perceived what they did not perceive, so I seized a handful from the track of the messenger and threw it [in]. Thus my soul prompted me'*. (*Ta Ha*, 20:96) ❂ *Then his soul prompted him to slay his brother, so he slew him and became one of the losers.* (*Al-Ma'idah*, 5:30)

Indeed, this soul is like Satan, *'who whispers in the breasts of mankind'* (*Al-Nas*, 114:5), save that it is a constant 'consort' of human beings.

In love, the 'soul which incites evil' is the soul that dies, whilst the 'soul at peace' is the soul that remains after this death, for God says: *O soul at peace! / Return to your Lord, pleased, pleasing. / Then enter among My servants! / And enter My Paradise!* (*Al-Fajr*, 89:27-30)

Thus the 'soul at peace', after returning to God and entering Paradise, does not hear anything more from the 'soul which incites evil'; there is no longer any incitement to evil, nor any prompting, nor any enticing, nor any attempt to compel, nor even any whispering. Rather, all that the soul hears in Paradise is peace, and greetings of peace. God says:

They will not hear therein any vain talk or any sinful words, / but only the saying, 'Peace!' 'Peace!' (*Al-Waqi'ah*, 56:25-26) ❂ *Therein they shall not hear anything that is trifling, but only [a greeting of] 'Peace!' And therein they will have their provision morning and evening. / That is the Paradise which We shall give as inheritance those of Our servants who are God-fearing.* (*Maryam*, 19:62-63) ❂ *And God summons to the Abode of Peace, and He guides whomever He wills to a straight path.* (*Yunus*, 10:25) ❂ *'Peace!'—the word from a Lord [Who is] Merciful.* (*Ya Sin*, 36:58) ❂ *Those, they will be rewarded with the sublime abode, forasmuch as they were steadfast, and they will be met therein with a greeting and [words of] peace.* (*Al-Furqan*, 25:75) ❂ *Their prayer therein: 'Glory be to You, O God!', and their greeting therein will be: 'Peace'. And their final prayer will be: 'Praise be to God, Lord of the Worlds'.* (*Yunus*, 10:10)

When the 'soul at peace' returns to its Lord, the 'soul which incites evil' dies automatically.[338] The Messenger of God ﷺ said: 'There is not one of you but he is assigned a consort of the jinn.' 'Even you, O Messenger of God?' they said. 'Even I,' he said, 'save that God aided me against him and he surrendered, and enjoins upon me only what is good.'[339]

Thus, after the inner 'consort' surrenders, the 'soul which incites evil' dies, and the believer becomes an internally unanimous[340] person who listens only to the voice of goodness, and is dead to incitements of evil. God says: *God strikes a similitude: a man shared by several [masters], quarrelling, and a man belonging exclusively to one man. Are the two equal in comparison? Praise be to God! Nay, but most of them do not know. / You will indeed die, and they [too] will indeed die.* (Al-Zumar, 39:29–30)

Accordingly, God indicates that there is a tremendous reward for the slaying of the evil soul. God says:

And had We prescribed for them: 'Slay yourselves' or 'Leave your habitations', they would not have done it, save a few of them; yet if they had done what they were admonished to do, it would have been better for them, and stronger in establishing. And then, We would have surely given them from Us a great wage. And We would have guided them to a straight path. / Whoever obeys God and the Messenger, they are with those whom God has blessed of the prophets and the truthful, and the martyrs, and the righteous. What fine companions they are! That is bounty from God. God suffices as Knower. (Al-Nisa', 4:66–70) ❋ *And when Moses said to his people, 'My people, you have done wrong against yourselves by your taking the [golden] calf; now turn to your Creator and slay one another; That, will be better for you in your Creator's sight'; He will turn to you [relenting]; truly He is the Relenting, the Merciful.* (Al-Baqarah, 2:54) ❋ *You were longing for death before you met it. Now you have seen it, looking on.* (Aal 'Imran, 3:143)

We may understand from these Qur'anic verses that dying for God is of two kinds: physical death, and psychological death. We can also see an allusion to psychological death, in addition to physical death, in the martyrdom mentioned in the following verses:

And if you are slain in God's way, or die, forgiveness from God and mercy are better than what they amass. / And if you die or are slain, it is to God you shall be mustered. (Aal 'Imran, 3:157–158) ❋ *Whoever emigrates in the way of God will find in the earth many refuges and abundance; whoever goes forth from his house as an emigrant to God and His Messenger, and then death overtakes him, his wage is then incumbent upon God; surely God is ever Forgiving, Merciful.* (Al-Nisa', 4:100) ❋ *And those who emigrated in the way of God, and then were slain, or died, God shall provide them with a good provision. Truly God is the best of providers. / Assuredly He will admit them into a place. And truly God is Knowing, Forbearing.* (Al-Hajj, 22:58–59) ❋ *Among the believers are men who are true to the covenant they made with God. Some of them have fulfilled their vow, and some are still awaiting; and they have not changed in the least.* (Al-Ahzab, 33:23) ❋ *Go forth, light and heavy! Struggle in the way of God with your possessions and your lives: that is better for you, if only you knew.* (Al-Tawbah, 9:41) ❋ *Indeed God has purchased from the believers their lives and their possessions, so that theirs will be [the reward of] Paradise: they shall fight in the way of God and they shall kill and be killed; that is a promise which is binding upon Him in the Torah and the Gospel and the Qur'an; and who fulfils his covenant better than God? Rejoice then in this bargain of yours which you have made, for that is the supreme triumph.* (Al-Tawbah, 9:111) ❋ *So let them fight in the way of God those who sell the life of this world for the Hereafter; and whoever fights in the way of God and is slain or conquers, We shall give him a great wage.* (Al-Nisa', 4:74)

The death in God's way of the ego or the *'soul which incites evil'* is the ultimate aim of the inner struggle, just as physical death in God's way is the ultimate martyrdom in the outer struggle against the enemy. Thus the Messenger of God ﷺ said: 'The treasure of the believer is death.'³⁴¹

And he ﷺ said: 'Be in this world as if you were a stranger or a passer-by.'³⁴²

THE DEATH OF THE 'SOUL WHICH INCITES EVIL' BY MEANS OF GOD'S LOVE

We have just seen that the 'soul which incites evil' dies in love in God's cause and thus how love is connected to this kind of death. We saw previously (in Chapter 21: The Different Kinds of Love) that 'protecting friendship' (*wilayah*) is a kind of love. Thus it should come as no surprise that the definition of a 'friend' of God or 'saint' (*wali Allah*) is someone who longs for death (in order to meet God). God says: *Say: 'O you of Jewry, if you claim that you are the [favoured] friends of God, to the exclusion of other people, then long for death, if you are truthful'. / But they will never long for it, because of what their hands have sent ahead; and God is Knower of the evildoers.* (Al-Jumu'ah, 62:6–7)

God also says: *Say: 'If the Abode of the Hereafter with God is purely yours, and not for other people, then long for death—if you speak truly'. / But they will never long for it, because of that which their own hands have sent before them. God knows the evildoers.* (Al-Baqarah, 2:95–96)

Thus the 'friends' of God love Him, and in their love for Him they long for physical death. Their 'souls which incite evil' have already died, so they are safe from all fear and grief. God says: *Assuredly God's friends, no fear shall befall them, neither shall they grieve.* (Yunus, 10:62)

And after that they become, by God's leave, like the Messenger of God ﷺ in their pure love for God, both in life and in death:

Say: 'As for me, my Lord has guided me to a straight path, a right religion, the creed of Abraham, a hanif; and he was not of the idolaters'. Say: 'My prayer and my rituals, and my living, and my dying, are all for God, the Lord of the Worlds. / No associate has He. And to this, I have been commanded, and I am the first of those who submit'. (Al-An'am, 6:161–162)

This state—or a state approaching it—is the state of those who truly love God and seek to please God to the point where they are completely ready to be martyred in His way because of the ardour of their love for Him. Indeed, this was the state of 'Ali ؓ when he took the place of the Messenger of God in his bed the night the idolaters tried to assassinate him; some scholars consider that the following verse is a reference to this: *But there are other men who sell themselves, desiring God's pleasure; and God is Gentle with His servants.* (Al-Baqarah, 2:207)

Fakr al-Din al-Razi says: 'There are several accounts of the circumstances of the revelation of this verse … The third account is that it was revealed about 'Ali bin Abi Talib ※, who spent the night in the Messenger of God's ※ bed on the night he left for the Cave'.[343]

THE TORMENT OF THE SOUL WHICH LOVES BUT DOES NOT DIE IN GOD

What we have just discussed above applies to those who love God. What happens to those who love things other than God, as their love grows ever more ardent? Do they die? And how do their 'souls which incite evil' die if they only love something like adultery or idolatry? God says:

> *Yet there be people who take to themselves rivals besides God, loving them as God is loved; but those who believe love God more ardently. If those who did evil could but see, as they shall when they behold the chastisement, that power altogether belongs to God, and that God is terrible in chastisement.* (Al-Baqarah, 2:165)[344]

God makes it clear in this Qur'anic verse that if people love things other than God with a degree of love that should be reserved only for God ('*loving them as God is loved*'), their egos do not die like those who love God. Rather their souls suffer a terrible chastisement ('*God is terrible in chastisement*'). By this we do not understand that God visits upon them an additional, external 'terrible chastisement', but rather that their own love makes them suffer terribly. They suffer because they are deprived of the object of their love (as in romantic love, as with Potiphar's wife loving Joseph ※) either because their love is unrequited, or simply because ultimately separation and death are inevitable in this world. However, even in adulterous love, if the love is ardent enough and / or there is sufficient suffering, this leads to something noble and beautiful, because it causes the lover to forget about their own ego for the sake of their beloved, and thus it can cause the lover to transcend himself or herself to a certain extent. Thus Potiphar's wife stayed loyal to Joseph ※, became more virtuous, and confessed to her sin, because of her ardent love. God says: *… The Chief of the Court's wife said, 'Now the truth is out; it was I who attempted to seduce him and he is indeed of the truthful'. / 'That is so that he may know I did not betray him in his absence, and that truly God does not guide [to success] the guile of the treacherous.* (Yusuf, 12:51–52)

The love of those who love God, however, is yet more ardent than this.

Love and Death

Because '*power altogether belongs to God*', they die and they are given new life in God, as we will see shortly, God willing.

LIFE IN GOD AFTER THE SOUL'S DEATH

It is obvious and certain that every human being will taste death. God says:

> *You will indeed die, and they [too] will indeed die.* (Al-Zumar, 39:30) ❋ *Every soul shall taste of death; you shall surely be paid in full your wages on the Day of Resurrection. Whoever is moved away from the Fire and admitted to Paradise, will have triumphed, the life of this world is but the comfort of delusion.* (Aal 'Imran, 3:185) ❋ *Every soul shall taste death, and We will try you with ill and good as an ordeal. And then unto Us you shall be brought back.* (Al-Anbiya', 21:35) ❋ *Every soul shall taste death. Then to Us you shall be returned.* (Al-'Ankabut, 29:57) ❋ *Wherever you may be, death will overtake you, though you should be in raised-up towers'. And if a good thing befalls them, they say, 'This is from God'; but if an evil thing befalls them, they say, 'This is from you'. Say, 'Everything is from God'. What is wrong with this people that they do not understand?* (Al-Nisa', 4:78)

However, 'the taste of death' differs from one person to another. For those whose 'souls which incite evil' have already died, they (physically) die in a 'goodly' state and then enter Paradise. God says: *Those whom the angels take away [in death] while they are goodly, saying: 'Peace be on you!; Enter Paradise because of what you used to do'.* (Al-Nahl, 16:32)

The word 'goodly' ('*tayyibin*') in Arabic may have a subtle symbolic meaning in addition to its plain meaning of 'purified from unbelief'.[345] The word '*tayyib*' also means 'alive'. Thus the death in the aforementioned verse can mean the death of the 'soul which incites evil' and not necessarily physical death. But then how can a person whose 'soul which incites evil' (the 'ego', roughly speaking) has died enter Paradise if he or she has not physically died?

We know that the Messenger of God ﷺ entered Paradise whilst he was physically alive on the Night of the Ascension (*Lailat Al-Mi'raj*). We also know that his Companion Bilal ؓ was in Paradise—or at least his spirit was in Paradise—whilst his body was still alive in the normal way in this world. The Messenger of God ﷺ said:

> 'O Bilal, tell me what deed you have done, since you entered Islam, in which you have most hope; for I have heard your footsteps before me in Paradise.' Bilal said: 'I have done no deed for which I have more hope than that whenever I made ablutions, by night or by day, I always followed this ablution with whatever amount of prayer I was destined to pray.'[346]

We also know that all those who 'draw nigh' unto God with voluntary deeds may attain something even greater than Paradise itself, for God says in a *Hadith Qudsi*:

'Whosoever shows enmity to a friend of Mine, I declare war upon him. My servant does not draw nigh unto Me with anything more beloved to Me than what I have made obligatory upon him; and My servant continues to draw nearer unto Me with voluntary deeds until I love him—and when I love him, I am his hearing wherewith he hears, his sight wherewith he sees, his hand wherewith he grasps³⁴⁷, and his foot wherewith he walks. If he asks Me, I will surely give unto him; if he seeks My refuge, I will surely give him refuge. I hesitate in nought of all that I do as I hesitate in taking the believer's soul: he hates to die, and I hate to hurt him.'³⁴⁸

We know, furthermore, that ʿUmar ibn al-Khattab ﷺ was 'dead' and then God brought him back to life and gave him a light with which he walked among the people. God says: *Why, is he who was dead, and We gave him life, and appointed for him a light by which to walk among people, as him whose likeness is in darkness whence he cannot emerge? So, what the disbelievers have been doing has been adorned for them.* (Al-Anʿam, 6:122)

Ibn Kathir says in his Commentary on this verse: 'Some say that two specific men are meant by this parable; it is said that ʿUmar ibn al-Khattab is the one who was dead, and then God gave him life, and appointed for him a light by which to walk among the people.'³⁴⁹

It is clear from all this that the friend (*wali*) of God can—by God's leave—live in God after his 'soul which incites evil' dies, and thus can enter Paradise whilst his body is still physically alive in the normal way in this world. In love there is death in God, and in love there is a life in God after this death. God says: *And say not of those slain in God's way: 'They are dead'; rather they are living; but you are not aware.* (Al-Baqarah, 2:154) ❊ *Count not those who were slain in God's way, as dead, but rather, living with their Lord, provided for [by Him].* (Aal ʿImran, 3:169)

Thus God says that there is *a new creation* after absolute poverty (and hence death of the 'ego') towards God (who is *the Independent, the Praised*, and hence the Beloved): *O mankind! You are the ones who are indigent to God. And God, He is the Independent, the Praised. / If He wishes, He can take you away and bring about a new creation. / And that is not an arduous thing for God.* (Fatir, 35:15–17)³⁵⁰

Indeed, even if a person does not realize it at first, the end of love is death in God and then life in God and Paradise³⁵¹, whilst the life of this world still continues. This is 'annihilation' and 'subsistence' in God, and it is the ultimate end of love, and perhaps of life itself. It was towards this ultimate end in God that God commanded His Messenger ﷺ to entirely devote his life and his death. God says:

Say: 'My prayer and my rituals, and my living, and my dying, are all for God, the Lord of the Worlds. / No associate has He. And to this, I have been commanded, and I am the first of those who submit'. / Say: 'Shall I seek any other than God for a lord, when He is the Lord of all things?' Every soul earns only against itself; and no burdened soul shall bear the burden of another. Then to your Lord shall you return, and He will inform you of that over which you differed. (Al-Anʿam, 6:162–164)

Indeed, God calls all believers to that which gives them (true) life, and reminds them that it is He who comes between them and their own hearts: *O you who believe, respond to God and the Messenger, when He calls you to that which will give you life; and know that God comes in between a man and his heart; and that it is to Him that you shall be gathered.* (Al-Anfal, 8:24)

To be called to true life, is to be called to God by a true death—a death of the ego through love of God.

CHAPTER THIRTY-SEVEN

THE MEETING WITH GOD AND BEATITUDE

In a healthy marriage between a man and a woman there are two kinds of 'meeting' with one's spouse: looking upon the beloved, and being with the beloved.[352]
Indeed, God says:

Tell believing men to lower their gaze and to guard their private parts. That is purer for them. Truly God is Aware of what they do. And tell believing women to lower their gaze and to guard their private parts, and not to display their adornment except for what is apparent, and let them draw their veils over their bosoms and not reveal their adornment, except to their husbands or their fathers, or their husbands' fathers, or their sons, or their husbands' sons, or their brothers, or their brothers' sons, or their sisters' sons, or their women, or what their right hands own, or such men who are dependant, not possessing any sexual desire, or children who are not yet aware of women's private parts. And do not let them thump with their feet to make known their hidden ornaments. And rally to God in repentance, O believers, so that you might be prosperous. (Al-Nur, 24:30)

And the Prophet ﷺ said: 'Look upon her, for it is more likely that you will bond with each other.'[353]

From this it is clear that in a healthy marriage the two kinds of 'meeting'—looking upon the beloved, and being with the beloved (and of course the essence of this conjugal 'being' is the conjugal act)—are immensely and mysteriously important and constitute the pillars of marriage.

In Paradise, the individual partakes of two immensely important kinds of meeting with God:

(a) The first kind is to look upon God. God says: *Some faces on that day will be radiant, / looking upon their Lord.* (Al-Qiyamah, 75:22–23)

(b) As for the second kind, we saw previously (in Chapters 7: God's Love for Humanity and 22: The Stages of Love) that between God and human beings there is a 'general companionship' and a 'special companionship'. As regards the 'general companionship', God says that He is 'with the believers'. God says: *If you have sought a judgement, the judgement has now come to you; and if you desist, it will better for you. But if you return, We shall return, and your host will*

The Meeting with God and Beatitude

not avail you in any way, however numerous it be; and verily God is with the believers. (Al-Anfal, 8:19)

However, God does not say even once in the Holy Qur'an that the believers—or even the Messenger of God ﷺ—are 'with God'. Rather, the greatest blessing in Paradise of which God speaks is the blessing of 'beatitude' ('*ridwan*'). God says: *God has promised the believers, both men and women, Gardens underneath which rivers flow, to abide therein, and blessed dwellings in the Gardens of Eden, and beatitude (ridwan) from God is greater. That is the supreme triumph.* (Al-Tawbah, 9:72)[354]

Thus God says that '*beatitude (ridwan) from God*' is '*greater*': it can be understood from this that God's beatitude is greater than anything else, and thus that God's beatitude is a kind of 'special companionship' with God in Paradise, for there can be nothing greater than 'companionship' with God. The Messenger of God ﷺ affirms this in the following *Hadith*:

> God will say to the denizens of Paradise: 'Denizens of Paradise!' They will say, 'At Your service and Your pleasure, Lord; all goodness is in Your hands!' He will say: 'Are you content?' They will say: 'How could we not be content, Lord, when You have given us what You never gave any of Your creatures?' He will say: 'Shall I not give you what is better?' They will say: 'Lord, what could be better than that?' He will say: 'I will enfold you in My beatitude, and will never be angry with you thereafter.'[355]

The Arabic word for 'beatitude' ('*ridwan*'), comes from '*rida*', meaning 'contentment'—and thus love—but it is greater than mere 'contentment', for God will enfold His creatures in this 'beatitude', and this will be the end of the Hereafter which has no end; and it will be the end of love which has no end—we can say no more than this! God knows best.

In the last Chapter (36: Love and Death), we said that a friend (*wali*) of God may enter Paradise whilst still alive in this world, as the Messenger of God ﷺ did during the Night of the Ascension (*Laylat al-Miʿraj*). But can a friend of God actually look upon God in this world? Vision cannot encompass God: *Vision cannot encompass Him, but He encompasses [all] vision. And He is the Subtle, the Aware.* (Al-Anʿam, 6:103)

And even the messengers did not see God with their eyes; for God says:

> *And when Moses came at Our appointed time, and his Lord spoke with him, he said, 'My Lord! Show me that I may behold You!' Said He, 'You shall not see Me, but behold the mountain, and if it remains, in its place, then you shall see Me'. And when his Lord revealed Himself to the mountain He levelled it to the ground and Moses fell down senseless. And when he recovered his senses*

he said, 'Glory be to You! I repent to You, and I am the first of the believers'. (Al-A'raf, 7:143)

But the 'inner heart' ('*fu'ad*') can see the 'great signs' ('*ayat*') of God, as God says: *The inner heart (fu'ad) denied not what it saw.* (Al-Najm, 53:11) *The eye did not swerve, nor did it go beyond [the bounds]. / Verily he saw, of the signs of his Lord, the greatest.* (Al-Najm, 53:17–18)

Since this happened during the earthly life of the Messenger of God ﷺ, we can deduce from this that the 'inner heart' ('*fu'ad*') of a friend (*wali*) of God or saint *can* behold the signs of God in his or her earthly life.

Does this mean that God enfolds people in His beatitude whilst they are still alive? The answer is that we do not know this for certain, but we do know that God may give to a person, in his or her earthly life, a (sublime) 'mercy from Him', and teach him or her (sublime) 'knowledge from Him'. God says: *So [there] they found one of Our servants to whom We had given mercy from Us and We had taught him knowledge from Us.* (Al-Kahf, 18:65)

Moreover, God sends the Spirit to whomever of His creatures He wills. God says:

> *He sends down the angels with the Spirit of His command to whomever He will of His servants, [saying]: Warn that there is no God save Me: so fear Me* (Al-Nahl, 16:2) ❊ *Exalter of ranks, Lord of the Throne, He casts the Spirit of His command upon whomever He wishes of His servants, that he may warn them of the Day of Encounter.* (Ghafir, 40:15)

Thus human beings must heed the words of Jacob ﷺ, and never despair of God's Spirit—in this world or in the Hereafter—for God says: *O my sons, go and enquire about Joseph and his brother, and do not despair of the Spirit of God. Indeed none despairs of the [gracious] Spirit of God save the disbelieving folk'.* (Yusuf, 12:87)

And He says: *But for those who feared the station of their Lord, there will be two gardens.* (Al-Rahman, 55:46)

Ibn 'Arabi says in his Commentary (which is said by some to actually be the work of 'Abd al-Razzaq Kashani) the following about this verse: ' "*Two gardens*": one is the Paradise of the soul, and the other is the Paradise of the heart.'[356]

Perhaps there is thus an allusion in this verse to the two kinds of meeting with the Lord, namely the beholding of God in the Hereafter, and the 'special companionship' of God in the Hereafter; and God knows best.

CHAPTER THIRTY-EIGHT

THE TRUE INTENDED OBJECT BEHIND ALL LOVE

We saw previously (in Chapter 6: The Universe and Love) that everything loves God naturally and innately, except disbelievers, hypocrites and evildoers. To this we must add that whatever people strive for, they are, in reality, striving for God, even if they do not realise it. This is true even for the disbelievers, hypocrites and evildoers. We see this even in the very roots of unbelief, hypocrisy and evildoing, in the false promise Satan first made to Adam ﷺ to tempt him. God says: *Then Satan whispered to him saying, 'O Adam, shall I guide you to the Tree of Immortality, and a kingdom that does not waste away?'* (*Ta Ha*, 20:120)

'Immortality' belongs only to God, and 'the kingdom that does not waste away' is also His Alone. Yet Satan promised to lead Adam ﷺ to them both. Thus when Adam ﷺ obeyed Satan, he wanted Satan to show him how he could attain the Qualities of God and the kingdom of God. Adam ﷺ wanted to obtain that which only God should have. His error was that he wanted to share what God has, or to possess the like of that which God possesses. Nevertheless, in both cases, what Adam ﷺ ultimately wanted was God Himself, since he wanted His Qualities: desiring qualities actually means desiring the reality and being of those qualities, whether one realizes it or not. Thus Adam ﷺ only wanted God and His Qualities and nothing else.

God says: *Adorned for mankind is love of lusts—of women, children, stored-up heaps of gold and silver, horses of mark, cattle, and tillage. That is the pleasure of the life of this world; but God—with Him is the most excellent abode.* (*Aal ʿImran*, 3:14)

In loving 'women, children, stored-up heaps of gold and silver, horses of mark, cattle, and tillage', mankind desires beauty, might, wealth, power and provision. Ultimately, all these things come from God, and manifest His Qualities and Most Beautiful Names. Whoever wants them wants nothing other than the Qualities and Acts of God, even though he or she mistakenly loves them for themselves instead of loving God, faith, and what God enjoins. God says: *I found her and her people prostrating to the sun instead of God, and Satan has adorned for them their deeds and he has barred them from the Way, so that they are not guided.* (*Al-Naml*, 27:24)

By prostrating to the sun instead of God, the Queen of Sheba (referred to here) was searching for the truth of God, and she thought that the sun was God. All this can clearly be seen in the story of Abraham ﷺ when he was trying to guide his people to God, first by pointing to a star; then to the moon; then to the sun; and then by telling them that God is the One who created the heavens and the earth, and that He is neither star, nor moon, nor sun. God says:

> *When night descended upon him he saw a star and said, 'This is my Lord'. But when it set, he said, 'I love not those that set'. / And when he saw the moon rising, he said, 'This is my Lord'. But when it set he said, 'Unless my Lord guides me, I shall surely become one of the folk who are astray'. / And when he saw the sun rising, he said, 'This is my Lord; this is greater!' But when it set, he said, 'O my people, surely I am innocent of what you associate. / Verily I have turned my face to Him Who originated the heavens and the earth; a hanif, and I am not of those that associate others'. / But his people disputed with him. He said, 'Do you dispute with me concerning God when He has guided me? I have no fear of what you associate with Him, unless my Lord wills something. My Lord encompasses all things through His knowledge; will you not remember? / How should I fear what you have associated, and you fear not, that you have associated with God that for which He has not revealed to you any warrant?' Which of the two parties has more right to security if you have any knowledge? / Those who believe and have not confounded their belief with evildoing, theirs is security; and they are rightly guided. (Al-An'am, 6:76–82)*

Thus all that people want in reality is God and His Qualities and Most Beautiful Names, but they do not realise this because, in their ignorance, they only see the outward appearance of things. This is not good enough before God. God says:

> *They know [merely] an outward aspect of the life of this world; but they, of the Hereafter, they are oblivious. (Al-Rum, 30:7)* ❂ *So shun him who turns away from Our Remembrance, and desires nothing but the life of this world. / That is the full extent of their knowledge. Truly your Lord knows best those who have strayed from His way, and He knows best those who are [rightly] guided. (Al-Najm, 53:29–30)* ❂ *And most of them follow nothing but conjecture; truly conjecture avails nothing against truth. Surely God is Knower of what they do. (Yunus, 10:36)*

What is astonishing about all this is how people do not realise that, at the heart of every one of their desires, lies the desire for God and His Qualities. This is astonishing because how can anything possibly veil God? God says: *O man! What has deceived you with regard to your generous Lord, / who created you, then made you upright, then proportioned you, / assembling you in whatever form He wishes? (Al-Infitar, 82:6–8)*

In fact, nothing can veil God, but people's sins veil them *from* God. God says: *No indeed! Rather, that which they earned is on their hearts as rust. (Al-Mutaffifin, 83:14)*

The True Intended Object behind All Love

God says: *And your Lord has decreed that you worship none save Him, and kindness to parents. If they should reach old age with you, one of them or both then do not say to them 'Fie' nor repulse them, but speak to them gracious words. (Al-Isra', 17:23)*

Ibn ʿAjibah comments on this verse: 'I say that 'decreed' here means 'ruled', 'obliged' and 'commanded'; it does not mean a decree of fate, for were that the case then nothing but God would ever have been worshipped'.[357]

Ibn ʿAjibah raises an important point here, which is the meaning of the word 'decreed'. According to his commentary, the word 'decreed' here is not being used in its usual meaning, because he considers the words *'your Lord has decreed'* to be a religious commandment, as he feels that to consider it as a description of God's decree of fate would be impossible since, as he says, 'were that the case then nothing but God would ever have been worshipped'. God says: *When the hypocrites come to you they say: 'We bear witness that you are indeed the Messenger of God'. And God knows that you are indeed His Messenger, and God bears witness that the hypocrites truly are liars. (Al-Munafiqun, 63:1)*

Now the statement the hypocrites make in this verse (that: 'Muhammad ﷺ is the Messenger of God') is true in itself, yet God declares that it was a lie when they spoke it, because they spoke it with a false intention, not believing it. God says: *…They say with their tongues what is not in their hearts… (Al-Fath, 48:11)*

And the Messenger of God ﷺ said: 'Actions are defined by their intentions, and each man has but what he intends…'[358]

Therefore, is it not possible for us to understand God's words *'your Lord has decreed'* to be an ontological description of God's decree of fate rather than a religious commandment, contrary to what Ibn ʿAjibah said? In other words, can we consider the words of this Qur'anic verse (*Al-Isra'*, 17:23) an allusion to the fact that the true intended object of all love is God Alone? In this case, the idolaters would intend by their worship nothing but idolatry, and not the worship of God—and thus their worship would remain idolatry—but God and His Qualities would be behind their intention without their knowing it; and God knows best. Indeed, this is the actual lexical meaning of 'decree' ('*qada*'). Moreover, God says: *Why, surely to God belongs all who are in the heavens and all who are in the earth. Those who call upon besides God are not following associates: they are following nothing but conjecture, and they are only telling lies. (Yunus, 10:66)*

And the *Tafsir al-Jalalayn* explains: ' "*Why, surely to God belongs all who are in the heavens and all who are in the earth*" as slaves, subjects and creatures. "*Those who call upon*", i.e. worship, "*besides God*" i.e. false gods instead of Him "*are not following associates*" of His in reality, for He is far above such things; "*they are following nothing*" when they do this "*but conjecture*", i.e. their conjecture that these beings are gods who can intercede for them; *"and they are only telling lies"*, i.e. they are false in asserting this.'³⁵⁹

Therefore the idols of the idolaters have no reality or existence to begin with—and thus their worship of them is purely conjecture—and so the object of their worship must necessarily be something other than what they think it is. All who are in the heavens and the earth belong to God, and this means that the thing the idolaters worship is either God—and of course '*There is nothing like Him*' (*Al-Shura*, 42:11)—or it *belongs to* God, and thus to His Qualities or their manifestations.

God says: *The hypocrites seek to trick God, but He is tricking them. When they stand up to pray, they stand up lazily and to be seen by people, and they do not remember God save a little.* (*Al-Nisa'*, 4:142)

Perhaps there is another allusion here to this concept in His words '*but He is tricking them*'; and God knows best.

In any case, God is the true intended object of all love—whether the individual realises it or not. How could it be otherwise, when: *He is the First and the Last, and the Manifest and the Hidden and He has knowledge of all things.* (*Al-Hadid*, 57:3)

And how could God not be the true intended object of all love, when He says: *To God belong the East and the West; whithersoever you turn, there is the Face of God. Lo! God is Embracing, Knowing.* (*Al-Baqarah*, 2:115)

And perhaps this is one of the secrets of His words:

And to the three who were left behind when the earth was straitened for them, for all its breadth, and their souls were straitened for them; until they thought that there is no refuge from God except in Him. Then He turned [relenting] to them that they might also turn [in repentance]. Truly God is the Relenting, the Merciful. (*Al-Tawbah*, 9:118)

In other words, God is the true intended Object of all love—*there is no refuge from God except in Him*—so there is no escape whatsoever from Him except to Him. Thus there is no escape from loving Him unknowingly and unwillingly except to love Him knowingly and willingly; and God knows best.

SUMMARY

CHAPTER THIRTY-NINE

CONCLUSION

To conclude: God (*Allah*) is the Compassionate (*Al-Rahman*), the Merciful (*Al-Rahim*), and the Loving (*Al-Wadud*). He created the world and human beings through mercy and through love. He placed beauty in all that He created, and He loves His Own Beauty via the universe in which He created beauty. Through love, human beings can return to God and Paradise. Through love, too—but through a base love—human beings can take the path to hell. Hence God says: '*We guided him to the two paths*' (*Al-Balad*, 90:10). Thus human beings must choose, throughout their lives in this world, between a higher love and a lower love; between the kind of love which leads to God and happiness, and the kind of love which leads to hell and to suffering. God asks all human beings to consider: '*Where, then, are you going?*' (*Al-Takwir*, 81:26). Thus the Messenger of God ﷺ said: 'The firmest bond of faith is to love for God's sake and to abhor for God's sake.'[360]

The Messenger of God ﷺ also said: 'Whosoever loves for God, and hates for God, and gives for God, and withholds for God, has perfect faith.'[361]

Equally, the Messenger of God said: 'And is religion anything other than love (*hubb*) and abhorrence (*bughd*)? God ﷺ says: *Say: 'If you love God, follow me, and God will love you more, and forgive you your sins; God is Forgiving, Merciful.'* (*Aal 'Imran*, 3:31).'[362]

Human beings must choose love of God, and place their hopes in Him in this life and the next. They must not choose passions and lusts. God says:

> *Truly those who do not expect to encounter Us, and are content with the life of this world, and feel reassured in it, and those who are heedless of Our signs, those, their abode will be the Fire because of what they used to earn. / Truly those who believe and perform righteous deeds, their Lord will guide them through their faith. Rivers will flow beneath them in the Gardens of Bliss, / their prayer therein: 'Glory be to You, O God!', and their greeting therein will be: 'Peace'. / And their final prayer will be: 'Praise be to God, Lord of the Worlds'.* (*Yunus*, 10:7–10)

CHAPTER FORTY

SYNOPSIS

(of key points in *Love in the Holy Qur'an* for teaching and discussion)

INTRODUCTION

THE MYSTERY OF LOVE
- Most of life's activity and effort is expended on the search for love, without people even perceiving what they are doing, and why.

THE DEFINITION OF LOVE
- Love can be defined as 'an inclination towards beauty after being pleased by it.'
- God's love is: first, the free gift of existence and of countless other favours (including beauty of various kinds) to every created thing, and, second, love of beauty as such.

DIVINE LOVE

GOD AND LOVE
- Love is not merely one of God's acts or actions, but one of God's very Own Divine Qualities.
- God's Loving is inseparable from His Mercy.... Love comes with Mercy, and Mercy comes with Love.
- Divine Mercy is of the very Divine Essence Itself.
- Divine Love, like Divine Mercy, is of the very Divine Essence Itself.
- God's Love is twice implied—along with the double mention of Divine Mercy—at the beginning of the Holy Qur'an itself and the beginning of every one of its one hundred and fourteen chapters except the ninth.

LOVE IS THE ROOT OF CREATION
- God created human beings out of His mercy.
- God created humankind for His mercy.
- God created human beings and the world out of mercy and for mercy.... This means that the world and human beings were created out of love and for love too.

THE UNIVERSE AND LOVE
- Everything in the heavens and the earth innately and naturally both glorifies and praises God with their very beings.

Synopsis

- The entire universe innately loves God.
- Even the most evil person committing the most evil deed—with his or her consciousness rejecting or hating God at that moment—nevertheless loves God in every atom of their being and in their deepest heart.
- God loves all beings and all things—apart from evildoers as such—before and more than they could possibly love Him.

GOD'S LOVE FOR HUMANITY

- God's great favour to human beings is a result of His Love for them in general.
- It is as though God were saying that He particularly loves those who adorn themselves with virtue or beauty of soul, in varying degrees.
- God particularly loves those whose souls are beautiful and virtuous according to the very measure of the level of their beauty of soul and virtue.
- God's mercy embraces all things ... to this it may be added that God's generous bounty reaches all things, whether they deserve it or not.

GOD'S LOVE FOR HIS MESSENGERS AND PROPHETS

- God favours his prophets more than the rest of humanity; God favours His messengers more than the Prophets; God especially loves the five 'resolute' messengers; and God made the Prophet Muhammad ﷺ His beloved.

THOSE WHOM GOD DOES NOT LOVE

- God never states—not even once—in the Holy Qur'an that He hates anyone or any type of evildoer. God only says that He hates evil deeds, or the evil that they cause.

THE MESSENGER OF GOD'S ﷺ LOVE

THE MESSENGER OF GOD'S ﷺ LOVE FOR GOD

- The Messenger of God's ﷺ love for God went beyond mere emotion ... he was completely immersed with all his being in the ocean of God's love.... God is the Beloved of His Messenger.

THE MESSENGER OF GOD'S ﷺ LOVE FOR THE BELIEVERS

- The Messenger of God ﷺ almost consumed himself with worry for humanity; ... he was full of pity and mercy for the believers; ... he was so tender with the believers that he was shy of them ... the Messenger of God ﷺ felt a great love for the believers especially, and for all humanity in general.

HUMAN LOVE

HUMANITY'S LOVE FOR GOD

- God's Qualities include Absolute Beauty, Mercy and Generosity, and He has graced human beings with gifts and blessings beyond measure, and is always answering their needs and prayers; so how could human beings not love God?

* Human beings' love for God begins as an emotion, and then—by following the Messenger of God ﷺ through righteous deeds, virtuous character and remembrance of God—it becomes part of the believer's very being and soul.... This love becomes then stronger and more ardent than any worldly love, and stronger and more ardent than any love which anyone who does not believe in God could ever experience, or even imagine.
* If one truly loves God, one cannot help but love what leads to God as well, as part of that love of God.

THE BELIEVER'S LOVE FOR THE MESSENGER OF GOD ﷺ

* Understanding and loving the Messenger of God ﷺ is the first step towards truly understanding and loving virtue as such, because, precisely, the Messenger of God was the embodiment of perfect virtue; and understanding and loving virtue is the first step towards practicing virtue and being virtuous.
* The mere emotion of love towards the Messenger of God ﷺ is not sufficient in itself ... It must be accompanied by invoking blessings and peace upon the Messenger ﷺ.

LOVE FOR THE FAMILY AND KIN OF THE MESSENGER OF GOD ﷺ

* It is obligatory to love the family and kin of the Messenger of God ﷺ according to the different degrees of their proximity to him. This love is obligatory for all those who love the Messenger of God ﷺ, and thus it is obligatory for all those who love God.

THE EFFECTS OF THE LOVE OF GOD ON HUMAN BEINGS

* Those whom God loves and who love Him are pious and humble but proud of their faith; they struggle constantly against their egos and obey none but God. And these attributes can be concretely recognised by others, for God says: '... *Their mark is on their faces...*'

FAMILY LOVE

* God has established a natural, licit, good and praiseworthy love between every human being and his or her family. God has established this love in accordance with the degree of closeness between family members: the closer they are to each other by blood, the stronger the love should be. However, God stresses that people's love for God must remain greater and stronger than all family love.

LOVE OF OTHERS (ALL HUMANITY; THE 'PEOPLE OF THE SCRIPTURE'; BELIEVERS, AND FRIENDS)

* God has given each and every human being inalienable rights, and has obliged Muslims to have respect for all human beings; not to commit aggression against anyone; to be peaceful and to be just; to be merciful; to empathize with all human beings; to forgive them; to pardon them; to restrain themselves from anger; and even to repay evil deeds with kindness and 'turn the other

cheek'—and to do this with all people, whoever they may be and regardless of their faith (or lack of it) all the time, so long as they are not first waging war against Muslims.
* God enjoins upon Muslims—in addition to having respect, justice and mercy in general towards all humanity—to have affection and admiration for the People of the Scripture in general (notably Christians and Jews).
* In addition to respect, justice, mercy, affection and kindness, God requires believers to love one another more than they love themselves.
* God mentions four different degrees of 'friendship' in the Holy Qur'an: (1) 'Company' or 'companionship' ('*suhbah*'); (2) 'friendship' ('*sadaqah*'); (3) 'close friendship' ('*sadaqah hamimiyya*'), and (4) 'intimate friendship' ('*khullah*'). These constitute, in ascending order, the gamut of friendship between believers, and the highest degrees of (non-sexual) love between those who are not related.

CONJUGAL AND SEXUAL LOVE
* Human beings cannot be complete without each other. Males need females, and females need males, and without each other they are generally incomplete. This need for each other can be clearly seen in three things: (a) the need males and females have for each other in order to procreate; (b) the need males and females have for each other psychologically and emotionally during marriage; and (c) conjugal and sexual love between spouses.
* Every soul has a particular spouse—a unique, individual 'soulmate'—which was created for it either by a Divine 'creation' ('*khalq*') a priori, or by a special Divine 'making' ('*ja'al*') ordained after creation. Sometimes, people are able to find their soulmate in this worldly life. Sometimes they never find him or her.
* Between some people, and between some spouses, there is a perfect relationship such that each person completes the other, as though they are a single person or a single soul. In such a case, we could call this 'a marriage of souls'. Other spouses, however, may enjoy peace, affection and mercy without their relationship being perfect and complete, even though they have been married for many years.
* God affirms that in marriage there is a love which can be entirely separate from physical relations, and that the souls of both spouses naturally need this love just as much as their bodies need physical love.
* The secrets ... of conjugal relations ... are symbolically alluded to a number of times in the Holy Qur'an.
* God holds the sexual act an irrevocable bond of sorts—even when the act, or the marriage in which it occurs, has come to end—and that this bond necessitates kindness and respect forever.
* Is there also a spiritual experience in the sexual act, in addition to the physical one?

- Beholding physical beauty can sometimes be—or bring about—a spiritual state of contemplation, which is diametrically opposed to physical lust.
- Can the annihilation in sexual climax lead—for certain people at least—to a spiritual experience and 'meeting'?
- Physical beauty may be the cause of remembrance of God and contemplation of a 'proof' of God, and thus there may be, for certain people, a profound spiritual element to sexual beauty.

LOVE AND EXTRA-MARITAL SEX
- There is—or can be—love in fornication, in addition to the passion and the physical desire.
- Extra-marital love can sometimes become so ardent and intense that it almost reaches the level of worship, although it can never actually reach the level of true worship of God.

LOVE AND THE EYES
- There is something special—a great mystery—about a person's eyes which may: (1) express love; or (2) engender love in the beholder himself or herself, or (3) engender love in the one who looks into another's eyes. In other words, love may: (1) be seen by others in a person's eyes; (2) 'enter' a person through his or her eyes into his or her soul and heart as they look at someone else, or (3) cause another person to love them as a result of a meeting of the eyes—of 'eye-contact'.

LOVE

THE DIFFERENT KINDS OF LOVE
- God mentions at least thirty-eight different kinds of 'hubb'—'love' or 'liking'—in the Holy Qur'an. Each one of these thirty-eight kinds of *hubb* differs subtly in meaning from each of the others so that there is no tautology in Arabic and each word means something unique and precise but subtly different. In English translation, however, we often are forced to resort to reusing the same word for different Arabic terms for *hubb* (but in these cases we generally provide accompanying transliterations in brackets). The different kinds of '*hubb*' mentioned in the Holy Qur'an include: 1. love (*hubb*); 2. love (*mahabba*); 3. preference (*istihbab*); 4. mercy (*rahmah*); 5. pity (*ra'fah*); 6. love (*wudd*); 7. affection (*mawaddah*); 8. love (*widad*); 9. will or desire (*iradah*); 10. to be smitten (*shaghaf*); 11. impulse (*hawa*); 12. infatuation (*istihwa'*); 13. to stray (*ghawa*); 14. desire (*hamm*); 15. longing (*raghab*); 16. to draw near (*taqarrub*); 17. anguish (*gharam*); 18. to wander distracted (*huyam*); 19. close friendship (*khullah*); 20. friendship (*sadaqah*); 21. companionship (*suhbah*); 22. preference to another over oneself (*ithar*); 23. going astray (*dalal*); 24. contentment (*rida*); 25. compassion (*hanan*); 26. admiration (*iʿjab*); 27. inclination (*mayl*); 28. lust (*shahwah*); 29. tendency towards (*saba*); 30. seeking (*ibtigha'*); 31. favour

(*tafdil*); 32. extra-marital sex (*zina*); 33. graciousness (*hafawah*); 34. concern (*shafaqah*); 35. protecting friendship (*wilayah*); 36. inclination (*sagha*); 37. intimate friendship/'penetrating' friendship (*walijah*) and 38. affinity (*ulfah*).

THE STAGES OF LOVE

● God mentions at least one hundred stages of human love in the Holy Qur'an:

(a) Stages of love that occur in both human beings' love for God and human beings' love for each other: (1. Emptiness (*al-Faragh*); 2. Neediness (*al-Faqr*); 3. Adornment (*al-Tazayyun*); 4. Admiration (*al-I'jab*); 5. Love (*al-Hubb*. and Intense Love (*al-Ihbab*); 6. Contentment (*al-Rida*); 7. Drawing Near (*al-Taqarrub*); 8. Will or Desire (*al-Iradah*); 9. Seeking (*al-Ibtigha'*); 10. Longing (*al-Raghab*); 11. Protecting Friendship (*al-Wilayah*); 12. Close Friendship (*al-Khullah*); 13. Joy (*al-Farah*); 14. Tranquillity (*al-Sakan*); 15. Hope or Expectancy (*al-Raja'*); 16. Action (*al-ʿAmal*); 17. Remembrance (*al-Dhikr*); 18. Communion (*al-Najwa*); 19. Trial (*al-Ibtila'*); 20. Serenity (*al-Itmi'nan*); 21. Knowledge (*al-ʿIlm*); 22. Recognition (*al-Maʿrifah*); 23. Will or Wish (*al-Mashi'ah*); 24. Fear (*al-Khawf*); 25. Grief (*al-Huzn*); 26. Suffering (*al-Alam*); 27. Weeping (*al-Buka'*); 28. Change (*al-Taghyir*); 29. Contraction (*al-Qabd*); 30. Expansion (*al-Bast*); 31. Need for Seclusion (*al-Hajah ila al-Khalwah*); 32. Patience (*al-Sabr*); 33. Hope (*al-Amal*); 34. Jealousy (*al-Ghirah*); 35. Meeting (*al-Liqa'*); 36. Company (*al-Ma'iyyah*); 37. Comfort of the Eye (*Qurrat al-ʿAyn*).

(b) Stages of love that occur in human beings' love for God (and may or may not apply to human love for other human beings): 38. Love (*al-Wudd*); 39. Concern (*al-Shafaqah*); 40. Comfortable Familiarity (*al-Uns, al-Isti'nas*); 41. Peace (*al-Salam*); 42. Sufficiency (*al-Iktifa'*); 43. Gratitude or Thankfulness (*al-Shukr*); 44. Trust (*al-Tawakkul*); 45. 'Expansion of the Breast' (*Inshirah al-Sadr*); 46. 'Softening of Skin' (*Layn al-Jild*); 47. 'Softening of the Heart' (*Layn al-Qalb*); 48. 'Quivering of the Skin' (*Qash'arirat al-Jild*); 49. 'Trembling of the Heart' (*Wajl al-Qalb*); 50. Devotion (*al-Tabattul*); 51. Humble Obedience (*al-Ikhbat*); 52. Turning in Penitence (*al-Inabah*); 53. Humility (*al-Tadarru'*); 54. Repentance (*al-Tawbah*); 55. Asking Forgiveness (*al-Istighfar*); 56. 'Hastening to Please' (*al-ʿAjal lil-Tardiyah*); 57. Calling upon or Supplication (*al-Duʿa'*); 58. Remembrance (*al-Tadhakkur*); 59. Following (*al-Ittiba'*); 60. 'Proving what is in the Heart' (*Tamhis al-Qalb*); 61. Uncertainty (*al-Shakk*); 62. Doubt (*al-Rayb*); 63. Entertaining Thoughts (*al-Zhann*); 64. Looking (*al-Nazhar*); 65. Contemplation (*al-Tafakkur*); 66. Meditation (*al-Tadabbur*); 67. 'Using Reason' (*Isti'mal al-ʿAql*); 68. Perception (*al-Tabassur*); 69. Certainty (*al-Yaqin*): Certain Knowledge (*ʿIlm al-Yaqin*); Certain Vision (*ʿAyn al-Yaqin*); Certain Truth (*Haqq al-Yaqin*); 70. Ardent Hope (*al-Tama*); 71. Need for Human Company (*al-Hajah ila al-Jalwah*); 72. Imploring or Tender-heartedness (*al-Ta'awwuh*); 73. Penitence (*al-Awb*); 74. Devoutness (*al-Qunut*); 75. Being Overwhelmed (*al-Qahr*); 76. Submission (*al-Islam*); 77. Faith (*al-Iman*); 78. Virtue (*al-Ihsan*); 79. Sincerity (*al-Ikhlas*).

(c) Stages of love that occur in human beings' love for each other (and may or may not apply to human love for God): 80. Love (*al-Mahabbah*); 81. 'The Presence of (physical) Beauty' (*Wujud al-Jamal*); 82. Mutual Knowledge (*al-Taʿaruf*); 83. Inclination (*al-Mayl*); 84. Affection (*al-Mawaddah*); 85. Pity (*al-Raʾfah*); 86. Lust (*al-Shahwah*); 87. Impulse (*al-Hawa*); 88. Desire (*al-Hamm*); 89. Pleasure (*al-Mutʿah*); 90. Enjoyment (*al-Istimtaʿ*); 91. Generosity (*al-Karam*); 92. Mercy (*al-Rahmah*); 93. Tenderness (*al-Lutf*); 94. Forgiveness (*al-Maghfirah, al-Ghufran*); 95. Pardoning (*al-ʿAfu*); 96. Overlooking (*al-Safh*); 97. Kindness (*al-Maʿruf*); 98. Seduction (*al-Murawadah*); 99. Shyness (*al-Istihyaʾ*); 100. Obliviousness to Oneself (*ʿAdam al-Ihsas bil-Hal*).

● In its totality, human love is composed of (at least) one hundred stages … these one hundred stages constitute most of the main stages of love. They provide a definite idea of how love develops, and thus also of what happens when someone falls in love.

FALLING IN LOVE

● Falling in love is 'the systematic inclination of a person's constituent parts and faculties towards beauty, after having been pleased by it'. All the stages of love are nothing but the workings of the body, soul and spirit's faculties as they incline towards, and attach themselves to, the object of love.

THE GROWTH OF LOVE

● Love increases as the other faculties incline towards the beloved. Love for God increases when the Sunnah (and thus virtue) is adhered to.

● How can a person choose and control what to love and what not to love? The key to strengthening a beneficial love is to perform righteous deeds and hence to behave virtuously. Virtue is truly its own reward. … Weakening a negative love is not so easy. It is, nevertheless, possible with God's help. [It] requires three key virtues or practices, namely: (1) patience; (2) humility; (3) prayer and remembrance of God.

THE TWO CIRCLES OF LOVE

● Those who truly believe and those who completely disbelieve are each in a state of constant increase of their own situation. True believers are always ascending and attaining ever higher degrees; and the opposite is true for complete disbelievers: they are constantly sinking to lower and lower levels. … There are thus two closed, self-perpetuating circles of love: a higher one of licit love or love for God; and a lower circle of illicit love, or at least negative, love.

THE TRIANGLE OF LOVE

● Since they know nothing when they are born … human beings require things to be 'adorned' for them beforehand—or rather, in them—before they can love them.

* The lover does not at first really know their beloved; the lover loves the beloved because he or she imagines that their beloved is identical to an internal image they already love, whether it is so in reality or not.
* Knowledge of God increases through faith, humility, love, good deeds, and meditating and contemplating upon everything inside the soul and the world. In other words, knowledge of God grows in a similar way to love of God, by the gradual exercise and concentration of the heart and soul and all their many faculties and constituent parts upon the object of knowledge—or rather, upon the Object of knowledge.
* People first love God through the faith which God adorns to them in their hearts. After this, they begin to come to know God and His Names and Qualities by means of considering God's acts and signs ... After knowledge of the Beloved and virtue increase, love becomes direct and no longer acts through the triangle of adornment.

THE HIERARCHIES OF BEAUTY AND OF LOVE
* The highest beauty is Divine Beauty; then sacred beauty (starting with the beauty of the Messenger of God ﷺ); then inner beauty; then outer beauty; then inner lusts; then outer lusts. Thus not every love is praiseworthy, and not every beauty should be loved.

THE OPPOSITES OF BEAUTY AND OF LOVE
* The word 'ugliness' (*basha'ah*) is not found in the Holy Qur'an at all, which indicates that everything in creation has some kind of beauty, even if some things are less beautiful than other things ... ugliness or vileness is a privation or absence of beauty and not a thing in itself.
* Hatred seems to depend on the state of the individual: believers and the good hate evil, and the disbelievers and the evil hate good, but it is possible that those believers who have not completely overcome their egos might love something that is bad for them or hate something that is good for them ... Hatred emerges from love of the thing opposite to what one loves.

THE END OF LOVE
* God's love for people never changes and never ends, unless of course those loved by God change and reject God's love.
* If a person changes and his or her faith lessens, it follows that his or her love for God will also lessen. Similarly, if a person's faith increases, it follows that his or her love for God will also increase ... In summary, a person's love for God may change, not because his or her Beloved has changed (for God never changes), but because the person themself has changed, in heart and soul.
* Conjugal love—like all the other natural or positive kinds of inter-human love that are ultimately love for God's sake—should not ever change in this life or the next, and will not, unless the inner state of the lover or the beloved changes

for the worst. Certainly it should not change merely because the beloved has become less beautiful physically, as all bodies naturally do over time.

THE NATURE OF LOVE

- All lovers are in a state of continuous change, constantly passing between the states of contraction and expansion of love, in this world at least … but this change does not cause them to grow weary of love.
- Love necessarily means need, and the lover needs his or her beloved.
- 'Ardent love' fills people completely and does not allow anything else to enter the heart.
- Love has a tremendous power, for love conquers lovers and then leads them on through the stages of love until their deaths through love. In the case of lovers of God, love leads them from death through love to eternity in their Beloved.

LOVE AND HAPPINESS

- There is no true happiness without the love of God … Worldly love is not sufficient to lead to happiness, because it does not fill one completely, perfectly and eternally … Nothing can completely suffice human beings and fill them except the love of God.

LOVE AND BEAUTY IN PARADISE

- Paradise contains all that its inhabitants love, and all those whom they love. There is love in Paradise, but the love of Paradise differs from the love of this world. Thus love in Paradise is all the soul desires and everything in which the eye rejoices, but without the imperfection, need, suffering and contraction of the love of this world.

THE BELOVED

BEAUTY AND ITS COMPONENTS

- The components of beauty are majesty, munificence and the harmony between them, all these together constituting the perfection of beauty.

TASTE

- Beauty is objective, whereas taste is … subjective, and personal.

THE NATURE OF BEAUTY

- Beauty is present in things themselves.
- Beauty can distract those who see it from everything around them; even from their own selves; even from their own senses; even from pain.
- Beauty has a tremendous power that works in two alternative ways: either it draws its beholder out of himself or herself, or returns its beholder back into himself or herself.
- Beauty (and love) may have the power to make even the hardship of death easier to endure.

LOVE AND DEATH

- The death in God's way of the ego or the 'soul which incites evil' is the ultimate aim of the inner struggle, just as physical death in God's way is the ultimate martyrdom in the outer struggle against the enemy.
- The definition of a 'friend' of God or 'saint' (*wali Allah*) is someone who longs for death (in order to meet Him) … the 'friends' of God love Him, and in their love for Him they long for physical death. Their 'souls which incite evil' have already died, so they are safe from all fear and grief.
- If people love things other than God with a degree of love that should be reserved only for God, their egos do not die like those who love God. Rather, their souls suffer a terrible chastisement.
- The friend (*wali*) of God can—by God's leave—live in God after his 'soul which incites evil' dies, and thus can enter Paradise whilst his body is still physically alive in the normal way in this world. In love there is death in God, and in love there is a life in God after this death.

THE MEETING WITH GOD AND BEATITUDE

- God's beatitude is greater than anything else, and thus God's beatitude is a kind of 'special companionship' with God in Paradise, for there can be nothing greater than 'companionship' with God.

THE TRUE INTENDED OBJECT BEHIND ALL LOVE

- God is the true intended Object of all love, so there is no escape whatsoever from Him except to Him. Thus there is no escape from loving Him unknowingly and unwillingly except to love Him knowingly and willingly.

CONCLUSION

- God (*Allah*) is the Compassionate (*Al-Rahman*), the Merciful (*Al-Rahim*), and the Loving (*Al-Wadud*). He created the world and human beings through mercy and through love. He placed beauty in all that He created, and He loves His Own Beauty via the universe in which He created beauty. Through love, human beings can return to God and Paradise. Through love, too—but through a base love—human beings can take the path to hell. Hence God says: '*We guided him to the two paths*' (*Al-Balad*, 90:10). Thus human beings must choose, throughout their lives in this world, between a higher love and a lower love; between the kind of love which leads to God and happiness, and the kind of love which leads to hell and to suffering.

NOTES

CHAPTER 1: PROLOGUE: THE GOALS AND METHODOLOGY OF THIS WORK

1 Throughout this book we use italics for Qur'anic quotes but not for *Hadith* (the sayings of the Messenger of God ﷺ). We have not dared to translate the Qur'an ourselves, but rather have selected translations from the following superior, well-known English translations: Abdel Haleem, M.A.S., *The Qur'an, A New Translation*; Ali, Abdullah Yusuf, *The Holy Qur'an*; Arberry, A.J., *The Koran Interpreted*; Asad, Muhammad, *The Message of the Holy Qur'an*; Lings, Dr. Martin, *The Holy Qur'an: Translations of Selected Verses*; Nasr, Seyyed Hossein, et al, *The Study Qur'an*; Pickthall, Mohammed Marmeduke, *The Meaning of the Glorious Koran*, and The Royal Aal al-Bayt Institute for Islamic Thought, *Translation of the Holy Qur'an*, (see Bibliography).

2 Abu Ja'far Muhammad bin Jarir al-Tabari, *Tafsir al-Tabari*, p. 325. There may be a subtle difference between the Divine words '*the details for all things*', as the Holy Qur'an says of itself in *Surat Yusuf* (12:111), and the Divine words '*a detailing of all things*', which in the Holy Qur'an describe the (first) Tablets of Moses ﷺ in *Surat Al-An'am* (6:154) and *Surat Al-A'raf* (7:145). Perhaps God's words '*the details for all things*' mean that God made a complete image of all things in the Holy Qur'an, whilst His words '*a detailing of all things*' mean that God placed a description of all things in the Tablets of Moses ﷺ. On the other hand, it will be noticed that whereas God's words about the Holy Qur'an—'*the details for all things*'—are unqualified, God's words about the Tablets of Moses ﷺ—'*a detailing of all things*'—are in reference to moral guidance:

> *Then We gave Moses the Scripture, complete for him who does good, and a detailing of all things, and as a guidance and a mercy, that perhaps they might believe in the encounter with their Lord.* (*Al-An'am*, 6:154) ❉ *And We inscribed for him in the Tablets about all things, as an admonition and a detailing of all things. 'Take it then firmly, and enjoin your people to adhere to the fairest [precepts] in it. I shall show you the abode of the wicked.* (*Al-A'raf*, 7:145) ❉ *Verily there is in their stories a lesson for people of cores. It is not a fabricated discourse but a confirmation of what was [revealed] before it, and the details for all things, and a guidance, and a mercy for a folk who believe.* (*Yusuf*, 12:111)

3 Fakhr al-Din al-Razi, *Al-Tafsir al-kabir*, vol. 7, p. 258. Al-Razi also says: 'God says: '*We have neglected nothing in the Book*' (*Al-An'am* 6:38), and there are two opinions about what is meant by 'the Book' here. The first is that it means the Book which is preserved in the realm of the Throne of God and the heavens, and which contains every last detail of the affairs of created beings, as (the Prophet) ﷺ said: 'The Pen has dried after [writing] all that will be until the Day of Resurrection.' The second opinion is that it means the [Arabic] Qur'an, and this is more plausible, because when a noun is prefixed by the definite article it refers to an established meaning, and for Muslims the established meaning of 'the Book' is the Qur'an; therefore the meaning of 'the Book' in this verse must be the Qur'an'. (Fakhr al-Din al-Razi, *Al-Tafsir al-kabir*, vol. 4, p. 526).

4 Abu al-Qasim Mahmud ibn 'Umar al-Zamakhshari al-Khawarizmi, *Al-Kashshaf*, p. 586.

5 The word 'philosophy' is originally a Greek word comprised of two terms: '*philo*', which means 'love', and '*sophia*', which means 'wisdom.' 'Philosophy', then, with respect to its linguistic origin, means 'love of wisdom.' Muslim scholars have defined philosophy in several ways, but we ourselves use it here to mean the wisdom which is 'below' the level of doctrine and the level of *Shari'ah* (Islamic sacred law); or to put it differently, 'philosophy' refers to all wisdom and

intellectual knowledge aside from doctrine, theology and sacred law. For example, love is a philosophical topic, as are time, logic, cognition, ethics, psychology, anthropology, epistemology, hermeneutics, oneirology, cosmology, numerology, metaphysics, soteriology, eschatology, jurisprudence, politics, sociology, comparative religion and so on. Of course these topics might have legal or doctrinal sides, but an understanding of them which is neutral as far as doctrine or law is concerned may be considered 'philosophical knowledge', as long as it is spiritually or intellectually beneficial or useful does not draw one into unbelief or sin. This is why philosophy was known in the past as '*ancilla theologiae*', 'the servant of theology.' Indeed, wisdom ('*hikmah*') as such—which though not exactly the same thing as philosophy perhaps, nevertheless must include it—is extremely highly regarded in the Qur'an, for God says: *He gives wisdom to whomever He will, and he who is given wisdom, has been given much good; yet none remembers, but the people of core.* (Al-Baqarah, 2:269)

6 Without delving into the complex Asha'rite theological discussions about the philosophical status of 'thingness' ('*shayyiyah*') and whether 'nothing' is a 'thing', we will just say that this question can be easily resolved by understanding the linguistic derivation—and, consequently, meaning—of the word '*shayy*' ('thing'): a '*shayy*' is not a mere fact, a detail, an idea or a piece of information: it is: 'a [thing] that can be known and spoken of. Among many theologians it is a name that can be used and that can be applied in common to God and to other than God, to things that exist and things that do not exist. However, some of them say [rather] that it is an expression of something that exists and its roots is '*sha'a*' [to will] ... and in the case of what is other than God, it means 'what is willed' ('*al-mashi*') [such as in God's words:] ... Say: 'God is the Creator of all things' ... (Al-Ra'd, 13:16)'. (Raghib al-Isfahani, *Al-Mufradat fi gharib al-Qur'an*, p. 204.)

Thus a '*shayy*' is a thing that God has willed and thus has either created as such, or commanded human beings to do, or commended to human beings, to know. The last of these includes wisdom ('*hikmah*') in the Qur'an, where it is given as one of the four reasons for the very revelation of the Qur'an itself (along with the recitation of its verses, understanding them and the purification of souls). God says:

Truly God was gracious to the believers when He sent to them a messenger from among their own to recite to them His verses, and to purify them, and to teach them the Book and wisdom, though before, they were in clear error. (Aal-'Imran, 3:164) ❋ *It is He Who sent to the unlettered [folk] a messenger from among them to recite to them His signs, and to purify them, and to teach them the Book and wisdom, though indeed before that they had been in clear error.* (Al-Jum'a, 62:2)

This is the reason why we maintain that since the Qur'an is *a clarification of all things* (*shayy*) (Al-Nahl, 16:89) then it must necessarily contain 'not only all forms of religious knowledge, but all the principles of the sciences of philosophy as well'.

To this argument, it could be objected (as some Islamic scholars have done) that the Qur'an uses the expression 'all things' or 'everything' ('*kulli shayy*') in a way that cannot be taken literally (and thus should be understood either metaphorically or metonymically—i.e. with '*majaz*') as in the verses:

Then, when they saw it as a sudden cloud heading towards their valleys, they said, 'This is a cloud that will bring us rain!' Nay, but it is what you sought to hasten a hurricane containing a painful chastisement, / destroying everything by the command of its Lord. So they became such that nothing could be seen except their dwellings. Thus do We requite guilty folk. (Al-Ahqaf, 46: 24–25)

The answer to this is of course first that there is a difference between metaphor and metonomy (symbolic replacement, e.g. 'the crown' for 'the king and his government') on the one hand, and implied synechdoche (substituting a part for the whole, or vice versa, e.g. 'face' for a 'person') on the other hand, and second that anyway in the verses cited above there is no need to suppose any *'majaz'* at all, since the Qur'an is quite specific and has given the exception itself (the *dwellings*, and all that comes with them). Moreover, as cited earlier, as regards religious knowledge, the Qur'an gives *the details for all things* (*Yusuf*, 12:111 and see also *Al-Isra'*, 17:12) and there are no exceptions given in these verses, and thus no way to understand them metaphorically.

7 Suyuti, *Al-Durr al-manthur*, vol. 5, p. 610.

CHAPTER 3: THE DEFINITION OF LOVE

8 The opinions of Muslim scholars about love generally fall into two categories. In the first category are those who say that love cannot be precisely defined because it is indescribable, so that only its effects can be described. In the second category are those who describe love as a kind of inclination towards something beautiful or desirable, notwithstanding of course that God does not 'incline'. This means that, as regards God, love is a form of grace that He shows to some of His servants. Some scholars combine these two approaches to defining love.

Al-Jahizh (d. 255 AH) quotes a poet as saying: 'The eye reveals what the soul contains of love or hate, if they are there; the eye speaks whilst the mouth is still, until the heart is laid bare.' (Jahizh, *Kitab al-bayan wa al-tabyin*, vol. 1, p. 62)

Al-Kalabadhi (d. 380 AH) says: 'Junayd said that love means the *inclination of the heart*, meaning that *the heart inclines towards God and towards the responsibilities which God has ordained*. Others said that love is acquiescence, meaning to obey [God's] commandments and pay heed to His prohibitions, and to be content with all He has decreed and ordained. Muhammad bin Ali al-Kattani said that *love means to prefer the beloved [to oneself]*. Others have said that love means to put the one you love first... Man's love of God is a glorification which unveils many mysteries, and thus cannot be combined with glorification for anything other than Him. God's love of human beings means that He marks him so that he is unfit for anyone else; this is the meaning of His words *And I chose you for Myself* (*Ta Ha*, 20:41). 'So that he is unfit for anyone else' means that he no longer cares to observe others or pay heed to them... The Folk [of mysticism] have many unique expressions and terms which almost no one else uses, some of which we might convey and explain briefly, but in doing this we only seek to give the meaning of the expression, not its content, *for its content cannot even be alluded to, never mind revealed*. As for the nature of their states, it cannot be spoken of, although those who have experienced it know it well.' (Kalabadhi, *al-Ta'arruf li-madhhab ahl al-tasawwuf*, pp. 109–110)

Ibn Sina (d. 428 AH) says: '*Love in reality is nothing but a strong preference for that which is beautiful and seemly.*' Ibn Hazm (d. 456 AH) says, defining love: '*I prefer to say that it is the connection of souls which are divided in this creation but connected in their pristine origin.*' (Ibn Hazm, *Tawq al-hamamah*, p. 7) He also defined it by saying: '*Love is the connection of souls in their original higher realm.*' (Ibn Hazm, *Tawq al-hamamah*, p. 27)

Al-Qushayri (d. 465 AH) says: '*Love is a noble condition to which the Real has attested many experiences, as well as speaking of His own love for man. The Real may be described as loving man, and man may be described as loving the Real.* For the scholars, *love means desire*, though for the Folk love is not desire, since desire cannot be attached to the Eternal, unless it means the desire to draw near to Him and glorify Him. In investigating this matter we will discuss two elements, God willing. The love of God for human beings is His will to bless them with a certain favour, just as His mercy for them is the will to give them a certain favour. Now mercy is more specific than will, and in turn love is more specific than mercy. God's will to reward and favour human beings is called 'mercy', and His will to grant human beings 'nearness' and high rank is called 'love'. His will is a single Quality which has different names depending on its different manifestations. If it is manifested in punishment it is called 'wrath'; if it is manifested through general favours it is called 'mercy', and if it is manifested through special favours it is called 'love'.... Some early Muslims said God's love is a Quality about which He has informed us, but which we cannot explain. As for the other kinds of love that man experiences such as the inclination to something and familiarity with it, or the feeling that one experiences when he is with his loved ones, the Eternal is beyond all this. As for man's love for God, it is a feeling in his heart too subtle to be expressed. This feeling may inspire him to glorify God, prefer His pleasure, have no time for anything other than Him, feel rapture in Him, find no peace in anything but Him, and take comfort in constantly invoking Him in his heart.... People have said many things about love, and spoken of its lexical origin. Some say that love is the name for pure affection... As for what the [Sufi] masters have said about it, some have said that *love is constant inclination with a passionate heart*. It is said that *love is to put one's beloved before everything else*. It is said that *it means to acquiesce to one's beloved in his presence and his absence*. It is said that *it means to efface one's own attributes and affirm the being of one's beloved*. It is said that *it means to surrender the heart to the Lord's will*. It is said *it means to fearfully uphold reverence and constant service*. Abu Yazid al-Bistami said that love *is to deem a lot of oneself as little, and a little of one's beloved as a lot*. Sahl bin Abdullah [al-Tustari] said that *love means to embrace obedience and stay clear of disobedience*. Junayd was asked about love, and replied that *it is when the attributes of the beloved replace those of the lover*. By this, he meant that the lover continues to make remembrance of the beloved until the attributes of the beloved overwhelm his heart, and he completely disregards his own attributes. Abu Ali Ahmad al-Rudhabari said that *love means acquiescence*. Abu Abdullah al-Qurashi said that *the reality of love is to give yourself completely to the one you love, so that nothing of yourself remains for you*. Shibli said that *love is called 'love'(mahabbah) because it effaces from the heart everything but the beloved....*' (Abu al-Qasim al-Qushayri, *al-Risalah al-qushayriyyah*, pp. 317–327)

Al-Ghazali (d. 505 AH) says: 'Regarding the reality of love and its causes, and the meaning of man's love for God: ... it is unimaginable that an inanimate object could be said to feel love, but rather it is specific to living, sentient beings... *Love is an expression of the disposition's inclination to something pleasant*, and if this inclination deepens and strengthens it is called 'devotion.' In its ordinary use, *love means the soul's inclination to something which suits it and pleases it*. Such a thing can only be envisaged for an imperfect being, which inclines towards something it lacks and is made complete by attaining it, and delights in having attained it; and this is impossible for God.... *God's love for man, then, is for Him to draw him nearer to Himself by warding off distractions and sins from him, and purifying his inner being from the turbidity of this worldly life, and drawing back the veil from his heart so that he may behold Him, as though he sees Him with his heart*. As for man's love for God, *it is his inclination towards attaining the perfection which he utterly lacks and needs, for he will doubtless yearn for what he lacks, and delight in attaining any part of it*. This kind of yearning and love is impossible for God.' (Abu Hamid al-Ghazali, *Ihya' 'ulum al-din*, vol. 4 pp. 378–454)

Ibn al-Arif (d. 536 AH) says: '*As for love, it is the first valley of extinction [in God], and the first step towards the stages of self-effacement*; and it is the final stage wherein the best of ordinary people meet with the lesser of the elite.' (Ibn al-Arif, *Al-Nafa'is wa mahasin al-majalis*, p. 695)

Ibn al-Jawzi (d. 597 AH) says: 'Know that *desire (hawa) means the disposition's inclination to what pleases it*, and this inclination was created in man because it was necessary for his preservation; for were it not for his inclination to food, he would not eat, and the same is true of drink, marriage, and all else he desires. Desire brings him what benefits him, just as hate keeps from him what harms him. Thus desire is not inherently blameworthy, but only excessive desire is blameworthy, namely all that which goes beyond the bounds of getting what is beneficial and warding off what is harmful.' (Ibn al-Jawzi, *Dhamm al-hawa*, p. 18)

The '*Sheikh al-Akbar*', Muhyi al-Din ibn al-Arabi (d. 638 AH) says (in Chapter 178—'The Station of Love'—of his magnum opus, *The Meccan Openings*): 'Know—may God give you success—that *love is a divine station*, for He ascribed it to Himself, and called Himself 'the Loving' (*Al-Wadud*).... This station has four names: there is *hubb* ('love'), which means its pure presence in the heart, purified from the turbidity of distractions, so that one seeks nothing and desires nothing from his beloved. The second name is *wudd* ('affection' or 'love'), from which the Divine Name *Al-Wadud* ('the Loving') is derived; it is one of His Qualities, and is affirmed in Him, and this is where the word *wudd* comes from, because of how firmly established it is on earth. The third name is '*ishq* ('devotion'), which means intense love; the Qur'an speaks of it as 'ardent love' when it says: '...*but those who believe love God more ardently*...' (*Al-Baqarah* 2:165), and speaks of it when it says: '...*Indeed he has smitten (shaghafa) her heart with love*...' (*Yusuf* 12:30); in other words, her love for Joseph has become like the skin which covers the heart ('*shaghaf*'), containing it and surrounding it. The Real also described Himself as having ardent love, although one cannot say that God has 'devotion'. Devotion means that love penetrates the lover so that it becomes intermixed with every part of him and covers him like a robe; it is derived from the word '*ashaqa* ('a convolvulus tree'). The fourth name is *hawa* ('desire' or 'impulse'), which means total concentration of the will on the beloved, and total attachment to him (or her) whenever anything comes to the heart. No Divine Name is derived from this word. It occurs because of specific causes, such as a look, a story, a kindness, or many other things. In the realm of sound God-given disclosure, it means God's love for a man when he does many good deeds and follows the Messenger in all that he conveyed; we call this station *hawa*... People differ as to its definition, and I have never seen anyone give it an essential definition; indeed, such a thing is unimaginable. All those who gave it definitions defined only its effects and results. This is especially true when we consider that it is a quality of God Himself. The best I ever heard said about it is what more than one person told me. Abu al-ᶜAbbas ibn al-Arif al-Sanhaji said when he was asked about love: "*Jealousy is part of love, and jealousy demands secrecy—do not define it.*" Know that all that can be known is of two kinds: what can be defined, and what cannot be defined. Those who know love and speak of it hold that it cannot be defined; those who experience it know it, though they do not know what it is, and they do not deny that it exists... *Love is a special manifestation of the will.*' (Ibn Arabi, *Al-Futuhat al-makkiyyah*, vol. 2 pp. 317–322)

Ibn Qayyim al-Jawziyya (d. 751 AH) says: '*Love cannot be defined with any definition clearer than love itself*, for other definitions only make it vaguer and colder. Love is its own definition, and love cannot be described with any adjective clearer than 'love.' People only speak about its causes, means, signs, indications, fruits and laws; their definitions and descriptions all centre on these six. Their expressions and allusions vary according to the individual's level and station, and his power of expression. The lexical root of the word *hubb* ('love') centres on five concepts, which are: (1) purity and whiteness, (2) loftiness and prominence, (3) adherence and constancy, (4) centrality; meaning the core of a thing and its origin, and (5) protection and preservation. Doubtless, these five things are all key constituents of love. (Ibn Qayyim al-Jawziyya, *Madarij al-salikin*, vol. 3 p. 10)

9 Abu Hamid Ghazali, *Ihya' 'ulum al-din*, vol. 4 pp. 378–454.

10 Muslim, *Sahih*, Hadith no. 99, *Kitab al-iman*.

11 Abu Hurayrah ﷺ narrated that the Messenger of God ﷺ said:

> 'Verily God has ninety-nine Names, one hundred less one. Verily, God is Odd and He loves the odd number. Whoever commits them to memory enters Paradise. And they

are: God (*Allah*), The One (*Al-Wahid*), the Eternally Besought (*Al-Samad*), the First (*Al-Awwal*), the Last (*Al-Akhir*), the Outward (*Al-Zhahir*), the Inward (*Al-Batin*), the Creator (*Al-Khaliq*), the Maker (*Al-Bari'*), the Fashioner (*Al-Musawwir*), the King (*Al-Malik*), the Truth (*Al-Haqq*), the Source of Peace (*Al-Salam*), the Preserver of Security (*Al-Mu'min*), the Protector (*Al-Muhaymin*), the Mighty (*Al-'Aziz*), the Overpowering (*Al-Jabbar*), the Great in Majesty (*Al-Mutakabbir*), the Compassionate (*Al-Rahman*), the Merciful (*Al-Rahim*), the Gentle (*Al-Latif*), the All-Aware (*Al-Khabir*), the All-Hearing (*Al-Sami'*), the All-Seeing (*Al-Basir*), the All-Knowing (*Al-'Alim*) the Great (*Al-'Azhim*), the Good (*Al-Barr*), the Sublime (*Al-Muta'al*), the Majestic (*Al-Jalil*), the Beautiful (*Al-Jamil*), the Living (*Al-Hayy*), the Self-Existing (*Al-Qayyum*), the Omnipotent (*Al-Qadir*), the Supreme (*Al-Qahir*), the Most High (*Al-'Ali*), the Wise (*Al-Hakim*), the Near (*Al-Qarib*), the Answerer (*Al-Mujib*), the All-Sufficient (*Al-Ghani*), the Plentiful Giver (*Al-Wahhab*), the Loving (*Al-Wadud*), the Appreciative (*Al-Shakur*), the Glorified (*Al-Majid*), the Self-Sufficient (*Al-Wajid*), the Governor (*Al-Wali*), the Guide (*Al-Rashid*), the Pardoner (*Al-'Afuw*), the Forgiving (*Al-Ghafur*), the Forbearing (*Al-Halim*), the Generous (*Al-Kareem*), the Granter and Accepter of Repentance (*Al-Tawwab*), the Lord (*Al-Rabb*), the Glorious (*Al-Majid*), the Patron (*Al-Wali*), the Witness (*Al-Shahid*), the Manifest (*Al-Mubin*), the Proof (*Al-Burhan*), the Kind (*Al-Raouf*), the Merciful (*Al-Rahim*), the Originator (*Al-Mubdi'*), the Restorer to life (*Al-Mu'id*), the Resurrector (*Al-Ba'ith*), the Inheritor (*Al-Warith*), the Strong (*Al-Qawi*), the Severe (*Al-Shadid*), the Harmer (*Al-Darr*), the Benefiter (*Al-Nafi'*), the Enduring (*Al-Baqi*), the Protector (*Al-Waqi*), the Abaser (*Al-Khafid*), the Exalter (*Al-Rafi'*), the Withholder (*Al-Qabid*), the Expander (*Al-Basit*), the Honourer (*Al-Mu'izz*), the Humiliator (*Al-Mudhill*), the Equitable (*Al-Muqsit*), the Provider (*Al-Razzaq*), the Possessor of Strength (*Dhul-Quwwah*), the Firm (*Al-Matin*), the Self-Sustaining (*Al-Qa'im*), the Everlasting (*Al-Da'im*), the Preserver (*Al-Hafizh*), the Trustee (*Al-Wakil*), the Originator (*Al-Fatir*), the All-Hearing (*Al-Sami'*), the Giver (*Al-Mu'ti*), the Giver of life (*Al-Muhyi*), the Giver of death (*Al-Mumit*), the Preventer of Harm (*Al-Mani'*), the Gatherer (*Al-Jami'*), the Guide (*Al-Hadi*), the Sufficient (*Al-Kafi*), the Eternal (*Al-Abad*), the Knower (*Al-'Alim*), the Truthful (*Al-Sadiq*), the Light (*Al-Nur*), the Illuminating (*Al-Munir*), the Perfect (*Al-Tamm*), the Pre-Existing (*Al-Qadim*), the Single (*Al-Witr*), the Unique (*Al-Ahad*), the Eternally Besought (*Al-Samad*) of all who *neither begets nor is He begotten, and there is none like unto Him.* (Ibn Majah, *Sunan, Bab al-Du'a*, Hadith no. 3994; there is another similar—and perhaps better known—*Hadith* wherein the Messenger of God ﷺ names a slightly different collection of God's Ninety-Nine Names to be found in: Al-Tirmidhi, *Sunan, Kitab al-Da'wat, Bab Asma' Allah al-Husna*, Hadith no. 3849. That collection, however, does not contain the Divine Name *Al-Jamil*.)

12 The Giver (*Al-Mu'ti*) is Itself one of the Divine Names (see previous endnote).

13 God created humanity, and indeed the universe out of His Mercy (*Rahmah*), for He says (as we will later discuss in more detail in Chapter 5: Love is the Root of Creation): *The Compassionate One (Al-Rahman) / has taught the Qur'an. / He created man, / teaching him [coherent] speech.* (*Al-Rahman*, 55:1–4)

And He says: *Had your Lord willed, He would have made humankind one community, but they continue to differ, / except those on whom your Lord has mercy; and for that did He create them...* (*Hud*, 11:118–119)

However, it will be noticed that whilst God's Mercy 'embraces' all things, it is 'prescribed' only *for those who are God-fearing and pay the alms, and those who believe in Our signs*:

'And prescribe for us in this world good and in the Hereafter. We have turned to You'. He says: 'My chastisement—I smite with it whom I will, and My mercy embraces all things, and so I

shall prescribe it for those who are God-fearing and pay the alms, and those who believe in Our signs. (Al-Aʿraf, 7:156)

Therefore God's Mercy is first of all to create everything and give everything its particular creation (and countless other favours), and, second, to show even more Mercy to *those who are God-fearing and pay the alms, and those who believe in Our signs*. Thus we can say that God's Mercy is first of all to the (free) gift of existence to everything in creation, and then the further Mercy to all those human beings who accept to receive God's mercy, and be guided back to God.

Thus God's Mercy is defined—or at least known—in a similar way to God's Love (as discussed above). This is of course to be expected because, as we will see later (in Chapter 4: God and Love), Divine Love is a Divine Quality that is inseparable from Divine Mercy, since God says: *And ask forgiveness of your Lord, then repent to Him. Truly my Lord is Merciful, Loving. (Hud, 11:90)* ❋ *And He is the Forgiving, the Loving. (Al-Buruj, 85:14)*

14 Al-Qushayri says: 'People have said many things about love, and spoken of its lexical origin. Some say that love is the name for pure affection, because the Arabs call white, shining teeth '*habab*'. It is said that '*hubab*' means the bubbles which float on the surface of water during heavy rain, which suggests that love is the boiling and agitation of the heart when it yearns and aches to meet its beloved. It is said that it is derived from the word '*habab*', which means the greatest part of a quantity of water, because love is the ultimate goal of most of the heart's desires. It is said it means stability and constancy, derived from the verb '*ahabba*', which describes how the camel sits and refuses to stand; it is as though the lover refuses to remove thoughts of his beloved from his heart. It is said that the word '*hubb*' is derived from '*habb*', which means 'earring.' A poet said:

> "The hissing snake spent the night next to him
> In the place where an earring (*habb*) might hang,
> so that he heard its whispers."

The earring is called '*habb*' either because of how it adheres fast to the ear, or because of how it swings unsteadily; both of these concepts are features of love. It is also said that it is derived from '*habba*', meaning the centre of the heart, since love resides in the heart. It is said it is derived from '*hibba*', meaning 'seed', because it is the core of life just as seeds are the cores of plants. It is said that '*hubb*' means the four pieces of wood upon which a two-handled jar is placed, which signifies that the lover will carry whatever burden his beloved gives him, noble or ignoble. It is said that it is named after a water-jug, because it holds onto what fills it but cannot accommodate anything else, just as when the heart is filled with love it has no room for anything but its beloved.' (Al-Qushayri, *Al-Risalah al-qushayriyyah*, p. 320)

CHAPTER 4: GOD AND LOVE

15 Abu Hamid al-Ghazali (d. 505 AH) says the following about God's Name 'the Loving': 'The Loving (*Al-Wadud*) is He who loves goodness for all creation, treats them with kindness and blesses them. *It is similar to the meaning of 'the Merciful'*, save that mercy is shown to those who are in dire need of mercy, and the actions of the Merciful require one who is weak and in need of mercy, whilst the actions of the Loving do not require this; rather, blessing in the first place is a fruit of love.' (Abu Hamid al-Ghazali, *Al-Maqsad al-asna fi sharh maʿani asma' Allah al-husna*, p. 122.

And Fakhr al-Din al-Razi (d. 606 AH) said about God's Name 'the Loving': 'The Almighty says: '*And He is the Forgiving, the Loving*', and '*wudd*' means 'love.' The word *Wadud* has two possible meanings: it may be an active participle, meaning 'He who loves', meaning that He loves them, as He says: '*...a people whom He loves and who love Him...*' (Al-Maʾidah, 5:54) When we say that He loves His servant, this means that He wants to send good things to him. Know that according to this understanding, love is similar to mercy; the difference between them is that mercy requires someone who is weak and in need of mercy, whilst love does not; rather, blessing in the first place is a fruit of love. The second possible meaning is that He is loving in the sense that He causes men to love one another, as He says: '...*for them the Compassionate One shall appoint love.*' (*Maryam*, 19:96). A third possibility is that it ['*Wadud*'] is a passive participle, morphologically similar to the words '*hayub*' ('afraid') or '*rakub*' ('mounted', as on a horse); in this case, God Almighty is beloved to the hearts of His friends because of the great favour He shows them.' (Fakhr al-Din al-Razi, *Sharh asma' Allah al-husna*, pp. 273–274)

16 *Al-Baqarah*, 2:143; *Al-Baqarah*, 2:207; *Aal ʿImran*, 3:30; *Al-Tawbah* 9:117; *Al-Nahl* 16:7; *Al-Nahl* 16:47; *Al-Mu'minun* 23:65; *Al-Nur* 24:20; *Al-Hadid* 57:9; and *Al-Hashr* 59:10.

17 Al-Tirmidhi, *Sunan*, Hadith no. 1907, *Kitab al-birr wa al-sila, Bab ma ja' fi qati'at al-rahim*.

18 It is important to carefully consider the meaning of the precise references to God's Self ('*Nafs*' which—as will be discussed in Chapter 18—means [in a human context] 'soul' as well as 'self'), and God's Face ('*Wajh*') in the Qur'an. In human beings, the soul is the human being himself (or herself) and it is hidden to the sight, but its qualities become apparent on the human face (which can also nevertheless veil those qualities). In the Qur'an, God's *Nafs* is beyond the knowledge of even Jesus Christ ﷺ, who says: ... *You know what is in my self, but I do not know what is within Your Self: You are the Knower of things unseen.* (*Al-Maidah*, 5: 116)

Moreover, God says elsewhere in the Qur'an: ... *God warns you of His Self....* (*Aal ʿImran*, 3:28; see also 3:30)

These words can also be understood as *God warns of His Self*.

On the other hand, as regards His Face, God says: ...*whithersoever you turn, there is the Face of God* (*Al-Baqarah*, 2:115).

And: *You are not responsible for guiding them; but God guides whomever He will. And whatever good you expend is for yourselves; for then you are expending, desiring only God's Face, and whatever good you expend, shall be repaid to you in full, and you will not be wronged.* (*Al-Baqarah*, 2:272).

These verses thus clearly show the specific differing implications of the Qur'an's references to God's Self and His Face.

19 In his book *Al-Insan al-kamil*, the Muslim scholar ʿAbd al-Karim Jili (d. 805 AH) suggests that Mercy is the origin of God's Names and Qualities, and that God's Names proceed from the Quality of Mercy.

'The Mercy from the Divine Essence (*Al-Rahmaniyyah*) is the manifestation of the realities of the Names and Qualities; it lies *between His essential qualities, such as the Names of the Essence, and those qualities which are directed towards created beings*, such as His being the Knower, the Omnipotent, the All-Hearing, and the other Qualities which have a connection to temporal beings.... The Name which is directly derived from the level of Mercy from the Divine Essence (*Al-Rahmaniyyah*) is *Al-Rahman*, the Compassionate—a Name which refers to the Names of His Essence (*al-Asma' al-Dhatiyyah*) and the Qualities of His Person (*al-Awsaf al-Nafsiyyah*), which are seven in number: life, knowledge, omnipotence, will, speech, hearing and seeing... This level [of Being] has this name because of how this all-enveloping mercy covers all the levels of Reality and creation; and it was because of its manifestation in the levels of Reality that the levels of creation came into existence. Thus mercy became universally present in all beings, from the Merciful Presence.' (Abd Al-Kareem al-Jili, *Al-Insan al-Kamil*, p. 73)

20 We have been deliberately very careful in our language here and have stuck to the exact language of the Qur'an and the Hadith (this theological practice is called '*tafwid*' in Arabic): we note that we have said that 'Divine Mercy is *of* (Arabic: '*min*') the Divine Essence' and that *Al-Rahman* is a Name *of* the Divine Essence. We have not said that the Divine Essence 'is' Mercy

(or Love). Without delving into theological controversies here, we will say that the previous two footnotes suffice to explain the reasons for this.

21 Muslim, *Sahih*, Hadith no. 810, *Kitab salat al-musafirin wa qasraha, Bab fadl surat al-kahf wa ayat al-kursi*.

22 God's Names *'the Compassionate'* (*Al-Rahman*) and *'the Merciful'* (*Al-Rahim*):

Muslim scholars have said many things about the meaning of God's Names *'the Compassionate'* and *'the Merciful'*. The following are amongst the most pertinent:

Ibn Kathir says: *'The Compassionate* and *the Merciful* are two Divine Names derived from the word *rahmah* ('mercy'); both are intensive morphological forms, but *'the Compassionate'* is more intensive than *'the Merciful'*. It is related that Jesus ﷺ said: "The Compassionate is Compassionate in this life and the next, while the Merciful is Merciful in the next life." ... Abu Ali Farisi said: "The Compassionate" is a universal name which encompasses all the forms of mercy, and only God may be called by this Name. *'The Merciful'* refers solely to the mercy God shows the believers, as He says: *...And He is Merciful to the believers. (Al-Ahzab, 33:43)"* Ibn Abbas ؓ said that: they are two gentle Names, one of which is gentler than the other: that is, suggestive of yet more mercy ... Ibn Mubarak said that 'the Compassionate' is the One who gives when He is asked, whilst 'the Merciful' is the One who becomes wrathful when He is not asked; this is derived from a *Hadith* .... The Messenger of God ﷺ said: "If one does not ask of God, He becomes angry with one."

I heard 'Azrami say of the Names *'the Compassionate', 'the Merciful'* that God is Compassionate with all His creatures, and Merciful to the believers. They say that this is why God says: *...Then [He] presided upon the Throne. The Compassionate One (Al-Furqan, 25:59)*, and says: *The Compassionate One presided upon the Throne (Taha, 20:5)*. God thus links His presiding [over the Throne] to His Name *'the Compassionate'* to indicate how His mercy envelops all His creation; and He says: *...And He is Merciful to the believers. (Al-Ahzab, 33:43)*, singling them out with His Name *'the Merciful'*. They say that this implies that *'the Compassionate'* denotes the higher degree of mercy because it applies in both worlds to all His creatures, whilst *'the Merciful'* applies to the believers alone ... And His Name *'the Compassionate'* (*Al-Rahman*) is for Him alone, and no one else may be called this ... As for *'the Merciful'*, He describes another with this attribute when He says: *Verily there has come to you a messenger from among yourselves for whom it is grievous that you should suffer; who is full of concern for you, to the believers full of pity, merciful (rahim). (Al-Tawbah, 9:128)"* (Ibn Kathir, *Tafsir al-Qur'an al-ʿAthim*, pp. 65–66)

Al-Ghazali says: *'The Compassionate (Al-Rahman)* and *the Merciful (Al-Rahim)* are both derived from the word "mercy" (*rahmah*), and mercy requires an object, and the object of mercy must be needy. Someone who meets a needy person's need unintentionally and without caring about the needy person is not called 'merciful'. The one who wishes to meet the needy person's need but does not do so when he is able to do is not called "merciful", because if he really wanted to do it, he would. If he is unable to do so, he might be called "merciful" because of his sympathy, but his mercy is incomplete. Perfect mercy means to shower the needy with goodness having the intention to take care of them. Universal mercy is that which is given to the deserving and the undeserving alike. God's mercy is thus both perfect and universal; it is perfect in that He wishes to meet the needs of the needy, and does so; and it is universal in that it encompasses both the deserving and the undeserving—in this lower world and in the Hereafter—and it meets both dire needs and ordinary needs, as well as additional matters beyond this. He is truly the Absolutely Merciful.' (Ghazali, *Al-Maqsad al-asna fi sharh maʿani asma' Allah al-husna*, p. 62)

Al-Razi says:'Which of them is more intensive: *'the Compassionate'*, or *'the Merciful'*? Abu Salih related that Ibn Abbas ؓ said: " *'The Compassionate'* and *'the Merciful'* are two gentle Names, one of which is gentler than the other"; yet he did not state which is the gentlest. But

Husayn bin Fadl al-Balkhi said: "This is a mistake on the part of the narrator, for gentleness (*riqqah*) is not a Divine Quality. The Prophet ﷺ said: 'God is Kind (*rafiq*), and He loves kindness, and He gives for it that which He does not give for violence.'

Know that there is no doubt that both '*The Compassionate*' (*Al-Rahman*) and '*the Merciful*' (*Al-Rahim*) are derived from the word 'mercy' (*rahmah*), and if one were not more intensive than the other they would be exact synonyms in every way without any distinction between them; and this is unlikely. Therefore we must understand that one of them is more intensive in meaning than the other. Beyond this, they differ: most say that '*the Compassionate*' implies greater mercy than '*the Merciful*', and they give several arguments to support this.' (Al-Razi, *Sharh asma' Allah al-husna*, p. 162)

The common elements between all these definitions are:

(1) that '*The Compassionate*' (*Al-Rahman*) can only be used to describe God, whilst '*Merciful*' (*Al-Rahim*) can be used to describe both God and human beings.

(2) that the Name '*the Compassionate*' linguistically implies a greater 'amount' of mercy.

(3) that '*the Merciful*' requires an object, whilst '*the Compassionate*' does not require an object.

(4) that '*the Compassionate*' always comes before '*the Merciful*' whenever the two Names are mentioned together.

(5) that '*the Compassionate*' is virtually a synonym for the Name 'God'('*Allah*') for God says: Say: *'Invoke God or invoke the Compassionate One, whichever you invoke, to Him belong the Most Beautiful Names'*... (*Al-Isra*', 17:110)

(6) and, finally, that since ...*He has prescribed for Himself mercy*... (*Al-An'am* 6:12), and since '*the Compassionate*' implies greater mercy than '*the Merciful*' and does not require an object, this means that '*the Compassionate*' is one of the Names of God's Essence, whilst '*the Merciful*' is one of the Names of His Qualities. And God knows best.

23 Al-Razi, *Al-Tafsir al-kabir, Mafatih al-ghayb*, vol. 5 p. 379.

24 Al-Qurtubi, *Tafsir al-Qurtubi*, vol. 7 p. 261.

CHAPTER 5: LOVE IS THE ROOT OF CREATION

25 Al-Razi, *Al-Tafsir al-kabir*, vol. 6 p. 412.

26 Bukhari, *Sahih*, Hadith no. 7403; *Kitab al-Tawhid, Bab: Qawlihi ta'ala 'Wa laqad sabaqat kalimatuna li-'ibadina al-mursalin'.*

27 We should not neglect to mention here the *Hadith Qudsi*: '*I was a hidden treasure, and I loved to be known, so I created humankind and made Myself known to them, and they knew Me.*'

The *Hadith* scholar 'Ajluni said about this *Hadith*: 'Ibn Taymiyah said it is not a saying of the Prophet ﷺ and that he did not know any chain or narration for it, whether strong or weak. Zarkashi, Hafiz Ibn Hajar (in *al-Lali*'), Suyuti and others concurred. Al-Qari said: "But its meaning is correct and can be derived from God's words: *And I did not create the jinn and humankind except that they may worship Me*, that is, that they may know God, as Ibn 'Abbas ؓ and others understood it. The way it is generally reported is: '*I was a hidden treasure and I loved to be known, so I created men, and through Me they knew Me.*' It is quoted very often by the Sufis, and they rely on it and have based some of their fundamental ideas on it.' ('Ajluni, *Kashf al-khafa*', vol. 1, p. 132)

However, Ibn Arabi declared—controversially perhaps—the *Hadith* to be 'authentic according to personal disclosure' ('*sahih kashfan*'); these are his words from *Al-Futuhat al-Makkiyyah*: 'In a *Hadith* which is authentic based on personal disclosure, but lacking an established chain of narration, the Messenger of God ﷺ reported that his Lord says words to the effect of: "I was a hidden treasure, and I loved to be known, so I created humankind and made Myself known to them, and they knew Me." ' (Muhyi al-Din Ibn al-Arabi, *Al-Futuhat al-Makkiyyah*, vol. 2 p. 393)

We do not wish to get into a discussion about the authenticity or weakness of this *Hadith*—all the other *Hadiths* that we quote in this work are sound—but we will say that the meaning of the *Hadith* is sound, as maintained above by the *Hadith* scholar ʿAli Al-Qari. And its meaning is that God created Human beings first of all out of His love ('and I loved to be known'), and secondly out of His mercy ('so I created humankind and made Myself known to them, and they knew Me'). There is no contradiction here between God's love and God's mercy, because as previously discussed (in Chapter 4: God and Love), Divine love and Divine Mercy are inseparable

28 See also: *Al-Baqarah*, 2:185–187; *Al-Anʿam*, 6:165; *Al-Aʿraf*, 7:156; *Yunus*, 10:5, 14, 67; *Ibrahim*, 14:32–34; *Al-Hijr*, 15:16–50; *Al-Nahl*, 16:78–81; *Ta Ha*, 20:15, 53–54; *Al-Hajj*, 22:65; *Al-Mu'minun*, 23:78–80; *Al-Furqan*, 25:10; *Al-Naml*, 27:60–64, 86; *Al-Qasas*, 28:70–73; *Al-Rum*, 30:46; *Luqman*, 31:10–11, 31–32; *Al-Sajdah*, 32:7–9; *Fatir*, 53:12–13; *Ya Sin*, 36:80; *Ghafir*, 40:64, 79–80; *Al-Fath*, 48:4–9; *Al-Talaq*, 65:12, 23–24; *Nuh*, 71:14–20.

29 In Chapters 7: God's Love for Humanity and 23: Falling in Love, we explain at length and in detail how and with what God blesses human beings.

30 Bukhari, *Sahih*, Hadith no. 1385, *Kitab al-Jana'iz, Bab Ma qil fi awlad al-mushrikin*; Muslim, *Sahih*, Hadith no. 2658, *Kitab al-Qadr, Bab Ma'na kull mawlud yulad ʿala al-fitra*.

31 Muslim, *Sahih*, Hadith no. 2865, *Kitab al-Janna, Bab al-Sifat allati yu'raf biha fi al-dunya ahl al-janna wa ahl al-nar*.

CHAPTER 6: THE UNIVERSE AND LOVE

32 Ibn Kathir says in his *Tafsir* (p. 67): 'Ibn ʿAbbas said that 'Praise be to God [*Al-HamduLillah*]' are the words of every thankful person. Qurtubi cites Ibn Jarir as affirming that it is correct for one to say 'Praise be to God' by way of giving thanks…, *Praise is more universal than thanks*, in terms of the circumstances when they are offered.'

33 In Arabic, this is called '*tasbih bil-hal*' (literally, 'glorification through state'), whereas deliberately and consciously glorifying God is called '*tasbih bil-qaul*' (literally, 'glorification through speech').

34 Bukhari, *Sahih*, Hadith no. 3584, *Kitab al-Manaqib, Bab ʿAlamat al-nubuwwah fi al-islam*.

35 Bukhari, *Sahih*, Hadith no. 3583, *Kitab al-Manaqib, Bab ʿAlamat al-nubuwwah fi al-islam*.

36 Jalal al-Din Mahalli and Jalal al-Din Suyuti, *Tafsir al-Jalalayn*, p. 35.

CHAPTER 7: GOD'S LOVE FOR HUMANITY

37 It will be noted here that whereas God favours or prefers (*faddala*) each one of the Prophets *above all the worlds* (*Al-Anʿam*, 6:85), and at one time preferred the Children of Israel *above all the worlds* (*Al-Jathiyah*, 45:16–17; see also: *Al-Dukhan*, 44:32–33; *Al-Ma'idah*, 5:20; *Al-Aʿraf*, 7:140), He only prefers humanity *above many of those whom We created* (*Al-Isra'*, 17:70). God sheds light on this elsewhere in the Holy Qur'an, when He asks Iblis (Satan) why he did not prostrate himself before Adam: *He [God] said, 'O Iblis! What prevents you from prostrating before that which I have created with My own hands? Are you being arrogant, or are you of the Exalted (al-ʿAalin)?*' (*Sad*, 38:75)

There are thus those who are too exalted to prostrate to Adam (*al-ʿAalin*). These are perhaps themselves *above the world* since God refers elsewhere to the '*muqarrabun*'—the angels 'close to God'—(*Al-Nisa*, 4:172). This perhaps explains why God says that He preferred the

Children of Adam to *many of those whom We created* and not 'all' of those whom He created; and God knows best.

38 See also: *Al-A'raf*, 7:12–27; *Al-Isra'*, 17:61–65; *Al-Kahf*, 18:50; *Ta Ha*, 20:115–116; *Sad*, 38:71–85; *Yunus*, 10:14; *Al-An'am*, 6:165; *Fatir*, 35:39; *Al-Ahzab*, 33:73.

39 At first glance the inclusion of *'those who fight for His cause in ranks, as if they were a solid structure'* among the kinds of people whom God loves might seem a little puzzling, especially given the more obvious virtues of the other seven kinds. However, this is easily understood if the verses preceding this verse are remembered. God says:

> O you who believe, why do you say what you do not do? / It is greatly loathsome to God that you say what you do not do. / Indeed God loves those who fight for His cause in ranks, as if they were a solid structure. (*Al-Saff*, 61:2–4)

Thus fighting in God's cause *in ranks, as if they were a solid structure* is linked to doing 'what we say we will do'. In other words, it is linked to being completely sincere; having no trace of hypocrisy or hesitation, and thus being 'unanimous' (literally: 'of one soul'). Hence the *ranks* and *solid structure* are above all in people's own selves, in their own souls (*anfus*). God says: *Will you bid others to piety and forget yourselves (anfusakum), while you recite the Book? Do you not understand?* (*Al-Baqarah*, 2:44)

40 Because of this, God loves thoroughness in acts and work. The Messenger of God ﷺ said: 'God loves that, when one of you does any work, he does it well.' (Tabarani, *Al-Mu'jam al-awsat*, vol. 1 p. 275)

Thoroughness is thus the work of the beautiful soul; and beautiful work comes from a beautiful soul. And God knows best

41 Muslim, *Sahih*, Hadith no. 99, *Kitab al-Iman*.

42 Muslim, *Sahih*, Hadith no. 1, *Kitab al-Iman*.

43 Zabidi, *Taj al-'arus*, vol. 18 p. 14.

44 And the eight kinds of people whom God loves are those who follow the way of the Messenger of God ﷺ, and they are all included in the general sense of this Qur'anic verse.

45 Raghib Al-Isfahani says: 'The meaning of "I greatly love (*hababtu*) so-and-so" is "I reached the core (*habbah*) of his heart"; there are other expressions [in Arabic] with similar meanings, such as "I reached the skin of his heart", "I reached his liver", I reached his inner heart".' (*Al-Mufradat fi gharib al-Qur'an*, p. 112)

46 Naturally the fact of God's being 'with' these categories of people can be considered a special kind of love, for the Messenger of God ﷺ explained the relationship of love to company when he said: 'A person is with those they love'. (Bukhari, *Sahih*, Hadith no. 6168, *Kitab al-Adab, Bab 'Alamat hubb Allah*),

And also when he ﷺ replied to someone who said to him, 'I have prepared nothing for the Hour save that I love God and His Messenger': 'You shall be with those you love.' (Bukhari, *Sahih*, Hadith no. 3688, *Kitab al-Manaqib, Bab Manaqib 'Umar ibn al-Khattab*.)

47 Al-Qushayri says in his *Risalah*, p. 46: 'Ibn Shahin asked Junayd what 'with [God]' means, and he said: " 'With' has two meanings; God is with the prophets in the sense that He gives succour and protection, as God says: '*He said, 'Do not fear, for I shall be with the two of you, hearing and seeing'*; and He is with all people in the sense that He has complete knowledge of them, as God says: '*No secret conversation of three takes place but He is their fourth*.''' Ibn Shahin replied, "Someone such as you is fit to guide the Community to God!" '

48 Perhaps the fact that God says four times in the Holy Qur'an that He is 'with' the patient

indicates that patience requires perseverance before the patient person ('*al-sabir*') reaches the level of virtue ('*ihsan*'); God knows best.

49 It is extremely instructive to consider how the three virtues of *taqwah, sabr* and *ihsan* are depicted in the Holy Qur'an. In general, we may say that: (1) *taqwah* is the very reason for the creation (see: *Al-Baqarah*, 2:21); that it is the essential message of the Prophets (see: *Al-Shu'ara*, 26:87, 106, 124, 142, 161, 177, and *Al-Saffat*, 37:124) and that the *muttaqin* (those who have *taqwah*) are those who will be in Paradise (this is repeated many times in the Holy Qur'an—see:7:128; 11:49; 15:45; 16:30-31; 19:85; 26:90; 28:31; 38:49; 44:51; 50:31; 51:17; 52:17; 54:55; 68:34; 77:41; 87:31). As regards: (2) *sabr*, it is also a virtue of those who will be in Paradise (see *Al-Ra'd*, 13:43), but it is more often described as the virtue of the 'resolute' among the Messengers (see: *Al-Ahqaf*, 46:35, see also *Al-Nahl*, 16:2 and *Al-Ma'arij*, 70:5) and the greatest of the saints (see: *Al-Kahf*, 18:68, 72, 75, 78, 82 and *Fussilat*, 41:35). Finally, as regards *ihsan*, whilst it also obviously a virtue of those who will be in Paradise (see: *Al-Ma'idah*, 5:85 and *Al-Dhariyat*, 51:16), it is more often described as a sublime and unsurpassable virtue (see: *Al-Nisa*, 4:125) for which there is an unfailing Divine reward (see: *Al-Rahman*, 55:60); that is *the firmest handle* ('*urwa wuthqa*—see *Luqman*, 31:22); that is never lost (see:9:120; 12:56; 12:90; 37:80, 105, 110, 121, 131; 39:34; 51:16); and that leads to perpetual increase (see: *Al-Baqarah*, 2:58). Because it is the sum of virtue, it is also the virtue to be exercised towards parents, who in the Holy Qur'an are accorded the highest respect and consideration (see: *Al-Baqarah*, 2:83; *Al-An'am*, 6:151 and *Al-Isra*, 17:23). One might also say that *taqwah* is the sum total of piety—how a human being should be towards God; *ihsan* is the sum of virtue—how human beings should be before other human beings, and *sabr* is how human beings should be in themselves—how they should face the human condition (although obviously all three virtues necessarily largely overlap). From a different point of view, one might even say that *sabr* relates more to the will and hence to fear (*makhafah*) of God; *taqwah* relates more to the intelligence and hence knowledge (*ma'rifah*) of God, and *ihsan* relates more to sentiment and hence love (*hubb*) of God, and God knows best.

50 In his commentary on this verse (in *Mafatih al-ghayb*), Fakhr al-Din al-Razi relates God's 'binding promise' (*wa'dan masula*) back to the supplication of the believers, and the supplication of the angels:

> '*Our Lord, grant us what You have promised us through Your messengers, and abase us not on the Day of Resurrection. You will not fail the tryst*' (*Aal'Imran*, 3:194), ☻ ….'*Our Lord, You embrace all things in [Your] mercy and knowledge. So forgive those who repent and follow Your way and shield them from the chastisement of Hell-fire. / Our Lord, and admit them into the Gardens of Eden that which You have promised them, along with whoever were righteous among their fathers and their wives and their descendants. Surely You are the One Who is the Mighty, the Wise.* (*Ghafir*, 40:7-8).

However, the extraordinary forwardness of these prayers—'reminding' God of His own promise, as it were, and cited by God Himself in the Holy Qur'an—only prove how God's own Essence has made His own promise binding upon Himself, if one may be permitted to phrase these things in such a manner; and God know best.

CHAPTER 8: GOD'S LOVE FOR HIS MESSENGERS AND PROPHETS

51 Abu Dharr ☙ is reported to have said: 'O Messenger of God, how many prophets have there been?' He said: 'One hundred and twenty-four thousand.' He said, 'How many of them were messengers?' He said, 'Three hundred and fifteen; a large group!' (Ahmad, *Musnad*, vol. 5, p. 265-266; Ibn Hibban, *Sahih*, vol. 2, p. 7)

52 Ibn Abi Sharif says: 'Three things have been said about the meaning of prophet and messenger:

The difference between them centres on whether they are commanded to preach the message or not, which is the most widely-held opinion; or the difference is that the messenger brings a law, a scripture or an abrogation of a law which came before him; or, they both mean the same thing, which is what those who have studied the matter in most depth prefer—[but] this would mean that the number of prophets and messengers is the same.' (Ibn Abi Sharif, *Al-Musamara fi al-aqa'id*, p. 194)

However, Prof. 'Abd al-Qadir al-Baghdadi says, in the course of his study of all those things upon which Sunni Muslims are agreed (*Al-Farq bayn al-firaq*), concerning the definition of 'messenger' and 'prophet': 'Everyone who received Revelation from God by means of an angel, and was aided with some kind of miracle, was a prophet; and those among them who were, in addition to all this, given a new law or an abrogation of certain laws which existed before him, was a messenger.' (Prof. 'Abd al-Qadir al-Baghdadi, *Al-Farq bayn al-firaq*, p. 342)

The correct and accurate definition of 'prophet' and 'messenger' and the difference between them, then, is that a messenger is 'one who has had revealed unto him a new law and been commanded to convey it', and a prophet is 'one who has had the law of a messenger revealed unto him, and been commanded to convey it.' They are both sent by God and commanded to convey His message; for He says:

> *And We did not send before you any messenger or prophet but that when he recited [the scripture] Satan cast into his recitation. Thereat God abrogates whatever Satan had cast, then God confirms His revelations. And God is Knower, Wise.* (Al-Hajj, 22:52) ● *And We did not send a prophet to any city but that We seized its people with misery and hardship so that they might be humble.* (Al-A'raf, 7:94)

And nothing indicates this more clearly than His words:

> *And mention in the Book Moses. Indeed he was devoted [to God] and he was a messenger, a prophet. And We called him from the right side of the Mount and We brought him near in communion. And We gave him out of Our mercy his brother Aaron, [likewise] a prophet.* (Maryam, 19:51–53)

God makes clear here the difference between the role of the messenger and the role of the prophet; for the Prophet Moses ﷺ was the messenger who was sent with a new law in the Torah, and the Prophet Aaron ﷺ was the prophet who was commanded to convey the Torah and the law of the Prophet Moses ﷺ as well. But God nevertheless honoured Aaron ﷺ with a certain part of the role of a messenger, by his brother Moses' ﷺ request, as God says:

> *'And that anguish will constrain my breast, and that my tongue will not utter clearly. So give the Mission to Aaron. / And I have sinned against them and I fear they will slay me.' / Said He, 'Certainly not! Go both of you with Our signs. We will indeed be with you, hearing.'* (Al-Shu'ara', 26:13–15)

The conclusive proof that the Prophet Aaron ﷺ was a messenger in a certain sense when he was sent forth alongside the Prophet Moses ﷺ is that God says:

> *So go to him and say, "Truly we are two messengers of your Lord, so let the Children of Israel go with us and do not [continue to] chastise them. We have verily brought you a sign from your Lord, and may peace be upon him who follows [right] guidance.'* (Ta Ha, 20:47)

53 Since the word '*mursal*' means the same as *rasul*, namely 'messenger', we can say that the Prophets Elijah ﷺ and Jonah ﷺ were messengers.

54 It is unclear to us whether the Prophet David ﷺ was a prophet or a messenger; this depends on whether his book, the Psalms, was independent from the Law of Moses ﷺ or a support and affirmation of it. It might be said that if the Prophet David ﷺ was only a prophet, then he was the only prophet we know to whom God revealed a book, the Psalms. Perhaps the following verse

indicates God's preference of him above all the other prophets (and by implication that he was not a messenger): *And your Lord knows best all who are in the heavens and the earth. And verily We have preferred some of the prophets above others; and We gave David the Psalms.* (Al-Isra', 17:55)

55 See: Hakim, *Al-Mustadrak 'ala al-sahihayn*, Hadith no. 400.

56 God says that some messengers (and prophets) brought forth signs by God's leave (see *Al-Ra'd*, 13:38 and *Ghafir*, 40:78). They included Salih (*Al-A'raf*, 7:43; *Hud*, 11:64), Zachariah (*Aal 'Imran*, 3:41; *Maryam*, 19:10); Noah (*Al-'Ankabut*, 29:15), Abraham (*Aal 'Imran*, 3:97), and Moses and Aaron together (*Ta Ha*, 20:47)—may peace be upon them all. Moses, however, was given more than one sign (see *Al-Isra'*, 17:101; *Ta Ha*, 20:22; *Al-A'raf*, 7:133). Perhaps the greatest sign was the one given to the Prophet Muhammad ﷺ, namely the splitting of the moon (see: *Al-Qamar*, 54:1–2)

57 Another thing which shows the difference between them is that the Prophet Moses said to God: '*and I hastened to You, my Lord, that You may be pleased*' (*Ta Ha*, 20:84), whereas God says to the Prophet Muhammad ﷺ: '*And verily your Lord shall give you and you shall be pleased*' (*Al-Duha*, 93:5). This means that the Prophet Moses ﷺ had to seek God's good pleasure, whilst God's good pleasure was a gift to the Prophet Muhammad ﷺ.

58 Raghib al-Isfahani, *Al-Mufradat fi gharib al-Qur'an*, p. 184 (see: '*dhikr*').

59 Darimi, *Sunan*, Hadith no. 47; Tirmidhi, *Sunan*, Hadith no. 3616, *Kitab al-Manaqib*.

CHAPTER 9: THOSE WHOM GOD DOES NOT LOVE

60 We should also not neglect to mention here that God is 'displeased' by certain things, such as ingratitude: *...while they plot at night with discourse displeasing to Him...* (*Al-Nisa'*, 4:108) *...He is not pleased with ingratitude for His servants...* (*Al-Zumar*, 39:7) *...God will surely not be pleased with the wicked folk.* (*Al-Tawbah*, 9:96)

61 Some Muslim scholars disagree with this view and say that God indeed does hate evildoers and disbelievers. One such scholar is the former Grand Mufti of Egypt, Sheikh Hasanayn Muhammad Makhluf—God rest his soul—who said: 'God's hatred of His servant means His wrath for him, His loathing of him, His anger with him and His displeasure with him; it means that He seals his [the servant's] heart, his hearing and his sight, brands him, curses him, debases him, chastises him in the Hereafter, and denies him His guidance and good fortune in this worldly life, and denies him His blessings and aid, save to let him be misled temporarily. This is the punishment for his unbelief or hypocrisy, or his evil and sin, or his corruption and tyranny, or his injustice and enmity, or his arrogance and pride, or his self-delusion and haughtiness, and so on.... [As for] the signs of those whom God hates: the Holy Qur'an tells of many signs of those of His slaves whom God hates, loathes, curses, and who incur His wrath and punishment as a recompense for their unbelief, sin, denial of their Lord's rights and waging war against Him.' (Sheikh Hasanayn Muhammad Makhluf, *Min wahy al-Qur'an al-Karim, fiman yuhibbihum Allah ta'ala wa fiman yakrahuhum Allah ta'ala min 'ibadih*, p. 5)

However, our view is that since it is not stated in the Holy Qur'an that God hates anyone, it is not appropriate for anyone to describe God in a way that He does not describe Himself.

Indeed, God speaks of His Face: *Yet there will remain the Face of your Lord, [the Face] of majesty and munificence* (*Al-Rahman*, 55:27) and: *...whithersoever you turn, there is the Face of God* (*Al-Baqarah*, 2:115),

And God speaks of His Hand: *... the Hand of God is above their hands* (*Al-Fath*, 48:10)

And God speaks of His Eyes: *And submit patiently to the judgement of your Lord, for surely you are bfore Our Eyes* (*Al-Tur*, 52:48)

And God speaks of His Words: *And God will vindicate the Truth by His Words* (*Yunus*, 10:82)

Regardless of how these Qur'anic phrases can be understood, can it be concluded from them that God also has a mouth? Absolutely not! Therefore when God says that He does not love the disbelievers; that He hates some of their actions; that He is angry with them; that He curses them, and that He has prepared hell for them wherein there is a stern chastisement—but despite all this He does not say that He hates the evildoers themselves—Muslims still cannot, of their own accord, ascribe something to God which He does not mention in His Book. Indeed, as we pointed out above, God says: *So do not strike any similitude for God. Truly God knows, and you do not know.* (Al-Nahl, 16:74)

There is also a second issue here: as already mentioned, God's mercy embraces all things, and His mercy outstrips His wrath; so logically speaking how could God hate people themselves? As we will, God willing, see later in Chapter 28. The Opposites of Love and Beauty, hatred is 'aversion'. How could God in His Mercy have aversion for anything (as we would expect if God hated it in particular), and yet this thing remain in existence? In other words, if God were to hate something, how could this thing continue to exist, when its very existence comes only from God's mercy and love? To express this in another way, we could say: if God cuts off His mercy from something, how could it remain in existence, and how could it occur? This is precisely the principle that can be observed in God's words: *If they had desired to go forth, they would have made some preparation for it, but God hated that they should be sent forth, so He slowed them down, and it was said: 'Stay back with those who stay back!'* (Al-Tawbah, 9:46)

Here, God hated that the hypocrites go forth, and so He slowed them down, and the thing which God hated did not come to pass.

If, on the other hand, it is countered that sins occur even though God says: *And do not walk in the earth exultantly. Indeed you will not rend the earth, nor attain the mountains in height. / All of that—the evil of it is hateful in the sight of your Lord.* (Al-Isra', 17:37–38),

In this case we respond that God says that the *evil* of sin is hateful to Him, not its existence as such, otherwise the sin would indeed never occur; and God knows best.

62 This is all despite the fact that disbelievers are 'injurious towards' (*yu'thun*) God and His Messenger: *Indeed those who are injurious to God and His Messenger, God has cursed them in this world and the Hereafter, and has prepared for them a humiliating chastisement.* (Al-Ahzab, 33:57)

And that they oppose (*yuhadid; yuhadun; hadda*) God and His Messenger:

Do they not know that, whoever opposes God and His Messenger, for him shall be the fire of Hell to abide therein? That is the great abasement. (Al-Tawbah, 9:63) ❊ *Indeed those who oppose God and His Messenger will be abased, just as those before them were abased. And verily We have revealed clear signs, and for those who disbelieve there is a humiliating chastisement.* (Al-Mujadilah, 58:5) ❊ *You will not find a people who believe in God and the Last Day loving those who oppose God and His Messenger, even though they were their fathers or their sons or their brothers or their clan. [For] those He has inscribed faith upon their hearts and reinforced them with a spirit from Him, and He will admit them into gardens underneath which rivers flow, wherein they will abide, God being pleased with them, and they being pleased with Him. Those [they] are God's confederates. Assuredly it is God's confederates who are the successful.* (Al-Mujadilah, 58:22)

And that they defy (*shaqqu*) God and His Messenger:

That is because they defied God and His Messenger; and whoever defies God, indeed God is severe in retribution. (Al-Hashr, 59:4) ❊ *That, because they had defied God and His Messenger: whoever contends with God and with His Messenger, surely God is severe in retribution.* (Al-Anfal, 8:13)

Or that they defy (*yushaqiq*) God's Messenger:

> But whoever defied the Messenger after guidance has become clear to him, and follows other than the way of the believers, We shall turn him over to what he has turned to, and We shall expose him in Hell—an evil journey's end. (Al-Nisa, 4:115) ❋ Indeed those who disbelieve and bar from way of God, and defy the Messenger after the guidance has become clear to them, they will not hurt God in any way, and He will make their works fail. (Muhammad, 47:32)

And that they fight (*yuqatiluna*) and wage war (*yuharibuna*) against God and His Messenger:

> Truly the only requital of those who fight against God and His Messenger, and hasten about the earth to do corruption there is that they shall be slaughtered, or crucified, or have their hands and feet cut off on opposite sides, or be banished from the land. That is a degradation for them in this world; and in the Hereafter theirs will be a great chastisement. (Al-Ma'idah, 5:33) ❋ And those who have chosen a mosque by way of harm, and disbelief, and to cause division among the believers, and as an outpost for those who waged war against God and His Messenger before, they will swear: 'We desired nothing but good'; and God bears witness that they are truly liars. (Al-Tawbah, 9:107) ❋ And fight in the way of God with those who fight against you, but aggress not; God loves not the aggressors. / And slay them wherever you come upon them, and expel them from where they expelled you; sedition is more grievous than slaying. But fight them not by the Sacred Mosque until they should fight you there; then if they fight you, slay them—such, is the requital of disbelievers. (Al-Baqarah, 2:190–191)

And that God, in turn, wages war (*harb*) upon the disbelievers: *But if you do not, then be warned of war from God, and His Messenger. Yet if you repent, you shall have your principal sums, not being unjust, and no injustice being done to you.* (Al-Baqarah, 2:279)

And that God says of the idolaters and hypocrites: '… *God assail them (qatalahum Allah)!* …':

> The Jews say: Ezra is the son of God; and the Christians say: The Messiah is the son of God. That is the utterance of their mouths, imitating the utterances of those who disbelieved before [them]. God assail them! How they are deviated! (Al-Tawbah, 9:30) ❋ And when you see them, their figures please you; and if they speak, you listen to their speech. [Yet] they are like blocks of timber [that have been] propped-up. They assume that every cry is [directed] against them. They are the enemy, so beware of them. May God assail them! How can they deviate? (Al-Munafiqun, 63:4)

And that God slew (*qatala*) some of the disbelievers: *You did not slay them, but God slew them, and you threw not when you threw, but God threw, and that He might try the believers with a fair test; surely God is Hearing, Knowing.* (Al-Anfal, 8:17)

Hence despite the injuriousness, defiance and war which the disbelievers direct towards God—and despite God's fighting and slaying them—this does not mean that God hates the disbelievers themselves as such.

Perhaps the secret of this mystery is that God fights and wages war upon them in the form of their own warring against God; for the worst punishment with which God requites the disbelievers with is merely to allow them to defy Him, seek to injure Him, and wage war against Him. God says:

> They would deceive God and the believers; and only themselves they deceive; and they are not aware. (Al-Baqarah, 2:9) ❋ The hypocrites seek to trick God, but He is tricking them. When they stand up to pray, they stand up lazily and to be seen by people, and they do not remember God save a little. (Al-Nisa', 4:142) ❋ And those who deny Our signs, We will draw them on by degrees, whence they do not know. (Al-A'raf, 7:182) ❋ So leave Me [to deal] with those who deny this discourse. We will draw them on by degrees, whence they do not know. (Al-Qalam, 68:44)

Thus the war waged by the evildoers, disbelievers and idolaters against God is in reality nothing but God's war against them, but they do not perceive this. It is not God who hates them, but they who hate themselves without knowing it. Human freedom necessarily means being free to harm oneself.

CHAPTER 10: THE MESSENGER OF GOD'S ﷺ LOVE FOR GOD

63 Narrated with this wording in Bayhaqi, *Al-Sunan al-kubra*, vol. 7, p. 78. Nisa'i, narrates it with the following wording:

'Beloved to me have been made perfume and women, and the coolness of my eye is in the prayer.' (Nisa'i, *Al-Sunan al-sughra*, *Hadith* no. 3940, *Kitab 'Ashrat al-nisa*'; see also: Ahmad Ibn Hanbal, *Musnad*, volume 3, p. 128 and p. 199.

CHAPTER 11: THE MESSENGER OF GOD'S ﷺ LOVE FOR THE BELIEVERS

64 Abu Ja'far Muhammad Ibn Jarir Al-Tabari, *Tafsir Al-Qur'an*, vol. 10, p. 200.

65 This is to say then that the Messenger of God ﷺ loved even his enemies. Did he ﷺ then love them as they were actually physically fighting against God's way? God says:

You will not find a people who believe in God and the Last Day loving (yuwaddun) those who oppose God and His Messenger, even though they were their fathers or their sons or their brothers or their clan. [For] those He has inscribed faith upon their hearts and reinforced them with a spirit from Him, and He will admit them into gardens underneath which rivers flow, wherein they will abide, God being pleased with them, and they being pleased with Him. Those [they] are God's confederates. Assuredly it is God's confederates who are the successful. (Al-Mujadilah, 58:22)

We note that *'yuwaddun'* which we have translated here as 'love' (see Chapter 21) is a particular kind of love (*'widad'*) and closely related to the word 'affection' (*'mawaddah'*), not love in a general way (*'hubb'*) or mercy (*'rahmah'*). However, when one is trying to defend oneself or one's religion it is necessary to love God first, and then preserve oneself, before caring for one's enemy. Nevertheless, it could be said perhaps that the Messenger of God ﷺ even when he fought his enemies (and indeed was ordered in the Qur'an to fight those who fought him first) may have loved them—not, obviously, insofar as they were God's enemies but rather insofar as they were still people. For all people—at least until they die and exit the terrestrial human state—have the potential to change, to become beautiful in soul, and thus to become loveable. Indeed, God says precisely this: *It may be that God will bring about between you and those of them with whom you are at enmity, affection. For God is Powerful, and God is Forgiving, Merciful.* (Al-Mumtahanah, 60:7)

Certainly, this fits with our definition of human love as 'an inclination towards beauty after being pleased by it': in all people there is the potential for beauty of soul, and in all but a very few people some beauty of soul is clearly perceivable. This would also explain why the Messenger of God ﷺ was always as merciful to his (and God's) enemies as he possibly could be, even whilst seeking to defend himself and the Muslim community from them. It even explains in some part why and how he was *a mercy to all the worlds* (Al-Anbiya', 21:107). At any rate, it could certainly be said that the Messenger of God ﷺ never hated anyone for personal reasons, and that his example (*Sunnah*) was to love all people insofar as they were people but not insofar as they were enemies of God (and physically fighting against God's way), and God knows best.

Notes

CHAPTER 12: HUMANITY'S LOVE FOR GOD

66 See also other verses on this theme, such as: *Al-Baqarah*, 2:37, 160-162, 187, 221, 268; *Al-Nisa'*, 4:17-18, 28-29, 31; *Al-An'am*, 6:165; *Al-Anfal*, 8:38; *Al-Tawbah*, 9:74, 118; *Ta Ha*, 20:82; *Ghafir*, 40:3; *Al-Dhariyat*, 51:50; *Al-Najm*, 53:35; *Al-Hadid*, 57:13; *Al-Tahrim*, 66:8; and there are many other verses in the Holy Qur'an which speak of God's Mercy towards human beings besides those we have mentioned here.

67 The translation of the Qur'an we have used gives the phrase *'however cherished,'* for the Qur'anic words "*ala hubihi*" which literally means 'on [or 'for', or 'despite'] its love'. According to Fakhr al-Din al-Razi's *Mafatih al-ghayb* (vol. 5, p. 36) there are three different (valid) interpretations for this phrase: the majority of scholars understand the meaning 'despite its love' ('its', here, referring back to the word 'substance'), in which case our translation—*and who gives of his substance, however cherished, to kinsmen and orphans and the needy and the traveller and beggars, and for slaves*—correctly conveys the sense of the verse. However, he gives two other interpretations: (1) 'for the love of it' where 'it' refers to 'giving', and (2) 'for the love of Him', where 'Him' refers to God. In other words, that true piety involves loving God and giving to others out of love of God—and loving to do so. The last interpretation is especially significant not only because it confirms that all good acts must be done, ideally, out of love of God, and that this is the example of the Messenger of God ﷺ—as mentioned earlier in connection with verse *Al-An'am* 6:161-164—but also that true love of God necessarily involves loving good actions towards the neighbor. Indeed, as will later be discussed (in Chapter 17), the Messenger of God ﷺ emphasized precisely this when he said:

> 'By Him in whose hand is my soul, no servant believes until he loves for his neighbour (or he said: 'his brother') what he loves for himself.' (Muslim, *Sahih; Kitab al-Iman; Bab al-Dalil 'ala anna min khisal al-iman an yuhibb li-akhihi al-Muslim ma yuhibb li-nafsih min khayr*; Hadith no. 45).

68 Jalal al-Din Mahalli and Jalal al-Din Suyuti, *Tafsir al-Jalalayn*, p. 35.

69 Abu al-Fida' Isma'il ibn Kathir al-Dimashqi, *Tafsir al-Qur'an al-'azim*, p. 363. Moreover, in the case of the Blessed Virgin Mary, God continued this miraculous grace even after she left the solitude of the sanctuary, as seen in God's words (for no one—let alone a woman giving birth—is strong enough to shake a palm tree and cause its dates to drop):

> *And the birth pangs brought her to the trunk of the palm-tree. She said, 'O would that I had died before this and become a forgotten thing, beyond recall!' / Then he called her from below her, 'Do not grieve. Your Lord has made below you a rivulet. / And shake the trunk of the palm-tree towards you—there will drop on you dates fresh and ripe.* (*Maryam*, 19:23-25)

70 The Messenger of God ﷺ himself was granted both God's spirit of peace (*al-sakinah*) and supernatural graces (*legions you did not see*, who delivered him from those trying to kill him) when he was in isolation with Abu Bakr ؓ in the Cave of Thawr—as well God's being (lovingly) with him! God says:

> *If you do not help him, [know that] God has already helped him, when the disbelievers drove him forth—the second of two; when the two were in the cave—when he said to his companion, 'Do not despair; verily God is with us'. Then God sent down His spirit of peace (sakinatahu) upon him and supported him with legions you did not see; and He made the word of those who disbelieved the nethermost, and the Word of God was the uppermost. And God is Mighty, Wise.* (*Al-Tawbah*, 9:40)

71 Tirmidhi, *Sunan*, Hadith no. 3490, *Kitab al-Da'awat*

72 Tirmidhi, *Sunan*, Hadith no. 3491, *Kitab al-Da'awat, Bab Ma ja' fi 'aqd al-tasbih bil-yad*.

73 *Sahih Muslim, Kitab Al-Imarah, Hadith* no. 5032.

74 See also: 2:139; 4:146; 7:29; 15:40; 37:40, 74, 128, 160, 169; 38:83 and 98:5.

75 *Sahih Al-Bukhari, Kitab Bad' al-Wahy, Hadith* no.1; *Sahih Muslim, Kitab al-Imarah, Hadith* no. 5036.

76 God also mentions humility and fear together at the end of *Surat Al-A'raf*, together 'with not being heedless' or 'not too proud' (and therefore being aware of God, and loving God), albeit that the exhortation ends with a reference to *those* [angels] *who are with your Lord*:

> And remember your Lord within yourself, humbly, and fearfully, and more quietly than speaking out loud at morning and evening. And do not be among the heedless. / Surely those who are with your Lord are not too proud to worship Him; they glorify Him, and to Him they prostrate. (Al-A'raf, 7:205–206)

77 *Sahih Bukhari, Kitab Tafsir Al-Qur'an, Bab ma Ja'a fi Fatihat Al-Kitab* (Hadith no. 1); also: *Sahih Bukhari, Kitab Fada'il Al-Qur'an Bab Fadl Fatihat Al-Kitab* (Hadith no. 9), no. 5006.

78 Nisa'i, *Sunan*, Hadith no. 3929; *Kitab 'Ashrat al-nisa'; Bab Hubb al-nisa'*.

79 It will be noted that these verses in the Qur'an which show that there is a certain 'mirroring' of God's portents ('*ayat*') between those in human beings and those in the universe—and thus also with the Qur'an itself which relates these portents—imply that the universe (the 'macrocosm') is a kind of massive cosmic mirror image of a human being (the 'microcosm'). Indeed, God further says: *Assuredly the creation of the heavens and the earth is greater (akbar) than the creation of mankind; but most people do not know.* (Ghafir, 40:57)

The word '*akbar*' can mean 'greater', but can also mean 'bigger', implying: 'the same, but bigger'. In other words, 'man is a small universe and the universe is a large man'. Thus in Arabic, the universe is sometimes called 'God's visible book' ('*kitab Allah al-manzhur*'); human beings are called 'God's destined book' ('*kitab Allah al-maqdur*') and the Qur'an is called 'God's enscribed book' ('*kitab Allah al-mastur*').

CHAPTER 13: THE BELIEVER'S LOVE FOR THE MESSENGER OF GOD

80 Abu al-Fida' Isma'il ibn Kathir al-Dimashqi, *Tafsir al-Qur'an al-'azim*, pp. 1131–1132.

81 Bukhari, *Sahih*, Hadith no. 15, *Kitab al-iman*; Muslim, *Sahih*, Hadith no. 44, *Kitab al-Iman*.

82 Bukhari, *Sahih*, Hadith no. 16, *Kitab al-Iman, Bab Halawat al-iman*; Muslim, *Sahih*, Hadith no. 43, *Kitab al-Iman, Bab Bayan khisal man ittasafa bihinna wajada halawat al-iman*.

83 Bayhaqi, *Al-Sunan al-kubra*, vol. 10, p. 191; see also: Ahmad Ibn Hanbal, *Musnad*, vol. 2, p. 381; Al-Hakim, *Mustadrak*, vol. 2, p. 613.

84 Muslim, *Sahih*, Hadith no. 408, *Kitab al-Salat, Bab al-Salat 'ala al-nabi ba'd al-tashahhud*.

85 Tirmidhi, *Sunan*, Hadith no. 2457, *Kitab Sifat yawm al-qiyamah*.

86 Bukhari, *Sahih*, Hadith no. 6167, *Kitab al-Adab*.

CHAPTER 14: LOVE FOR THE FAMILY AND KIN OF THE MESSENGER OF GOD

87 Ibn Kathir, *Tafsir al-Qur'an al-'azim*, vol. 4, p. 142.

88 Qurtubi, *Al-Jami' li-ahkam al-Qur'an al-karim*, vol. 16, p. 20.

89 Fakhr al-Din al-Razi, *Mafatih al-ghayb*, vol. 13, p. 433.

Notes

90 It is worth mentioning that the 'relatives' (by which we mean here blood relations) of the Messenger of God ﷺ does not necessarily mean the same as his 'kinsfolk' (by which we mean here the word used in the verse *Al-Shura*, 42:23, as cited above), because God says:

> And Noah called out to his Lord and said, 'My Lord, lo! my son is of my family, and truly Your promise is the Truth, and You are the Most Just of Judges'. / He said: 'O Noah, lo! he is not of your family; lo! it is not a righteous deed. So do not ask of Me that whereof you have no knowledge. I admonish you lest you be among the ignorant'. (Hud, 11:45–46) ❊ And when his Lord tested Abraham with certain words, and he fulfilled them, He said: 'I make you a leader for the people'. Said he, 'And of my seed?' He said, 'My covenant shall not reach the evildoers'. (Al-Baqarah, 2:124) ❊ And no burdened soul shall bear the burden of another [sinful soul]. And should one burdened heavily call for its burden to be borne, nothing of it will be borne, even if [he] be a relative. You can only warn those who fear their Lord in secret and observe the prayer. For whoever purifies himself is purifying himself only for [the sake of] his own soul. And to God is the [end of the] journeying. (Fatir, 35:18)

We should not fail to mention here that Abu Lahab, the Messenger's paternal uncle, went to hell because of his unbelief, for God says:

> Perish the hands of Abu Lahab and perish he! / His wealth will not avail him, nor what he has earned. / He will [soon] enter a Fire of flames, / and his wife the carrier of firewood/ with a rope of palm-fibre around her neck. (Al-Masad, 111:1–5)

So the true kinsfolk of the Messenger of God ﷺ are those who are connected to him by blood on the one hand, and by love, character and state on the other hand.

91 Muslim, *Sahih*, Hadith no. 2424, *Kitab Fada'il al-Sahaba, Bab Fada'il ahl bayt al-nabi*.

92 Tirmidhi, *Sunan*, Hadith no. 3787, *Kitab al-Manaqib; Bab Ahl bayt al-Nabi*.

93 Fakhr al-Din al-Razi, *Mafatih al-ghayb*, vol. 13 p. 433.

94 Fakhr al-Din al-Razi, *Mafatih al-ghayb*, vol. 4, p. 383.

95 This narration is authentic by its multiple transmitters (*mutawatir*); it was narrated in Ibn Hibban's *Sahih* (vol. 15, p. 376); in Ahmad Ibn Hanbal's, *Musnad*, vol. 4 p. 370; and in Nisa'i's, *Khasa'is*, p. 93. In Ahmad Ibn Hanbal's *Musnad*, vol. 1 p. 119 it is transmitted by multiple transmitters on the authority of twelve Companions. It is thus an authentic *Hadith* with multiple transmitters, as affirmed by many scholars of *Hadith*, including Dhahabi (*Siyar a'lam al-nubala*, vol. 8, p. 335).

96 Bukhari, *Sahih*, no. 4416, *Kitab al-Maghazi*; Muslim, *Sahih*, no. 4416, *Kitab Fada'il al-Sahaba*.

97 Fakhr al-Din al-Razi, *Mafatih al-ghayb*, vol. 2, p. 350.

98 Ahmad, *Musnad*, vol. 5, p. 391; Tirmidhi, *Sunan*, Hadith no. 3768, *Kitab al-Manaqib, Bab: Manaqib al-Hasan wa al-Husayn*. Tirmidhi considered this *Hadith* 'sound and authentic' ('*hasan sahih*'), and it is considered by the *Hadith* scholars to be 'authentic by multiple transmission' ('*mutawatir*').

99 Tirmidhi, *Sunan*, Hadith no. 3788, *Kitab al-Manaqib, Bab Ahl Bayt al-Nabi*; Muslim, *Sahih* (slightly different wording), Hadith no. 2408, *Kitab Fada'il al-Sahaba, Bab Min fada'il ʿAli ibn Abi Talib*.

100 Bukhari, *Sahih*, Hadith no. 111, *Kitab al-ʿIlm, Bab Kitabat al-ʿilm*.

101 Bukhari, *Sahih*, Hadith no. 3713, *Kitab al-Manaqib, Bab Manaqib qarabat Rasul Allah*.

102 Bukhari, *Sahih*, Hadith no. 6788, *Kitab al-Hudud*; Muslim, *Sahih*, Hadith no. 1688, *Kitab al-Hudud*.

103 See: *Al-Nahl*, 16:103; *Ta Ha*, 20:113; *Al-Zumar*, 39:28; *Fussilat*, 41:3; *Al-Shura*, 42:7; *Al-Zukhruf*, 43:3; *Al-Ahqaf*, 46:12.

104 Bukhari, *Sahih, Hadith* no. 3370, *Kitab Ahadith al-anbiya'*; Muslim, *Sahih, Hadith* no. 406, *Kitab al-Salat*.

CHAPTER 15: THE EFFECTS OF THE LOVE OF GOD ON HUMAN BEINGS

105 Faith is a mercy from God, because no one can have faith without God's leave. God Almighty says:

> And it is not for any soul to believe save by the permission of God, and He causes abomination to fall upon those who have no understanding. (Yunus, 10:100) ● *This is indeed a reminder. Let him who will, then, choose a way to his Lord. / But you will not, unless God wills. Assuredly God is ever Knower, Wise. / He admits whomever He will into His mercy, and as for the evildoers, He has prepared for them a painful chastisement.* (Al-Insan, 76:29–31)

106 *Tafsir Al-Jalalayn*, p. 28.

107 The verses which precede this Qur'anic verse indicate that this verse (*Aal ʿImran*, 3:31) is addressed to the believers especially. God says:

> Let not the believers take the disbelievers as patrons, rather than the believers—for whoever does that, does not belong to God in anyway—unless you protect yourselves against them, as a safeguard. God warns you of His Self; and to God is the journey's end. / Say: 'Whether you hide what is in your breasts, or disclose it, God knows it and knows what is in the heavens and what is in the earth; and God is Able to do all things. / The day every soul shall find what it has done of good present before it, and what it has done of evil, it will wish that between it and that there were a great distance. God warns you of His Self, and God is Kind to His servants. (Aal ʿImran, 3:28–30)

Fakr al-Din al-Razi affirms that these verses are addressed to the believers, saying: 'After the Almighty says how the believer must glorify Him, He then says how the believer should interact with other people ... Concerning the word 'servants' (' *ibad*') in the Qur'an, God says: *And the [true] servants of the Compassionate One are those who walk upon the earth modestly, and who, when the ignorant address them, say [words of] peace* (Al-Furqan, 25:63). And He says: *[A] spring from which the servants of God drink* (Al-Insan, 76:6). This means that after mentioning the warning that He has given to the disbelievers and the iniquitous, God then mentions the promise He makes to those who obey Him, saying: *[A]nd God is Kind to His servants*. That is to say then that just as God requites the iniquitous, He is Kind to the obedient and the virtuous.' (Fakr al-Din al-Razi, *Al-Tafsir al-kabir*), vol. 3, pp. 191–197).

108 And 'hope' ('*raja*') is a kind of love, as we will see later God willing, in Chapter 21: The Different Kinds of Love

109 Bukhari, *Sahih, Hadith* no 5602, *Kitab al-Riqaq; Bab al-Tawadu'*.

110 Fakhr al-Din al-Razi says in *Al-Tafsir al-kabir*: 'What this means is that he gives of his wealth despite how cherished this wealth is to him. Ibn ʿAbbas ؓ and Ibn Masʿud ؓ said that it means to give when you are healthy but somewhat covetous, hoping for wealth and fearing poverty, and you do not delay until death is upon you to say, "This is for so-and-so, and this is for so-and-so"...' (Fakhr al-Din al-Razi, *Mafatih al-ghayb*, vol. 2 p. 215)

111 In *Surat Al-Waqiʿah*, God speaks of 'those on the right' and 'the ones brought near', and described 'the ones brought near' as drinking from a cup from a flowing stream, but does not describe 'those on the right' as doing this. God says: *They will be waited on by immortal youths with goblets and ewers and a cup from a flowing spring.* (Al-Waqiʿah, 56:17–18)

And in *Surat Al-Mutaffifin*, God mentions both 'the pious' ('*al-abrar*') and 'the ones brought near' ('*al-muqarrabun*'), and describes the latter as drinking from a spring of *Tasneem* in Paradise. As for the pious, God describes them in this *Surah* as drinking from a sealed nectar mixed with *Tasneem*, and not pure *Tasneem*. God says:

> Nay! The record of the pious is in 'Illiyyun; / and what will tell you, what 'Illiyyun is?, / [It is] a sealed book, / witnessed by those brought near. / Assuredly the pious will be amid bliss, / upon couches, gazing. / You will perceive in their faces the radiancy of bliss, / as they are given to drink a nectar [that is] sealed, / whose seal is musk—so for such [bliss] let the viers vie /—and whose mixture is of Tasneem: / a spring from which those brought near will drink. (Al-Mutaffifin, 83:18–28)

These verses make it clear that there are three classes of people in Paradise, namely: 'Those on the right', 'the pious' and 'those brought near'; the highest ranked are 'those brought near', and the lowest are 'those on the right', and 'the pious' are in between the other two, lower than 'those brought near' and higher than 'those on the right'.

As for those of whom God says '*He loves [them] and [they] love Him*', they have attained to all piety, as we said above; this means that they are at least at the level of 'the pious', and higher than 'those on the right'. At the end of this chapter, God willing, we will examine the question as to whether those of whom God says '*He loves [them] and [they] love Him*' are among 'those brought near', and thus whether they are among God's righteous 'friends'.

112 Narrated by Tabarani from 'reliable transmitters', according to Al-Hafiz Haythami in *Majma' al-zawa'id*, vol. 8, p. 18.

113 Bukhari, *Sahih*, Hadith no. 604, *Kitab al-Adab*.

114 Tabari comments, with reference to God's words—*[S]truggle against them therewith with a great endeavour* (Al-Furqan, 25:52)—that this means: 'But struggle against them, with the aid of this Qur'an, with a mighty struggle.' (Tabari, *Jami' al-bayan fi ta'wil al-Qur'an*, vol. 9 p. 397)

And Ibn Kathir says, in his *Tafsir*: 'And struggle against them with it, i.e. with the Qur'an, as Ibn 'Abbas ﷺ said.' (Ibn Kathir, *Tafsir al-Qur'an al-'azim*, p. 1360)

115 Jabir ﷺ reported that the Messenger of God ﷺ returned from a battle and said to the people: 'You have made a fine step: you have stepped from the Lesser Struggle to the Greater Struggle.' They said, 'And what is the Greater Struggle, O Messenger of God?' He said: 'The servant's struggle against his desire.' (Narrated by Bayhaqi, [though he said that its chain of transmission was somewhat weak], *Kitab al-zuhd al-kabir*, p. 165; and by al-Khatib al-Baghdadi, *Tarikh Baghdad*, vol. 13 p. 523.)

And Fadala ibn 'Ubayd reported that the Messenger of God ﷺ said: 'The struggler is the one who struggles against his ego [*nafs*].' (Tirmidhi, *Sunan*, Kitab: *Fada'il al-jihad; Bab Ma ja' fi fadl man mat murabita*; Tirmidhi declared it to be sound and authentic; also narrated in Ibn Hibban, *Sahih*, vol. 10 p. 484, and elsewhere.)

116 It is worth mentioning that God protects the believer who loves Him and struggles in His cause from this world, despite the gravity of his struggle. Qatadah ibn al-Nu'man reported that the Messenger of God ﷺ said: 'When God loves a servant, He protects him from this world just as one of you keeps protecting the sick person in his care from [fetid] water.' (Tirmidhi, *Sunan*, Hadith no. 2036, *Kitab al-Tibb*)

117 God also says: *When you have performed the prayer, remember God, standing and sitting and on your sides. Then, when you are reassured, observe the prayer, surely the prayer is for believers a prescription at specific times.* (Al-Nisa', 4:103)

118 Ibn Hibban, *Sahih*, vol. 3, p. 99.

119 Therefore the Messenger of God ﷺ described the sweetness of faith by saying, according to Anas ibn Malik ﷺ:

> 'Three [things] which, if they are found in someone, he [or she] tastes the sweetness of faith: For God and His Messenger to be more beloved to him than anything else; for him to love a servant for no one's sake but God Almighty; and for him to hate to return to unbelief, after God saved him from it, just as he would hate to be cast into fire.' (Bukhari, *Sahih*, Hadith no. 21, *Kitab al-Iman*)

120 Abu Hurayrah reported that the Messenger of God ﷺ said: 'I shall be the master of humankind on Resurrection Day...' (Bukhari, *Sahih*, Hadith no. 4712, *Kitab Tafsir al-Qur'an; Bab Dhurriyyat man hamalna ma' Nuh*; Muslim, *Sahih*, Hadith no. 194, *Kitab al-Iman, Bab Adna ahl al-janna manziluhu fiha*.)

And also: 'I shall be the master of the sons of Adam on Resurrection Day, and [I say this] without pride ... Adam and all who came after him shall be beneath my banner, and [I say this] without pride.' (Ahmad, *Musnad*, vol. 1, p. 281; Ibn Hibban, *Sahih*, vol. 14, p. 398).

121 There is something in human beings which can truly and sincerely long for death. God says: *You were longing for death before you met it. Now you have seen it, looking on.* (Aal 'Imran, 3:143)

And there is an actual example of this from the life of the Messenger of God ﷺ in the story of 'Umayr ibn al-Humam al-Ansari: Anas ibn Malik reported that the Messenger of God ﷺ said, before the battle of Uhud:

> 'Stand for a paradise as vast as the heavens and the earth!' 'Umayr ibn al-Humam al-Ansari said: 'O Messenger of God, a Paradise as vast as the heavens and the earth?' 'Yes', he said. 'Ah, ah!', cried 'Umayr. The Messenger of God ﷺ said: 'What makes you say "Ah, ah"?' He said: 'Nothing, O Messenger of God, save that I long to be among its inhabitants.' He said: 'Then you are among its inhabitants.' ['Umayr] then took some dates from his pack and began to eat them. He then said, 'Were I to live to eat all these dates of mine, such a life would be too long!' So he flung down the dates and went to fight, until he was killed. (Muslim, *Sahih*, Hadith no. 1901, *Kitab al-Imarah; Bab Thubut al-jannah lil-shahid*).

But there is another *Hadith* which says that there is something in human beings that hates death:

> The Messenger of God ﷺ said: 'Whosoever loves to meet God, God loves to meet him; and whosoever hates to meet God, God hates to meet him.' It was said, 'O Messenger of God, to hate to meet God means to hate to meet death; and we all hate death.' He said: 'Nay, this means at the hour of his death: if he is given tidings of God's mercy and forgiveness, he loves to meet God and God loves to meet him; and if he is given tidings of God's chastisement, he hates to meet God and God hates to meet him.' (Muslim, *Sahih*, Hadith no. 2685, *Kitab al-dhikr wa al-du'a'; Bab Man ahabba liqa' Allah*. The wording here is that of Ibn Majah, *Sunan*, Hadith no. 4264, *Kitab al-Zuhd; Bab Dhikr al-mawt wa al-isti'dad lah*.)

Therefore we conclude that perhaps there are two elements in human beings: one part of his nature always hates death, and another part can love death and long for it (if he or she is a true 'friend' of God); perhaps the first element is the 'ego' or 'lower soul' (*nafs*), and the second element is the spirit (*ruh*); and God knows best.

122 Perhaps in the following Qur'anic verses, there are also allusions to God's 'friends':

> *So let them fight in the way of God those who sell the life of this world for the Hereafter; and whoever fights in the way of God and is slain or conquers, We shall give him a great wage.* (Al-Nisa', 4:74) *Indeed God has purchased from the believers their lives and their possessions, so that theirs will be [the reward of] Paradise: they shall fight in the way of God and they shall kill and be killed...* (Al-Tawbah, 9:111)

Notes

CHAPTER 16: FAMILY LOVE

123 It is worth mentioning here that God also made laws for folk (*ahl*). God says:

And whoever has not the means wherewith to be able to marry believing women in wedlock, let him take believing maids whom your right hands own. God knows very well your faith; the one of you is as the other. So marry them, with the permission of their folk, and give them their wages, honourably, as women in wedlock, not illicitly, or taking lovers. But when they are given in wedlock, if they commit lewdness, they shall be liable to half the chastisement, of married women. That is for those of you who fear the distress of sin, yet it is better for you to be patient. God is Forgiving, Merciful. (Al-Nisa', 4:25) ❋ *And if you fear a breach between the two, send forth an arbiter from his folk, and an arbiter from her folk, if they desire to set things right, God will grant them success. Surely God is ever Knower, Aware.* (Al-Nisa', 4:35)

And God also mentions the rights of relatives (*dhul qurba*) in a general way: *And give the kinsman (dhul qurba) his due, and the needy and the traveller [as well]; and do not squander. / Indeed squanderers are brothers of devils, and the Devil was ever ungrateful to his Lord.* (Al-Isra', 17:26–27)

124 See also: Al-An'am, 6:140; Al-An'am, 6:151; Al-Anfal, 8:31; Al-Mumtahanah, 60:12; Al-Takwir, 81:8–9.

125 Abu al-Fida' Isma'il ibn 'Umar ibn Kathir al-Qurashi al-Dimashqi, *Tafsir al-Qur'an al-'azim*, p. 1345.

126 In this regard, the following *Hadith* is related:

Abu Hurayrah reported that a man said: 'O Messenger of God, which person most deserves to be treated well?' He said ﷺ: 'Your mother; then your mother; then your mother; then your father; then the next nearest to you, and then the next nearest.' (Muslim, *Sahih*, *Hadith* no. 2548, *Kitab al-Birr wa al-silah*; *Bab Birr al-walidayn wa annahuma ahaqqu bih*.) Another narration has it that a man came to the Messenger of God ﷺ and said: 'O Messenger of God, which person most deserves good treatment from me?' He said: 'Your mother.' The man said, 'Then who?' He said: 'Then your mother.' He said, 'Then who?' He said, 'Then your mother.' He said, 'Then who?' He said: 'Then your father.' (Bukhari, *Sahih*, *Hadith* no. 5971, *Kitab al-Adab*; *Bab Man ahaqqu al-nas bi-husn al-suhbah*.)

127 Jalal al-Din Mahalli and Jalal al-Din Suyuti, *Tafsir al-Jalalayn*, p. 668.

128 It will be noted that loving relatives in accordance to their proximity to ourselves means loving them, if not in accordance with the (inner) beauty they manifest to us (in principle at least), then certainly in accordance with our knowledge of their inner beauty, because we naturally know those closest to us more. In other words, even in family love we are loving beauty and goodness: in general we love those closest to us more, for they show us more goodness and beauty (or should, all other things being equal).

CHAPTER 17: LOVE OF OTHERS (ALL HUMANITY; THE 'PEOPLE OF THE SCRIPTURE'; BELIEVERS, AND FRIENDS)

129 This also means, naturally, that every human being is essentially God's vicegerent on earth, into which God breathed 'something' of His spirit (as we saw in Chapter 7: God's Love for Humanity).

130 That is not to say obviously that the religion of Islam is sympathetic towards idolatry in any way—it is absolutely against it and refutes it completely in the very first Testimony of Faith

(the *Shahadah*) that *There is no god but God* (*La illaha illa Allah*)—but nevertheless, God allows everyone to choose their own religion freely, whatever it be, for He says:

> *There is no compulsion in religion. Rectitude has become clear from error; so whoever disbelieves in the false deity, and believes in God, has laid hold of the most firm handle, unbreaking; God is Hearing, Knowing.* (Al-Baqarah, 2:256) ❋ *And say, 'The truth [that comes] from your Lord; so whoever will, let him believe, and whoever will, let him disbelieve'....* (Al-Kahf, 18:29) ❋ *Say: 'O disbelievers! / I do not worship what you worship, / and you do not worship what I worship, / nor will I worship what you have worshipped, / nor will you worship what I worship. / You have your religion and I have a religion'.* (Al-Kafirun, 109:1–6) ❋ *So leave them to indulge and to play, until they encounter that day of theirs, which they are promised;* (Al-Ma'arij, 70:42)

131 God says:

> *Indeed God protects those who believe. Indeed God does not love the treacherous, the ungrateful. / Permission is granted to those who fight because they have been wronged. And God is truly able to help them; / those who were expelled from their homes without right, only because they said: 'Our Lord is God'. Were it not for God's causing some people to drive back others, destruction would have befallen the monasteries, and churches, and synagogues, and mosques in which God's Name is mentioned greatly. Assuredly God will help those who help Him. God is truly Strong, Mighty.* (Al-Hajj, 22:38–40)

132 Fakr al-Din al-Razi, *Al-Tafsir al-kabir*, vol. 10, p. 747.

133 These two verses (10:85 and 60:5) can also be understood as a supplication not to lose to the unbelievers in combat. The *Tafsir al-Jalalayn* comments as follows (on verses 10:85 and 60:5 respectively): 'So they said, *'In God we have put our trust. Our Lord, make us not a [cause of] temptation for the evildoing folk*, that is, do not make them prevail over us, lest they then think that they are upon the right path and so end up succumbing to [the] temptation [of thinking that they are upon the right path] because of us.' (p.218)

'*Our Lord, do not make us a cause of beguilement for those who disbelieve*, that is to say, do not make them prevail over us, lest they think that they are following the truth and are beguiled as a result, in other words, [lest] they lose their reason because of us; *and forgive us. Our Lord, You are indeed the Mighty, the Wise*', in Your kingdom and Your actions.' (p.549)

134 Jalal al-Din Mahalli and Jalal al-Din Suyuti, *Tafsir al-Jalalayn*, p. 106.

135 Al-Qurtubi, *Tafsir al-Qurtubi*, vol. 5, p. 171.

136 Muslim, *Sahih*, Hadith no. 45, (related on the authority of Anas ibn Malik) *Kitab al-Iman; Bab al-Dalil 'ala anna min khisal al-iman an yuhibb li-akhihi al-Muslim ma yuhibb li-nafsih min khayr.* In another narration on the authority of Anas ibn Malik ﷺ the Messenger of God ﷺ said: 'None of you believes until he loves for his brother what he loves for himself.' (Bukhari, *Sahih*, Hadith, no. 13, *Kitab al-Iman; Bab Min al-iman an yuhibb li-akhihi ma yuhibb li-nafsih*)

137 Tirmidhi, *Sunan*, Hadith no. 1924, (related on the authority of 'Abdullah ibn 'Amr) *Kitab al-Birr wa al-silah; Bab Ma ja' fi rahmat al-nas.*

138 Bukhari, *Sahih*, Hadith no. 7376, (related on the authority of Jarir ibn 'Abdullah) *Kitab al-Tawhid; Bab Qawluhu ta'ala qul ud'⊕ Allah aw ud'⊕ al-Rahman.*

139 Bayhaqi, *Al-Sunan al-kubra*, vol. 9, p. 118.

140 Abu al-Fida' Isma'il ibn 'Umar ibn Kathir al-Qurashi al-Dimashqi, *Tafsir al-Qur'an al-'azim*, p. 480.

141 Qurtubi, *Tafsir al-Qurtubi*, vol. 19, p. 257. The story of the Christians of Najran is also

mentioned in Muslim's *Sahih*, *Hadith* no. 3005, *Kitab al-Zuhd wa al-raqa'iq; Bab Qissat ashab al-ukhdud, qissat al-rahib wa al-ghulam.*

142 It is very important to point out here also that God addresses His Messenger ﷺ individually in this verse ('*You* ['*innaka*', which means 'you' in the second person singular] *will truly find*'), and not the believers in general; that is to say then, that this hostility does not extend to all Jews and all Muslims, but rather between certain Jewish tribes and the Messenger of God ﷺ during his own lifetime.

143 Thus God says:

> So, for their breaking their covenant and disbelieving in the signs of God, and slaying the prophets wrongfully, and for their saying, 'Our hearts are covered up'—nay, but God sealed them for their disbelief; so they do not believe, except for a few. (*Al-Nisa'*, 4:155) ❉ And verily you know that there were those among you who transgressed the Sabbath, and We said to them, 'Be apes, despised!' (*Al-Baqarah*, 2:65)

(See also: *Al-Baqarah*, 2:78, 91; *Al-Ma'idah*, 5:60; *Al-A'raf*, 7:166; and others verses in this regard.)

144 Indeed, God says:

> And let not those who possess dignity and ease among you swear not to give to the near of kin and to the needy, and to fugitives for the cause of God. Let them forgive and show indulgence. Yearn ye not that God may forgive you? God is Forgiving, Merciful. (*Al-Nur*, 24: 22).

145 As such, Muslims are not even allowed to morally judge their fellow believers, much less drive them away. God says (relating the story of Noah ﷺ):

> The council of his people who disbelieved, said: 'We see you but a mortal like us, and we see not that any follow you save the vilest among us, [through] rash opinion. We do not see that you have any merit over us; nay, we deem you liars'. / He said, 'O my people, have you considered if I am [acting] upon a clear proof from my Lord and He has given me mercy from Him, and it has been obscured from you, can we compel you to it, while you are averse to it? / And O my people, I do not ask of you any wealth for this. My wage falls only upon God and I will not drive away those who believe; they shall surely meet their Lord. But I see you are a people who are ignorant. / And O my people, who would help me against God if I drive them away? Will you not then remember? / And I do not say to you, "I possess the treasure houses of God" nor, 'I have knowledge of the Unseen; nor do I say, "I am an angel". Nor do I say to those whom your eyes scorn that God will not give them any good—God knows best what is in their souls. Lo! then indeed I would be of the evildoers'. (*Hud*, 11:27–31) ❉ They said, 'Shall we believe in you, when it is the lowliest people who follow you?' / He said, 'And what do I know of what they may have been doing? / Their reckoning is only my Lord's concern, if only you were aware. / And I am not about to drive away the believers. / I am just a plain warner'. (*Al-Shu'ara*, 26:111–5)

Accordingly, God tells the Prophet Muhammad ﷺ:

> And do not drive away those who call upon their Lord at morning and evening desiring His countenance. You are not accountable for them in anything; nor are they accountable for you in anything, that you should drive them away and be of the evildoers. (*Al-An'am*, 6:52)

146 See also the description of 'intimate friend' in the following verses: *Ghafir*, 40:18; *Fussilat*, 41:34; *Al-Haqqah*, 69:35; *Al-Ma'arij*, 70:10.

147 This kind of friendship might perhaps also be called a '*walijah*'—an intimate friendship, or literally a 'penetrating friendship'—which is only appropriate between believers (as we will

discuss further, God Willing, in Chapter 21: The Different Kinds of Love). God says: *Or did you suppose that you would be left [in peace] when God does not yet know those of you who have struggled and have not taken, besides God and His Messenger and the believers, an intimate friend? And God is aware of what you do*. (*Al-Tawbah*, 9:16)

148 It will be noted that we become friends in accordance with the goodness and inner beauty people show us, as we understand it at least—that is, if the friendship is sincere—and in accordance with the time we have spent with our friends (and thus in accordance with our experience of their inner beauty and their experience of ours).

CHAPTER 18: CONJUGAL AND SEXUAL LOVE

149 We say 'generally speaking' because perhaps God's words '*Or He combines them, males and females; and He makes whomever He will infertile. Surely He is Knower, Powerful*' (*Al-Shura*, 42:50) allude to the existence of 'hermaphrodites' wherein male and female are combined in a single person, or wherein the person is neither male nor female.

150 Raghib Al-Isfahani says, about the word 'mate' ('*zawj*') the following: 'Each one of the two genders of male and female in all animals which breed is called a 'mate', and each individual in a pair of any kind has a corresponding 'mate', just like shoes and socks come in pairs. Everything which has a complement or opposite with which it is always linked may be called a 'mate.' God says: '*And He made of it the two mates, the male and the female*' (*Al-Qiyamah*, 75:39), and He says: '*…dwell with your mate in the Garden…*' (*Al-Baqarah*, 2:35). (Raghib Isfahani, *Al-Mufradat*, p. 220)

151 Jalal al-Din Mahalli and Jalal al-Din Suyuti, *Tafsir al-Jalalayn*, p. 802.

152 Fakhr al-Din al-Razi, *al-Tafsir al-kabir*, vol. 9, p. 91.

153 Raghib al-Isfahani says about the word '*gone in*' ('*afda*'): '*Fada* means 'a wide open space', and from this is derived the verb *afda*, which means 'to go in', as in to put one's hand into something, or to go into one's wife; it is a more direct euphemism than to say 'he lay with her'. God says: '*when each of you has gone in unto the other*', and the poet said: Their food is open (*fawda*) and placed inside (*fada*) their packs.… That is, it is like it has been placed in an open space into which anyone may place his hand.' (Raghib al-Isfahani, *Al-Mufradat fi gharib al-Qur'an*, p. 383)

154 Narrated with this wording by Bayhaqi (*Al-Sunan al-kubra*, vol. 7, p. 87); also narrated by Nisa'i (*Al-Sunan al-sughra*, Hadith no. 394, *Kitab 'Asharat al-nisa'*) with the wording: 'Beloved to me have been made women and perfume, and the coolness of my eye is in prayer.' Also narrated by Ahmad Ibn Hanbal in his *Musnad* (vol. 3, pp. 128, 199).

155 See also: *Al-Baqarah*, 2:46; *Al-Tawbah*, 9:77; *Yunus*, 10:7, 11, 15; *Hud*, 11:29; *Al-Ra'd*, 13:2; *Al-Kahf*, 18:105, 110; *Al-Mu'minun*, 23:33; *Al-Furqan*, 25:21; *Al-'Ankabut*, 29:5, 23; *Al-Rum*, 30:5, 16; *Al-Sajdah*, 32:10, 14, 23; *Al-Zumar*, 39:71; *Fussilat*, 41:54; *Al-Jathiyah*, 45:34.

156 Ibn Hibban, *Sahih*, vol. 9, p.428; see also: Al-Hakim, *Al-Mustadrak*, vol.4, p.174.

157 Ibn Hibban, *Sahih*, vol. 10, p.503.

CHAPTER 19: LOVE AND EXTRA-MARITAL SEX

158 Jalal al-Din Mahalli and Jalal al-Din Suyuti, *Tafsir al-Jalalayn*, p. 105.

159 Thus illicit love harms the lover and can also harm—with eternal consequences; consequences that may affect their afterlife—their beloved, who they feel, or claim, they love (and therefore should want the best for them). Hence not all love benefits the lover or the beloved! Some kinds of love can ruin them both, eternally.…

CHAPTER 20: LOVE AND THE EYES

160 Tirmidhi, *Hadith* no. 3127, *Kitab Tafsir al-Qur'an; Bab Wa min Surat al-Hijr.*

161 We also see from God's words that happiness and pleasure can result from a glance of the eye. God says:

> They said, 'Pray to your Lord for us, that He make clear to us what her colour may be'. He said, 'He says she shall be a golden cow, bright in colour, gladdening to beholders'. (Al-Baqarah, 2:69) ⚫ They will be served from all around with [large] dishes of gold and goblets and therein will be whatever souls desire and eyes delight in, and you will abide in it [forever]. (Al-Zukhruf, 43:71)

162 Al-Hakim, *Al-Mustadrak*, (he considered it 'authentic') vol. 4, p. 349; Al-Tabarani, *Al-Mu'jam al-kabir*, vol. 10, p. 173.

163 Tirmidhi, *Sunan*, *Hadith* no. 277, *Kitab al-Adab, Bab Ma ja' fi nazrat al-mufaja'ah*; Ibn Hibban, *Sahih*, vol. 12, p. 381.

164 Tirmidhi, *Sunan*, *Hadith* no. 1087, *Kitab al-Nikah, Bab: Ma ja' fi al-nazr ila al-makhtubah.*

165 The power and danger of the eyes is also manifested in a different way, namely in envy or 'the evil eye'. God says: *And from the evil of an envier when he envies.* (Al-Falaq, 113:5)

And the Messenger of God ﷺ said: 'The [evil] eye is real.' (Bukhari, *Sahih*, Hadith no. 5740, *Kitab al-Tibb; Bab al-ʿAyn haqq.*)

CHAPTER 21: THE DIFFERENT KINDS OF LOVE

166 The word '*hubb*' in Arabic—which we discussed previously in Chapter 3: The Definition of Love—is translated throughout this work as 'love'. Thus the English title of this work is *Love in the Holy Qur'an*, and its Arabic title is: *Al-Hubb fil-Qur'an al-Kareem*. However, '*hubb*' does not only mean 'love' in Arabic, it also means 'like'. In fact, there is no proper word for 'to like' other than '*hubb*'. This is to say then that, linguistically speaking in Arabic, 'love' and 'liking' are indistinguishable—much like the French word '*aimer*'—except from the context and from the degree of intensity implied in that context. In English, however, the degrees of intensity of love are kept separate by having two separate words denoting two clearly different orders of intensity, though it is generally understood that 'liking' is a lesser degree of 'loving', and that 'loving' is a greater intensification of 'liking'. Arabic makes up for this, however, by having—as we shall see throughout this chapter, God Willing—many more words (and concepts) for the different kinds of love. This means that what are defined in this chapter as different kinds of love might appear to the English reader to be actually different kinds of 'liking' only. Nevertheless, since in Arabic this distinction does not apply, we define them as kinds of 'love', however weak their intensity or degree.

167 The different kinds of love according to Muslim scholars: What we mention above are the different kinds of love that are mentioned in the Holy Qur'an, and their lexical semantic and etymological definitions. In what follows below we mention what some Muslim scholars have said about the kinds of love (some of which we have already discussed in previous endnotes).

Abu Hamid Al-Ghazali, says in his *Ihya'*, in the chapter on 'Love, Devotion, Familiarity and Contentment' (p. 379): '*Love* ('*al-hubb*') is an expression of the disposition's inclination to something pleasant, and if this inclination deepens and strengthens it is called '*devotion*' ('*ishq*').'

He also says (p. 414): 'Know that whoever denies that *love* for God is possible will certainly also deny that '*yearning*' ('*al-shawq*') is possible, for there can be no yearning without a beloved as its object; and we affirm that it is possible to be *devoted* to God...'

And also (p. 421): '*Yearning* ('*al-shawq*') means to seek and look for something. Now what is already present cannot be sought, but this may be explained by saying that *yearning* is only directed to that which is known in one way and unknown in another; that which is not known at all cannot be yearned for ... We have said that man's love for God is real, and not merely allegorical, for when people say '*love*' they mean the soul's inclination to something which suits it, and *devotion* means an especially powerful inclination ... As for God's love for man, it cannot be described in this way ... *God's love for man, then, is for Him to draw him nearer to Himself by warding off distractions and sins from him, and purifying his inner being from the turbidity of the life of this world, and drawing back the veil from his heart so that he may behold Him, as though he sees Him with his heart.* As for man's love for God, it is his *inclination towards attaining the perfection which he utterly lacks and needs*, for he will doubtless yearn for what he lacks, and delight in attaining any part of it. This kind of yearning and love is impossible for God'.

And also (p. 436): 'If [the lover] is overwhelmed by joy at the nearness and direct witnessing which is given to him by way of mystical unveiling, and he looks to nothing else but the beauty which has been shown to him, and does not look for that which he has not yet seen, the heart rejoices in what it sees, and this rejoicing is called '*familiarity*' ('*uns*'). And if his attention is turned to the Qualities of might and self-sufficiency, and lack of need for anything but God, then the notion crosses his mind that this state might end and he might be distanced from God, the heart feels the pain of this sensation, and its pain is called '*fear*' ('*khawf*'). These states are provoked by observations, and the observations are provoked by innumerable causes. *Familiarity* (*uns*) means the heart's rejoicing upon beholding beauty; and when it reaches the point where it completely overcomes the lover and he does not pay any heed to what he does not have, and casts off all his worries that he might lose what he has, his bliss and joy become mighty indeed. One of those who experienced such a state was asked, "Do you yearn?" "No," he said, "only absent things are yearned for; and since what was absent is now present, for whom should I yearn?" These are the words of one who is immersed in joy at what he has attained, and who pays no heed to any other delights there may be'.

Finally, he says (p. 441): 'Know that '*contentment*' ('*rida*') is one of the fruits of love, and one of the highest levels reached by those who are drawn near to God and a truth which is veiled from most people. Other things resemble it and are falsely supposed to be it, but they can only be recognised by those unto whom God has imparted right understanding, and given deep comprehension of the religion.' (Abu Hamid Al-Ghazali, *Ihya 'ulum al-din*, vol. 4, pp. 141–441)

And Sheikh Muhyi al-Din Ibn al-ʿArabi says that love is a divine station with four names, as follows: 'Know—may God give you success—that love (*hubb*) is a divine station, for He ascribed it to Himself, and called Himself 'the Loving' (*Al-Wadud*)... This station has four names: there is *hubb* ('*love*'), which means its pure presence in the heart, purified from the turbidity of distractions, so that one seeks nothing and desires nothing from his beloved. The second name is *wudd* ('*affection*' or '*love*'), from which the Divine Name *Al-Wadud* ('the Loving') is derived; it is one of His Qualities, and is affirmed in Him, and this is where the word '*wudd*' comes from, because of how firmly established it is on earth. The third name is ' *ʿishq*' ('*devotion*'), which means *intense love*; the Qur'an speaks of it as 'ardent' love when it says: '*...but those who believe love God more ardently...*' (*Al-Baqarah* 2:165), and speaks of it when it says: '*...Indeed he has smitten (shaghafa) her heart with love...*' (*Yusuf* 12:30), that is, her love for Joseph has become like the skin which covers the heart ('*shaghaf*'), containing it and surrounding it. The Real also described Himself as having ardent love, although one cannot say that God has '*devotion*'. '*Devotion*' (' *ʿishq*') means that the love penetrates the lover so that it becomes intermixed with every part of him and covers him like a robe; it is derived from the word '*ashaqa* ('a wilting tree'). The fourth name is *hawa* ('*desire*' or '*impulse*'), which means total concentration of the will on the beloved, and total attachment to him whenever anything comes to the heart. No

Divine Name is derived from this word. It occurs for specific reasons, such as a look, a story, a kindness, or many others. With reference to sound God-given disclosure, it means God's love for a man when he does many good deeds and follows the Messenger in all that he conveyed; we call this station *'hawa'* ... People differ as to its definition, and I have never seen anyone give it an essential definition; indeed, such a thing is unimaginable. All those who gave it definitions defined only its effects and results. This is especially true when we consider that it is a Quality of God Himself. The best I ever heard said about it is what more than one person told me Abu al-ʿAbbas ibn al-Arif al-Sanhaji said when he was asked about love: "Jealousy (*'ghira'*) is part of love, and jealousy demands secrecy—do not define it." Know that all that can be known is of two kinds: what can be defined, and what cannot be defined. Those who know love and speak of it hold that it cannot be defined; those who experience it know it, though they do not know what it is, and they do not deny that it exists... Love is a special manifestation of the will'. (Ibn Al-Arabi, *Al-Futuhat al-makkiyyah*, vol. 2 pp. 317–322)

Al-Ansari al-Harawi (d. 481 AH) says: 'As for the section of [spiritual] states, it has ten s, which are: *Love ('mahabbah'); jealousy ('ghira'); yearning ('shawq'); worry ('qalaq'); thirst ('atash'); ecstasy ('wajd'); astonishment ('dahsh'); overwhelming ('hayman'); lightning ('barq'), and taste ('dhawq').*' (Harawi, *Manazil al-saʾirin*, p. 88)

Ibn al-ʿArif (d. 536 AH) says: 'As for *ordinary love*, it sprouts from the observation of [God's] blessings and from following the Sunnah, and is cultivated by being shown proper care ... As for *the love of the elite*, it is a penetrating love which cuts through all expressions and goes beyond all allusions; it cannot be exhausted by descriptions, and it can only be known through perplexity and silence.' (Ibn al-ʿArif, *al-Nafaʾis wa mahasin al-majalis*, p. 696)

Ibn Qayyim al-Jawziyya (d. 751 AH) says: '...All these three notions are combined in love, to which they have given almost sixty names, including: *Love, relation, desire, passion, ardour, thrall, tenderness, ecstasy, fondness, infatuation, devotion, lovesickness, fervour, anxiousness, yearning, bewitchment, concern, torment, grief, infatuation, dismay, distress, burning, melancholy, suffering, sadness, sorrow, hurt, scorching, insomnia, sleeplessness, fretting, longing, yielding, sickness, rapture, captivation, madness, derangement, stupor, obsession, intoxication, affection, amity, forbearance, engrossment, zeal, attachment, bewilderment, and worship.* It has been given other names besides these which are not really its names, but rather its causes and effects, so we did not include them here.' (Ibn Qayyim Jawziyya, *Rawdat al-majin wa nuzhat al-mushtaqin*, p. 20)

168 Raghib al-Isfahani, *Al-Mufradat*, p. 112.

169 Ibn Manzhur, *Lisan al-ʿArab*, vol. 1, p. 289.

170 Al-Zabidi, *Taj al-ʿArus*, vol. 1, p. 391.

171 **A Question:** Are '*hubb*' and '*mahabbah*' the same thing?

From what the scholars say above about the root word *hubb*, we can ascertain that the difference between *hubb* and *mahabbah* is that *hubb* is deeper and stronger then *mahabbah*, and on a higher level.

Ibn Manzhur said: '*Hubb* means affection (*widad*) and *mahabbah*, and the same is the case for *hibb*.' (Ibn Manzhur, *Lisan al-ʿArab*, vol. 1, p. 289).

Raghib al-Isfahani says in *Al-Mufradat* that the meaning of *hibb* is: 'One whose love is excessive'.

Al-Razi says in *Mukhtar al-Sihah*: '*Hubb* is also called *mahabbah* and *hibb*; and *hibb* also means the one who loves. And *mahabbah* has been defined as: 'a desire for what you see or deem to be good', which they say is comprised of three things: Love for pleasure, love for benefit, and love for favour. As for *hubb*, as can be seen from their words, it means love for the sake of the object itself. All this shows that the word *hubb* is stronger and higher than the word *mahabbah*.'

Thus certain scholars have said that the meaning of God's words '*...And I cast upon you a love* (*mahabbah*) *from Me...*' (*Ta Ha*, 20:39) is that God cast upon the Prophet Moses ﷺ a special kind of beauty which made all who saw him love him. Fakhr al-Din al-Razi says: '*And I cast upon you a love from Me* that was engendered in My creatures, and this is why Pharaoh's wife loved you and said: "*...A joyous sight for me and you. Do not slay him...*" (*Al-Qasas*, 28:9). It is related that there was a kind of beauty in his face and a sparkle in his eyes which would enthral those who looked upon him ... Qadi said: '...The meaning of this is that just as his physical form was pleasing and attractive, as we said, this was also how he was viewed by Pharaoh and his wife. Thus God facilitated for him an unparalleled upbringing at their hands."' (Fakhr al-Din al-Razi, *Al-Tafsir al-Kabir* (*Mafatih al-ghayb*), vol. 8, p. 48).

On the other hand, Al-Zamakhshari suggests it might mean that God loved Moses ﷺ: '*And I cast upon you a love from Me*—{*from Me*} ... either it refers back to {*cast upon*} in which case it means: 'I loved you and whosoever God loves, hearts love also', or it means: 'love is occurring [i.e. from God] or coming from Me: I have concentrated it in hearts and planted it there, and because of that Pharaoh loved you, as did all who saw you.' (Abu al-Qasim Mahmud ibn ʿUmar al-Zamakhshari al-Khawarizmi, *Al-Kashshaf*, from the commentary on *Ta Ha*, 20:39).

172 *Al-Mufradat*, p. 113.

173 *Lisan al-ʿArab*, vol. 1, p. 289.

174 *Taj al-ʿarus*, vol. 1, p. 392.

175 **A Question**: How can *preference* (*istihbab*) be considered to be a kind of love?

From what the scholars say above about *preference* (*istihbab*), we can ascertain that it means to pursue something to gain its love. Ibn Hazm speaks of this when he says: 'You see that the lover does not take his eyes off his beloved, following wherever his beloved goes, and aping his beloved's every move.' (Ibn Hazm, *Tawq al-Hamamah*, p. 13)

176 *Al-Mufradat*, p. 197.

177 *Lisan al-ʿArab*, vol. 12, p. 230.

178 *Taj al-ʿarus*, vol. 16, p. 274.

179 *Al-Mufradat*, p. 189.

180 *Lisan al-ʿArab*, vol. 9, p. 112.

181 *Taj al-ʿarus*, vol. 12, p. 221

182 **A Question**: How can *pity* be considered a kind of love?

From what the scholars say above about *pity* (*raʾfah*), we can ascertain that it is stronger and more tender than *mercy*. Now *mercy* is a tenderness which engenders kindness and compassion, and tenderness usually goes hand in hand with love, because it is unlikely that one would have *pity* on someone he hates or does not love. Thus *pity* must be a kind of love. Indeed, if a heart has love for someone, it also will have mercy and pity for them.

183 *Al-Mufradat*, p. 532.

184 *Lisan al-ʿArab*, vol. 3, p. 453.

185 *Taj al-ʿarus*, vol. 5, p. 304.

186 *Al-Mufradat*, p. 517.

187 *Al-Mufradat*, p. 516.

188 *Lisan al-ʿArab*, vol. 3, p. 453.

189 *Taj al-ʿarus*, vol. 2, p. 529.

190 Strictly speaking, '*iradah*' means 'desire' and '*mashiʾah*' is 'will', but we are forced here (and elsewhere) to translate it inconsistently as 'will or desire'—and indeed the Qurʾanic translators

tend to use both—because we cannot in English use the phrase 'God desires' for the reason that the word 'desire' in English has come to be too closely associated with physical or sexual desire, and obviously that cannot apply to God. For that reason also, sometimes (as in verse *Al-Ahzab*, 33:33) Qur'anic translators have even translated '*yurid Allah*' as 'God wishes', since 'God wills' sounds awkward in English in the present tense.

191 *Al-Mufradat*, p. 206–207.

192 *Lisan al-ʿArab*, vol. 3, p. 191.

193 *Taj al'arus*, vol. 2, p. 358.

194 **A Question:** How can *will* be considered a kind of love?

From what the scholars say above about *will* or *desire* (*iradah*), we can ascertain that, as Ibn Manzhur says, 'To will something means to love it and be concerned with it.' Thus Ibn Hazm says: 'The lover is keen to hear the name of his beloved, and enjoys speaking about her, and he does this habitually ... Were it possible for the lover to speak only of his beloved at all times, he would do so.' (Ibn Hazm, *Tawq al-hamamah*, pp. 15–17)

In other words, to love someone or something inevitably means 'willing' them, and so there is a kind of will that is also a kind of love.

195 *Al-Mufradat*, p. 263.

196 *Lisan al-ʿArab*, vol. 9, p. 179.

197 *Taj al-ʿarus*, vol. 6, p. 157.

198 *Al-Mufradat*, p. 548.

199 *Lisan al-ʿArab*, vol. 15, p. 373.

200 *Taj al-ʿarus*, vol. 10, p. 415.

201 *Al-Mufradat*, p. 548.

202 *Lisan al-ʿArab*, vol. 15, p. 371.

203 *Taj al-ʿarus*, vol. 10, p. 415.

204 *Al-Mufradat*, p. 369.

205 *Lisan al-ʿArab*, vol. 15, p. 140.

206 *Taj al-ʿarus*, vol. 10, p. 273.

207 **A Question:** How can *straying* be considered a kind of love?

From what the scholars say above about *straying* (*ghawa*), especially as regards God's words 'As for the poets, [only] the stray follow them' (*Al-Shuʿara*', 26:224) it is: *a kind of love, namely that people love the poet when he satirises others in an unlawful manner, or they love him for praising them*, as Zabidi says in *Taj al-ʿarus* (Zabidi, *Taj al-ʿarus*, vol. 10, p. 273). Indeed, Ibn Manzhur describes *straying* (*ghawa*) as 'when the poet composes satire in an unlawful manner, people desire this and love him for it'.

208 *Al-Mufradat*, p. 545.

209 *Lisan al-ʿArab*, vol. 12, p. 620.

210 *Taj al-ʿarus*, vol. 9, p. 109.

211 *Al-Mufradat*, p. 198.

212 *Lisan al-ʿArab*, vol. 1, p. 422.

213 *Taj al-ʿarus*, vol. 1, p. 273.

214 *Al-Mufradat*, p. 398

215 *Lisan al-ʿArab*, vol. 1, p. 667.

216 Qurtubi says, in his Commentary on God's words '*Truly its chastisement is abiding anguish*': 'That is, perpetual and unending; the *gharim* ('creditor' or 'foe') is named after this, because of how zealously he follows his target. The word *mughram* means someone who is obsessed and passionately in love with something.' (*Tafsir al-Qurtubi*, vol. 13, p. 71)

217 *Al-Mufradat*, p. 360.

218 *Lisan al-ʿArab*, vol. 12, p. 436.

219 *Taj al-ʿarus*, vol. 9, p. 3.

220 *Al-Mufradat*, p. 547.

221 *Lisan al-ʿArab*, vol. 12, p. 626.

222 *Taj al-ʿarus*, vol. 9, p. 112.

223 *Al-Mufradat*, p. 153.

224 *Lisan al-ʿArab*, vol. 11, p. 211.

225 *Taj al-ʿarus*, vol. 7, p. 308.

226 *Al-Mufradat*, p. 278.

227 *Lisan al-ʿArab*, vol. 10, p. 193.

228 *Taj al-ʿarus*, vol. 6, p. 404.

229 *Al-Mufradat*, p. 275.

230 *Lisan al-ʿArab*, vol. 1, p. 519.

231 *Taj al-ʿarus*, vol. 1, p. 332.

232 **A Question:** How can *companionship (suhbah)* be considered a kind of love?

From what the scholars say above about *companionship (suhbah)*, we can ascertain that it means *constant nearness*, which may be physical or with care and concern. A common euphemism for 'women' is 'the *companions* of Joseph', i.e. those who love him. Because of this, Ibn Hazm says: 'You may see two lovers reach such a level of animosity that it seems could not be resolved for a balanced and rancour-free person save over a long period of time, and that for a rancorous person could never be resolved; and then behold, the next moment they have once more become the closest of companions and all their disputes and animosities have vanished, and suddenly they are all smiles and jokes; and this may happen many times over and again from one instant to the next. If you see two people act this way, do not doubt that the love they share is deep and profound.' (Ibn Hazm, *Tawq al-hamamah*, p. 15)

233 *Al-Mufradat*, p. 10.

234 *Lisan al-ʿArab*, vol. 4, p. 5.

235 *Taj al-ʿarus*, vol. 3, p. 6.

236 **A Question:** How can *preferring another to oneself* be considered a kind of love?

From what the scholars say above about *preferring another to oneself (ithar)*, we can ascertain that lovers prefer their beloveds to themselves, putting them first and preferring them to all others they hold dear. Ibn Hazm says:

'You see that the lover loves the family, relatives and dear ones of his beloved, preferring them to his own family, himself, and all others he holds dear'. (Ibn Hazm, *Tawq al-hamamah*, p. 12) This shows how love is what drives one to put others first, such as when God says: '*they prefer [others] to themselves, though they be in poverty*' (*Al-Hashr*, 59:9)'.

237 *Al-Mufradat*, p. 297.

238 *Lisan al-ʿArab*, vol. 11, p. 390.

239 *Taj al-ʿarus*, vol. 7, p. 410.

240 **A Question:** How can *going astray* be considered a kind of love?

From what the scholars say above, we can ascertain that *going astray* (*dalal*) linguistically means to be smitten with love and longing for one's beloved; an example of this is found in God's words: '...*Indeed he has smitten her heart with love. Lo! we see her to be plainly astray*' (*Yusuf*, 12:30). This makes it clear that going astray is a kind of love. Ibn Manzhur said: 'Farra' said that to be smitten with love means for love to penetrate one's heart' (Ibn Manzhur, *Lisan al-ʿArab*, vol. 9, p. 178). Thus we can see that going astray is a kind of love which reaches the innermost region of the heart. Ibn Hazm says:

'When things are taken to their ultimate extremes, they begin to resemble their opposites, as a result of God Almighty's power, which baffles the mind. If you take a handful of ice and squeeze it, it burns you like fire ... And we find if two people love one another equally and extremely intensely, they will turn against each other for no reason at all.' (Ibn Hazm, *Tawq al-hamamah*, p. 15)

241 *Al-Mufradat*, p. 203.

242 *Lisan al-ʿArab*, vol. 14, p. 324.

243 *Taj al-ʿarus*, vol. 19, p. 462.

244 *Al-Mufradat*, p. 133.

245 *Lisan al-ʿArab*, vol. 13, p. 129.

246 *Taj al-ʿarus*, vol. 9, p. 184.

247 *Al-Mufradat*, p. 322.

248 *Lisan al-ʿArab*, vol. 1, p. 580.

249 *Taj al-ʿarus*, vol. 1, p. 368.

250 *Al-Mufradat*, p. 478.

251 *Lisan al-ʿArab*, vol. 11, p. 635.

252 *Taj al-ʿarus*, vol. 8, p. 122.

253 **A Question:** How can *inclination* be considered a kind of love?

From what the scholars say above about *inclination* (*mayl*), we can ascertain that it means 'to turn towards something and approach it'; and naturally we find that lovers incline towards their beloved. One of the stages of love through which lovers pass is to incline more and more towards their beloved, until they become as Ibn Hazm describes: 'He addresses all his words to his beloved, even when he purports earnestly to address another; the affectation is clear to anyone who has eyes to see. And he listens attentively to every word his beloved speaks ... And he hurries towards the spot where his beloved is, and endeavours to sit as close to her as possible, and lays aside all occupations which might oblige him to leave her company, and makes light of any matter, however worthy, which might demand that he part company with her. And when he must take his leave, he is very slow in doing so.' (Ibn Hazm, *Tawq al-hamamah*, p. 13)

254 *Al-Mufradat*, p. 270.

255 *Lisan al-ʿArab*, vol. 14, p. 445.

256 *Taj al-ʿarus*, vol. 10, p. 205.

257 **A Question:** How can *lust* be considered a kind of love?

From what the scholars say above about *lust* (*shahwa*), we can ascertain that lusting is having an object of desire and lust; so lust means to desire one's beloved. Ibn Manzhur's words

'To lust for something means to love it and desire it' imply that the beloved is an object of lust; lovers lust after their beloveds in many ways, including how they lust and desire to sit with them, converse with them, and look upon them. Ibn Hazm said of this: 'Love, may God strengthen you, is a fatal disease which contains within it its own cure according to how one handles it; it is a delightful malady and a most desirable sickness. The one who is free of it does not wish to be immune, and the one who is stricken by it does not wish to be cured. It makes you deem glamorous what you once disdained, and makes easy for you what you once found difficult, transforming even established temperaments and inborn dispositions ... I often hear people say that only men are able to subjugate their lusts, and not women. I never cease to wonder at this assertion. My opinion is unwavering: men and women incline towards these things in exactly the same way. (Ibn Hazm, *Tawq al-hamamah*, p. 12)

258 *Al-Mufradat*, p. 274.

259 *Lisan al-ʿArab*, vol. 14, p. 449.

260 *Taj al-ʿarus*, vol. 10, p. 206.

261 **A Question:** How can *tendency* (*saba*) be considered a kind of love?

From what the scholars say above about *tendency* (*saba*), we can ascertain that it means, as Raghib says, 'to incline and yearn as children do'. Ibn Hazm explains this further in his book *Tawq al-hamamah*, describing what love does to people:

'How often has the miser become generous, the scowler become cheery, the coward become brave, the dullard become sharp-witted, the boor become well-mannered, the stinker become elegant, the tramp smartened up, the decrepit recaptured his youth, the penitent become wild, and the upright gone off the rails ... Another of its signs and tokens which all who have eyes may clearly see is an abundance and excess of cheerfulness ... and much clandestine winking, and leaning sideways and supporting oneself against the object of one's love, and endeavouring to touch his or her hand or any part of the body when conversing, and drinking the remainder of what is left in the beloved's cup, seeking out the spot where his or her lips touched it'. (Ibn Hazm, *Tawq al-hamamah*, pp. 14–15.

262 *Al-Mufradat*, p. 65.

263 *Lisan al-ʿarab*, vol. 14, p. 75.

264 *Taj al-ʿarus*, vol. 19, p. 204.

265 **A Question:** How can *seeking* (*ibtigha*) be considered a kind of love?

From what the scholars say above about *seeking* (*ibtigha*), we can ascertain that it means to search for something avidly, and of course lovers avidly seek their beloveds. Ibn Hazm says of this: 'Another sign of love is the care which lovers show for their beloveds, and how they pay attention to everything they do, and seek out news of them so that they do not miss even a single minute, and how they follow their every move.' (Ibn Hazm, *Tawq al-hamamah*, p. 20)

266 *Al-Mufradat*, p. 383.

267 *Lisan al-ʿArab*, vol. 11, p. 524.

268 *Taj al-ʿarus*, vol. 8, p. 61.

269 *Al-Mufradat*, p. 220.

270 *Lisan al-ʿArab*, vol. 14, p. 359.

271 *Taj al-ʿarus*, vol. 19, p. 497.

272 **A Question:** How can *extra-marital sex* (*zina*) be considered a kind of love?

From what scholars cited above say about *extra-marital sex* (*zina*), we can ascertain that it means for love between the male and female sexes to lead them into a position which contradicts and opposes sacred law and religion; but were it not for love and desire, in addition to unbridled lust, *extra-marital sex* would never occur. Ibn Hazm says about this kind of relationship: 'Many people obey their own egos and disobey their intelligence, and follow their passions and defy their religions, disdaining the decency, righteousness, and self-control which God has instilled in all healthy minds. They disobey God, their Lord, and collude with Satan in his love for ruinous lust, thus sinning through their love ... In their inclination to these things, men and women are alike. No [such] man to whom a beautiful woman offers herself without there being any impediment to him can long resist falling into Satan's net and being seduced by sin, excited by desire and led astray by concupiscence. Similarly there is no [such] woman who, if invited by a man in the same way, will not eventually surrender to him. This is the absolute law and inescapable decree of destiny'. (Ibn Hazm, *Tawq al-hamamah*, p. 120)

273 *Al-Mufradat*, p. 132.

274 *Lisan al-ʿArab*, vol. 14, p. 188.

275 *Taj al-ʿarus*, vol. 19, p. 330.

276 *Al-Mufradat*, p. 267.

277 *Lisan al-ʿArab*, vol. 10, p. 180.

278 *Taj al-ʿarus*, vol. 13, p. 244.

279 *Al-Mufradat*, p. 547.

280 *Lisan al-ʿArab*, vol. 15, p. 409.

281 *Taj al-ʿarus*, vol. 20, p. 310.

282 *Al-Mufradat*, p. 285.

283 *Lisan al-ʿArab*, vol. 14, p. 461.

284 *Taj al-ʿarus*, vol. 10, p. 210.

285 *Al-Mufradat*, p. 533.

286 *Lisan al-ʿArab*, vol. 2, p. 399.

287 *Taj al-ʿarus*, vol. 6, p.262.

288 *Al-Mufradat*, p. 516.

289 *Lisan al-ʿArab*, vol. 9, p.9.

290 *Taj al-ʿarus*, vol. 8, p.180.

CHAPTER 22: THE STAGES OF LOVE

291 A number of Classical Muslim scholars describe the stages of love (as they see them), but none of them (to our knowledge) base these stages exclusively on the words, phrases and verses of the Holy Qur'an. Among the Muslim scholars who wrote on this subject are:

Al-Ansari al-Harawi (d. 481 AH), who says: 'Love is the defining characteristic of the folk (of God), the name of the path they follow, and the bond which holds them together. It has three levels: The *first level* is the love which silences all misgivings, sweetens all toil and consoles all misfortunes. It is a love which takes root with the beholding of grace, strengthens with following of the *Sunnah*, and grows with continuous experience. The *second level* is a love which provokes one to prefer the Real above all else, inspires the tongue to invoke Him, and instils in the heart the longing to behold Him. This love emerges through studying the Divine Qualities, beholding signs, and passing through spiritual stations. The *third level* is enthralling love which defies all expression, outdoes all allusion, and exhausts all description. This love is the very axis of the affair; all that lies beneath are but desires of which tongues chatter, human nature makes claims, and human minds affirm. (Al-Harawi, *Manazil al-salikin*, pp. 89–90)

Ibn Jawzi (d. 597 AH) says: The first stage [of love] is *preference* (*istihsan*) of a person, and this leads to *a desire to be near* (*iradat al-qurb*) him or her; then comes *affection* (*mawaddah*), which means a desire to possess. Then this affection gets stronger and becomes *love* (*mahabbah*), and then *strong need* (*khula*), and then *desire* (*hawa*), such that its object is desired and loved without there being any possession; then it becomes *passionate love* (*'ishq*), and then *thrall* (*tatayyum*), wherein the lover becomes the possession of the beloved, and the lover's heart is emptied of all else besides the beloved; we speak of the 'thrall of God'. Then the resolve becomes *infatuation* (*walaha*), which means to be so madly in love as to go beyond the bounds of reason and sense. (Ibn Jawzi, *Dhamm al-hawa*, pp. 230–231)

Ibn Taymiyyah (d. 728 AH) says: The love of the human heart has several stages. The first is *attachment*, wherein the heart is attached to the beloved; then comes *longing* (*'ilaqah*), wherein the heart longs for the beloved; then comes *ardour* (*sababah*), which means firm love; then comes *devotion* (*gharam*); then comes passionate love (*'ishq*) and then the final stage is *thrall* (*tatayum*), which means utter adoration and worship of the beloved; 'God's thrall' means God's slave and worshipper. The lover constantly thinks of the beloved, and worships and adores him or her. Another term for it is *fervour* (*inabah*), and there are many others besides, as was mentioned before. (Ibn Taymiyyah, *Al-Tuhfah al-'iraqiyyah*, p. 88)

292 See also: *Al-An'am*, 6:43, 108, 122, 137; *Al-Anfal*, 8:48; *Al-Nahl*, 16:63; *Al-Naml*, 28:4, 24; *Al-'Ankabut*, 29:38; *Fussilat*, 41:25; *Al-Tawbah*, 9:37; *Yunus*, 10:12, 24; *Al-Ra'd*, 13:33; *Fatir*, 35:8; *Ghafir*, 40:37; *Muhammad*, 47:14.

293 **A Question:** How can 'seduction' be considered to be a stage of love?

Ibn Manzhur says: 'To seduce, whether it is done by a man or a woman, means to attempt to make someone engage in sexual intercourse with oneself, such as is found in God's words: '... *The Chief of the Court's wife has been seducing her boy...*'; the verb here is ascribed to the woman. To seduce (*rawada*) can also mean 'to desire'.' (Ibn Manzhur, *Lisan al-'Arab*, vol. 3, p. 187)

Fayruzabadi says: 'Petition (*muraja'ah*) is akin to seduction'; and elsewhere he said: '*rawada* also means to deceive'; and again elsewhere he said: 'to employ deceitful artifice (*murawaghah*) is akin to seduction'. Defining the word *farghal*, he said: 'it means to woo and seduce'. He also said: 'seduction means to petition and attempt to convince'. (Fayruzabadi, *Al-Qamus al-muhit*)

Al-Razi says: 'To seduce ... means to desire'. (Al-Razi, *Mukhtar al-Sihah*, p. 110)

Thus we see that 'seduction' ('*murawadah*') has many meanings, one being invitation to sexual intercourse, and another being a petition and attempt to make one's beloved return one's love. Another of its meanings is to woo, and wooing is an expression of love. Seduction, in this case, means repeated attempts to win the heart of one's beloved; it is thus one of the stages of love and one of the means of reaching the beloved.

Thus seduction is part of love just as jealousy is part of love, and it indicates the presence of love. Jealousy occurs because of the lover's love for the beloved. Seduction, however, has a sexual side to it. If it takes place between a married couple, it is permitted or licit. If it takes place between an unmarried couple it is blameworthy and forbidden.

One of the lexical meanings of '*murawadah*' is 'petition', meaning a desire to win the love and good pleasure of one's beloved. In human love of God, the lover *petitions* his or her Lord by fulfilling all He commands and by repeatedly offering supererogatory acts of worship, until he or she reaches the point where God loves him or her. Concerning this, the *Hadith Qudsi* says:

'Whosoever shows enmity to a friend of Mine, I declare war upon him. My servant does not draw nigh unto Me with anything more beloved to Me than what I have made obligatory upon him; and My servant continues to draw nearer unto Me with voluntary

Notes

deeds until I love him—and when I love him, I am his Hearing wherewith he hears, his Sight wherewith he sees, his Hand wherewith he grasps, and his Foot wherewith he walks. If he asks Me, I will surely give unto him; if he seeks refuge in Me, I will surely give him refuge. I hesitate in nought of all that I do as I hesitate in taking the believer's soul: he hates to die, and I hate to hurt him.' (Bukhari, *Sahih*, Hadith no. 6502, 'Kitab al-riqaq, bab al-tawadu')

CHAPTER 23: FALLING IN LOVE

294 Jalal al-Din Mahalli and Jalal al-Din Suyuti, *Tafsir al-Jalalayn*, p. 709.

295 Al-Ghazali discusses—and this is perhaps the best text ever written on this subject—the different meaning of the 'soul', 'heart', 'intelligence' and 'spirit' in his book *Kitab sharh 'aja'ib al-qalb* ('An Explanation of the Wonders of the Heart'), Part 21 of his *opus magnus*, *Ihya 'ulum al-din*. We will discuss the subject here, however, based solely upon the Holy Qur'an.

296 Al-Ghazali says—in his philosophical work *Maqasid al-falsafah*, in the third section 'On Matters of Nature'—that the 'inner faculties' of human beings are: common sense, the power of recollection, the power of imagination, the power of supposition, and the power of memory (p. 356). He also mentions two other powers of the soul, namely: the powers of knowledge and of action (p. 359). We will discuss the subject here, however, based solely upon the Holy Qur'an.

297 Hakim Al-Tirmidhi explains in detail—and this is perhaps the best text ever written on this subject—the defintions and natures of the breast, heart, inner heart and heart's core in his book *Bayan al-farq bayn al-sadr wal-qalb wal-fu'ad wal-lubb*. We will discuss the subject here, however, based solely upon the Holy Qur'an.

298 The stages of love are sometimes painful and sometimes pleasurable; sometimes successive and sometimes simultaneous, according to (as we will see later, God willing, in Chapter 30: The Nature of Love) the lover's states of 'contraction' and 'expansion' and the influence of these on the lover's various faculties. God says: *Who is he that will lend God a loan that is good, and He will multiply it for him manifold? God contracts and expands; and to Him you shall be returned.* (Al-Baqarah, 2:245)

However, after 'contraction', there will always be—for the believer at least, God willing—'expansion'. God says:

> *...And whoever fears God, He will make matters ease for him.* (Al-Talaq, 65:4) ❋ *...God will assuredly bring about ease after hardship.* (Al-Talaq, 65:7) ❋ *For truly with hardship comes ease. / Truly with hardship comes ease. / So when you are finished, toil and seek your Lord.* (Al-Sharh, 94:5–7)

299 This is also the reason why modern thought cannot understand love: modern science reduces human beings to biology, physics and chemistry such that human love becomes, in its view, only a chemically or electrically induced state of heightened and / or sublimated lust. Modern science does not identify human beings' faculties as such, and denies the very existence of the higher human 'constituent parts' such as the soul, the (spiritual) heart and the spirit. Therefore it cannot see the process whereby the human faculties and 'constituent parts' systematically incline towards a beloved. Hence it cannot correctly identify or understand love or falling in love. We do not, of course, deny the chemical, biological and physically processes manifest in the body when a person is falling love; we only maintain that these are—at least in the case of those human beings whose souls dominate their bodies to whatever extent—the *effects* of love, and not their cause.

CHAPTER 24: THE GROWTH OF LOVE

300 We discussed this verse in Chapter 21: The Different Kinds of Love and saw that one of the meanings of this verse is that God cast His love upon Moses ※.

301 See also: *Al-Baqarah*, 2:200; *Al-A'raf*, 7:55–56, 180, 205; *Al-Anfal*, 8:45; *Al-Nur*, 24:37; *Al-Jumu'ah*, 62:9–10; *Al-A'la*, 87:14–15.

302 See also: *Al-Baqarah*, 2:114; *Al-Nisa'*, 4:142; *Al-A'raf*, 7:179–180; *Al-Kahf*, 18:28, 100–101; *Ta Ha*, 20:99–101, 124–127; *Al-Furqan*, 25:18; *Al-Zumar*, 39:22–23; *Al-Najm*, 29:30; *Al-Mujadilah*, 58:19; *Al-Jinn*, 72:17; *Al-Ma'un*, 107:4–6.

CHAPTER 25: THE TWO CIRCLES OF LOVE

303 A similar situation lies in God's address to His Messenger: *'And did He not find you astray, and guide you?'* (*Al-Duha*, 93:7): we know that the Messenger of God ※ was not 'astray' as such in the sense that he was not misguided and errant, nor did he ever indulge in evil deeds. All the books of prophetic biography (*Sirah*) show that he was known in the days of pagan ignorance as 'the Honest and Trusted One' ('al-Ameen') because of his noble qualities and virtuous character. Moreover, angels washed his breast and heart when he was a child—this is how Muslim scholars interpret God's words: *'Did We not expand your breast for you'* (*Al-Sharh*, 94:1). It is also related in the authentic *Hadith* collections that the Messenger of God ※ (before he became a Messenger) used to spend many nights in ascetic vigil in the cave of Hira, in spiritual meditation and contemplation. He was thus absolutely distant from all the sins and frivolities which the pagans of his time indulged in, and God Himself attests to all this at the very beginning of the Prophet's mission by saying: *'And assuredly you possess a magnificent nature'* (*Al-Qalam*, 68:4), and then by saying about him that: *'your companion has neither gone astray, nor has he erred'* (*Al-Najm*, 53:2). This proves that the Messenger of God ※ was not 'astray' in the sense of being misguided as such, but rather that the meaning of 'astray' here is that the Prophet ※ had not yet attained the rank of Prophet and the rank of the Seal of the Messengers which he would later attain. Thus relative to the great station which he eventually would attain, his earlier state was akin to the difference between being astray and being guided, or between shadows and light.

304 God says: *If you avoid the grave sins that are forbidden you, We will absolve you of your evil deeds and admit you by an honourable gate.* (*Al-Nisa'*, 4:31) ● *And those who avoid grave sins and indecencies and [who], when they are angry, forgive.* (*Al-Shura*, 42:37)

CHAPTER 26: THE TRIANGLE OF LOVE

305 See also: *Al-An'am*, 6:43, 108, 122, 137; *Al-Anfal*, 8:48; *Al-Nahl*, 16:63; *Al-Naml*, 28:4, 24; *Al-'Ankabut*, 29:38; *Fussilat*, 41:25; *Al-Tawbah*, 9:37; *Yunus*, 10:12, 24; *Al-Ra'd*, 13:33; *Fatir*, 35:8; *Ghafir*, 40:37; *Muhammad*, 47:14.

306 Ibn Kathir explained this verse in the following way: 'God tells us here that He took the children of Adam from his loins, and they bore witness before themselves that God is their Lord and their Sovereign, and that there is no god besides Him'. (Ibn Kathir, *Tafsir al-Qur'an al-'azim*, p. 797)

This Qur'anic verse is also explained by the *Hadith* reported by Ibn 'Abbas y wherein the Messenger of God ※ says:

> 'God took a firm pledge from the seed of Adam at Nu'man [meaning Mt. 'Arafah], removing from his loins every seed He had planted therein, and scattering them before Him like powder. He then spoke to them directly, saying: *'Am I not your Lord?'* They

Notes

said, 'Yea, indeed we testify', lest they should say on the Day of Resurrection, 'Truly, of this we were unaware'. (Ahmad, *Musnad*, vol. 1, p. 272.)

307 A *Hadith* in both *Sahih* collections of Bukhari and Muslim states that three people were exceptions to this rule, speaking when they were still infants. They were: Jesus Christ ﷺ; a child who spoke to proclaim the innocence of Jarij the Monk, and an Israelite baby. Abu Hurayrah ؓ reports that the Messenger of God ﷺ said:

> 'None spoke in the cradle save three: Jesus; and there was a man of the Israelites named Jarij ... And a woman of the Israelites was nursing her baby ... And he said: "O God, make me like her!" ...' (Bukhari, *Sahih*, Hadith no. 3436, *Kitab ahadith al-anbiya', bab qawl Allah wadhkur fi kitab Maryam*; Muslim, *Sahih*, Hadith no. 2550, *Kitab al-birr was-silah, bab taqdim birr al-walidayn 'ala al-tatawwu' bis-salat wa ghayriha*)

308 See also: *Aal 'Imran*, 3:46; *Maryam*, 19:29.

309 Indications of God are Found in His Actions in Creation:

A very important issue raised here is that when Pharaoh asks Moses ﷺ 'What is the Lord of the worlds?', Moses ﷺ does not answer by giving any description of God's Essence (if that were possible) but rather alludes to God's acts that can be seen in creation and nature. This means that creation and nature offer the best guide to knowledge of God. God says:

> Pharaoh said, 'And what is the Lord of the Worlds?' He said, 'The Lord of the heavens and the earth and all that is between them should you have conviction'. He said to those who were around him, 'Did you not hear?!' He said, 'Your Lord and the Lord of your forefathers'. He said, 'Verily this messenger of yours sent to you is a madman!' He said, 'The Lord of the east and the west and all that is between them—should you comprehend'. He said, 'If you choose any god other than me, I will surely make you a prisoner!' (*Al-Shu'ara'*, 26:23–29)

Thus contemplation of creation and nature directs towards God and also leads to guidance. This is confirmed in another Qur'anic verse wherein Moses ﷺ directs Pharaoh even more explicitly towards the existence of God and towards guidance by referring to nature. God says: *He said, 'So who is your Lord, O Moses?' He said, 'Our Lord is He Who gave to every thing its [particular] nature and then guided [them]'*. (*Ta Ha*, 20:49–50)

Similarly, the Messenger of God ﷺ was commanded, in many verses, to point others towards God, and to derive evidence for His existence based on both rational and intuitive examinations of creation and nature. These verses include:

> Say: 'Behold what is in the heavens and in the earth!' But signs and warners do not avail a folk who will not believe. (*Yunus*, 10:101) ❀ Say: 'Shall I take as a protector other than God, the Originator of the heavens and the earth, He Who feeds and is not fed?' Say: 'I have been commanded to be the first to submit, and: "Do not be among those who associate others"'. (*Al-An'am*, 6:14) ❀ Say: 'Who is the Lord of the heavens and the earth?' Say: 'God'. Say: 'Then have you taken beside Him protectors, who have no power to benefit or harm themselves?' Say: 'Are the blind one and the seer equal? Or are darkness and the light equal? Or have they set up for God associates who have created the like of His creation, so that creation seems alike to them?' Say: 'God is the Creator of all things; and He is the One, the Subjugator'. (*Al-Ra'd*, 13:16) ❀ Say: 'Who is the Lord of the seven heavens and the Lord of the Great Throne?' (*Al-Mu'minun*, 23:86) ❀ *Or He Who created the heavens and the earth, and sends down for you water from the heaven, whereby We cause to grow splendid gardens whose trees you could never cause to grow? Is there a god with God? Nay, but they are a people who ascribe equals [to Him]. / Or He Who made the earth an abode [of stability] and made rivers [to flow] throughout it and set firm mountains for it, and set an isthmus between the two seas. Is there a god with God? Nay, but most of them have no knowledge. /*

Or He Who answers the desperate one when he calls to Him and Who removes [his] distress and makes you successors in the earth. Is there a god with God? Little do you remember. / Or He Who guides you in the darkness of the land and the sea and Who sends forth the winds as harbingers of His mercy. Is there a god with God? Exalted be God [high] above what they associate [with Him]. / Or He Who originates creation then brings it back again, and Who provides for you from the heaven and [from] the earth. Is there a god with God? Say: 'Produce your proof if you are truthful'. (Al-Naml, 27:60–64) ❈ *Glory be to the Lord of the heavens and the earth, the Lord of the Throne above what they allege! (Al-Zukhruf, 43:82)*

(See also: *Al-Baqarah*, 2:164–165; *Aal ʿImran*, 3:189–191, and *Al-Rahman*, 55:1–13.)

Likewise, the Prophet Abraham ﷺ pointed towards the existence of God through creation and nature:

'Verily I have turned my face to Him Who originated the heavens and the earth; a hanif, and I am not of those that associate others'. / But his people disputed with him. He said, 'Do you dispute with me concerning God when He has guided me? I have no fear of what you associate with Him, unless my Lord wills something. My Lord encompasses all things through His knowledge; will you not remember?' (Al-Anʿam, 6:79–80) ❈ *He said, 'Nay, but your Lord is the Lord of the heavens and the earth, [the One] Who originated them, and to that I am a witness. (Al-Anbiya', 21:56)*

The same is true of other prophets such as Noah ﷺ, Hud ﷺ and Salih ﷺ: they were all commanded to point towards the existence of God, and knowledge of Him, through creation and nature. God says:

Their messengers said, 'Can there be doubt concerning God, the Originator of the heavens and the earth? He calls you so that He might forgive you your sins and defer you to an appointed term'. They said, 'You are but mortals like us, desiring to bar us from that which our fathers used to worship. So bring us a clear warrant'. (Ibrahim, 14:10)

The 'People of the Cave', too, came to know God through nature: *And We strengthened their hearts when they stood up and said, 'Our Lord is the Lord of the heavens and the earth. We will not call on any god besides Him, for then we shall certainly have uttered an outrage. (Al-Kahf, 18:10)*

Moreover, God Himself says to humanity, directly:

So behold the effects of God's mercy, how He revives the earth after it has died. Surely He is the Reviver of the dead, and He has power over all things. (Al-Rum, 30:50) ❈ *So let man consider his [source of] food / that We pour down water plenteously; / then We split the earth into fissures, / and cause the grains to grow therein, / and vines and herbs, / and olives and date-palms, / and gardens of dense foliage, / and fruits and pastures, / as sustenance for you and your flocks. (ʿAbasa, 80:24–32)* ❈ *Will they not consider the camels, how they are created? / And the heaven, how it was raised? / And the mountains, how they were set? / And the earth, how it was laid out flat?, / So remind. For you are only an admonisher; (Al-Ghashiyah, 88:17–21)*

Indeed, it is the manifest world that indicates the unmanifest (extended shade being a symbol of the unmanifest since it is promised in Paradise, as in *Al-Waqiʿah*, 56:30: *[A]nd extended shade*): *Have you not seen your Lord, how He extends the [twilight] shadow? For had He willed, He would have made it still. Then We made the sun an indicator of it. / Then We retract it to Us by gentle retraction. (Al-Furqan, 25:45–6)*

Finally, we should also not neglect to mention that God alludes to the magnificence of creation and nature when He swears oaths on them, such as in His words:

By the Mount, (Al-Tur, 52–1) ❈ *By the sun and her morning light, / and [by] the moon when it follows her, / and [by] the day when it reveals her, / and [by] the night when it* enshrouds her. / By the heaven and the One Who built it, / and [by] the earth and the One Who spread it, / and [by] the soul and the One Who proportioned it. (Al-Shams, 97:1-7) ❊ By the dawn, / and [by] the ten nights, / and [by] the even and the odd, / and [by] the night in motion: / Is there in that an oath for one of sense? (Al-Fajr, 89:1-5) ❊ By Time! (Al-ʿAsr, 103:1) ❊ By the chargers panting. (Al-ʿAdiyat, 100:1) ❊ By the fig and the olive, and [by] the Mount Sinai. (Al-Tin, 95:1-2) ❊ By the night as it enshrouds, / and [by] the day as it unveils. (Al-Layl, 92:1-2) ❊ By the forenoon, / and [by] the night when it is still. (Al-Duha, 93:1-2) ❊ Nay, I swear by the setting-places of the stars! / And indeed it is a tremendous oath, if you only knew. (Al-Waqiʿah, 56:75-76)

And God even swears an oath by Himself as Lord of creation and nature: *So by the Lord of the heaven and the earth, it is as assuredly true as [the fact] that you have [power of] speech.* (Al-Dhariyat, 51:23)

310 God says: *Say: 'O people, if you are in doubt of my religion, then [know that] I do not worship those whom you worship besides God; but I worship God Who will take you to Him, and I have been commanded to be of the believers.'* (Yunus, 10:104)

311 Ibn Hajar Al-ʿAsqalani says, in *Fath al-Bari*, that some differ with Ibn Kathir over his assertion that many scholars do not consider Khadir a prophet, including Qurtubi and Ibn ʿAtiyyah. (Ibn Hajar, *Fath al-Bari*, vol. 6, p. 434)

312 Abu al-Fida' Isma'il ibn ʿUmar ibn Kathir Qurashi Dimashqi, *Tafsir al-Qur'an al-ʿazim*, p. 1169.

313 God says: *And they will question you concerning the Spirit. Say: 'The Spirit is of the command of my Lord. And you have not been given knowledge except a little'.* (Al-Isra', 17:85)

CHAPTER 27: THE HIERARCHIES OF BEAUTY AND OF LOVE

314 It is very telling to note that Surat Yusuf is the only Surah in the Holy Qur'an which contains a complete tale from beginning to end in one Surah; which contains a tale which is never taken up again in other Surahs; and which does not contain elements of the tales of other prophets save that of its main subject matter (the story of Joseph). And we have not even begun to discuss, as some esoteric Qur'anic Commentaries do, its microcosmic symbolism as being the story of the intellect (ʿaql—Joseph himself), the son of the spirit and heart (Jacob and his wife); being trapped in a well by the physical senses (his ten evil brothers); tempted by the lower soul (Potiphar's wife); put in prison, and freed by the higher soul (the King)—in other words, being the story of the very human condition itself in the earthly state, and therefore, by definition, the truest and most beautiful story possible.

315 Bukhari, *Sahih*, Hadith no. 5090, *Kitab al-nikah, bab al-akfa' fid-din*; Muslim, *Sahih*, Hadith no. 1466, *Kitab al-rida', bab istahbab nikah dhat al-din*.

CHAPTER 28: THE OPPOSITES OF BEAUTY AND OF LOVE

316 Raghib defines 'vileness' ('*qubh*') as follows: 'It is what the eye disdains (in terms of visible things) and what the soul disdains (in terms of actions and states). A vile person or thing is said to be *qabih*. The Almighty's words '*they will be among the reviled*' means they will be among those who are in an unpleasant state, alluding to the way God describes the disbelievers as unclean, filthy, and so on, and how their faces will be blackened and their eyes dimmed on the Day of Resurrection, and how they will be dragged in shackles and chains, and so on. The verb *qabaha*, when ascribed to God with a person as its object, means that He draws them away from goodness. The word *qabih* also means the extremity of the bone of the upper half of the arm, next to the elbow.' (Raghib Isfahani, *al-Mufradat fi gharib al-Qur'an*, p. 391).

Al-Razi defines vileness as follows: 'Beauty (*jamal*) means goodness (*husn*) ... and vileness is the opposite of beauty, whether in appearance or action.' (Al-Razi, *Mukhtar al-Sihah*, p. 59)

Ibn Manzhur defines vileness as follows: 'Vileness is the opposite of beauty, whether in appearance or action ... Azhari said it is the opposite of beauty in a universal sense.' (Ibn Manzhur, *Lisan al-ᶜArab*, vol. 2, p. 552).

In summary, vileness is what makes one feel revulsion, for it is the opposite of beauty and goodness, in appearances and in actions.

CHAPTER 29: THE END OF LOVE

317 Muslim, *Sahih*, *Hadith* no. 144, *Kitab al-iman, bab bayan ann al-islam badaa ghariba*.

318 Tirmidhi, *Sunan*, *Hadith* no. 3334, *Kitab al-tafsir, bab surat al-mutaffifin*. Tirmidhi declared it to be a sound and authentic *Hadith*.

319 Al-Qurtubi, *Tafsir al-Qurtubi*, vol. 7, p. 321.

320 Needless to say, love for family and relatives—and *a fortiori* love for believers; love for people of the Scripture, and love for all humanity—comes to end in the next life if it is not based on love for God. God says:

And when the Trumpet is blown, there will be no more ties [of kinship] between them on that day, nor will they question one another. (Al-Muminun, 23:101) ❋ *Your relatives and your children will not avail you. On the Day of Resurrection you will be separated. And God is Seer of what you do. (Al-Mumtahanah, 60:3)* ❋ *And no friend will inquire about his friend. / They will [however] be made to see them. The guilty one will desire to ransom himself from the chastisement of that day at the price of his children, / and his companion, and his brother, / and his kin that had sheltered him, / and all who are on earth, if it might then deliver him. (Al-Maᶜarij, 70:10–14)* ❋ *The day when a man will flee from his [own] brother, / and his mother and his father, / and his wife and his sons, / every person that day will have a matter to preoccupy him. (ᶜAbasa, 80:34–37)*

321 Abu Dawud, *Sunan*, *Hadith* no. 2178, *Kitab al-talaq, ma fi karahiyat al-talaq*; Ibn Majah, *Sunan*, *Hadith* no. 2018, *Kitab al-talaq, bab talaq al-sunnah*.

CHAPTER 32: LOVE AND BEAUTY IN PARADISE

322 Obviously, Paradise is the abode of perfect contentment (*rida*), joy (*farah*), happiness (*saadah*) and peace (*salam*) in Paradise. God says about contentment (*rida*) in Paradise:

So he will enjoy a pleasant living (radiah), (Al-Haqqah, 69:21) ❋ *Other faces on that day will be joyful (na'imah), / pleased by their efforts (radiah); (Al-Ghashiyah, 88:8–9)* ❋ *'O soul at peace! / Return to your Lord, pleased, pleasing (radiyatan mardiyah). / Then enter among My servants! / And enter My Paradise!' (Al-Fajr, 89:27–30)* ❋ *[H]e will enjoy a pleasant life (radiah), (Al-Qar'iah, 101:7)*

Equally, God says about joy (*farah*) in Paradise: *Rejoicing (farahin) in what God has given them of His bounty, and rejoicing, for the sake of those who have not joined them but are left behind, that no fear shall befall them, neither shall they grieve. (Aal ᶜImran, 3:170)*

Similarly, God says about happiness (*saadah*) in Paradise:

The day it comes, no soul shall speak except by His permission. Some of them will be wretched, and [some] happy (sa'id). / As for those who are damned, they will be in the Fire; their lot therein will be wailing and sighing; / abiding therein for as long as the heavens and the earth endure, except what your Lord may will. Truly your Lord is Doer of what He desires. / And as for those who are happy (su'idu) they shall be in Paradise, abiding therein for as long as the heavens and the earth endure except what your Lord may will, an endless bounty. (Hud, 11:105–8)

Finally, God says about peace (salam) in Paradise:

'Peace (salam)!'—the word from a Lord [Who is] Merciful. (Yasin, 36:58) ❋ They will not hear therein any vain talk or any sinful words, / but only the saying, 'Peace (salam) !' 'Peace (salam)!' (Al-Waqi'ah, 56:25–26) ❋ Truly the God-fearing shall be amidst gardens and springs'. / 'Enter them in peace (salam), secure!' (Al-Hijr, 15:45–46) ❋ Theirs will be the abode of peace (dar al-salam) with their Lord, and He will be their Friend because of what they used to do. (Al-An'am, 6:127) (See also:10:10; 14:23; 16:32; 19:62; 25:75; 33:43; 50:34; 56:91)

Now we have seen previously (in Chapters 21: The Different Kinds of Love and 22: The Stages of Love) that rida (contentment) is both a kind of love and a stage of love, and that farah (joy) and salam (peace) are stages of love. This means that there must be love of sorts in Paradise, since without love there is no happiness, and thus it would not be Paradise

323 Furthermore, every rancour or imperfection in love will be removed in Paradise, so that Paradisiacal love will become pure and perfect. God says:

We shall strip away all rancour that is in their breasts; and beneath them flow rivers; and they will say, 'Praise be to God, Who guided us to this; for we would surely never have been guided if God had not guided us. Verily the messengers of our Lord did bring the truth.' And it is cried to them: 'This is your Paradise; you have inherited it for what you used to do'. (Al-A'raf, 7:43) ❋ 'Enter them in peace, secure!' / And We remove whatever rancour may be in their breasts. As brethren, [they shall recline] upon couches, facing one another. / No toil will touch them, nor will they be expelled from thence. (Al-Hijr, 15:46–48)

CHAPTER 33: BEAUTY AND ITS COMPONENTS

324 Al-Mufradat, p. 97.

325 Taj al-'arus, vol. 7, p. 263.

326 Al-Mufradat, p. 118.

327 Taj al-'arus, vol.7, p. 263.

328 Yusuf, 12:83.

329 Al-Nahl, 16:6.

330 See: Al-A'raf, 7:18; Al-Isra', 17:100; Ta Ha, 20:8; Al-Hashr, 59:24.

331 Jalal al-Din Mahalli and Jalal al-Din Suyuti, Tafsir al-Jalalayn, p. 709.

332 Bayhaqi, Hadith no. 2/490, Kitab shu'ab al-iman, bab ta'zhim al-Qur'an.

333 Al-Fakhr al-Razi, Sharh Asma' Allah al-husna, p. 30.

CHAPTER 34: TASTE

334 Muslim, Sahih, Hadith no. 2638, Kitab al-birr wal-silah wal-abad, bab al-arwah junud mujannadah.

335 God says: And they shall be presented before your Lord in ranks: 'Verily you have come to Us just as We created you the first time; rather you claimed that We would not appoint for you a tryst'. (Al-Kahf, 18:48)

Al-Razi says in his *Tafsir*: 'God then says: '*Verily you have come to Us just as We created you the first time*'; this does not mean that they are alike in every way, because they were created babies with no intelligence or responsibility. Rather, the meaning is that God will say to the idolaters who deny the Resurrection and are proud of the material and military advantages they enjoy in this world, over the believers: '*Verily you have come to Us just as We created you the first time*', naked and barefoot with neither wealth nor helpers. It is akin to the Almighty's words: '*And now you have come to Us singly, as We created you the first time, and you have left what We conferred on you behind your backs...*' (Al-An'am, 6:94), and His words: '*Have you seen him who disbelieves in Our signs and says, 'I shall assuredly be given wealth and children?*" up until: '*and he shall come to Us, alone*'. (Maryam, 19:77–80)' (Al-Razi, *Al-Tafsir al-kabir: Mafatih al-ghayb*, vol. 7, p. 470).

The reason al-Razi explains God's words '*the first time*' as meaning 'naked and barefoot' rather than '*in ranks*' is that he sees there is a contradiction between the notion of God's having created human beings in ranks, and what the other verse says about God's having created them '*singly*'. However, we say that there is no contradiction here, for perhaps God created us in ranks so vastly wide that each person seems to come alone. In any case, the realities and affairs of the Hereafter are not like those of this world, as the authentic *Hadith* says: '[Such things] as have never occurred to any human heart.' (Bukhari, *Sahih*, Hadith no. 3244, *Kitab bad' al-kahlq, bab ma ja' fi sifat al-jannah*).

The point of this discussion is to say that God Himself alludes to the very same thing as the *Hadith*: 'Spirits are conscripted soldiers'. In other words, the spirits of people were created in ranks, and each spirit has its own special nature; and God knows best.

CHAPTER 35: THE NATURE OF BEAUTY

336 The Lady Aishah (may God be pleased with her) said:

> 'When the Messenger of God ﷺ became ill and lost consciousness, I took hold of his hand to do what used to be done, and he pulled his hand from mine and said: 'O God, forgive me and enter me into the supreme communion!' So I looked upon him, and found that it was over.' (Muslim, *Sahih*, Hadith no. 2191, *Kitab al-salam, bab istahbab riqyat al-marid*.)

337 The Lady Aishah, (may God be pleased with her) said:

> 'Fatimah (may God be pleased with her) came along, walking just as the Prophet ﷺ walked. The Prophet ﷺ said to her: 'I deem naught save that my time has come, and that you shall be the first of my household to join me.' She wept, and he said: 'Are you not content to be the Lady of the women of Paradise [or: 'the women of the believers']?' Then she smiled.' (Bukari, *Sahih*, Hadith no. 3624, *Kitab al-manaqib, bab 'alamat al-nuwubbah fil-islam*; Muslim, *Sahih*, Hadith no. 2450, *Kitab fada'il al-Sahabah, bab fada'il Fatima bint al-Nabi 'alayhima al-salat wal-salam*.)

And to give another example, Anas ibn Malik ؓ is reported to have said that when his uncle Haram ibn Milhan was stabbed at the battle of Bi'r Ma'unah, he sprinkled blood upon his face and head and said, 'I have triumphed, by the Lord of the Ka'bah!' (Bukhari, *Sahih*, Hadith no. 4072, *Kitab al-maghazi, bab ghazwat al-raji' ... wa bi'r ma'unah*).

CHAPTER 36: LOVE AND DEATH

338 And perhaps there is an allusion to this in God's words: *Those who deny Our signs and scorn*

them, *indeed the gates of heaven shall not be opened for them, nor shall they enter Paradise until the camel passes through the eye of the needle. So, We requite those who are sinful.* (Al-Aʿraf, 7:40)

Perhaps the 'camel' symbolises the 'soul which incites evil', and the passing through the 'eye of the needle' symbolises the entrance into Paradise; therefore this symbolises that the 'camel' must die and be effaced before it can pass through the 'eye of the needle', i.e. into Paradise; and God knows best.

339 Muslim, *Sahih*, Hadith, no. 2814, *Kitab sifat al-qiyamah wal-jannah, bab tahrish al-shaytan wa baʾthihi sarayahu li-fitnat al-nas*.

340 This is in fact the original meaning of the word 'unanimous' in English (stemming from the Latin): literally, 'of one soul'.

341 Hakim, *Mustadrak*, vol. 4, p. 355.

342 Bukhari, *Sahih*, Hadith no. 6416, *Kitab al-riqaq, bab qawl al-Nabi kun fil-dunya kaʾannaka gharib*.

343 Fakhr al-Din al-Razi, *al-Tafsir al-kabir*, vol. 2, p. 350.

344 This verse is one of only six verses in the Holy Qur'an that contains five mentions of the Divine Name *Allah* in a single verse (the other five being:2:283; 4:171; 9:40; 33:37; 58:22). There is only one verse in the Holy Qur'an that has more mentions of the Divine Name *Allah* than this in a single verse (*Al-Muzammil*, 73:20—it has seven mentions). However, this verse (2:165) is the shortest of these verses, and in Arabic it creates a very powerful effect on the listener or reciter of the verse—a powerful effect which presents and mirrors the power of love mentioned in the verse.

345 Jalal al-Din Mahalli and Jalal al-Din Suyuti, *Tafsir al-Jalalayn*, p. 349.

346 Bukari, *Sahih*, Hadith no. 1149, *Kitab al-jumuʿah, bab fadl al-tuhur bil-layl wal-nahar wa fadl al-salat baʾd al-wudu*.

347 Of course this was *a fortiori* the state of the Messenger of God ﷺ himself, and perhaps we see an allusion to this in the following holy verse (which was revealed in connection with the Battle of Badr): *You did not slay them, but God slew them, and you threw not when you threw, but God threw, and that He might try the believers with a fair test; surely God is Hearing, Knowing.* (Al-Anfal, 8:17)

348 Bukhari, *Sahih*, Hadith no 6502, *Kitab al-riqaq, bab al-tawaduʾ*.

349 Abu al-Fida' Ismaʾil ibn ʿUmar ibn Kathir Qurashi Dimashqi, *Tafsir al-Qur'an al-ʿazim*, p. 718; but Ibn Kathir also says that this Qur'anic description can apply to any true believer who used to be a disbeliever.

350 God also alludes to this 'new creation' in His words: *Were We then wearied by the first creation? Nay, yet they are in doubt about a new creation.* (Qaf, 50:15)

351 We can also understand this from the following Qur'anic verse: *That which is with you will come to an end, but that which is with God remains. And He shall surely pay those who were patient, their reward according to the best of what they used to do.* (Al-Nahl, 16:96)

And see also: *Hud*, 11:86; *Al-Kahf*, 18:48; *Ta Ha*, 20:73, 131; *Al-Qasas*, 28:60, 88; *Al-Aʿla*, 87:17.

CHAPTER 37: THE MEETING WITH GOD AND BEATITUDE

352 And of course, sex is a foundational part of marital companionship.

353 Tirmidhi, *Sunan*, Hadith no. 1087, *Kitab al-nikah, bab ma jaʾ fil-nazhr ila al-makhtubah*.

354 See also: *Aal ʿImran*, 3:15, 162, 174; *Al-Ma'idah*, 5:2, 16; *Al-Tawbah*, 9:21, 109; *Muhammad*, 47:28; *Al-Fath*, 48:29; *Al-Hadid*, 57:20, 27; *Al-Hashr*, 59:8.

355 Bukhari, *Sahih*, *Hadith* no. 6549, *Kitab al-riqaq, bab sifat al-jannah wal-nar*; Muslim, *Sahih*, *Hadith* no. 2829, *Kitab al-jannah wa sifat na'imaha, bab ihlal al-ridwan ala ahl al-jannah*.

356 Muhyi al-Din ibn 'Arabi, *Tafsir Ibn 'Arabi*, vol. 2, p. 283.

CHAPTER 38: THE TRUE INTENDED OBJECT BEHIND ALL LOVE

357 Abu al-ʿAbbas Ahmad ibn Muhammad ibn ʿAjibah, *al-Bahr al-madid fitafsir al-Qur'an al-majid*, vol. 3, p. 192.

358 Bukhari, *Sahih*, *Kitab al-iman*, *Hadith* no. 1; Muslim, *Sahih*, *Kitab al-imarah*, *Hadith* no. 5036.

359 Jalal al-Din Mahalli and Jalal al-Din Suyuti, *Tafsir al-Jalalayn*, p. 276.

CHAPTER 39: CONCLUSION

360 Abu Dawud, *Sunan*, *Hadith* no. 101, on the authority of al-Barra' ibn 'Azib (it is a sound *Hadith*).

361 Abu Dawud, *Sunan*, *Hadith* no. 4681, *Kitab al-sunnah, bab al-dalil 'ala ziyadat al-iman wa naqsanih*.

362 Al-Hakim, *Al-Mustadrak*, vol. 2, p. 319, on the authority of the Lady 'Aisha (it is considered a rigorously sound *Hadith*).

BIBLIOGRAPHY

The main sources and resources read or used during the writing of this work are as follows:

(A) THE HOLY QUR'AN

TRANSLATIONS OF THE HOLY QUR'AN INTO ENGLISH

Abdel Haleem, M.A.S., *The Qur'an, A New Translation*, (Oxford World Classics; Oxford University Press, U.K., 2008).

Ali, Abdullah Yusuf, *The Holy Qur'an*, (available at: www.altafsir.com).

Arberry, A.J., *The Koran Interpreted*, (available at: www.altafsir.com).

Asad, Muhammad, *The Message of the Holy Qur'an*, (available at: www.altafsir.com).

Lings, Dr. Martin, *The Holy Qur'an: Translations of Selected Verses*, (available at: www.altafsir.com).

Nasr, Seyyed Hossein, et al, *The Study Qur'an*, (Manuscript).

Pickthall, Mohammed Marmeduke, *The Meaning of the Glorious Koran*, (available at: www.altafsir.com).

The Royal Aal al-Bayt Institute, *Translation of the Holy Qur'an*, (available at www.altafsir.com).

(B) PRIMARY SOURCES IN ARABIC

(Sources are in Arabic alphabetical order according to the author's family name)

(I) WORKS OF QUR'ANIC COMMENTARY AND EXEGESIS (*TAFSIR*)

Barusuwi, Isma'il Haqqi (d. 1137 AH), *Tafsir ruh al-bayan* (*The Spirit of Elucidation*); Dar Ihya' al-Turath al-'Arabi, 1st ed., 2001, Beirut, 10 volumes.

Baghawi, Abu Muhammad Husayn ibn Mas'ud (d. 516 AH), *Ma'alim al-tanzil* (*The Signposts of Revelation*); Dar Tayyibah, 4th ed., 1997, Riyad, 8 volumes.

Baqa'i, Burah al-Din Abu Hasan Ibrahim ibn 'Umar (d. 885 AH), *Nazhm a darar fi tanasub al-ayat wal-suwar* (*The String of Pearls*); Dar al-Kutub al-'Ilmiyyah, 1st ed., 1995, Beirut, 8 volumes.

Baydawi, Qadi Nasir al-Din Abu Sa'id 'Abd Allah Abu 'Umar ibn Muhammad Shirazi (d. 791 AH), *Tafsir*; Dar al-Fikr, 1996, Beirut, 5 volumes.

Tustari, Abu Muhammad Sahl ibn 'Abd Allah (d. 283 AH), *Tafsir*; Dar al-Kutub al-'Ilmiyyah, 1st ed., 2002, Beirut, 10 volumes.

Tha'alabi, Abu Zayd 'Abd al-Rahman ibn Muhammad ibn Makhluf (d. 875 AH), *Al-Jawahir al-hisan fi tafsir al-Qur'an* (*The Resplendent Gems*); Dar Ihya' al-Turath al-'Arabi, 1st ed., 1997, Beirut, 5 volumes.

Tha'labi, Abu Ishaq Ahmad ibn Muhammad ibn Ibrahim Nisapuri (d. 427 AH), *Al-Kashf wal-Bayan* (*Unveiling and Illumination*); Dar Ihya' al-Turath al-'Arabi, 1st ed., 2002, Beirut, 10 volumes.

Tabari, Abu Ja'far Muhammad ibn Jarir (d. 310 AH), *Tafsir*; Dar al-Kutub al-'Ilmiyyah, 4th ed., 2005, Beirut, 12 volumes.

Kalbi, Abu Qasim Muhammad ibn Ahmad ibn Juzayy Ghirnati (d. 741 AH), *Al-Tashil fi 'ulum al-tanzil* (*Facilitating the Studies of Revelation*); Dar Ihya' al-Turath al-'Arabi, 1st ed., 2004, Beirut, 2 volumes.

Ibn Jawzi, Abu Faraj 'Abd al-Rahman ibn 'Ali (d. 567 AH), *Zad al-masir* (*The Wayfarer's Provision*); Dar al-Kitab al-'Arabi, 1st ed., 2003, Beirut, 13 volumes.

Ibn Abi Hatim Razi, Abu Muhammad ʿAbd al-Rahman ibn Muhammad ibn Idris ibn al-Mundhir al-Hanahali, (d. 327 AH), *Tafsir al-Qur'an al-azhim* (*Tafsir of the Glorious Qur'an*); Dar al-Fikr, 2003, Beirut, 14 volumes.

Hakim Tirmidhi, Abu ʿAbd Allah Muhammad ibn ʿAli ibn Hasan ibn Bishr (d. 320 AH), *Bayan al-farq bayn al-sadr wal-qalb wal-fu'ad wal-lubb* (*The Difference Between the Breast, the Heart, the Inner Heart and the Core*), 10 volumes.

Andalusi, Muhammad ibn Yusuf al-Shahir bi-Abi Hayyan Ghirnati (d. 753 AH), *Al-Bahr al-muhit fil-tafsir* (*The Vast Ocean*); Dar al-Fikr, 1929, Beirut, 11 volumes.

Andalusi, Muhammad ibn Yusuf al-Shahir bi-Abi Hayyan Ghirnati (d. 753 AH), *Tafsir al-nahr al-madd* (*The Long River*); Dar al-Jinan, 1st ed., 1987, Beirut, 3 volumes.

Zamakhshiri, Abu Qasim ibn ʿUmar Khwarizmi (d. 538 AH), *Tafsir al-kashshaf* (*The Lifter of Veils*); Dar Ihya' al-Turath al-ʿArabi, 1st ed., 1997, Beirut, 4 volumes.

Abu Sa'ud, Qadi Muhammad ibn Muhammad ibn Mustafa Umadi Hanafi (d. 928 AH), *Tafsir*; Dar al-Kutub al-ʿIlmiyyah, 1st ed., 199, Beirut, 6 volumes.

Samarqandi, Jalal al-Din Muhammad ibn Ahmad al-Mahalli, and Suyuti, Imam Jalal al-Din ʿAbd al-Rahman ibn Abi Bakr, *Tafsir al-Jalalayn*; Dar al-Maʿrifah, 1995, Beirut, 1 volume.

Suyuti, Jalal al-Din ʿAbd al-Rahman ibn Abu Bakr (d. 911 AH), *Al-Dur al-manthur fi tafsir al-ma'thur* (*The Scattered Pearls*); Dar al-Kutub al-ʿIlmiyyah, 1st ed., 2000, Beirut, 7 volumes.

Shawkani, Muhammad ibn ʿAli ibn Muhammad (d. 1250 AH), *Fath al-Qadir al-jami' fil-riwayah wal-dirayah min ʿilm al-tafsir* (*The Almighty's Succour*); Dar al-Maʿrifah, 2nd ed., 1997, Beirut, 5 volumes.

Shirazi, Abu Muhammad Sadr al-Din Ruzaban ibn Abi Nasr Baqali (d. 606 AH), *Tafsir 'ara'is al-aayan fi haqa'iq al-Qur'an* (*The Brides of Elucidation*); manuscript.

Sabuni, Muhammad ʿAli, *Safwat al-tafasir* (*The Cream of the Commentaries*); Dar al-Sabuni, ninth ed., Cairo, 3 volumes.

Sawi, Ahmad ibn Muhammad Masri Khalwati Maliki (d. 1241 AH), *Hashiyat al-Sawi ʿala tafsir al-Jalalayn* (Interlinear Commentary on *Tafsir al-Jalalayn*); Dar al-Fikr, 1st ed., 2005, Beirut, 6 volumes.

Tabarani, Abu Qasim Sulayman ibn Ahmad ibn Ayyub (d. 360 AH), *Al-Tafsir al-kabir* (*Great Tafsir*); Dar al-Kitab al-Thaqafi, 1st ed., 2008, Irbid (Jordan), 6 volumes.

Ibn ʿAdil Hanbali, Abu Hafs ʿUmar ibn ʿAli Dimashqi (d. 880 AH), *Al-Lubab fi 'ulum al-Qur'an* (*The Kernel of Qur'anic Sciences*); Dar al-Kutub al-ʿIlmiyyah, 1st ed., 1998, Beirut, 20 volumes.

Ibn ʿAshur, Muhammad Tahir (contemporary), *Al-Tahrir wal-tanwir* (*Examination and Illumination*); Mu'assasat al-Tarikh, 1st ed., 2000, Beirut, 30 volumes.

Ibn ʿAjibah, Abu ʿAbbas Ahmad Muhammad (d. 1224 AH), *Al-Bahr al-madid fi tafsir al-Qur'an al-majid* (*The Vast Ocean*); 1999, Cairo, 6 volumes.

Ibn ʿArabi, Muhyi al-Din, *Tafsir*; al-Maktabah al-Tawfiqiyyah, Cairo, 2 volumes. (Actual author is ʿAbd al-Razzaq al-Qashani.)

'Izz ibn ʿAbd al-Salam, ʿAbd al-ʿAziz Sulmi Dimashqi Shafiʿi (d. 660 AH), *Tafsir* (Abridgement of Mawardi's exegesis); Dar Ibn Hazm, 1st ed., 2002, Beirut, 1 volume.

Ibn ʿAtiyyah, Abu Muhammad ʿAbd al-Haqq Andalusi (d. 541 AH), *al-Muharrar al-wajiz fi tafsir al-kitab al-ʿaziz* (*The Concise Document*); 1st ed., 1977, Doha, 10 volumes.

Ghazali, Abu Hamid Muhammad ibn Muhammad ibn Muhammad (d. 505 AH), *Jawahir al-Qur'an* (*Gems of the Qur'an*); Maktabat al-Jundi, 1964, Cairo, 1 volume.

Fakhr al-Din al-Razi, Abu ʿAbd Allah Muhammad ibn ʿUmar ibn Husayn Bakri Tabrastani (d. 606 AH), *Al-Tafsir al-Kabir* (*Great Tafsir*) Dar Ihya' al-Turath al-ʿArabi, 4th ed., 2001, Beirut, 11 volumes.

Farra', Abu Zakariya Yahya ibn Ziyad (d. 207 AH), *Maʿani al-Qur'an* (*Meanings of the Qur'an*); Dar al-Surur, 3 volumes.

Bibliography

Qurtubi, Abu ʿAbd Allah Muhammad ibn Ahmad Ansari (d. 671 AH), *Al-Jami' li-ahkam al-Qur'an* (*Collected Rulings of the Qur'an*); Dar al-Hadith, 1st ed., 1994, 2nd ed., 1996, Cairo, 22 volumes.

Qushayri, Abu Qasim ʿAbd al-Karim ibn Hawazin ibn ʿAbd al-Malik Nisapuri Shafi'i (d. 465 AH), *Lata'if al-Isharat* (*Subtle Allusions*); Dar al-Kutub al-ʿIlmiyyah, 1st ed., 2000, Beirut, 3 volumes.

Ibn Kathir, Abu Fida Isma'il ibn ʿUmar Qurashi Dimashqi (d. 774 AH), *Tafsir al-Qur'an al-ʿAzhim* (*Tafsir of the Magnificent Qur'an*); Dar Ibn Hazm, 1st ed., 2000, Beirut, 1 volume.

Mawardi, Abu Hasan ʿAli ibn Muhammad ibn Habib Basri (d. 450 AH), *al-Nukat wal-ʿUyun* (*Insights and Wellsprings*); Mu'assasah al-Kutub al-Thaqafiyah, Beirut, 6 volumes.

Mujahid ibn Jabr, Abu Hajjaj Qurashi Makhzumi (d. 104 AH), *Tafsir*; Dar al-Kutub al-ʿIlmiyyah, 1st ed., 2005, Beirut, 1 volume.

Muqatil ibn Sulayman, Abu Hasan ibn Bashir (d. 150 AH), *Tafsir*; Dar al-Kutub al-ʿIlmiyyah, 1st ed., 2003, Beirut, 3 volumes.

Nasafi, Jalil ʿAbd Allah ibn Ahmad ibn Mahmud, *Tafsir*; Dar al-Maʿrifah, 1st ed., 200, Beirut, 1 volume.

Wahidi, Abu Hasan ʿAli ibn Ahmad (d. 468 AH), *Asbab nuzul al-Qur'an* (*Circumstances of the Qur'an's Revelation*); Dar al-Kutub al-ʿIlmiyyah, 1998, Beirut, 1 volume.

Wahidi, Abu Hasan ʿAli ibn Ahmad (d. 468 AH), *Al-Wajiz fi tafsir al-Kitab al-ʿaziz* (*The Concise Tafsir*); Dar al-Qalam, Damascus/Dar al-Shamiyah, Beirut, 1st ed., 1995, 2 volumes.

(II) PROPHETIC SAYINGS LITERATURE (HADITH)

Bukhari, Abu ʿAbd Allah Muhammad ibn Isma'il ibn Ibrahim ibn Mughirah ibn Bardazbah, *Sahih*; Dar al-Kutub al-ʿIlmiyyah, 1st ed., 1992, Beirut, 8 volumes.

Bayhaqi, Abu Bakr Ahmad ibn Husayn ibn ʿAli (d. 458 AH), *Al-Sunan al-Kubra*; Dar al-Kutub al-ʿIlmiyyah, 1999, Beirut, 11 volumes.

Bayhaqi, Abu Bakr Ahmad ibn Husayn ibn ʿAli (d. 458 AH), *Kitab al-zuhd al-kabir* (*Asceticism*); Mu'assasah al-Kutub al-Thaqafiyah, 3rd ed., 1996, Beirut, 1 volume.

Tirmidhi, Abu ʿIsa Muhammad ibn ʿIsa ibn Surah (d. 279 AH), *Al-Jami' al-Sahih*; Dar al-Kutub al-ʿIlmiyyah, Beirut, 5 volumes.

Hakim, Abu ʿAbd Allah Nisapuri (d. 405 AH), *Al-Mustadrak 'ala al-sahihayn* (*Addendum to Bukhari and Muslim*); Dar Ihya' al-Turath al-ʿArabi, 1st ed., 2002, Beirut, 1 volume.

Ibn Hibban, Abu Hatim Muhammad Basti (d. 354), *Sahih*; Mu'assasah al-Risalah, 2nd ed., 1993, Beirut, 18 volumes.

Ibn Hajar, Abu Fadl Ahmad ibn ʿAli ibn Hajr Asqalani (d. 852 AH), *Fath al-Bari* (*Commentary on Bukhari*); Dar al-Maʿrifah, 1960, 14 volumes.

Ibn Hanbal, Ahmad, *Musnad*; Al-Maktabah al-Islamaiyah, 1st ed., 1993, Amman, 8 volumes.

Khatib Baghdadi, Abu Bakr Ahmad ibn ʿAli (d. 463), *Tarikh Baghdad* (*The History of Baghdad*); Dar al-Kutub al-ʿIlmiyyah, Beirut, 13 volumes.

Sajistani, Abu Dawud Sulayman ibn Ash'ath (d. 275), *Sunan*; Dar al-Jinan and Mu'assasah al-Kutub al-Thaqafiyah, 1st ed., 1988, Beirut, 2 volumes.

Tabarani, Abu Qasim Sulaymn ibn Ahmad ibn Ayyub (d. 360 AH), *Al-Mu'jam al-kabir*); Maktabah al-ʿUlum wal-Hikam, 2nd ed., 1983, Mosul, 20 volumes.

Al-Kitab al-jami' li-fada'il al-Qur'an al-karim (*Collected Virtues of the Holy Qur'an*), Mu'assasah Aal al-Bayt al-Malakiyah lil-Fikr al-Islami; Matba'ah al-Amn al-ʿAm, 2nd ed., 2008, Amman, 1 volume.

Muslim, Abu Hasan ibn Hajjaj Qushayri Nisapuri (d. 261 AH), *Sahih*; Dar ibn Hazm, 1st ed., 2002, Beirut, 1 volume.

Ibn Majah, Abu ʿAbd Allah Muhammad ibn Yazid Qazwini (d. 275 AH), *Sunan*; Dar Ihya' al-

Turath, 1st ed., Egypt, 2 volumes.

Malik, Malik ibn Anas (d. 179 AH), *Al-Mawatta'*; Dar al-gharb al-Islami, 1st ed., 1996, Beirut, 2 volumes.

Nisa'i, Abu ʿAbd al-Rahman Ahmad ibn Shu'ayb ibn ʿAli ibn Bahr ibn Sinan ibn Dinar (d. 303 AH), *Sunan*; Maktabah al-Matbu'at al-Islamiyah, 1994, Aleppo, 5 volumes.

(III) PROPHETIC BIOGRAPHY (*SEERAH*)

Ibn Hisham, ʿAbd al-Malik (d. 218 AH), *Sirah*; Dar Ihya' al-Turath al-ʿArabi, 1st ed., 1994, Beirut, 4 volumes.

Waqidi, Muhammad ibn ʿUmar ibn Waqid, *Kitab al-maghazi*; Oxford University Press, London, 1 volume.

(IV) QUR'ANIC STUDIES

Dhahabi, Muhammad Husayn (Azhar University), *Al-Tafsir wal-mufassirun (Tafsir and its Authors)*; 1976, 3 volumes.

Zarakshi, Badr al-Din Muhammad ibn ʿAbd Allah (d. 794 AH), *Al-Burhan fi 'ulum al-Qur'an (The Proof)*; Dar al-Maʿrifah, 1st ed., 1990, Beirut, 4 volumes.

Suyuti, Jalal al-Din ʿAbd al-Rahman ibn Abu Bakr (d. 911 AH), *Al-Itqan fi 'ulum al-Qur'an (Precision in Qur'anic Studies)*; Dar Ibn Kathir, 4th ed., 2000, Damascus, 2 volumes.

Muhammad Fu'ad ʿAbd al-Baqi, *Al-Muʿjam al-mufahras li-alfazh al-Qur'an al-karim (Concordance of the Qur'an)*; Dar al-Fikr/Dar al-Maʿrifah, 4th ed., 1994, Beirut, 1 volume.

Ibn Nahhas, Abu Jaʿfar Ahmad ibn Muhammad ibn Ismaʾil (d. 338 AH), *I'rab al-Qur'an (Grammatical Parsing of the Qur'an)*; Dar al-Kutub al-ʿIlmiyyah, 1st ed., 2001, Beirut, 5 volumes.

(V) LEXICONS

Akhfash, Sa'id ibn Mas'adah Balkhi Majashi'i, *Ma'ani al-Quran (The Meanings of the Qur'an)*; Alam al-Kutub, 1st ed., 1985, Beirut, 2 volumes.

Razi, Muhammad ibn Abi Bakr ibn ʿAbd Allah (d. 666 AH), *Muktar al-Sahhah (Abridgement of the Sahhah dictionary)*; Dar al-Basa'ir, Mu'assasah al-Risalah, 1985, Beirut, 1 volume.

Raghib al-Isfahani, Abu Qasim Husayn ibn Muhammad (d. 502 AH), *Al-Mufradat fi gharib al-Qur'an (Dictionary of rare words found in the Qur'an)*; Dar al-Maʿrifah, 4th ed., 2005, Beirut, 1 volume.

Zabidi, Muhibb al-Din Abu Fayd Sayyid Muhammad Murtada Husayni Wasiti Hanafi, *Taj al-a'rus min jawahir al-qamus (Dictionary)*; Dar al-Fikr, 1994, Beirut, 20 volumes.

Fayruzabadi, Majd al-Din Muhammad ibn Yaʿqub (d. 817 AH), *Al-Qamus al-muhit (Dictionary)*; Dar Ihya' al-Turath al-ʿArabi, 2nd ed., 2003, Beirut, 1 volume.

Ibn Manzhur, Abu Fadl Jamal al-Din Muhammad ibn Mukrim Afriqi Masri (d. 711 AH), *Lisan al-ʿArab (Dictionary)*; Dar Sadir, Beirut, 15 volumes.

(C) SECONDARY SOURCES IN ARABIC

(Sources are in Arabic alphabetical order according to the author's family name)

(I) OTHER BOOKS BY MUSLIM SCHOLARS

Askadari, Mahmud ibn Fadl Allah (d. 1038 AH), *Habbat al-mahabbah (The Essence of Love)*; manuscript.

Juwayni, Imam al-Haramayn, Abu Ma'ali ʿAbd al-Malik ibn ʿAbd Allah ibn Yusuf (d. 478 AH), *Al-Irshad (Guidance)*; Matba'ah al-Sa'adah, 1950, Cairo, 1 volume.

Bibliography

Tawhidi, Abu Hayan ʿAli ibn Muhammad ibn Abbas (d. circa 400 AH), *Al-Imta' wal-Muʾanasah (Pleasure and Consolation)*; Dar al-Kutub al-ʿIlmiyyah, 1st ed., 2007, Beirut, 1 volume.
Ibn Taymiyyah, Abu Abbas Ahmad ibn ʿAbd al-Halim ibn ʿAbd al-Salam Harani (d. 728 AH), *Al-Nubuwwat (Matters of Prophethood)*; Dar al-Qalam, Beirut, 1 volume.
Ibn Taymiyyah, Abu Abbas Ahmad ibn ʿAbd al-Halim ibn ʿAbd al-Salam Harani (d. 728 AH), *Al-Tuhfah al-ʿIraqiyyah (The Iraqi Treasure)*; Maktabah al-Manar, 1st ed., 1987, Zarqa (Jordan), 1 volume.
Jahizh, Abu ʿUthman ʿAmr ibn Bahr (d. 255), *Al-Bayan wal-tabyin (Elucidation and Clarification)*; Dar al-Kutub al-ʿIlmiyyah, 2nd ed., 2003, Beirut, 2 volumes.
Jahizh, Abu ʿUthman ʿAmr ibn Bahr (d. 255), *Rasa'il (Letters)*; Dar al-Kutub al-ʿIlmiyyah, 1st ed., 2000, Beirut, 4 volumes.
Ibn Jawzi, Abu Faraj ʿAbd al-Rahman ibn ʿAli (d. 567 AH), *Dhamm al-hawa (The Blameworthiness of Desire)*; Dar al-Kitab al-ʿArabi, 1st ed., 1999, Beirut, 1 volume.
Jili, ʿAbd al-Karim ibn Ibrahim (d. 508 AH), *Al-Insan al-kamil fi maʿrifat al-awakhir wal-awa'il (The Universal Man)*; Dar al-Kutub al-ʿIlmiyyah, 2nd ed., 2001, Beirut, 1 volume.
Ibn Hazm, Abu Muhammad ʿAli ibn Ahmad ibn Sa'id Andalusi (d. 456 AH), *Tawq al-hamamah fil-alfah wal-ullaf (The Ring of the Dove)*; Dar al-Kutub al-ʿIlmiyyah, 3rd ed., 2003, Beirut, 1 volume.
Fakhr al-Din al-Razi, Imam Abu ʿAbd Allah Muhammad ibn ʿUmar ibn Husayn Bakri Tabrastani (d. 606 AH), *Lawamiʿ al-bayyinat sharh asma' Allah taʿala wal-sifat (Explanation of God's Names and Qualities)*; al-Maktabah al-Azhariyah lil-Turath, new edition, 2000, Cairo, 1 volume.
Ibn Sina, Abu ʿAli Husayn ibn ʿAbd Allah (d. 428 AH), *Risalah fi Dimashq (Letter from Damascus)*; Dar al-Fikr, 1st ed., 2002, Beirut, 1 volume.
Ibn Abi Sharaf, Kamal al-Din Muhammad ibn Muhammad ibn Abi Bakr Marri Maqdasi Shafi'i (d. 905 AH), *Al-Musamarah sharh al-musayarah fil-ʿaqaid al-manjiyya min al-akhirah (The Discourse)*; Dar al-Kutub al-ʿIlmiyyah, 1st ed., 2002, Beirut, 1 volume.
Halabi, Shihab al-Din Mahmud ibn Sulayman (d. 725 AH), *Kitab manazil al-ahbab wa manazih al-albab (The Stations of the Lovers and the Pastures of the Intellects)*; Dar Sadir, 1st ed., 2000, Beirut, 1 volume.
Makki, Abu Talib Muhammad Abu Hasan ʿAli ibn ʿAbbas (d. 386 AD), *Qut al-qulub fi maʿamalt al-mahbub (Nourishment for the Heart)*; Dar al-Fikr, Beirut, 2 volumes.
Tahawi, Abu Jaʿfar Ahmad ibn Muhammad ibn Salamah Masri Hanafi, *Sahih sharh al-aqidah al-Tahawiyah bi-sharh Hassan Saqqaf* (Hassan Saqqaf's commentary on Tahawi's creed); Dar Imam Nawawi, 3rd ed., 2006, Beirut, 1 volume.
Baghdadi, ʿAbd al-Qadir ibn Tahir ibn Muhammad Tamimi (d. 429 AH), *Al-Farq bayn al-firaq (The Difference Between the Sects)*; Dar Maʿrifah, Beirut, 1 volume.
'Ajlouni, Isma'il ibn Muhammad Jarrahi (d. 1162 AH), *Kashf al-khafa' wa mazil al-ilbas 'amma ishtahara min al-Hadith 'ala alsinat al-nas (Clearing up Confusion about Certain Famous Hadiths)*; Dar al-Kutub al-ʿIlmiyyah, 3rd ed., 1988, Beirut, 2 volumes.
Ibn 'Arabi, Muhyi al-Din Muhammad ibn ʿAli ibn Muhammad Hatimi Ta'i Andalusi (d. 638 AH), *Al-Futuhat al-Makkiyah (The Meccan Revelations)*; Dar Ihya' al-Turath al-ʿArabi, 1st ed., Beirut, 4 volumes.
Ibn 'Arif, Sheikh Ahmad ibn Muhammad Sanhaji (d. 536 AH), *Kitab al-nafa'is wa mahasin al-majalis (Treasures and Good Counsels)*; al-Mawrid magazine, vol. 9, 1980, pp. 681–706.
Sakandari, Ibn 'Ata Illah Ahmad ibn Muhammad ibn ʿAbd al-Karim (d. 709 AH), *Al-Hikam (Aphorisms)*; Dar al-Fikr, 2ne ed., 2005, Beirut, 4 volumes.
Ghazali, Abu Hamid Muhammad Tusi (d. 505 AH), *Ihya' 'ulum al-din (Revival of Religious Sciences)*; Dar al-Arqam ibn Abi al-Arqam, 1st ed., 1998, Beirut, 5 volumes.
Ghazali, Abu Hamid Muhammad Tusi, *Maqasid al-falsafah (The Intentions of Philosophy)*; Dar

al-Ma'arif, 1961, Cairo, 1 volume.

Ghazali, Abu Hamid Muhammad Tusi, *Al-Maqsad al-asna fi sharh ma'ani asmla' Allah al-husna* (*Explanation of the Divine Names*); Dar Ibn Hazm, 1st ed. 2003, Beirut, 1 volume.

Qushayri, Abu Qaim ʿAbd al-Karim ibn Hawazin Nisapuri (d. 465 AH), *Al-Risalah fi ʿilm al-tasawwuf* (*The Epistle*); Dar al-Khayr, 2nd ed., 1995, Damascus/Beirut, 1 volume.

Jawziyya, Ibn Qayyim Abu ʿAbd Allah Muhammad ibn Abi Bakr Zar'i Dimashqi (d. 751 AH), *Al-Ruh* (*The Spirit*); Dar Ibn Kathir, 7th ed., 2008, Damascus/Beirut, 1 volume.

Jawziyya, Ibn Qayyim Abu ʿAbd Allah Muhammad ibn Abi Bakr Zar'i Dimashqi (d. 751 AH), *Madarij al-salikin* (*The Stages of the Wayfarer*); Dar Ihya' al-Turath al-ʿArabi, 2nd ed., 2001, Beirut, 3 volumes.

Jawziyya, Ibn Qayyim Abu ʿAbd Allah Muhammad ibn Abi Bakr Zar'i Dimashqi (d. 751 AH), *Rawdat al-muhibbin wa nuzhat al-mushtaqin* (*The Pasture of the Lovers and the Garden of the Yearners*); Dar al-Bayan al-ʿArabi, Egypt, 1 volume.

Kalabadhi, Abu Bakr Muhammad ibn Ishaq (d. 380), *Al-Ta'arruf li-madhhab al-tasawwuf* (*Introduction to Sufism*); Maktabah al-Thaqafah al-Diniyah, 1st edition, 2004, Cairo, 1 volume.

Makhluf, Grand Mufti of Egypt Hasanayn Muhammad (Twentieth Century CE), *Min wahi al-Qur'an fi man yuhibbuhum Allah wa fi man la yuhibbuhum Allah min 'ibadih* (*What the Qur'an Says about those whom God Loves and those whom He does not Love*); Matba'ah al-Madani, 3rd ed., 1979, Cairo, 1 volume.

Niffari, Muhammad ibn ʿAbd al-Jabbr ibn al-Hasan, *Al-Mawaqif* (*The Stations*); Dar al-Kutub al-Masriyah, 1934, Cairo, 1 volume.

Hujwayri, *Kashf al-mahjub* (*Unveiling the Veiled*); manuscript.

Harawi, ʿAbd Allah Ansari (d. 481 AH), *Manazil al-sa'irin* (*The Stations of the Wayfarers*); Dar al-Kutub al-ʿIlmiyyah, 1988, Beirut, 1 volume.

(II) OTHER SOURCES

'Ajluni, Kamil Muhammad Salih, *Al-Jins fil-Yahudiyah wal-Masihiyah wal-Islam* (*Sex in Judaism, Christianity and Islam*); Jordan University Press, 2007, Amman, 1 volume.

Ghazi bin Muhammad bin Talal, *Al-Haqiqa wal-Maʿrifah* (*Truth and Knowledge*); Kitab al-Thaqafah al-ʿAmmah lil-Marhalah al-Thanawiyyah, 1st ed., 2004, Ministry of Education, Jordan.

Various scholars, *Al-Hubb fil-Qur'an al-Karim* (*Love in the Holy Qur'an*), Mu'assasah Aal al-Bayt al-Malakiyah lil-Fikr al-Islami, 2007, Amman/Jordan, 2 volumes.

(D) PRIMARY SOURCES ON LOVE IN ENGLISH AND FRENCH

(I) (RELIGIOUS AND SECULAR) ANCIENT SOURCES ON LOVE IN ENGLISH AND FRENCH

Ficino, Marsilio, *Commentary on Plato's Symposium of Love*, trans. Sears Jayne (2nd ed.) (Dallas, 1985)

Plato, *Phaedrus* and *The Seventh Letter*, trans. Walter Hamilton (London, 1973)

Plato, *Phaedo*, in *Five Dialogues*, trans. G.M.A.Grube (Indianapolis, 1984)

Plato, *The Republic*, trans. G.M.A.Grube (Indianapolis, 1984)

Plato, *The Symposium of Love*, trans. A.Nehemas and P.Woodruff (New York, 1989)

Plotinus, *The Enneads*, Intro. J.Dillon, trans. S.Mackenna (London, 1991)

Rumi, Jalaludin, *The Mathnawi*, Volumes I-VI, trans. Reynold Nicholson, (Reprinted Great Britain, 1960)

(ii) (Religious) Modern Sources on Love in English and French

Lewis, C.S., *The Allegory of Love*, (London, 1972)

Bibliography

Lewis, C.S., *The Four Loves*, (London, 1972)
Nasr, Seyyed Hossein, *The Garden of Truth, The Vision and Promise of Sufism, Islam's Mystical Tradition*, (New York, 2007)

(III) (SECULAR) MODERN SOURCES ON LOVE IN ENGLISH AND FRENCH
De Rougemont, Denis, *L'Amour et L'Occident*, (Paris, 1939)
Ghazi Ben Mohammed, *What is Falling in Love?*, (Cambridge University, U.K., PhD, 1993)
Stendhal, *De L'Amour*, (Paris 1965); Stendhal, *De L'Amour*, Intro. Jean Stewart, trans. Gilbert and Suzanne Sale (London, 1975).

(E) SECONDARY SOURCES ON LOVE IN ENGLISH AND FRENCH

(I) (RELIGIOUS) ANCIENT SOURCES ON LOVE IN ENGLISH AND FRENCH
Aquinas, St. Thomas, *Summa Theologia*, in Great Books of the Western World, Volume XIX and Volume XX, trans. W.O.Ross (Chicago, 1989)
Climacus, John, *The Ladder of Divine Ascent*, trans. Colm Luibheid and Norman Russell (The Classics of Western Spirituality, NJ, 1982)
Maimonides, Moses, *The Guide of the Perplexed*, in 2 Volumes, trans. Shlomo Pines (Chicago, 1963)
Mechthild of Magdeburg, *The Flowing Light of the Godhead* (selected writings from), trans. Lucy Menzies in German Mystical Writings ed. Karen Campbell (New York, 1991)
Porphyry, *On the Cave of the Nymphs*, trans. Thomas Taylor, (Grand Rapids, Michigan, 1991)
Proclus, Diadochus, *Commentary on the First Alcibiades of Plato*, trans. L.G.Westernick (Amsterdam, 1954)
Pseudo-Dionysius Aeropogite, *The Divine Names and Mystical Theology*, trans. J.D.Jones (Milwaukee, 1980)
Rolle, Richard, *The Fire of Love*, trans. Clifton Walters (London, 1972)
St. Augustine, *Confessions*, trans. R.S.Pine-Coffin (Middlesex, U.K., 1985)
St. Bernard of Clairvaux, *On the Song of Songs*, in 4 Volumes, trans. K.Walsh and I.M.Edmunds (Kalamazoo, Michegan 1979)
St. John of the Cross, *Dark Night of the Soul*, trans. E.Allison Peers (New York, 1990)
St. Julian of Norwich, *Showings*, trans. E.Colledge and J.Walsh (New York, 1978)
St. Nicholas of Cusa, *The Vision of God*, trans. E.Gurney-Salter (London, 1928)
St. Teresa of Avila, *The Life of St.Teresa of Avila* by Herself, trans. J.M.Cohen (London, 1957)
The Holy Bible, King James Translation (H.M. Printers, London)
The Philokalia, (Writings from the Philokalia on the Prayer of the Heart) trans. E.Kadlouboudsky and G.E.H.Palmer (London, 1992)
The Zohar, Moses de Léon, attributed to Rabbi Simeon ben Yohai, trans. H.Sperling and M.Simon (London, 1949)
Theologia Germanica (selected writings from), trans. Bengt Hoffman in German Mystical Writings ed. Karen Campbell (New York, 1991)

(II) (SECULAR) ANCIENT SOURCES ON LOVE IN ENGLISH AND FRENCH
Aristotle, *Nicomachean Ethics*, in Great Books of the Western World, Volume IX, trans. W.O.Ross (Chicago, 1989)
Capellanus, Andreas, *The Art of Courtly Love*, trans. John Jay Parry, (New York, 1969)
Capellanus, Andreas, *On Love*, trans. P.G. Walsh, (U.K., 1982)
De Lorris, Guillaume, and De Meun, Jean, *The Romance of the Rose*, trans. Charles Dahlberg (Hanover, New Hampshire, 1983)

(III) (RELIGIOUS) MODERN SOURCES ON LOVE IN ENGLISH AND FRENCH

Burckhardt, T., *Moorish Culture in Spain*, trans. Alisa Jaffa (New York, 1972)
Burckhardt, T., *Alchemy. Science of the Cosmos, Science of the Soul*, trans. William Stoddart (Dorset, U.K., 1986)
Chittick, William C., *The Sufi Path of Love: The Spiritual Teachings of Rumi*, (New York, 1983)
Coomaraswamy, A.K., *Traditional Art and Symbolism*, Volume I, ed. Roger Lipsey (Oxford, U.K., 1977)
Evola, Julius, *Eros and the Mysteries of Love*, (Rochester, Vermont, 1991)
Greeley, Andrew M. and Mary G. Durkin, *The Book of Love*, (New York, 2002)
Happold, F.C., *Mysticism: A Study and an Anthology*, (London, 1990)
Mahmutcehajic, Rusmir, *On Love in the Muslim Tradition*, (New York, 2007)
Schuon, Frithjof, *The Essential Writings of Frithjof Schuon*, ed. S.H.Nasr (New York 1986)
Schuon, Frithjof, *Esoterism as Principle and Way*, (Kent, U.K., 1981)
Schuon, Frithjof, *Gnosis—Divine Wisdom*, (Middlesex, U.K., 1959)
Schuon, Frithjof, *Logic and Transcendence*, (London, 1975)
Schuon, Frithjof, *Roots of the Human Condition*, (Bloomington, Indiana 1990)
Schuon, Frithjof, *Spiritual Perspectives and Human Facts*, (Middlesex, U.K., 1987)
Smith, Huston, *The World's Religions*, (New York, 1986)
Staveley, Lilian, *The Golden Fountain: On the Soul's Love for God*, (Bloomington, Indiana 1982)
Underhill, Evelyn, *Mysticism*, (London, 1957)
Vaughn-Lee, Llewellyn, *The Paradoxes of Love*, (California, 1996)
Arthur Verslius, *The Mysteries of Love*, (Minn., USA, 1996)
Warren, Rick, *The Purpose Driven Life*, (Michegan, 2002)
The Way of a Pilgrim and *The Pilgrim Continues his Way*, trans. J.M.French (San Francisco, 1991

(IV) (SECULAR) MODERN SOURCES ON LOVE IN ENGLISH AND FRENCH

Bell, Joseph Norment, *Love Theory in Later Hanbalite Islam*, (New York, 1979)
Boase, Roger, *The Origin and Meaning of Courtly Love*, (Manchester, U.K., 1977)
Campbell, Joseph, *The Hero with a Thousand Faces*, (London, 1988)
D'Arcy, M.C., *The Mind and Heart of Love*, (London, 1954)
Dawkins, Richard, *The Selfish Gene*, (London, 1979)
Fisher, Helen E., *Anatomy of Love*, (New York, 1992)
Freud, Sigmund, *On Sexuality: Three Essays on the History of Sexuality and Other Works* trans. James Strachey (London, 1987)
Fromm, Erich, *The Art of Loving*, (New York, 1956)
Girard, René, *Deceit, Desire and the Novel*, trans. Yvonne Freccero (London, 1984)
Hazo, Robert G., *The Idea of Love* (New York, 1967)
Menocal, Maria Rosa, *The Arabic Role in Medieval Literary History*, (Philadelphia, 1990)
Morris, Desmond, *The Naked Ape*, (London, 1967)
Nygren, Anders, *Agape and Eros*, trans. P.S.Walton (London, 1953)
Parker, A.A., *The Philosophy of Love in Spanish Literature, 1480–1680*, (Edinburgh, 1985)
Peck, Scott M., *The Road Less Travelled: A New Psychology of Love, Traditional Values and Spiritual Growth* (New York, 1978)
Raglan, Lord Fitzroy, *The Hero*, (London, 1936)
Solovyev, Vladimir, *The Meaning of Love*, (London, 1945)
Singer, Irving, *The Nature of Love*, Volumes I-III, (Chicago, 1984)
Wolf, Naomi, *The Beauty Myth*, (New York, 1992)

INDEX OF QUR'ANIC VERSES CITED BY CHAPTER*

* This list does not include those verses referred to but not actually cited.

INTRODUCTORY CHAPTERS

Chapter 1: Prologue: The Goals and Methodology of this Work
Al-Baqarah, 2:23–24, 147, 176, 269 [endnote]
Aal 'Imran, 3:164 [endnote]
Al-Nisa', 4:82
Al-An'am, 6:38, 154
Al-A'raf, 7:52, 145,
Yunus, 10:36–39, 37
Hud, 11:1, 13–14, 88
Yusuf, 12:111
Al-Nahl, 16:89
Al-Isra', 17:12, 88, 89, 105
Al-Kahf, 18:1, 29, 54, 109
Al-Rum, 30:58
Luqman, 31:27
Al-Zumar, 39:27–28
Al-Ahqaf, 46:24–25 [endnote]
Al-Tur, 52:33–34
Al-Jum'a, 62:2 [endnote]

Chapter 2: Introduction: The Secret of Love
Al-Baqarah, 2:17–18
Aal 'Imran, 3:14
Al-Rum, 30:7

Chapter 3: The Definition of Love
Al-Baqarah, 2:165, 261
Al-Nisa', 4:129
Al-Ma'idah, 5:54
Al-A'raf, 7:156
Hud, 11:90 [endnote]; 118–119 [endnote]
Ta Ha, 20:49–50
Al-Sajdah, 32:7
Al-Ahzab, 33:4, 52
Muhammad, 47:38
Al-Rahman, 55:1–5 [endnote]
Al-Buruj, 85:14–15

PART ONE: DIVINE LOVE

Chapter 4: God and Love
Al-Baqarah, 2:115 [endnote], 165, 255, 272 [endnote]
Aal 'Imran, 3:28 [endnote], 159
Al-Nisa', 4:93
Al-Ma'idah, 5:18, 54, 116 [endnote]
Al-An'am, 6:12, 51, 54,
Al-A'raf, 7:156
Hud, 11:90
Al-Isra', 17:110
Al-Naml, 27:30
Al-Rum, 30:21
Al-Sajdah, 32:4
Al-Zumar, 39:43–44
Ghafir, 40:7
Al-Shura, 42:19
Al-Najm, 53:26
Al-Buruj, 85:14–15

Chapter 5: Love is the Root of Creation
Al-Baqarah, 2:21, 30–31
Al-An'am, 6:12, 54
Al-A'raf, 7:156
Yunus, 10:4
Hud, 11:28, 118–119

Al-Ra'd, 13:2
Al-Nahl, 16:3–16
Al-Furqan, 25:77; 62
Al-Ahzab, 33:73
Ghafir, 40:64, 67
Fussilat, 41:17
Al-Jathiyah, 45:12–13, 22
Al-Hujurat, 49:13
Qaf, 50:8
Al-Dhariyat, 51:56
Al-Najm, 53:31
Al-Rahman, 55:1–4, 1–9
Al-Taghabun, 64:3
Al-Mulk, 67:2, 12
Al-Insan, 76:2–3, 3
Al-Nazi'at, 79:27–33
Al-Infitar, 82:6–8
Al-Balad, 90:10
Al-Tin, 95:1–8

Chapter 6: The Universe and Love
Aal 'Imran, 3:83
Al-A'raf, 7:156
Yunus, 10:55, 66
Al-Ra'd, 13:15
Al-Isra', 17:44
Al-Hajj, 22:18
Al-Nur, 24:24
Al-Rum, 30:26
Al-Sajdah, 32:7
Fatir, 35:15
Ya Sin, 36:65
Fussilat, 41:20–21
Al-Shura, 42:11, 19
Muhammad, 47:38
Al-Rahman, 55:29
Al-Hashr, 59:24
Al-Ikhlas, 112:1–2

Chapter 7: God's Love for Humanity

Al-Baqarah, 2:29–34, 44, 153, 194, 195, 212, 222, 249
Aal 'Imran, 3:37, 31, 76, 134, 146, 148, 159, 194 [endnote]
Al-Nisa', 4:108
Al-Ma'idah, 5:12, 13, 42, 54. 93
Al-A'raf, 7:7, 11, 56
Al-Anfal, 8:19, 46, 66
Al-Tawbah, 9:4, 7, 36, 40, 109, 123
Yusuf, 12:90
Ibrahim, 14:34
Al-Hijr, 15:28–34
Al-Nahl, 16:18, 53, 61, 127–128
Al-Isra', 17:20, 70
Ta Ha, 20:46
Al-Nur, 24:37–38
Al-Furqan, 25:15–16
Al-Shu'ara', 26:15, 62, 88–89
Al-Qasas, 28:70
Al-'Ankabut, 29:69
Al-Rum, 30:29–30
Luqman, 31:20
Al-Sajdah, 32:7–9
Al-Ahzab, 33:72
Fatir, 35:45
Sad, 38:72, 75
Al-Zumar, 39:10
Ghafir, 40:7–8 [endnote], 40, 64
Muhammad, 47:35
Al-Hujurat, 49:9
Al-Hadid, 57:4
Al-Mujadilah, 58:7
Al-Mumtahanah, 60:8
Al-Saff, 61:2–3, 4
Al-Taghabun, 64:3
Al-Qalam, 68:4
Al-Infitar, 82:6–8
Al-Tin, 95:1–8

Chapter 8: God's Love for His Messengers and Prophets

Al-Baqarah, 2:136, 253, 285
Aal 'Imran, 3:31, 36–39, 45, 50, 84
Al-Nisa', 4:113, 125, 150–152, 158, 163, 171
Al-Ma'idah, 5:15, 46, 110, 114
Al-An'am, 6:14, 83–87, 85
Al-A'raf, 7:94 [endnote], 143, 150, 154
Al-Tawbah, 9:40, 114
Hud, 11:37, 79
Al-Hijr, 15:87
Al-Nahl, 16:63
Al-Isra', 17:55
Maryam, 19:21, 51–53 [endnote], 52, 54
Ta Ha, 20:39, 41, 47 [endnote], 84 [endnote]
Al-Anbiya', 21:91, 107
Al-Hajj, 22:52 [endnote]
Al-Mu'minun, 23:27, 50
Al-Shu'ara', 26:13–15 [endnote], 15, 62, 124–125, 142–143, 161–162, 177–178, 208
Al-Ahzab, 33:7, 21, 40, 45–46, 56, 69
Fatir, 35:24
Al-Saffat, 37:123, 139
Al-Zumar, 39:12
Ghafir, 40:34, 78
Fussilat, 41:43
Al-Shura, 42:13
Al-Zukhruf, 43:59, 81
Al-Ahqaf, 46:9, 35
Al-Fath, 48:10
Al-Tur, 52:48
Al-Najm, 53:36
Al-Hadid, 57:27
Al-Mumtahanah, 60:4
Al-Talaq, 65:10–11
Al-Qalam, 68:4
Al-Haqqah, 69:40
Al-A'la, 87:18–19
Al-Duha, 93:5 [endnote]
Al-Sharh, 94:4

Chapter 9: Those whom God does not Love

Al-Baqarah, 2:9 [endnote], 115 [endnote], 190, 191 [endnote], 205, 276, 279 [endnote]
Aal 'Imran, 3:32, 57, 140
Al-Nisa', 4:36, 93, 107, 108 [endnote], 115 [endnote], 142 [endnote], 145, 148
Al-Ma'idah, 5:33 [endnote], 60, 64, 87, 91
Al-An'am, 6:141, 161–164 [endnote]
Al-A'raf, 7:31, 55, 182 [endnote]
Al-Anfal, 8:13 [endnote], 17 [endnote], 58
Al-Tawbah, 9:30 [endnote], 46, 63 [endnote], 92, 96 [endnote], 107 [endnote]
Yunus, 10:82 [endnote]
Al-Nahl, 16:23, 74 [endnote]
Al-Isra', 17:22–39, 37–38 [endnote]
Al-Hajj, 22:38
Al-Qasas, 28:76, 77
Al-Rum, 30:45
Luqman, 31:18
Al-Ahzab, 33:57 [endnote]
Fatir, 35:39
Al-Zumar, 39:7 [endnote]
Ghafir, 40:10, 35
Al-Shura, 42:40
Muhammad, 47:32 [endnote]
Al-Fath, 48:6, 10 [endnote]
Al-Tur, 52:48 [endnote]
Al-Rahman, 55:27 [endnote]
Al-Hadid, 57:23
Al-Mujadilah, 58:5 [endnote], 22 [endnote]
Al-Hashr, 59:4 [endnote]
Al-Saff, 61:3
Al-Munafiqun, 63:4 [endnote]
Al-Qalam, 68:44 [endnote]

PART TWO: THE

Index of Qur'anic Verses Cited by Chapter*

MESSENGER OF GOD'S ※ LOVE

Chapter 10: The Messenger of God's ※ Love for God
Al-Baqarah, 2:165
Al-Ma'idah, 5:54
Al-An'am, 6:14, 161–164
Al-Ahzab, 33:21, 56
Al-Zumar, 39:12
Al-Zukhruf, 43:81

Chapter 11: The Messenger of God's ※ Love for the Believers
Aal 'Imran, 3:159
Al-Tawbah, 9:61, 80, 103, 123
Al-Hijr, 15:88
Al-Kahf, 18:6
Al-Anbiya', 21:107
Al-Nur, 24:62
Al-Shu'ara', 26:3, 215
Al-Ahzab, 33:45, 53
Fatir, 35:7
Muhammad, 47:19
Al-Fath, 48:8
Al-Hashr, 59:9
Al-Mumtahanah, 60:7 [endnote], 12
Al-Munafiqun, 63:6

PART THREE: HUMAN LOVE

Chapter 12: Humanity's Love for God
Al-Fatihah 1: 5–7
Al-Baqarah, 2:156, 164–165, 165,177, 186, 284
Aal 'Imran, 3:31–32, 37, 92, 97, 133–136, 189–191
Al-Nisa', 4:32, 48, 110, 165–166
Al-An'am, 6:41, 161, 162
Al-A'raf, 7:54–58, 180, 196, 205–206 [endnote]
Al-Anfal, 8:2, 35
Al-Tawbah, 9:24, 40 [endnote], 59, 102–104, 111, 124
Yunus, 10:12, 101, 103
Hud, 11:5, 90
Yusuf, 12:33
Al-Ra'd, 13:6, 28
Ibrahim, 14:8, 34
Al-Hijr, 15:49
Al-Nahl, 16: 53, 54, 97
Al-Isra', 17:25, 110
Maryam, 19:23–25 [endnote], 96
Ta Ha, 20:8
Al-Anbiya', 21:89–90
Al-Hajj, 22:30, 32
Al-Naml, 27:62
Al-'Ankabut, 29:6, 45
Al-Rum, 30:47, 50
Luqman, 31:20
Al-Sajdah, 32:15–19
Al-Ahzab, 33:21
Saba, 34:46
Fatir, 35:15
Al-Zumar, 39:2–3, 7, 9, 14, 22–23, 36, 53–55
Ghafir, 40:14, 57, 60, 65
Fussilat, 41:53
Al-Shura, 42:19, 25–26
Muhammad, 47:38
Al-Fath, 48:4, 29
Qaf, 50:16
Al-Dhariyat, 51:20–21, 50
Al-Mulk, 67:12–14
Al-Qalam, 68:4
Al-Muzzammil, 73:8–10
Al-Insan, 76:8
Al-Buruj, 85:14
Al-Sharh, 94:7–8
Al-Ma'un, 107:1–7
Al-Nasr, 110:3

Chapter 13: The Believer's Love for the Messenger of God ※
Al-An'am, 6:160
Al-Tawbah, 9:120, 128
Al-Isra', 17:79
Al-Ahzab, 33:6, 56
Al-Shura, 42:23
Al-Fath, 48:29
Al-Hujurat, 49:1–5
Al-Qalam, 68:4

Chapter 14: Love for the Family and Kin of the Messenger of God ※
Al-Baqarah, 2:124 [endnote], 207
Aal 'Imran, 3:61, 110, 121
Al-Ma'idah, 5:55–56
Al-Anfal, 8:74–75
Al-Tawbah, 9:40, 99, 100, 117
Hud, 11:45–46 [endnote], 73
Ibrahim, 14:37
Ta Ha, 20:132
Al-Shu'ara', 26:214
Al-Ahzab, 33:6, 32–33, 33, 37, 40
Fatir, 35:18 [endnote]
Al-Shura, 42:23
Al-Fath, 48:29
Al-Hashr, 59:8–10
Quraysh, 106:1–4
Al-Kawthar, 108:1–3
Al-Masad, 111 :1–5 [endnote]

Chapter 15: The Effects of Love of God on Human Beings
Al-Baqarah, 2:94–96, 136–138, 177, 189
Aal 'Imran, 3:28–30 [endnote], 31, 92, 143 [endnote], 191
Al-Nisa', 4:74 [endnote], 103 [endnote]
Al-Ma'idah, 5:54
Al-An'am, 6:52, 161–164
Al-Anfal, 8:2–4
Al-Tawbah, 9:24, 38, 72, 91–92, 111 [endnote], 123
Yunus, 10:62–65, 100 [endnote]
Al-Kahf, 18:28
Maryam, 19:96
Al-Hajj, 22:32–35
Al-Mu'minun, 23:1–11, 57–63
Al-Furqan, 25:52,

Al-Rum, 30:50
Al-Ahzab, 33:21, 23
Al-Zukhruf, 43:36
Al-Fath, 48:29
Al-Waqi'ah, 56:17–18 [endnote]
Al-Hashr, 59:9
Al-Jumu'ah, 62:6–7
Al-Munafiqun, 63:8
Al-Tahrim, 66:9
Al-Insan, 76:29–31 [endnote]
Al-Mutaffifin, 83:18–28 [endnote]

Chapter 16: Family Love
Al-Baqarah, 2:83, 177, 215, 233
Al-Nisa', 4:11, 22–24, 25 [endnote], 35 [endnote], 36, 135
Al-An'am, 6:151
Al-Anfal, 8:28, 75
Al-Tawbah, 9:24, 114
Al-Nahl, 16:72
Al-Isra', 17:23–25, 26–27 [endnote], 26–28
Al-Kahf, 18:46
Al-Nur, 24:31, 58, 61
Al-Furqan, 25:54
Al-'Ankabut, 29:8
Luqman, 31:14–15
Al-Ahzab, 33:6
Al-Shura, 42:23, 49–50
Al-Ahqaf, 46:15–18
Al-Hadid, 57:20
Al-Mujadilah, 58:22
Al-Munafiqun, 63:9
Al-Taghabun, 64:14–15

Chapter 17: Love of Others (All Humanity; the 'People of the Scripture'; Believers, and Friends)
Al-Baqarah, 2:47, 65 [endnote], 177, 190, 265
Aal 'Imran, 3:113–115, 133–136,159
Al-Nisa', 4:1, 36, 155 [endnote]
Al-Ma'idah, 5:2, 8, 20, 32, 82
Al-An'am, 6:52, 98, 108, 151

Al-A'raf, 7:38–39, 142, 156, 170
Al-Tawbah, 9:7, 16, 40
Yunus, 10:85
Hud, 11:27–31
Yusuf, 12:39, 90–92
Al-Ra'd, 13:21–24
Ibrahim, 14:31, 36
Al-Hijr, 15:85–86
Al-Nahl, 16:126
Al-Isra', 17:33
Al-Kahf, 18:9, 29, 76
Al-Hajj, 22:38–40
Al-Mu'minun, 23:96
Al-Nur, 24:22 [endnote], 61
Al-Furqan, 25:63
Al-Shu'ara', 26:101, 111–115
Al-Rum, 30:1–4, 22
Luqman, 31:28
Al-Sajdah, 32:23–25
Fussilat, 41:34–35
Al-Shura, 42:36–42, 43
Al-Zukhruf, 43:67, 89
Al-Dukhan, 44:32–33
Al-Jathiyah, 45:14, 16–17
Al-Hujurat, 49:10, 13
Al-Hashr, 59:9
Al-Mumtahanah, 60:5–6, 7–8
Al-Ma'arij, 70:40
Al-Insan, 76:8
Al-Buruj, 85:4–8
Al-Humazah, 104:1
Al-Fil, 105:1
Al-Ma'un, 107:1–7
Al-Kafirun, 109:1–6

Chapter 18: Conjugal and Sexual Love
Al-Baqarah, 2:187, 222–223, 223, 228–237, 249–250
Aal 'Imran, 3:36, 195
Al-Nisa', 4:1, 19–21, 21, 24, 34, 35, 73, 147
Al-An'am, 6:154, 162–163
Al-A'raf, 7:179, 189
Al-Tawbah, 9:71
Yunus, 10:45
Yusuf, 12:24
Al-Nahl, 16:72
Ta Ha, 20:131

Al-Mu'minun, 23:12–14
Al-Nur, 24:6–9, 32–33
Al-Furqan, 25:74
Al-Rum, 30:21, 50
Al-Ahzab, 33:21, 32, 35
Ya Sin, 36:36
Al-Zumar, 39:6
Al-Shura, 42:11, 49–50, 50 [endnote]
Muhammad, 47:12
Al-Dhariyat, 51:49
Al-Najm, 53:45
Al-Mujadilah, 58:1
Al-Munafiqun, 63:4
Al-Taghabun, 64:14
Al-Talaq, 65:6
Al-Tahrim, 66:5
Al-Qiyamah, 75:39
Al-Mursalat, 77:20–23
Al-Inshiqaq, 84:6
Al-Tariq, 86:5–7
Al-Tin, 95:4

Chapter 19: Love and Extra-marital Sex
Al-Baqarah, 2:165, 216, 221
Aal 'Imran, 3:14
Al-Nisa', 4:19, 27
Yusuf, 12:24, 25, 32, 52
Al-Isra', 17:32
Al-Nur, 24:1–5

Chapter 20: Love and the Eyes
Al-Baqarah, 2:69 [endnote]
Al-Hijr, 15:88
Ta Ha, 20:131
Al-Nur, 24:30–31
Ghafir, 40:19
Al-Zukhruf, 43:71 [endnote]
Muhammad, 47:30
Al-Falaq, 113:5 [endnote]

PART FOUR: LOVE

Chapter 21: The Different Kinds of Love
Al-Baqarah, 2:144, 186, 207, 221, 228, 254, 257

Index of Qur'anic Verses Cited by Chapter*

Aal ʿImran, 3:14
Al-Nisaʾ, 4:27, 125, 127, 129, 172
Al-Maʾidah, 5:70, 82, 119
Al-Anʿam, 6:71, 113, 114, 164
Al-Aʿraf, 7:81
Al-Tawbah, 9:16, 23, 40, 59, 96, 128
Hud, 11:73, 90
Yusuf, 12:24, 30, 33, 91, 95
Al-Nahl, 16:107
Al-Israʾ, 17:21, 32, 70
Maryam, 19:13, 47, 52, 55, 96
Ta Ha, 20:39
Al-Anbiyaʾ, 21:28, 90
Al-Muʾminun, 23:57
Al-Nur, 24:2, 61
Al-Furqan, 25:43, 65
Al-Shuʿaraʾ, 26:101, 224, 225
Al-Rum, 30:21, 29
Al-Ahzab, 33:52
Fussilat, 41:34
Al-Shura, 42:23
Al-Zukhruf, 43:67
Al-Najm, 53:23
Al-Waqiʿah, 56:66
Al-Hadid, 57:27
Al-Mujadilah, 58:22
Al-Hashr, 59:9
Al-Munafiqun, 63:4
Al-Jinn, 72:1
Al-Aʿla, 87:16
Al-Sharh, 94:8

Chapter 22: The Stages of Love

Al-Baqarah, 2:23, 46, 124, 137, 146, 152, 164, 165, 186, 200, 207, 212, 221, 223, 228, 230, 245, 249, 254, 260
Aal ʿImran, 3:14, 28, 31, 141, 154, 170, 191
Al-Nisaʾ, 4:9, 24, 27, 104, 125, 127, 129
Al-Maʾidah, 5:82, 83, 119
Al-Anʿam, 6:14, 52, 104, 125, 162
Al-Aʿraf, 7:55, 56, 143, 156, 189, 196, 201, 205
Al-Anfal, 8:2, 19

Al-Tawbah, 9:92, 96, 100, 114, 128
Yunus, 10:7, 25, 45, 58, 62, 94, 101
Hud, 11:3, 73, 75, 90, 121
Yusuf, 12:8–9, 15, 18, 24, 25, 26, 30, 31, 32, 33, 39, 40, 51, 52, 53, 83, 84, 85, 86–87, 101
Al-Raʿd, 13:26, 27, 28
Ibrahim, 14:7
Al-Hijr, 15:3, 39
Al-Nahl, 16:50, 128
Al-Israʾ, 17:23, 25, 47
Al-Kahf, 18:28, 46
Maryam, 19:52, 58, 65, 96
Ta Ha, 20:39, 84, 114, 131
Al-Anbiyaʾ, 21:90
Al-Hajj, 22:5, 34, 35
Al-Muʾminun, 23:53, 57, 68
Al-Nur, 24:60
Al-Furqan, 25:43, 74
Al-Naml, 27:43–44, 44
Al-Qasas, 28:10, 24–25
Al-ʿAnkabut, 29:23, 69
Al-Rum, 30:8, 21, 50
Al-Ahzab, 33:4, 10, 11, 21, 41, 51, 52, 53
Fatir, 35:15
Ya Sin, 36:58
Sad, 38:24, 29
Al-Zumar, 39:2–3, 22, 34, 36, 54–5
Ghafir, 40:7, 60
Al-Shura, 42:19, 22
Al-Zukhruf, 43:67, 81
Al-Ahqaf, 46:15
Muhammad, 47:38,
Al-Fath, 48:12, 29
Al-Hujurat, 49:7, 13, 14
Qaf, 50:32
Al-Dhariyat, 51:56
Al-Tur, 52:48
Al-Najm, 53:3, 11
Al-Qamar, 54:37
Al-Waqiʿah, 56:25–26, 95
Al-Mujadilah, 58:22
Al-Munafiqun, 63:4
Al-Taghabun, 64:14
Al-Talaq, 65:3, 6
Nuh, 71:10

Al-Jinn, 72:1
Al-Muzzammil, 73:8, 20
Al-Duha, 93:11
Al-Sharh, 94:1, 7, 8
Al-Qadr, 97:3–5
Al-Bayyinah, 98:8
Al-Takathur, 102:5, 7

Chapter 23: Falling in Love

Al-Baqarah, 2:20, 33, 44, 75, 197, 245 [endnote], 247, 269
Al-Nisaʾ, 4:4–6, 43, 128
Al-Maʾidah, 5:54, 100
Al-Anʿam, 6:104, 113, 125
Al-Tawbah, 9:45
Hud, 11:120
Yusuf, 12:45, 53, 86–87, 87
Al-Raʿd, 13:4
Ibrahim, 14:37, 43, 52
Al-Nahl, 16:106
Al-Israʾ, 17:19, 85
Ta Ha, 20:66
Al-Hajj, 22:46
Al-Muʾminun, 23:20
Al-Furqan, 25:32
Al-Shuʿaraʾ, 26:113
Al-Naml, 27:7
Al-Qasas, 28:10, 29
Al-Rum, 30:30
Al-Sajdah, 32:9
Sad, 38:29
Ghafir, 40:15
Al-Fath, 48:4
Al-Hujurat, 49:14
Al-Najm, 53:11
Al-Rahman, 55:1–4, 12
Al-Hashr, 59:9, 10
Al-Munafiqun, 63:4
Al-Taghabun, 64:16
Al-Talaq, 65:4 [endnote], 7 [endnote]
Al-Tahrim, 66:3
Al-Mulk, 67:10
Al-Qiyamah, 75:2
Al-Fajr, 89:27
Al-Sharh, 94:5–7 [endnote]
Al-ʿAlaq, 96:3–5

Chapter 24: The Growth of Love
Al-Baqarah, 2:44–46, 165, 216, 265, 282, 285
Aal 'Imran, 3:31, 139, 190–191
Al-Nisa', 4:19, 103, 118–120
Al-Ma'idah, 5:100
Al-An'am, 6:91
Al-A'raf, 7:201
Al-Anfal, 8:29
Al-Tawbah, 9:69, 125
Yunus, 10:9
Yusuf, 12:22
Al-Ra'd, 13:27–28
Al-Nahl, 16:128
Al-Isra', 17:64–65
Al-Kahf, 18:23–24, 28
Maryam, 19:96
Ta Ha, 20:39, 42, 124
Al-'Ankabut, 29:45, 69
Al-Ahzab, 33:41–42
Fatir, 35:28
Fussilat, 41:30–32
Al-Zukhruf, 43:36
Muhammad, 47:17
Al-Tur, 52:11–12
Al-Rahman, 55:60
Al-Hadid, 57:16, 28
Al-Mujadilah, 58:11
Al-Munafiqun, 63:9–10
Al-Taghabun, 64:9, 11, 16
Al-Talaq, 65:2–3
Al-Muzzammil, 73:8
Al-Qiyamah, 75:14–15
Al-Insan, 76:25
Al-Nazi'at, 79:40–41
Al-Layl, 92:5–7
Al-Nas, 114:5

Chapter 25: The Two Circles of Love
Al-Baqarah, 2:165, 212, 245, 257, 261
Aal 'Imran, 3:13–16, 27, 37
Al-Nisa', 4:31 [endnote], 40
Al-An'am, 6:160
Al-Tawbah, 9:102
Yunus, 10:26
Yusuf, 12:33
Al-Isra', 17:32

Ta Ha, 20:39
Al-Nur, 24:31, 38
Al-Ahzab, 33:59
Saba, 34:37
Al-Zumar, 39:10
Ghafir, 40:40
Al-Shura, 42:37 [endnote]
Al-Fath, 48:6
Al-Najm, 53:2 [endnote]
Al-Rahman, 55:60
Al-Hadid, 57:11, 18, 28
Al-Taghabun, 64:17
Al-Qalam, 68:4 [endnote]
Al-Duha, 93:7 [endnote]
Al-Sharh, 94:1 [endnote]

Chapter 26: The Triangle of Love
Al-Baqarah, 2:115, 186, 212
Aal 'Imran, 3:14
Al-Ma'idah, 5:110
Al-An'am, 6:14 [endnote], 79–80 [endnote], 103, 137
Al-A'raf, 7:62, 7:172
Al-Anfal, 8:48
Yunus, 10:85 [endnote], 101, 104 [endnote]
Hud, 11:17
Yusuf, 12: 24, 26, 56, 76, 86–87, 101
Al-Ra'd, 13:16 [endnote]
Ibrahim, 14:10 [endnote]
Al-Hijr, 15:39
Al-Nahl, 16:2, 63, 78
Al-Isra', 17:85
Al-Kahf, 18:10 [endnote], 65
Ta Ha, 20:49–50 [endnote]
Al-Anbiya', 21:56 [endnote]
Al-Mu'minun, 23:86 [endnote]
Al-Furqan, 25:45–46 [endnote], 59
Al-Shu'ara', 26:23–29 [endnote]
Al-Naml, 27:4, 24, 60–64 [endnote]
Al-'Ankabut, 29:38
Al-Rum, 30:50
Fatir, 35:8
Ghafir, 40:15

Fussilat, 41:25
Al-Zukhruf, 43:82 [endnote]
Muhammad, 47:14
Al-Fath, 48:12
Al-Hujurat, 49:7
Al-Dhariyat, 51:23 [endnote]
Al-Tur, 52:1
Al-Waqi'ah, 56:30 [endnote], 75–76 [endnote]
Al-Tahrim, 66:3
Al-Nazi'at, 79:40–41
'Abasa, 80:24–32 [endnote]
Al-Ghashiyah, 88:17–20 [endnote]
Al-Fajr, 89:1–5 [endnote]
Al-Layl, 92:1–2 [endnote]
Al-Duha, 93:1–2 [endnote]
Al-Shams, 91:1–7 [endnote]
Al-Tin, 95:1–2 [endnote]
Al-'Adiyat, 100:1 [endnote]
Al-'Asr, 103:1 [endnote]

Chapter 27: The Hierarchies of Beauty and of Love
Al-Baqarah, 2:165, 221
Aal 'Imran, 3:14, 195
Al-Ma'idah, 5:15, 54, 100
Al-An'am, 6:137
Al-A'raf, 7:31–32, 180
Al-Anfal, 8:2
Al-Tawbah, 9:111, 128
Yunus, 10:88
Yusuf, 12:3, 18, 83
Al-Nahl, 16:6
Al-Isra', 17:18, 32, 110
Al-Kahf, 18:19
Ta Ha, 20:8, 131
Al-Mu'minun, 23:14
Al-Nur, 24:31
Al-Shu'ara', 26:224–226
Al-Qasas, 28:60
Al-Sajdah, 32:7
Al-Ahzab, 33:6, 21, 28, 45–46, 49, 52
Fatir, 35:12
Sad, 38:1, 30–32
Al-Zumar, 39:22–23
Ghafir, 40:64
Fussilat, 41:25

Index of Qur'anic Verses Cited by Chapter*

Al-Fath, 48:29
Al-Hujurat, 49:7
Al-Hashr, 59:9
Al-Taghabun, 64:3
Al-Maʿarij, 70:5
Al-Muzzammil, 73:8–10
Al-Qiyamah, 75:20–21
Al-Fajr, 89:20
Al-Sharh, 94:7–8
Al-Tin, 95:4

Chapter 28: The Opposites of Beauty and of Love
Al-Baqarah, 2:216, 285
Al-Maʾidah, 5:14, 19, 91
Al-Anfal, 8:2, 8
Al-Tawbah, 9:32, 72, 81, 102
Al-Qasas, 28:42
Al-Sajdah, 32:7
Muhammad, 47:9, 28
Al-Hujurat, 49:7, 12
Al-Hashr, 59:9
Al-Taghabun, 64:16

Chapter 29: The End of Love
Al-Baqarah, 2:167, 260
Aal ʿImran, 3:76, 173
Al-Nisaʾ, 4:20–21, 73, 119
Al-Anʿam, 6:34, 115
Al-Aʿraf, 7:16, 175–176, 182
Al-Anfal, 8:2
Al-Tawbah, 9:124
Yunus, 10:64
Yusuf, 12:68
Al-Hijr, 15:39
Al-Israʾ, 17:34, 53, 62–64, 77
Al-Kahf, 18:13, 27
Maryam, 19:76
Al-Muʾminun, 23:101
Al-Furqan, 25:28
Al-ʿAnkabut, 29:25
Al-Ahzab, 33:22, 62
Fatir, 35:43
Sad, 38:82
Fussilat, 41:34
Al-Zukhruf, 43:67
Muhammad, 47:17
Al-Fath, 48:4, 10, 23
Qaf, 50:29

Al-Najm, 53:37
Al-Mumtahanah, 60:3, 4–5, 7
Al-Qalam, 68:44
Al-Maʿarij, 70:10–14
Al-Muddathir, 74:31
ʿAbasa, 80:34–37
Al-Mutaffifin, 83:14

Chapter 30: The Nature of Love
Al-Baqarah, 2:154–156, 245
Al-Nisaʾ, 4:129
Al-Anʿam, 6:162–163
Al-Anfal, 8:53
Al-Tawbah, 9:111
Yusuf, 12:39
Al-Raʿd, 13:11
Ibrahim, 14:19–20
Al-Hijr, 15:48
Al-Ahzab, 33:4
Fatir, 35:15
Fussilat, 41:49
Muhammad, 47:38
Qaf, 50:15, 38
Al-Rahman, 55:29
Al-Sharh, 94:5–6

Chapter 31: Love and Happiness
Al-Baqarah, 2:25, 137, 165
Aal ʿImran, 3:14
Al-Anʿam, 6:128
Al-Tawbah, 9:81–82
Yunus, 10:7
Hud, 11:105–108
Al-Raʿd, 13:28
Ta Ha, 20:124
Al-ʿAnkabut, 29:64
Al-Ahzab, 33:4
Al-Zumar, 39:36
Al-Bayyinah, 98:8

Chapter 32: Love and Beauty in Paradise
Al-Baqarah, 2:25
Aal ʿImran, 3:170 [endnote]
Al-Nisaʾ, 4:69
Al-Anʿam, 6:127 [endnote]
Al-Aʿraf, 7:32, 43[endnote]
Hud, 11:105–108 [endnote]

Al-Raʿd, 13:23
Al-Hijr, 15:45–48, 45–46 [endnote]
Fatir, 35:34–35
Ya Sin, 36:56, 58 [endnote]
Al-Saffat, 37:22, 48
Sad, 38:52
Ghafir, 40:8
Al-Zukhruf, 43:66–67, 66–72, 70
Al-Dukhan, 44:54
Muhammad, 47:15
Al-Tur, 52:20, 21
Al-Rahman, 55:56, 72
Al-Waqiʿah, 56:22–23, 25–26 [endnote], 36–37
Al-Haqqah, 69:21 [endnote]
Al-Qiyamah, 75:22–23
Al-Nabaʾ, 78:33
Al-Ghashiyah, 88:8–9 [endnote]
Al-Fajr, 89:27–30 [endnote]
Al-Zalzalah, 99:7
Al-Qariʿah, 101:7 [endnote]

PART FIVE: THE BELOVED (BEAUTY; THE MEETING WITH GOD; BEATITUDE)

Chapter 33: Beauty and its Components
Al-Naml, 27:88
Al-Sajdah, 32:7
Al-Rahman, 55:1–13, 78

Chapter 34: Taste
Al-Anʿam, 6:76–78
Yusuf, 12:31
Al-Israʾ, 17:84
Al-Kahf, 18:48 [endnote153]
Al-Muʾminun, 23:52–53
Al-Rum, 30:32
Al-Hujurat, 49:13

Chapter 35: The Nature of Beauty
Al-Baqarah, 2:115
Aal ʿImran, 3:124–6

Al-A'raf, 7:31
Yusuf, 12:23–25, 31, 83, 86–87
Al-Hijr, 15:88
Al-Nahl, 16:6–7
Ta Ha, 20:131
Al-Naml, 27:88
Al-Sajdah, 32:7
Al-Fath, 48:10, 18
Al-Hadid, 57:3
Al-Infitar, 82:6–8
Al-Layl, 92:5–7

Chapter 36: Love and Death
Al-Baqarah, 2:54, 95–96, 154, 165, 207
Aal 'Imran, 3:143, 157–158, 169, 185
Al-Nisa', 4:66–70, 74, 78, 100
Al-Ma'idah, 5:30
Al-An'am, 6:122, 161–162, 162–164
Al-A'raf, 7:40 [endnote]
Al-Anfal, 8:17 [endnote], 24
Al-Tawbah, 9:41, 111
Yunus, 10:10, 25, 51–52, 62
Yusuf, 12:18, 31, 53, 83
Al-Nahl, 16:32, 96 [endnote]
Maryam, 19:62–63
Ta Ha, 20:96
Al-Anbiya', 21:35
Al-Hajj, 22:58–59
Al-Furqan, 25:75
Al-'Ankabut, 29:57
Al-Ahzab, 33:23
Fatir, 35:17–19

Ya Sin, 36:58
Al-Zumar, 39:29–30
Qaf, 50:15 [endnote]
Al-Waqi'ah, 56:25–26
Al-Jumu'ah, 62:6–7
Al-Fajr, 89:27–30
Al-Nas, 114:5

Chapter 37: The Meeting with God and Beatitude
Al-An'am, 6:103
Al-A'raf, 7:143
Al-Anfal, 8:19
Al-Tawbah, 9:72
Yusuf, 12:87
Al-Nahl, 16:2
Al-Kahf, 18:65
Al-Nur, 24:30
Ghafir, 40:15
Al-Najm, 53:11, 17–18
Al-Rahman, 55:46
Al-Qiyamah, 75:22–23

Chapter 38: The True Intended Object behind Love
Al-Baqarah, 2:115
Aal 'Imran, 3:14
Al-Nisa', 4:142
Al-An'am, 6:76–82
Al-Tawbah, 9:118
Yunus, 10:36, 66
Al-Isra', 17:23
Ta Ha, 20:120
Al-Naml, 27:24
Al-Rum, 30:7

Al-Shura, 42:11
Al-Fath, 48:11
Al-Najm, 53:29–30
Al-Hadid, 57:3
Al-Munafiqun, 63:1
Al-Infitar, 82:6–8
Al-Mutaffifin, 83:14

SUMMARY

Chapter 39: Conclusion
Al-Baqarah, 2:165
Aal 'Imran, 3:31
Al-Ma'idah, 5:54
Al-An'am, 6:14, 85
Yunus, 10:7–10
Al-Hijr, 15:88
Al-Isra', 17:32, 44
Al-Shu'ara', 26:3
Al-Zumar, 39:12
Ghafir, 40:7
Al-Jumu'ah, 62:6–7
Al-Qalam, 68:4
Al-Takwir, 81:26
Al-Balad, 90:10

Epigraph
Al-Fatihah, 1:1–7
Al-Baqarah, 2:165

Postscript
Saba, 34:1
Al-Safaat, 37:180–182

INDEX OF QUR'ANIC VERSES CITED BY QUR'ANIC CHAPTER

Al-Fatihah, 1:1–7 (It has 7 verses in total.)

Al-Baqarah, 2:9, 17–18, 20, 21, 23–24, 25, 29–34, 44, 45, 46, 47, 54, 65, 69, 75, 83, 94–96, 115, 124, 136, 137, 138, 144, 146, 147, 152, 153, 154–156, 164, 165, 167, 176, 177, 186, 187, 189, 190, 191, 194, 195, 197, 200, 205, 207, 212, 215, 216, 221, 222, 223, 228–237, 245, 247, 249, 250, 253, 254, 255, 256, 257, 260, 261, 265, 269, 272, 276, 279, 282, 284, 285 (It has 286 verses in total.)

Aal ʿImran, 3:3, 13–16, 27, 28–30, 31, 32, 36–39, 45, 50, 57, 61, 76, 83, 84, 92, 97, 104, 110, 113–115, 121, 124–126, 133–136, 139, 140, 141, 143, 146, 148, 154, 157–158, 159, 164, 169–170, 173, 185, 189–191, 194, 195 (It has 200 verses in total.)

Al-Nisaʾ, 4:1, 4–6, 9, 11, 19, 20–21, 22–24, 25, 27, 31, 32, 34, 35, 36, 40, 43, 48, 66–70, 73, 74, 78, 82, 93, 100, 103, 104, 107, 108, 110, 113, 115, 116, 118–120, 125, 127, 128, 129, 135, 142, 145, 147–148, 150–152, 155, 158, 163, 165–166, 171, 172 (It has 176 verses in total.)

Al-Maʾidah, 5:2, 8, 12, 13, 14, 15, 18, 19, 20, 30, 32, 33, 42, 46, 54, 55–56, 60, 64, 70, 82, 83, 87, 91, 93, 100, 110, 114, 116, 119 (It has 120 verses in total.)

Al-Anʿam, 6:12, 14, 34, 38, 41, 51, 52, 54, 71, 76–82, 83–87, 91, 98, 103–104, 108, 113, 114, 115, 122, 125, 127, 128, 137, 141, 151, 154, 160, 161–164 (It has 165 verses in total.)

Al-Aʿraf, 7:7, 11, 16, 31, 32, 38–39, 40, 43, 52, 54, 55, 56, 57, 58, 62, 81, 94, 140, 143, 145, 150, 154, 156, 170, 172, 175–176, 179, 180, 182, 189, 196, 201, 205, 206 (It has 206 verses in total.)

Al-Anfal, 8:2–4, 8, 13, 17, 19, 24, 28, 29, 35, 46, 48, 53, 58, 66, 74–75 (It has 75 verses in total.)

Al-Tawbah, 9:4, 7, 16, 23, 24, 30, 32, 36, 38, 40, 41, 45, 46, 59, 61, 69, 71, 72, 80, 81, 82, 91, 92, 96, 97, 99, 100, 102–104, 107, 109, 111, 114, 117, 118, 120, 123, 124, 125, 128 (It has 129 verses in total.)

Yunus, 10:4, 7, 9, 10, 12, 24, 25, 26, 36–39, 45, 55, 58, 62–65, 66, 82, 85, 88, 94, 100, 101, 103, 104 (It has 109 verses in total.)

Hud, 11:1, 3, 5, 7, 13–14, 17, 27–31, 37, 45–46, 73, 75, 79, 88, 90, 105–108, 118–119, 120, 121 (It has 123 verses in total.)

Yusuf, 12:3, 8–9, 15, 18, 22, 23–25, 26, 30, 31, 32, 33, 39, 40, 45, 51, 52, 53, 56, 68, 76, 83, 86–87, 90–92, 95, 101, 111 (It has 111 verses in total.)

Al-Raʿd, 13:2, 4, 6, 11, 15, 16, 21–24, 26, 27, 28 (It has 43 verses in total.)

Ibrahim, 14:7, 8, 10, 19–20, 31, 34, 36–37, 43, 52 (It has 52 verses in total.)

Al-Hijr, 15:3, 28–34, 39, 45–48, 49, 85–86, 87, 88, 99 (It has 99 verses in total.)

Al-Nahl, 16:2, 3–16, 18, 23, 32, 50, 53–54, 61, 63, 72, 74, 78, 89, 96, 97, 106–107, 126, 127–128 (It has 128 verses in total.)

Al-Israʾ, 17: 12, 18, 19, 20, 21, 22–39, 44, 47, 53, 55, 62–64, 65, 70, 77, 79, 84, 85, 88, 89, 105, 110 (It has 111 verses in total.)

Al-Kahf, 18:1, 6, 9, 10, 13, 19, 23–24, 27, 28, 29, 46, 48, 54, 65, 76, 109 (It has 110 verses in total.)

Maryam, 19:13, 21, 47, 23–25, 51–53, 54, 55, 58, 62–63, 65, 76, 96 (It has 98 verses in total.)

Ta Ha, 20:8, 39, 41, 42, 46, 47, 49–50, 66, 84, 96, 114, 120, 124, 131, 132 (It has 135 verses in total.)

Al-Anbiyaʾ, 21:28, 35, 56, 89, 90, 91, 107 (It has 112 verses in total.)

Al-Hajj, 22:5, 18, 30, 32–35, 38–40, 46, 52, 58–59 (It has 78 verses in total.)

Al-Muʾminun, 23:1–11, 12–14, 20, 27, 50, 52, 53, 57–63, 68, 86, 96, 101 (It has 118 verses in total.)

Al-Nur, 24:1–5, 6–9, 22, 24, 27, 30–31, 32–33,

37–38, 58, 60, 61, 62 (It has 64 verses in total.)
Al-Furqan, 25:15–16, 28, 32, 43, 45–46, 52, 54, 59, 62, 63, 65, 74, 75, 77 (It has 77 verses in total.)
Al-Shuʿara', 26:3, 13–15, 23–29, 62, 88–89, 101, 111–115, 124–125, 142–143, 161–162, 177–178, 208, 214, 215, 224–226 (It has 227 verses in total.)
Al-Naml, 27:4, 7, 24, 30, 44, 60–64, 88 (It has 93 verses in total.)
Al-Qasas, 28:10, 24, 25, 29, 42, 60, 70, 76, 77 (It has 88 verses in total.)
Al-ʿAnkabut, 29:6, 8, 25, 38, 45, 57, 64, 69 (It has 69 verses in total.)
Al-Rum, 30:1–4, 7, 8, 21, 22, 26, 29–30, 32, 45, 47, 50, 58 (It has 60 verses in total.)
Luqman, 31:14–15, 18, 20, 27, 28 (It has 34 verses in total.)
Al-Sajdah, 32:4, 7–9, 15–19, 23–25, 32 (It has 30 verses in total.)
Al-Ahzab, 33:4, 6, 7, 10–11, 21, 22–23, 28, 32–33, 35, 37, 40, 41, 42, 43, 45–46, 49, 51, 52, 53, 56, 57, 59, 62, 69, 72–73 (It has 73 verses in total.)
Saba, 34:1, 37, 46 (It has 54 verses in total.)
Fatir, 35:8, 12, 15, 18, 24, 28, 34–35, 39, 43, 45 (It has 45 verses in total.)
Ya Sin, 36:36, 56, 58, 65 (It has 83 verses in total.)
Al-Saffat, 37:22, 48, 123, 139, 180–182 (It has 182 verses in total.)
Sad, 38:1, 24, 29, 30–32, 52, 72, 75, 82 (It has 88 verses in total.)
Al-Zumar, 39:2–3, 6, 7, 9, 10, 12, 14, 22–23, 27–28, 29–30, 34, 36, 38, 53–55 (It has 75 verses in total.)
Ghafir, 40:7, 8, 10, 14, 15, 17, 19, 34, 35, 40, 57, 60, 64, 65, 67, 78 (It has 85 verses in total.)
Fussilat, 41:17, 20–21, 25, 30–32, 34, 35, 43, 49, 53 (It has 54 verses in total.)
Al-Shura, 42:11, 13, 19, 22, 23, 25–26, 36–42, 43, 49–50 (It has 53 verses in total.)
Al-Zukhruf, 43:36, 59, 66–72, 81–82, 89 (It has 89 verses in total.)
Al-Dukhan, 44:32–33, 54 (It has 59 verses in total.)
Al-Jathiyah, 45:12–13, 14, 16–17, 22 (It has 37 verses in total.)
Al-Ahqaf, 46:9, 15–18, 24–25, 35 (It has 35 verses in total.)
Muhammad, 47:9, 12, 14, 15, 17, 19, 28, 30, 32, 35, 38 (It has 38 verses in total.)
Al-Fath, 48:4, 6, 8, 10, 11, 12, 18, 23, 29 (It has 29 verses in total.)
Al-Hujurat, 49:1–5, 7, 9–10, 12, 13, 14 (It has 18 verses in total.)
Qaf, 50:8, 15, 16, 29, 32, 38 (It has 45 verses in total.)
Al-Dhariyat, 51:20–21, 23, 49, 50, 56 (It has 60 verses in total.)
Al-Tur, 52:1, 11–12, 20–21, 33–34, 48 (It has 49 verses in total.)
Al-Najm, 53:2, 3, 11, 17–18, 23, 26, 29, 30, 31, 36, 37, 45 (It has 62 verses in total.)
Al-Qamar, 54:37 (It has 55 verses in total.)
Al-Rahman, 55:1–13, 27, 29, 46, 56, 60, 72, 78 (It has 78 verses in total.)
Al-Waqiʿah, 56:17–18, 22–23, 25–26, 30, 36–37, 66, 75–76, 95 (It has 96 verses in total.)
Al-Hadid, 57:3, 4, 11, 18, 16, 20, 23, 27, 28 (It has 29 verses in total.)
Al-Mujadilah, 58:5, 7, 11, 22 (It has 22 verses in total.)
Al-Hashr, 59:4, 5, 8–10, 24 (It has 24 verses in total.)
Al-Mumtahanah, 60:1; 3, 4, 5–6, 7–8, 12 (It has 13 verses in total.)
Al-Saff, 61:2–4 (It has 14 verses in total.)
Al-Jumuʿah, 62: 2, 6–7 (It has 11 verses in total.)
Al-Munafiqun, 63:1, 4, 6, 8, 9, 10 (It has 11 verses in total.)
Al-Taghabun, 64:3, 9, 11, 14, 15, 16, 17 (It has 18 verses in total.)
Al-Talaq, 65:2, 3, 4, 6–7, 10, 11 (It has 12 verses in total.)
Al-Tahrim, 66:3, 5, 9 (It has 12 verses in total.)
Al-Mulk, 67:2, 10, 12–14, 15 (It has 30 verses in total.)
Al-Qalam, 68:4, 44 (It has 52 verses in total.)
Al-Haqqah, 69:21, 40, 51 (It has 52 verses in total.)
Al-Maʿarij, 70:5, 10–14, 42 (It has 44 verses in total.)
Nuh, 71:10 (It has 28 verses in total.)
Al-Jinn, 72:1 (It has 28 verses in total.)
Al-Muzzammil, 73:8–10, 20 (It has 20 verses in total.)
Al-Muddathir, 74:31 (It has 56 verses in total.)
Al-Qiyamah, 75:2, 14–15, 20–21, 22–23, 39 (It has 40 verses in total.)

Index of Qur'anic Verses Cited by Qur'anic Chapter

Al-Insan, 76:2-3, 6, 8, 25, 29-31 (It has 31 verses in total.)
Al-Mursalat, 77:20-23 (It has 50 verses in total.)
Al-Naba', 78:33 (It has 40 verses in total.)
Al-Nazi'at, 79:27-33, 40-41 (It has 46 verses in total.)
'Abasa, 80:24-32, 34-37 (It has 42 verses in total.)
Al-Takwir, 81:26 (It has 29 verses in total.)
Al-Infitar, 82:6-8 (It has 19 verses in total.)
Al-Mutaffifin, 83:14, 18-28 (It has 36 verses in total.)
Al-Inshiqaq, 84:6 (It has 25 verses in total.)
Al-Buruj, 85:4-8, 14-15 (It has 22 verses in total.)
Al-Tariq, 86:5-7 (It has 17 verses in total.)
Al-A'la, 87:16, 18-19 (It has 19 verses in total.)
Al-Ghasiyah, 88:8-9, 17-21 (It has 26 verses in total.)
Al-Fajr, 89:1-5, 20, 27-30 (It has 30 verses in total.)
Al-Balad, 90:10 (It has 20 verses in total.)
Al-Shams, 91:1-7 (It has 15 verses in total.)
Al-Layl, 92:1-2, 5-7, 20 (It has 21 verses in total.)
Al-Duha, 93:1-2, 5, 7, 11 (It has 11 verses in total.)
Al-Sharh, 94:1, 4, 5-6, 7- 8 (It has 8 verses in total.)
Al-Tin, 95:1-8 (It has 8 verses in total.)
Al-'Alaq, 96:3-5 (It has 19 verses in total.)
Al-Qadr, 97:3-5 (It has 5 verses in total.)
Al-Bayyinah, 98:8 (It has 8 verses in total.)
Al-Zalzalah, 99:7 (It has 8 verses in total.)
Al-'Adiyat, 100:1 (It has 11 verses in total.)
Al-Qari'ah, 101:7 (It has 11 verses in total.)
Al-Takathur, 102:5, 7 (It has 8 verses in total.)
Al-'Asr, 103:1 (It has 3 verses in total.)
Al-Humazah, 104:1 (It has 9 verses in total.)
Al-Fil, 105:1 (It has 5 verses in total.)
Quraysh, 106:1-4 (It has 4 verses in total.)
Al-Ma'un, 107:1-7 (It has 7 verses in total.)
Al-Kawthar, 108:1-3 (It has 3 verses in total.)
Al-Kafirun, 109:1-6 (It has 6 verses in total.)
Al-Nasr, 110:3 (It has 3 verses in total.)
Al-Masad, 111:1-5 (It has 5 verses in total.)
Al-Ikhlas, 112:1-2 (It has 4 verses in total.)
Al-Falaq, 113:5 (It has 5 verses in total.)
Al-Nas, 114:5 (It has 6 verses in total.)

(1345 verses cited in total, nearly all in their entirety, and many of them more than once.)

N.B.: The Holy Qur'an has 114 Chapters or *Surahs*. These are not arranged in any thematic or chronological order but rather (excluding the first and most important *Surah*, *Al-Fatihah*—the 'Opening' of the Book—which has seven verses) roughly in order of length. Thus the second *Surah*—*Surat Al-Baqarah*—has 286 verses, and the shortest *Surahs* at the end of the Holy Quran (*Surat Al-'Asr* [*Surah* no.103], *Surat Al-Kawthar* [*Surah* no. 108] and *Surat Al-Nasr* [*Surah* no. 110]) have only 3 verses. In total, there are 6236 verses (of varying lengths) in the standard Kufic division of verses of Abu 'Abd Al-Rahman Al-Sulami (used herein).

INDEX OF PROPHETIC HADITHS CITED BY CHAPTER

Hadith	Cited
God is Beautiful, and He loves beauty.	Ch. 3
Verily God has ninety-nine Names…	Ch. 3, endnote
I am God (*Allah*), I am the…	Ch. 4
[*Ayat al-Kursi* is] the greatest verse…	Ch. 4
If one does not ask God…	Ch. 4, endnote
God is Kind and He loves…	Ch. 4, endnote
The greatest *Surah* in the Holy Qur'an…	Ch. 4
When God created the world…	Ch. 5
I was a hidden treasure,…	Ch. 5, endnote
Every child is born primordially pure,…	Ch. 5
God Almighty says: "…And I created all…	Ch. 5
A person is with those they love.	Ch. 5, endnote
You weep for the remembrance you used…	Ch. 6
The Prophet gave a sermon…	Ch. 6
God is beautiful, and He loves beauty.	Ch. 7
Virtue (*al-ihsan*) means to worship God…	Ch. 7
One hundred and twenty-four thousand…	Ch. 8, endnote
I am God's beloved, and…	Ch. 8
There have been made beloved to me,…	Ch. 10
Beloved to me have been…	Ch. 10, endnote
I hear that my Lord has given me leeway…	Ch. 11
O God, make Your love more beloved…	Ch. 12
O God, provide me with Your love…	Ch. 12
There have been made beloved to…	Ch. 12
The first person to be judged…	Ch. 12, endnote
Actions are defined by their intentions…	Ch. 12
The believers will be gathered…	Ch. 13
None of you believes until I am…	Ch. 13
Three [things] there are which,…	Ch. 13
I have been sent to complete…	Ch. 13
Whosoever invokes one blessing…	Ch. 13
O People! Remember God,…	Ch. 13

You shall be with those you love.	Ch. 13
You shall be with those you love.	Ch. 13, endnote
O God, these are my Household,…	Ch. 14
Whose master I am,…	Ch. 14
Are you not content to have…	Ch. 14
Hasan and Al-Husayn are the lords…	Ch. 14
I leave with you that which…	Ch. 14
Say: O God, bless Muhammad…	Ch. 14
Whosoever shows enmity to a friend…	Ch. 15
If God loves a servant, He gives…	Ch. 15
If God loves a servant, He calls Gabriel…	Ch. 15
You have made a fine step…	Ch. 15, endnote
The struggler is the one who…	Ch. 15, endnote
When God loves a servant, He protects…	Ch. 15, endnote
Invoke God until they say: …	Ch. 15
Three [things] which, if they are…	Ch. 15, endnote
I shall be the master of humankind…	Ch. 15, endnote
I shall be the master of the sons…	Ch. 15, endnote
Stand for a paradise as vast…	Ch. 15, endnote
Whosoever loves to meet God,…	Ch. 15, endnote
They are not filthy; for they are…	Ch. 16
Your mother; then your mother; then…	Ch. 16, endnote
By Him in whose hand is my soul…	Ch. 17
The Compassionate One has mercy…	Ch. 17
God does not have mercy on those…	Ch. 17
None of you believes until he loves…	Ch. 17, endnote
What say you, and what think you…	Ch. 17
The best money is the money…	Ch. 18
The best of you is the best to his wife…	Ch. 18
Whosoever shows enmity to a friend…	Ch. 18, endnote
Beware the insight of the believer,…	Ch. 20
Beloved to me have been…	Ch. 20, endnote
The glance of the eye is a poison…	Ch. 20
O 'Ali, do not follow one glance…	Ch. 20
Look upon her, for it is more likely…	Ch. 20
The [evil] eye is real…	Ch. 20, endnote
There are two groups…	Ch. 21
Be upright though…	Ch. 21

Index of Prophetic Hadiths Cited by Chapter

Lord, be a friend…	Ch. 21
God will say to the denizens of Paradise…	Ch. 21
Whosoever shows enmity to a friend…	Ch. 22, endnote
God took a firm pledge from…	Ch. 26, endnote
None spoke in the cradle save three…	Ch. 26, endnote
A woman is married for four things…	Ch. 27
Temptations come to hearts like…	Ch. 29
When the servant commits a sin…	Ch. 29
The most hateful of all permitted…	Ch. 29
Everything has a bride,…	Ch. 33
Spirits are conscripted soldiers…	Ch. 34
[Such things] as have never occurred…	Ch. 34, endnote
O God, forgive me and enter…	Ch. 35, endnote
I deem naught save that…	Ch. 35, endnote
There is not one of you but…	Ch. 36
The treasure of the believer is death.	Ch. 36
Be in this world as if you were…	Ch. 36
O Bilal, tell me what deed…	Ch. 36
Whosoever shows enmity to a friend…	Ch. 36
Look upon her for it is more likely…	Ch. 37
God will say to the denizens…	Ch. 37
Actions are defined by their intentions…	Ch. 38
The firmest bond of faith is …	Conclusion
Whosoever loves for God…	Conclusion
And is religion anything other than love …	Conclusion

ALPHABETICAL INDEX OF PROPHETIC HADITHS CITED

Hadith	Cited
A person is with those they love.	Chapter 5, endnote
A woman is married for four things…	Chapter 27
Actions are defined by their intentions…	Chapter 12; Chapter 38
And is religion anything other than love …	Conclusion
Are you not content to have…	Chapter 14
Be in this world as if you were…	Chapter 36
Be upright though …	Chapter 21
Beloved to me have been…	Chapter 10, endnote; Chapter 20, endnote
Beware the insight of the believer,…	Chapter 20
By Him in whose hand is my soul…	Chapter 17
Every child is born primordially pure,…	Chapter 5
Everything has a bride,…	Chapter 33
God Almighty says: "…And I created all…	Chapter 5
God does not have mercy on those…	Chapter 17
God is Beautiful, and He loves beauty.	Chapter 3; Chapter 7
God is Kind and He loves…	Chapter 4, endnote
God took a firm pledge from…	Chapter 26, endnote
God will say to the denizens…	Chapter 21; Chapter 37
Hasan and Al-Husayn are the lords…	Chapter 14
I am God (*Allah*), I am the…	Chapter 4
I am God's beloved, and…	Chapter 8
I deem naught save that…	Chapter 35, endnote
I have been sent to complete…	Chapter 13
I hear that my Lord has given me leeway…	Chapter 11
I leave with you that which…	Chapter 14
I shall be the master of humankind…	Chapter 15, endnote
I shall be the master of the sons…	Chapter 15, endnote
I was a hidden treasure,…	Chapter 5, endnote
If God loves a servant, He gives,…	Chapter 15
If God loves a servant, He calls Gabriel…	Chapter 15
If one does not ask God…	Chapter 4, endnote

Alphabetical Index of Prophetic Hadiths Cited

Invoke God until they say: …	Chapter 15
Look upon her, for it is more likely…	Chapter 20; Chapter 37
Lord, be a friend…	Chapter 21
None of you believes until I am…	Chapter 13
None of you believes until he loves…	Chapter 17, endnote
None spoke in the cradle save three…	Chapter 26, endnote
O ʿAli, do not follow one glance…	Chapter 20
O Bilal, tell me what deed…	Chapter 36
O God, forgive me and enter…	Chapter 35, endnote
O God, make Your love more beloved…	Chapter 12
O God, provide me with Your love…	Chapter 12
O God, these are my Household,…	Chapter 14
O People! Remember God,…	Chapter 13
One hundred and twenty-four thousand…	Chapter 8, endnote
Say: O God, bless Muhammad…	Chapter 14
Spirits are conscripted soldiers…	Chapter 34
Stand for a paradise as vast…	Chapter 15, endnote
[Such things] as have never occurred…	Chapter 34, endnote
Temptations come to hearts like…	Chapter 29
The believers will be gathered…	Chapter 13
The best money is the money…	Chapter 18
The best of you is the best to his wife…	Chapter 18
The Compassionate One has mercy…	Chapter 17
The [evil] eye is real…	Chapter 20, endnote
The firmest bond of faith is …	Conclusion
The first person to be judged…	Chapter 12
[*Ayat al-Kursi* is] the greatest verse…	Chapter 4
The glance of the eye is a poison…	Chapter 20
The greatest *Surah* in the Holy Qur'an…	Chapter 4
The greatest verse…	Chapter 12
The most hateful of all permitted…	Chapter 29
The Prophet gave a sermon…	Chapter 6
The struggler is the one who…	Chapter 15, endnote
The treasure of the believer is death.	Chapter 36
There are two groups…	Chapter 21
There have been made beloved to me,…	Chapter 10; Chapter 12
There is not one of you but…	Chapter 36
They are not filthy; for they are…	Chapter 16

Three [things] there are which,…	Chapter 13
Three [things] which, if they are…	Chapter 15, endnote
Verily God has ninety-nine Names…	Chapter 3, endnote
Virtue (*al-ihsan*) means to worship God…	Chapter 7
What say you, and what think you…	Chapter 17
When God created the world…	Chapter 5
When God loves a servant, He protects…	Chapter 15, endnote
When the servant commits a sin…	Chapter 29
Whose master I am,…	Chapter 14
Whosoever invokes one blessing…	Chapter 13
Whosoever loves for God…	Conclusion
Whosoever loves to meet God,…	Chapter 15, endnote
Whosoever shows enmity to a friend…	Chapter 15, endnote; Chapter 22, endnote; Chapter 36
You have made a fine step…	Chapter 15, endnote
You shall be with those you love.	Chapter 13; Chapter 13, endnote
You weep for the remembrance you used…	Chapter 6
Your mother; then your mother; then…	Chapter 16, endnote

GENERAL INDEX

Aaron (*Harun*), 39, 44, 46, 48, 92
al-ʿAbbas, 90
ʿAbdullah b. Salam, 92
abhorrence (*bughd*), 58, 287
Abraham (*Ibrahim*), 44, 45, 46, 47, 51–2, 85, 97, 111–12, 117, 172, 186, 188, 243, 263, 281–2; God's close friend/*khalil*, 47, 155, 156; prayer of, 96
Abu Bakr al-Siddiq, 39, 51, 91, 92, 93, 94–5
Abu Dharr, 92
Abu Hurayrah, 27, 101, 161, 240, 264
Abu Ishaq, 119
Abu Juhayfa, 93
Abu Tufayl, 92
Abu ʿUbaydah, 153, 155, 166
action (*ʿamal*), xxix, 173, 194, 203
Adam, 23–4, 32–3, 85, 113, 124, 125, 127, 198, 219, 281
ʿadam al-ihsas bil-hal, see obliviousness to oneself
admiration (*iʿjab*), xxix, 12, 160–1, 167, 169, 170, 194, 203, 245
adornment, 230, 249; love's requirement of prior adornment/triangle of adornment, 219–23, 226; *tazayyun*, xxix, 169, 194, 203, 219
adultery, see extra-marital sex
affection (*mawaddah*), xxvii, 18, 149–50, 166, 167, 191, 195, 203, 245; conjugal love, 129, 135; *hubb*, 148
affinity (*ulfah*), 8, 166–7
ʿafu, see pardoning
aggression, 40, 114, 117, 118
Ahmad b. Hanbal, 85, 86, 108
ʿAishah, 91, 94
al-ʿajal lil-tardiyah, see 'hastening to please'
alam, see suffering
ʿAli b. Abi Talib, 90, 91, 92, 93, 115, 142, 261, 273–4

ʿAli b. Husayn, 90
alms, 38, 41, 64, 70, 73, 92, 93, 94, 97, 100, 107, 109, 115, 138, 159, 192, 215
ʿamal, see action
ʿAmr b. Shuʿayb, 90
Anas b. Malik, 85, 86
angel, 23–4, 32, 33, 49, 154, 163, 204, 207, 226, 243, 267; intercession by, 18, 19; invoking blessings upon the Prophet Muhammad, 50–1, 62, 88; see also Gabriel
anger, 117–18
anguish (*gharam*), 155, 167
animal, 108 128, 138, 230, 259, 268, 281
apostasy, xxii
Arabic language, 14, 96, 147, 167
Arabs, 91, 96
al-Asma al-Husna, see Divine Names
ʿAsmaʾi, 158, 259
ʿAtaʾ b. Yasar, 92
ʿatifah, see sentiment
awb, see penitence
awliyaʾ, see saints
Azhari, 151, 259

Balʿam b. Baʿura, 240
basira, see insight
basmalah, xv, 18–19, 20
beatitude (*ridwan*), xxxiv, 88, 89, 100, 236, 279, 280
beauty, xxxi–xxxii; beauty of faith, 220, 234; beauty of the Qurʾan, 227–8, 234; Divine Beauty, xxiii, 31, 69, 72, 234, 239, 287; Divine Love for beauty, xx, xxi, xxii, 13–14, 31, 36, 37; free gift from God, 13–14, 31; 'God is beautiful and He loves beauty', xvi, xxii, 13, 31, 36, 37, 259; hierarchy of, xxiii, 227–31, 234, 235; *husn*, 259–60; *jamal*, 259; Paradise, 234, 253; patience, beauty of, 228–9, 259;

physical beauty, xxiii, 129, 132–3, 135, 230, 243 (a reminder of God, xxxiii, 133, 134, 267); 'presence of beauty'/*wujud al-jamal*, 190, 195, 203; sacred beauty, xxiii, 234; sexual beauty, xxvi, 134, 267; *Surat Al-Rahman*, 261; universe, beauty in, 31, 227, 287; woman, 229–30, 260, 268; see also *the entries below for* beauty; ugliness and vileness

beauty, components of, xxxii, 260–3; balance/*mizan*, 260–1; harmony, 261–2; majesty/*jalal*, 261–2; munificence/*jamal*, 261–2; see also beauty

beauty, nature of, xxxii, 265–9; exteriorising/interiorising power of beauty, xxxii–xxxiii, 265–8; objective reality of, 263, 264, 265; see also beauty

beauty of soul, xxi, 13, 36, 37, 42, 56, 208; conjugal love, 129, 135, 243; Prophet Muhammad, xxiii, 85, 87–8, 228, 234, 253, 267; see also beauty; virtue

Bedouins, 87, 96, 189, 201

being smitten (*shaghaf*), xxviii, 151, 158, 167, 194

believer, 97–9, 214, 229, 235, 237; circle of love for God, 213–16, 217; God's love for, 215–16; happiness, 251; humility towards believers, 100–101, 103; love for, 91, 121, 233, 234, 241; Prophet Muhammad, love for the believers, 64–5, 85–6; reward, 214–16

beloved: benefit/harm of love, 217–18; constant need for the beloved, 246; death 'in' the beloved/death of the ego, xxx–xxxi, 247–8, 270, 275–7; falling in love, 204; requirement of prior adornment, 221–2

Bilal, 275

breast (*sadr*), xxix, 200, 202, 203; 'expansion of the breast'/*inshirah al-sadr*, 182, 195, 200; see also heart

bughd, see abhorrence

buka', see weeping

al-Bukhari, Muhammad, 29, 86

certainty (*yaqin*), 187, 195, 203; certain knowledge/*'ilm al-yaqin*, 187, 195, 203;

certain truth/*haqq al-yaqin*, 187–8, 195, 203; certain vision/*'ayn al-yaqin*, 187, 195, 203

change: internal change, 209; *taghyir*, 177, 194, 203

child, 27, 107–108, 110, 125, 205, 231, 281; child/parents' love, 108, 136; rights, 108, 110; a trial, 112; see also family love

Christians, xvi, 20, 119–20, 140, 148, 154, 165, 171, 236

comfortable familiarity (*al-uns, al-isti'nas*), 181, 195, 203

communion (*najwa*), xxix, 174, 194, 203, 251

Companions of the Prophet, 90, 91, 94–5, 96, 102, 130, 267

company: *ma'iyyah*, 180, 195; need for human company/*al-hajah ila al-jalwah*, 188, 195, 203

compassion (*hanan*), 159–60, 167

concern (*shafaqah*), 164, 167, 181, 195, 203

conjugal and sexual love, xxiii, xxv–xxvi, 124–38, 179–80, 241, 243–4, 278; affection, 129, 135; beauty of soul, 129, 135, 243; changes in love, 243–4; fidelity, 243–4; gender distinction, 124–5; ideal spouse, 129; love and the eyes, 142–3; marriage, 107–108, 131; 'a marriage of souls', xxvi, 128; meeting with God, xxvi, 133–4, 267; mercy, 129, 135; need for each other, 125–6; need of, in order to procreate, 126; non-physical conjugal love, 126–9; Paradise, 135, 254; physical beauty, 129, 132–3, 134, 135; prayer, 127, 135; preservation of conjugal love, 135–8; protecting friendship/*wilayah*, 135, 138; psychological/emotional needs, 126–9; sexual act, xxvi, 130–2, 134, 154, 267, 278; sexual beauty, xxvi, 134, 267; sexual conjugal love, xxvi, xxxiii, 129–31, 134, 196; soulmate, xxv–xxvi, 127–8, 243; spiritual conjugal love, 132–4; ten principles to be observed in marriage, 135–8; see also extra-marital sex

contemplation (*tafakkur*), 187, 195, 203, 224

contentment (*rida*), xxxiv, 249, 251, 279;

General Index

kind/stage of love, xxx, 159, 167, 170, 194, 203, 245
contraction (*qabd*), 177, 194, 203
corruption, xxii, 55, 56
creation, xv, 13–14, 19, 32, 79, 80, 227, 245; beauty in, 227, 260–1, 287; Divine Love as root of, xv, xx, 22–8, 287; Divine Mercy as root of creation, 22–8, 69, 287; *hadith*, xv; human beings, creation of, 23–6, 27, 32–3, 124, 126, 227, 260; love for nature as God's creation, 82, 83–4; worship, 22, 23, 24–5; see also universe

Dahhak, 119
dalal, see going astray
David (*Dawud*), 44, 46, 186, 232, 233
death, 224, 249, 250, 270–7; beauty and love: lightening the hardship of death, 268–9; death 'in' the beloved/death of the ego, xxx–xxxi, 247–8, 270, 273, 275–7; entering Paradise whilst physically alive, 275–6, 279; life in God after the soul's death, 275–7; love for God, 61, 104–105, 273–7; martyrdom, 272–3; physical death, 270, 272, 273, 275; Prophet Muhammad, 269, 276–7; psychological death, 270, 272; 'soul at peace', 271; 'soul which incites to evil', 270–2, 273; suicide, xxxi; torment of the soul which loves but does not die in God, 274–5
desire (*hamm*), 153, 167, 191–2, 195, 203
devotion (*tabattul*), 183, 195, 203, 245
devoutness (*qunut*), 188, 195, 203
dhakirah, see memory
dhikr, see remembrance
disbeliever, 82, 150, 214, 236, 237; circle of illicit/negative love, 213–14, 216–17; God's lack of love for, xxi, 27, 31, 43, 54, 56–7; happiness, 251; love for God, xx, 236, 239–40, 281; mercy towards, 115, 116; sternness towards, 100, 101, 102, 103, 104
disobedience, 30, 56; see also obedience
Divine Attributes, see Divine Names
Divine Love, xv–xvi, xix–xxii; creation, Divine Love as root of, xv, xx, 22–8, 287; definition, 14; Divine Essence, xx, 19–20; a Divine Quality 17–18, 19, 238; love for beauty, xx, xxi, xxii, 13–14, 31, 36, 37; love/mercy connection, xix, 17–18, 19; *mahabbah*, 13; Qur'an, xv–xvi, xix–xx; see also God's love for humanity
Divine Mercy (*Rahmah*), xv–xvi, xix–xx, 18, 69, 148, 192; creation, Divine Mercy as root of, xx, 22–8, 69, 287; Divine Essence, xx, 18–20, 42; *hadith*, 17, 23; love/mercy connection, xix, 17–18, 19; 'My mercy embraces all things', xv, 18, 20, 23, 31, 42, 113, 192; punishment and mercy, 20–1; Qur'an, xix–xx; tenderness/mercy distinction, 20–1, 31; worship, 23, 26; see also mercy
Divine Names (*al-Asma al-Husna*), xvii, xxxii, 69, 223, 224, 227, 234, 259, 262, 281, 282; *al-ʿAfu*, xix, 17; *Allah*, 18, 287; *al-Barr*, xix, 17; *Dhul Jalal wal-Ikram*, 261; *al-Ghaffar*, xix, 17; *al-Ghafur*, xix, 17; *al-Haleem*, xix, 17; *al-Hannan*, 160; *al-Hayy*, 19; *al-Jamil*, xvi, 13, 75; *al-Kareem*, xix, 17; *al-Latif*, xix, 17, 31, 193; *al-Mannan*, 160; *al-Qayyum*, 19; *al-Rahman*, xix, xx, xxxiv, 17, 18, 77, 210, 287; *al-Rahman/al-Rahim* distinction, 19–20; *al-Rahim*, xix, xxxiv, 210, 287; *al-Raouf*, xix, 17, 149; *al-Samad*, 29; *al-Tawwab*, xix, 17; *al-Wadud*, xv, xix, xxxiv, 17, 150, 287; *al-Wakil*, xix, 17, 74; *al-Wali*, xix, 17
divorce, 135–8, 150, 179, 229, 244
doubt (*rayb*), 186, 195, 203
duʿa', see supplication

Elijah (*Elias*), 44, 45
Elisha, 44
the Emigrants, 87, 91, 94, 95, 106, 170, 232
emotion, xxiii, 61, 77, 88, 89, 159, 160
emptiness (*faragh*), xxix, 168, 194, 203
enjoyment (*istimtaʿ*), 192, 195, 203
Enoch (*Idris*), 45
entertaining thoughts (*zhann*), 186, 195

Eve, 113, 124, 127
evil deed, xxiii, 221, 231, 237, 243; disliked by God, xxii, 27, 28, 56, 57, 235; 'turn the other cheek', xxv, 118; utterance of evil words, xxii, 56; see also corruption
evildoer, 26; God's lack of love for, xx, xxii, 27–8, 31, 43, 55, 56–7; love for God, xx, 30, 281; ugliness of soul, 37, 56
expansion: *bast*, 177, 194, 203; 'expansion of the breast'/*inshirah al-sadr*, 182, 195
extra-marital sex (*zina*), xxvii, 139–41, 163–4, 167; adultery, 63, 132, 216, 266, 274; condemned, 139, 233, 234; fornication, xxvii, 57, 140, 163, 216, 233; lust, 139, 140
eyes/looking, 142, 197, 223; comfort of the eye/*qurrat al-ʿayn*, 180, 195, 203; controling one's gaze, 107, 142–3, 216, 230, 266, 268, 278; looking/*nazhar*, 186–7, 195, 203, 278; looking upon God, 278, 279–80; overlooking/*safh*, 193, 195
Ezekiel (*Dhul-Kifl*), 45

faith (*iman*), xxx, 87, 205–206, 208, 209, 224, 287; beauty of faith, 220, 234; changes in, 239, 240; effects of, 97–8; love for faith, 232, 234; love for God, 76, 77, 80, 81, 223; stage of love, 189, 195, 203
falling in love, xxix–xxx, 196, 202–204, 222; body, 203, 204; constituent parts and faculties of human beings, xxix, 82, 197–204; definition, xxix, 204, 205; fear, 82; hope, 82; knowledge, 82; secret of, 204; soul, 203, 204; spirit 203, 204; stages of love, 203–204; triangle of love, 221–2
family, 10, 106; love for the family and kin of Prophet Muhammad, 90–6; see also family love
family love, xxiii, xxiv–xxv, 17–18, 106–12, 241; affection for kinsfolk, 106; child, 107–108, 110, 112; child/parents' love, 108, 136; degrees of blood relations, 106, 112; idolatry 111; marriage, 107–108; mother, 109; parents' rights 108–109,

110–11, 116; see also child
faragh, see emptiness
farah, see joy
Fatimah, 91–2, 115, 269
favour (*tafdil*), 163, 167; God's favour/*fadl*, 13–14, 22, 32–4, 51, 163
fear (*khawf*), 101, 206–207; motives for loving God, 79, 80–1, 82, 209; stage of love, xxix, 176, 194, 203, 245; see also God-fearing; piety
feelings (*shuʿur*), 199, 200
fidelity (*wafaʾ*), 243–4
following (*ittibaʿ*), 185, 195, 203
forgiveness (*maghfirah*, *ghufran*): asking forgiveness/*istighfar*, 184, 195, 203, 240, 245; between human beings, xxv, 116–18; from God, 18, 70–1; invoking blessings upon the Prophet Muhammad, 88–9; prayer for, 63–4; Prophet Muhammad, 117; stage of love, 193, 195, 203
fornication, see extra-marital sex
freedom, 23, 27, 28
friend/friendship, 116, 119, 121–3, 241; brotherhood, 122; changes in love, 242–3; close friend/*khalil*, 47, 85, 155–6; close friendship/*khullah*, 123, 155–6, 167, 172, 194, 254; companionship/*suhbah*, 121–2, 123, 156–7, 167; friendship/*sadaqah*, 122, 123, 156, 167; 'friendship in evil', 242; 'friendship in goodness', 242–3; God's special companionship, 38–9, 51, 278, 279, 280; intimate friendship/*walijah*, 165–6, 167; protecting friendship/*wilayah*, 135, 138, 164–5, 167, 172, 194, 203, 213, 224, 226, 273; see also saints

Gabriel, 36, 101, 243
generosity (*karam*), 192, 195, 203, 229
gentleness, 20, 29, 31, 101
gharam, see anguish
ghawa, see straying in love
al-Ghazali, Abu Hamid, 6, 13
ghirah, see jealousy
God, xvi–xvii; absolute independence, 71–2; Divine Beauty, xxiii, 31, 234, 239,

287; Divine Essence, xx, 18–20, 42; hatred, impossible in God, xxii, 56, 57, 58, 235; Spirit, 32, 49, 86, 199, 200, 202, 226, 252, 280; see also Divine Love; Divine Mercy; Divine Names; love for God; meeting with God

God-fearing (*muttaqin*), 23, 25, 40, 41, 73–4, 89, 113, 212; God's Companionship 38; God's love for, xxi, 35–6, 37–8, 40, 41–2; love in Paradise, 254; see also fear

God's love for humanity, xx, xxi–xxii, 12–13, 27–8, 32–43; attributes of 'those whom He loves and who love Him', 99–104; beauty of soul, xxi, 13, 36, 42; believer, 215–16; Divine Companionship 38–9, 51, 278, 279, 280; effects, 97–105; eight categories of people whom God loves particularly, xxi, 13, 34–7, 56; God's Beloved/*Habib Allah*, xv, xx, xxi, xxiv, 34, 37, 50–3, 61; God's bounty to all human beings, 42–3; God's favour/*fadl*, 13–14, 22, 32–4, 51, 163; God's 'nearness', 42, 48, 62, 71–2, 154, 223, 276; kinds of people that God does not love, xxi–xxii, 54–8; never changes/ends in itself, 238–9; rewarding without reckoning, 40–1, 75, 215–16; see also Divine Love; God-fearing; just; messengers and prophets; patient; virtuous

going astray (*dalal*), 158, 167

Gospel, 48–9, 76, 88, 95, 100, 101, 148, 180, 220, 229, 232, 247, 272

graciousness (*hafawah*), 164, 167

gratitude (*shukr*), 24, 25, 26, 71–2, 84, 224; stage of love, 181–2, 195, 203, 245; see also praise of God

grief (*huzn*), xxix, 176, 194, 203, 245

growth of love, 205–12, 213, 226, 239, 241, 247; knowledge of God, 224; love's requirement of prior adornment/triangle of adornment, 221–2; strengthening a beneficial love, 208–209; weakening a negative love, 208, 209–12, 222–3; see also love

hadith, xv, 5, 6, 7, 17, 23; 'God is beautiful and He loves beauty', xvi, xxii, 13, 31, 36, 37, 259; *Hadith al-Nawafil*, 99, 276; Hadith of Gabriel, 36

hafawah, see graciousness

hamd, see praise of God

hamm, see desire

Hammad b. Salamah, 86

hanan, see compassion

happiness, 6, 10, 251, 264; love and happiness, xxx, 6, 249–52; only in Paradise, xxx, 250–1

al-Hasan, 91, 93, 115

'hastening to please' (*al-ʿajal lil-tardiyah*), 184, 195, 203

hatred: impossible in God, xxii, 56, 57, 58, 235; opposite of love, 56, 235–7

hawa, see impulse

heart (*qalb*), xxix, 196, 200–202, 203, 246–7, 249; heart's core/*lubb*, xxix, 196, 201–202, 203; inner heart/*fuʾad*, xxix, 196, 200, 201, 202, 203, 280; 'proving what is in the heart'/*tamhis al-qalb*, 185, 195, 203; rest of the heart, 129; serenity of heart, 75; sickness of the heart, 94, 132, 207, 213; 'softening of the heart'/*layn al-qalb*, 182, 195, 203; sound/spiritual heart, 42; 'trembling of the heart'/*wajl al-qalb*, 183, 195, 203, 245

hell, 57, 86, 122, 128, 161, 255, 287

Helpers, 29, 91, 95, 170

Hereafter, 10, 11, 105, 252; beauty of, 228, 233; meeting with God, 133, 134; see also Paradise

hope, 203; *amal*, 178, 195; motives for loving God, 79, 80–1, 82, 209; *rajaʾ*, xxix, 173, 194; *tamaʿ*, 81, 188, 195

hubb, see love

Hud, 45

Hudhayfah, 142, 240

human being, 125; constant change in, 238, 245, 246; constituent parts and faculties of, xxix, 82, 197–204 (body/*jism*, xxix, 197–8, 200, 203, 204; soul/*nafs*, xxix, 197, 198–200, 204; spirit/*ruh*, xxix, 197, 200, 202, 203, 204); Divine creation of, 23–6, 27, 32–3, 124, 126, 227, 229, 260; gender distinction, 124–5; human life, goal of, xv, xvi; human nature, 125, 221; innate knowledge of God, 219; see also falling in love; God's love for humanity; human love

human love, xxii–xxvii, 69–143, 241–4; beauty, xxiii; changes in, 241–4, 245; definition, xxiii, 12–14, 205, 239; God as the true object behind all love, 281–4; see also conjugal and sexual love; family love; love; love for God; love for others

humility (tadarruʿ), 56, 80, 81, 109, 203, 209, 211, 224, 245, 293, 294, 295; humble obedience/ikhbat, 183, 195, 203, 245; stage of love, 183–4, 195, 203, 245; towards believers, 100–101, 103

al-Husayn, 91, 93, 115

huyam, see wandering distracted

huzn, see grief

hypocrite, 25, 281, 283, 284; God's lack of love for, 31, 43, 56, 57–8, 216; prayer for forgiveness, 63–4

Iblis, see Satan
Ibn ʿAbbas, ʿAbd Allah, 7, 22, 23, 92, 151
Ibn Abi Hatim, 7
Ibn ʿAjibah, 283
Ibn Anbari, 150
Ibn ʿArabi, Muhyi al-Din Muhammad, xvii, 6, 156, 159, 160, 280
Ibn ʿAwf, 165
Ibn Hazm, 6
Ibn Kathir, 85, 90, 108, 119, 225, 276
Ibn Manzhur, 147–67 passim
Ibn Masʿud, 142
Ibn al-Mundhir, 7
Ibn Qattaʾ, 150
Ibn Sayyidih, 149, 151, 152, 159
Ibn Sina, 6
Ibn ʿUmar, ʿAbd Allah, 29
ibtighaʾ, see seeking
ibtilaʾ, see trial
idolater, 25, 36, 111, 119, 250–1, 284; God's lack of love for, 43, 57–8; marriage, 141, 160, 229; see also idolatry

idolatry, 70–1, 111, 140–1, 206, 231, 233, 281–2, 283–4; see also idolater

ihsan, see virtue

ihsas, see intuition

iʿjab, see admiration

ikhlas, see sincerity

ʿIkrimah b. Abi Jahl, 92, 119

iktifaʾ, see sufficiency

imagination (khayal), 199, 200, 203, 204

iman, see faith

imploring (taʾawwuh), 188, 195, 203

impulse (hawa), xxviii, 151–2, 167, 191, 195, 203

inas, see sense

inclination: mayl, 12–13, 14, 140, 161, 165, 167, 190–1, 195, 203; sagha, 165, 167

infatuation (istihwaʾ), xxviii, 152, 167, 204

insight (basira), 25–6, 196, 199–200, 201, 203, 209

intelligence (ʿaql), 81, 82, 198, 200, 204, 205

intention, 78; motives for loving God, 77–82, 200, 209

intuition (ihsas), 199, 200, 203

iradah, see will/desire

Isaac, 44, 46, 97

Ishmael (Ismail), 44, 45, 46, 96, 97

islam, see submission

Islamic Law (Shariʿah), 179, 241

istihbab, see preference

istihwaʾ, see infatuation

istihyaʾ, see shyness

istimtaʿ, see enjoyment

ithar, see preference to another over oneself

itmiʾnan, see serenity

ittibaʿ, see following

ʿIyad b. Majashiʾi, 27

Jabir b. ʿAbdullah, 29
Jacob, 44, 46, 97, 158, 225, 242, 266, 280
Jarir b. ʿAbdullah, 7, 101
jealousy (ghirah), 178–9, 195, 203, 247
Jesus Christ (ʿIsa), 44, 45, 46, 47, 48–50, 52, 86, 97, 119, 125, 148, 154, 220

General Index

Jethro (*Shuʿayb*), 45
Jews, 20, 119–20, 140, 154, 165, 171
jihad, see struggle
al-Jili, ʿAbd al-Karim b. Ibrahim, 262
jinn, 5, 22, 23, 27, 110, 122, 128, 152, 160, 169, 179, 200, 221, 231, 249, 253, 271
Job, 44, 46
John (*Yahya*), 44, 50, 80, 153, 172
Jonah (*Yunus*), 44, 45, 46
Joseph (*Yusuf*), xxxii, xxxiii, 40, 44, 45, 117, 158, 175, 195, 223–8 *passim*, 247, 263, 265–9 *passim*, 270; retreat, 75, 178, 224; Zulaykhah, Potiphar's wife, xxxii–xxxiii, 132, 139–40, 151, 153, 158, 175, 177, 193–4, 218, 266, 267, 274
joy (*farah*), xxix, xxx, 172–3, 194, 203, 245, 249, 251
just (*muqsitin*), xxi, 35, 38
justice, 26, 118, 120, 121, 260, 261

Kaʿb b. ʿAjaza, 96
Kaʿbah, 96, 108, 122; Pilgrimage, 71, 202
kalam, see speech
karam, see generosity
Khadir, 45, 225
khaʾinin, see treacherous
khawf, see fear
khayal, see imagination
khufyatan, see secrecy
killing, 114
kindness (*maʿruf*), 193, 195, 203
knowledge, 206, 219–20; certain knowledge/*ʿilm al-yaqin*, 187, 195, 203; *ʿilm*, stage of love, 174–5, 190, 194, 195, 203; knowledge of God, 219, 223, 224–6, 267, 280; motives for loving God, 80–1, 82; mutual knowledge/*taʿaruf*, 190, 195, 203; religious knowledge, 4–5; self-knowledge, 209; spiritual knowledge, 202, 206, 225–6

Layth, 151, 162
learning and imitation (*taʿlim*), 198, 200, 203, 220
life of this world, 161, 214, 220, 230, 233, 234, 249–51

liqaʾ, see meeting
loathing (*maqt*), 58
longing (*raghab*), 74, 75, 81, 153–4, 167, 171–2, 194, 203, 269
Lot (*Lut*), 44, 45
love: benefit/harm, 217–18; contraction, 245, 247, 253, 255; definition, xxiii, 12–14, 205, 239; exclusiveness, 246–7; expansion, 245; God as the true object behind all love, 281–4; hierarchy of, xxiii, 10, 231–4; higher/beneficial and lower/negative love, 213–18, 227, 234, 241, 287; kinds of, xvi, xxiii, xxvii–xxviii, xxx, 147–67, 204; love for the sacred, xxiii, xxiv; metaphysical love xvi; nature of love, 245–8; power of, 247–8, 265; secret of, 6, 10–11; see also *the entries below for* love; beauty; Divine Love; falling in love; family love; growth of love; human love
love (*hubb*), 287; kind of love, xxvii, 13, 147, 148, 167, 203; *habb*, 14; *mahabbah/hubb* distinction 13
love (*mahabbah*): kind of love, xxvii, 12–13, 122, 147–8, 167; *mahabbah/hubb* distinction 13; stage of love, 190, 195, 203
love (*widad*), xxvii–xxviii, 148, 149, 150, 167
love (*wudd*): kind of love, xxvii, 77, 149, 150, 167, 181; stage of love, 180–1, 195, 203
love for God, xv, xxiii–xxiv, 12–13, 69–84, 234, 241; attributes of 'those whom He loves and who love Him', 99–104; difference between human love for God and love of other beings and inanimate objects for God, 204; difference between love for God and love for others, 196; disbeliever, xx, 236, 239–40, 281; Divine Beauty, 69, 72; emulating the Prophet, xxiv–xxv, 34, 52, 73–4, 76, 77, 82, 99, 208, 287; end of, 239–40; evildoer, xx, 30, 281; faith, 76, 77, 80, 81, 223; greater and stronger than any other love, xxv, 77, 112, 217, 231–2; *Hadith al-Nawafil*, 99, 276; how to love God, 73–7; increase in, xxx, 74; intentions and motives for loving

God, 77–82, 200, 209; love for the Holy Qur'an, xvi, xxiv, 82, 83, 232, 234; loving God *most ardently*, xxiv, 61, 76, 77, 179, 196, 205, 273; loving that what reminds one of God, 82–4; reasons for loving God, 69–72; returning to God through love, xxxiv, 287; supplication for, 77; universe, love for God, xx, 29–31, 69, 204, 239, 246, 281; virtue, xxiii, xxiv, 73; worship of God, xxiv, 75; see also human love

love for others, xxiii, xxv, 113–23, 241–2; all humanity, 113–18, 241 (ethnic/linguistic differences, 113–14); believer, 91, 121; difference between love for God and love for others, 196; forgiveness, 116–18; inner beauty, xxiii; the needy, 115, 116, 118, 147; neighbour, 116, 118, 119; orphan, 73, 115, 116, 118, 147, 153, 172; see also Christians; friend/friendship; Jews

love, stages of, xxviii–xxix, xxx, 168–96, 204; falling in love, 203–204; love for God, 180–9, 195; love for God and love for others, 168–80, 194–5; love for others, 189–94, 195

lust (*shahwah*), 161–2, 167, 169, 191, 195, 203, 249, 287; impulse, 151; love for, xxiii, 6, 10, 233, 241, 242; love in, xxvii; see also extra-marital sex

lutf, see tenderness

maghfirah, ghufran, see forgiveness
mahabbah, see love
al-Mahalli, Jalal al-Din: *Tafsir al-Jalalayn*, 30, 74, 97, 116, 119, 126, 140, 260, 283
Malik b. Anas, 108
maqt, see loathing
maʿrifah, see recognition
marriage, 107–108, 131; idolater, 141, 160, 229; 'a marriage of souls', xxvi, 128; ten principles to be observed in marriage, 135–8; see also conjugal and sexual love; divorce
maʿruf, see kindness
Mary, the Blessed Virgin, 41, 46, 47, 48–50, 75, 124–5, 148, 215, 220

mashiʾah, see will/wish
Maymun b. Mahran, 119
Mecca, 96, 165; see also Kaʿbah
meditation (*tadabbur*), 187, 195, 203
meeting (*liqaʾ*), 179–80, 195, 203
meeting with God, 105, 133–4, 278–80; beatitude/*ridwan*, 279, 280
memory (*dhakirah*), 199, 200, 203
mercy (*rahmah*), 17–18, 148, 167, 192, 203; Arabic language, 22–3 (*rahim*/womb, xix, 17–18, 129; root R-H-M, xix; conjugal love, 129, 135); pity, 149; Prophet Muhammad, 52, 64–5, 85, 89; see also Divine Mercy
messengers and prophets, 44–53, 81, 225, 237, 279–80; Divine Companionship 38–9; forgiveness, 117; God's love for, xx, 44–53; *hadith*, 45, 47; messenger/prophet distinction, 45, 53; 'the resolute' messengers, 47, 53
modesty, xxxiii, 107, 142–3, 216, 230; controlling one's gaze, 107, 142–3, 216, 230, 266, 268, 278
Moses (*Musa*), 13, 39, 44, 45, 46, 47–8, 50, 71, 85, 92, 97, 120, 121, 133, 168, 179, 184, 199, 201, 208, 231, 272, 279–80
muhsinin, see virtuous
Mujahid, 119
Muqatil b. Hayyan, 119
muqsitin, see just
murawadah, see seduction
Muslim b. al-Hajjaj, 86
mutʿa, see pleasure
Muʿtazilite, 22
muttaqin, see God-fearing

nafs, see soul
najwa, see communion
Nawf Bakkali, 119
nearness: drawing near/*taqarrub*, 154, 167, 171, 194, 203, 276; God's 'nearness', 42, 48, 62, 71–2, 154, 223, 276; *Hadith al-Nawafil*, 99, 276
need: neediness/*faqr*, xxix, 168, 194, 203; the needy, 73, 100, 107, 109, 115, 116, 118, 147

General Index

neighbour, 54, 116, 118, 119
Noah (*Nuh*), 28, 44, 45, 46, 47, 50, 85, 176, 225

obedience, 30, 82, 103, 159, 237; creation's obedience of God, 30; humble obedience/*ikhbat*, 183, 195, 203, 245; see also disobedience
obliviousness to oneself (*'adam al-ihsas bil-hal*), 194, 195, 203
orphan, 73, 100, 107, 109, 115, 116, 118, 147, 153, 172
overwhelming: being overwhelmed/*qahr*, 188, 195, 203

pain, 12, 20-1, 203, 265, 268, 269
Paradise, xxxiii–xxxiv, 10, 62, 212, 253–5, 287; beatific vision, xxxiii, 253; beatitude/*ridwan*, xxxiv, 279; beauty, 234, 253; conjugal love, 135, 254; entering Paradise, xxxi, 76, 77, 86, 272; entering Paradise whilst physically alive, 275–6; happiness, xxx, 250–1; houris, 253; love for, xxiv, 232, 234; love in, xxxiii, 246, 253–5; Prophet Muhammad, 275, 279; see also Hereafter; meeting with God
pardoning (*'afu*), 193, 195, 203
patience (*sabr*), 178, 195, 203, 209, 210; beauty of, 228-9, 259
patient (*sabirin*), 38, 41; God's love for, xxi, 35, 39–40, 41, 42
peace (*salam*), xxx, 249, 250, 251; 'soul at peace', 127, 198, 203, 270; stage of love, xxx, 181, 195, 203, 245
penitence (*awb*), 26; stage of love, 188, 195, 203, 245; turning in penitence/*inabah*, 183, 195, 203
People of the Cloak, 91; see also 'Ali b. Abi Talib; Fatimah; al-Hasan; al-Husayn
People of the Scripture, 51, 95, 120, 236, 241; see also Christians; Jews
perception (*tabassur*), 187, 195
piety, 73, 74, 82, 98, 100–101, 103, 107, 115, 206, 234, 240; see also fear
pity (*ra'fah*), 148–9, 167, 191, 195, 203

pleasure (*mut'a*), xxx, 192, 195, 203, 249, 251
praise of God (*hamd*), 7, 29, 30; see also gratitude
prayer, 38, 41, 73, 74, 82, 92, 97, 103, 209, 210, 224, 275; Abraham, 96; answered by God, 71, 72, 224; *Fatihah*, 81–2; invoking blessings upon the Prophet Muhammad, 50–1, 62, 88–9; invoking blessings upon the Prophet Muhammad's family and kin, 96; love for prayer and invocation, 82, 83, 232, 234; marriage, 127, 135; prayer for forgiveness, 63–4; prayer said when a man reaches forty, 109–10; praying for parents, 109; Prophet Muhammad, 61, 62, 77, 83 (intercession, 63–4, 85–6); see also remembrance; supplication; worship
preference (*istihbab*), xxvii, 148, 167
preference to another over oneself (*ithar*), 157–8, 167
primordial state of purity (*fitra hanifa*), 33, 61, 73, 155, 204, 273, 282
Prophet Muhammad, xxiv, 45, 50–3, 267–8; a 'beautiful example', 51–2, 99; beauty of soul, xxiii, 85, 87–8, 228, 234, 253, 267; Cave of Thawr, 39, 51, 92, 274; death, 269; Divine Companionship 38–9, 51; following the Prophet, xxiv–xxv, 4, 34, 52, 73–4, 76, 77, 82, 99, 208, 241, 287; God's Beloved/*Habib Allah*, xv, xx, xxi, xxiv, 34, 37, 50–3, 61; *hadith*, 53, 62, 85–6; Household/*Ahl Bayt*, 91, 93–4; invoking blessings upon, 50–1, 62, 88–9; invoking blessings upon his family and kin, 96; love for his family and kin, 90–6; love for humanity, 63–5, 85–6; love for God, 61–2, 77; love for the Prophet Muhammad, xv, xx–xxi, xxiii, xxiv, 85–9, 232, 234; *a magnificent nature*, 37, 51, 73, 87, 208; mercy of, 52, 64–5, 85, 89; Night of the Ascension/*Lailat Al-Mi'raj*, 275, 279; 'praiseworthy station', 85–6; prayer, 61, 62, 63, 77, 83 (intercession, 63–4, 85–6); Qur'an, xvi,

51; remembrance of God, 52, 73, 74, 103; Seal of the prophets, xx, 50, 93; virtue, xxiii, 87–8, 228; wives, 87, 91, 93–4, 132; woman, 62, 83, 132, 138, 153; see also *Sunnah*
punishment and Divine Mercy, 20–1

qabd, see contraction
qalb, see heart
Qatada, 119
Queen of Sheba, 281
qunut, see devoutness
Qur'an, xvi, xix, 3–5; *basmalah*, xv, 18–19, 20; beauty of, 227–8, 234; exegesis, 7, 100; *Fatihah*, 81–2; happiness, xxx; love for the Holy Qur'an, xvi, xxiv, 82, 83, 232, 234; philosophy, 5; Prophet Muhammad, xvi, 51; reading and reciting, xvi, 224; revelation of, xv–xvi, 51; *Surat Al-Rahman*, 261; the Truth, 3–5
Quraysh, 90, 91, 94, 96
al-Qurtubi, Abu ʿAbdullah, 20, 90, 116, 119

raʾfah, see pity
raghab, see longing
Raghib al-Isfahani, 52, 53, 147–65 *passim*, 259
rahmah, see Divine Mercy; mercy
Ramadan, fasting, 130–1
rayb, see doubt
al-Razi, Fakhr al-Din, 4, 20, 22–3, 90, 91–2, 115, 128, 149, 159, 262, 274
reason: 'using reason'/*istiʿmal al-ʿaql*, 187, 195, 203
recognition (*maʿrifah*), xxix, 175, 194, 203
religion, 82–3, 204, 236; see also worship
remembrance (*dhikr*), xxiv, 25–6, 41, 77, 207, 250; invocation, 9, 69, 74, 103, 211, 227, 228; love for prayer and invocation, 82, 83, 232, 234; overcoming temptation, 209, 210–12; Prophet Muhammad, 52, 73, 74, 103; spirit of peace, 75; stage of love, 174, 185, 194, 195, 203; see also prayer
repentance (*tawbah*), 184, 195, 203
retreat/seclusion, 74–5, 224; beauty of, 228; need for/*al-hajah ila al-khalwah*, 177–8, 194, 203; parting from people in a beautiful manner/*hajran jamilan*, 74–5, 228
ridwan, see beatitude
righteous deeds, xxx, 76, 77, 80, 98, 206, 208, 224, 251; *Hadith al-Nawafil*, 99, 276; reward for, 214–16; strengthening a beneficial love, 209
rights, 107, 113, 118, 124; child, 108, 110; parents 108–109, 110–11, 116; woman, 135, 150, 171
ruh, see spirit
Rumi, Jalal al-Din, xvii

saba, see tendency towards
sabirin, see patient
sabr, see patience
Saʿd b. Abi Waqqas, 92
sadr, see breast
Saʿid b. Abi ʿAruba, 85
Saʿid b. Jubayr, 7
saints (*awliyaʾ*), 44, 53, 104–105, 225, 237, 238, 240, 273, 276, 279, 280
sakan, see tranquillity
sakinah, see spirit of peace
salam, see peace
Salih, 45
Satan (Iblis), 20, 32, 33, 44, 49–50, 58, 125, 142, 185, 210–11, 234, 236, 240–1, 271, 281; adornment of things, 220–1
Saul, 39, 133, 179, 197
secrecy (*khufyatan*), 80
seduction (*murawadah*), 193–4, 195, 203
seeking (*ibtighaʾ*), 162, 167, 171, 194, 203
sense (*inas*), 199, 200, 203
sentiment (*ʿatifah*), xxiv, 73, 81, 82, 121, 199, 200, 203, 205
serenity (*itmiʾnan*), 174, 194, 203, 245, 250, 267
shafaqah, see concern
shaghaf, see being smitten
shahwah, see lust
shakk, see uncertainty
Shariʿah, see Islamic Law
shukr, see gratitude

General Index

shuʿur, see feelings
shyness (*istihya'*), 194, 195, 203
sin, xxii, 56, 57, 206, 240, 282
sincerity (*ikhlas*), 103, 105; sincere worship, 77–81; stage of love, 189, 195, 203
skin: 'quivering of the skin'/*qashʿarirat al-jild*, 183, 195, 203; 'softening of skin'/*layn al-jild*, 182, 195, 203
Solomon (*Sulayman*), 44, 46, 175, 189, 232, 233
soul (*nafs*), xxv, xxix, 127, 128, 197, 198–200, 204; conscience, xxix; ego, xxiii, xxix, 102, 208, 247 (death of, xxx–xxxi, 247–8, 270, 273, 275–7); faculties of, 81–2, 198–200; 'self-reproaching soul', 127, 198, 203, 270; 'soul at peace', 127, 198, 203, 270; 'soul which incites to evil', 127, 198, 203, 255, 270–2, 273; soulmate, xxv–xxvi, 127–8, 243; ugliness of, 37, 56; see also beauty of soul
speech (*kalam*), 198, 200, 203, 230
spirit (*ruh*), xxix, 197, 200, 202, 203, 204
spirit of peace (*sakinah*), 75, 157, 201, 267
spiritual life, xxvi, xxvii, xxxi, 210
straying in love (*ghawa*), 152–3, 167
struggle (*jihad*), 40, 99, 189, 207; Greater Struggle, 102, 273; Lesser Struggle, 102, 273; struggle in the way of God, 100, 102–103, 272
submission (*islam*), 188–9, 195, 203, 224
Suddi, 90
suffering (*alam*), xxix, 20–1, 176, 194, 203, 245
sufficiency (*iktifa'*), 181, 195, 203, 245
Sufism, 7
Sunnah, xv, 5, 37, 74, 90, 208; see also Prophet Muhammad
supplication (*duʿa'*), 25, 71, 77, 82, 224, 246; stage of love, 184–5, 195, 203, 246; see also prayer
al-Suyuti, Jalal al-Din, 7; *Tafsir al-Jalalayn*, 30, 74, 97, 116, 119, 126, 140, 260, 283

taʿawwuh, see imploring
al-Tabari, Muhammad b. Jarir, 4

tabassur, see perception
tabattul, see devotion
tadabbur, see meditation
tadarruʿ, see humility
tafakkur, see contemplation
tafdil, see favour
taghyir, see change
taʿlim, see learning and imitation
taste: subjectivity in the perception of beauty, xxxii, 263–4, 265
tawakkul, see trust
tawbah, see repentance
tawhid (unity), xvi
temptation, 116, 210–11, 240, 241, 281
tendency towards (*saba*), 162, 167
tenderness (*lutf*), 69, 148, 193, 195, 203; tenderness/mercy distinction, 20–1, 31
Torah, 47–9, 76, 85, 88, 95, 100, 101, 109, 180, 220, 229, 232, 247, 272
tranquillity (*sakan*), 173, 194, 203, 245, 250
treacherous (*kha'inin*): God's lack of love for, xxii, 54–5, 56
trial (*ibtila'*), xxix, 174, 194, 203
trust (*tawakkul*), 182, 195, 203

Ubayy b. Kaʿb, 88
ugliness and vileness, 235, 237, 243, 259; definition, 235; ugliness of soul, 37, 56
ulfah, see affinity
ʿUmar b. Abi Salamah, 91
ʿUmar b. al-Khattab, 276
Umm Salamah, 91, 160
uncertainty (*shakk*), 185–6, 195, 203
unity, see *tawhid*
universe, 80; beauty in, 31, 227, 287; glorification and praise of God, 29; love for God, xx, 29–31, 69, 204, 239, 246, 281; the weeping tree-trunk, 29; see also creation
al-uns, al-istiʾnas, see comfortable familiarity
uprightness, 27, 32, 111, 114, 158, 207, 265

virtue (*ihsan*), 36–7, 42, 77, 87–8, 207, 209, 225, 226; beauty of soul, 37, 42; *Hadith of Gabriel*, 36; love for God, xxiii, xxiv, 73; Prophet Muhammad, xxiii, 87-8, 228; stage of love, 189, 195, 203; strengthening a beneficial love, 209; see also virtuous

virtuous (*muhsinin*), 41, 87, 259-60; beauty of soul, xxi, 13, 36, 42, 56; God's Companionship 38; God's love for, xx, xxi, 34-7, 40, 41, 42, 56, 231; hierarchy of, 37-42; see also virtue

wafa', see fidelity

wandering distracted (*huyam*), 155, 167

war, xxv, 114-15, 116, 118, 119

wealth, 74, 100-101, 138, 231, 234; love for, xxiii, xxvii, 10, 74, 233, 281

weeping (*buka'*), 176-7, 194, 203, 245

will/desire (*iradah*), 81, 82, 198, 200, 205; kind of love, 150-1, 167, 204; stage of love, xxix, 171, 194, 203

will/wish (*mashi'ah*), 175-6, 194

woman, 106, 125, 281; beauty of, 229-30, 260, 268; bride, 261; gender distinction, 124-5; ideal spouse, 129, 234; mother, 109, 136, 137; motherly love, 17-18; Prophet Muhammad, 62, 83, 132, 138, 153 (wives, 87, 91, 93-4, 132); rights, 135, 150, 171; wife, 12, 106, 125; see also modesty

worship, xxv, 10, 22, 23, 24-5, 283-4; creation, worship in the, 22, 23, 24-5; Divine Mercy, 23, 26; *Hadith* of Gabriel, 36; love for God, xxiv, 75; love for religion and worship, 82-3; Prophet Muhammad, 61; sincere worship, 77-81; spirit of peace, 75; see also prayer

wudd, see love

Yahya b. Saʿid, 85

yaqin, see certainty

Zabidi, Muhibb al-Din, 147-56 *passim*, 159-65 *passim*, 259

Zachariah (*Zakariyya*), 41, 44, 50, 80, 153, 215

Zajjaj, 152, 153, 156, 164

al-Zamakhshari, Abu al-Qasim 4-5

Zayd b. Arqam, 93

Zayd b. Aslam, 119

Zayd b. Harithah 94

zhann, see entertaining thoughts

zina, see extra-marital sex

*In the Name of God,
the Compassionate, the Merciful.*

*Praise be to God to Whom belongs whatever is
in the heavens and whatever is in the earth.
And to Him belongs all praise
in the Hereafter. And
He is the Wise,
the Aware.*

Saba, 34:1

*In the Name of God,
the Compassionate, the Merciful.*

*Glory be to your Lord, the Lord of Might,
above what they allege! / And
peace be to the messengers. /
And praise be to God,
Lord of the
Worlds!*

Al-Saffat,
37: 180–2

REVIEWS OF THE ENGLISH EDITION

'The Open Letter 'A Common Word Between Us and You' (2007) was probably the single most important initiative ever taken by Muslim scholars and authorities towards Christians. Its subject was love of God and love of neighbour, and now Prince Ghazi has produced the ideal follow-up: a definitive study of love in the Qur'an. Ghazi has achieved not only an account of the subject that engages with and goes beyond what others have said; he explores too the many-splendoured reality of love itself. So this remarkable volume is not just for scholars, but is also for anyone who values love.'

*David F. Ford,
Regius Professor of Divinity, University of Cambridge, U.K.
Director, Cambridge Inter-faith Programme.*

'A masterwork of scholarship and of inspiration.'

*H.E. Cardinal Theodore E. McCarrick,
Distinguished Senior Scholar,
The Library of Congress.*

'*Love in the Holy Qur'an* was a joy to read. [T]he book is a real inspiration and a rare insight into the hidden feelings within the Holy Qur'an ... shedding light on the values preached by Islam.'

*H.B. Orthodox Patriarch Theophilos III
Patriarch of Jerusalem*

'[T]his book will open up to you that which stands theologically behind *Shari'ah* law. And for those delving deeper than *Shari'ah* for the first time, you may well be astounded to find that, behind *Shari'ah* stands love. The love of God for humanity. ... You will find this book easy to enter into and inviting to read, but after you read it, you will find yourself sitting in deep thought, surprised by the depth of the theology of love that exists in the Qur'an. And the more you read the book, the more you will find yourself immersed in the breadth and depth of the ocean of love, invited to swim further and deeper than ever before.

As an Arab Christian, who has lived amidst Muslims my whole life, this book reminds me of our commonalities, where the world so often only sees our differences. And, while delving deeper into the Qur'an in this book, I find myself reminded of passages from the Christian Bible. Passages such as St. John's teaching that God is love—to know God is to know love, and to know love is to know God: "Beloved, let us love one another, because love is from God; everyone who loves is born of God and knows God. Whoever does not love does not know God, for God is love." – 1 John 4:7–8

And it reminds me of Jesus' answer in St. Matthew 22 when asked, "Teacher, which commandment in the law is greatest?":

Jesus said to him, "'You shall love the Lord your God with all your heart, and with all your soul, and with all your mind.' This is the greatest and first commandment. And a second is like it: 'You shall love your neighbor as yourself.' On these two commandments hang all the law and the prophets." – Matthew 22:36–40

This book is a powerful continuation of the work that began in the 2007 'A Common Word Between Us and You.' And I hope that, through this new work, more people will come to understand that the core principle of religion is love of God and love of neighbor. For I truly believe that our world needs this message of love today.'

The Rt. Rev. Dr. Munib A. Younan
The President of the Lutheran World Federation
The Bishop of the Evangelical Lutheran Church in Jordan and the Holy Land

'Deeply learned, wise, compassionate and humane, it testifies to the qualities of its author and his devotion to God. It is a superb book from which I have learned much and for which I profoundly thank God.'

Very Rev. Professor Iain R. Torrance,
President of Princeton Theological Seminary,
Former Moderator of the Church of Scotland

'*Love in the Holy Qur'an*' is, to my knowledge, the first systematic treatment of the recurrent theme of love—both Divine and human—in the Qur'an. It reflects classical training in Islamic sciences, yet is a prime example of the contemporary genre of thematic *tafsirs*. As such, it is of extraordinary importance for our time. Both inspiring and reassuring, the text focuses on love and mercy as reciprocals of more commonly discussed themes of justice and judgment. '*Love in the Holy Qur'an*' is bound to become a classic.'

Tamara Sonn
Kenan Professor of Humanities; Department of Religious Studies;
College of William & Mary

'In this translation of the sixth edition of Prince Ghazi's al-Azhar dissertation (undertaken after a first doctorate at Cambridge), English readers are helped to explore love in the Qur'an, assisted by extensive resources of a rich Islamic tradition bearing on the Qur'anic texts. Displaying an organization friendly to western readers and redolent of the author's academic journeys to Princeton and Cambridge before al-Azhar, this study respects the parameters of academia while moving beyond them to engage searchers in other faith traditions.

Though this work (with homage to its co-translator, Khalid Williams) readers will discover the poignancy of Qur'anic expression as well as a rich commentary tradition. Non-Muslim readers will be treated to what Islamic tradition celebrates as the 'inimitability' of the Qur'an ... [which] could address all human beings, allowing those in diverse stages of intellectual and spiritual development each to profit from its teaching. And Ghazi's work shares some of that amplitude: readers will be inspired, and by virtue of that be moved to ponder more deeply the realities of human existence—in this case, of human love—so as to allow those very realities to become signs of the presence of the creating God.'

David Burrell, C.S.C.
Professor of Comparative Theology, Tangaza College, Nairobi, Kenya
Hesburgh Professor Emeritus Philosophy and Theology,
University of Notre Dame, IN, USA

REVIEWS OF THE ARABIC EDITION

Leading Islamic Scholars said the following about *Love in the Holy Qur'an* (in its original Arabic):

'An outstanding work, worthy of praise and esteem for its method, its content and its language.'

H.E. Imam Prof. Dr. Ahmad Muhammad al-Tayyib,
Grand Sheikh of al-Azhar and Supervisor of the thesis at al-Azhar University

'The word '*hubb*' ('love') is composed of two letters: the pronunciation of the '*h*' evokes expansion, and the enunciation of the '*b*' evokes union. After the heart has become attached to the beloved and encompassed him (or her) according to its knowledge of him (or her), it grows like a sheaf of goodness which God multiplies for whom He wills. What a magnificent thing it is when love is constant and undying, and enduring without end... Love is the way in the Qur'an in which man is connected to his Creator, and none of the Pillars of Islam reach God save by way of the heart, as the Messenger of God ﷺ said: "Indeed, in the body is a morsel which, if it is sound the whole body is sound, and if it is corrupt the whole body is corrupt."

And if the heart is the locus of God Almighty's manifestations, then love is the light which shines forth from this heart.

[This] study of love in the Qur'an has gathered together all the many pearls of the meanings of love and strung them on the cord of [the author's] own love, making them into a most precious necklace, resplendent with beauty, which takes deep root in the heart, inspires the mind, and moves the soul. We see in this study breadth and power of knowledge, the love and humility of the author, lofty insight, beautiful language, perfect style, and fine rhetoric. May these efforts be blessed and recompensed with abundant goodness, and may God benefit humanity by it; and may my Lord shower His favours upon [the author], manifestly and secretly.'

H.E. Sheikh Prof. Dr. Ahmad Badr al-Din Hassoun,
Grand Mufti and Chief of the High Council for Ifta', Syrian Arab Republic

'Love is the essential branch of the mercy with which God began His Book, and it is the connection between the Creator and His creation, and between parents and children in human relations and also in the animal world, and in all beings. Love in the Holy Qur'an is the name of a beautiful and marvellous study by our

Reviews Of The Arabic Edition

beloved Prince Ghazi bin Muhammad, may God reward him well, in which he has shown what the world should understand when it hears the Qur'an. He has produced a fine and worthy work, and we ask God to benefit the world by its means—Amen!'

H.E. Sheikh Prof. Dr. Ali Gomaa,
Grand Mufti of Egypt

'A book which plunges into the depths of the truth and retrieves its hidden pearl; for it presents to people what they did not understand about the sanctity of love and its place in the Qur'an .... [The author] has produced in this work something which no one has ever done before; and why not, for it is not unusual to find a thing at its source, and fine pearls are only found in plentiful seas. It is enough that [this book] has raised love to the highest virtue, and sanctified it from being sullied with any kind of baseness; and this is a virtue which anyone who reads this book, and studies it well, will recognize in the author.'

H.E. Sheikh Ahmad bin Hamad al-Khalili,
Grand Mufti of the Sultanate of Oman

'*Love in the Holy Qur'an* ... is a timely work given the circumstances in which the Islamic community currently finds itself. It is an unprecedented work which promises to promote love among the members of individual communities on the one hand, and among different communities on the other.... This work is the result of a sound understanding of love in the Holy Qur'an and the presence of love in the heart of its author, who has been able to present Qur'anic verses and prophetic *Hadiths* which reveal the secret of God's love for man and man's love for God and his neighbour. All this has come from a sound heart which loves humanity. Everyone should read this book, in order to learn about love in the Qur'an, and to witness the love which pervades the work.'

H.E. Sheikh Mustafa Ceric,
Chief Scholar and Grand Mufti, Bosnia-Herzegovina

'This is a work of a mystical and philosophical bent, which I found to contain many beautiful concepts which the author—God keep him—derived by gathering [Qur'anic] verses in a way which has perhaps never been done before, but which does not contradict the principles of Islamic doctrine.'

H.E. Sheikh Prof. Dr. Nuh Ali Salman al-Qudah
Grand Mufti of the Hashemite Kingdom of Jordan,

'This book, '*Love in the Holy Qur'an*', is the fruit of blessed intellectual efforts, and the culmination of a spiritual journey, enlightened by the illuminations of God-given knowledge. It is a blessed and gratifying work which will be well rewarded, God willing, and which will inspire every well-intentioned and resolved believer to increase his love for God and His Messenger ﷺ. May God reward [the author] on behalf of all who read this blessed book, and revive their spirits and enrich their souls in doing so, because of the treasures of knowledge and subtle wisdom it contains.'

H.E. Prof. Dr. Bu Abdullah Ghulam Allah,
Minister of Religious Affairs and Endowments, Algeria

'[Love] is the key to happiness in both lives, and the Book of God is the way to this happiness and the guide for those who seek it. Whoever reads this book will find a generous presentation of the truth of this matter, and details of its every aspect, in a style which is agreeable and pleasing to the reader.'

H.E. Sheikh Abdullah bin Muhammad bin Abdullah al-Salimi
Minister of Endowments and Religious Affairs, Sultanate of Oman

'In the midst of my fruitless searching for someone who has treated the subject of love in the Book of God and wrote about it or spoke about it, I received glad tidings in the mail giving me exactly what I was looking for: '*Love in the Qur'an*' by H.R.H. Prince Ghazi bin Muhammad bin Talal al-Hashemi. I set aside everything I was doing and began reading it at once. The value of this book, and this subject, is immense.... This book is wonderful... I congratulate [the author] for the love which inspired [him] to write it, and which [he] took as a guide leading to knowledge of God and the universe, and which then settled firmly in [his] heart. And I ask the Almighty to make our hearts vessels of His love, that we may be drawn from ourselves to Him, and use it to reach Him.'

Sheikh Prof. Dr. Muhammad Sa'id Ramadan al-Buti,
Dean of the College of Shariah, Damascus University

In the Name of God, the Compassionate, the Merciful
We cause to grow splendid gardens whose trees you could never cause to grow (Al-Naml, 27:60) ❊ *And We send down from the heaven blessed water with which We cause to grow gardens and the grain that is harvested, and the date-palms that stand tall with piled spathes (Qaf, 50:9–10)*

'[This book is] a journey into the depths of the soul. Its arena is the garden of love; its roots have been nourished by the water of wisdom; its branches extend into the sky of knowledge; its flowers are perfumed with the scent of the Sacred Law; its fruit is happiness. A beneficial work, and a wonderful arrangement.'

H.E. Sheikh Prof. Dr. Abdullah bin Mahfuz bin Bayyah,
President of the International Union of Muslim Scholars, and
President and Founder of the Global Centre for Renewal and Guidance

Reviews Of The Arabic Edition

'This wonderful book *Love in the Holy Qur'an* contains a beautiful arrangement of complimentary [Qur'anic] verses.... What is particularly pleasing is the concentration on the mutual love between God Almighty and His servants, and between humanity themselves, and indeed between all created beings. It is also wonderful how the verse of the *basmallah* implies that the entire universe subsists through the Name of God ﷻ—who has the Most Beautiful Names—and through the manifestation of His vast mercy.'

Ayatollah Muhammad Ali al-Taskhiri,
Secretary General of the Forum for the Rapprochement of Islamic Schools in the World

'I am delighted that the esteemed Professor Ghazi bin Muhammad bin Talal—that man in whom radiates clearly his proud heritage as a scion of the Messenger of God ﷺ—has done such a fine job of researching this subject in the Holy Qur'an, choosing to devote his doctorate at al-Azhar to studying this subject. He has been fully successful in this endeavour, and has made a valuable addition to the annals of Islamic literature by concentrating his work on the foundation of wisdom in Islam.'

Ayatollah Prof. Dr. Sayyid Mustafa Muhaqqiq Damad,
Professor in the Faculty of Law and Islamic Philosophy, Shahid Beheshti University,
President of the Islamic Studies Department, Academy of Sciences, Iran

'I consider this work a precious treasure because of its detailed study of one of the most important human values and emotions, one which is shared by individuals and peoples alike.... [This] valuable study has gathered together all elements of ethics, philosophy and spirituality, most of it previously unavailable in any studies.... The book contains many beacons of light. These are presented in an interconnected way, making it easy for the reader to understand the subject and connect with it emotionally.... There is enough in it to satisfy the student; convince the doubter; increase the faith of the believer, and evoke in everyone a sense of the importance of the direct experience of love and the higher human emotions.'

H.E. Grand Ayatollah Sayyid Husayn Isma'il al-Sadr

'By God's grace this study is illuminated by the light of the Holy Qur'an and the lamps of the *Sunnah*, and deals with a highly relevant subject which is one of the most important issues of all. It is based on completely Qur'anic foundations and a precise use of the prophetic *Hadith* literature, showing that love ... is the most important axis around which circle all the different relationships of existence, including the relationship between God, His creation and His creatures, and among the creatures themselves. This work has detailed all of this very thoroughly, showing the effects this love has—according to the Qur'anic guidance—on man's being and his behaviour in all aspects of his life. It is indeed a unique work, original in its method and style, greatly beneficial and effective, and worthy of all praise and esteem.'

H.E. Prof. Dr. 'Abd al-Salam Abbadi,
Secretary General of the International Academy of Islamic Jurisprudence

'This work, characterized by its depth, analysis and authenticity, is further adorned with a fluent and attractive style. It captivated me as soon as I began to read it, so that I finished it in one sitting. This valuable work must be seen by the media and by the people—all people, so that love will spread among them and so that their connection with God, the Compassionate and Merciful, will be strengthened. It would be wonderful if an institution were to have the book translated into every living language and then distribute it, for it contains such noble concepts that deserve to be seen by all.'

H.E. Dr. 'Ikrimah Sabri
Imam of the al-Aqsa Mosque, President of the Islamic High Committee;
President of the Committee of Scholars and Preachers, Jerusalem

'This book contains just the sort of God-given counsel that the Muslims require today, leading to dignified behaviour, building bridges of communication, and paving the way for social harmony, all through lofty advice and sound guidance.'

Habib 'Umar bin Muhammad bin Hafiz,
Dean of Dar al-Mustafa for Islamic Studies, Yemen

'An important addition to Islamic thought in modern times because of how it deals with the subjects of love and beauty in great depth in the light of the Holy Qur'an, without clashing with modern man's needs. Moreover, the book aids in removing the suspicion that there is a conflict between religion and love, and between faith and an appreciation of beauty.'

Dr. 'Amr Khalid,
Chairman of the Board of Trustees, Right Start Foundation International

'I find this to be an innovative work which clarifies the meaning of love and its forms, components and secrets, deriving all this from the Holy Qur'an. It shows which kinds of love are praiseworthy and which are blameworthy, and the different degrees of love, lovers and beloveds—and it does all this with a creative and engaging style of exposition. We ask God Almighty to accept this effort from the author, and make it a cause of benefit for the world.'

Mufti Muhammad Taqi Uthmani,
Vice President of Darul Uloom Karachi, Pakistan

Reviews Of The Arabic Edition

'There is a large philosophical gap in Qur'anic studies. Muslim scholars have spent centuries producing competing studies of the Qur'anic text in terms of recitation, doctrine, jurisprudence, exegesis, and history—and this competition has been very fruitful—but unfortunately they have neglected many understandings, concepts, values, realities and proofs which potentially could solve many problems and philosophical issues of great importance. This, despite the fact that this neglected portion [of the Holy Qur'an] actually constitutes the greater part of this revealed text.... Therefore I say: the virtue of this book is that it tackles philosophical Qur'anic subjects which have not been covered before. It presents moral philosophy through precise arrangement but subtle understanding, concentrating on its special place in the Holy Qur'an, in a high and easy style. It enters unexplored territory in Islamic philosophy, inspiring us to reread the Book of God in the light of essential moral concepts.'

Prof. Dr. Taha Abdurrahman,
Chairman of the Wisdom Forum for Thinkers and Researchers, Morocco;
Managing Editor of al-Ummah magazine;
Member of the International Union of Muslim Scholars

'The book before us is a moving narrative of Qur'an's self-expression on love and how the love of God animates every aspect of His creation. Love is vividly shown as the governing principle of Islam and of God's relationship with the prize of His creation, humankind. The author skilfully lets the Qur'an speak for itself, a hallmark of credibility that also espouses the author's intimate knowledge of the Holy Book.

It is a comprehensive and self-contained text on the subject that aspires to high standards of scholarship, [and] one that is imbued with the strength and conviction of Iman (faith).'

Prof. Dr. Mohammad Hashim Kamali,
Founding Chairman & CEO,
International Institute of Advanced Islamic Studies (IAIS), Malaysia

'This book—the first of its kind—is unique in its style and its methodology, precise in its detail, and consistent in its thought. It should be a resource for all those who study the subject of love at university and research level. It covers the subject in all its aspects, concepts, and values, drawing them all from the Book of God.'

H.E. Prof. Dr. Kamel 'Ajlouni,
Chairman of the Board of Trustees, Jordan University

'Love in the Holy Qur'an is a study characterized by sound scholarship and spiritual insight. This is a compelling and subtle presentation of a topic which has not been given adequate attention in previous literature.'

Prof. Dr. Ingrid Mattson,
Director, Macdonald Center for the
Study of Islam and Christian-Muslim Relations Hatford Seminary;
President, Islamic Society of North America (ISNA)

'Prince Ghazi gives a masterly exposition of love. Drawn from the words of the Qur'an itself, this long-needed work is a nuanced treatment of a subject that deserves the regard of anyone who wants to understand the real 'fundamentalism' of the Qur'an, which speaks to the very core of the human being.'

Shaykh Nuh Ha Mim Keller